CAMBRIDGE TEXTS IN THE
HISTORY OF POLITICAL THOUGHT

MONTESQUIEU
The Spirit of the Laws

CAMBRIDGE TEXTS IN THE HISTORY OF POLITICAL THOUGHT

Cambridge Texts in the History of Political Thought is now firmly established as the major student textbook series in political theory. It aims to make available to students all the most important texts in the history of western political thought, from ancient Greece to the early twentieth century. All the familiar classic texts will be included, but the series seeks at the same time to enlarge the conventional canon by incorporating an extensive range of less well-known works, many of them never before available in a modern English edition. Wherever possible, texts are published in complete and unabridged form, and translations are specially commissioned for the series. Each volume contains a critical introduction together with chronologies, biographical sketches, a guide to further reading and any necessary glossaries and textual apparatus. When completed the series will aim to offer an outline of the entire evolution of western political thought.

For a list of titles published in the series, please see end of book.

MONTESQUIEU

The Spirit of the Laws

TRANSLATED AND EDITED BY

ANNE M. COHLER

BASIA CAROLYN MILLER

HAROLD SAMUEL STONE

PUBLISHED BY THE PRESS SYNDICATE OF THE UNIVERSITY OF CAMBRIDGE
The Pitt Building, Trumpington Street, Cambridge, United Kingdom

CAMBRIDGE UNIVERSITY PRESS
The Edinburgh Building, Cambridge CB2 2RU, UK www.cup.cam.ac.uk
40 West 20th Street, New York, NY 10011–4211, USA www.cup.org
10 Stamford Road, Oakleigh, Melbourne 3166, Australia
Ruiz de Alarcón 13, 28014 Madrid, Spain

First published 1989
Reprinted 1990, 1992, 1994, 1995, 1997, 1999

Printed in the United Kingdom at the University Press, Cambridge

British Library Cataloguing in Publication data
Montesquieu, Charles de Secondat, *baron de. 1689–1755*
The spirit of the laws. –
(Cambridge texts in the history of political thought).
1. Government
I. Title II. De l'esprit de lois.
English
350

Library of Congress Cataloging in Publication data
Montesquieu, Charles de Secondat, baron de, 1689–1755.
[De l'esprit des lois. English]
The spirit of the laws / Montesquieu: translated by
Anne M. Cohler, Basia C. Miller, Harold Stone.
p. cm. –
(Cambridge texts in the history of political thought)
Translation of: De l'esprit des lois.
Bibliography.
ISBN 0–521–36183–4. ISBN 0–521–36974–6 (pbk.)
1. Political science. 2. State, The. 3. Law – Philosophy.
4. Jurisprudence. I. Cohler, Anne M. II. Miller, Basia C.
III. Stone, Harold, 1949– . IV. Title. V. Series.
JC179.M74 1989
320 – dc19 88–30006 CIP

ISBN 0 521 36183 4 hard covers
ISBN 0 521 36974 6 paperback

WV

Prolem sine matre creatum

Ovid, *Metamorphoses* 2.553

Contents

Part 5

Part 6

Introduction

In a letter written in 1748 when *The Spirit of the Laws* was first published Montesquieu wrote, "I can say that I have worked on it my whole life: I was given some law books when I left my *collège*; I sought their spirit, I worked, but I did nothing worthwhile. I discovered my principles twenty years ago: they are quite simple; anyone else working as hard as I did would have done better. But I swear that this book nearly killed me; I am going to rest now; I shall work no more" (*Oeuvres de Montesquieu*, ed. André Masson (3 vols., Paris, 1950–1954), vol. 3, p. 1200).

The publication of *The Spirit of the Laws* did mark the end of Montesquieu's work. He was, like La Bruyère and Montaigne before him, a man who put all he knew into his one book. Although it was published as Diderot, d'Alembert, and Rousseau were imagining the Enlightenment in the coffee houses and salons of Paris, and although the first volume of the *Encyclopedia* and Rousseau's *Discourse on the Arts and Sciences* appeared just three years later, these facts suggest the wrong context. Rather, *The Spirit of the Laws* belongs to the first half of the eighteenth century – to a period of relative quiet when one could think of reform, muddling through, or marking time. Montesquieu, for example, wrote of Cromwell, "It was a fine spectacle in the last century to see the impotent attempts of the English to establish democracy among themselves. As those who took part in public affairs had no virtue at all, as their ambition was excited by the success of the most audacious one and the spirit of one faction was repressed only by the spirit of another, the government was constantly changing; the people, stunned, sought democracy and found it nowhere. Finally, after much motion and many shocks and jolts, they had to come to rest on the very government that had been proscribed" (3.3). Here Montesquieu lectured the English, as Burke was later to lecture the French, for forgetting the need to preserve the forms as they changed toward a popular government.

In retrospect we have identified three different ways of life in France before the revolution: that of the orders of the feudal monarchy, that of the absolute king and his servants, the bureaucrats, and their equal subjects, and that of those corners of society which supported the new thought and freedom. But in Montesquieu's time the distinction was not so clear. An examination of Montesquieu's life provides a view of the eighteenth century as it impinged upon Montesquieu; he was a feudal proprietor, wine merchant, parliamentarian, academician, man of letters. Although he took his place briefly in the Parliament of Bordeaux and toyed with the notion of serving the king in foreign relations, he principally worked to maintain his family and took part in the academies and other less formal gatherings of like-minded men and women. Here we shall first consider Montesquieu's life as a noble landowner, then as an eighteenth-century man of letters, and finally as the author of *The Spirit of the Laws*. Then we shall proceed to the book itself and its reception.

The noble landowner

Montesquieu's family first appears among the provincial nobility of Bordeaux, when Jean de Secondat, whose wife was related to the Plantagenets, was ennobled in 1562. The title was raised to a barony in 1606 by Henry IV. Two generations later, Montesquieu's grandfather, whose wife was the daughter of the First President of the parliament, became Président à Mortier in the Parliament of Bordeaux. (The office of president was bought, sold, and inherited; there were, in the parliament, a number of Présidents à Mortier who served on various panels as judges and administrators and one First President.) This family offered its members the choice of either the parliamentary nobility of the robe or the military nobility of the sword; at the same time it saw to it that the family lands and goods all stayed within the family, that the children beyond those needed to continue the family joined religious orders, and that those who took up either robe or sword married well. This was a noble family, carefully built and maintained, depending on no single notion of honor or prosperity. Montesquieu was to write to his son, "You are of the robe or the sword. It is up to you to choose when you have to answer as to your estate" (*Oeuvres*, vol. 2, *Pensées* 5(69)).

Montesquieu's uncle, his father's oldest brother, became Baron de Montesquieu and Président à Mortier, but he had no surviving children. Montesquieu's father, a younger son, took up arms as a profession, finally fighting the Turks in Hungary, where "he must have been somewhat well regarded," said Montesquieu, "because, when I was in Vienna, I still found former officers who remembered having seen him" (*Oeuvres*, vol. 3, p. 1564). When Montesquieu's father returned to Bordeaux, he married a rich noblewoman, who inherited the barony of La Brède, as well as many debts that he spent much of the rest of his life retiring. His three other brothers became ecclesiastics, and his three sisters, nuns. Our Montesquieu, Charles Louis de Secondat, stood to inherit both from his uncle, the Baron de Montesquieu and President à Mortier, and his father, the Baron de La Brède, becoming finally Charles Louis de Secondat, Baron de La Brède et de Montesquieu and Président à Mortier of the Parlement of Bordeaux. Eventually Montesquieu sold the *présidence* he had inherited from his uncle, but he remained the careful steward of the family lands.

Montesquieu was born in 1689 at La Brède. His early life moved smoothly toward preparing him for his position both as noble landowner and as parliamentary magistrate. His first experiences were of everyday rural life, and he continued to feel at home on his estates. It is said that, like Montaigne, he was given a beggar as godfather and spent his earliest years being cared for in the mill near La Brède. Much later in his life, he was taken for a worker in his own vineyards by visitors who addressed him as a peasant and asked him the way to Montesquieu's château.

At age eleven Montesquieu was sent to the Collège de Juilly near Paris, an excellent and aristocratic institution, to begin the education that was to prepare him for the *présidence*. There he was given a thorough grounding in history, both ancient and modern. That education seems to have encouraged reading and comparing a wide variety of sources and keeping notebooks of reflections and of observations on a variety of topics, habits which Montesquieu maintained from then on. There is no record of Montesquieu's time at the Collège, and Montesquieu, typically, remarks not upon the academic content of his education, but upon the moral education embedded in the practices of everyday life of a school which forced a young man "to betray his comrades every day in a hundred petty ways" and ruined "the hearts of all those within" (*Oeuvres*, vol. 2, *Pensées* 218 (1758)). After graduating, Montesquieu was sent to study law at the University of Bordeaux, taking a licentiate after three years. He then returned to Paris, continuing his study of law in the courts of Paris, keeping notes as always. Little is known about this period of his life (1708–13), but he maintained an acquaintance with Père Desmolets and Nicholas Fréret, both of whom were probably known to him from Collège (*Oeuvres*, vol. 3, p. 729). He spoke extensively about China with a Chinese visitor, writing a summary in his notebooks that points toward both the *Persian Letters* and *The Spirit of the Laws* (*Oeuvres*, vol. 2, pp. 924–63). In 1713, just after his father's death, Montesquieu returned to Bordeaux to take up his inheritance. He bought himself a place in the parliament as a counsellor and married a woman who brought considerable lands and wealth with her. Little is known of her except that she was a practicing Protestant and the trusted steward of his lands during his absences. In 1716 his uncle died, leaving Montesquieu the family estates and the *présidence à mortier*. In three years Montesquieu, now twenty-seven years old, had become a provincial nobleman of some consequence.

These were very quiet years in the Parlement of Bordeaux; the ordinary judicial and administrative activities were primary. There were few moves made to revive and exercise the right of remonstrance, that is, the right to judge the legality of new laws, and no claim to be in any way the representatives of the nation, unlike some of the parliaments in the later period closer to the revolution. Montesquieu began in the court at its lowest rank, as a counsellor in the criminal court, and moved up as far as the senior president in that court. He served as the commissioner of prisons, was one of the counsellors charged with overseeing the assignment of those condemned to the galleys, and could not have avoided participating in interrogations that relied upon torture. His activities were always as a member of a panel of judges. The chief issues in the parliament in those years had to do with the complicated rules of precedence, both as they applied to relations between counsellors and presidents, and in respect to the disregard of those same rules by the governor of the region, the Maréchal Berwick, who was to become a life-long friend of Montesquieu's. Montesquieu's attendance in the sessions, never among the best, became so infrequent after the publication of the *Persian Letters* in 1721 that there appear even to have been murmurs of discontent in the parliament. When Montesquieu sold the life interest in his *présidence* in 1728, his friend the Président Barbot tried to persuade him to remain by arguing that, although the work was not pleasant, it was routine and easy, that it "scarcely distracts you from your other occupations or amusements" (*Oeuvres*, vol. 3, p. 819). Montesquieu answered that not the questions but the proceedings were incomprehensible to him and that it was tiresome "to see fools in possession of the very talent that fled me, so to speak" (*Oeuvres*, vol. 2, *Pensées* 213(4)). There is no suggestion on either man's part that the parliament could be anything more than a law court and a job.

As a great landowner, Montesquieu took care to maintain his customary rights and to increase his land-holding. He was constantly involved in complicated legal actions and in buying land near his own. He advised his daughter to invest her money in land and that legal actions were a part of being a great lady with much land (*Oeuvres*, vol. 3, pp. 1271, 1344). But Montesquieu was a modern farmer concerned with the market for his goods as well as a nobleman collecting his feudal goods. He was concerned with his vines, his wine, and the course of international trade in wine. In 1727 he found himself in conflict with the Intendant, writing a memorandum arguing that he knew best what to do with his land and wine, and objecting to the controls on production and export. The Intendant responded in a note to his superior with scorn for the excessive cleverness of the enlightened landowner (*Oeuvres*, vol. 3, p. 264). Here the nobleman's presumption of independence, even while defending economic freedoms, runs against the planning, and even the egalitarianism, of the king's servant. When the market for his wine collapsed, largely because wars made it impossible to ship it to England, he stayed in La Brède and did not spend his customary time in Paris. Thus, he wrote in 1742, "But I am afraid that if the war continues I shall be forced to go and plant cabbages at La Brède. In Guyenne, our commerce will soon be on its last legs; our wine will be left on our hands, and you know that it is our entire wealth" (*Oeuvres*, vol. 3, p. 1017). In sum, in a letter to a woman friend in Paris from La Brède, he wrote, "I hear people talk of nothing but grapevines, hard times, and lawsuits, and fortunately I am fool enough to enjoy all that, that is, to be interested in it" (*Oeuvres*, vol. 3, p. 1383). He did not conduct his life as a man of letters at the expense of his life as a landowner.

Montesquieu followed the family tradition in his arrangements for his children and estates. He educated his son to take over the *présidence* when it returned to his family upon the death of the man to whom he had sold his life-interest. Although his son briefly became a counsellor, he wanted to be a naturalist and refused to take up the *présidence*, which Montesquieu subsequently sold altogether. When it became clear to Montesquieu that his son was not likely to have any children, he married his daughter Denise to a distant cousin, Godefroy de Secondat, and arranged for the bulk of the estate to go to her children so that it would stay in the family.

The man of letters

In 1715, soon after returning to Bordeaux to take up the life of a provincial nobleman, Montesquieu was elected to the Academy of Bordeaux and remained active in it for the rest of his life, becoming its mainstay and its connection to Paris. The provincial academies offered a protected institutional environment in which the urban, educated nobles, the clergy, and the members of the third estate met to conduct altogether secular discussions of scientific, moral, and literary questions. Papers were presented and discussed by the members of the Academy. Montesquieu reported primarily on scientific observations, but his discontent with this science is illustrated by his remarks that "these systems" are "no sooner set up than they are overthrown" (*Oeuvres*, vol. 3, p. 52). He also offered a number of papers on social practices in other countries and times, and on duties and natural law, contrasting the performance of duties in accordance with natural law to a totally disordered pursuit of the desire of the moment. In one of the sections that remains from the *Traîté des devoirs*, which Montesquieu never finished for publication, he again follows the traditional formula, saying that the monarchy is based on the spirit of obedience (*Oeuvres*, vol. 3, p. 169). This last comment indicates the distance his thought was to travel before he wrote *The Spirit of the Laws*, where honor is said to be the principle of action in a monarchy.

In 1721 Montesquieu published the *Persian Letters* anonymously and began to move increasingly in Parisian and European literary society.

The *Persian Letters* purport to be letters by two Persian gentlemen visiting Europe from 1710 to 1720 written to their friends, to each other, to a miscellany of other figures, and to and from the harem of the protagonist, Usbek. As they set out, Usbek praises sincerity and claims that his troubles in Persia began with his decision to speak honestly to the king. In response to a request from his friends in Persia to remind them of their conversations about virtue, he writes the story of the Troglodytes, whose inclination to help each other became an inclination to follow their own desires, or self-interest, until all but one virtuous family had died. Their morality remained a consequence of inclinations, not of contemplation. The central portion of the *Persian Letters* offers a cool dissection of the foibles of eighteenth-century, particularly French, society and politics. In the last series of letters Usbek reacts increasingly despotically to his wives' evasion of their confinement, of their enforced virtue. As a charming and pointed commentary on French mores, the book is part of the long tradition of writing by French moralists, often particularly reminiscent of La Bruyère's *Caractères*. But in its concluding pages Montesquieu undermines the position of the moralist, the observer, through his description of the collapse of the harem and the violence of Usbek's response. This conclusion gives the book its peculiar allure, makes it into a puzzle, and points away from the moralizing works of his youth.

From 1721 to 1728, Montesquieu's visits to Paris became longer and more frequent. He became a part of court society, devoting himself to various ladies and offering no disapproval of the morals of the court. He also became a regular in the salon of Mme. Lambert. In this salon, as in the others that Montesquieu was to attend when he returned to Paris after 1733, conversation was based not on rank and manners, but upon character, wit, and knowledge. Montesquieu seems also to have attended the Club de l'Entresol, where those invited often had particular expertise; each session was formally divided into a time for general discussion of government and international events and a time when a paper was read and considered. The chief concern behind these discussions seems to have been both the history and the reform of institutions. Boulainvilliers, whose work Montesquieu discusses extensively in Book 30 of *The Spirit of the Laws*, had attended this club, as did the Abbé de Saint Pierre and Bolingbroke. It was suppressed by the government, as was another such club that Montesquieu attended; Montesquieu saw the dissolution of these kinds of little free academies as a real loss for men of letters (*Oeuvres*, vol. 3, pp. 1343–1344). He seems to have taken advantage of social environs in which the rules and hierarchy of the absolute monarchy were not enforced. In 1728, he arranged to become a member of the French Academy with the help of his friends and what must have been a politic interview with Cardinal Fleury, the First Minister of Louis XV. He was not to become an active member of that academy until he resumed his regular visits to Paris after his European tour.

Those of Montesquieu's writings that seem to have been directed to this Parisian audience portray exotic settings, pretty women, harmless adventure, and Roman virtue. Only Rousseau took offence, saying of one such piece, "If, for example, there is any moral purpose in the *Temple de Gnide* it is thoroughly obfuscated and spoiled by the voluptuous details and lascivious images. What has the author done to cover it with a gloss of modesty? He has pretended that this work was the translation of a Greek manuscript and has fashioned the story about the discovery of this manuscript in the manner most likely to persuade his readers of the truth of his tale. . . . But who has thought to accuse the author of a crime for this lie or to call him a deceiver for it?" (Rousseau, *Reveries* (New York, 1982), p. 49). The only paper of Montesquieu's found in the files of the Club de l'Entresol is the *Dialogue de Sylla et d'Eucrate*, but its only imaginable connection with the interests of the club is the criticism Montesquieu implies by joining Sulla's noble-sounding talk of social reform with his great violence and self-delusion.

The author of *The Spirit of the Laws*

Montesquieu set forth on an extended trip in 1728, traveling primarily to Italy and England, and he did not return to La Brède until 1731, when he began the work that led directly to writing *The Spirit of the Laws*. What precisely, if anything, Montesquieu originally expected from this tour is not clear. He might already have had the writing of *The Spirit of the Laws* in mind. In 1747 he wrote in his Preface that he had discovered his principles twenty years previously, that is, before setting out. There is no direct evidence for this, but parts of Book 3 on the principles of governments have been identified as among the first written in the only existing manuscript (*Oeuvres*, vol. 3, pp. 567–576). In addition, there is also some evidence that at the beginning of his trip Montesquieu harbored the idea of employment in foreign affairs.

Montesquieu's first lengthy stop on his trip was in Vienna. There he began to keep a diary of his journey; he kept notes on and recorded his impressions of the art objects, personalities, and governments he encountered, and he kept reminders of books to be bought or people to see. The journal still exists for the trip to Italy and Germany, but not for the trip to England. In Vienna, he met Prince Eugene of Savoy and spent time with his circle, which was notorious for its so-called libertines and free-thinkers. In Venice, his next major stop, he sought out Antonio Conti, a churchman and one of the most effective popularizers of Newton's theories in Italy. Conti was in close contact with the circle of Prince Eugene and with the leading scientists and scholars of Italy. Conti, in turn, gave Montesquieu letters of introduction to the leading biologists of northern Italy and to the scholars Ludovico Muratori, a literary critic and historian of the Italian Middle Ages, and Scipione Maffei, a dramatist and classicist. In Naples Montesquieu was led to converse with Costantino Grimaldi, an aged jurist known for his defenses of Cartesian philosophy and his advocacy of the priority of civil over ecclesiastical jurisdiction. Montesquieu's interests in Italy seem to have been in modern thought rather than ancient history.

Montesquieu spent two years in England. This was the England of George II, whom Montesquieu first met in Hanover; of Swift, Defoe, Pope, and of bitter, violent public discussion and satire; where the Whig, Walpole, was the king's minister and the Tory, Bolingbroke, defended Parliament against what was called corruption, that is the influence of the king and his minister. British political freedom attracted visiting Frenchmen, whereas the disorder of its public debate was upsetting to them. Montesquieu's interests in England seem to have been primarily political; he was acquainted with figures on all sides of the issues and with the court, and he observed Parliament in action. In England he found what was scarcely imaginable in France – a politics where the question was the proper understanding of the relation, or balance, between the representative Parliament and the king, or the king's minister, and the reigning issue was the constitutional propriety of the actions of the king and Parliament.

Montesquieu's famous description of English politics and of the possibility of a government based on separated and balanced powers has its source in his observation of this government. His assessment in *The Spirit of the Laws* of the way the balance operated is carefully neutral between Walpole, who controlled Parliament through his patronage, and Bolingbroke, who disapproved of the minister's invasion of the independence of Parliament: "And, as the executive power, which has all the posts at its disposal, could furnish great expectations but not fears, all those who would obtain something from it would be inclined to move to that side, and it could be attacked by all those who could expect nothing from it" (*Spirit of the Laws*, 19.27). For the English balance of power to work, people must be able to move between allegiance to the executive and the legislature. The posts available to the executive make that possible.

The years between 1731, when he returned to France, and 1748, when *The Spirit of the Laws* was finished, were occupied with the serious and extensive reading and writing required to produce first his *Considerations on the Causes of the Greatness of the Romans and their Decline* and then *The Spirit of the Laws*. The quality of Montesquieu's scholarship has been a perennial question. Shackleton has traced evidence of Montesquieu's extensive reading in his *Pensées*, notebooks, and journals. The search for sources of his thought is handicapped, however, by an excess of evidence. He seems to have read everything. In *The Spirit of the Laws*, Montesquieu cites some 300 works in over 3,000 references. Muriel Dodds had located many of Montesquieu's references to the travel literature. Iris Cox has investigated the works cited in his analysis of French law, concluding that Montesquieu used the best sources available to him, critically and with judgment. In our experience, if one is attentive to the point Montesquieu is trying to make, and to the possibility of irony, his use of his sources is plausible and responsible.

Montesquieu's life showed little external change during the seven years he lived after his great work was completed; he continued to travel between La Brède and Paris, to care for his family and estates, and to visit with his friends in the "republic of letters." He wrote the *Défense de l'esprit des lois*, tried to keep his work from being censored by the Sorbonne and from being put on the Index, and wrote an article, "Du goût," for the *Encyclopedia*. In 1755, he died of a fever in Paris, confessing and taking communion, but without surrendering his papers to the priest.

The Spirit of the Laws and its reception

The Spirit of the Laws, in spite of Montesquieu's request to the contrary, has been read piecemeal. As in his life, Montesquieu did not seem to require any clear, overt, organizing device. The best analogy for the book is the complex mosaic and embroidery of the eighteenth century, or even rococo painting. Although there is no over-arching, organizing image, there are similarities and contrasts that send the viewer, or reader, across the painting, or through the book. The elements that have attracted the attention of those who have read and thought about Montesquieu are: the law and the spirit of the law; the division of governments into republics, monarchies, and despotisms; the notion of a free government of divided and balanced powers, and the examination of the conditions of the existence of such a government; and the distinction between moderate and despotic government. Here, I can give only a brief notion of the standing and ramifications of each notion and point out the thinkers who have responded to each.

Montesquieu begins the book with the distinction between the law and the spirit of the law. He refuses in effect to use the great organizing principle of his predecessors, the natural law – however it was understood. As a legal principle, the spirit points away from an assessment of individual laws in terms of some universal principle and toward some particular, unifying principle. In Book 28 Montesquieu takes up the question of the development of civil law in France from the time of the conquest by the Germanic tribes through the reign of Saint Louis and then forward to Charles VII. This is the kind of material that seems to validate the claim of the Enlightenment that the "Middle Ages" were a period of senseless barbarism. But Montesquieu finds a kind of order in them: "One will perhaps be curious to see the monstrous usage of judicial combat reduced to principles and to find the body of so singular a jurisprudence. Men who are fundamentally reasonable place even their prejudices under rules. Nothing was more contrary to common sense than judicial combat, but once this point was granted, it was executed with a certain prudence" (28.23). Later, he speaks of the spirit of a warrior nation governed solely by the point of honor (28.27). The problem in approaching Montesquieu from this point of view has always been in ascertaining the kind of thing the spirit of a government, or country, is – natural, political, or even divine?

Montesquieu does offer a typology of government, presenting the reader with the distinction between monarchies, despotisms, and republics. He distinguishes between the nature of a government, its source of rule, and its principle, the passions that keep it going. This permits him to make a distinction between monarchy and despotism; both are ruled by one person, but in the first the honor of political men ensures the rule of law and in the second the fear of the prince is virtually the only passion. In monarchies, there is a complicated, even confusing, hierarchy of institutions; in despotisms, there is only the prince, or his agent, and everyone else. Everyone is a slave, and in effect the slave of the prince, who in turn is the slave of his passions. Thus, Montesquieu claims that, because of the complex of institutions that do or do not support it, the same source of rule can be exercised in such different ways that the governments must be said to be different. This notion that the kinds of governments are a consequence of the way rule is exercised, which in turn is due to the entire complex of political and social groupings and institutions, marks a new way of viewing government, which is identified by Durkheim and Raymond Aron as the beginning of sociology, although they express their distress at Montesquieu's continued use of political categories.

However, his first readers in France did not follow him. Dupin explicitly objected to this distinction between despotism and monarchy, claiming, as is traditional, that the form of a government determines its end and the way its people act. He was further horrified that it was not the spirit of submission but a monstrous, odious, and false notion of a monarchy based on honor that was put forward. Voltaire objected that Montesquieu's distinctions among governments, particularly the one between monarchy and despotism, were not accurately drawn. They were, he claimed, based on inaccurate information, on mere stories. His view that Montesquieu used his sources uncritically became a commonplace.

In the first eight books, Montesquieu presents a moderate, or regular and law-abiding, monarchy. However, the intermediate powers that make it a monarchy resemble those of the French – a military nobility of the sword, a parliamentary nobility of the robe, and a clergy. The suggestion then, is that the moderation of the French monarchy was a consquence of its intermediate powers. During both the religious wars of the sixteenth century and the wars of the Fronde of the seventeenth, the institutions independent of the king defended their place in the monarchy. The parliaments pushed their claim to assess the appropriateness of new laws issued by the king. Claude de Seyssel in *La Monarchie de France* pictured a monarchy held in check by the brakes or reins on the king of religion, justice, and the police (the everyday life and habits of a people). But Montesquieu's notion is that the political bodies create ways of acting and thinking, that in a monarchy, for example, honor channels and regularizes the actions of a king. It does so because each noble conceives of himself as a separately responsible political actor, however unfortunate his notion of honor may be. Politics in this monarchy is no longer the private business of the king, even of a king who must be advised and sometimes curbed.

Montesquieu offers an explicit discussion of the history and revolutions of the French monarchy in Books 30 and 31, and thus concludes his text with a discussion of the actual condition of France. Here he joins the argument over what the constitution of France was or had been, if indeed it had had, or still had, a constitution. Each of these visions of the constitution and of its history pointed to a different future for France, making the discussion of the status of its constitution in effect a discussion of the possibilities for change in France. Here one can see the beginning of the discussion that led directly to the French Revolution.

An informed historical argument had become possible because the laws of the Germanic tribes and the practices of the Merovingians and Carolingians as well as the Capetians and the Valois had been published and edited during the seventeenth century. Henri de Boulainvilliers argued that the Frankish king and his nobles conquered Gaul and ruled it together as conquerors, but that this noble rule had dissolved into despotism. Jean-Baptiste Dubos argued that Clovis, the Frankish king, took the place of the Roman emperor and ruled Franks and Romans alike, creating a pattern followed by the contemporary monarch. Montesquieu argued that there were distinctions among both the Franks and the Romans that were worked into the law and practice of a new kingdom in a number of different ways. In each case, the question was the shape or constitution of the monarchy, that is of the relation between the king and the other political bodies, which could be identified by a consistent historical practice or development. The variety of possible constitutions and revolutions over the course of French history makes the very existence of any French constitution problematic. Later Mably claimed that there had been no consistent relation between the parts of the monarchy: in effect, that there had been no constitution for the monarchy. He makes both the king and the nobility usurpers at different times, and in so doing he takes Montesquieu's intermediate position one step further and makes an altogether new start more plausible.

Marat, in 1785, offered a formal *éloge* of Montesquieu which praises his "delicate satire," while attributing to him the outrage that was to fuel the revolution. He wrote, "he was the first among us to carry the torch of philosophy into legislation, to avenge outraged humanity, to defend its rights, and in a way, to become the legislator for the whole world." Montesquieu's own willingness to offer thoughts about legislation to the public, rather than to the king, as was proper in the absolute monarchy, is taken by Marat as a model not only for statesmen but for everyone.

Republics, in addition to monarchies and despotisms, are the topic for the first eight books. These governments, small, pagan, and based on slavery, seemed to offer little to eighteenth-century France, but the image of political virtue had great charm in spite of Montesquieu's characterization of the environment that a republic required. He claimed that republics were based on virtue as a principle, understood as love of country. They were maintained by a whole way of life that established equality among the citizens and left them little or nothing other than that country to love or identify with. Put this way, the virtue of Montesquieu's republican government and the virtue celebrated by Rousseau bear a remarkable resemblance. (Rousseau was the secretary to Mme. Dupin when she and her husband, the Fermier Général, wrote, published, and withdrew from publication the first critical assessment of *The Spirit of the Laws*.) In each case the passions that could be invested in an individual's well-being are directed toward that of the society as a whole; virtue is that single-minded devotion to country.

In the United States, Jefferson and the Anti-Federalists took seriously Montesquieu's account of the social conditions that make republican government possible. In arguing that Americans ought not to take up manufacturing, Jefferson wrote, "It [corruption] is the mark set on those, who, not looking up to heaven, to their own soil and industry, as does the husbandman, for their subsistence, depend for it on casualties and caprice of customers. Dependence begets subservience and venality, suffocates the germ of virtue, and prepares fit tools for the designs of ambition" (Jefferson, *Notes on Virginia* (New

York, 1964), p. 157). The Anti-Federalists worried constantly that the proposed new U.S. Constitution did not encourage civic virtue, that it both ignored the question of virtue and set up conditions, such as large size, complex representation, and encouragement of commerce, that positively discouraged the development of such virtue.

In addition to the paradigms of republics, monarchies, and despotisms, Montesquieu offered the model of a government whose end was political liberty, the English government of his time (11.6; 19.27). His analysis of that liberty and that government affected the way both Englishmen and Americans came to think of their political institutions and of the social and economic underpinnings of those institutions. According to Montesquieu, political liberty is the result of the separation of powers. In England, the orders of the old regime, commons, lords, and king, each take up a function in the new division of rule into legislative and executive functions, with the judicial function set aside in juries. The functions of government are not entirely separated, as each branch participates to some extent in the task of the others, making the balance a result of an interaction between the branches. However, the question remains of the separation of the three orders. That is, does the king properly have some part in the choice of members of Parliament? Is the king, or his minister in Parliament, the executive, and what is the meaning of that term? Is it proper to dilute the old nobility by creating new nobles? Montesquieu is quoted approvingly by both Blackstone and Burke. Blackstone defends the separation of powers in their sources, while Burke is quite willing to find reasons for all the ways of electing members of Parliament that made it possible for the executive to have some control over them. Still, for Blackstone and Burke, as for Montesquieu, the structure of the government itself, not some appeal to first principles, is the defense of liberty.

In France, during and after the French Revolution, Montesquieu's concern to balance power led to the question of whether there remained any independent political body, king, or noble, that could be used to moderate the sovereignty of the people. Burke, a careful student of Montesquieu, berated the French in his *Reflections on the Revolution in France* for not attaching themselves to the institutions of their old regime, as the English had. Tocqueville replied that those institutions were no longer viable in France. Using Montesquieu's analysis of monarchy, he offered the argument that the loss of intermediate powers made possible the revolutionary move from royal to popular tyranny. England did not offer a plausible model: "The European revolution continues among the English, but it continues there by assuming forms that are entirely English" (Tocqueville, *Oeuvres complètes* (Paris, 1967), 8.1, p. 157). Only in America could one see that there were democratic intermediate institutions that could moderate democratic sovereignty.

The second half of *The Spirit of the Laws* is a consideration of the conditions of government – of climate, temperament, family structure, commerce, religion and history. Here we come upon the conditions that could support a modern free government, like that of England. It is hard to see how these conditions can be managed to the benefit of the governments, as direct governmental control seems to be precluded by the principle of freedom. In Book 12 on freedom as personal security Montesquieu takes up treason, sexual crimes, and heresy, and in each case he moves the government toward punishment only for the most overt, visible acts. His suggestions for the reform of criminal law appealed to the Milanese intellectual Cesare Beccaria, the author of the most famous book of the Italian Enlightenment, *Of Crimes and Punishments* (1764), and came to circulate widely.

The Spirit of the Laws was received with praise by much of the Scottish Enlightenment, including David Hume, Adam Ferguson, and Adam Smith, and was incorporated into their thought and work. Hume wrote Montesquieu a letter upon reading the book that praises by commenting carefully on some passages about English republicanism and commercial policy (*Oeuvres*, vol. 3, pp. 1217–1222). Ferguson wrote in *An Essay on Civil Society* (Philadelphia, A. Finley, 1819), pp. 119–120, "When I recollect what the President Montesquieu has written I am at a loss to tell, why I should treat of human affairs; . . . In his writings will be found, not only the original of what I am now, for the sake of order, to copy from him, but likewise probably the source of many observations, which, in different places, I may, under the belief of invention, have repeated, without quoting their author." The parts of Montesquieu of most interest to these writers were those reflecting on such conditions as temperament, family structure, commerce, religion, and legal history, which made possible free governments such as England's. These writers amplified and restructured the second half of *The Spirit of the Laws* so that it illustrated the development of the conditions of a modern free government. Unlike Montesquieu, they were not interested in the complex of passions, beliefs, and practices that supported other kinds of governments, or in a comparative politics based on the possibility of fundamentally different governments.

James Madison, one of the architects of the U.S. Constitution at the Convention where it was written, and one of its great defenders in *The Federalist*, was an inheritor of this intellectual tradition. Madison attended Princeton, where John Witherspoon, a Scotsman who followed the tradition of thought exemplified by Ferguson and Smith's *Lectures on Jurisprudence*, was president and gave the lectures on moral philosophy. Witherspoon, however, added the quality of moral earnestness and anti-aristocratic self-reliance that can lead to political action as well as to the ministry. In *Federalist* 10, Madison argues that a large republic could halt the republican tendency to develop majority and minority factions that dominate political life. The effort to disperse large divisions and the confidence in large, modern governments follows in the Scottish tradition.

But Madison's analysis of how a government of balanced powers could be expected to work reflects a contemplation of Montesquieu's book itself. In Montesquieu's England and the U.S. Constitution as Madison defended it in *The Federalist*, the balance of power is a result both of the division of power and of its sharing. The positions within the government are shaped by a notion of the character of good government. As in Montesquieu's monarchy, those who hold the positions are shaped by them. They identify themselves with the importance of the place they hold and the task it gives them. These habits of mind defend the division of powers and form the character of the rule.

The distinction between moderate and despotic governments permeates Montesquieu's book. In despotic governments, people are isolated from each other; their only rule is the will or whim of the ruler; they relate to each other only through fear. In moderate governments, people can count on regularity in the rule; they can relate to each other without fear insofar as they rely on the things they hold in common; they share something other than just fear of the ruler. Moderation and despotism are characteristics that can be found in virtually any government – in differing proportions. From this point of view, the egalitarian, bureaucratizing impulse of the absolute king was despotic, however well intentioned. Tocqueville made this notion the cornerstone of his analysis of the *Old Regime and the French Revolution*, and the severity of this criticism of the absolute monarchy was more influential than Montesquieu's analysis of the moderate monarchy. In *Democracy in America*, Tocqueville seems to have patterned his despotic democracy after Montesquieu's despotic king. But there the character of the ruler and the people became identical, leading to a new quiet, calm despotism. Tocqueville suspected that Madison's infinitely divided, shapeless population was inherently despotic and that the formal governmental institutions of the Federal government and even of the state governments could not teach the use of political freedom. Rather he sought out the equivalent of Montesquieu's intermediate institutions within the society, finding local governments, voluntary associations, and religious and familial habits and practices that shaped free democratic politics.

In turning his attention to the principles of a variety of governments and to the social, economic, and historical foundations of each, Montesquieu turned his readers away from the consideration of political right and toward an analysis of how to make particular governments work. Readers were directed to think of the possibilities – to become a small republic like those of the ancients, a monarchy with ranks and orders, a free government of divided powers, or a despotism of one or many. Each government, other than the despotisms, is a particular arrangement of equalities and inequalities. Montesquieu's thought has been most carefully attended to by those who, like the members of the provincial French academies of his time, tried to use institutional structures to work out a balance. Montesquieu's perspicacity about the possibilities for such balances and the reasons they are essential for any decent politics has made and continues to make him worth reading.

ANNE M. COHLER
Chicago, Illinois

Principal events in Montesquieu's life

1685 Revocation of the Edict of Nantes, the end of French toleration for Protestantism.

1688 Glorious revolution in England.

1689 Montesquieu was born, January 18, at the Château of La Brède.

1700 Montesquieu went to Collège de Juilly.

1708 Montesquieu studied law in Bordeaux and Paris.

1713 The Papal Bull Unigenitus was promulgated condemning some propositions from P. Quesnel's *Reflexions morales*, and thus supporting the Jesuits at the expense of the Jansenists.

1714 Montesquieu became a Counsellor in the Parlement of Bordeaux.

1715 Montesquieu married Jeanne Lartique, a Protestant; they had three children.
Louis XIV died.

1716 Montesquieu became a member of the Academy of Bordeaux and, when his uncle died, inherited the barony of Montesquieu and became Président à Mortier in the Parlement of Bordeaux.

1721 The *Persian Letters* was published, anonymously.

1725 Montesquieu published *Le Temple de Gnide*, anonymously, and sold a life interest in his *présidence*.

1728 Montesquieu was elected to the French Academy and set out on trip to Germany, Italy, and England.

1729 Montesquieu traveled to England.

1731 Montesquieu returned to France.

1734 Publication of the *Considerations on the Causes of the Greatness of the Romans and their Decline.*

1747 Montesquieu's son refused to take up the Présidence and it was sold altogether.

1748 Publication of *The Spirit of the Laws.*

1750 Publication of the *Défense de l'esprit des lois.*
Thomas Nugent published an English translation of *The Spirit of the Laws.*

1751–1765 Diderot and d'Alembert edit the *Encyclopedia.*

1751 *The Spirit of the Laws* was put on the Index.
Rousseau published the *Discourse on the Arts and Sciences.*

1754 Montesquieu wrote the *Essay on Taste*, which appeared in the *Encyclopedia.*
Rousseau published the *Discourse on the Origins of Inequality.*

1755 Montesquieu died in Paris of a fever.

1757 A new, revised edition of *The Spirit of the Laws* was published under the direction of Montesquieu's son from notes left by Montesquieu at his death.

1771 Maupeou dissolved the parlements and substituted another system of courts, whose members were to be appointed. The parlements were reestablished when Louis XVI became king in 1774. This is often used as a date to mark the beginning of the pre-revolutionary thrust in French history.

Bibliographical note

For a general introduction to eighteenth-century France, Alfred Cobban, *A History of Modern France*, vol. 1 and *The Old Regime and the French Revolution*, ed. Keith Michael Baker, vol. 7 of *Readings in Western Civilization* (Chicago, 1987) serve admirably. William Doyle, *The Parlement of Bordeaux and the End of the Old Regime* (New York, 1974) and Daniel Roche, *Le Siècle des lumières en Province* (Paris, 1978) provide a picture of provincial life before the revolution. The collected essays in *The Political Culture of the Old Regime*, ed. Keith Michael Baker (Oxford, 1987) give an idea of contemporary historians' assessment of this period. The references are extremely useful.

The standard reference for Montesquieu's biography is Robert Shackleton, *Montesquieu* (Oxford, 1961). Jean Starobinski's little book *Montesquieu* (Paris, 1979) collects the autobiographical information and has wonderful pictures. Judith N. Shklar, *Montesquieu* (Oxford, 1987) presents yet another version of Montesquieu's personality and work. Jean Dalat, *Montesquieu magistrat*, *Archives des lettres modernes*, ns. 132, 139 and Jean Dalat, *Montesquieu, chef de famille*, *Archives des lettres modernes*, n. 217, give a closer view of Montesquieu's actual activities than was previously available.

Nannerl O. Keohane, *Philosophy and the State in France* (Princeton, 1980), sees Montesquieu in the light of earlier French constitutionalist thought. Franklin Ford, *Robe and Sword* (New York, 1965) identifies Montesquieu with the parliamentary revolt, and A. Lloyd Moote, *The Revolt of the Judges, the Parlement of Paris and the Fronde, 1643–1652* (Princeton, 1971) gives a good notion of the way the parliamentarians thought. E. Carcassone, *Montesquieu et le problème de la constitution française au XVIIIe siècle* (Paris, 1927) places Montesquieu within eighteenth-century constitutionalism.

H. Roddier, "De la composition de *L'Esprit des Lois*: Montesquieu et les Oratorien de L'Académie de Juilly," *Revue d'histoire littéraire de la France*, 52 (1952) connects Montesquieu's use of historical sources to the way he was taught. The essays in the *Oeuvres complètes de Montesquieu* (Paris, 1950–1954) are also useful. There are three books which take particular topics and try and assess Montesquieu's use of his sources: Iris Cox, *Montesquieu and the History of French Laws* (Oxford, 1983); Muriel Dodds, *Les Recits de voyages: sources de L'Esprit des lois de Montesquieu* (Paris, 1929); and Catherine Volpilhac-Auger, *Tacite et Montesquieu* (Oxford, 1985). François Furet and Mona Ouzuf, "Two Historical Legitimations of Eighteenth-Century French Society: Mably and Boulainvilliers," in François Furet, *In the Workshop of History* (Chicago, 1985) helps place the final historical chapters in context.

For accounts of Montesquieu and English politics see: J. Dedieu, *Montesquieu et la tradition anglaise en France* (Paris, 1909); F. T. H. Fletcher, *Montesquieu and English Politics* (Philadelphia, 1980, reprint of 1939 edn); John Plamenatz, *Man and Society* (Harlow, Essex, 1963), vol. 1, pp. 284–291; and C. P. Courtney, *Montesquieu and Burke* (Oxford, 1963).

Emile Durkheim, *Montesquieu and Rousseau: Forerunners of Sociology* (Ann Arbor, Michigan, 1965); Raymond Aron, "Montesquieu," in *Main Currents in Sociological Thought* (New York, 1965), pp. 11–56; Louis Althusser, *Politics and History* (London, 1972), pp. 12–109; and Henry J. Merry, *Montesquieu's System of Natural Government* (W. Lafayette, Indiana, 1970) take Montesquieu as the beginning of modern sociology and history. For David Carrithers, in "Montesquieu's Philosophy of History," *Journal of History of Ideas* (1986), pp. 61–80 the question is the way Montesquieu looked for underlying causes in history. Albert O. Hirschman, *The Passions and the Interests* (Princeton, N.J., 1977), pp. 70–80 connects Montesquieu to the development of economic thought.

Destutt de Tracey, *A Commentary and Review of Montesquieu's "Spirit of the Laws"*, tr. Thomas Jefferson (New York, 1969, reprinted from 1811 edn), Mark Waddicor, *Montesquieu and the Philosophy of Natural Law* (The Hague, 1970), and Thomas L. Pangle, *Montesquieu's Philosophy of Liberalism* (Chicago, 1974) have placed Montesquieu's book within the tradition of natural law, or right, as they understand it. For an assessment see Bernard Manin, "Montesquieu et la politique moderne," *Cahiers de Philosophie Politique*, n. 2–3, and Michael A. Mosher, "The Particulars of a Universal Politics: Hegel's Adaptation of Montesquieu's Typology," *American Political Science Review* (1984), pp. 179–188.

Another approach explores the patterns of overlapping categories and concerns: Georges Benrekassa, *Montesquieu* (Paris, 1968); Anne M. Cohler, *Montesquieu's Comparative Politics and the Spirit of American Constitutionalism* (Kansas, 1988); Suzanne Gearhart, *The Open Boundary of History and Fiction* (Princeton, 1984); Bernard Groethuysen, *Philosophie de la Révolution Française précédé de Montesquieu* (Paris, 1956); Mark Hulliung, *Montesquieu and the Old Regime* (Berkeley, California, 1976); Catherine Larrère, "Les Typologies des gouvernments chez Montesquieu," in *Etudes sur le XVIIIe Siècle* (Clermont, 1979); Jacques Proust, *L'Objet et le texte, pour une poétique de la prose française du XVIIIe siècle* (Genève, 1980); Paul Vernière, *Montesquieu et l'esprit des lois ou la Raison impure* (Paris, 1977).

Translators' preface

The Spirit of the Laws offers a genial surface that carries the reader from one idea to the next; its array of paradoxes, anecdotes, metaphors, witty phrases and *saillies*, which leads the reader deeper into the text, also amuses. As much as possible of this civilized surface with its light touches is retained here, permitting Montesquieu to help the reader even through the English translation. In Montesquieu's apparent digressions the reader often finds echoes or applications of general principles Montesquieu has already enunciated, sometimes several hundred pages earlier. With this in mind, we have, as often as practicable, chosen the language of each part of the translation in terms of the entire book rather than in terms of the more limited context of the paragraph or chapter. This results in a stabilized core of terminology, which conveys some of the resonance of the original text.

Although in the Foreword to the *Spirit of the Laws* Montesquieu says that he has had to find new words or give new meanings to old ones, it is the conservatism of his vocabulary that is striking. Though he plays with the varied meanings of *vertu*, "virtue," *principe*, "principle," *esprit*, "spirit," and *constitution*, "constitution," he does so against a background of rigorously correct French usage. In *Considerations on the Causes of the Greatness of the Romans and their Decline*, Sainte-Beuve observes that Montesquieu "excels in returning expressions to all their primitive strength, which permits his style to be both succinct and strong, and to appear simple." Accordingly, we have respected Montesquieu's use of various distinctions, for instance between *prononcer*, "to pronounce," and *statuer*, "to enact," between *peine*, "penalty," and *supplice*, "punishment," between *ville*, "town," and *cité*, "city."

The greatest problems for the translators were presented by those French words whose broad meaning is not easily rendered into modern English. We have had to translate *affaires* as "business," "public business," "affairs," "public affairs," and even "suits" and "law suits;" but we have been able to maintain *biens* as "goods." We use "right" for *droit*, "law" for *loi*, and "money" for *monnaie*, all terms whose meanings have changed over time and have been the subject of much discussion. The translators' notes are largely concerned with these problems.

Montesquieu's discussion of feudal law raises the additional question of the difference between feudal French and feudal English institutions. Once the threshold of simple equivalents is passed with *seigneur*, "lord," *comte*, "county," and *prince*, "prince," modern English words tend to be inseparable from the English institutions to which they refer. Such words as *fisc*, *cens*, and *police*, which can be translated as "exchequer," "head-tax," and "administration," are rendered here by the more literal, if obsolete, English forms, "fisc," "census," and "police." The very obsoleteness of the terms will remind the reader that these institutions and categories differ from the English ones.

Paragraph divisions and virtually all the sentences are divided as they are in our French text. Where there are curiosities – for example, capital letters following a colon, or question-marks followed by a lower-case letter – we have followed the punctuation rather than the capitalization when possible. Within the sentences we have altered the punctuation to conform with English usage. We have kept as much of the structure of the sentences as is compatible with readable English and have used the first person when it appears in the text.

The first edition of *The Spirit of the Laws* was published in 1748 under the supervision of Jacob Vernet in Geneva. In 1749 an edition was published with some minor revisions and a map. In 1750 another edition was published with some additional corrections and the division into six parts that had been left out of the first edition. A version with a few substantial revisions and a new Author's Foreword appeared in 1757 as a separate volume and in 1758 as a part of a complete works. This version was published by Richer under the directions of Montesquieu's son from notes for a new edition left at Montesquieu's death in 1755 (*Oeuvres*, vol. 3, pp. 691–692). For the preparation of this translation, as there is no critical edition of the *Spirit of the Laws*, we used the text of the facsimile edition of the *Oeuvres complètes* of 1758, *Oeuvres complètes de Montesquieu*, ed. André Masson (Paris, Nagel,

1950–1955), vol. 1. We have taken the liberty of returning the Invocation to the Muses, which appears in the Masson edition immediately following the editor's introduction, to its original place at the opening of Book 20, and of reintroducing the division into six parts.

The only other translation of the entire book, by Thomas Nugent, was first published in 1750. Although it was based on the first edition, some of the later changes were incorporated in later editions of the translation. We have profited from Nugent's grasp of eighteenth-century French and have been immensely grateful to have had a predecessor with whom we could argue.

Montesquieu's text also contains some 2,000 footnotes. It has seemed appropriate to present his documentation in a format accessible to the modern reader. Our aim has been to make it possible for the specialist and non-specialist alike to evaluate Montesquieu's use of evidence. Montesquieu's references can be grouped under four general headings: (1) references to the classical texts of the Greeks and Romans; (2) to Roman law; (3) to the laws, law codes and public documents of the barbarian tribes and the French monarchy, primarily in the early Middle Ages; (4) to the travel literature which he consulted for information about contemporary non-European cultures.

For the first category, whereas Montesquieu refers to classical texts with book and chapter numbers, or with page numbers to editions which are no longer in print, we have used the present-day standard form. When a classical text may prove difficult to locate, the specific edition used is identified; otherwise we have relied on the Oxford, Loeb, or Teubner edition. For the second, Montesquieu refers to the laws in the Roman law codes by title. Although this is an efficient and elegant system of reference, it may put off a reader without Latin. We have identified, therefore, the name of the law-code and the book, title, law (imperial rescripts, extracts from the classical jurists), and paragraph numbers. For the third, while Montesquieu used the best editions available in his time for citations of the law codes of the barbarians, and of those of the Middle Ages, these are no longer in print. They have been superseded by texts prepared under the auspices of the *Monumenta Germaniae historica*. References are traced to this work since these volumes represent the best modern editions. Finally, in respect to the travel literature, as a number of these works have been republished in this century, we have used them whenever possible; otherwise, we have attempted to find the most recent printing.

All information appearing in brackets in the footnotes is that of the translators. We have preserved the original information of Montesquieu's citations, adding full author and title where needed. Although there are often incongruities between the numbers in Montesquieu's citations and those in our own, these differences should not be interpreted as his errors. They reflect typographical mistakes, differences in editions, changes in the form of citation, etc. Factual errors and incorrect citations are indicated. These instances are rare. Montesquieu was scrupulous about his references.

In earlier editions, many errors in the printing of the documentation resulted from the confusion, or transposition, of roman and arabic numerals. Mindful of this, and despite certain traditional forms of citation, we have used arabic numerals for all the numbers in the notes, except when roman numerals identify specific pages, as in a preface.

Our additions to the footnotes follow two basic forms. The first is for classical texts and for works for which there exists a specific standard form of citation. Each element of the citation – book number, chapter or title number, sentence or line number – is set off by a period. The second form of citation is to a particular edition; these citations contain three elements, each set off by semicolons. The first element contains information such as book, part, or chapter number, and the title of a specific section is given where it may be helpful in locating the information in a different edition. The second element contains volume and page number, separated by a comma, for the edition cited. The third and last element identifies the specific edition.

A bibliography follows the translation. When the form of citation differs from that of the National Union Catalog, the form of the National Union Catalog main entry appears in parentheses. The author's name and the title as they appear in the footnotes correspond to their form in the Bibliography. Montesquieu gallicized names and followed the convention of citing all books by a French title, whether or not the one he used was in French. It is often clear that Montesquieu in fact was referring to a Latin, and sometimes even to an English, original.

Evidence cited by Montesquieu in Latin, Italian, and Old French has been translated; we indicate in brackets the language of the original when it is not French (e.g. [O.F.], [L.]). Translation of the Medieval Latin and Old French presents special problems because the meaning of certain phrases and words remains uncertain. Montesquieu appears to recognize these difficulties, for he leaves certain phrases in the original in the footnote while translating the rest into French, or omits words and phrases when offering a translation in the text of a quotation in a footnote. Since Montesquieu's time much substantial scholarship has grown up around these problems and frequently their interpretation has remained controversial. In our translations we attempt to find a middle ground between intelligibility and the real opaqueness of certain of his citations.

We wish to thank those who have helped us with this project. The work could not have been done without the assistance of the staff of the research collections of the Newberry Library, Regenstein Library of the University of Chicago, the libraries of Northwestern University, and the libraries of Harvard University. Both the Bibliothèque Nationale and the British Library were helpful to visiting strangers. The ARTFL Project at the University of Chicago has provided us with periodic reassurance as to our accuracy. We are especially grateful for the support given Harold Stone by the National Endowment for the Humanities, the Travel to Collections Program of the Division of Research Programs, for work on the project of completing the documentation. We are immensely grateful for the generosity of our friends in Hyde Park, at the University of Chicago, at Shimer College, and Colgate University. They have put their learning at our disposal. Thanks again to Mary Hynes-Berry, Joan Grimbert, and George Anastaplo. Keith Baker and Charles Grey have invited us to their seminars and workshops; they, their students, and colleagues have given us an education in eighteenth-century history. To Keith Baker we are particularly indebted for the encouragement and assistance that has brought this project to a successful conclusion. Our friends and families have been generous enough not to enquire too often when our project would be completed. We, of course, bear the responsibility for the final product.

ANNE M. COHLER
BASIA C. MILLER
HAROLD S. STONE

Abbreviations

Cass. Dio	Cassius Dio Cocceianus
CRF	Capitularia regum Francorum (part of *MGH* series)
CSHB	Corpus scriptorum historiae Byzantinae
Dion. Hal.	Dionysius of Halicarnassus
Ant. Rom.	*Antiquitates Romanae*
FGrH	F. Jacoby, *Fragmenta der greichischen Historiker*
FIRA	S. Riccobono, *Fontes iuris Romani AnteIustiniani*
I.	Italian
L.	Latin
Livy	Livy, *Ab urbe condita*
M.	Montesquieu
MGH	*Monumenta Germaniae historica*
Auct.	*Auctorum antiquissimiorum*
Epp.	*Epistolae Karolini aevi*
LL.	*Leges* (series in folio)
LL. Form.	*Legum sectio V. Formulae*
LL. Nat.	*Legum sectio I. Leges nationum Germanicarum*
SS.	*Scriptores*
SS. Lang.	*Scriptorum rerum Langobardicarum*
SS. Merov.	Scriptores rerum Merovingicarum
NA	Aulus Gellius, *Noctes Atticae*
Migne PG	Migne, Patrologiae Cursus, series Graeca
Migne PL	Migne, Patrologiae Cursus, series Latina
O.F.	Old French
Pol.	*Aristotle*, Politics
Vit.	Plutarch, *Vitae parallelae*

For an explanation of the abbreviations used with *Leges Langobardorum* and Jean Baptiste Du Halde's *Description de l'Empire de la Chine et de la Tartarie Chinoise* consult the entries in the bibliography.

Author's foreword

In order to understand the first four books of this work, one must note that what I call *virtue* in a republic is love of the homeland, that is, love of equality.[a] It is not a moral virtue or a Christian virtue; it is *political* virtue, and this is the spring that makes republican government move, as *honor* is the spring that makes monarchy move. Therefore, I have called love of the homeland and of equality, *political virtue*. I have had new ideas; new words have had to be found or new meanings given to old ones. Those who have not understood this have made me say absurdities that would be outrageous in every country in the world, because in every country in the world morality is desired.

2. It should be observed that there is a very great difference between saying that a certain quality, modification of the soul, or virtue is not the spring that makes a government act and saying that it is not present in that government. If I were to say that a certain wheel, a certain gear, is not the spring that makes this watch move, would one conclude that it is not present in the watch? Far from excluding moral and Christian virtues, monarchy does not even exclude political virtue. In a word, honor is in the republic though political virtue is its spring; political virtue is in the monarchy though honor is its spring.

Finally, the good man discussed in Book 3, chapter 5, is not the Christian good man, but the political good man, who has the political virtue I have mentioned. He is the man who loves the laws of his

In the translators' notes, references such as 3.4 are to books and chapters in *The Spirit of the Laws*.

[a] The Foreword was first printed in the 1757 edition.

country and who acts from love of the laws of his country. I have put all these matters in a new light in the present edition by further specifying the ideas, and in most places where I have used the word *virtue*, I have written *political virtue*.

Preface

If, among the infinite number of things in this book, there is any that, contrary to my expectations[a] might give offense, at least there is none that has been put here with ill intent. By nature, I have not at all a censorious spirit. Plato thanked heaven that he was born in Socrates' time, and as for me, I am grateful that heaven had me born in the government in which I live and that it wanted me to obey those whom it had me love.

I ask a favor that I fear will not be granted; it is that one not judge by a moment's reading the work of twenty years, that one approve or condemn the book as a whole and not some few sentences. If one wants to seek the design of the author, one can find it only in the design of the work.

I began by examining men, and I believed that, amidst the infinite diversity of laws and mores, they were not led by their fancies alone.

I have set down the principles, and I have seen particular cases conform to them as if by themselves, the histories of all nations being but their consequences, and each particular law connecting with another law or dependent on a more general one.

When I turned to antiquity, I sought to capture its spirit in order not to consider as similar those cases with real differences or to overlook differences in those that appear similar.

I did not draw my principles from my prejudices but from the nature of things.

[a] In Montesquieu *espoir* usually implies the concreteness of "expect" more than the wishfulness of "hope," so we have translated it consistently as "expect" and "expectation" rather than "hope" in order to avoid interpreting the standing of the hope or expectation.

Many of the truths will make themselves felt here only when one sees the chain connecting them with others. The more one reflects on the details, the more one will feel the certainty of the principles. As for the details, I have not given them all, for who could say everything without being tedious?

The sallies[b] that seem to characterize present-day works will not be found here. As soon as matters are seen from a certain distance, such sallies vanish; they usually arise only because the mind attaches itself to a single point and forsakes all others.

I do not write to censure that which is established in any country whatsoever. Each nation will find here the reasons for its maxims, and the consequence will naturally be drawn from them that changes can be proposed only by those who are born fortunate enough to fathom by a stroke of genius the whole of a state's constitution.

It is not a matter of indifference that the people be enlightened. The prejudices of magistrates began as the prejudices of the nation. In a time of ignorance, one has no doubts even while doing the greatest evils; in an enlightened age, one trembles even while doing the greatest goods. One feels the old abuses and sees their correction, but one also sees the abuses of the correction itself. One lets an ill remain if one fears something worse; one lets a good remain if one is in doubt about a better. One looks at the parts only in order to judge the whole; one examines all the causes in order to see the results.

If I could make it so that everyone had new reasons for loving his duties, his prince, his homeland and his laws and that each could better feel his happiness in his own country, government, and position, I would consider myself the happiest of mortals.

If I could make it so that those who command increased their knowledge of what they should prescribe and that those who obey found a new pleasure in obeying, I would consider myself the happiest of mortals.

I would consider myself the happiest of mortals if I could make it so that men were able to cure themselves of their prejudices. Here I call prejudices not what makes one unaware of certain things but what makes one unaware of oneself.

By seeking to instruct men one can practice the general virtue that includes love of all. Man, that flexible being who adapts himself in

[b] *traits saillants*. These *traits* are prominent features, as in architecture, not witticisms.

society to the thoughts and impressions of others, is equally capable of knowing his own nature when it is shown to him, and of losing even the feeling of it when it is concealed from him.

Many times I began this work and many times abandoned it; a thousand times I cast to the winds the pages I had written;[1] every day I felt my paternal hands drop;[2] I followed my object without forming a design; I knew neither rules nor exceptions; I found the truth only to lose it. But when I discovered my principles, all that I had sought came to me, and in the course of twenty years, I saw my work begin, grow, move ahead, and end.

If this work meets with success, I shall owe much of it to the majesty of my subject; still, I do not believe that I have totally lacked genius. When I have seen what so many great men in France, England, and Germany have written before me, I have been filled with wonder, but I have not lost courage. "And I too am a painter,"[3] have I said with Correggio.

[1]"A sport to the winds" [L.] [Vergil, *Aeneid* 6.75].
[2]"Twice the paternal hand had fallen" [L.] [Vergil, *Aeneid* 6.33].
[3]"And I too am a painter" [I.]. [An apocryphal remark attributed to Correggio on seeing, in 1515, Raphael's *St. Cecilia*; the story was first published by Sebastiano Resta, a seventeenth-century Italian writer on art.]

SUPPLÉMENT POUR
LA CARTE DU LIVRE
intitulé
DE L'ESPRIT DES LOIX
Par le S. Robert de Vaugondy
Géog. ord. du Roi, de S.M.té Polonoise
Duc de Lorraine et de Bar,
et de l'Acad. R.le des Sc. et B.L. de Nancy.
1756.
Ouest
ECOSSE
Edimbourg
IRLANDE
Dublin
ANGLETERRE
Londre
Pays Bas
Hollande
Bonn
Hanover
DANEMARK
NORWEGE
Normandie
Paris
Rheims
Laon
Beauvais
GAULE
Orleans
Loire R.
Poitiers
Fontevrau
FRANCE
Bourgogne
SUISSES
Lombardie
Verone
Genes
Garonne R.
Bayonne
Narbonne
Monts Pyrenées
Arles
Marseille
Rhone Fl.
Leon
Saragosse
Douro R.
Madrid
Tage R.
Toledo
Valence
Lisbonne
PORTUGAL
Carthagene
Betique
Cadix
Colonnes d'Hercule
Alger
Carthage
Corse
Bastia
Bonifacio
Sardaigne
Cagliari
Palerme
Sicile
Rome
Naples
MER
AFRIQUE
Echelle
Mille pas géometriques de 60 au deg.
100 200 300 400 500 600
Lieues d'une heure de 20 au degré
50 100 150 200
5 10 15 20 25 30
60 55 50 45 40 35
15 20 25 30
Sud

Figure 1

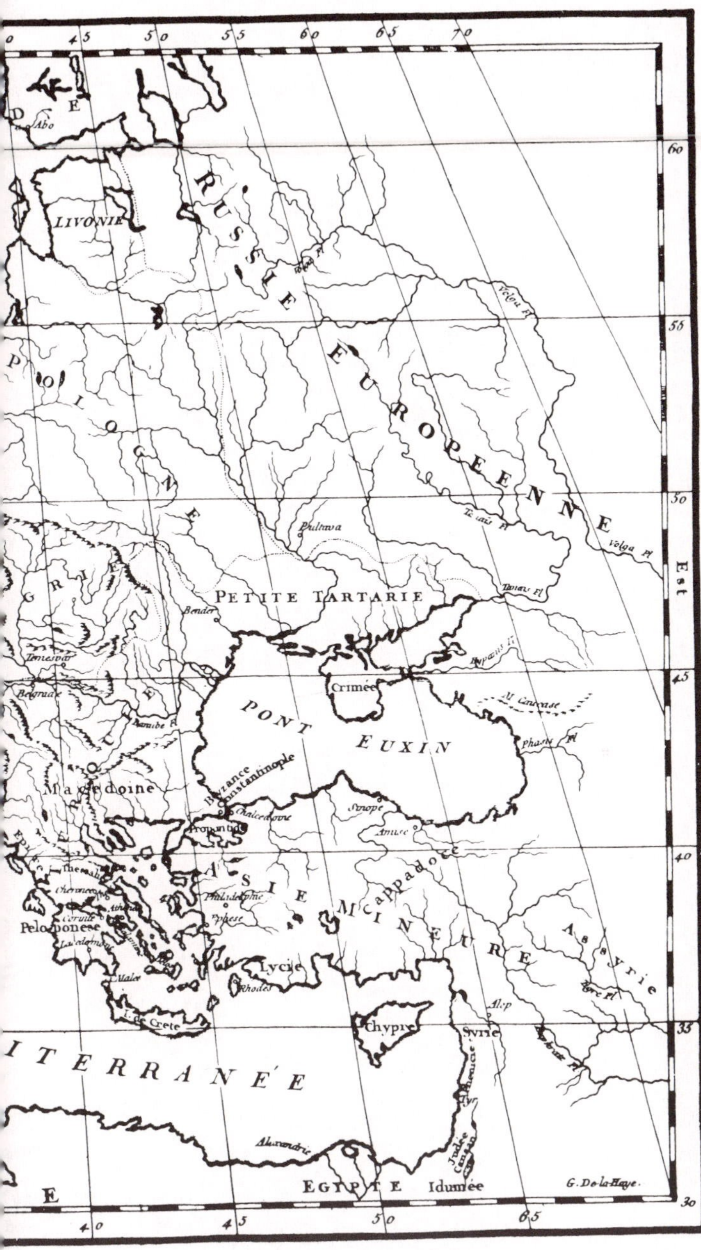
RUSSIE EUROPEENNE
LIVONIE
POLOGNE
PETITE TARTARIE
Crimée
PONT EUXIN
Byzance
Constantinople
Chalcedoine
Propontide
Macedoine
ASIE MINEURE
Cappadoce
Assyrie
Lycie
Rhodes
Chypre
Syrie
Peloponese
I. de Crete
ITERRANÉE
EGYPTE
Idumée
Alexandrie
G. De-la-Haye.
Est

Part 1

BOOK 1
On laws in general

CHAPTER I

On laws in their relation with the various beings

Laws, taken in the broadest meaning, are the necessary relations deriving from the nature of things; and in this sense, all beings have their laws: the divinity[1] has its laws, the material world has its laws, the intelligences superior to man have their laws, the beasts have their laws, man has his laws.

Those who have said that *a blind fate has produced all the effects that we see in the world* have said a great absurdity; for what greater absurdity is there than a blind fate that could have produced intelligent beings?

There is, then, a primitive[a] reason; and laws are both the relations that exist between it and the different beings, and the relations of these various beings to each other.

God is related to the universe, as creator and preserver; the laws according to which he created are those according to which he preserves; he acts according to these rules because he knows them; he knows them because he made them; he made them because they are related to his wisdom[b] and his power.

As we see that the world, formed by the motion of matter and devoid of intelligence, still continues to exist, its motions must have invariable laws; and, if one could imagine another world than this, it would have consistent[c] rules or it would be destroyed.

[1] "The law," Plutarch says in [*Moralia*] *Ad principem ineruditum* [780c], "is the queen of all, mortal and immortal." [Plutarch is quoting Pindar, fragment 169 (151).]

---

[a] We have rendered Montesquieu's *primitive* as "primitive," thus retaining the distinction between that term and *premier*, "first," which is used repeatedly in 1.2.

[b] We have translated *sage* and its various forms with "wise" and its various forms. The meaning is generally prudence, calm, sobriety.

[c] Montesquieu uses *constant*, *constamment*, and *constance* to refer both to a fixed rule and

Thus creation, which appears to be an arbitrary act, presupposes rules as invariable as the fate claimed by atheists. It would be absurd to say that the creator, without these rules, could govern the world, since the world would not continue to exist without them.

These rules are a consistently established relation. Between one moving body and another moving body, it is in accord with relations of mass and velocity that all motions are received, increased, diminished, or lost; every diversity is *uniformity*, every change is *consistency*.[d]

Particular intelligent beings can have laws that they have made, but they also have some that they have not made. Before there were intelligent beings, they were possible; therefore, they had possible relations and consequently possible laws. Before laws were made, there were possible relations of justice.[e] To say that there is nothing just or unjust but what positive laws ordain or prohibit is to say that before a circle was drawn, all its radii were not equal.

Therefore, one must admit that there are relations of fairness[f] prior to the positive law that establishes them, so that, for example, assuming that there were societies of men, it would be just to conform to their laws; so that, if there were intelligent beings that had received some kindness from another being, they ought to be grateful for it;[g] so that, if one intelligent being had created another intelligent being, the created one ought to remain in its original dependency; so that one intelligent being who has done harm to another intelligent being deserves the same harm in return, and so forth.

But the intelligent world is far from being as well governed as the physical world. For, though the intelligent world also has laws that are invariable by their nature, unlike the physical world, it does not follow its laws consistently. The reason for this is that particular intelligent beings are limited by their nature and are consequently subject to error; furthermore, it is in their nature to act by themselves. Therefore, they

to multiple actions that conform to the rule. We have chosen to translate them by "consistent" and "consistency," which have both of these implications.

[d] Here translating *constance* as "consistency" conveys the meaning of changing according to a rule, as "constancy" with its static implication would not. See note [b], above.

[e] Here Montesquieu takes advantage of the range of meaning of the French *juste*, which includes both the notion of "correct" and that of "just." It leads him to the arithmetic notion of justice in the next paragraph.

[f] *Equité* is translated throughout as "fairness," because it implies a much wider sphere than the English term "equity" with its almost exclusively legal implications. Here Montesquieu's *équité* reminds the reader of the *égal*, "equal," at the end of the preceding sentence and of the arithmetic relation.

[g] *avoir de la reconnaissance*, See 31.33 (note [q], bk. 31).

do not consistently follow their primitive laws or even always follow the laws they give themselves.

It is not known whether beasts are governed by the general laws of motion or by a movement particular to themselves. Be that as it may, they do not have a more intimate relation with god[h] than the rest of the material world has, and feeling is useful to them only in their relation to one another, either with other particular beings, or with themselves.[i]

By the attraction of pleasure they preserve their particular being; by the same attraction they preserve their species. They have natural laws because they are united by feeling; they have no positive laws because they are not united by knowledge. Still, they do not invariably follow their natural laws; plants, in which we observe neither knowledge nor feeling, better follow their natural laws.

Beasts do not have the supreme advantages that we have; they have some that we do not have. They do not have our expectations,[j] but they do not have our fears; they suffer death as we do, but without recognizing it; most even preserve themselves better than we do and do not make such bad use of their passions.

Man, as a physical being, is governed by invariable laws like other bodies. As an intelligent being, he constantly violates the laws god has established and changes those he himself establishes; he must guide himself, and yet he is a limited being; he is subject to ignorance and error, as are all finite intelligences; he loses even the imperfect knowledge he has. As a feeling creature, he falls subject to a thousand passions. Such a being could at any moment forget his creator; god has called him back to him by the laws of religion. Such a being could at any moment forget himself; philosophers have reminded him of himself by the laws of morality. Made for living in society, he could forget his fellows; legislators have returned him to his duties by political and civil laws.

[h] Montesquieu never capitalizes *dieu*, "god."

[i] *dans le rapport qu'elles ont entre elles, ou avec d'autres êtres particuliers, ou avec elles-mêmes.* The middle term was added after 1748. This addition suggests that the meaning is that relations among animals may be either with members of other species or with other members of their own species.

[j] Whether men's having purposes beyond those of the animals leads to hopes or expectations is, of course, not clear from the French. (See note [a] in Preface.)

CHAPTER 2

On the laws of nature

Prior to all these laws are the laws of nature, so named because they derive uniquely from the constitution of our being. To know them well, one must consider a man before the establishment of societies. The laws he would receive in such a state will be the laws of nature.

The law that impresses on us the idea of a creator and thereby leads us toward him is the first of the *natural laws* in importance, though not first in the order of these laws. A man in the state of nature would have the faculty of knowing rather than knowledge. It is clear that his first ideas would not be speculative ones; he would think of the preservation of his being before seeking the origin of his being. Such a man would at first feel only his weakness; his timidity would be extreme: and as for evidence, if it is needed on this point, savages have been found in forests;[2] everything makes them tremble, everything makes them flee.

In this state, each feels himself inferior; he scarcely feels himself an equal. Such men would not seek to attack one another, and peace would be the first natural law.

Hobbes gives men first the desire to subjugate one another, but this is not reasonable. The idea of empire and domination is so complex and depends on so many other ideas, that it would not be the one they would first have.

Hobbes asks, *If men are not naturally in a state of war, why do they always carry arms and why do they have keys to lock their doors?*[k] But one feels that what can happen to men only after the establishment of societies, which induced them to find motives for attacking others and for defending themselves, is attributed to them before that establishment.

Man would add the feeling of his needs to the feeling of his weakness. Thus another natural law would be the one inspiring him to seek nourishment.

I have said that fear would lead men to flee one another, but the marks of mutual fear would soon persuade them to approach one

[2] Witness the savage who was found in the forests of Hanover and who lived in England in the reign of George I.

[k] See Thomas Hobbes, *Leviathan*, bk. I, chap. 13.

another. They would also be so inclined by the pleasure one animal feels at the approach of an animal of its own kind. In addition, the charm that the two sexes inspire in each other by their difference would increase this pleasure, and the natural entreaty[l] they always make to one another would be a third law.

Besides feelings, which belong to men from the outset, they also succeed in gaining knowledge; thus they have a second bond, which other animals do not have. Therefore, they have another motive for uniting, and the desire to live in society is a fourth natural law.

[l] *prière.*

CHAPTER 3

On positive laws

As soon as men are in society, they lose their feeling of weakness; the equality that was among them ceases, and the state of war begins.

Each particular society comes to feel its strength, producing a state of war among nations. The individuals within each society begin to feel their strength; they seek to turn their favor the principal advantages of this society, which brings about a state of war among them.

These two sorts of states of war bring about the establishment of laws among men. Considered as inhabitants of a planet so large that different peoples are necessary, they have laws bearing on the relation that these peoples have with one another, and this is the RIGHT OF NATIONS.[m] Considered as living in a society that must be maintained, they have laws concerning the relation between those who govern and those who are governed, and this is the POLITICAL RIGHT.[n] Further, they have laws concerning the relation that all citizens have with one another, and this is the CIVIL RIGHT.

The *right of nations* is by nature founded on the principle that the various nations should do to one another in times of peace the most good possible, and in times of war the least ill possible, without harming their true interests.

[m] *le droit des gens* is translated "right of nations" throughout.

[n] We have translated *droit* as "right" and *loi* as "law." Although the French *droit* is usually closer to the meaning of "law" in English, we have kept Montesquieu's usage so that his distinction and his version of the changes in meaning would not be obscured.

The object of war is victory; of victory, conquest; of conquest, preservation. All the laws that form the *right of nations* should derive from this principle and the preceding one.

All nations have a right of nations; and even the Iroquois, who eat their prisoners, have one. They send and receive embassies; they know rights of war and peace: the trouble is that their right of nations is not founded on true principles.

In addition to the right of nations, which concerns all societies, there is a *political right* for each one. A society could not continue to exist without a government. "*The union of all individual strengths*," as Gravina aptly says, "forms what is called the POLITICAL STATE."[o]

The strength of the whole society may be put in the hands of *one alone* or in the hands of *many*.[p] Since nature has established paternal power, some have thought that government by one alone is most in conformity with nature. But the example of paternal power proves nothing. For, if the power of the father is related to government by one alone, then after the death of the father, the power of the brothers, or after the death of the brothers, the power of the first cousins, is related to government by many. Political power necessarily includes the union of many families.

It is better to say that the government most in conformity with nature is the one whose particular arrangement best relates to the disposition of the people for whom it is established.[q]

Individual strengths cannot be united unless all wills are united. *The union of these wills*, as Gravina again aptly says, *is what is called the* CIVIL STATE.[r]

Law in general is human reason insofar as it governs all the peoples of the earth; and the political and civil laws of each nation should be only the particular cases to which human reason is applied.

Laws should be so appropriate to the people for whom they are made that it is very unlikely that the laws of one nation can suit another.

Laws must relate to the nature and the principle of the government that is established or that one wants to establish, whether those laws form it as do political laws, or maintain it, as do civil laws.

[o] Giovanni Vincenzo Gravina, *Origine Romani juris* (1739), bk. 2, chap. 18, p. 160.

[p] The eighteenth-century meaning of *plusieurs* was "many." The opposition is between "one" and "many," as between monarchies or despotisms and republics in Book 2.

[q] *Il vaut mieux dire que le gouvernement le plus conforme à la nature est celui dont la disposition particulière se rapporte mieux à la disposition du peuple pour lequel il est établi.* No English word covers all the disparate topics Montesquieu joins with the word *disposition*.

[r] Giovanni Vincenzo Gravina, *Origine Romani juris* (1739), bk. 3, chap. 7, footnote, p. 311.

They should be related to the *physical aspect* of the country; to the climate, be it freezing, torrid, or temperate; to the properties of the terrain, its location and extent; to the way of life of the peoples, be they plowmen, hunters, or herdsmen; they should relate to the degree of liberty that the constitution can sustain, to the religion of the inhabitants, their inclinations, their wealth, their number, their commerce, their mores and their manners; finally, the laws are related to one another, to their origin, to the purpose of the legislator, and to the order of things on which they are established. They must be considered from all these points of view.

This is what I undertake to do in this work. I shall examine all these relations; together they form what is called THE SPIRIT OF THE LAWS.[5]

I have made no attempt to separate *political* from *civil* laws, for, as I do not treat laws but the spirit of the laws, and as this spirit consists in the various relations that laws may have with various things, I have had to follow the natural order of laws less than that of these relations and of these things.

I shall first examine the relations that laws have with the nature and the principle of each government, and, as this principle has a supreme influence on the laws, I shall apply myself to understanding it well; and if I can once establish it, the laws will be seen to flow from it as from their source. I shall then proceed to other relations that seem to be more particular.

[5] L'ESPRIT DES LOIX. Whenver possible, we translate *esprit* as "spirit," but "mind" and "wit" also appear.

BOOK 2

On laws deriving directly from the nature of the government

CHAPTER I

On the nature of the three varieties of governments

There are three kinds of government: REPUBLICAN, MONARCHICAL, and DESPOTIC. To discover the nature of each, the idea of them held by the least educated of men is sufficient. I assume three definitions, or rather, three facts: one, *republican government is that in which the people as a body, or only a part of the people, have sovereign power; monarchical government is that in which one alone governs, but by fixed and established laws; whereas, in despotic government, one alone, without law and without rule, draws everything along by his will and his caprices.*

That is what I call the nature of each government. One must see what laws follow directly from this nature and are consequently the first fundamental laws.

CHAPTER 2

On republican government and on laws relative to democracy

In a republic when the people as a body have sovereign power, it is a *democracy*. When the sovereign power is in the hands of a part of the people, it is called an *aristocracy*.

In a democracy the people are, in certain respects, the monarch; in other respects, they are the subjects.

They can be the monarch only through their votes which are their wills. The sovereign's will is the sovereign himself. Therefore, the laws establishing the right to vote are fundamental in this government. Indeed, it is as important in this case to regulate how, by whom, for whom, and on what issues votes should be cast, as it is in a monarchy to know the monarch and how he should govern.

Libanius[1] says that *in Athens a foreigner who mingled in the people's assembly was punished with death*. This is because such a man usurped the right of sovereignty.

It is essential to determine the number of citizens that should form assemblies; unless this is done it cannot be known if the people have spoken or only a part of the people. In Lacedaemonia, there had to be 10,000 citizens. In Rome, which started small and became great, Rome, made to endure all the vicissitudes of fortune, Rome, which sometimes had nearly all its citizens outside its walls and sometimes all Italy and a part of the world within them, the number was not determined;[2] this was one of the great causes of its ruin.

A people having sovereign power should do for itself all it can do well, and what it cannot do well, it must do through its ministers.

Ministers do not belong to the people unless the people name them; therefore it is a fundamental maxim of this government that the people should name their ministers, that is, their magistrates.

The people, like monarchs and even more than monarchs, need to be guided by a council or senate. But in order for the people to trust it, they must elect its members, either choosing the members themselves, as in Athens, or establishing some magistrate to elect them as was occasionally the practice in Rome.

The people are admirable for choosing those to whom they should entrust some part of their authority. They have only to base their decisions on things of which they cannot be unaware and on facts that are evident to the senses. They know very well that a man has often been to war, that he has had such and such successes; they are, then, quite capable of electing a general. They know that a judge is assiduous, that many people leave the tribunal[a] satisfied with him, and

[1] [Libanius] *Declamations* 17 [*Hyperides oratio* 18.5–6] and 18 [*Strategi apologia* 44.15].

[2] See [M.'s] *Considerations on the Causes of the Greatness of the Romans and their Decline*, chap. 9, Paris, 1755 [chap. 9, p. 92; 1965 Eng. edn.].

[a] For *tribunal* we use "tribunal," and for *cour*, "court"; by keeping this distinction, we make the history of the development of tribunals as separate from the court of some king or nobleman easier to follow.

that he has not been convicted of corruption; this is enough for them to elect a praetor.[b] They have been struck by the magnificence or wealth of a citizen; that is enough for them to be able to choose an aedile. All these things are facts that they learn better in a public square than a monarch does in his palace. But will the people know how to conduct the public business,[c] will they know the places, the occasions, the moments, and profit from them? No, they will not.

If one were to doubt the people's natural ability to perceive merit, one would have only to cast an eye over that continuous series of astonishing choices made by the Athenians and the Romans; this will doubtless not be ascribed to chance.

It is known that in Rome, though the people had given themselves the right to elevate plebeians to posts, they could not bring themselves to elect them; and in Athens, although, according to the law of Aristides, magistrates could be drawn from any class, Xenophon[3] says that it never happened that the common people turned to those classes that could threaten their well-being or glory.

Just as most citizens, who are competent enough to elect, are not competent enough to be elected, so the people, who are sufficiently capable to call others to account for their management, are not suited to manage by themselves.

Public business must proceed, and proceed at a pace that is neither too slow nor too fast. But the people always act too much or too little. Sometimes with a hundred thousand arms they upset everything; sometimes with a hundred thousand feet they move only like insects.

In the popular state, the people are divided into certain classes. Great legislators have distinguished themselves by the way they have made this division, and upon it the duration and prosperity of democracies have always depended.

Servius Tullius followed the spirit of aristocracy in the composition of his classes. In Livy[4] and Dionysius of Halicarnassus[5], we see how he

[3] [Xenophon, "The Old Oligarch," *The Constitution of Athens*] pp. 691, 692, Wechelius edition of 1596 [1.3].
[4] [Livy] bk. 1 [1.43].
[5] [Dion. Hal., *Ant. Rom.*] bk. 4, arts. 15ff. [4.15–21].

[b] See 11.14 (p. 173) for Montesquieu's explanation of the Roman magistracies.
[c] Montesquieu uses *affaire* to refer to law-suits, translated "suits"; to issues before legislative bodies or sovereigns, translated "public business"; and to commercial transactions, translated "business."

put the right to vote into the hands of the principal citizens. He divided the people of Rome into one hundred and ninety-three centuries, forming six classes. He put the rich men, but in smaller numbers, into the first centuries; he put the less rich, but in larger numbers, into the following ones; he put the entire throng of the poor into the last century; and, since each century had only one voice,[6] it was means and wealth that had the vote rather than persons.

Solon divided the people of Athens into four classes. Guided by the spirit of democracy, he made these classes in order to specify not those who were to elect but those who could be elected; and leaving to the citizens the right to elect, he wanted them[7] to be able to elect judges from each of those four classes but magistrates from the first three only, where the well-to-do citizens were found.

Just as the division of those having the right to vote is a fundamental law in the republic, the way of casting the vote is another fundamental law.

Voting by *lot* is in the nature of democracy; voting by *choice* is in the nature of aristocracy.

The casting of lots is a way of electing that distresses no one; it leaves to each citizen a reasonable expectation of serving his country.

But as it is imperfect by itself, the great legislators have outdone each other in regulating and correcting it.

In Athens, Solon established that all military posts would be filled by choice but that senators and judges would be elected by lot.

He wanted the civil magistrates that required great expenditures to be given by choice and the others to be given by lot.

But in order to correct the vote by lot, he ruled that one could elect only from the number of those who presented themselves, that he who had been elected would be examined by judges,[8] and that each judge could accuse him of being unworthy;[9] this derived from both lot and

[6] See [M.'s] *Considerations on the Causes of the Greatness of the Romans and Their Decline*, chap. 9, for how the spirit of Servius Tullius was preserved in the republic [chap. 8, pp. 86–87; 1965 Eng. edn.].

[7] Dion. Hal. [*De antiquis oratoribus*], "Isocrates," vol. 2, p. 97, Wechelius edition [Isocrates 8]. [Julius] Pollux [*Onomasticon*], bk. 8, chap. 10, art. 130 [8.10.130. Pollux does not mention election, only class divisions in accord with property evaluations and the tax to be paid. See below, bk. 13, n. 4].

[8] See Demosthenes, *Orationes*, *De falsa legatione* [19.1–8] and *Against Timocrates* [24.21–22].

[9] Two tickets were even drawn for each place, one assigning the place and the other naming the person who was to succeed to it in case the first was rejected.

choice. On completing his term, the magistrate had to go through a second judgment regarding the way in which he had conducted himself. People without ability must have been very reluctant to offer their names to be drawn by lot.

The law that determines the way ballots are cast is another fundamental law in democracy. Whether the votes should be public or secret is a great question. Cicero[10] writes that the laws[11] that made them secret in the late period of the Roman republic were one of the major causes of its fall. Given that this practice varies in different republics, here, I believe, is what must be thought about it.

When the people cast votes, their votes should no doubt be public;[12] and this should be regarded as a fundamental law of democracy. The lesser people must be enlightened by the principal people and subdued by the gravity of certain eminent men. Thus in the Roman republic all was destroyed by making the votes secret; it was no longer possible to enlighten a populace on its way to ruin. But votes cannot be too secret in an aristocracy when the body of nobles casts the votes,[13] or in a democracy when the senate does so,[14] for here the only issue is to guard against intrigues.

Intrigue is dangerous in a senate; it is dangerous in a body of nobles; it is not dangerous in the people, whose nature is to act from passion. In states where the people have no part in the government, they become as inflamed for an actor as they would for public affairs. The misfortune of a republic is to be without intrigues, and this happens when the people have been corrupted by silver; they become cool, they grow fond of silver, and they are no longer fond of public affairs; without concern for the government or for what is proposed there, they quietly await their payments.

Yet another fundamental law in democracy is that the people alone should make laws. However, there are a thousand occasions when it is necessary for the senate to be able to enact laws; it is often even

[10] [Cicero] *De legibus*, bks. 1 and 3 [e.g., 3.15.33–3.17.40].

[11] They were called ballotting laws. Each citizen was given two ballots, the first marked with an A, for *Antiquo* [to reject or to leave something in its former condition]; the other with U and R, for *uti rogas* [to ask for an opinion or vote]. [Refers to Cicero, *De legibus* 3.34.37.]

[12] In Athens, hands were raised.

[13] As in Venice.

[14] The thirty tyrants of Athens wanted the votes of the Areopagus to be public in order to direct them according to their fancy. Lysias, *Orationes*, *Against Agoratus*, chap. 8 [13.37].

appropriate to test a law before establishing it. The constitutions of Rome and Athens were very wise. The decrees of the senate[15] had the force of law for a year; they became permanent only by the will of the people.

[15]See Dion. Hal. [*Ant. Rom.*], bk. 4 [4.80.2 and 4.74.2] and bk. 9 [9.37.2].

CHAPTER 3

On laws relative to the nature of aristocracy

In aristocracy, sovereign power is in the hands of a certain number of persons. They make the laws and see to their execution, and the rest of the people mean at best no more to these persons than the subjects in a monarchy mean to the monarch.

Voting should not be by lot; this would have only drawbacks. Indeed, in a government that has already established the most grievous distinctions, though a man might be chosen by lot, he would be no less odious for it; the noble is envied, not the magistrate.

When there are many nobles, there must be a senate to rule on the affairs that the body of nobles cannot decide and to take the preliminary steps for those on which it decides. In the latter case, it may be said that aristocracy is, in a way, in the senate, that democracy is in the body of nobles, and that the people are nothing.

It is a very fine thing in an aristocracy for the people to be raised from their nothingness in some indirect way; thus, in Genoa, the Bank of St George, administered largely by the principal men among the people,[16] gives the people a certain influence in government, which brings about their whole prosperity.

Senators should not have the right to fill vacancies in the senate; nothing would be more likely to perpetuate abuses. In Rome, which was a kind of aristocracy in its early days, the senate did not name replacements; new senators were named by the censors.[17]

When an exorbitant authority is given suddenly to a citizen in a

[16][Joseph] Addison, *Remarks on Several Parts of Italy in the Years 1701, 1702, 1703*, p. 16 [2, 24–25; 1914 edn.].

[17]At first they were named by the consuls.

republic, this forms[d] a monarchy or more than a monarchy. In monarchies, the laws have protected the constitution or have been adapted to it; the principle of the government checks the monarch; but in a republic when a citizen takes exorbitant power,[18] the abuse of this power is greater because the laws, which have not foreseen it, have done nothing to check it.

The exception to this rule occurs when the constitution of the state is such that it needs a magistracy with exorbitant power. Such was Rome with its dictators, such is Venice with its state inquisitors; these are terrible magistracies which violently return the state to liberty. But how does it happen that the magistracies are so different in these two republics? It is because, whereas Venice uses its state inquisitors to maintain its aristocracy against the nobles, Rome was defending the remnants of its aristocracy against the people. From this it followed that the dictator in Rome was installed for only a short time because the people act from impetuosity and not from design. His magistracy was exercised with brilliance, as the issue was to intimidate, not to punish, the people; the dictator was created for but a single affair and had unlimited authority with regard to that affair alone because he was always created for unforeseen cases. In Venice, however, there must be a permanent magistracy: here designs can be laid, followed, suspended, and taken up again; here too, the ambition of one alone becomes that of a family, and the ambition of one family, that of several. A hidden magistracy is needed because the crimes it punishes, always deep-seated, are formed in secrecy and silence. The inquisition of this magistracy has to be general because its aim is not to check known evils but to curb unknown ones. Finally, the Venetian magistracy is established to avenge the crimes it suspects, whereas the Roman magistracy used threats more than punishments, even for those crimes admitted by their instigators.

In every magistracy, the greatness of the power must be offset by the brevity of its duration. Most legislators have fixed the time at a year; a longer term would be dangerous, a shorter one would be contrary to the nature of the thing. Who would want thus to govern his domestic

[18] This is what caused the overthrow of the Roman republic. See the *Considerations on the Causes of the Greatness of the Romans and their Decline*, Paris, 1755 [chap. 11, pp. 107–108; 1965 Eng. edn.].

[d] Montesquieu often uses the verb *former* in the old sense of establishing by giving shape.

affairs? In Ragusa,[19] the head of the republic changes every month; the other officers, every week; the governor of the castle, every day. This can take place only in a small republic[20] surrounded by formidable powers which could easily corrupt petty magistrates.

The best aristocracy is one in which the part of the people having no share in the power is so small and so poor that the dominant part has no interest in oppressing it. Thus in Athens when Antipater[21] established that those with less than two thousand drachmas would be excluded from the right to vote, he formed the best possible aristocracy, because this census[e] was so low that it excluded only a few people and no one of any consequence in the city.

Therefore, aristocratic families should be of the people as far as possible. The more an aristocracy approaches democracy, the more perfect it will be, and to the degree it approaches monarchy the less perfect it will become.

Most imperfect of all is the aristocracy in which the part of the people that obeys is in civil slavery to the part that commands, as in the Polish aristocracy, where the peasants are slaves of the nobility.

[19] [Joseph Pitton] Tournefort, *Relation d'un voyage du Levant*. [Not in Tournefort; he did not write about Ragusa. A probable source is Louis Des Hayes Courmenin, *Voiage de Levant*, pp. 480, 484, 485; 1632 edn.].
[20] In Lucca, the magistrates are established for only two months.
[21] Diodorus Siculus [*Bibliotheca historica*], bk. 18, p. 601, Rhodoman edition [18.18.4].

[e] See 13.7 (p. 216) for a further discussion of the Athenian census.

CHAPTER 4

On laws in their relation to the nature of monarchical government[f]

Intermediate, subordinate, and dependent powers constitute the nature of monarchical government, that is, of the government in which one alone governs by fundamental laws. I have said intermediate, subordinate, and dependent powers; indeed, in a monarchy, the prince is the source of all political and civil power. These fundamental laws

[f] The awkwardness of some of the sentences and paragraphs in this chapter reflects the difficulties inherent in asserting, in the middle of the eighteenth century in France, that intermediate powers, however understood, were intrinsic to monarchy.

necessarily assume mediate channels through which power flows; for, if in the state there is only the momentary and capricious will of one alone, nothing can be fixed and consequently there is no fundamental law.

The most natural intermediate, subordinate power is that of the nobility. In a way, the nobility is of the essence of monarchy, whose fundamental maxim is: *no monarch, no nobility: no nobility, no monarch*; rather, one has a despot.

In a few European states, some people had imagined abolishing all the justices of the lords.[g] They did not see that they wanted to do what the Parliament of England did. If you abolish the prerogatives of the lords, clergy, nobility, and towns in a monarchy, you will soon have a popular state or else a despotic state.

For several centuries the tribunals of a great European state have been constantly striking down the patrimonial jurisdiction of the lords and the ecclesiastical jurisdiction. We do not want to censure such wise magistrates, but we leave it to be decided to what extent the constitution can be changed in this way.

I do not insist on the privileges of the ecclesiastics, but I would like their jurisdiction to be determined once and for all. It is a question of knowing not if one was right in establishing it but rather if it is established, if it is a part of the country's laws, and if it is relative to them throughout; if between two powers recognized as independent, conditions should not be reciprocal; and if it is not all the same to a good subject to defend the prince's justice or the limits that his justice has always prescribed for itself.

To the extent that the power of the clergy is dangerous in republics, it is suitable in monarchies, especially in those tending to despotism. Where would Spain and Portugal have been, after the loss of their laws, without the power that alone checks arbitrary power? Ever a good barrier when no other exists, because, as despotism causes appalling ills to human nature, the very ill that limits it is a good.

Just as the sea, which seems to want to cover the whole earth, is checked by the grasses and the smallest bits of gravel on the shore, so monarchs, whose power seems boundless, are checked by the slightest obstacles and submit their natural pride to supplication and prayer.

In order to favor liberty, the English have removed all the intermedi-

[g]In French *justice* denotes both the abstract notion and the institution which judges. See 30.20 and note [bb] for Montesquieu's account of the justices of the lords.

ate powers that formed their monarchy. They are quite right to preserve that liberty; if they were to lose it, they would be one of the most enslaved peoples on earth.

Mr. Law, equally ignorant of the republican and of the monarchical constitutions, was one of the greatest promoters of despotism that had until then been seen in Europe.[h] Besides the changes he made, which were so abrupt, so unusual, and so unheard of, he wanted to remove the intermediate ranks and abolish the political bodies;[i] he was dissolving[22] the monarchy by his chimerical repayments and seemed to want to buy back the constitution itself.

It is not enough to have intermediate ranks in a monarchy; there must also be a depository of laws.[j] This depository can only be in the political bodies, which announce the laws when they are made and recall them when they are forgotten. The ignorance natural to the nobility, its laxity, and its scorn for civil government require a body that constantly brings the laws out of the dust in which they would be buried. The prince's council is not a suitable depository. By its nature it is the depository of the momentary will of the prince who executes, and not the depository of the fundamental laws. Moreover, the monarch's council constantly changes; it is not permanent; it cannot be large; it does not sufficiently have the people's trust: therefore, it is not in a position to enlighten them in difficult times or to return them to obedience.

In despotic states, where there are no fundamental laws, neither is there a depository of laws. This is why religion has so much force in these countries; it forms a kind of permanent depository, and if it is not religion, it is customs that are venerated in the place of laws.

[22] Ferdinand, King of Aragon, made himself Grand Master of the Orders, and that alone spoiled the constitution.

---

[h] John Law (1671–1729). See 22.10 and note [e] for Montesquieu's account of Law's System.

[i] *corps politiques*, "political bodies," refers to political entities, including the *parlements*.

[j] The laws were in effect kept, held, by an entity whose responsibility was both to preserve and to use and interpret them. In English we retain something of this meaning in the term "deposition," or sworn evidence taken outside the court for later submission to the court. See 28.45 and note [v] for Montesquieu's explanation of the depository of the laws.

CHAPTER 5

On laws relative to the nature of the despotic state

A result of the nature of despotic power is that the one man who exercises it has it likewise exercised by another. A man whose five senses constantly tell him that he is everything and that others are nothing is naturally lazy, ignorant, and voluptuous. Therefore, he abandons the public business. But, if he entrusted this business to many people, there would be disputes among them; there would be intrigues to be the first slave; the prince would be obliged to return to administration. Therefore it is simpler for him to abandon them to a vizir[23] who will instantly have the same power as he. In this state, the establishment of a vizir is a fundamental law.

It is said that a certain pope, upon his election, overcome with his inadequacy, at first made infinite difficulties. Finally, he agreed to turn all matters of business over to his nephew. He was awestruck and said, "I would never have believed that it could be so easy." It is the same for the princes of the East. When, from that prison where eunuchs have weakened their hearts and spirits and have often left them ignorant even of their estate, these princes are withdrawn to be put on the throne, they are stunned at first; but when they have appointed a vizir, when in their seraglio they have given themselves up to the most brutal passions, when in the midst of a downtrodden court they have followed their most foolish caprices, they would never have believed that it could be so easy.

The more extensive the empire, the larger the seraglio, and the more, consequently, the prince is drunk with pleasures. Thus, in these states, the more peoples the prince has to govern, the less he thinks about government; the greater the matters of business, the less deliberation they are given.

[23] Eastern kings always have vizirs, says [John] Chardin [*Voyages*, "Description du gouvernement"; chap. 5, "Des charges"; 5, 339–340; 1811 edn.].

BOOK 3
On the principles of the three governments

CHAPTER I
The difference between the nature of the government and its principle

After having examined the laws relative to the nature of each government, one must look at those that are relative to its principle.

There is this difference[1] between the nature of the government and its principle: its nature is that which makes it what it is, and its principle, that which makes it act. The one is its particular structure, and the other is the human passions that set it in motion.

Now, the laws should be no less relative to the principle of each government than to its nature. Therefore, this principle must be sought. I shall do so in this book.

[1] This difference is very important, and I shall draw many consequences from it; it is the key to an infinity of laws.

CHAPTER 2
On the principle of the various governments

I have said that the nature of republican government is that the people as a body, or certain families, have the sovereign power; the nature of monarchical government is that the prince has the sovereign power, but that he exercises it according to established laws; the nature of despotic government is that one alone governs according to his wills and caprices. Nothing more is needed for me to find their three principles; they derive naturally from this. I shall begin with republican government, and I shall first speak of the democratic government.

CHAPTER 3

On the principle of democracy

There need not be much integrity for a monarchical or despotic government to maintain or sustain itself. The force of the laws in the one and the prince's ever-raised arm in the other can rule or contain the whole. But in a popular state there must be an additional spring, which is VIRTUE.

What I say is confirmed by the entire body of history and is quite in conformity with the nature of things. For it is clear that less virtue is needed in a monarchy, where the one who sees to the execution of the laws judges himself above the laws, than in a popular government, where the one who sees to the execution of the laws feels that he is subject to them himself and that he will bear their weight.

It is also clear that the monarch who ceases to see to the execution of the laws, through bad counsel or negligence, may easily repair the damage; he has only to change his counsel or correct his own negligence. But in a popular government when the laws have ceased to be executed, as this can come only from the corruption of the republic, the state is already lost.

It was a fine spectacle in the last century to see the impotent attempts of the English to establish democracy among themselves. As those who took part in public affairs had no virtue at all, as their ambition was excited by the success of the most audacious one[2] and the spirit of one faction was repressed only by the spirit of another, the government was constantly changing; the people, stunned, sought democracy and found it nowhere. Finally, after much motion and many shocks and jolts, they had to come to rest on the very government that had been proscribed.

When Sulla wanted to return liberty to Rome, it could no longer be accepted; Rome had but a weak remnant of virtue, and as it had ever less, instead of reawakening after Caeser, Tiberius, Caius,[a] Claudius, Nero, and Domitian, it became ever more enslaved; all the blows were struck against tyrants, none against tyranny.

The political men of Greece who lived under popular government recognized no other force to sustain it than virtue. Those of today speak

[2] Cromwell.

---

[a] Caligula.

to us only of manufacturing, commerce, finance,[b] wealth, and even luxury.

When that virtue ceases, ambition enters those hearts that can admit it, and avarice enters them all. Desires change their objects: that which one used to love, one loves no longer. One was free under the laws, one wants to be free against them. Each citizen is like a slave who has escaped from his master's house. What was a *maxim* is now called *severity*; what was a *rule* is now called *constraint*;[c] what was *vigilance* is now called *fear*. There, frugality, not the desire to possess, is avarice. Formerly the goods of individuals made up the public treasury; the public treasury has now become the patrimony of individuals. The republic is a cast-off husk, and its strength is no more than the power of a few citizens and the license of all.

There were the same forces in Athens when it dominated with so much glory and when it served with so much shame. It had 20,000 citizens[3] when it defended the Greeks against the Persians, when it disputed for empire with Lacedaemonia, and when it attacked Sicily. It had 20,000 when Demetrius of Phalereus enumerated them[4] as one counts slaves in a market. When Philip dared dominate in Greece, when he appeared at the gates of Athens,[5] Athens had as yet lost only time. In Demosthenes one may see how much trouble was required to reawaken it; Philip was feared as the enemy not of liberty but of pleasures.[6] This town, which had resisted in spite of so many defeats, which had been reborn after its destructions, was defeated at Chaeronea and was defeated forever. What does it matter that Philip returns all the prisoners? He does not return men. It was always as easy to triumph over the forces of Athens as it was difficult to triumph over its virtue.

How could Carthage have sustained itself? When Hannibal, as praetor, wanted to keep the magistrates from pillaging the republic, did

[3] Plutarch [*Vit.*], *Pericles* [37.4]; Plato, *Critias* [112d].

[4] There were 21,000 citizens, 10,000 resident aliens, and 400,000 slaves. See Athenaeus [Naucratia] [*Deipnosophistae*], bk. 6 [272c].

[5] It had 20,000 citizens. See Demosthenes, [*Orationes*] *Against Aristogeiton* [25.51].

[6] They had passed a law to punish by death anyone who might propose that the silver destined for the theatres be converted to the uses of war.

[b] *Finance*, "finance," refers to both the debts and the receipts of the state; "finance" is linked with "fisc." See note [h], bk. 30.

[c] The meaning of *gêne* goes as far as "torture," but "constraint" gets at the central meaning of something imposed from outside.

they not go and accuse him before the Romans? Unhappy men, who wanted to be citizens without a city and to owe their wealth to the hand of their destroyers! Soon Rome asked them to send three hundred of the principal citizens of Carthage as hostages; Rome made them surrender their arms and ships and then declared war on them. Given the things that a disarmed Carthage did from despair,[7] one may judge what it could have done with its virtue when it had its full force.

[7] This war lasted three years.

CHAPTER 4

On the principle of aristocracy

Just as there must be virtue in popular government, there must also be virtue in the aristocratic one. It is true that it is not as absolutely required.

The people, who are with respect to the nobles what the subjects are with respect to the monarch, are contained by the nobles' laws. Therefore, they need virtue less than the people of a democracy. But how will the nobles be contained? Those who should see to the execution of the laws against their fellows will instantly feel that they act against themselves. Virtue must, therefore, be in this body by the nature of the constitution.

Aristocratic government has a certain strength in itself that democracy does not have. In aristocratic government, the nobles form a body, which, by its prerogative and for its particular interest, represses the people; having laws is enough to insure that they will be executed.

But it is as easy for this body to repress the others as it is difficult for it to repress itself.[8] Such is the nature of this constitution that it seems to put under the power of the laws the same people it exempts from them.

Now such a body may repress itself in only two ways: either by a great virtue that makes the nobles in some way equal to their people, which may form a great republic; or by a lesser virtue, a certain moderation that renders the nobles at least equal among themselves, which brings about their preservation.

[8] Public crimes can be punished there because they are the business of all; private crimes will not be punished there, because it is not the business of all to punish them.

Therefore, *moderation* is the soul of these governments. I mean the moderation founded on virtue, not the one that comes from faintheartedness and from laziness of soul.

CHAPTER 5

That virtue is not the principle of monarchical government

In monarchies, politics accomplishes great things with as little virtue as it can, just as in the finest machines art employs as few motions, forces, and wheels as possible.

The state continues to exist independently of love of the homeland, desire for true glory, self-renunciation, sacrifice of one's dearest interests, and all those heroic virtues we find in the ancients and know only by hearsay.

The laws replace all these virtues, for which there is no need; the state excuses you from them: here an action done noiselessly is in a way inconsequential.

Though all crimes are by their nature public, truly public crimes are nevertheless distinguished from private crimes, so called because they offend an individual more than the whole society.

Now, in republics private crimes are more public, that is, they run counter to the constitution of the state more than against individuals; and, in monarchies, public crimes are more private, that is, they run counter to individual fortunes more than against the constitution of the state itself.

I beg that no one be offended by what I have said; I have followed all the histories. I know very well that virtuous princes are not rare, but I say that in a monarchy it is very difficult for the people to be virtuous.[9]

Read what the historians of all times have said about the courts of monarchs; recall the conversations of men from every country about the wretched character of courtiers: these are not matters of speculation but of sad experience.

Ambition in idleness, meanness in arrogance, the desire to enrich oneself without work, aversion to truth, flattery, treachery, perfidy, the

[9] I speak here about political virtue, which is moral virtue in the sense that it points toward the general good, very little about individual moral virtues, and not at all about that virtue which relates to revealed truths. This will be seen in book 5, chap. 2 [below].

abandonment of all one's engagements, the scorn of the duties of citizens, the fear of the prince's virtue, the expectation of his weaknesses, and more than all that, the perpetual ridicule cast upon virtue, these form, I believe, the character of the greater number of courtiers, as observed in all places and at all times. Now, it is very awkward for most of the principal men of a state to be dishonest people and for the inferiors to be good people, for the former to be deceivers and the latter to consent to be no more than dupes.

If there is some unfortunate honest man among the people,[10] hints Cardinal Richelieu in his *Political Testament*, a monarch should be careful not to employ him.[11] So true is it that virtue is not the spring of this government! Certainly, it is not excluded, but it is not its spring.

[10] To be understood in the sense of the preceding note.

[11] There it is said, "One must not employ people of low degree; they are too austere and too difficult" [Cardinal Richelieu, *Testament politique*, pt. 1, chap. 4, sec. 1; pp. 237–238; 1947 edn.].

CHAPTER 6

How virtue is replaced in monarchical government

I hasten and I lengthen my steps, so that none will believe I satirize monarchical government. No; if one spring is missing, monarchy has another. HONOR, that is, the prejudice of each person and each condition, takes the place of the political virtue of which I have spoken and represents it everywhere. It can inspire the finest actions; joined with the force of the laws, it can lead to the goal of government as does virtue itself.

Thus, in well-regulated monarchies everyone will be almost a good citizen, and one will rarely find someone who is a good man; for, in order to be a good man,[12] one must have the intention of being one[13] and love the state less for oneself than for itself.

[12] These words, *good man*, are to be taken here only in a political sense.

[13] See note 9.

CHAPTER 7
On the principle of monarchy

Monarchical government assumes, as we have said, preeminences, ranks, and even a hereditary nobility. The nature of *honor* is to demand preferences and distinctions; therefore, honor has, in and of itself, a place in this government.

Ambition is pernicious in a republic. It has good effects in monarchy; it gives life to that government; and it has this advantage, that it is not dangerous because it can constantly be repressed.

You could say that it is like the system of the universe, where there is a force constantly repelling all bodies from the center and a force of gravitation attracting them to it. Honor makes all the parts of the body politic move; its very action binds them, and each person works for the common good, believing he works for his individual interests.

Speaking philosophically, it is true that the honor that guides all the parts of the state is a false honor, but this false honor is as useful to the public as the true one would be to the individuals who could have it.

And is it not impressive that one can oblige men to do all the difficult actions and which require force, with no reward other than the renown of these actions?

CHAPTER 8
That honor is not the principle of despotic states

Honor is not the principle of despotic states: as the men in them are all equal, one cannot prefer oneself to others; as men in them are all slaves, one can prefer oneself to nothing.

Moreover, as honor has its laws and rules and is incapable of yielding, as it depends on its own caprice and not on that of another, honor can be found only in states whose constitution is fixed and whose laws are certain.

How could honor be endured by the *despot*? It glories in scorning life, and the despot is strong only because he can take life away. How could honor endure the despot? It has consistent rules and sustains its caprices; the despot has no rule, and his caprices destroy all the others.

Honor, unknown in despotic states where even the word to express it is often lacking,[14] reigns in monarchies; there it gives life to the whole body politic, to the laws, and even to the virtues.

[14]See [John] Perry [*The State of Russia under the Present Czar*], p. 447 [262] [p. 217; 1967 edn.].

CHAPTER 9

On the principle of despotic government

Just as there must be *virtue* in a republic and *honor* in a monarchy, there must be FEAR in a despotic government. Virtue is not at all necessary to it and honor would be dangerous.

The prince's immense power passes intact to those to whom he entrusts it. People capable of much self-esteem would be in a position to cause revolutions. Therefore, *fear* must beat down everyone's courage and extinguish even the slightest feeling of ambition.

A moderate government can, as much as it wants and without peril, relax its springs. It maintains itself by its laws and even by its force. But when in despotic government the prince ceases for a moment to raise his arm, when he cannot instantly destroy those in the highest places,[15] all is lost, for when the spring of the government, which is *fear*, no longer exists, the people no longer have a protector.

Apparently it was in this sense that the cadis claimed that the Grand Signior was not obliged to keep his word or his oath if by doing so he limited his authority.[16d]

The people must be judged by the laws, and the important men by the prince's fancy; the head of the lowest subject must be safe, and the pasha's head always exposed. One cannot speak of these monstrous governments without shuddering. The Sophi of Persia, deposed in our time by Myrrweis, saw his government perish before it was conquered because he had not spilled enough blood.[17]

[15]As often happens in military aristocracy.

[16][Paul] Rycaut, *The History of the Present State of the Ottoman Empire* [bk. 1, chap. 2; pp. 4–5; 1703 edn.].

[17]See Father [Jean Antoine] du Cerceau's [translation of Judasz Tadeusz Krusinski's] *Histoire de la dernière révolution de Perse* [1, 135–136; 1740 Eng. edn.].

[d]The Grand Signior was the Turkish sultan.

History tells us that Domitian's horrible cruelties so frightened the governors that the people revived somewhat during his reign.[18] In the same way, a flood, destroying everything on one bank, leaves stretches of land on the other where meadows can be seen in the distance.

[18] His was a military government, which is one of the kinds of despotic government. [For example, Suetonius, *Vitae duodecim Caesarum*, *Domitian*, 10–14, 23.1; and Tacitus, *Agricola*.]

CHAPTER 10

The difference in obedience between moderate governments and despotic governments

In despotic states the nature of the government requires extreme obedience, and the prince's will, once known, should produce its effect as infallibly as does one ball thrown against another.

No tempering, modification, accommodation, terms, alternatives, negotiations, remonstrances, nothing as good or better can be proposed. Man is a creature that obeys a creature that wants.

He can no more express his fears about a future event than he can blame his lack of success on the caprice of fortune. There, men's portion, like beasts', is instinct, obedience, and chastisement.

It is useless to counter with natural feelings, respect for a father, tenderness for one's children and women, laws of honor, or the state of one's health; one has received the order and that is enough.

In Persia, when the king has condemned someone, no one may speak to him further about it or ask for a pardon. If he were drunken or mad, the decree would have to be carried out just the same;[19] if it were not, he would be inconsistent, and the law cannot be inconsistent. This has always been their way of thinking: as the order given by Ahasuerus to exterminate the Jews could not be revoked, it was decided to give them permission to defend themselves.[e]

There is, however, one thing with which one can sometimes counter

[19] See [John] Chardin [*Voyages*, "Description du gouvernement," chap. 2, "De la nature du gouvernement"; 5, 229; 1811 edn.].

[e] Ahasuerus is the Hebrew form of Xerxes (Xerxes I in this instance).

the prince's will:[20] that is religion. One will forsake one's father, even kill him, if the prince orders it, but one will not drink wine if the prince wants it and orders it. The laws of religion are part of a higher precept, because they apply to the prince as well as to the subjects. But it is not the same for natural right; the prince is not assumed to be a man.

In monarchical and moderate states, power is limited by that which is its spring; I mean honor, which reigns like a monarch over the prince and the people. One will not cite the laws of religion to a courtier: he would feel it was ridiculous; instead one will incessantly cite the laws of honor. This results in necessary modifications of obedience; honor is naturally subject to eccentricities, and obedience will follow them all.

Though the way of obeying is different in these two governments, the power is nevertheless the same. In whatever direction the monarch turns, he prevails by tipping the balance and he is obeyed. The whole difference is that, in the monarchy, the prince is enlightened and the ministers are infinitely more skillful and experienced in public affairs than they are in the despotic state.

[20] Ibid. [John Chardin, *Voyages*, "Description du gouvernement des Persans"; 5, 233–235; 1811 edn.].

CHAPTER 11

Reflections on all this

Such are the principles of the three governments: this does not mean that in a certain republic one is virtuous, but that one ought to be; nor does this prove that in a certain monarchy, there is honor or that in a particular despotic state, there is fear, but that unless it is there, the government is imperfect.

BOOK 4

That the laws of education should be relative to the principles of the government

CHAPTER 1

On the laws of education

The *laws of education* are the first we receive. And as these prepare us to be citizens, each particular family should be governed according to the plan of the great family that includes them all.

If there is a principle for the people taken generally, then the parts which compose it, that is, the families, will have one also. Therefore, the laws of education will be different in each kind of government. In monarchies, their object will be *honor*; in republics, *virtue*; in despotisms, *fear*.

CHAPTER 2

On education in monarchies

In monarchies the principal education is not in the public institutions where children are instructed; in a way, education begins when one enters the world. The world is the school of what is called *honor*, the universal master that should everywhere guide us.

Here, one sees and always hears three things: that *a certain nobility must be put in the virtues, a certain frankness in the mores, and a certain politeness in the manners*.

The virtues we are shown here are always less what one owes others than what one owes oneself; they are not so much what calls us to our fellow citizens as what distinguishes us from them.

One judges men's actions here not as good but as fine, not as just but as great; not as reasonable but as extraordinary.

As soon as honor can find something noble here, honor becomes either a judge who makes it legitimate or a sophist who justifies it.[a]

It allows gallantry when gallantry is united with the idea of an attachment of the heart or the idea of conquest; and this is the true reason mores are never as pure in monarchies as in republican governments.

It allows deceit when deceit is added to the idea of greatness of spirit or greatness of business, as in politics, whose niceties do not offend it.

It forbids adulation only when adulation is separated from the idea of a great fortune and is joined only with the feeling of one's own meanness.

I have said that, in monarchies, education should bring a certain frankness to the mores. Therefore, truth is desired in speech. But is this for the love of truth? Not at all. It is desired because a man accustomed to speaking the truth appears to be daring and free. Indeed, such a man seems dependent only on things and not on the way another receives them.

This is why, commending this kind of frankness here, one scorns that of the people, which has for its aim only truth and simplicity.

Finally, education in monarchies requires a certain politeness in manners. Men, born to live together, are also born to please each other; and he who does not observe the proprieties offends all those with whom he lives and discredits himself so much that he becomes unable to do any good thing.

But politeness does not customarily have its origin in such a pure source. It arises from the desire to distinguish oneself. We are polite from arrogance; we flatter ourselves that our manners prove that we are not common and that we have not lived with the sort of people who have been neglected through the ages.

In monarchies, politeness is naturalized at court. One excessively great man makes all others small. Hence the regard owed to everyone else and the politeness that flatters as much those who are polite as those to whom they are polite, because that politeness makes it understood that one belongs to the court or that one is worthy of belonging to it.

[a] *Dès que l'honneur y peut trouver quelque chose de noble, il est ou le juge qui les [le] rend legitimes, ou le sophiste qui les [le] justifie.*

The courtly air consists in putting away one's own greatness for a borrowed greatness. This greatness is more flattering to a courtier than is his own. It gives a certain haughty modesty that spreads afar but whose arrogance diminishes imperceptibly in proportion to its distance from the source of greatness.

At court one finds a delicacy of taste in all things, which comes from continual use of the excesses of a great fortune, from the variety, and especially the weariness, of pleasures, from the multiplicity, even the confusion, of fancies, which, when they are pleasing, are always accepted.

Education bears on all these things to make what is called the *honnête homme*,[b] who has all the qualities and all the virtues required in this government.

Honor, meddling in everything, enters into all the modes of thought and all the ways of feeling and even directs the principles.

This eccentric honor shapes the virtues into what it wants and as it wants: on its own, it puts rules on everything prescribed to us; according to its fancy, it extends or limits our duties, whether their source be religion, politics, or morality.

There is nothing in monarchy that laws, religion, and honor prescribe so much as obedience to the wills of the prince, but this honor dictates to us that the prince should never prescribe an action that dishonors us because it would make us incapable of serving him.

Crillon refused to assassinate the Duke of Guise, but he proposed to Henry III that he engage the duke in battle. After Saint Bartholomew's Day, when Charles IX had sent orders to all the governors to have the Huguenots massacred, the Viscount of Orte, who was in command at Bayonne, wrote to the king,[1] "Sire, I have found among the inhabitants and the warriors only good citizens, brave soldiers, and not one executioner; thus, they and I together beg Your Majesty to use our arms and our lives for things that can be done." This great and generous courage regarded a cowardly action as an impossible thing.

For the nobility, honor prescribes nothing more than serving the prince in war: indeed, this is the preeminent profession because its risks, successes, and even misfortunes lead to greatness. But honor

[1] See [Théodore Agrippa] d'Aubigné's *Histoire universale* [bk. 6, chap. 5; 3.364; 1985 edn.].

[b] In the seventeenth century *honnête homme* came to refer to a gentleman of courtly manner who was not necessarily noble by birth.

wants to be the arbiter in imposing this law; and if honor has been offended, it permits or requires one to withdraw to one's home.

It wants one to be able indifferently to aspire to posts or to refuse them; it regards this liberty as greater than fortune itself.

Honor, therefore, has its supreme rules, and education is obliged to conform to them.[2] The principal rules are that we are indeed allowed to give importance to our fortune but that we are sovereignly forbidden to give any to our life.

The second is that, when we have once been placed in a rank, we should do or suffer nothing that might show that we consider ourselves inferior to the rank itself.

The third is that, what honor forbids is more rigorously forbidden when the laws do not agree in proscribing it, and that what honor requires is more strongly required when the laws do not require it.

[2]These comments refer to what is and not to what should be; honor is a prejudice, which religion sometimes works to destroy and sometimes to regulate.

CHAPTER 3
On education in despotic government

Just as education in monarchies works only to elevate the heart, education in despotic states seeks only to bring it down. There, education must bring about servility. It will be a good, even for the commander, to have had such an education, since no one is a tyrant there without at the same time being a slave.

Extreme obedience assumes ignorance in the one who obeys; it assumes ignorance even in the one who commands; he does not have to deliberate, to doubt, or to reason; he has only to want.

In despotic states, each household is a separate empire. Therefore, education, which comes mainly from living with others, is quite limited there; it is reduced to putting fear in the heart and in teaching the spirit a few very simple religious principles. Knowledge will be dangerous, rivalry deadly; and, as for the virtues, Aristotle cannot believe that any are proper to slaves;[3] this would indeed limit education in this government.

[3][Aristotle] *Pol.*, bk. 1 [1260a34–1260b8].

Therefore, education is, in a way, null there. One must take everything away in order to give something and begin by making a bad subject in order to make a good slave.

Well! Why would education be intent upon forming a good citizen to take part in the public unhappiness? If he loved the state, he would be tempted to relax the springs of the government; if he failed, he would be ruined; if he succeeded, he would run the risk of ruining himself, the prince, and the empire.

CHAPTER 4

The difference in the effect of education among the ancients and among ourselves

Most of the ancient peoples lived in governments that had virtue for their principle, and when that virtue was in full force, things were done in those governments that we no longer see and that astonish our small souls.

Their education had another advantage over ours; it was never contradicted. In the last year of his life, Epaminondas said, heard, saw, and did the same things as at the time that he was first instructed.

Today we receive three different or opposing educations: that of our fathers, that of our schoolmasters, and that of the world. What we are told by the last upsets all the ideas of the first two. This comes partly from the opposition there is for us between the ties of religion and those of the world, a thing unknown among the ancients.

CHAPTER 5

On education in republican government

It is in republican government that the full power of education is needed. Fear in despotic governments arises of itself from threats and chastisements; honor in monarchies is favored by the passions and favors them in turn; but political virtue is a renunciation of oneself, which is always a very painful thing.

One can define this virtue as love of the laws and the homeland. This love, requiring a continuous preference of the public interest over one's own, produces all the individual virtues; they are only that preference.

This love is singularly connected with democracies. In them alone, government is entrusted to each citizen. Now government is like all things in the world; in order to preserve it, one must love it.

One never hears it said that kings do not love monarchy or that despots hate despotism.

Therefore, in a republic, everything depends on establishing this love, and education should attend to inspiring it. But there is a sure way for children to have it; it is for the fathers themselves to have it.

One is ordinarily in charge of giving one's knowledge to one's children and even more in charge of giving them one's own passions.

If this does not happen, it is because what was done in the father's house is destroyed by impressions from the outside.

It is not young people who degenerate; they are ruined only when grown men have already been corrupted.

CHAPTER 6

On some Greek institutions

The ancient Greeks, persuaded that peoples who lived in a popular government must of necessity be brought up to be virtuous, made singular institutions to inspire virtue. When you see, in the *Life of Lycurgus*, the laws he gave the Lacedaemonians, you believe you are reading the history of the Sevarambes. The laws of Crete were the originals for the laws of Lacedaemonia, and Plato's laws were their correction.

I pray that one pay a little attention to the breadth of genius of those legislators who saw that by running counter to all received usages and by confusing all virtues, they would show their wisdom to the universe. Lycurgus, mixing larceny with the spirit of justice, the harshest slavery with extreme liberty, the most heinous feelings with the greatest moderation, gave stability to his town. He seemed to remove all its resources, arts, commerce, silver, walls: one had ambition there without the expectation of bettering oneself; one had natural feelings but was neither child, husband, nor father; modesty itself was removed from chastity. In these ways, Sparta was led to greatness and glory, with such an infallibility in its institutions that nothing was gained by winning battles against it, until its police was taken away.[4c]

Crete and Laconia were governed by these laws. Lacedaemonia was the last to yield to the Macedonians, and Crete[5] was the last prey of the Romans. The Samnites had these same institutions and they provided the occasion for twenty-four triumphs for the Romans.[6]

We can see that which was extraordinary in the Greek institutions in the dregs and corruption of modern times.[7] A legislator, an *honnête homme*,[d] has formed a people in whom integrity seems as natural as bravery was among the Spartans. Mr. Penn is a true Lycurgus; and, though he has had peace for his object as Lycurgus had war, they are alike in the unique path on which they have set their people, in their ascendancy over free men, in the prejudices they have vanquished, and in the passions they have subdued.

Paraguay can furnish us with another example. Some have wanted to use it to level charges against the Society,[e] which considers the pleasure of commanding the only good in life, but governing men by making men happier will always be a fine thing.[8]

It is fortunate for the Society that it was the first to show in these countries the idea of religion joined with that of humanity. By repairing the pillages of the Spaniards, it has begun to heal one of the greatest wounds mankind has yet received.

The Society's exquisite feeling for all it calls honor and its zeal for a religion that humbles those who listen far more than those who preach have made it undertake great things, and it has been successful. It has

[4]Philopoemen forced the Lacedaemonians to give up their way of raising children, knowing that if he did not, the Lacedaemonians would always have great souls and lofty hearts. Plutarch [*Vit.*], *Philopoemen* [16.5]. See Livy, bk. 38 [38.34.9].

[5]Crete defended its laws and its liberty for three years. See books 98, 99, and 100 of Livy in the *Epitome* of Florus [1.42.1; 3.7.1]. [In Johann Freinsheim, *Supplementorum Livianorum* 97.14–15; 98.80–84; 99.47; 100.10.] It put up more resistance than the greatest kings.

[6]Florus [*Epitome rerum Romanorum*], bk. 1 [1.11.8–1.16.8].

[7]"Among the dregs of Romulus" [L.]. Cicero [*Epistolae ad Atticum* 2.1.8].

[8]The Indians of Paraguay do not depend on a particular lord; their tributes are but one-fifth, and they have firearms for protection.

[c]We have translated *police* as "police." In the eighteenth century, in both French and English, *police* meant the administration, or order, of everyday things. See note [c], bk. 26.

[d]See note [b], bk. 4.

[e]The Jesuits were called the *Société*.

brought dispersed peoples out of the woods; it has assured their sustenance; it has clothed them; and if, in so doing, it had done no more than increase industry among men, it would have accomplished much.

Those who want to make similar institutions will establish the community of goods of Plato's *Republic*, the respect he required for the gods, the separation from strangers in order to preserve the mores, and commerce done by the city,[f] not by the citizens; they will produce our arts without our luxury and our needs without our desires.

They will proscribe silver, whose effect is to fatten the fortune of men beyond the limits nature has set for it, to teach men to preserve vainly what has been amassed vainly, to multiply desires infinitely and to supplement nature, which has given us very limited means to excite our passions and to corrupt one another.

"The Epadamnians,[9] feeling that their communication with the barbarians corrupted their mores, elected a magistrate to do all their trading in the name of the city and for the city." In this way commerce does not corrupt the constitution, and the constitution does not deprive the society of the advantages of commerce.

[9] Plutarch [*Moralia*], *Quaestiones Graecae* [chap. 29, 297f–298a].

[f] By and large Montesquieu seems to use *cité*, "city," when speaking of a political organization and *ville*, "town," when speaking of a collection of inhabitants, however large.

CHAPTER 7

In what case these singular institutions can be good

These sorts of institutions can be suitable in republics, because political virtue is their principle, but less care is needed to induce honor in monarchies or to inspire fear in despotic states.

Furthermore, they can have a place only in a small state,[10] where one can educate the general populace and raise a whole people like a family.

The laws of Minos, Lycurgus, and Plato assume that all citizens pay a singular attention to each other. This cannot be promised in the confusion, oversights, and extensive business of a numerous people.

As has been said, silver must be banished from these institutions.

[10] As were the Greek towns.

But in large societies, the number, the variety, the press and the importance of business, the ease of purchases, and the slowness of exchanges, all these require a common measure. In order to carry one's power everywhere or defend it everywhere, one must have that to which men everywhere have attached power.

CHAPTER 8

Explanation of a paradox of the ancients in relation to mores

Polybius, judicious Polybius, tells us that music was necessary to soften the mores of the Arcadians, who lived in a country where the weather is gloomy and cold, that the inhabitants of Kynaithes, who neglected music, surpassed all the other Greeks in cruelty and that never had so much crime been seen in a town.[g] Plato is not afraid to say that no change can be made in music which is not a change in the constitution of the state. Aristotle, who seems to have written his *Politics* only in order to oppose his feelings to Plato's, nevertheless agrees with him about the power of music over mores. Theophrastus,[h] Plutarch,[11] and Strabo,[12] all the ancients, have thought likewise. This is not an opinion proffered without reflection; it is one of the principles of their politics.[13] It is thus that they gave laws; it is thus that they wanted the cities to be governed.

I believe I can explain this. One must keep in mind that in the Greek towns, especially in those whose principal aim was war, all work and all professions that could lead to earning silver were regarded as unworthy of a free man. "Most arts," said Xenophon,[14] "corrupt the body of the one who practices them; they oblige one to sit in the shade or near the

[11] [Plutarch, *Vit.*], *Pelopidas* [19.1].

[12] [Strabo, *Geographica*] bk. 1 [1.2.3,8].

[13] Plato, *Laws*, bk. 4 [6.765e], says that the prefectships of music and gymnastics are the most important employments of the city; and in his *Republic*, bk. 3 [400b]: "Damon will tell you," he said, "what sounds are capable of giving rise to baseness of soul, to insolence, and to the contrary virtues."

[14] [Xenophon] bk. 5, *Oeconomicus* [4.2–3].

[g] Polybius 4.20–21.

[h] Theophrastus, *Fragments* 87, 88, 89, 90.

fire: one has no time for one's friends, no time for the republic." It was only when some democracies became corrupted that craftsmen managed to become citizens. Aristotle[15] teaches us this, and he holds that a good republic will never give them citizenship.[16i]

Agriculture, too, was a servile profession, and it was ordinarily some conquered people who followed it: the Helots farmed for the Lacedaemonians, the Perioikoi for the Cretans, the Penestai for the Thessalians, and other[17] slave peoples in other republics.

Finally, all common commerce[18] was disgraceful to the Greeks. A citizen would have had to provide services for a slave, a tenant, or a foreigner; this idea ran counter to the spirit of Greek liberty; thus Plato[19] in his *Laws* wants any citizen who engages in commerce to be punished.

In the Greek republics, one was, therefore, in a very awkward position. One did not want the citizens to work in commerce, agriculture, or the arts; nor did one want them to be idle.[20] They found an occupation in the exercises derived from gymnastics and those related to war.[21] The institutions gave them no others. One must regard the Greeks as a society of athletes and fighters. Now, these exercises, so

[15] [Aristotle] *Pol.*, bk. 3, chap. 4 [1277b1–3].

[16] "Diophantes," says Aristotle in *Pol.* [bk. 2], chap. 7 [1267b15–19], "formerly established in Athens that the artisans would be slaves of the public."

[17] Thus Plato and Aristotle want slaves to cultivate the land. [Plato] *Laws*, bk. 7 [806e]; [Aristotle] *Pol.*, bk. 7, chap. 10 [1330a25–26]. It is true that agriculture was not everywhere the work of slaves; on the contrary, as Aristotle says [*Pol.* 1318b9–10], the best republics were those in which it was undertaken by the citizens, but this happened only through the corruption of the ancient governments, which had become democratic, for in the earliest times, the towns of Greece lived as aristocracies.

[18] *Cauponatio* [shopkeeping or innkeeping].

[19] [Plato, *Laws*] bk. 2 [919d–920a].

[20] Aristotle, *Pol.*, bk. 10. [This refers to the "completion" of Aristotle's *Politics* prepared by the Florentine scholar Cyriacus Stroza (1504–1565). It was first published in 1563. Stroza prepared two books, 9 and 10, providing a Greek text and a Latin translation. His supplement later appeared in Casaubon's edition of Aristotle, and was published into the eighteenth century. A French translation, prepared in the late sixteenth century, was appended to Le Roy's translation of the *Politics*. Book 9 concerns the education and training of soldiers; book 10 describes the role of princes and of priests. Both book 9 and book 10 address the issues of gymnastics, agriculture, commerce, and the best life.]

[21] "Gymnastic art is to exercise the body; the trainer's art is for the activities of different sports contests" [L.]. Aristotle, *Pol.*, bk. 8, chap. 3 [1338b6–8].

---

[i] *droit de la cité.* We translate several expressions as "citizenship"; because of the variety of meanings, the reader will find the French in these notes.

appropriate for making people harsh and savage,[22][j] needed to be tempered by others that might soften the mores. Music, which enters the spirit through the organs of the body, was quite suitable. It is a mean between the physical exercises that render men harsh and the speculative sciences that render them savage. One cannot say that music inspired virtue; it would be inconceivable; but music curbed the effect of the ferocity of the institution and gave the soul a part in education that it would not otherwise have had.

I assume among ourselves a society of people so enamored of hunting that they did nothing else; they would surely acquire a certain roughness. If these same people were also to develop a taste for music, one would soon find a difference in their manners and in their mores. In short, the exercises practiced by the Greeks aroused in them only one type of passion: roughness, anger, and cruelty. Music arouses them all and can make the soul feel softness, pity, tenderness, and sweet pleasure. Those who write on morality for us and so strongly proscribe the theaters make us feel sufficiently the power of music on our souls.

If one gave only drums and trumpet fanfares to the society I have mentioned, would not one fall shorter of one's goal than if one gave it a tender music? The ancients were right, therefore, when, under certain circumstances, they preferred one mode of music to another for the sake of mores.

But, one will say, why should music be preferred? Of all the pleasures of the senses, none corrupts the soul less. We blush to read in Plutarch[23] that the Thebans, in order to soften the mores of their young people, established by their laws a love that ought to be proscribed by all nations in the world.

[22] Aristotle says that the children of the Lacedaemonians, who began these exercises when very young, became too ferocious as a result. Aristotle, *Pol.*, bk. 8, chap. 4 [1338b12–14].
[23] [Plutarch, *Vit.*] *Pelopidas* [18–19.2].

[j] The meaning in French of *sauvage* covers both the notion of the brutal and savage and that of the shy and wild; it means something asocial.

BOOK 5

That the laws given by the legislator should be relative to the principle of the government

CHAPTER I

The idea of this book

We have just seen that the laws of education should have a relation to the principle of each government. It is the same for the laws the legislator gives to the society as a whole. This relation between the laws and the principle tightens all the springs of the government, and the principle in turn receives a new force from the laws. Thus, in physical motion, an action is always followed by a reaction.

We shall examine this relation in each government, and we shall begin with the republican state, which has virtue for its principle.

CHAPTER 2

What virtue is in the political state

Virtue, in a republic, is a very simple thing: it is love of the republic; it is a feeling and not a result of knowledge; the lowest man in the state, like the first, can have this feeling. Once the people have good maxims, they adhere to them longer than do those who are called *honnêtes gens*.[a] Corruption seldom begins with the people; from their middling enlightenment they have often derived a stronger attachment to that which is established.

Love of the homeland leads to goodness in mores, and goodness in mores leads to love of the homeland. The less we can satisfy our

[a] See note [b], bk. 4.

particular passions, the more we give ourselves up to passions for the general order. Why do monks so love their order? Their love comes from the same thing that makes their order intolerable to them. Their rule deprives them of everything upon which ordinary passions rest; what remains, therefore, is the passion for the very rule that afflicts them. The more austere it is, that is, the more it curtails their inclinations, the more force it gives to those that remain.

CHAPTER 3
What love of the republic is in a democracy

Love of the republic in a democracy is love of democracy; love of democracy is love of equality.

Love of democracy is also love of frugality. As each one there should have the same happiness and the same advantages, each should taste the same pleasures and form the same expectations; this is something that can be anticipated only from the common frugality.

Love of equality in a democracy limits ambition to the single desire, the single happiness, of rendering greater services to one's homeland than other citizens. Men cannot render it equal services, but they should equally render it services. At birth one contracts an immense debt to it that can never be repaid.

Thus distinctions in a democracy arise from the principle of equality, even when equality seems to be erased by successful services or superior talents.

Love of frugality limits the *desire to possess* to the mindfulness required by that which is necessary for one's family, and even by that which is superfluous for one's homeland. Wealth gives a power that a citizen cannot use for himself, for he would not be equal. It also procures delights that he should not enjoy, because these would likewise run counter to equality.

Thus by establishing frugality in domestic life, good democracies opened the gate to public expenditures, as happened in Athens and Rome. Magnificence and abundance had their source in frugality itself; and, just as religion requires unsullied hands so that one can make offerings to the gods, the laws wanted frugal mores so that one could give to one's homeland.

The good sense and happiness of individuals largely consists in their having middling talents and fortunes. If a republic whose laws have formed many middling people is composed of sober people, it will be governed soberly;[b] if it is composed of happy people, it will be very happy.

[b]See note [b], bk. I. Here *sage* must mean a quality available to *médiocre*, "middling," people.

CHAPTER 4

How love of equality and frugality is inspired

Love of *equality* and love of *frugality* are strongly aroused by equality and frugality themselves, when one lives in a society in which both are established by the laws.

In monarchies and despotic states, no one aspires to equality; the idea of equality does not even occur; in these states everyone aims for superiority. The people of the lowest conditions desire to quit those conditions only in order to be masters of the others.

It is the same for frugality; in order to love it, one must practice it. Those who are corrupted by delights will not love the frugal life; and if this had been natural and ordinary, Alcibiades would not have been the wonder of the universe. Nor will those who envy or admire the luxury of others love frugality; people who have before their eyes only rich men, or poor men like themselves, detest their poverty without loving or knowing what puts an end to poverty.

Therefore, it is a very true maxim that if one is to love equality and frugality in a republic, these must have been established by the laws.

CHAPTER 5

How the laws establish equality in democracy

Some legislators of ancient times, like Lycurgus and Romulus, divided the lands equally. This could happen only at the founding of a new republic; or when the old one was so corrupt and spirits so disposed that the poor believed themselves obliged to seek, and the rich obliged to suffer, such a remedy.

If the legislator who makes such a division does not give laws to maintain it, his is only a transitory constitution; inequality will enter at the point not protected by the laws, and the republic will be lost.

One must, therefore, regulate to this end dowries, gifts, inheritances, testaments, in sum, all the kinds of contracts. For if it were permitted to give one's goods to whomever one wanted and as one wanted, each individual will would disturb the disposition of the fundamental laws.[c]

In Athens, Solon[1] acted inconsistently with the old laws, which ordered that goods should remain in the family of the testator,[2] when he permitted one to leave one's goods to whomever one wanted by testament provided one had no children. He acted inconsistently with his own laws; for, by cancelling debts, he had sought equality.

The law that forbade one to have two inheritances was a good law for democracy.[3] It originated in the equal division of the lands and portions given to each citizen. The law did not want any one man to have several portions.

The law ordering the closest male relative to marry the female heir arose from a similar source. Among the Jews, this law was given after a similar division. Plato,[4] who founds his laws on this division, gives it also, and it was an Athenian law.

There was a certain law in Athens of which, so far as I know, no one has understood the spirit. Marriage was permitted to the step-sister on the father's side, but not to the step-sister on the mother's side.[5] This usage originated in republics, whose spirit was to avoid giving two portions of land and consequently two inheritances to one person. When a man married the step-sister on the father's side, he could

[1] Plutarch [*Vit.*] *Solon* [21.2].
[2] Ibid. [Plutarch, *Vit.*, *Solon* 21.2.]
[3] Philolaus of Corinth established in Athens that the number of portions of land and that of inheritances would always be the same. Aristotle, *Pol.*, bk. 2, chap. 12 [1274b4–5].
[4] [Plato] *Republic*, bk. 8. [See *Laws* 924e–925e.]
[5] Cornelius Nepos [*Liber de excellentibus ducibus exterrarum gentium*], "Preface" [4]; this usage belonged to earliest times. Thus Abraham says of Sarah [Genesis 20.12]: "She is my sister, daughter of my father and not of my mother." The same reasons had caused the same law to be established among different peoples.

[c] Montesquieu distinguishes here, and at note [a], bk. 27, between *volontés*, "wills," and *testaments*, "testaments," which may or may not be guided by those wills.

receive only one inheritance, that of his father; but, when he married the step-sister on the mother's side, it could happen that the father of this sister, in the absence of male children, might leave her the inheritance, and that the brother, who had married her, might consequently receive two of them.

Let not what Philo says be proposed to me as an objection:[6] that, although in Athens one might marry a step-sister on the father's side and not on the mother's side, in Lacedaemonia one could marry a step-sister on the mother's side and not on the father's side. For I find in Strabo[7] that in Lacedaemonia when a step-sister married a brother, she had half the brother's portion for her dowry. It is clear that this second law was made to curb the bad consequences of the first. In order to prevent the goods of the step-sister's family from passing to the brother's, half the brother's goods were given to the step-sister as a dowry.

Seneca,[8] speaking of Silanus, who had married his step-sister, says that such permission had restricted application in Athens and was applied generally in Alexandria. In the government of one alone, the question of maintaining the division of goods hardly arose.

In order to maintain this division of lands in a democracy, it was a good law that wanted the father of several children to choose one to inherit his portion[9] and have his other children adopted by someone who had no children, so that the number of citizens might always be maintained equal to the number of shares.

Phaleas of Chalcedon[10] devised a way of rendering fortunes equal in a republic where they were not equal. He wanted the rich to give dowries to the poor and to receive none from them, and the poor to receive silver for their daughters and to give none. But I know of no republic that adopted such a rule. It places the citizens under such strikingly different conditions that they would hate the very equality that one sought to introduce. It is sometimes good for laws not to appear to go so directly toward the end they propose.

Although in a democracy real equality is the soul of the state, still this

[6] [Philo Judaeus] *De specialibus legibus* [III.22; chap. 4].

[7] [Strabo, *Geographica*] bk. 10 [10.4.20].

[8] "In Athens it [marriage] was permitted to a half [sister]; in Alexandria to a full [sister]" [L.]. Seneca, *De morte Claudii* [*Apokolokyntosis* (*The Pumpkinification of the Divine Claudius*) 9.2].

[9] Plato makes a similar law. Bk. 3 of the *Laws* [740b–c].

[10] Aristotle, *Pol.*, bk. 2, chap. 7 [1266a39–1266b5].

equality is so difficult to establish that an extreme precision in this regard would not always be suitable. It suffices to establish a census[11] that reduces differences or fixes them at a certain point; after which, it is the task of particular laws to equalize inequalities, so to speak, by the burdens they impose on the rich and the relief they afford to the poor. Only wealth of middling size can give or suffer these kinds of adjustments, because, for men of immoderate fortunes, all power and honor not accorded them is regarded as an affront.

Every inequality in a democracy should be drawn from the nature of democracy and from the very principle of equality. For example, it can be feared there that people who need steady work for their livelihood might become too impoverished by a magistracy, or that they might neglect its functions; that artisans might become arrogant; that too-numerous freed men might become more powerful than the original citizens. In these cases, equality among the citizens[12] in the democracy can be removed for the utility of the democracy. But it is only an apparent equality that is removed; for a man ruined by a magistracy would be in a worse condition than the other citizens; and this same man, who would be obliged to neglect its functions, would put the other citizens in a condition worse than his, and so forth.

[11] Solon made four classes: the first, those who had five hundred minas of income, whether in grain or in liquid products; the second, those who had three hundred and could keep a horse; the third, those who had only two hundred; the fourth, all those who lived by their hands. Plutarch [*Vit.*], *Solon* [18.1–2].

[12] Solon excludes from burdens all those in the fourth census [hundred]. [Plutarch, *Vit.*, *Solon* 18.2.]

CHAPTER 6

How laws should sustain frugality in democracy

It is not sufficient in a good democracy for the portions of land to be equal; they must be small, as among the Romans. Curius said to his soldiers,[13] "God forbid that a citizen should esteem as little that land which is sufficient to nourish a man."

As the equality of fortunes sustains frugality, frugality maintains the

[13] They asked for a larger portion of the conquered land. Plutarch, *Moralia*, *Regum et imperatorum apophthegmata* [194e].

equality of fortunes. These things, although different, are such that they cannot continue to exist without each other; each is the cause and the effect; if one of them is withdrawn from democracy, the other always follows.

Certainly, when democracy is founded on commerce, it may very well happen that individuals have great wealth, yet that the mores are not corrupted. This is because the spirit of commerce brings with it the spirit of frugality, economy, moderation, work, wisdom, tranquillity, order, and rule. Thus, as long as this spirit continues to exist, the wealth it produces has no bad effect. The ill comes when an excess of wealth destroys the spirit of commerce; one sees the sudden rise of the disorders of inequality which had not made themselves felt before.

In order for the spirit of commerce to be maintained, the principal citizens must engage in commerce themselves; this spirit must reign alone and not be crossed by another; all the laws must favor it; these same laws, whose provisions divide fortunes in proportion as commerce increases them, must make each poor citizen comfortable enough to be able to work as the others do and must bring each rich citizen to a middle level such that he needs to work in order to preserve or to acquire.

In a commercial republic, the law giving all children an equal portion in the inheritance of the fathers is very good. In this way, whatever fortune the father may have made, his children, always less rich than he, are led to flee luxury and work as he did. I speak only of commercial republics, because, for those that are not, the legislator has to make many other regulations.[14]

In Greece there were two sorts of republics. Some were military, like Lacedaemonia; others, commercial, like Athens. In the former, one wanted the citizen to be idle; in the latter, one sought to instill a love for work. Solon made idleness a crime and wanted each citizen to account for the way he earned his living. Indeed, in a good democracy where spending should be only for necessities, each person should have them, for from whom would he receive them?

[14]Women's dowries should be much restricted there.

CHAPTER 7
Other means of favoring the principle of democracy

An equal division of lands cannot be established in all democracies. There are circumstances in which such an arrangement would be impractical and dangerous and would even run counter to the constitution. One is not always obliged to take extreme courses. If one sees that this division, which should maintain the mores, is not suitable in a democracy, one must have recourse to other means.

If a fixed body is established that is in itself the rule in mores, a senate to which age, virtue, gravity and service give entrance, the senators, who are seen by the people as simulacra of gods, will inspire feelings that will reach into all families.

The senate must, above all, be attached to the old institutions and see that the people and the magistrates never deviate from these.

With regard to mores, much is to be gained by keeping the old customs. Since corrupt peoples rarely do great things and have established few societies, founded few towns, and given few laws; and since, on the contrary, those with simple and austere mores have made most establishments, recalling men to the old maxims usually returns them to virtue.

Furthermore, if there has been some revolution and one has given the state a new form, it could scarcely have been done without infinite pain and work, and rarely with idleness and corrupt mores. The very ones who made the revolution wanted it to be savored, and they could scarcely have succeeded in this without good laws. Therefore, the old institutions are usually correctives, and the new ones, abuses. In a government that lasts a long time, one descends to ills by imperceptible degrees, and one climbs back to the good only with an effort.

It has been asked whether the members of the senate of which we are speaking should be members for life or chosen for a set time. They should doubtless be chosen for life, as was done in Rome,[15] Lacedaemonia,[16] and even Athens. The senate in Athens, a body that

[15]There the magistracies were for one year and the senators for life.

[16]"Lycurgus," says Xenophon, *The Constitution of the Lacedaemonians* [10.1–2], "wanted the senators elected from among the old men so that they should not be neglected even at the end of their lives; and by establishing them as judges of the courage of the young people, he made the old age of the former more honorable than the strength of the latter."

changed every three months, must not be confused with the Areopagus, whose members were established for life, a permanent model, as it were.

Here is a general maxim: in a senate made to be the rule, and, so to speak, the depository of the mores, senators should be elected for life; in a senate made to plan public business, the senators can change.

The spirit, says Aristotle, ages like the body. This reflection is good only in regard to a single magistrate and cannot be applied to an assembly of senators.

Besides the Areopagus, Athens had guardians of the mores and guardians of the laws.[17] In Lacedaemonia all the old men were censors. In Rome, two of the magistrates were the censors. Just as the senate keeps watch over the people, the censors must keep their eyes on the people and the senate. They must reestablish all that has become corrupted in the republic, notice slackness, judge oversights, and correct mistakes just as the laws punish crimes.

The Roman law that wanted the accusation of adultery to be made public maintained the purity of mores remarkably well; it intimidated the women and also intimidated those who kept watch over them.

Nothing maintains mores better than the extreme subordination of the young to the elderly. Both are contained, the former by the respect they have for the elderly, the latter by the respect they have for themselves.

Nothing gives greater force to the laws than the extreme subordination of the citizens to the magistrates. "The great difference Lycurgus set up between Lacedaemonia and other cities," says Xenophon,[18] "consists above all in his having made the citizens obey the laws; they hasten when the magistrate calls them. But in Athens, a rich man would despair if one believed him dependent on the magistrate."

Paternal authority is also very useful for maintaining mores. We have already said that none of the forces in a republic is as repressive as those in other governments. The laws must, therefore, seek to supplement them; they do so by paternal authority.

In Rome fathers had the right of life and death over their own

[17] The Areopagus itself was subject to the censorship.

[18] [Xenophon] *The Constitution of the Lacedaemonians* [8.2]. [Athens is not explicitly mentioned in the original.]

children.[19] In Lacedaemonia each father had the right to correct the child of another.

In Rome paternal power was lost along with the republic. In monarchies, where there is no question of such pure mores, one wants each person to live under the power of magistrates.

The laws of Rome, which accustomed young people to dependency, delayed their coming of age. Perhaps we were wrong to take up this usage; this much constraint is not needed in a monarchy.

The same subordination in a republic could make it possible for the father to remain the master of his children's goods during his life, as was the rule in Rome. But this is not in the spirit of monarchy.

[19] One can see in Roman history with what advantage to the republic this power was used. I shall speak only of the time of the greatest corruption. Aulus Fulvius was on his way to find Catilina; his father called him back and put him to death. Sallust, *Catilina* [39.5]. Several other citizens did the same. Cass. Dio [*Historia Romana*], bk. 37 [37.36.4].

CHAPTER 8

How laws should relate to the principle of the government in aristocracy

In an aristocracy, if the people are virtuous, they will enjoy almost the same happiness as in popular government, and the state will become powerful. But, as it is rare to find much virtue where men's fortunes are so unequal, the laws must tend to give, as much as they can, a spirit of moderation, and they must seek to reestablish the equality necessarily taken away by the constitution of the state.

The spirit of moderation is what is called virtue in aristocracy; there it takes the place of the spirit of equality in the popular state.

If the pomp and splendor surrounding kings is a part of their power, modesty and simplicity of manners are the strength of nobles in an aristocracy.[20] When the nobles affect no distinction, when they blend

[20] In our time the Venetians, who in many respects behaved very wisely, decided in a dispute between a Venetian nobleman and a gentleman of the mainland over precedence in a church that, outside of Venice, a Venetian nobleman had no preeminence over another citizen.

with the people, dress like them, and share all their pleasures with them, the people forget their own weakness.

Each government has its nature and its principle. The aristocracy must, therefore, not assume the nature and principle of monarchy, which would happen if the nobles had any personal and particular prerogatives distinct from those of the body to which they belong: privileges should be for the senate, and simple respect for the senators.

There are two principal sources of disorders in aristocratic states: extreme inequality between those who govern and those who are governed, and a similar inequality between the different members of the governing body. Hatreds and jealousies that the laws should prevent or check result from these two inequalities.

The first inequality is found chiefly when the privileges of the principal men are considered honorable only because they bring shame to the people. Such was the law in Rome that prohibited patricians from marrying plebeians,[21] which had no other effect than to render the patricians, on the one hand, more haughty, and on the other, more odious. Witness the advantages the tribunes drew from this in their harangues.

This inequality will again be found if the conditions of citizens differ in relation to payments, which happens in four ways: when the nobles give themselves the privilege of not paying them; when they exempt themselves fraudulently;[22] when they recover them for themselves on the pretext of remunerations or stipends for the tasks they do; finally, when they make the people their tributaries and divide among themselves the imposts they levy upon them. This last case is rare; when it occurs, an aristocracy is the harshest of all governments.

While Rome leaned toward aristocracy, it avoided these defects very well. The magistrates never drew stipends from their magistracies. The principal men of the republic were assessed like all others; they were assessed even more; and sometimes they were the only ones assessed. Finally, far from dividing the revenues of the state among themselves, they distributed all that could be drawn from the public treasury, all the wealth that fortune sent them, to the people, to be pardoned for their honors.[23]

[21] The decemvirs include it in the last two Tables. See Dion. Hal. [*Ant. Rom.*], bk. 10 [10.60.5].

[22] As in some aristocracies of our time. Nothing so weakens the state.

[23] See in Strabo [*Geographica*], bk. 14 [14.2.5], how the Rhodians behaved in this respect.

It is a fundamental maxim that distributions made to the people have pernicious effects in democracy to the same extent that they have good effects in aristocratic government. The former cause the loss of the spirit of citizenship,[d] the latter lead back to it.

If the revenues are not distributed to them, the people must be shown that they are well administered; displaying them to the people is a way of letting the people enjoy them. The gold chain that was hung in Venice, the wealth carried in Rome during the triumphs, and the treasures kept in the temple of Saturn, all were truly the people's wealth.

In aristocracy it is essential above all that the nobles not levy taxes.[e] In Rome, the highest order of the state had nothing to do with levying taxes; the second was charged with it, and even that led to serious drawbacks. If the nobles were to levy taxes in an aristocracy, all private individuals would be taxed at the discretion of the men concerned with matters of public business; there would be no higher tribunal to correct them. The nobles appointed to relieve the abuses would prefer to enjoy the abuses. Nobles would be like princes of despotic states, who confiscate the goods of whomever they please.

Soon these profits would be regarded as a patrimony, which avarice would extend according to its fancy. Tax farming[f] would collapse; public revenues would be reduced to nothing. In this way some states, without having received an observable setback, fall into a weakness that surprises their neighbors and stuns the citizens themselves.

The laws must also prohibit nobles from engaging in commerce; merchants with such rank would set up all sorts of monopolies. Commerce is the profession of equal people, and the poorest despotic states are those whose prince is a merchant.

The laws of Venice[24] prohibit nobles from engaging in any commerce, for it could give them, even innocently, exorbitant wealth.

The laws should use the most effective means to make the nobles render justice to the people. If the laws have not established a tribune, they must themselves be the tribune.

[24] [Abraham Nicolas] Amelot de la Houssaye, *Histoire du gouvernement de Venise*, part III [*Loix du gouvernement de Venise*, II; p. 25; 1740 edn]. The Claudian law forbade senators to have any vessel at sea holding more than forty barrels. Livy, bk. 21 [21.63].

---

[d] *ésprit de citoyen*. [e] *les tributs*.

[f] *les fermes*. In tax-farming, the job of collecting taxes was given, farmed out, to people who retained some of the taxes they collected. See 30.19.

Every sort of refuge from the execution of the laws ruins aristocracy, and tyranny is very near.

The laws should always humble the arrogance of domination. There must be, for a time or forever, a magistrate to make the nobles tremble, like the ephors in Lacedaemonia and the state inquisitors in Venice, whose magistracies are subject to no formalities. This government needs violent springs: in Venice, a stone mouth[25] is open for every informer; you might say it is the mouth of tyranny.

These tyrannical magistracies in aristocracies are related to censorship in democracy, which is no less independent by its nature. Indeed, the censors should not be examined about the things they have done during their censorship; they must be trusted, never daunted. The Romans were remarkable; all the magistrates[26] except the censors could be required to explain their conduct.[27]

Two things are pernicious in aristocracy: the extreme poverty of the nobles and their exorbitant wealth. To curb their poverty, they must above all be obliged to pay their debts promptly. To moderate their wealth, provisions must be made that are wise and imperceptible, in contrast to confiscations, agrarian laws, or the abolition of debts, which produce infinite evils.

The laws should remove the right of primogeniture from the nobles[28] so that fortunes are always restored to equality by the continual division of inheritances.

There must be no substitutions, no redemptions by one of the lineage, no entailed property, and no adoptions.[g] The means invented to perpetuate the greatness of families in monarchical states cannot be used in aristocracy.[29]

When the laws have equalized families, it remains for them to

[25] Informers throw their notes into it.

[26] See Livy, bk. 49 [45.15.7–8]. One censor could not even be bothered by another; each made his notation without consulting his colleague; and when it was done otherwise, the censorship was, so to speak, overthrown.

[27] In Athens, the Logistae, who had all the magistrates give account of themselves, did not do the same themselves.

[28] It is established in this way in Venice. [Abraham Nicolas] Amelot de la Houssaye [*Histoire du gouvernement de Venise*], pp. 30–31 [*Lois du gouvernement de Venise*, XII; 32–34; 1740 edn].

[29] It seems that the purpose of some aristocracies is less to maintain the state than to maintain what they call their nobility.

[g] *Il ne faut point de substitutions, de retraits lignagers, de majorats, d'adoptions.*

maintain the union between families. Disagreements among nobles should be resolved promptly; failing this, disputes between persons become disputes between families. Arbiters can end proceedings or keep them from arising.

Finally, the laws must not favor the distinctions that vanity puts between families on the pretext that some are nobler or older; this should rank with the pettinesses of private individuals.

One has only to cast an eye at Lacedaemonia; one will see how the ephors were able to humble the weaknesses of the kings, those of the important men, and those of the people.

CHAPTER 9

How laws are relative to their principle in monarchy

Since honor is the principle of this government, the laws should relate to it.

In monarchy they must work to sustain that nobility for whom honor is, so to speak, both child and father.

They must render it hereditary, not in order to be the boundary dividing the power of the prince from the weakness of the people, but to be the bond between them.

Substitutions, which keep goods in families, will be very useful in this government, though they are not suitable in the others.

Redemption by one of the lineage will return to the noble families the lands that a prodigal relative has transferred.

Noble lands, like noble persons, will have privileges. One cannot separate the dignity of the monarch from that of the kingdom; one can scarcely separate the dignity of the noble from that of his fief.

All these prerogatives will be peculiar to the nobility and will not transfer to the people, unless one wants to run counter to the principle of the government, unless one wants to diminish the force of the nobility and the force of the people.

Substitutions hamper commerce; redemption by one of the lineage makes an infinite number of proceedings necessary; and all the lands that are sold in the kingdom are more or less without a landlord for at least a year. Prerogatives attached to fiefs give a very burdensome power to those who hold them. These are the peculiar drawbacks of a nobility, which disappear in the face of the general utility it procures. But if these are extended to the people, one uselessly runs counter to all principles.

In monarchies, a man can be permitted to leave most of his goods to one of his children; this permission is good only there.

The laws must favor all the commerce[30] that the constitution of this government can allow, so that the subjects can, without being ruined, satisfy the ever-recurring needs of the prince and his court.

The laws must put a certain order in the manner of levying taxes so that the manner is not heavier than the burdens themselves.

The weight of burdens at first produces work; work, dejection; dejection, the spirit of laziness.

[30] The constitution permits commerce only to the people. See Law 3 in the *Code* [*Corpus Juris Civilis*, *Code* 4.63.3]; *de commerciis et mercatoribus*, which is full of good sense.

CHAPTER 10

On the promptness of execution in monarchy

Monarchical government has a great advantage over republican; as public business is led by one alone, execution is more prompt. But, since this promptness could degenerate into haste, here the laws will introduce a certain slowness. They should not only favor the nature of each constitution, but also remedy the abuses that can result from this same nature.

In monarchies Cardinal Richelieu[31] wants one to avoid the intricacies of corporations, which form difficulties at every point. Even if this man's heart was not filled with despotism, his head was.

The bodies that are the depository of the laws never obey better than when they drag their feet and bring into the prince's business the reflection that one can hardly expect from the absence of enlightenment in the court concerning the laws of the state and the haste of the prince's councils.[32]

What would have become of the finest monarchy in the world if the

[31] [Cardinal Richelieu] *Testament politique* (pt. 1, chap. 4, sec. 2; 243–247; 1947 edn).

[32] "For the barbarians, to delay is servile; immediate execution is proper to a king" [L.]. Tacitus, *Annales*, bk. 5 [6.32].

magistrates, by their slowness, their complaints, and their prayers, had not checked the course of even the virtues of its kings, when these monarchs, consulting only their generous souls, wanted to reward boundlessly services that were rendered with a similarly boundless courage and fidelity?

CHAPTER II

On the excellence of monarchical government

Monarchical government has a great advantage over despotic. As it is in its nature to have under the prince several orders dependent on the constitution, the state is more fixed, the constitution more unshakable, and the persons of those who govern more assured.

Cicero[33] believes that the establishment of tribunes in Rome saved the republic. "Indeed," he says, "the force of the people without a leader is more terrible. A leader feels that the business turns on him, he thinks about it; but the people in their impetuosity do not know the peril into which they throw themselves." One can apply this reflection to a despotic state, where the people have no tribunes, and to a monarchy, where the people do, in a way, have tribunes.

Indeed, one sees everywhere in the activities of despotic government that the people, led by themselves, always carry things as far as they can go; all the disorder they commit is extreme; whereas, in monarchies, things are very rarely carried to excess. The leaders fear for themselves; they fear being abandoned; the intermediate dependent powers[34] do not want the people to have the upper hand too much. Rarely are the orders of the state entirely corrupted. The prince depends on these orders; seditious men, who have neither the will nor the expectation of overturning the state, have neither the power nor the will to overthrow the prince.

In these circumstances, people of wisdom and authority intervene; temperings are proposed, agreements are reached, corrections are made; the laws become vigorous again and make themselves heard.

Thus all our histories are full of civil wars without revolutions; those of despotic states are full of revolutions without civil wars.

[33] [Cicero] *De legibus*, bk. 3 [3.10.23].

[34] See above, bk. 2, chap. 4, n. 22.

Those who have written the history of the civil war of some states, even those who have fomented them, have sufficiently proven how rarely princes should be suspicious of the authority they leave to certain orders in return for their service, for, even in their frenzy, these orders have longed only for the laws and their duty and have slowed the ardor and impetuousity of factious men more than they were able to serve them.[35]

Cardinal Richelieu, thinking perhaps that he had degraded the orders of the state too much, has recourse to the virtues of the prince and his ministers to sustain it,[36] and he requires so many things of them that, in truth, only an angel could have so much care, so much enlightenment, so much firmness, and so much knowledge; one can scarcely flatter oneself that, between now and the dissolution of monarchies, there could ever be such a prince and such ministers.

Just as the peoples who live under a good police[h] are happier than those who run about in the forest, without rule and without leaders, so monarchs who live under the fundamental laws of their state are happier than despotic princes, who have nothing to rule their people's hearts or their own.

[35] *Memoirs* of the Cardinal de Retz and other histories.
[36] [Cardinal Richelieu] *Testament politique* [pt. 1, chap. 6, sec. 8; 1947 edn].

[h] See note [c], bk. 4.

CHAPTER 12

Continuation of the same subject

Let one not seek magnanimity in despotic states; there, the prince could not give a greatness that he himself does not have: there is no glory there.

In monarchies one sees the subjects around the prince receive his light; there, as each one has, so to speak, a larger space, he can exercise those virtues that give the soul not independence but greatness.

CHAPTER 13
The idea of despotism

When the savages of Louisiana want fruit, they cut down the tree and gather the fruit.[37] There you have despotic government.

[37] *Lettres édifiantes et curieuses*, bk. 2, p. 315 [Lettre du P. Gabriel Marest, Cascaskias, Illinois, November 9, 1712; vol. 11, 315; 1715 edn].

CHAPTER 14
How the laws are relative to the principle of despotic government

Despotic government has fear as its principle; and not many laws are needed for timid, ignorant, beaten-down people.

Everything should turn on two or three ideas; therefore, there must be no new ones. When you instruct a beast you take great care not to let him change masters, training, or gait; you stamp his brain with two or three impulses and no more.

When the prince is enclosed, he cannot end his stay among sensual pleasures without distressing all those who keep him there. They cannot allow his person and his power to pass into other hands. Therefore, he rarely wages war in person and scarcely dares have it waged by his lieutenants.

Such a prince, accustomed to meeting no resistance in his palace, becomes insulted at that offered him by armed men; he is, therefore, usually moved by anger or vengeance. Besides, he cannot have an idea of true glory. Therefore, wars have to be waged there in all their natural fury, and the right of nations has to be less extensive than elsewhere.

Such a prince has so many faults that one must fear exposing his natural foolishness to the light of day. He is hidden, and one remains in ignorance of his condition. Fortunately, men in these countries are such that they need only a name to govern them.

Charles XII, meeting some resistance in the senate of Sweden while he was at Bender, wrote that he would send one of his boots to command it. The boot would have governed like a despotic king.

If the prince is taken prisoner, he is supposed dead, and another ascends the throne. The treaties made by the prisoner are null; his successor would not ratify them. Indeed, as he is the laws, the state, and the prince, and as from the moment he is no longer the prince, he is nothing, if he were not considered dead, the state would be destroyed.

One of the things that led the Turks to decide to make their separate peace with Peter I was that the Muscovites told the vizir that in Sweden another king had been put on the throne.[38]

The preservation of the state is only the preservation of the prince, or rather of the palace in which he is enclosed. Nothing which does not directly menace the palace or the capital makes an impression on ignorant, arrogant, and biased minds; and, as for the sequence of events, they cannot follow it, foresee it, or even think about it. Politics with its springs and laws should here be very limited, and political government is as simple as civil government.[39]

Everything comes down to reconciling political and civil government with domestic government, the officers of the state with those of the seraglio.

Such a state will be in the best situation when it is able to consider itself as alone in the world, when it is surrounded by deserts and separated from the peoples it calls barbarians. It will be good for the despotism, unable to count on the militia, to destroy a part of itself.

While the principle of despotic government is fear, its end is tranquillity; but this is not a peace, it is the silence of the towns that the enemy is ready to occupy.

Since force is not in the state but in the army that has founded it, that army must be preserved in order to defend the state; however, it is dangerous to the prince. How then is the security of the state to be reconciled with the security of the person?

I beg you to observe with what industry the Muscovite government seeks to escape the despotism which weighs on the government even more than it does on the peoples. Great bodies of troops have been disbanded; penalties for crimes have been lessened; tribunals have

[38] Continuation of Pufendorf, *Histoire universelle*, in the article on Sweden, chap. 10. [This is in Pufendorf's *Histoire de Suède*; 1711; 3, 125; 1748 edn, not *Introduction à l'histoire générale et politique de l'univers*; the boot story is told in Voltaire's *Histoire du Charles XII*, Book 7.]

[39] According to [John] Chardin [*Voyages*, "Description du gouvernement . . . des Persans," chap. 3, "De l'économie politique"; 5, 237; 1811 edn], there is no Council of State in Persia.

been established; some men have begun to be versed in the laws; the peoples have been instructed. But there are particular causes that will perhaps return it to the misfortune it had wanted to flee.

In these states, religion has more influence than in any other; it is a fear added to fear. In Mohammedan empires the peoples derive from religion a part of the astonishing respect they have for their prince.

It is religion that slightly corrects the Turkish constitution. Those subjects who are not attached to the glory and greatness of the state by honor are attached to it by force and by religious principle.

Of all despotic governments, none is more oppressive to itself than the one whose prince declares himself owner of all the land and heir to all his subjects. This always results in abandoning the cultivation of the land and, if the prince is a merchant, in ruining every kind of industry.

In these states, nothing is repaired, nothing improved.[40] Houses are built only for a lifetime; one digs no ditches, plants no trees; one draws all from the land, and returns nothing to it; all is fallow, all is deserted.

Do you think that laws that take away ownership of land and inheritance of goods will diminish the avarice and cupidity of the important men? No: such laws will excite their cupidity and avarice. The important men will be led to take a thousand oppressive measures because they will not consider anything their own but the gold or silver that they can steal or hide.

In order that all not be lost, it is well to moderate the greediness of the prince by some custom. Thus, in Turkey, the prince is usually satisfied to take 3 per cent from the inheritances of the people.[41] But, as the Grand Signior gives most of the land to his militia and disposes of it according to his fancy, as he seizes all the inheritances of the officers of the empire, as, when a man dies without male children, the Grand Signior becomes the owner and the daughters have only the usufruct, it happens that most of the goods of the state are held in precarium.[i]

According to a law of Bantam,[42] the king takes the inheritance,

[40] See [Paul] Rycaut, *The History of the Present State of the Ottoman Empire*, p. 196 [bk. 1, chap. 17, pp. 29–30; 1703 edn].

[41] Concerning inheritances among the Turks, see [Georges Guillet de Saint-Georges] *Lacédémone ancienne et nouvelle* [bk. 3; p. 463; 1676 edn]. See also [Paul] Rycaut, *The History of the Present State of the Ottoman Empire* [bk. 1, chap. 16; p. 28; 1703 edn].

[42] *Recueil des voyages qui ont servi à l'établissement de la Compagnie des Indes*, vol. 1 ["Premiers voiages des Hollandais aux Indes Orientales"; 1, 384; 1702 edn; 1, 348; 1725 edn]. The

[i] *d'une manière précaire*. This is a technical term for "obtained by entreaty or favor."

including the wife, the children, and the house. In order to elude the most cruel provision of this law, one is obliged to marry children at the age of eight, nine, or ten, and sometimes even younger, so that they do not remain an unfortunate part of the father's inheritance.

In states where there are no fundamental laws, the inheritance of the empire cannot be fixed. The prince elects from within his family or from outside it the one who is to wear the crown. It would be vain to establish inheritance by the eldest; the prince could always choose another. The successor is declared either by the prince himself, by his ministers, or by a civil war. Thus, this state has one more reason for dissolution than a monarchy.

As each prince of the royal family is equally entitled to be elected, it happens that the one who ascends to the throne immediately has his brothers strangled, as in Turkey; or blinded, as in Persia; or driven mad, as with the Moguls; and, if these precautions are not taken, as in Morocco, each time the throne is vacated a horrible civil war follows.

According to the constitutions of Muscovy,[43] the czar can choose whomever he wants as his successor, either from within his family or from outside it. The establishment of such a succession causes a thousand revolutions and renders the throne as unsteady as the succession is arbitrary. As one of the most important things for the people to know is the order of succession, the best one is that which is most obvious, such as birth and a certain order of birth. Such a provision checks intrigues and stifles ambition; the spirit of a weak prince is no longer captive, and the dying are not made to speak.

When a fundamental law establishes the order of succession, one prince alone is the successor, and his brothers have no real or apparent right to contend for the crown. One can neither presume nor bring to bear a particular will of the father. It is, therefore, no more a question of checking the king's brother or of killing him than it is of checking or killing any other subject at all.

But in despotic states, where the prince's brothers are equally his slaves and his rivals, prudence requires that they be imprisoned, especially in Mohammedan countries, where the religion regards

law of Pegu is less cruel: if one has children, the king inherits only two-thirds. Ibid., vol. 3, p. 1 ["Second voiage d'Etienne van der Hagan," 3, 73; 1705 edn; 3, 69; 1725 edn].

[43] See the different constitutions, particularly that of 1722. [*Polnoe sobranie zakovov Rossiiskoi imperii s 1649 goda*, no. 3893, February 5, 1722, 6, 496–497; 1830 edn.]

victory or success as a judgment of god, so that no one is sovereign there by right, but only in fact.

In states where the princes of the blood see that they will be enclosed or put to death if they do not ascend to the throne, ambition is excited much more than among ourselves, where princes of the blood enjoy a condition which, though not as satisfying to ambition, is perhaps more satisfying to moderate desires.

In despotic states princes have always abused marriage. They usually take several wives, especially in that part of the world, Asia, where despotism is, so to speak, naturalized. They have so many children that they can scarcely have any affection for them, nor can the children have any for their brothers.

The reigning family resembles the state; it is too weak, and its leader is too strong; it seems extensive, and it amounts to nothing. Artaxerxes[44] had all his children murdered for having plotted against him. It is not credible that fifty children would conspire against their father, and still less that they would conspire because he had refused to yield his concubine to his eldest son. It is simpler to believe that this was some intrigue in those seraglios of the East, those places where artifice, wickedness, and deceit reign in silence and are covered by the darkness of night, where an old prince who becomes more imbecilic every day is the first prisoner of the palace.

After all we have just said, it seems that human nature would rise up incessantly against despotic government. But, despite men's love of liberty, despite their hatred of violence, most peoples are subjected to this type of government. This is easy to understand. In order to form a moderate government, one must combine powers, regulate them, temper them, make them act; one must give one power a ballast, so to speak, to put it in a position to resist another; this is a masterpiece of legislation that chance rarely produces and prudence is rarely allowed to produce. By contrast, a despotic government leaps to view, so to speak; it is uniform throughout; as only passions are needed to establish it, everyone is good enough for that.

[44] See Justin [*Epitoma historiarum Philippicarum* 10.1].

CHAPTER 15

Continuation of the same subject

In hot climates, where despotism usually reigns, passions make themselves felt earlier and are also deadened sooner;[45] the spirit ages more quickly; the perils of dissipating one's goods are not as great; it is not as easy to distinguish oneself, and there is not as much commerce among the young, who are shut in at home; one marries younger; one can, therefore, come of age earlier than in our European climates. In Turkey, one reaches majority at the age of fifteen.[46]

The surrender of goods has no place there;[j] in a government where no one is assured of his fortune, one's lending is based on persons rather than on goods.

This surrender enters by nature into moderate governments,[47] and above all into republics, because there one should have greater trust in the citizens' integrity and because of the gentleness that should be inspired by a form of government that each seems to have given to himself.

If the legislators in the Roman republic had established the surrender of goods,[48] Rome would not have been thrown into so many seditions and civil discords and would have risked neither the dangers of those ills nor the perils of the remedies.

Poverty and the uncertainty of fortunes naturalizes usury in despotic states, as each one increases the price of his silver in proportion to the peril involved in lending it. Therefore, destitution is omnipresent in these unhappy countries; there everything is taken away including the recourse to borrowing.[k]

It follows that a merchant cannot engage in much commerce there;

[45] See [bk. 14], "On the laws in relation to the nature of the climate."

[46] [Georges] Guillet de Saint-Georges, *Lacédémone ancienne et nouvelle* [bk. 3], p. 463 [1676 edn].

[47] It is the same for extensions of credit in surrenders of goods [bankruptcies] in good faith.

[48] It was established only by the Julian law, *De cessione bonorum*; one avoided prison and the ignominious surrenders of one's goods. [See *Corpus Juris Civilis*, *Code* 7.71.4; *qui bonis cedere possunt*. See also Gaius, *Institutes* 3.78; this passage, however, was certainly unknown to M., for the manuscript containing it was not discovered until 1816 by Niebuhr. M. presumes, as we do today, that this is one of Julius Caesar's laws on the debtor problem.]

[j] *cession des biens*.

[k] See 22.19 (note [i], bk. 22) for a distinction between interest and usury.

he lives from day to day; if he burdened himself with many commodities, he would lose more on the interest owed on the purchase than he would make on the commodities. Thus the laws of commerce scarcely apply there; these laws amount only to a simple police.

Government could not be unjust without hands to exercise its injustices; now, it is impossible for these hands not to be used on their own behalf. Therefore, embezzlement is natural in despotic states.

As this is the ordinary crime there, confiscations are useful. In this way the people are consoled; the silver from confiscations amounts to a substantial tax that the prince would find difficult to levy on his downtrodden subjects; there is not even any family in this country one wants to preserve.

In moderate states, it is entirely different. Confiscations would render the ownership of goods uncertain; they would despoil innocent children; they would destroy a family man when it was only a question of punishing a guilty man. In republics, confiscations would have the ill effect of taking away the equality which is their soul, by depriving a citizen of his physical necessities.[49]

A Roman law[50] wants confiscation in only the most serious case of the crime of high treason. It would often be very wise to follow the spirit of this law and limit confiscation to certain crimes. In those countries where local custom has made provision for *goods by inheritance*, as Bodin[51] aptly states, one must confiscate only those that are *acquired*.[l]

[49] It seems to me that confiscations were too much loved in the republic of Athens.

[50] *Authentics*, *Bona damnatorum*, *Code* [*Corpus Juris Civilis*, *Code* 9.49.10; *Novel.* 134,c.13]; *de bonis proscriptorum seu damnatorum.*

[51] [Jean Bodin, *The Six Books of a Commonwealth*] bk. 5, chap. 3 [bk. 5, chap. 3; p. 581; 1962 edn].

[l] *propres* and *acquêtes*.

CHAPTER 16
On the communication of power

In despotic government, *power* passes entirely into the hands of the one to whom it is entrusted. The vizir is the despot himself, and each individual officer is the vizir. In monarchical government, power is not applied without some mediation; the monarch, in giving it, tempers it.[52] He distributes his authority in such a way that he never gives a part without retaining a greater part.

Thus, in monarchical states individual governors of towns are not so answerable to the governor of the province as not to be even more answerable to the prince, and individual officers of military units are not so dependent upon the general as not to have an even greater dependence upon the prince.

In most monarchical states it has wisely been established that those whose command is somewhat extensive are not attached to any body of militia, with the result that, as their command derives only from the particular will of the prince, who employs them or not, they are, in a way, in service and, in a way, outside it.

This is incompatible with despotic government. For, if those who had no current employment nevertheless had prerogatives and titles, there would be men in the state who were great in themselves, and this would run counter to the nature of this government.

If the governor of a town were independent of the pasha, there would have to be constant temperings to accommodate the two of them, an absurdity in a despotic government. And, in addition, if an individual governor could disobey, how could the pasha personally answer for his province?

In this government authority cannot be counter-balanced; neither that of the lowest magistrate nor that of the despot. In moderate countries law is everywhere wise; it is known everywhere, and the lowest of the magistrates can follow it. But in despotism, where law is only the will of the prince, even if the prince is wise, how can a magistrate follow a will that he does not know? He must follow his own.

Furthermore, as law is only what the prince wants, and the prince is able to want only what he knows, surely there must be an infinite number of people who want in his name and in the same way he does.

Finally, as law is the momentary will of the prince, those who want in his name necessarily want instantly as he does.

[52]"The light of Phoebus is usually sweeter/ As it sets" [L.]. [Seneca, *Tragedies*, *Troades* II.1140–1141.]

CHAPTER 17
On presents

In despotic countries the usage is that one does not approach a superior, even a king, without giving him a present. The emperor of the Moguls[53] does not accept requests from his subjects unless he has received something from them. These princes go so far as to corrupt their own pardons.

It should be this way in a government where no one is a citizen, in a government where one is filled with the idea that the superior owes nothing to the inferior, in a government where men believe themselves bound only by the chastisements that the former give the latter, in a government where there is little public business and where one is rarely introduced into the presence of an important man to request something of him, and even more rarely to complain to him.

Presents are an odious thing in a republic because virtue has no need of them. In a monarchy, honor is a stronger motive than presents. But in the despotic state, where there is neither honor nor virtue, one can decide to act only in anticipation of the comforts of life.

In accordance with his ideas about the republic, Plato[54] wanted those who received presents for doing their duty to be punished by death. *One must not accept them*, he states, *either for good things or for bad.*

It was a bad law of the Romans[55] that permitted magistrates to accept small presents[56] provided they did not exceed one hundred ecus per year. Those to whom nothing is given desire nothing; those to whom a little is given soon desire a little more and then a great deal. Besides, it is easier to convict the one who ought to take nothing but takes something than it is to convict the one who takes more when he ought to take less and who always finds plausible pretexts, excuses, causes and reasons for doing so.

[53] *Recueil des voyages qui ont servi à l'établissement de la Compagnie des Indes*, vol. 1, p. 80 ["Avis sur le Commerce des Indes Orientales. Description de leur maniere de vivre"; 1, LXXXVIII; 1725 edn].
[54] [Plato] *Laws*, bk. 12 [955c–d].
[55] Law 6, par. 2, *Digest* [*Corpus Juris Civilis, Digest* 48.11.6.2]; *de lege Julia repetundarum*.
[56] *Munuscula*: "A small gift."

CHAPTER 18

On rewards given by the sovereign

In despotic governments, where, as we have said, one decides to act only in anticipation of the comforts of life, the prince who gives rewards has only silver to give. In a monarchy, where honor alone reigns, the prince would reward only with distinctions were it not that the distinctions established by honor are joined with a luxury that necessarily produces needs; therefore, the prince rewards with honors that lead to fortune. But in a republic under the reign of virtue, a motive that suffices in itself and excludes all others, the state rewards only with testimonies to that virtue.

It is a general rule that great rewards in a monarchy and a republic are a sign of their decadence because they prove that the principles have been corrupted: on the one hand, the idea of honor no longer has as much force, on the other, citizenship has been weakened.[m]

The worst Roman emperors were those who gave the most: for example, Caligula, Claudius, Nero, Otho, Vitellius, Commodus, Heliogabulus, and Caracalla. The best, such as Augustus, Vespasian, Antoninus Pius, Marcus Aurelius, and Pertinax, were frugal. Under the good emperors, the state regained its principles; the treasure of honor replaced other treasures.

[m] *qualité de citoyen.*

CHAPTER 19

New consequences of the principles of the three governments

I cannot bring myself to finish this book without making some further applications of my three principles.

FIRST QUESTION. Should the laws force a citizen to accept public employments? I say that they should in republican government and not in monarchical. In the former, magistracies are testimonies to virtue; they are depositories entrusted by the homeland to a citizen who should live, act, and think only for its sake; he cannot, therefore, refuse them.[57]

[57] Plato, in his *Republic*, bk. 8 [557e], puts such refusals among the marks of corruption of the

In the latter, magistracies are testimonies to honor; now, such is the eccentricity of honor that it is pleased to accept magistracies only when it wants and in the manner it wants.

The late king of Sardinia[58] punished those who refused the dignities and employments of his state; unwittingly he followed republican ideas. His manner of governing, however, proves sufficiently that this was not his intention.

SECOND QUESTION. Is it a good maxim whereby a citizen can be obliged to accept a place in the army below one he has previously held? Among the Romans the captain often served the next year under his lieutenant.[59] This is because virtue here asks for the continuous sacrifice to the state of oneself and one's aversions. But in monarchies, honor, true or false, cannot suffer that which it calls degradation.

In despotic governments where honor, posts, and ranks are equally abused, it is indifferent whether a lout is made from a prince or a prince from a lout.

THIRD QUESTION. Shall civil and military employments be given to one person? They must be united in a republic and separated in a monarchy. In republics it would be very dangerous to make the profession of arms a particular estate distinct from that of civil functions; and, in monarchies, there would be no less peril in giving the two functions to the same person.

One takes up arms, in the republic, only to defend the laws and the homeland; it is because one is a citizen that one becomes, for a time, a soldier. If these were two distinct estates, the one who bore arms and believed himself a citizen would come to feel he was only a soldier.

In monarchies, the object of men of war is only glory, or at least honor or fortune. One should be very careful not to give civil employments to such men; they must, on the contrary, be contained by civil magistrates, and they must not have at the same time both the people's trust and the force to abuse it.[60]

republic. In his *Laws*, bk. 6 [756b–e], he wants to punish them by a fine. In Venice, they are punished by exile.

58 Victor Amedeus [Victor Amedeus II, 1666–1732].

59 When some centurions asked the people what employments they had had, one centurion said, "It is just, my companions, for you to esteem as honorable any post in which you defend the republic," Livy, bk. 42 [42.34.15].

60 "Lest political power be transferred to the best of the nobles, Gallienus forbade the senate military service, and even entry to the army" [L.]. Aurelius Victor, *De viris illustribus* [*De Caesaribus* 33.34].

In a nation where the republic hides under the form of monarchy, observe how a particular estate for fighting men is feared and how the warrior still remains a citizen or even a magistrate, so that these titles serve as a pledge to the homeland so that it is never forgotten.

That division of the magistracies into civil and military ones, which the Romans made after the loss of the republic, was not arbitrary. It followed from a change in the Roman constitution; it was in the nature of monarchical government. And in order to temper the military government, the emperors that succeeded Augustus[61] were obliged to finish what he had only begun.[62]

Thus Procopius, rival of Valens for the empire, failed to grasp this when, giving the dignity of proconsul[63] to Hormisdas, prince of the royal blood of Persia, he returned to this magistracy its former command of the armies; but perhaps he had particular reasons for this. A man who aspires to sovereignty seeks what is useful to the state less than what is useful to his cause.

FOURTH QUESTION. Is it suitable for posts to be sold? They should not be sold in despotic states, where the prince must place or displace subjects in an instant.

Venality is good in monarchical states, because it provides for performing as a family vocation what one would not want to undertake for virtue, and because it destines each to his duty and renders the orders of the state more permanent. Suidas[64] aptly says that Anastasius had made a kind of aristocracy of the empire by selling all the magistracies.

Plato[65] cannot endure such venality. "It is," he says, "as if, on a ship, one made someone a pilot or a sailor for his silver. Is it possible that the rule is good only for guiding a republic and bad in all other life employments?" But Plato is speaking of a republic founded on virtue, and we are speaking of a monarchy. Now, in a monarchy, where, if the posts were not sold by a public regulation, the courtiers' indigence and avidity would sell them all the same, chance will produce better

[61] Augustus removed from the senators, proconsuls, and governors, the right to bear arms. Cass. Dio [*Historia Romana*], bk. 33 [53.12.2–3].

[62] Constantine. See Zosimus [*Historiae*], bk. 2 [2.33].

[63] "In accord with ancient custom and the rule of war" [L.]. Ammianus Marcellinus [*Res gestae*], bk. 26 [26.8.12].

[64] Fragments drawn from the *Ambassades* of Constantine Porphyrogenitus [Suidas, *Lexicon*, "Anastasios," 1, 187; 1938 edn].

[65] [Plato] *Republic*, bk. 8 [551c].

subjects than the choice of the prince. Finally, advancing oneself by way of wealth inspires and maintains industry,[66] a thing badly needed in this kind of government.

FIFTH QUESTION. In which government must there be censors? There must be censors in a republic where the principle of government is virtue. It is not only crimes that destroy virtue, but also negligence, mistakes, a certain slackness in the love of the homeland, dangerous examples, the seeds of corruption, that which does not run counter to the laws but eludes them, that which does not destroy them but weakens them: all these should be corrected by censors.

It is astonishing that an Areopagite was punished for killing a sparrow that had taken refuge in his breast while in flight from a hawk. It is surprising that the Areopagus sent to his death a child who had put out the eyes of a bird. Notice that the question is not that of condemning a crime but of judging mores in a republic founded on mores.

In monarchies there must be no censors; monarchies are founded on honor, and the nature of honor is to have the whole universe as a censor. Every man who commits a breach of honor is subject to the reproaches of even those without honor.

There censors would be spoiled by the very men they ought to correct. Their opposition to the corruption of a monarchy would do no good; the corruption of a monarchy would be too strong for them.

It is manifest that there must be no censors in despotic governments. The example of China seems to be an exception to this rule, but in the course of this work we shall see the singular reasons for its establishment there.

[66] Laziness of Spain: all employments there are given out.

BOOK 6

Consequences of the principles of the various governments in relation to the simplicity of civil and criminal laws, the form of judgments, and the establishment of penalties

CHAPTER I

On the simplicity of civil laws in the various governments

Monarchical government does not admit of such simple laws as does despotic government. In monarchical government there must be tribunals. These tribunals give decisions. These decisions should be preserved; they should be learned, so that one judges there today as one judged yesterday and so that the citizens' property and life are as secure and fixed as the very constitution of the state.

In a monarchy, the administering of a justice[a] that hands down decisions not only about life and goods, but also about honor, requires scrupulous inquiries. The fastidiousness of the judge grows as more issues are deposited[b] with him and as he pronounces upon greater interests.

In the laws of these states, therefore, one must not be astonished to find so many rules, restrictions, and extensions that multiply particular cases and seem to make an art of reasoning itself.

The differences in rank, origin, and condition that are established in monarchical government often carry with them distinctions in the nature of men's goods, and the laws regarding the constitution of this state can increase the number of these distinctions. Thus, among ourselves, goods are inherited, acquired, or seized; dotal, paraphernal; paternal and maternal; those of personal estates of several kinds; free,

[a]See note [g], bk. 2. [b]See note [j], bk. 2.

substituted; those of the lineage or not; noble, freely held, or common goods; ground rents, or those given a price in silver. Each sort of goods is subject to particular rules; these must be followed in order to make disposition of the goods, which further removes simplicity.

In our governments fiefs became hereditary. The nobility had to have had a certain standing so that the owner of a fief would be in a position to serve the prince. This produced many variations; for example, there are countries in which fiefs could not be divided among brothers; in others, younger brothers could receive a more extensive provision of their own.

The monarch, who knows each of his provinces, can set up various laws or permit different customs. But the despot knows nothing and can attend to nothing; he must approach everything in a general way; he governs with a rigid will that is the same in all circumstances; all is flattened beneath his feet.

In monarchies, in proportion to the number of judgments made by tribunals, jurisprudence is responsible for decisions that are sometimes inconsistent, because successive judges think differently, or because suits are sometimes well and sometimes poorly defended, or finally, because an infinity of abuses slips into whatever is touched by the hands of men. This is a necessary ill that the legislator corrects from time to time, as being an ill that is contrary even to the spirit of moderate governments. For when one is obliged to turn to the tribunals, it must be because of the nature of the constitution and not because of the inconsistency and uncertainty of the laws.

There must be privileges in governments where there are necessarily distinctions between persons. This further diminishes simplicity and produces a thousand exceptions.

One of the privileges least burdensome to society and least of all to him who gives it is that of being allowed to plead before one tribunal rather than another. Otherwise there are new suits, that is, those which seek to ascertain the tribunal before which one must plead.

The peoples in despotic states present a very different case. I do not know on what matter the legislator could enact or the magistrate judge in these countries. It follows from the fact that the lands belong to the prince that there are scarcely any civil laws concerning the ownership of lands. It follows from the sovereign's right to inherit that there are no laws concerning inheritance. Because trade belongs exclusively to the despot in some countries, all sorts of laws concerning commerce are rendered useless. Because marriages are contracted there with female slaves, there are scarcely any civil laws about dowries or the privileges of wives. Another result of the prodigious multitude of slaves there is that scarcely anyone has a will of his own, and consequently scarcely anyone is answerable for his conduct before a judge. Most moral actions, which are nothing but the wills of the father, the husband, or the master, are regulated by them and not by magistrates.

I have almost forgotten to say that since what we call honor is scarcely known in these states, suits concerning honor, such an important subject among us, do not arise there. Despotism is self-sufficient; everything around it is empty. Thus when travelers describe countries to us where despotism reigns, they rarely speak of civil laws.[1]

Therefore, all occasions for disputes and proceedings are taken away there. This is, in part, what makes pleaders so mistreated; the injustice of their request appears baldly, being neither hidden, mitigated, nor protected by an infinity of laws.

[1] No written law has been discovered in Mazulipatam. See the *Recueil des voyages qui ont servi à l'établissement de la Compagnie des Indes*, vol. 4, pt. 1, p. 391 ["Voyage de Pierre Van den Broeck"; 4, 420; 1705 edn; 4, 392; 1725 edn]. In judgments, the Indians go only by certain customs. The *Veda* and other such books contain religious precepts but not civil laws. *Lettres édifiantes et curieuses*, 14 [Lettre du P. Bouchet, Pontichéry, October 2, 1714; 14, 326–332; 1720 edn].

CHAPTER 2

On the simplicity of criminal laws in the various governments

It is constantly said that justice should be rendered everywhere as it is in Turkey. Can it be that the most ignorant of all peoples have seen clearly the one thing in the world that it is most important for men to know?

If you examine the formalities of justice in relation to the difficulties a citizen endures to have his goods returned to him or to obtain satisfaction for some insult, you will doubtless find the formalities too many; if you consider them in their relation to the liberty and security of the citizens, you will often find them too few, and you will see that the penalties, expenses, delays, and even the dangers of justice are the price each citizen pays for his liberty.

In Turkey, where one pays very little attention to the fortune, life, or honor of the subjects, all disputes are speedily concluded in one way or another. The manner of ending them is not important, provided that they are ended. The pasha is no sooner informed than he has the pleaders bastinadoed according to his fancy and sends them back home.

And, for one to have the passions of pleaders would be quite dangerous there; these passions presuppose an ardent desire to see justice done, a hatred, an active spirit, and a steadfastness in pursuit of justice. All this should be avoided in a government where there must be no feeling other than fear and where everything leads abruptly and unforeseeably to revolutions. Each man should know that the magistrate must not hear of him and that he owes his safety only to his nothingness.

But in moderate states where the head of even the lowest citizen is esteemed, his honor and goods are removed from him only after long examination; he is deprived of his life only when the homeland itself attacks it; and when the homeland attacks his life, it gives him every possible means of defending it.

Thus, when a man makes himself more absolute,[2] his first thought is to simplify the laws. In these states he begins by being struck more by particular drawbacks than by the liberty of the subjects, with which he is not concerned.

One can see that there must be at least as many formalities in republics as in monarchies. In both governments, formalities increase in proportion to the importance given to the honor, fortune, life, and liberty of the citizens.

Men are all equal in republican government; they are equal in despotic government; in the former, it is because they are everything; in the latter, it is because they are nothing.

[2]Caesar, Cromwell, and so many others.

CHAPTER 3

In which governments and in which cases one should judge according to a precise text of the law

The more the government approaches a republic, the more the manner of judging becomes fixed; and it was a vice of the Lacedaemonian republic that the ephors judged arbitrarily without laws to guide them. In Rome, the first consuls judged like the ephors; the drawbacks of this were felt, and precise laws were made.

In despotic states there is no law; the judge himself is the rule. In monarchical states there is a law; and, when it is precise, the judge follows it; when it is not, he seeks its spirit. In republican government, it is in the nature of the constitution for judges to follow the letter of the law. No law can be interpreted to the detriment of a citizen when it is a question of his goods, his honor, or his life.

In Rome, judges pronounced only that the accused was guilty of a certain crime, and the penalty was found in the law, as can be seen from various laws that were made. In England likewise, the jury decides whether the accused is guilty or not of the deed brought before it; and, if he is declared guilty, the judge pronounces the penalty imposed by law for this deed; and he needs only his eyes for that.

CHAPTER 4

On the manner of forming judgments

The different ways of forming judgments follow from this. In monarchies judges assume the manner of arbiters; they deliberate together, they share their thoughts, they come to an agreement; one modifies his opinion to make it like another's; opinions with the least support are incorporated into the two most widely held. This is not in the nature of a republic. In Rome and in the Greek towns, judges did not communicate with each other; each gave his opinion in one of three ways, *I absolve*, *I condemn*, *It is not evident to me*[3] because the people judged or were thought to judge. But the people are not jurists; the

[3] *Non liquet*: "It is not evident."

modifications and temperings of arbiters are not for them; they must be presented with a single object, a deed, and only one deed, and they have only to see whether they should condemn, absolve, or remand judgment.

The Romans, following the example of the Greeks, introduced formulae for actions at law,[4] and established that it was necessary for each suit to be managed by the action proper to it. This was necessary to their manner of judging; the state of the question had to be fixed in order to keep it before the people. Otherwise, in the course of an important suit, the state of the question would continually change and become unrecognizable.

Thus it followed that judges, among the Romans, would admit only the specific request without increasing, diminishing, or modifying anything. But the praetors imagined other formulae for the guidance of actions, which were called *in good faith*,[5] where the manner of pronouncing judgment was more at the disposition of the judge. This arrangement was more in agreement with the spirit of monarchy. Thus, French legal experts say: *In France, all actions are in good faith.*[6]

[4]"Such legal actions were instituted just as the people wished, for they wanted them to be both solemn and certain" [L.]. Law 2, para. 6, *Digest* [*Corpus Juris Civilis, Digest* 1.2.2.6]; *de origine juris*.

[5]In which these words were included: *ex bona fide*: "in good faith."

[6]There even the one of whom more is demanded than he owes is condemned to pay the expenses unless he has offered and consigned what he owes.

CHAPTER 5

In which governments the sovereign can be the judge

Machiavelli[7] attributes the loss of liberty in Florence to the fact that the people as a body did not judge the crimes of high treason committed against them, as was done in Rome. Eight judges were established for this: *But*, states Machiavelli, *few are corrupted by few*. I would gladly adopt this great man's maxim; but, as in these cases of treason, political interest forces civil interest, so to speak (for it is always a drawback if the people themselves judge their offenses), the laws must provide, as

[7][Niccolò Machiavelli] *Discourses on the First Ten Books of Livy*, bk. 1, chap. 7 [bk. 1, chap. 7].

much as they can, for the security of individuals in order to remedy this drawback.

Using this idea, the Roman legislators did two things: they permitted accused men to exile themselves[8] before the judgment[9] and they wanted the goods of condemned men to be made sacred so that the people could not confiscate them. Other limitations placed on the people's power to judge will be seen in Book 11.

Solon knew very well how to curb the people's abuses of their power when judging crimes; he wanted the Areopagus to review the suit, and if it believed the accused to be unjustly acquitted,[10] it accused him again before the people; and if it believed him unjustly condemned,[11] it checked the execution and had the suit judged again: an admirable law, which subjected the people to the censure of the magistracy they most respected and to their own censure as well!

It will be well to slow down such suits, especially after the accused is made a prisoner, so that the people will be calmed and will judge with cool heads.

In despotic states the prince himself can judge. He cannot judge in monarchies: the constitution would be destroyed and the intermediate dependent powers reduced to nothing; one would see all the formalities of judgments cease; fear would invade all spirits; one would see pallor on every face; there would be no more trust, honor, love, security, or monarchy.

Here are some other reflections. In monarchical states, the prince is the party who pursues those who are accused and has them punished or acquitted; if he himself judged, he would be both judge and party.

In these same states, the prince often receives what is confiscated; if he judged the crimes, he would again be both judge and party.

Moreover, he would lose the finest attribute of his sovereignty, which is that of pardoning.[12] It would be senseless for him both to make and unmake his own judgments; he would not want to contradict himself.

[8] This is well explained in the oration of Cicero, *Pro Caecina* [100], at the end.

[9] It was an Athenian law, as appears from Demosthenes. Socrates refused to use it.

[10] Demosthenes [*Orationes*], *De Corona*, p. 494, Frankfurt edition of 1604 [18.133].

[11] See Flavius Philostratus, *Vitae sophistarum*, *Aeschines*, bk. 1 [508 [Olearius]].

[12] Plato does not think that the kings, who are, as he says, priests, can be present at judgments in which condemnations to death, exile, or imprisonment are made [Plato, *Epistolae* 8, 356e–357a].

Beyond the confusion into which this would throw all ideas, one would not know if a man had been acquitted or pardoned.

Louis XIII wanted to be the judge in the case against the Duke de la Valette[13] and for this purpose called into his chambers some officers of the parlement and state councillors; as the king forced them to give an opinion on the warrant for arrest, the president of Bélièvre said "that he saw something strange in this business where a prince would give an opinion in the case of one of his subjects; that kings had kept only pardons for themselves and that they had left condemnations to their officers. And Your Majesty would be glad to see before him at the bar a man, who by your judgment would go to his death in an hour! That the countenance of the prince, who pardons, cannot endure this, that his visage alone suspended the interdicts of churches, and that one should never be anything but satisfied on leaving the presence of the prince." When the merits of the case were judged, the same president said in his opinion, "It is an unexampled judgment, not to say contrary to all examples from the past to the present, that a King of France as judge has, by his opinion, condemned a gentleman to death."[14]

Judgments rendered by the prince would be an inexhaustible source of injustices and abuses; the courtiers would extort his judgments by their badgering. Some of the Roman emperors had a craze for judging; no reigns stunned the universe more by their injustices than these.

Tacitus says,[15] "As Claudius had taken for himself the judgment of suits and the functions of the magistrates, he occasioned all sorts of rapine." Thus when Nero, on becoming emperor after Claudius, wanted to win over men's spirits, he declared "that he would take care not to be the judge of all suits so that the accusers and the accused, within the walls of a palace, should not be exposed to the iniquitous power of a few freed men."[16]

"In the reign of Arcadius," says Zosimus,[17] "the nation of slanderers increased, surrounded the court, and infected it. It was assumed, when a man died, that he had left no children;[18] his goods were given by a

[13] See the account of the case against the Duke de la Valette. It is printed in [Claude de Bourdeille, Comte de] Montrésor, *Memoirs*, vol. 2, p. 62 [2, 296–341; 1723 edn].

[14] This was later changed. See the same account [Claude de Bourdeille, Comte de Montrésor, *Memoirs*, 2, 307–308, 326; 1723 edn].

[15] [Tacitus] *Annales*, bk. 11 [11.5].

[16] Ibid. [Tacitus, *Annales*], bk. 13 [13.4].

[17] [Zosimus] *Historiae*, bk. 5 [5.24.17–19; 279–280 Bekker].

[18] There was the same disorder under Theodosius the Younger.

rescript of the emperor. For, as the prince was strangely dull-witted and the empress venturesome to excess, she served the insatiable avarice of her domestics and confidantes; so that for moderate people nothing was more desirable than death."

"Formerly," says Procopius,[19] "there were few people at court, but under Justinian, since the judges were no longer free to render justice, the tribunals were deserted, while the prince's palace resounded with the clamor of the parties soliciting suits." Everyone knows how judgments, and even laws, were sold there.

The laws are the prince's eyes; he sees with them what he could not see without them. Does he want to perform the function of the tribunals? Then he works not for himself, but for those who would deceive him.

[19] [Procopius] *Anecdota sive Historia arcana* [30.30–31].

CHAPTER 6

That, in a monarchy, the ministers should not judge

It is also a great drawback in a monarchy for the ministers of the prince themselves to judge contested suits. Today we still see states in which there are innumerable judges to decide suits concerning the fisc and the ministers (who would believe it!) still want to judge them.[c] Reflections on this subject crowd upon me; I shall offer just one.

There is, by the nature of things, a kind of contradiction between the monarch's council and his tribunals. The king's council should be composed of few persons, and the tribunals of the judiciary require many. The reason is that in the king's council one must undertake public business with a certain passion and pursue it likewise; this can be expected only from four or five men who make it their business. Tribunals of the judiciary must, on the contrary, be coolheaded and, in a way, neutral in all matters of business.

[c] Translators' parentheses.

CHAPTER 7
On the single magistrate

Such a magistrate can have a place only in despotic government. In Roman history one sees to what point a single judge can abuse his power. How could Appius in his tribunal not have despised the laws, since he violated even the law he had made?[20] Livy tells us of this decemvir's iniquitous distinction. He had induced a man to claim before him that Virginia was his slave; Virginia's relatives asked that, by virtue of his law, she be returned to them until final judgment. He declared that his law had been made only to benefit the father and that, as Virginius was absent, it was not applicable.[21]

[20] See Law 2, para. 24 [*Corpus Juris Civilis, Digest* 1.2.24]; *de origine juris et omnium magistratuum et successione prudentum.*

[21] "Since the father of the girl was absent, he thought it an opportune moment to commit an injustice" [L.]. Livy, decade 1, bk. 3 [3.44.5].

CHAPTER 8
On accusations in the various governments

In Rome[22] citizens were permitted to accuse one another. This was established in the spirit of the republic, where each citizen should have boundless zeal for the public good, where it is assumed that each citizen has all the rights of the homeland in his hands. The maxims of the republic were followed under the emperors, and one saw a dreadful kind of man, a band of informers, immediately appear. Whoever had many vices and many talents, a common soul and an ambitious spirit, would seek out a criminal whose condemnation might please the prince; this was the way to advance to honors and to fortune,[23] a thing that we never see among ourselves.

At present we have an admirable law; it wants the prince, who is established in order to see to the execution of the laws, to appoint an officer in each tribunal who will pursue all crimes in his name; thus the office of informer is unknown among us. And if this public avenger

[22] And in many other cities.

[23] See in Tacitus [*Annales* 4.30] the rewards granted to these informers.

were suspected of abusing his ministry, he would be obliged to name the one who had made the denunciation.

In Plato's *Laws*,[24] those who neglect to alert or aid magistrates are to be punished. This would not be suitable today. The party for the public keeps watch for the citizens; it acts, and they are tranquil.[d]

[24] [Plato, *Laws*] bk. 9 [856b–c].

[d] *partie publique*. For Montesquieu's understanding of the historical development of the public prosecutor see 28.36 (note [q], bk. 28).

CHAPTER 9

On the severity of penalties in the various governments

Severity in penalties suits despotic government, whose principle is terror, better than monarchies and republics, which have honor and virtue for their spring.

In moderate states, love of the homeland, shame, and fear of blame are motives that serve as restraints and so can check many crimes. The greatest penalty for a bad action will be to be convicted of it. Therefore in moderate states civil laws will make corrections more easily and will not need as much force.

In these states a good legislator will insist less on punishing crimes than on preventing them; he will apply himself more to giving mores than to inflicting punishments.

Chinese writers have perpetually observed[25] that, in their empire, the more severe the punishments, the nearer the revolution. This is the case because punishments increased in severity to the extent that mores were lost.

It would be easy to prove that in all or nearly all the states of Europe penalties have decreased or increased in proportion as one has approached or departed from liberty.

In despotic countries one is so unhappy that one fears death more than one cherishes life; therefore, punishments should be more severe there. In moderate states one fears the loss of life more than one dreads death as such; punishments that simply suppress life are sufficient there.

[25] I shall show later that China, in this respect, is a case of a republic or a monarchy.

Extremely happy men and extremely unhappy men are equally disposed to harshness: witness monks and conquerors. Only the middling sort, and the mixture of good fortune with bad, offer gentleness and pity.

One can find in the various nations what one sees in men taken individually. There is equal cruelty among savage peoples, who lead a hard life, and among the peoples of despotic governments where fortune favors only one man exorbitantly and abuses all the rest. Gentleness reigns in moderate governments.

When we read in histories the examples of the atrocious justice of the sultans, we feel with a kind of sorrow the ills of human nature.

In moderate governments a good legislator can form anything into penalties. Is it not quite extraordinary that in Sparta one of the principal penalties forbade a man to lend his wife to another or to receive that man's wife or ever to be in his own house except with virgins? In a word, whatever the law calls a penalty is in effect a penalty.

CHAPTER 10
On the old French laws

In the old French laws one surely finds the spirit of monarchy. In cases involving pecuniary penalties, non-nobles are punished less than nobles.[26] It is quite the contrary for crimes;[27] the noble loses his honor and his voice at court while the villein, who has no honor, is punished corporally.

[26] "When complying with a decree of the court, the non-noblemen owe a fine of forty sous and the noblemen sixty pounds." [Jean Boutillier], *Le Grand Coustumier La Somme rural*, bk. 2, p. 198; Got. edn of 1512 [197 v]; [bk. 2, tit. 40, "D'un nobles hommes meffaire"; pp. 864–865; 1621 edn]; and Beaumanoir [*Coûtumes de Beauvaisis*], chap. 61, p. 309 [#1720].

[27] See the *Conseil* of Pierre de Fontaines, chap. 13, chiefly art. 22 [chap. 13, art. 22; pp. 79–80; 1846 edn].

CHAPTER 11

That when a people is virtuous few penalties are needed

The Romans were a people of integrity. Their integrity was so strong that often the legislator needed only to show them the good to have them follow it. It seemed that it was enough to give them counsels instead of ordinances.

Almost all the penalties in the royal laws and in the laws of the Twelve Tables were removed during the republic, either in accordance with the Valerian law,[28] or as a consequence of the Porcian law.[29] One observes that the republic was no more poorly ruled and that no injury to its police resulted.

The Valerian law, which forbade the magistrates to attack in any way a citizen who had appealed to the people, inflicted on one who transgressed the law only the penalty of a reputation for wickedness.[30]

[28] It was made by Valerius Publicola soon after the expulsion of the kings; it was renewed twice, both times by magistrates of the same family, as Livy says, bk. 10 [10.9.3]. It was not a question of giving it more force, but of perfecting its provisions. "More thoroughly inviolate" [L.], Livy says, ibid. [10.9.3].

[29] "The Porcian Law was made to protect the citizens" [L.] [Livy 10.9.4]. It was made in Roman year 454 [300 B.C.].

[30] "It added nothing other than that it be deemed a wicked act" [L.], Livy [10.9.5].

CHAPTER 12

On the power of penalties

Experience has shown that, in countries where penalties are gentle, the citizen's spirit is struck by them as it is elsewhere by heavy ones.

Is some defect felt in a state? A violent government wants to correct it instantly; and, instead of considering that the old laws should be executed, one establishes a cruel penalty that checks the ill then and there. But the spring of the government wears down; the imagination becomes inured to this heavier penalty as it had to the lesser, and as fear of the lesser penalty diminishes, one is soon forced to establish the heavier in every case. Highway robberies were common in some states; one wanted to check them; the punishment of the wheel was invented, which halted them for a while. Since that time there have been robberies on the highways as before.

In our time desertion has been very frequent; the death penalty has been established against deserters, yet desertion has not diminished. There is a very natural reason for this: a soldier, accustomed to risking his life every day, despises danger or flatters himself that he despises it. He is accustomed to fearing shame every day; the penalty of marking him for life should have been kept.[31] It was claimed that the penalty had been increased and in reality it had been diminished.

Men must not be led to extremes; one should manage the means that nature gives us to guide them. If one examines the cause of every instance of laxity, one will see that it is unpunished crimes and not moderated penalties.

Let us follow nature, which has given men shame for their scourge, and let the greatest part of the penalty be the infamy of suffering it.

If there are countries in which shame is not an effect of punishment, it is a result of tyranny, which has inflicted the same penalties on scoundrels as on good people.

And, if you see other countries in which men are restrained only by cruel punishments, reckon again that this arises largely from the violence of the government, which has employed these punishments for slight transgressions.

A legislator who wants to correct an ill often thinks only of that correction; his eye is on that object and not on its defects. Once the ill has been corrected, only the harshness of the legislator is seen; but a vice produced by the harshness remains in the state; spirits are corrupted; they have become accustomed to despotism.

After Lysander[32] had won a victory over the Athenians, the prisoners were judged; the Athenians were accused of having hurled the captives from two galleys over a precipice and of having resolved, in full assembly, to cut off the hands of any prisoners they might take. The Athenians were all slaughtered except Adeimantus, who had opposed the Athenian decree. Before sending Philocles to his death, Lysander reproached him for depraving the spirit of the Athenians and for giving lessons in cruelty to all Greece.

"After the Argives had had fifteen hundred citizens put to death,"

[31] The nose was broken, and the ears cut off.

[32] Xenophon, *Hellenica*, bk. 2 [2.1.31–32].

says Plutarch,[33] "the Athenians ordered expiatory sacrifices so that the gods would turn the hearts of the Athenians from such a cruel thought."

There are two kinds of corruption: one, when the people do not observe the laws, the other, when they are corrupted by the laws; the latter is an incurable ill because it lies in the remedy itself.

[33] [Plutarch] *Moralia, Praecepta gerendae republicae* [814b].

CHAPTER 13

Powerlessness of Japanese laws

Extravagant penalties can corrupt despotism itself. Let us look at Japan.

In Japan almost all crimes are punished by death[34] because disobedience to such a great emperor as Japan's is an enormous crime. It is not a question of correcting the guilty man but of avenging the prince. These ideas are drawn from servitude and derive chiefly from the fact that the emperor is the owner of all the goods and so almost all crimes are committed directly against his interests.

Lies told to the magistrates are punished by death;[35] a thing that is contrary to natural defense.

There, things that do not appear to be crimes are severely punished: for example, a man who risks silver at gaming is punished by death.

It is true that the astonishing character of these opinionated, capricious, determined, eccentric people, who brave every peril and every misfortune, seems at first sight to absolve their legislators for their atrocious laws. But, are people who naturally despise death and who disembowel themselves at the slightest fancy corrected or checked by the continual prospect of punishments? Or, do they not become accustomed to them?

On the subject of the education of the Japanese, accounts tell us that children must be treated gently because they resist penalties and that slaves should not be treated too roughly because they immediately take

[34] See [Engelbert] Kaempfer [*The History of Japan together with a Description of the Kingdom of Siam, 1690–1692*, appendix 6; 3, 325–326; 1906 edn].

[35] *Recueil des voyages qui ont servi à l'établissement de la Compagnie des Indes*, vol. 3, part 2, p. 428 ["Voiage de Hagenaar aux Indes Orientales"; 5, 343; 1706 edn; 5, 428; 1725 edn].

a defensive posture. From the spirit that should reign in domestic government, could one not judge what should be carried into political and civil government?

A wise legislator would have sought to lead men's spirits back by a just tempering of penalties and rewards; by maxims of philosophy, morality, and religion, matched to this character; by the just application of the rules of honor; by using shame as a punishment, and by the enjoyment of a constant happiness and a sweet tranquillity. And, if this legislator had feared that men's spirits, accustomed to being checked only by cruel penalties, could no longer be checked by a gentle one, he would have acted[36] silently and imperceptibly and would have moderated the penalty for the crime in the most pardonable particular cases until he could manage to modify it in every case.

But despotism does not know these springs; it does not lead in these ways. It may abuse itself, but that is all it can do. In Japan it has made an effort and has become more cruel than itself.

Souls that are everywhere startled and made more atrocious can be guided only by a greater atrocity.

This is the origin and spirit of the Japanese laws. But these laws had more fury than force. They have succeeded in destroying Christianity, but such unheard-of efforts are a proof of their powerlessness. The laws wanted to establish a good police, and their weakness has appeared even more clearly.

One must read the account of the meeting between the emperor and the deyro of Meaco.[37e] The number of people smothered or killed by rogues then was unbelievable: girls and boys were carried off; they were discovered in the following days exposed in public places, at all hours, entirely naked, sewed up in canvas bags so that they would not know where they had been; men stole what they wanted; horses' stomachs were split open to make their riders fall; coaches were overturned in order to plunder the ladies inside. The Dutch, who were told that they could not spend the night outdoors on the benches without being murdered, departed, and so forth.

I shall briefly mention another point. The emperor, given to

[36] Observe this as a practical maxim in cases where spirits have been spoiled by overly rigorous penalties.

[37] *Recueil des voyages qui ont servi à l'établissement de la Compagnie des Indes*, vol. 5, part 2 ["Visite du Dairo à l'Empereur du Japon"; 5, 438–440; 1706 edn; 5, 508–511; 1725 edn].

[e] Meaco is today's Kyoto.

infamous pleasures, had not married; he ran the risk of dying without an heir. The deyro sent him two beautiful girls; he married one of them out of respect but had no commerce with her. His nurse sent for the most beautiful woman in the empire. Nothing availed. The daughter of an armourer caught his fancy;[38] his decision was made; he had a son by her. The ladies of the court, outraged that he had preferred a person of such low birth to them, smothered the child. This crime was hidden from the emperor; he would have caused much bloodshed. Therefore, atrocity in the laws prevents their execution. When the penalty is excessive, one is often obliged to prefer impunity.

[38] Ibid. [*Recueil des voyages qui ont servi à l'établissement de la Compagnie des Indes*, vol. 5, "Voiage de Hagenaar aux Indes Orientales"; 5, 313; 1706 edn; 5, 392–393; 1725 edn.]

CHAPTER 14
On the spirit of the Roman senate

During the consulate of Acilius Glabrio and Piso, the Acilian law[39] was made in order to check intrigues. Dio[40] says that the senate engaged the consuls to propose it, because the tribune C. Cornelius had resolved to establish terrible penalties for this crime, which the people were strongly inclined to commit. The senate thought that immoderate penalties would certainly terrify men's spirits but that, as a result, no one could be found to accuse or condemn; whereas, with moderate penalties, there would be both judges and accusers.

[39] The guilty ones were condemned to a fine; they could no longer be admitted to the order of the senators or named to any magistracy. Cass. Dio, bk. 36 [*Historia Romana* 36.38.1].
[40] Ibid. [Cass. Dio, *Historia Romana* 36.38.4–5.]

CHAPTER 15
On the laws of the Romans in respect to penalties

I am strengthened in my maxims when I find the Romans on my side; and I believe that penalties depend on the nature of the government, when I see that, in step with the changes in their political laws, this great people made corresponding changes in the penalties of the civil laws.

The *royal* laws, made for a people composed of fugitives, slaves, and brigands, were very severe. The spirit of the republic would have required the decemvirs not to put these laws in the Twelve Tables, but those who aspired to tyranny cared nothing about following the spirit of the republic.

Concerning the punishment of Mettius Fufetius, the dictator of Alba, whom Tullus Hostilius condemned to be pulled apart by two chariots, Livy says[41] that this was the first and final punishment that bore witness to one's failure to remember humanity. He is mistaken: the law of the Twelve Tables is full of very cruel provisions.[42]

The provision that best reveals the design of the decemvirs is the pronouncement of the death penalty against authors of libels and against poets. That is scarcely in accord with the genius of the republic, where the people like to see important men humbled. But those who wanted to overthrow liberty feared writings that could call back the spirit of liberty.[43]

After the expulsion of the decemvirs, almost all of the laws with fixed penalties were removed. They were not expressly abrogated; but, as the Porcian law prohibited putting Roman citizens to death, they were no longer applicable.

To that time one can ascribe what Livy[44] says of the Romans, that never had a people more loved moderation in penalties.

If one adds, to the gentleness of penal laws, the right of the accused to depart before the judgment, one will see that the Romans followed that spirit which I have said is natural to a republic.

Sulla, who confused tyranny, anarchy, and liberty, made the Cornelian laws. His regulations seem to have been made only in order to establish crimes. Thus, defining an infinite number of actions as murder, he found murderers everywhere; and by a practice that was followed only too often, he laid snares, scattered thorns, and opened abysses in the path of all citizens.

Almost all of Sulla's laws stipulated only the interdiction of water and

[41] [Livy] bk. 1 [1.28.10].

[42] In it one finds the punishment by fire, penalties that are almost always capital, the theft punished by death, etc.

[43] Sulla, moved by the same spirit as the decemvirs, increased, as they did, the penalties against satirical writers.

[44] [Livy] bk. 1 [1.28.11].

fire.[f] Caesar added the confiscation of goods[45] because the rich, who kept their patrimony even in exile, were bolder in committing crimes.

After the emperors had established a military government, they soon felt that it was no less terrible for them than for their subjects; they sought to temper it; they believed they needed dignities and the respect accompanying them.

They drew somewhat nearer to monarchy and divided penalties into three classes:[46] those regarding the principal persons of the state,[47] which were gentle enough; those inflicted on persons of an inferior rank,[48] which were more severe; and finally, those penalties concerning only those of low condition,[49] which were the most strict.

The ferocious and senseless Maximinus excited, so to speak, the military government, which should have been gentle. The senate learned, says Capitolinus,[50] that some men had been hung on crosses, others thrown to beasts or wrapped in the skins of freshly killed beasts without regard to dignities. He seemed to want to exert military discipline, the model on which he intended to regulate civil business.

One can find in the *Considerations on the Grandeur of the Romans and Their Decadence* how Constantine changed the military despotism into a military and civil despotism and drew nearer to monarchy.[g] In that book one can follow the various revolutions of this state and see how it went from strictness to indolence, and from indolence to impunity.

[45] "He increased the penalties for crimes, since those with wealth were more apt to commit them, because, if they were found guilty, they would be exiled but their property would remain untouched" [L.]. Suetonius, *Vitae duodecim Caesarum, Julius Caesar* [42].

[46] See Law 3 [*Corpus Juris Civilis, Digest* 48.8.3.5]; *ad legem Corneliam de sicariis et veneficiis*; and a great number of others in the *Digest* and the *Code* [*Code* 9.16 *ad legem Corneliam de sicariis*].

[47] *Sublimiores*: "more distinguished."

[48] *Medios*: "middling."

[49] *Infimos*: "lowest, meanest." Law 3 [*Corpus Juris Civilis, Digest* 48.8.3.5]; *ad legem Corneliam de sicariis et veneficiis*.

[50] Julius Capitolinus, *Maximini duo* [8].

[f] The "interdiction of fire and water" was a decree prohibiting the return of an exiled person.

[g] See chapter 17 of M.'s *Considerations* (1965 edn, pp. 157–158).

CHAPTER 16

On the just proportion between the penalties and the crime

It is essential for penalties to be harmonious among themselves, because it is essential that the greater crime be avoided rather than the lesser one, the one that attacks society rather than the one that runs less counter to it.

"An impostor,[51] who called himself Constantine Ducas, sparked a great uprising in Constantinople. He was caught and condemned to be flogged, but, as he had accused eminent persons, he was condemned to be burned as a slanderer." It is singular that one should have apportioned penalties in this way between the crime of high treason and that of calumny.

This recalls a remark of Charles II, King of England. He passed a man in the pillory; he asked why he was there. *Sire*, he was told, *he has written libels against your ministers. The great fool*, said the king, *why didn't he write them against me? Nothing would have happened to him.*

"Seventy persons conspired against the emperor Basil;[52] he had them thrashed; their hair and beards were burned. When a stag caught the emperor's belt with his antlers, one of his attendants drew his sword, cut the belt, and freed him; the emperor had him beheaded, because, the emperor said, 'he had drawn his sword against him.' " Who could believe that these two judgments were rendered under the same prince?

Among ourselves, it is a great ill that the same penalty is inflicted on the highway robber and on the one who robs and murders. For the public safety, it is evident that there must be some difference in the penalties.

In China robbers who are cruel are cut to bits,[53] the others are not; because of this difference, one robs there but does not murder.

[51] *History* of Nicephorus, patriarch of Constantinople. [Not Nicephorus but Leo the Grammarian, *Chronographia*, "Constantinus," CSHB 47.321–322; M. is quoting from Louis Cousins, *Histoire de Constantinople* 3. 484; 1685 edn.]

[52] *History* of Nicephorus. [Not Nicephorus but Leo the Grammarian, *Chronographia*, "Basil," CSHB 47. 261–262; M. is quoting here from Louis Cousins, *Histoire de Constantinople*, 3. 438; 1685 edn.]

[53] Father [Jean Baptiste] du Halde [*Description de l'Empire de la Chine*], vol. 1, p. 6 ["Idée générale de l'Empire de la Chine"; 1, 5 P; 1, 6 H; 1, 6 L].

In Muscovy, where the penalty for robbery is the same as for murder, one always murders.[54] Dead men, they say, tell no tales.

When there is no difference in the penalty, there must be some difference in the expectation of pardon. In England robbers do not murder because, unlike murderers, they can expect to be transported to the colonies.

Letters of pardon are a great spring of moderate governments. The power of the prince to pardon, executed wisely, can have admirable results. The principle of despotic government, a government which does not pardon and which is never pardoned, deprives it of these advantages.[h]

[54] [John] Perry, *The State of Russia Under the Present Czar* [p. 229; 1967 edn].

[h] In this sentence the prince and the principle of despotic government are indistinguishable.

CHAPTER 17

On torture or the question for criminals

Because men are wicked, the law is obliged to assume them to be better than they are. Thus the deposition of two witnesses is enough in the punishment of all crimes. The law believes them as if they spoke with the mouth of truth. Also, every child conceived during marriage is judged legitimate; the law trusts the mother as if she were modesty itself. Though the law is forced to make the preceding assumptions, it is not forced to use the *question* in criminal cases. Today we see a well-policed nation[55] reject it without meeting drawbacks. The use of the question is, therefore, not necessary by its nature.[56]

So many clever people and so many men of genius have written

[55] The English nation.

[56] The citizens of Athens could not be put to the *question* (Lysias, *Orationes*, *Against Agoratus* [13.25–28]), except in the crime of high treason. The *question* was used thirty days after the condemnation: C. Chirius Fortunatianus, *Artis rhetoricae*, bk. 2 [1.15; 2.26, 30]. There was no preparatory *question*. As for the Romans, Laws 3 and 4 [*Corpus Juris Civilis*, *Digest* 48.4.3–4 *ad legem Juliam maiestatis*] show that birth, dignity, and the profession of the militia guaranteed protection from the *question*, if it were not a case of the crime of high treason. See the wise restrictions made by the *Lex Wisigothorum* [2.3.4] on this practice.

against this practice that I dare not speak after them. I was going to say that it might be suitable for despotic government, where everything inspiring fear enters more into the springs of the government; I was going to say that slaves among the Greeks and Romans . . . But I hear the voice of nature crying out against me.

CHAPTER 18

On pecuniary penalties and corporal penalties

Our fathers the Germans admitted almost none but pecuniary penalties. These men, who were both warriors and free, considered that their blood should be spilled only when they were armed. The Japanese,[57] by contrast, reject these sorts of penalties on the pretext that rich people would escape punishment. But do not rich people fear the loss of their goods? Cannot pecuniary penalties be proportionate to fortunes? And, finally, cannot infamy be joined with these penalties?

A good legislator takes a middle way;[i] he does not always order pecuniary penalties; he does not always inflict corporal penalties.

[57] See [Engelbert] Kaempfer [*The History of Japan together with a Description of the Kingdom of Siam, 1690–1692*, appendix 6, 3, 325–326; 1906 edn].

[i] *juste milieu.*

CHAPTER 19

On the law of retaliation

Despotic states, which prefer simple laws, make much use of the *law of retaliation*;[58] moderate states sometimes accept it. But the difference is that the former have it exercised strictly, while the others almost always temper it.

The law of the Twelve Tables admitted both; it sentenced in terms of retaliation only when the pleader could not be appeased.[59] After

[58] It is established in the Koran. See the chapter "On the Cow" [2.178].

[59] "If a limb has been broken, unless an agreement be made, there will be retaliation" [L.]. Aulus Gellius [*NA*], bk. 20, chap. 1 [20.1.14].

sentencing, one could pay damage and interest,[60] and the corporal penalty would be converted into a pecuniary penalty.[61]

[60] Ibid. [*NA* 20.1.14].
[61] See also the *Lex Wisigothorum*, bk. 6, tit. 4, paras. 3 and 5 [6.4.3, 5].

CHAPTER 20
On fathers being punished for their children

Fathers are punished in China for the offenses of their children. This was the usage in Peru.[62] It is another punishment derived from despotic ideas.

It is all very well to say that in China the father is punished for not having used that paternal power established by nature and augmented by the laws themselves; this always assumes that there is no honor among the Chinese. Among ourselves, fathers whose children are condemned to punishment and children[63] whose fathers have met the same fate are punished as much by shame as they would be in China by the loss of life.

[62] See Garcilaso [de la Vega, El Inca], *Royal Commentaries of the Incas and General History of Peru* [pt. 1, bk. 2, chap. 12; 1, 95; 1966 edn].
[63] Instead of being punished, said Plato, they must be praised for not resembling their father. [Plato] *Laws*, bk. 9 [855a].

CHAPTER 21
On the clemency of the prince

Clemency is the distinctive quality of monarchs. In a republic, which has virtue as its principle, it is less necessary. In a despotic state, where fear reigns, it is used less, because the important men of the state must be restrained by examples of severity. In monarchies, where one is governed by honor, which often requires what the law prohibits, it is more necessary. Disgrace there is equivalent to a penalty; even the formalities of judgments are punishments. There, shame comes from all sides and forms penalties particular to monarchies.

The important men there are so heavily punished by disgrace, by the often-imaginary loss of their fortune, their credit, their habits, and their pleasures, that strictness in respect to them is useless; it can serve only to take from the subjects the love they bear the person of their prince and the respect they should have for positions.

Just as the instability of important men is in the nature of despotic government, their security enters into the nature of monarchy.

Monarchs have so much to gain from clemency, it is followed by such love, and they draw such glory from it, that it is almost always a fortunate thing for them to have occasion to exercise it; and one can almost always do so in our countries.

There will perhaps be disputes over some branch of their authority but almost never over their whole authority; and, if they sometimes fight for the crown, they never fight for their lives.

But, one will ask, when is one to punish? When to pardon? This is something better felt than prescribed. Though clemency has dangers, they are visible. Clemency is easily distinguished from the weakness that leads the prince to scorn punishing and even to lack the power to do so.

The emperor Maurice[64] resolved never to shed the blood of his subjects. Anastasius[65] did not punish crimes. Isaac the Angel[j] swore that, during his reign, he would put no one to death. The Greek emperors had forgotten that they did not carry the sword in vain.

[64] Evagrius Scholasticus, *Historia ecclesiastica* [6,10; p. 228; 1979 edn].

[65] Suidas, in Constantine Porphyrogenitus [*Extracts of Virtues and Vices*]. [M.'s interpretation follows a Latin translation, not the Greek original. Suidas, *Lexicon*, "Anastasios," 1. 187; Teubner edn, 1938.]

[j] Isaac II Angelus.

BOOK 7

Consequences of the different principles of the three governments in relation to sumptuary laws, luxury, and the condition of women

CHAPTER I

On luxury

Luxury is always proportionate to the inequality of fortunes. If wealth is equally divided in a state, there will be no luxury, for luxury is founded only on the comforts that one can give oneself from the work of others.

For wealth to remain equally divided, the law must give each man only the physical necessities. If men have more than that, some will spend, others will acquire, and inequality will be established.

Assuming physical necessities equal to a given sum, the luxury of those who have only the necessary will be equal to *zero*: he who has its double will have a luxury equal to one; he who has double the goods of the latter will have a luxury equal to three; when the next has yet again the double, he will have a luxury equal to seven; so that, always assuming the goods of the next individual to be twice those of the previous one, luxury will increase by twice plus one, in this progression: 0, 1, 3, 7, 15, 31, 63, 127.

In the republic of Plato,[1a] it was possible to calculate luxury accurately. Four levels of census were established. The first was set precisely at the point where poverty ended; the second at double the first, the third triple, and the fourth, quadruple. In the first census, luxury was equal to *zero*: it was equal to one in the second, to two in the

[1] The first census was the hereditary based on amounts of land, and Plato wanted no one to have more than triple the hereditary lot in other effects. See his *Laws*, bk. 5 [744d–e].

[a] In the *Pensées*, 1378 (1452), Montesquieu speaks of "Plato's two *Republics*."

third, to three in the fourth; and it followed arithmetic proportion accordingly.

The luxury of the various peoples in regard to each other exists in each state as a compound ratio of the inequality of fortunes among the citizens and the inequality of wealth of the various states. In Poland, for example, there is an extreme inequality in fortunes, but the poverty of the whole prevents it from having as much luxury as would a richer state.

Luxury is also proportionate to the size of the towns and above all of the capital, so that luxury exists in a compound ratio of the wealth of the state, the inequality of the fortunes of individuals, and the number of men gathered together in certain places.

The more men there are together, the more vain they are, and the more they feel arise within them the desire to call attention to themselves by small things.[2] If their number is so great that most are unknown to one another, the desire to distinguish oneself redoubles because there is more expectation of succeeding. Luxury produces this expectation; each man takes the marks of the condition above his own. But, by dint of wanting to distinguish themselves, all became equal, and one is no longer distinct; as everyone wants to be looked at, no one is noticed.

The result of all this is a general distress. Those who excel in a profession put their own price on their art; the least talented follow this example; there is no longer harmony between needs and means. When I am forced to plead, I need to be able to pay a lawyer; when I am sick, I must be able to have a doctor.

Some people have thought that gathering of so many people in a capital has diminished commerce because men are no longer a certain distance apart. I do not believe it; men have more desires, more needs, and more fancies when they are together.

[2] In a great town, says [Bernard Mandeville] the author of *The Fable of the Bees*, vol. 1, p. 133 [1732 edn; Remark M; 1, 129–130; 1924 edn], one dresses above one's quality to be esteemed by the multitude as being more than one is. For a weak spirit this pleasure is nearly as great as that from the fulfillment of his desires.

CHAPTER 2

On sumptuary laws in democracy

I have just said that in republics where wealth is equally divided, there can be no luxury; and, as one has seen in Book 5[3] that this equality of distribution made the excellence of a republic, it follows that the less luxury there is in a republic, the more perfect it is. There was none among the first Romans; there was none among the Lacedaemonians; and in republics where equality is not altogether lost, the spirit of commerce, of work, and of virtue makes each one there able and willing to live from his own goods; consequently, there is little luxury.

Laws dividing the fields anew, demanded with such insistence in certain republics, were salutary by their nature. They are dangerous only as a sudden action. By abruptly removing wealth from some and increasing the wealth of others, they make a revolution in each family and must produce one generally throughout the state.

So far as luxury is established in a republic, so far does the spirit turn to the interest of the individual. For people who have to have nothing but the necessities, there is left to desire only the glory of the homeland and one's own glory. But a soul corrupted by luxury has many other desires; soon it becomes an enemy of the laws that hamper it. When those in the garrison at Rhegium became familiar with luxury, they slaughtered the town's inhabitants.

As soon as the Romans were corrupted, their desires became immense. This can be judged by the price they put on things. A jug of Falernian wine[4] sold for one hundred Roman deniers; a barrel of salt meat from the Black Sea cost four hundred deniers; a good cook, four talents; young boys were priceless. When everyone, by a common impulse,[5] was carried to voluptuousness, what became of virtue?

[3] Chaps. 3 and 4.

[4] Fragment of Diodorus Siculus [*Bibliotheca historica*], bk. 365 [37.3.5], reported by Constantine Porphyrogenitus, *Extracts of Virtues and Vices*.

[5] "As everyone strove for the greatest luxury" [L.]. Ibid. [Diodorus Siculus, *Bibliotheca historica*, 37.3.2.]

CHAPTER 3
On sumptuary laws in aristocracy

The misfortune of the badly constituted aristocracy is that its nobles have wealth but should not spend it; luxury, which is contrary to the spirit of moderation, should be banished from it. Therefore, there are only the very poor who cannot get anything and the very rich who cannot spend anything.

In Venice the laws force the nobles to be modest in their tastes. They are so accustomed to thrift that only courtesans can make them give up money. This course is taken to maintain industry: the most despised women spend without danger, while those who pay them tribute lead the most obscure lives in the world.

The good Greek republics had admirable institutions in this regard. The rich used their silver for festivals, musical choruses, chariots, race horses, and onerous magistracies. Wealth there was as burdensome as poverty.

CHAPTER 4
On sumptuary laws in monarchies

"The Suiones, a German nation, honor wealth," says Tacitus,[6] "which makes them live under the government of one alone." This means that luxury is singularly appropriate in monarchies and that they do not have to have sumptuary laws.

As wealth is unequally divided in accord with the constitution of monarchies, there must be luxury. If wealthy men do not spend much, the poor will die of hunger. There the rich must indeed spend in proportion to the inequality of fortunes, and, as we have said, luxury must increase in this proportion. Individual wealth has increased only because it has removed physical necessities from a part of the citizens; these must, therefore, be returned to them.

Thus, for the monarchical state to sustain itself, luxury has to increase from the laborer to the artisan, to the merchant, to the nobles,

[6] [Tacitus] *Germania* [44].

to the magistrates, to the great lords, to the principal revenue officers, to the princes; otherwise, all would be lost.

In the Roman senate, composed of serious magistrates, jurists, and men filled with the idea of the earliest times, one proposed, under Augustus, the correction of the mores and luxury of women. It is interesting to see in Dio[7] the art with which Augustus evaded the importunate demands of these senators. This is because he was founding a monarchy and dissolving a republic.

Under Tiberius, the aediles in the senate proposed the reestablishment of the old sumptuary laws.[8] This enlightened prince opposed it, saying, "The state could not continue to exist, given the present situation. How could Rome live? How could the provinces live? We were frugal when we were citizens of a single town; today we consume the wealth of the whole universe; masters and slaves are made to work for us." He saw clearly that they could no longer have sumptuary laws.

When, under the same emperor, it was proposed to the senate that governors be prohibited from taking their wives with them to the provinces because of the dissoluteness that accompanied them, the proposal was rejected. It was said *that the examples of the harshness of the ancients had been changed into a more pleasant way of living.*[9] One felt that there had to be different mores.

Luxury is, therefore, necessary in monarchical states; it is also necessary in despotic states. In the former, it is a use of the liberty one possesses; in the latter, it is an abuse of the advantages of one's servitude, when a slave, chosen by his master to tyrannize over the other slaves, uncertain of enjoying each day's fortune on the following day, has no other felicity than that of sating the arrogance, desires, and voluptuousness of each day.

All this leads to a reflection: republics end in luxury; monarchies, in poverty.[10]

[7] Cass. Dio [*Historia Romana*], bk. 54 [54.16.3–6].

[8] Tacitus, *Annales*, bk. 3 [3.53].

[9] "Much of the harshness of the ancients has been changed into a better and more pleasant manner" [L.]. Tacitus, *Annales*, bk. 3 [3.34].

[10] "Opulence soon gives rise to poverty" [L.]. Florus [*Epitome rerum Romanorum*], bk. 3 [1.47.12; 3.12.12].

CHAPTER 5

In which cases sumptuary laws are useful in a monarchy

In the middle of the thirteenth century in Aragon sumptuary laws were made in the spirit of the republic, if not for some particular cases. James I ordered that neither the king nor any of his subjects could eat more than two sorts of meat at any meal and that each meat would be prepared in only one way, unless it was game that one had killed oneself.[11]

In our time, sumptuary laws have been made in Sweden, but they have a different purpose from those of Aragon.

A state can make sumptuary laws with the purpose of an absolute frugality; this is the spirit of sumptuary laws in republics, and the nature of the thing shows that this was the purpose of the laws in Aragon.

Sumptuary laws can also have relative frugality for their purpose, when a state, feeling that foreign commodities are too highly priced and that so many exports of its own commodities are required that it would deprive itself of more of what it needs than these foreign commodities can satisfy, absolutely prohibits their entrance; and this is the spirit of the laws made in our time in Sweden.[12] These are the only sumptuary laws suitable to monarchies.

In general, the poorer the state, the more it is ruined by relative luxury, and the more, consequently, it must have relative sumptuary laws. The richer the state, the more its relative luxury enriches it, and one must be careful not to make relative sumptuary laws there. We shall explain this better in the book on commerce.[13] Here only absolute luxury is in question.

[11] Constitution of James I in [Pierre de Marca] *Marca Hispanica*, anno 1234, art. 6, p. 1429 [Appendix, chap. 513, art. 6, pp. 1429–1430; 1688 edn].

[12] Exquisite wines and other precious merchandise were forbidden there.

[13] See bk. 20, chap. 20 [below].

CHAPTER 6
On luxury in China

Particular reasons can require sumptuary laws in some states. The people can become so numerous through the force of the climate, and on the other hand, their means of subsistence can be so uncertain that it is well for all the people to cultivate the land. In these states luxury is dangerous and sumptuary laws should be strict. Thus, in order to know if luxury must be encouraged or proscribed, one should first observe the relation between the number of people and the ease of giving them enough to eat. In England the soil produces much more grain than is needed to feed both those who cultivate the land and those who provide clothing; there they can have frivolous arts and, consequently, luxury. In France enough wheat grows to feed both those who work the land and those employed in manufacture; in addition, commerce with foreigners can bring in return for frivolous things so many necessary things that luxury should scarcely be feared there.

In China, on the other hand, women are so fertile and humankind multiplies so fast that the fields, even heavily cultivated, scarcely suffice to produce enough food for the inhabitants. Consequently, luxury is pernicious there and the spirit of work and economy is as requisite as in any republic whatever.[14] One must apply oneself to the necessary arts and avoid those of voluptuousness.

This is the spirit of the fine ordinances of the Chinese emperors. "Our ancestors," says an emperor of the T'ang family,[15] "took it as a maxim that if there were a man who did not plow the fields, a woman who did not spin, someone in the empire would suffer from cold or hunger . . ." And on this principle he had an infinite number of the bonze monasteries destroyed.[b]

The third emperor of the twenty-first dynasty,[16] when given precious

[14] Luxury has always been checked there.

[15] In an ordinance reported by Father [Jean Baptiste] du Halde [*Description de l'Empire de la Chine*], vol. 2, p. 497 ["La cinquième des années nommées Ho i Tchang"; 2, 596–597 H; 2, 496–497 P].

[16] *Description de l'Empire de la Chine*, twenty-first dynasty, in the work of Father [Jean Baptiste] du Halde, vol. 1 ["21st Dynasty, Tching Tsou, 3rd Emperor"; 1, 447 H; 1, 509 P; 1, 455 L].

[b] The "bonze" were Buddhist monks.

stones found in a mine, had it closed, not wanting to tire his people with working for what could neither feed nor clothe them.

"Our luxury is so great," said Kia-y,[17] "that the people embroider the shoes of the boys and girls whom they are obliged to sell." Is it by occupying so many men with making garments for one that many people are kept from lacking clothes? For each plowman there are ten men who eat the yield of the lands: is this the way to keep many people from lacking food?

[17] In a speech reported by Father [Jean Baptiste] du Halde [*Description de l'Empire de la Chine*], vol. 2, p. 418 ["Discours ou memoire de Kia-y"; 2, 499–500 H; 2, 418 P].

CHAPTER 7

A fatal consequence of luxury in China

One sees in the history of China that it has had twenty-two dynasties in succession; that is, it has suffered twenty-two general revolutions, not counting an infinite number of particular ones. The first three dynasties lasted a long time, because they were wisely governed and because the empire was less extensive than it was to become. But in general, one can say that all these dynasties began well enough. Virtue, care, and vigilance are necessary for China; they were present at the beginning of the dynasties and missing at the end. Indeed, it was natural for emperors raised on the hardship of war and successful in forcing a family inundated by delights from the throne, to preserve the virtue they had found so useful and to fear the voluptuousness they had seen to be so fatal. But, after these first three or four princes, corruption, luxury, laziness, and delights master their successors; they shut themselves in the palace, their spirits grow weak, their lives are short, the family declines; the important men rise up, the eunuchs gain credit, children only are put on the throne; the palace becomes the enemy of the empire; the lazy people living there ruin those who work; the emperor is killed or destroyed by a usurper, who founds a family, whose successor in the third or fourth generation goes into the same palace and shuts himself in again.

CHAPTER 8

On public continence

So many imperfections are attached to the loss of virtue in women, their whole soul is so markedly degraded by this, and when this principal point is removed so many others fall, that in a popular state one can regard public incontinence as the last misfortune and as assurance of a change in the constitution.

Thus good legislators have required a certain gravity in the mores of women. They have proscribed from their republics not only vice but even the appearance of vice. They have banished even that commerce of gallantry that produces laziness, that causes women to corrupt even before being corrupted, that puts a high price on every trifle and reduces the price on what is important, and that makes one no longer conduct oneself by any but the maxims of ridicule that women understand so well how to establish.

CHAPTER 9

On the condition of women in the various governments

In monarchies women have so little restraint because, called to court by the distinction of ranks, they there take up the spirit of liberty that is almost the only one tolerated. Each man uses their charms and their passions to advance his fortune; and as their weakness allows them not arrogance but vanity, luxury always reigns there with them.

In despotic states women do not introduce luxury, but they are themselves an object of luxury. They should be kept in extreme slavery. Each man follows the spirit of the government and brings to his home what he sees established outside of it. As the laws in these states are severe and executed on the spot, one fears that women's liberty could be a cause for bringing suit. Women's quarrels, their indiscretions, their aversions, their inclinations, their jealousies, their spiteful remarks, in short that art by which narrow souls affect generous ones, cannot be without consequence there.

In addition, as the princes in these states trifle with human nature, they have several wives, and a thousand considerations oblige them to enclose their women.

In republics women are free by the laws and captured by the mores; luxury is banished there and with it, corruption and vices.

In the Greek towns where one did not live under the religion which established that even among men the purity of mores is a part of virtue; in the Greek towns where a blind vice reigned unbridled, where love took only a form one dare not mention while only friendship was to be found within marriages,[18] women's virtue, simplicity, and chastity were such that one has scarcely ever seen a people who had a better police in this regard.[19]

[18]"As for true love," says Plutarch in the *Moralia, Amatorius*, p. 600 [750c], "women have no part in it." He spoke as did his age. See Xenophon, in the dialog entitled *Hiero* [1.31–36].
[19]In Athens there was a particular magistrate who watched over the conduct of women.

CHAPTER 10

On the domestic tribunal among the Romans

Unlike the Greeks, the Romans had no special magistrates to inspect women's conduct. The censors paid no more attention to women than to the rest of the republic. The institution of a domestic tribunal[20] replaced the magistracy established among the Greeks.[21]

The husband assembled the wife's relatives and judged her before them.[22] This tribunal maintained mores in the republic. But these same mores maintained this tribunal. Its task was to judge not only the violation of laws but also the violation of mores. Now, in order to judge the violation of mores, one must have mores.

The penalties of this tribunal had to be arbitrary as, indeed, they

[20]Romulus instituted this tribunal, as appears in Dion. Hal. [*Ant. Rom.*], bk. 2, p. 96 [2.25.6].
[21]See Livy, bk. 39 [39.18.6], for the usage made of this tribunal at the time of the conspiracy of the Bacchantes; the assemblies which corrupted the mores of women and youth were deemed conspiracies against the republic.
[22]It appears from Dion. [*Ant. Rom.*], bk. 2 [2.25.6], that by the institution of Romulus, the husband, in ordinary cases, judged alone in the presence of the wife's relatives and that in great crimes, he judged along with five of them. Thus Ulpian [*Fragmenta*], tit. 6, para. 9, 12–13 [6.9.12–13] distinguishes in judgments on mores between those he calls serious and those that are less so: *mores graviores, mores leviores*.

were, for all that concerns mores and all that concerns the rules of modesty can scarcely be included in a code of laws. It is easy to regulate by laws what one owes others; it is difficult to include in them all that one owes oneself.

The domestic tribunal was concerned with the general conduct of women. But there was one crime which, besides being reproved by this tribunal, was also submitted to public accusation: this crime was adultery, either because such a serious violation of mores in a republic is of interest to the government, or because the profligacy of the wife might imply that of the husband, or finally, because one feared that even honest people might prefer hiding the crime to punishing it, might prefer ignorance to vengeance.

CHAPTER 11

How institutions changed in Rome with the government

Just as the domestic tribunal presupposed mores, public accusation also presupposed them; and this made both of them collapse along with the mores and come to an end with the republic.[23]

The establishment of perpetual questions, that is, the division of jurisdiction among the praetors, and the custom that was gradually introduced that the praetors themselves judged all suits,[24] weakened the use of the domestic tribunal; the evidence for this change is the surprise registered by the historians, who regard the judgments Tiberius rendered through this tribunal as singular facts and as the renewal of the old practice.

The establishment of the monarchy and the change in mores also brought public accusation to an end. One could fear that a dishonest man, stung by a woman's sneers, indignant at her refusals, outraged even by her virtue, might form the design of ruining her. The Julian law ordered that one could accuse a woman of adultery only after accusing her husband of encouraging her profligacies, a stipulation which

[23] "Judgments in accord with custom (which previously had had a place in the ancient laws, although not frequently used), are now entirely abolished" [L.; M.'s parentheses]. Law 11, para. 2, *Code* [*Corpus Juris Civilis*, *Code* 5.17.11.2 [2b]]; *de repudiis et judicio de moribus sublato*.

[24] *Judicia extraordinaria*: a judicial procedure that is not the ordinary one.

greatly restrained this accusation and reduced it, so to speak, to nothing.[25]

Sixtus V seemed to want to renew public accusation.[26] But one has to reflect only a little to see that this law, in a monarchy such as his, was even more out of place than in any other.

[25] Constantine removed it entirely: "It is an unworthy thing," he said, "that tranquil marriages should be disturbed by the audacity of strangers." [*Corpus Juris Civilis*, *Code* 9.9.29 (30); *ad legem Juliam de adulteriis et de stupro*.]

[26] Sixtus V ordered that a husband who would not complain of the debauches of his wife be punished with death. See [Gregorio] Leti [*The Life of Pope Sixtus V*, bk. 6; p. 273; 1779 Eng. edn].

CHAPTER 12

On the tutelage of women among the Romans

The Roman institutions put women under perpetual guardianship unless they were under the authority of a husband.[27] This guardianship was given to the closest male relative and it appears, according to a popular phrase,[28] that the women were very hemmed in by it. This was good for the republic, and was not necessary in the monarchy.[29]

It seems, according to the various law codes of the barbarians, that among the early Germans, women were also under perpetual guardianship.[30] This usage passed into the monarchies they founded but it did not continue to exist.

[27] "Except by marriage when she comes into the hands of her husband" [L.].

[28] "Verily, do not be a paternal uncle to me" [L.] [Horace, *Satires* 2.3.88].

[29] The Papian law ordained, under Augustus, that wives who had had three children would be exempt from this tutelage.

[30] Among the Germans this tutelage was called *mundeburdium*.

CHAPTER 13

On penalties established by the emperors against women's debaucheries

The Julian law established a penalty for adultery. But this law and those made later on the same subject were far from indicating the goodness of the mores; on the contrary, they indicated their debasement.

The whole political system with regard to women changed in the monarchy. It was no longer a question of establishing the purity of their mores but of punishing their crimes. New laws were made to punish these crimes only because the violations, which were not the same as the crimes, were no longer punished.

The dreadful excesses of the mores obliged the emperors to make laws to check immodesty at some point; but their intention was not to correct mores generally. Positive facts, reported by historians, are more a proof of this than all the laws could be proof of the contrary. One can see in Dio both the conduct of Augustus in this regard and his evasion of the demands that were made of him when he was praetor and censor.[31]

In the historians, one finds rigid judgments rendered under Augustus and Tiberius against the indecency of certain Roman ladies; but by acquainting us with the spirit of these reigns, they acquaint us with the spirit of these judgments.

Augustus and Tiberius thought principally of punishing the debauchery of their female relatives. They did not punish dissolute mores but a certain crime of impiety or of high treason[32] that they had invented, which was useful both for instilling respect and for taking revenge. Hence the strong protests of the Roman authors against this tyranny.

The penalty in the Julian law was light.[33] The emperors wanted the penalty they had put into the law to be increased in the judgments. This was an object of the historians' invective. They did not examine whether the women deserved to be punished, but whether the law had been violated in order to punish them.

[31] When a young man, who had had evil commerce with his wife before their marriage, was brought before Augustus, Augustus hesitated at length, daring neither to approve nor to punish these things. Finally, collecting his wits, he said, "Seditions have been the cause of great evils; let us forget them." Cass. Dio [*Historia Romana*], bk. 54 [54.16.6]. As the senators had asked him for rulings on the mores of women, he avoided this request, telling them to "correct their wives as he had corrected his own." At that they begged him to tell them how he dealt with his wife, a highly indiscreet question, it seems to me.

[32] "In calling what is a common fault between men and women by the serious names of sacrilege and treason, [Augustus] overstepped the clemency of our ancestors and that of his own laws" [L.]. Tacitus, *Annales*, bk. 3 [3.24].

[33] This law is reported in the *Digest*, but the penalty was not included. One judges it to have been exile by relegation, since that for incest was only exile by deportation [with loss of civil rights]. The law *si quis viduam* and following [*Corpus Juris Civilis*, *Digest* 48.18.5]; *de questionibus*.

One of the principal tyrannies of Tiberius[34] was his abuse of the old laws. When he wanted to push some Roman matron beyond the penalty set by the Julian law, he reestablished the domestic tribunal for her.[35]

These provisions in respect to women involved only the families of senators, not those of the people. One wanted pretexts for accusing the important men, and women's misconduct provided innumerable ones.

Finally, what I have said, that the goodness of mores is not the principle of the government of one alone, was never more verified than under these first emperors; and if there were any doubt about it, one would have only to read Tacitus, Suetonius, Juvenal, and Martial.

[34]"It was characteristic of Tiberius to conceal newly invented crimes by venerable words" [L.]. Tacitus [*Annales* 4.19].

[35]"For her [Appuleia Varilia, the grandniece of Augustus], he [Tiberius] deprecated the more severe penalty, and following ancestral precedent, recommended that she be removed by her relatives beyond the 200th milestone. The adulterer Manlius was outlawed from both Italy and Africa" [L.]. Tacitus, *Annales* bk. 2 [2.50].

CHAPTER 14

Sumptuary laws among the Romans

We have spoken of public incontinence because it is joined to luxury; it is always followed by luxury, and always follows luxury. If you leave the impulses of the heart at liberty, how can you hamper the weaknesses of the spirit?

In Rome, in addition to the general institutions, the censors had the magistrates make several particular laws to keep women frugal. The Fannian, Licinian, and Oppian laws had this purpose. One must see in Livy[36] how agitated the senate became when the women demanded the revocation of the Oppian Law. Valerius Maximus dates the epoch of luxury among the Romans from the time of the repeal of this law.

[36][Livy] decade 4, bk. 4 [34.1–8].

CHAPTER 15

On dowries and the advantages of marriage in the various constitutions

Dowries should be of a considerable size in monarchies so that married men can sustain their rank and its established luxury. They should be of medium size in republics, where luxury should not reign.[37] They should be nearly nothing in despotic states where women are, in a way, slaves.

The community of goods between husband and wife introduced by French laws is very suitable to monarchical government because it interests women in domestic business and recalls them, as if in spite of themselves, to the care of their households. It is less suitable in a republic, where wives are more virtuous. It would be absurd in despotic states, where wives are themselves almost always a part of the master's property.

Since women are, by their state, sufficiently inclined to marriage, the advantages the law gives them over their husbands' goods are useless. But such advantages would be very pernicious in a republic, because the individual wealth of wives produces luxury. In despotic states the advantages of marriage should be the wife's sustenance and nothing more.

[37] Marseilles was the wisest of the republics of her time; dowries could not exceed one hundred ecus in silver and five in clothing, says Strabo [*Geographica*], bk. 4 [4.1.5].

CHAPTER 16

A fine custom of the Samnites

The Samnites had a custom, which, in a small republic and especially one in the situation theirs had, produced admirable effects. All the young people were assembled and judged. The one who was declared best took for his wife the girl he wanted; he who had the next largest vote then chose; and so on.[38] It was admirable to consider among the

[38] *Fragments* of Nicholas of Damascus [*FGrH*, vol. 2A, 384], from Stobaeus [*Morum mirabilum collectio*, 109], in the collection by Constantine Porphyrogenitus.

goods of the boys only the fine qualities and the services rendered to the homeland. He who was richest in these sorts of goods would choose a girl from among the whole nation. Love, beauty, chastity, virtue, birth, even wealth, all were, so to speak, the dowry of virtue. It would be difficult to imagine a reward that was nobler, greater, less burdensome to a small state, or more able to have an effect on both sexes.

The Samnites were descendants of the Lacedaemonians; and Plato, whose institutions are only the perfection of the laws of Lycurgus, gave almost the same law.[39]

[39] He even permits them to see one another more frequently. [Plato, *Republic* 459d–460c; *Laws* 771e–772a.]

CHAPTER 17
On administration by women

It is against reason and against nature for women to be mistresses in the house, as was established among the Egyptians, but not for them to govern an empire. In the first case, their weak state does not permit them to be preeminent; in the second, their very weakness gives them more gentleness and moderation, which, rather than the harsh and ferocious virtues, can make for a good government.

In the Indies government by women turns out very well; it is established that, if the males do not come from a mother of the same blood, a daughter whose mother is of royal blood succeeds to the throne.[40] She is given a certain number of people to help her carry the weight of the government. According to Mr. Smith,[41] government by women also turns out very well in Africa. If one adds to this the examples of Muscovy and of England, one will see that they succeed equally well in moderate government and in despotic government.

[40] *Lettres édifiantes et curieuses*, 14 [Lettre du P. Bouchet, Pontichéry, October 2, 1714; 14, 382–389; 1720 edn].

[41] [William Smith] *A New Voyage to Guinea*, pt. 2, p. 165 of the translation [pp. 208–209; 1967 edn] on the kingdom of Angona on the Gold Coast.

BOOK 8

On the corruption of the principles of the three governments

CHAPTER 1

The general idea of this book

The corruption of each government almost always begins with that of its principles.

CHAPTER 2

On the corruption of the principle of democracy

The principle of democracy is corrupted not only when the spirit of equality is lost but also when the spirit of extreme equality is taken up and each one wants to be the equal of those chosen to command. So the people, finding intolerable even the power they entrust to the others, want to do everything themselves: to deliberate for the senate, to execute for the magistrates, and to cast aside all the judges.

Then there can no longer be virtue in the republic. The people want to perform the magistrates' functions; therefore, the magistrates are no longer respected. The senate's deliberations no longer carry weight; therefore, there is no longer consideration for senators or, consequently, for elders. And if there is no respect for elders, neither will there be any for fathers; husbands no longer merit deference nor masters, submission. Everyone will come to love this license; the restraint of commanding will be as tiresome as that of obeying had been. Women, children, and slaves will submit to no one. There will no longer be mores or love of order, and finally, there will no longer be virtue.

One sees in Xenophon's *Symposium* an artless depiction of a republic

whose people have abused equality. Each guest in turn gives his reason for being pleased with himself. "I am pleased with myself," says Charmides, "because of my poverty. When I was rich I was obliged to pay court to slanderers, well aware that I was more likely to receive ill from them than to cause them any; the republic constantly asked for a new payment; I could not travel. Since becoming poor, I have acquired authority; no one threatens me, I threaten the others; I can go or stay. The rich now rise from their seats and make way for me. Now I am a king, I was a slave; I used to pay a tax to the republic, today the republic feeds me; I no longer fear loss, I expect to acquire."[a]

The people fall into this misfortune when those to whom they entrust themselves, wanting to hide their own corruption, seek to corrupt the people. To keep the people from seeing their own ambition, they speak only of the people's greatness; to keep the people from perceiving their avarice, they constantly encourage that of the people.

Corruption will increase among those who corrupt, and it will increase among those who are already corrupted. The people will distribute among themselves all the public funds; and, just as they will join the management of business to their laziness, they will want to join the amusements of luxury to their poverty. But given their laziness and their luxury, only the public treasure can be their object.

One must not be astonished to see votes given for silver. One cannot give the people much without taking even more from them; but, in order to take from them, the state must be overthrown. The more the people appear to take advantage of their liberty, the nearer they approach the moment they are to lose it. Petty tyrants are formed, having all the vices of a single one. What remains of liberty soon becomes intolerable. A single tyrant rises up, and the people lose everything, even the advantages of their corruption.

Therefore, democracy has to avoid two excesses: the spirit of inequality, which leads it to aristocracy or to the government of one alone, and the spirit of extreme equality, which leads it to the despotism of one alone, as the despotism of one alone ends by conquest.

It is true that those who corrupted the Greek republics did not always become tyrants. They had applied themselves more to eloquence than to military arts; besides, there was in the hearts of all Greeks an

[a] Xenophon, *Symposium* 4.30–31.

implacable hatred for those who had overthrown the republican government, which made anarchy crumble into dissolution instead of turning into tyranny.

But Syracuse, situated among many little oligarchies that had become tyrannies,[1] Syracuse, whose senate[2] is scarcely ever mentioned in history, endured misfortunes not produced by ordinary corruption. This town, always licentious[3] or oppressed, equally tormented by its liberty and by its servitude, always receiving the one or the other like a tempest, and, in spite of its power abroad, always determined to revolution by the smallest foreign force, had an immense population whose only choice was the cruel one between giving itself to a tyrant and being one.

[1] See Plutarch in the lives of Timoleon and Dion [*Vit.*].
[2] It is the Six Hundred of which Diodorus [Siculus] speaks [*Bibliotheca historica* 19.5.6].
[3] After driving out the tyrants, they made citizens of foreigners and mercenary soldiers, which caused civil wars. Aristotle, *Politics*, bk. 5, chap. 3 [1303a38–1303b2]. As the people had been the cause of the victory over the Athenians, the republic was changed. Ibid., chap. 4 [1304a27–29]. The passion of two young magistrates, the first taking a boy away from the other, the latter debauching the wife of the former, made the form of this republic change. Ibid., bk. 7, chap. 4 [1303b17–26].

CHAPTER 3
On the spirit of extreme equality

As far as the sky is from the earth, so far is the true spirit of equality from the spirit of extreme equality. The former consists neither in making everyone command nor in making no one command, but in obeying and commanding one's equals. It seeks not to have no master but to have only one's equals for masters.

In the state of nature, men are born in equality, but they cannot remain so. Society makes them lose their equality, and they become equal again only through the laws.

The difference between the democracy that is regulated and the one that is not is that, in the former, one is equal only as a citizen, and, in the latter, one is also equal as a magistrate, senator, judge, father, husband, or master.

The natural place of virtue is with liberty, but virtue can no more be found with extreme liberty than with servitude.

CHAPTER 4

A particular cause of the corruption of the people

Great successes, especially those to which the people contribute much, make them so arrogant that it is no longer possible to guide them. Jealous of the magistrates, they become jealous of the magistracy; enemies of those who govern, they soon become enemies of the constitution. In this way the victory at Salamis over the Persians corrupted the republic of Athens;[4] in this way the defeat of the Athenians ruined the republic of Syracuse.[5]

The republic of Marseilles never underwent these great shifts from lowliness to greatness; thus, it always governed itself with wisdom; thus, it preserved its principles.

[4] Aristotle, *Pol.*, bk. 5, chap. 4 [1304a22–24].
[5] Ibid. [Aristotle, *Pol.* 1304a27–29].

CHAPTER 5

On the corruption of the principle of aristocracy

Aristocracy is corrupted when the power of the nobles becomes arbitrary; there can no longer be virtue either in those who govern or in those who are governed.

When the ruling families observe the laws, it is a monarchy that has many monarchs and is quite good by its nature; almost all these monarchs are bound by the laws. But when these families fail to observe the laws, it is a despotic state that has many despots.

In this case the republic continues to exist only with regard to the nobles and only among them. The body that governs is a republic and the body that is governed is a despotic state; they are the two most ill-matched bodies in the world.

Extreme corruption occurs when nobility becomes hereditary;[6] the nobles can scarcely remain moderate. If they are few in number, their power is greater, but their security diminishes; if they are greater in number, their power is less and their security greater; so that power

[6] The aristocracy changes into an oligarchy.

keeps increasing and security diminishing up to the despot in whose person lies the extreme of power and danger.

Therefore, a large number of nobles in an hereditary aristocracy will make the government less violent; but as there will be little virtue there, one will fall into a spirit of nonchalance, laziness, and abandon, which will make a state with neither force nor spring.[7]

An aristocracy can sustain the force of its principle if the laws are such that they make the nobles feel more strongly the perils and fatigues of command than its delights, and if the state is in such a situation that it has something to dread, and if security comes from within and uncertainty from without.

A certain kind of confidence is the glory and security of a monarchy, but, by contrast, a republic must dread something.[8] Fear of the Persians maintained the laws among the Greeks. Carthage and Rome intimidated one another and were mutually strengthened. How singular! The more secure these states are, the more, as with tranquil waters, they are subject to corruption.

[7] Venice is one of the republics which has best corrected, by its laws, the drawbacks of hereditary aristocracy.

[8] Justin attributes the extinction of virtue in Athens to the death of Epaminondas. No longer rivalrous, the Athenians spent their income on festivals, "more frequently in attendance at the table [theater is the reading in modern texts] than at the camp" [L.]. Then the Macedonians came out of obscurity. [Justin, *Epitoma historiarum Philippicarum*], bk. 6 [6.9.4].

CHAPTER 6

On the corruption of the principle of monarchy

Just as democracies are ruined when the people strip the senate, the magistrates, and the judges of their functions, monarchies are corrupted when one gradually removes the prerogatives of the established bodies[b] or the privileges of the towns. In the first case, one approaches the despotism of all; in the other, the despotism of one alone.

"What ruined the dynasties of Tsin and Sui," says a Chinese author, "is that the princes, instead of limiting themselves like the ancients to a general inspection, which is the only one worthy of a sovereign, wanted

[b] *prérogatives des corps.*

to govern everything by themselves without an intermediary."[9] Here the Chinese author gives us the cause for the corruption of almost all monarchies.

A monarchy is ruined when a prince believes he shows his power more by changing the order of things than by following it, when he removes the functions that are natural to some to give them arbitrarily to others, and when he is more enamoured of what he fancies than of what he wills.

A monarchy is ruined when the prince, referring everything to himself exclusively, reduces the state to its capital, the capital to the court, and the court to his person alone.

Finally, it is ruined when a prince misunderstands his authority, his situation, and his people's love, and when he does not realize that a monarch should consider himself secure, just as a despot should believe himself imperiled.

[9] "Compilation of works done under the Ming," reported by Father [Jean Baptiste] du Halde [*Description de l'Empire de la Chine* 2, 781 H; 2, 648 P].

CHAPTER 7

Continuation of the same subject

The principle of monarchy has been corrupted when the highest dignities are the marks of the greatest servitude, when one divests the important men of the people's respect and makes them into vile instruments of arbitrary power.

It has been corrupted even more when honor has been set in opposition to honors and when one can be covered at the same time with infamy[10] and with dignities.

It has been corrupted when the prince changes his justice into

[10] Under the reign of Tiberius statues were raised and the triumphal ornaments were given to informers, which so degraded these honors that those who had deserved them scorned them. Fragment of [Cass.] Dio [*Historia Romana*], bk. 58 [58.4.8], drawn from the *Extracts of Virtues and Vices* of Constantine Porphyrogenitus. See in Tacitus how Nero, on the discovery and punishment of a supposed conspiracy, gave Petronius Turpilianus, Nerva, and Tigellinus triumphal ornaments. [Tacitus] *Annales*, bk. 14 [15.72]. See also how the generals scorned to wage war because they despised the honors. "The distinction of the triumph having been debased" [L.]. Tacitus, *Annales*, bk. 13 [13.53].

severity, when he puts a Medusa's head on his breast[11] as did the Roman emperors, and when he takes on that menacing and terrible air which Commodus required in his statues.[12]

The principle of monarchy has been corrupted when some singularly cowardly souls grow vain from the greatness of their servitude and when they believe that what makes them owe everything to the prince makes them owe nothing to their homeland.

But, if it is true (as has been seen through the ages) that insofar as the monarch's power becomes immense, his security diminishes, is it not a crime of high treason against him to corrupt this power to the extent of changing its nature?

[11] In this state the prince well knew what the principle of his government was.
[12] Herodianus [*Ab excessu divi Marci* 1.14.9].

CHAPTER 8

A danger of the corruption of the principle of monarchical government

It is not a drawback when the state passes from moderate government to moderate government, as from republic to monarchy or from monarchy to republic, but rather when it falls and collapses from moderate government into despotism.

Most European peoples are still governed by mores. But if, by a long abuse of power or by a great conquest, despotism became established at a certain time, neither mores nor climate would hold firm, and in this fine part of the world, human nature would suffer, at least for a while, the insults heaped upon it in the other three.

CHAPTER 9

How much the nobility is inclined to defend the throne

The English nobility was buried with Charles I in the debris of the throne; and before that, when Philip II sounded the name of liberty in French ears, the crown had always been sustained by that nobility

which holds it an honor to obey a king but regards it as the sovereign infamy to share power with the people.

The house of Austria tried persistently to oppress the Hungarian nobility. It did not know how much it would one day prize that nobility. It sought among these peoples silver they did not have; it did not see the men who were there. When the many princes had divided the states of the Hungarian monarchy among themselves, all its pieces fell, so to speak, one on top of the other, immobile and inactive: the only life that then remained was in the nobility, which grew indignant, forgot everything in order to fight, and believed that its glory lay in dying and in forgiving.

CHAPTER 10

On the corruption of the principle of despotic government

The principle of despotic government is endlessly corrupted because it is corrupt by its nature. Other governments are destroyed because particular accidents violate their principle; this one is destroyed by its internal vice if accidental causes do not prevent its principle from becoming corrupt. Therefore, it can maintain itself only when circumstances, which arise from the climate, the religion, and the situation or the genius of the people, force it to follow some order and to suffer some rule. These things force its nature without changing it; its ferocity remains; it is, for a while, tractable.

CHAPTER 11

Natural effects of the goodness and of the corruption of the principles

Once the principles of the government are corrupted, the best laws become bad and turn against the state; when their principles are sound, bad laws have the effect of good ones; the force of the principle pulls everything along.

The Cretans, in order to keep the highest magistrates dependent on the laws, used a very singular means: that of *insurrection*. Part of the citizenry would rise up,[13] put the magistrates to flight, and oblige them to return to private life. This was supposedly done in pursuance of the law. Such an institution, which established sedition in order to prevent the abuse of power, seemed bound to overthrow any republic at all. It did not destroy that of Crete: here is why.[14]

When the ancients wanted to speak of a people who had the greatest love of the homeland, they cited the Cretans. *The homeland, a tender name among the Cretans*, said Plato.[15] They called it by a name that expresses a mother's love for her children.[16] Now, love of the homeland corrects everything.[c]

The laws of Poland have also their *insurrection*. But the drawbacks that result from it show clearly that only the people of Crete were in a state to use such a remedy successfully.

The gymnastic exercises established among the Greeks depended no less on the goodness of the principle of government. "The Lacedaemonians and the Cretans," said Plato,[17] "opened those famous academies that gave them such a distinguished rank in the world. At first modesty was alarmed, but it yielded to public usefulness." In Plato's time, these institutions were remarkable;[18] they were related to a great purpose, the military art. But when the Greeks were no longer virtuous, these institutions destroyed the military art itself; one no longer went down to the wrestling arena to be trained but to be corrupted.[19]

Plutarch tells us[20] that, in his time, the Romans thought these games were the principal cause of the servitude into which the Greeks had

[13] Aristotle, *Pol.*, bk. 2, chap. 10 [1272b1–15].

[14] One always united first against the enemies from the outside; this was called *syncretism*. Plutarch, *Moralia*, p. 88 [*De fraterno amore* 490b].

[15] [Plato] *Republic*, bk. 9 [575d].

[16] Plutarch, *Moralia*, in the treatise *An seni respublica gerenda sit* [792e].

[17] [Plato] *Republic*, bk. 5 [452c–d].

[18] Gymnastic was divided into two parts, dancing and wrestling. In Crete there were the armed dances of the Curettes; in Lacedaemonia, those of Castor and Pollux; in Athens, the armed dances of Pallas, quite proper for those who are not yet of an age to go to war. Wrestling is the image of war, says Plato, *Laws*, bk. 7 [814d; see also 795e–796d]. He praises in antiquity the establishment of only two dances, the pacific and the pyrrhic. See how the latter dance was applied to the military art. Plato, ibid. [*Laws* 814d–816d].

[19] ". . . Or the lustful wrestling arenas of the Lacedaemonians who are beloved of Leda" [L.]. Martial [*Epigrammaton*], bk. 4, epig. 55 [4.55.6–7].

[20] [Plutarch] *Moralia*, in the treatise *Quaestiones Romanae* [bk. 2, ques. 40, 274d–e].

[c] These observations are reinforced by the fact that the word *patrie*, "homeland," is a feminine noun, and easily lends itself to personification as a mother.

fallen. On the contrary: it was the Greeks' servitude that had corrupted these exercises. In Plutarch's time,[21] the parks, where one fought naked, and the wrestling matches, made the young people cowardly, inclined them to an infamous love and made only dancers of them; but in Epaminondas' time, wrestling had brought victory to the Thebans at the battle of Leuctra.[22]

There are few laws that are not good when the state has not lost its principles; and, as Epicurus said, speaking of wealth, "It is not the drink that is spoiled, it is the jar."

[21] Plutarch, ibid. [*Moralia, Quaestiones Romanae*, bk. 2, ques. 40; 274d–e].
[22] Plutarch, *Moralia, Quaestionum convivialium*, bk. 2 [bk. 2, ques. 5; 639f–640a].

CHAPTER 12
Continuation of the same subject

In Rome, judges were taken from the order of senators. The Gracchi transferred this prerogative to the knights. Drusus gave it to both senators and knights; Sulla, to senators alone; Cotta, to senators, knights, and public treasurers. Caesar excluded these last. Antony made decurions of senators, knights, and centurions.

When a republic has been corrupted, none of the ills that arise can be remedied except by removing the corruption and recalling the principles; every other correction is either useless or a new ill. So long as Rome preserved its principles, judgments could be in the hands of the senators without suffering abuse; but when it had been corrupted, regardless of the body to which judgments were transferred, whether to senators, knights, or public treasurers, or to two of these bodies, to all three together, or to any other body at all, the result was always bad. Knights had no more virtue than senators, public treasurers no more than knights, and the latter as little as centurions.

When the Roman people had secured their participation in the patrician magistracies, it was natural to think that their flatterers would be the arbiters of the government. No: one saw these people, who had opened the common magistracies to plebeians, always elect patricians. Because the people were virtuous, they were magnanimous; because they were free, they scorned power. But when they had lost their principles, the more power they had, the less carefully they managed it, until finally, having become their own tyrant and their own slave, they lost the strength of liberty and fell into the weakness of license.

CHAPTER 13

The effect of the oath on a virtuous people

There has never been a people, says Livy,[23] to whom dissoluteness came later than to the Romans and among whom moderation and poverty were honored longer.

The *oath* had so much force among these people that nothing attached them more to the laws. In order to observe an oath, they often did what they would never have done for glory or for the homeland.

When the consul Quinctius Cincinnatus wanted to raise an army against the Aequi and the Volscians, the tribunes objected. "All right, then," he said, "let all those who swore their oath to the consul last year march under my banner."[24] In vain the tribunes cried out that no one was still bound by that oath and that when it had been sworn, Quinctius was a private citizen: the people were more religious than those who attempted to guide them; the people would not listen to the distinctions and interpretations of the tribunes.

When these same people wanted to withdraw to the Mons Sacer, they felt restrained by the oath they had sworn to follow the consuls to war.[25] They formed the design of killing the consuls; they were made to understand that the oath would none the less continue to exist. One can judge their idea of the violation of an oath by the crime they wanted to commit.

After the battle of Cannae, the people were frightened and wanted to withdraw to Sicily; Scipio made them swear they would remain in Rome; the fear of breaking their oath overcame every other fear. Rome in the storm was a vessel held by two anchors: religion and mores.

[23] [Livy] bk. 1 [Preface; 11].
[24] Livy, bk. 3 [3.20.4].
[25] Livy, bk. 2 [2.32.1–2].

CHAPTER 14

How the slightest change in the constitution entails the ruin of the principles

Aristotle speaks to us of the republic of Carthage as a well-regulated republic. Polybius tells us that during the Second Punic War,[26] the trouble in Carthage was that the senate had lost almost all its authority. Livy teaches us that when Hannibal returned to Carthage, he found the magistrates and principal citizens turning the public revenues to their own profit and abusing their power. Therefore, the virtue of the magistrates fell along with the authority of the senate; everything flowed from the same principle.

The prodigious results of the censorship among the Romans are well known. At one time it became oppressive but was kept up because there was more luxury than corruption. Clodius weakened it; by that weakening, corruption became even greater than luxury; and the censorship[27] abolished itself, so to speak. Having been altered, demanded, resumed, and abandoned, it was entirely suspended until it became useless, I mean during the reigns of Augustus and Claudius.

[26] About a hundred years later [Polybius, *Historia* 6.51].

[27] See [Cass.] Dio [*Historia Romana*], bk. 38 [38.13.2]; Plutarch [*Vit.*], *Cicero* [29–30.2; 34.1–2]; Cicero, *Epistolae ad Atticum*, bk. 4, letters 10 and 15 [4.9 and 16]; [Pseudo] Asconius [Pedianus], *Scholia Sangallensis Ciceronis, In Divinationem* [3.8; 2.189; see also Freinsheim, *Supplementorum Livianorum*, 103.109].

CHAPTER 15

Some very effective means of preserving the three principles

I shall be able to be understood only when the next four chapters have been read.

CHAPTER 16

Distinctive properties of the republic

It is in the nature of a republic to have only a small territory; otherwise, it can scarcely continue to exist. In a large republic, there are large fortunes, and consequently little moderation in spirits: the depositories are too large to put in the hands of a citizen; interests become particularized; at first a man feels he can be happy, great, and glorious without his homeland; and soon, that he can be great only on the ruins of his homeland.

In a large republic, the common good is sacrificed to a thousand considerations; it is subordinated to exceptions; it depends upon accidents. In a small one, the public good is better felt, better known, lies nearer to each citizen; abuses are less extensive there and consequently less protected.

What made Lacedaemonia last so long is that, after all its wars, it always remained within its territory. Lacedaemonia's only goal was liberty; the only advantage of its liberty was glory.

It was in the spirit of the Greek republics for them to be as satisfied with their lands as they were with their laws. Athens was seized with ambition and transmitted it to Lacedaemonia; but this was in order to command free peoples rather than to govern slaves; to be at the head of the union rather than to shatter it. All was lost when a monarchy rose up, a government whose spirit tends more toward expansion.

It is difficult for any government other than the republican to continue to exist in a single town unless there are particular circumstances.[28] A prince of such a small state would naturally be inclined to oppression because he would have a great power and few ways to enjoy it or to make it respected; therefore he would trample his people greatly. Then again, such a prince would be easily oppressed by a foreign force or even by a domestic force; the people could come together and unite against him at any moment. Now, when the prince of a single town is driven from his town, the proceeding is finished; if he has several towns, it has just begun.

[28] As when a small sovereign maintains himself between two great states by their mutual jealousy; but he exists only precariously.

CHAPTER 17
Distinctive properties of monarchy

A monarchical state should be of a medium size. If it were small, it would form itself into a republic; if it were quite extensive, the principal men of the state, being great in themselves, away from the eyes of the prince, with their court outside of his court, and, moreover, secured by the laws and by the mores from hasty executions, could cease to obey; they would not fear a punishment that was so slow and so distant.

Thus, Charlemagne had scarcely founded his empire before it had to be divided, either because the governors of the provinces did not obey, or because they would obey better if the empire were divided into several kingdoms.

After Alexander's death, his empire was divided. How could those important men of Greece and Macedonia, who were once free or were at least leaders of conquering peoples then so scattered across that vast conquest, how could they have obeyed others?

After Attila's death, his empire was dissolved; the many kings who were no longer constrained could not take up their chains again.

In these cases, the quick establishment of unlimited power is the remedy which can prevent dissolution: a new misfortune after that of expansion!

Rivers run together into the sea; monarchies are lost in despotism.

CHAPTER 18
That the Spanish monarchy was a particular case

Let Spain not be cited as an example; rather, it proves what I say. In order to hold America, it did what despotism itself does not do; it destroyed the inhabitants. In order to preserve its colony Spain had to keep it dependent even for its subsistence.

Spain attempted despotism in the Low Countries, and, as soon as it had abandoned this attempt, it became more encumbered. On the one hand, the Walloons would not be governed by the Spaniards, and, on the other, the Spanish soldiers refused to obey the Walloon officers.[29]

[29] See [Jean] Le Clerc, *Histoire des Provinces-Unies des Pays-Bas* [e.g. 1, 81; 1737–1738 edn].

Spain maintained itself in Italy only by enriching Italy and ruining itself, for those who wanted to be rid of the king of Spain were nevertheless not in a humor to relinquish his money.

CHAPTER 19
Distinctive properties of despotic government

A large empire presupposes a despotic authority in the one who governs. Promptness of resolutions must make up for the distance of the places to which they are sent; fear must prevent negligence in the distant governor or magistrate; the law must be in a single person; and it must change constantly, like accidents, which always increase in proportion to the size of the state.

CHAPTER 20
Consequence of the preceding chapters

If the natural property of small states is to be governed as republics, that of medium-sized ones, to be subject to a monarch, and that of large empires to be dominated by a despot, it follows that, in order to preserve the principles of the established government, the state must be maintained at the size it already has and that it will change its spirit to the degree to which its boundaries are narrowed or extended.

CHAPTER 21
On the Chinese empire

Before completing this book, I shall answer an objection that may be raised about all I have said to this point.

Our missionaries speak of the vast empire of China as of an admirable government, in whose principle intermingle fear, honor, and virtue. I would therefore have made an empty distinction in establishing the principles of the three governments.

I do not know how one can speak of honor among peoples who can be made to do nothing without beatings.[30]

Moreover, our men of commerce, far from giving us an idea of the same kind of virtue of which our missionaries speak, can rather be consulted about the banditry of the mandarins.[31] I also call to witness the great man, Lord Anson.

Besides, Father Parennin's letters on the proceeding that the emperor caused to be brought against the neophyte princes of the blood[32] who had displeased him show us a tyrannical plan consistently followed and affronts to human nature done as a matter of rule, that is, in cold blood.

We also have letters from M. de Mairan and the same Father Parennin concerning the government of China. After some very sensible questions and answers, the aura of the marvelous vanishes.

Could it not be that the missionaries were deceived by an appearance of order, that they were struck by that continuous exercise of the will of one alone by which they themselves are governed and which they so like to find in the courts of the kings of India? For, as they go there only to make great changes, it is easier for them to convince princes that they can do everything than to persuade the peoples that they can suffer everything.[33]

Finally, there is often something true even in errors. Particular and perhaps unique circumstances may make it so that the Chinese government is not as corrupt as it should be. In this country causes drawn mostly from the physical aspect, climate, have been able to force the moral causes and, in a way, to perform prodigies.

The climate of China is such that it prodigiously favors the reproduction of mankind. Women there have such great fertility that

[30] The stick governs China, says Father [Jean Baptiste] du Halde [*Description de l'Empire de la Chine*, "Des prisons"; 2, 156–157 H; 2, 132–133 P; 2, 226 L].

[31] See, among others, the relation of Lange [*Recueil de voyages au Nord*, "Journal du Sieur Lange continuant ses négotiations à la cour de la Chine, 1721–1722"; vol. 8; 1727 edn].

[32] Of the family of Sourniama, *Lettres édifiantes et curieuses*, 18 [Lettre du P. Parennin, Pékin, July 20, 1726; 18, 33–122; Pékin, August 24, 1726; 18, 248–311; 1728 edn].

[33] In Father [Jean Baptiste] du Halde, see how the missionaries used the authority of Kang-hi to silence the mandarins who always said that by the laws of the country a foreign form of worship could not be established in the empire. [Jean Baptiste du Halde, *Description de l'Empire de la Chine*, "De l'établissement et du progrès de la religion chrétienne," 3, 126–136 H; 3, 104–111 P.]

nothing like it is seen elsewhere on earth. The cruellest tyranny cannot check the progress of propagation. The prince cannot say, with the Pharaoh, *Let us oppress them wisely*. He would be reduced, rather, to formulating Nero's wish that mankind should have only one head. Despite tyranny, China, because of its climate, will always populate itself and will triumph over tyranny.

China, like all countries where rice is grown,[34] is subject to frequent famines. When the people are starving, they scatter to seek something to eat. Everywhere bands of three, four, or five robbers form: most are immediately wiped out; others grow and are also wiped out. But, in such a great number of distant provinces, a group may meet with success. It maintains itself, grows stronger, forms itself into an army, goes straight to the capital, and its leader comes to the throne.

The nature of the thing is such that bad government there is immediately punished. Disorder is born suddenly when this prodigious number of people lacks subsistence. What makes it so hard to recover from abuses in other countries is that the effects are not felt; the prince is not alerted as promptly and strikingly as in China.

He will not feel, as our princes do, that if he governs badly, he will be less happy in the next life, less powerful and less rich in this one; he will know that, if his government is not good, he will lose his empire and his life.

As the Chinese people become ever more numerous despite exposing their children,[35] they must work tirelessly to make the lands produce enough to feed themselves; this demands great attention on the part of the government. It is in its interest for everyone at every moment to be able to work without fear of being frustrated for his pains. This should be less a civil government than a domestic government.

This is what has produced the rules that are so much discussed. Some have wanted to have laws reign along with despotism, but whatever is joined to despotism no longer has force. This despotism, beset by its misfortunes, has wanted in vain to curb itself; it arms itself with its chains and becomes yet more terrible.

Therefore, China is a despotic state whose principle is fear. In the first dynasties, when the empire was not so extensive, perhaps the government deviated a little from that spirit. But that is not so today.

[34] See bk. 23, chap. 14, below.

[35] See the memoir of one Tsongtu, *Lettres édifiantes et curieuses*, 21 "Expédients pour faire défricher les terres incultes" [22.210–223; 1736 edn].

Part 2

BOOK 9

On the laws in their relation with defensive force

CHAPTER I

How republics provide for their security

If a republic is small, it is destroyed by a foreign force; if it is large, it is destroyed by an internal vice.

This dual drawback taints democracies and aristocracies equally, whether they are good or whether they are bad. The ill is in the thing itself; there is no form that can remedy it.

Thus, it is very likely that ultimately men would have been obliged to live forever under the government of one alone if they had not devised a kind of constitution that has all the internal advantages of republican government and the external force of monarchy. I speak of the federal republic.

This form of government is an agreement by which many political bodies consent to become citizens of the larger state that they want to form. It is a society of societies that make a new one, which can be enlarged by new associates that unite with it.

Such associations made Greece flourish for so long. By using them, the Romans attacked the universe, and with their use alone, the universe defended itself from the Romans; and when Rome had reached its greatest height, the barbarians were able to resist it by associations made beyond the Danube and the Rhine, associations made from fright.

Because of them, Holland,[1] Germany, and the Swiss leagues are regarded in Europe as eternal republics.

Associations of towns were more necessary formerly than they are today. A city without power risked greater perils. Conquest made it lose

[1] It is formed of about fifty republics, all of them different from one another. [François Michel] Janiçon, *Etat présent de la République des Provinces-Unies* [1, 76; 1729 edn].

not only executive and legislative power, as today, but also all property among men.[2]

This sort of republic, able to resist external force, can be maintained at its size without internal corruption: the form of this society curbs every drawback.

One who might want to usurp could scarcely have equal credit in all the confederated states. If he became too strong in one state, he would alarm all the others; if he subjugated a part, the part still free could resist him with forces independent of those he had usurped and overwhelm him before he had completely established himself.

If a sedition occurs in one of the members of the confederation, the others can pacify it. If some abuses are introduced somewhere, they are corrected by the healthy parts. This state can perish in one place without perishing in another; the confederation can be dissolved and the confederates remain sovereign.

Composed of small republics, it enjoys the goodness of the internal government of each one; and, with regard to the exterior, it has, by the force of the association, all the advantages of large monarchies.

[2] Civil liberty, goods, women, children, temples, and even sepulchers.

CHAPTER 2

That the federal constitution should be composed of states of the same nature, above all of republican states

The Canaanites were destroyed because they were small monarchies that had not confederated and did not have a common defense. This is because it is not in the nature of small monarchies to confederate.

The federal republic of Germany is composed of free towns and small states subject to princes. Experience shows that it is more imperfect than the federal republics of Holland and Switzerland.

The spirit of monarchy is war and expansion; the spirit of republics is peace and moderation. The only way these two sorts of governments can continue to exist together in one federal republic is by force.

Thus we see in Roman history that when the Veientes chose a king, all the small republics of Tuscany abandoned them. In Greece all was lost when the Macedonian kings gained a place among the Amphictiones.

The federal republic of Germany, composed of princes and free towns, continues to exist because it has a leader who is, in a way, the magistrate of the union and, in a way, the monarch.

CHAPTER 3

Other things required in the federal republic

In the republic of Holland, one province cannot make an alliance without the consent of the others. This law is good and even necessary in the federal republic. It is missing from the German constitution, where it would curb the misfortunes that can come to all the members from the imprudence, ambition, or avarice of one alone. A republic united in a political confederation has given itself entirely and has nothing more to give.

It is unlikely that the states that associate will be of the same size and have equal power. The republic of the Lycians[3] was an association of twenty-three towns; the large ones had three votes in the common council; the medium-sized ones, two; the small ones, one. The republic of Holland is composed of seven provinces, large and small, each having one vote.

The towns of Lycia[4] paid the costs in proportion to their votes. The provinces of Holland cannot follow this proportion; they must follow that of their power.

In Lycia,[5] the judges and magistrates of the towns were elected by the common council in the proportion that we have said. In the republic of Holland, they are not elected by the common council, and each town names its magistrates. If one had to propose a model of a fine federal republic, I would choose the republic of Lycia.

[3] Strabo [*Geographica*], bk. 14 [14.3.3].
[4] Ibid. [Strabo, *Geographica*, 14.3.3].
[5] Strabo [*Geographica*], bk. 14 [14.3.3].

CHAPTER 4

How despotic states provide for their security

Just as republics unite to provide for their security, despotic states separate and hold themselves, so to speak, apart. They sacrifice a part of the country, ravage the frontiers, and leave them deserted; the main part of the empire becomes inaccessible.

It is accepted in geometry that the larger a body, the smaller, relatively, its circumference. Therefore, this practice of laying waste the frontiers is more tolerable in large states than in medium-sized ones.

This state does to itself all the ill that could be done by a cruel enemy, but an enemy that could not be checked.

The despotic state preserves itself by another kind of separation, by which the distant provinces are put in the hands of a feudatory prince. The Moguls, the Persians, and the emperors of China have their feudatory princes; and the Turks are very well off for having put the Tartars, the Moldavians, the Walachians, and formerly the Transylvanians between their enemies and themselves.

CHAPTER 5

How monarchy provides for its security

Monarchy does not destroy itself as does the despotic state; but a state of medium size may quickly be invaded. Therefore, it has strongholds that protect its frontiers and armies that defend these strongholds. There one disputes artfully, courageously, and opinionatedly over the smallest area. Despotic states make invasions; only monarchies make war.

Strongholds belong to monarchies; despotic states are afraid to have them. They dare not entrust them to anyone; for no one there loves the state or the prince.

CHAPTER 6

On the defensive force of states in general

For a state to be at its full force, its size must be such that there is a relation between the speed with which one can execute an undertaking against it and its promptness in rendering this ineffective. As the one who attacks can suddenly appear everywhere, the one who defends must also be able to appear everywhere; consequently, the state must be of a medium extent so as to be proportionate to the degree of speed nature has given men to move from one place to another.

France and Spain are precisely the requisite size. Their forces communicate so well that they go immediately where they are wanted; the armies join together and go rapidly from one frontier to the other; and one fears none of the things that need a certain amount of time for their execution.

It is remarkably fortunate for France that its capital is closer to the different frontiers in proportion to their greater weakness; and the prince here sees each part of his country the better as it is the more exposed.

But when a vast state, such as Persia, is attacked, several months must pass before the dispersed troops can assemble, and there can be no forced march for this length of time, as there can be for two weeks. If the army on the frontier is beaten, it will surely disperse because its places of retreat are not nearby; the victorious army, finding no resistance, advances by long daily marches, appears at the capital, and besieges it, when the governors of the provinces have just been alerted to send help. Those who judge the revolution at hand hasten it by not obeying. For people, faithful only because punishment is at hand, are no longer faithful when it is distant; they work for their own particular interests. The empire dissolves, the capital is taken, and the conqueror disputes the provinces with the governors.

The true power of a prince consists not so much in the ease he has in conquering as in the difficulty there is in attacking him, and, if I dare put it this way, in the immutability of his condition. But the expansion of states makes them expose new sides from which they can be taken.

Thus, just as monarchs should be wise in increasing their power, they should be no less prudent in limiting it. While they put an end to the drawbacks of being small, they must always have an eye out for the drawbacks of being large.

CHAPTER 7

Reflections

The enemies of a great prince who has long reigned have accused him a thousand times, more from fears than from reasons, I believe, of having formed and pursued the project of universal monarchy.[a] If he had succeeded in it nothing would have been more fatal to Europe, to his first subjects, to himself, and to his family. Heaven, which knows the true advantages, has better served him by defeats than it would have by victories. Instead of making him the only king in Europe, it has favored him more by making him the most powerful of all.

The people of his nation, who, in foreign countries, are affected only by that which they have left behind, who, on leaving their home, regard glory as the sovereign good, and in distant countries, as an obstacle to their return, who antagonize even by their good qualities because they seem to join scorn to them, who can bear wounds, perils, or exhaustion, but not the loss of their pleasures, who love nothing so much as their gaiety and are consoled for the loss of a battle by singing of their general, would never have completed such an undertaking, which cannot fail in one country without failing in all others, or fail for a moment without failing forever.

[a] This prince was Louis XIV.

CHAPTER 8

A case where the defensive force of a state is inferior to its offensive force

The comment of Sir De Coucy to King Charles V was that "the English are never so weak or so easy to defeat as at home." This is what was said of the Romans; this is what the Carthaginians experienced; it is what will happen to any power that has sent its armies far away in order to bring together by force of discipline and of military power those who are divided among themselves by political or civil interests. The state is weak because of the ill that remains and has been further weakened by the remedy.

The maxim of Sir De Coucy is an exception to the general rule by which one is never to undertake distant wars. And this exception indeed proves the rule, because it applies only to those who have themselves broken the rule.

CHAPTER 9
On the relative force of states

All size, all force, all power is relative. One must take care that in seeking to increase real size, one does not diminish relative size.

Toward the middle of the reign of Louis XIV, France was at the highest point of its relative size. Germany did not yet have the great monarchs it has since had. Italy was in the same situation. Scotland and England had not formed a monarchy. Aragon had not formed one with Castile; and the separate parts of Spain were weakened by this and weakened Spain. Muscovy was as yet no better known in Europe than was the Crimea.

CHAPTER 10
On the weakness of neighboring states

When a neighboring state is in its decline, one should take care not to hasten its ruin, because this is the most fortunate situation possible; there is nothing more suitable for a prince than to be close to another who receives in his stead all the blows and outrages of fortune. By conquering such a state, one rarely increases as much in real power as one loses in relative power.

BOOK 10
On laws in their relation with offensive force

CHAPTER I
On offensive force

Offensive force is regulated by the right of nations, which is the political law of the nations considered in their relation with each other.

CHAPTER 2
On war

The life of states is like that of men. Men have the right to kill in the case of natural defense; states have the right to wage war for their own preservation.

In the case of natural defense, I have the right to kill, because my life is mine, as the life of the one who attacks me is his; likewise a state wages war because its preservation is just, as is any other preservation.

Among citizens, the right to natural defense does not carry with it a necessity to attack. Instead of attacking they have the recourse of the tribunals. Therefore, they can exercise that right of defense only in cases that occur so suddenly that one would be lost if one waited for the aid of the laws. But among societies, the right of natural defense sometimes carries with it a necessity to attack, when one people sees that a longer peace would put another people in a position to destroy it and that an attack at this moment is the only way to prevent such destruction.

Hence small societies more frequently have the right to wage wars than large ones, because they are more frequently in a position to fear being destroyed.

Therefore, the right of war derives from necessity and from a strict justice. If those who direct the conscience or the councils of princes do not hold to these, all is lost; and, when that right is based on arbitrary principles of glory, of propriety, of utility, tides of blood will inundate the earth.

Above all, let one not speak of the prince's glory; his glory is his arrogance; it is a passion and not a legitimate right.

It is true that his reputation for power could increase the forces of his state, but his reputation for justice would increase them in any case.

CHAPTER 3

On the right of conquest

From the right of war derives that of conquest, which is its consequence; therefore, it should follow the spirit of the former.

When a people is conquered, the right of the conqueror follows four sorts of laws: the law of nature, which makes everything tend toward the preservation of species; the law of natural enlightenment,[a] which wants us to do to others what we would want to have done to us; the law that forms political societies, which are such that nature has not limited their duration; lastly, the law drawn from the thing itself. Conquest is an acquisition; the spirit of acquisition carries with it the spirit of preservation and use, and not that of destruction.

One state that has conquered another treats it in one of these four ways: the state continues to govern its conquest according to its own laws and takes for itself only the exercise of the political and civil government; or it gives its conquest a new political and civil government; or it destroys the society and scatters it into others; or, finally, it exterminates all the citizens.

The first way conforms to the right of nations we follow at present; the fourth is more in conformity with the right of nations among the Romans; on this point, I leave others to judge how much better we have become. Here homage must be paid to our modern times, to contemporary reasoning, to the religion of the present day, to our philosophy, and to our mores.

[a] Montesquieu uses *lumières*, which we translate as "enlightenment"; it also implies insight or illumination.

When the authors of our public right, for whom ancient histories provided the foundation, have no longer followed cases strictly, they have fallen into great errors. They have moved toward the arbitrary; they have assumed among conquerors a right, I do not know which one, of killing; this has made them draw consequences as terrible as this principle and establish maxims that the conquerors themselves, when they had the slightest sense, never adopted. It is clear that, once the conquest is made, the conqueror no longer has the right to kill, because it is no longer for him a case of natural defense and of his own preservation.

What has made them think in this way is that they have believed the conqueror had the right to destroy the society; thus they have concluded that he had the right to destroy the men composing it, which is a consequence wrongly drawn from a wrong principle. For, from the annihilation of the society, it would not follow that the men forming that society should also be annihilated. The society is the union of men and not the men themselves; the citizen may perish and the man remain.

From the right to kill during conquest, political men have drawn the right to reduce to servitude, but the consequence is as ill founded as the principle.

One has the right to reduce a people to servitude only when it is necessary for the preservation of a conquest. The purpose of conquest is preservation; servitude is never the purpose of conquest, but it is sometimes a necessary means for achieving preservation.

In this case, it is against the nature of the thing for this servitude to be eternal. It must be possible for the enslaved people to become subjects. Slavery is accidental to conquest. When, after a certain length of time, all the parts of the conquering state are bound to those of the conquered state by customs, marriage, laws, associations, and a certain conformity of spirit, servitude should cease. For the rights of the conqueror are founded only on the fact that these things do not exist and that there is a distance between the two nations, such that the one cannot trust the other.

Thus, the conqueror who reduces a people to servitude should always reserve for himself means (and these means are innumerable) for allowing them to leave it.

I am not saying vague things here. Our fathers who conquered the Roman Empire acted in this way. They softened the laws that they made in the heat, impetuosity, and arrogance of victory; their laws had been hard, they made them impartial. The Burgundians, the Goths, and the Lombards wanted the Romans to continue to be the vanquished people; the laws of Euric, of Gundobad, and of Rotharis made the barbarian and the Roman fellow citizens.[1b]

To subdue the Saxons, Charlemagne deprived them of their freeborn status and of the ownership of goods. Louis the Pious freed them;[2] he did nothing better during his reign. Time and servitude had softened their mores; they were forever faithful to him.

[1] See the law codes of the barbarians, and book 28 below.

[2] See the anonymous author ["Astronomous"] of the life of Louis the Pious in the Duchesne collection, vol. 2, p. 296 [*Vita Hludowici Imperatoris*, *MGH*, SS. 2; chap. 24, anno 814].

[b] See 28.5 for an elaboration of the personal law of the barbarians.

CHAPTER 4

Some advantages for the conquered peoples

Instead of drawing such fatal consequences from the right of conquest, political men would have done better to speak of the advantages this right can sometimes confer on a vanquished people. They would have been more sensitive to these advantages if our right of nations were followed exactly and if it were established around the earth.

Ordinarily states that are conquered do not have the force they had at their institution: corruption has entered them; their laws have ceased to be executed; the government has become an oppressor. Who can doubt that there would be gain for such a state and that it would draw other advantages from the conquest itself, if the conquest were not destructive? What would the government lose by being recast, if it had reached the point of being unable to reform itself? A conqueror who comes to a people among whom the rich, by a thousand ruses and a thousand tricks, have imperceptibly practiced an infinite number of usurpations; where the unfortunate man who trembles as he watches what he believed to be abuses become laws is oppressed and believes himself wrong to feel so; a conqueror, I say, can change the course of everything, and muffled tyranny is the first thing which is liable to violence.

For example, one has seen states whose oppression by tax-collectors was relieved by the conqueror, who had neither the engagements nor the needs of the legitimate prince. Abuses were corrected even without the conqueror's correcting them.

The frugality of the conquering nation has sometimes put it in a position to leave the vanquished people the necessities that had been taken from them under the legitimate prince.

A conquest can destroy harmful prejudices, and, if I dare speak in this way, can put a nation under a better presiding genius.

What good could the Spanish not have done the Mexicans? They had a gentle religion to give them; they brought them a raging superstition. They could have set the slaves free, and they made freemen slaves. They could have made clear to them that human sacrifice was an abuse; instead they exterminated them. I would never finish if I wanted to tell all the good things they did not do, and all the evil ones they did.

It is for the conqueror to make amends for part of the evils he has done. I define the right of conquest thus: a necessary, legitimate, and unfortunate right, which always leaves an immense debt to be discharged if human nature is to be repaid.

CHAPTER 5
Gelon, King of Syracuse

The finest peace treaty mentioned in history is, I believe, the one Gelon made with the Carthaginians. He wanted them to abolish the custom of sacrificing their children.[3] Remarkable thing! After defeating three hundred thousand Carthaginians, he exacted a condition useful only to them, or rather, he stipulated one for mankind.

The Bactrians had their elders eaten by large dogs; Alexander forbade them to do this,[4] and this was a triumph he gained over superstition.

[3] See the collection by [Jean] Barbeyrac [*Histoire des anciens traitez*], art. 112 [art. 113; 1739 edn].

[4] Strabo [*Geographica*], bk. 2 [11.11.3].

CHAPTER 6

On a republic that conquers

It is against the nature of the thing for one confederated state under a federal constitution to conquer another, as we have seen among the Swiss in our own time.[5] In mixed federal republics, with an association of small republics and small monarchies, such conquest is less shocking.

It is also against the nature of the thing for a democratic republic to conquer towns that could not enter the sphere of the democracy. As the Romans had established from the beginning, the conquered people must be able to enjoy the privileges of sovereignty. The limit to conquest should be the number of citizens fixed for the democracy.

If a democracy conquers a people in order to govern it as a subject, it will expose its own liberty, because it will entrust too much power to the magistrates whom it sends out to the conquered state.

What danger would not the republic of Carthage have run if Hannibal had taken Rome? Having caused so many revolutions in his own town after his defeat, what might he not have done there after that victory?[6]

Hanno could never have persuaded the senate not to send aid to Hannibal if he had let only his jealousy speak. That senate, which Aristotle tells us was very wise (something the prosperity of that republic proves very well),[c] could reach a decision only for sensible reasons. One would have had to be dull-witted not to see that an army three hundred leagues away had had necessary losses that had to be repaired.

Hanno's party wanted Hannibal to surrender to the Romans.[7] At that time, one could not have feared the Romans; therefore, one feared Hannibal.

Hannibal's successes, they say, could not be believed; but how could they be doubted? Were the Carthaginians, scattered around the earth,

[5] Of Tockenburg.

[6] He was at the head of a faction.

[7] Hanno wanted to surrender Hannibal to the Romans, as Cato wanted Caesar to be surrendered to the Gauls.

---

[c] Aristotle, *Politics* 1272b24–41.

unaware of what was happening in Italy? It was because they were aware of it that they did not want to send help to Hannibal.

Hanno became firmer after Trebia, after Trasimene, after Cannae; it is not their incredulity that grows, it is their fear.

CHAPTER 7
Continuation of the same subject

There is still another drawback to conquests made by democracies. Their kind of government is always odious to subject states. It is monarchical only by a fiction; but, in truth, it is harsher than monarchy, as the experience of all times and all countries has shown.

The conquered peoples are in a sad state; they enjoy the advantages neither of the republic nor of the monarchy.

What I have said of the popular state can be applied to aristocracy.

CHAPTER 8
Continuation of the same subject

Thus, when a republic holds a people dependent, it must seek to make amends for the drawbacks that arise from the nature of the thing by giving this people a good political right and good civil laws.

An Italian republic held certain islanders obedient to it, but its political and civil right in their regard was faulty. One recalls the act of amnesty[8] that stipulated that they would no longer be condemned to corporal penalties *on the privy knowledge of the governor.*[d] Peoples have often asked for privileges; here it is the sovereign who grants what is the right of all nations.

[8] Of October 18, 1738, printed at Genoa by Franchelli. "We forbid our Governor-general in this said Island [Corsica] to condemn to grievous punishment any person based solely on his own privy information [*ex informata conscientia*]. He will certainly be able to arrest and imprison such persons who are suspect, provided that he render to us a speedy account" [It.], art. 6. [This reference has not been verified.]

[d] The "corporal penalties" are *peines afflictives*, meaning imprisonment or death.

CHAPTER 9

On a monarchy that conquers its neighbors

If a monarchy can have an influence long before its expansion weakens it, it will become formidable; and its force wil last as long as neighboring monarchies continue to press it.

Therefore it should conquer only up to the limits natural to its government. Prudence wants it to check itself as soon as it exceeds these limits.

In this sort of conquest, things must be left as they were found: the same tribunals, the same laws, the same customs, the same privileges. Nothing should be changed but the army and the sovereign's name.

When the monarchy has extended its limits by the conquest of a few neighbouring provinces, it must treat them very gently.

In a monarchy that has worked long for conquest, the provinces of its first domain will ordinarily be badly trampled. They have to suffer both the new abuses and the old ones, and often a vast capital that engulfs everything has decreased their population. Now if, after the conquest of the area around this domain, the vanquished peoples were treated as were the first subjects, the state would be lost; what the conquered provinces would send in tribute to the capital would no longer return to them; the frontiers would be ruined, and consequently weaker; the peoples would be badly affected by this; the sustenance of armies that were to remain there and have influence would be more precarious.

Such is the necessary state of a conquering monarchy: frightful luxury in the capital, poverty in the provinces at some distance from it, abundance at the farthest points. It is as it is with our planet: fire is in the center, greenery on the surface, and between them an arid, cold, and sterile land.

CHAPTER 10

On a monarchy that conquers another monarchy

Sometimes one monarchy conquers another. The smaller the latter is, the better it will be contained by strongholds; the larger, the better preserved by colonies.

CHAPTER 11

On the mores of the vanquished people

In these conquests, it is not enough to leave the vanquished nation its laws; it is perhaps more necessary to leave it its mores, because a people always knows, loves, and defends its mores better than its laws.

The French were driven out of Italy nine times because, say the historians,[9] they were insolent to women and girls. It is too much for a nation to have to suffer not only the conqueror's pride but also his incontinence; not only both these but also his indiscretion, probably the more trying because it multiplies outrages to infinity.

[9] See [Samuel] Pufendorf, *Introduction à l'histoire générale et politique de l'univers* [see, for example, p. 358; 1700 Latin edn; bk. 1, chap. 4; 1, 343; 1743 Fr. edn].

CHAPTER 12

On a law of Cyrus

I do not consider good the law that Cyrus made: that the Lydians could exercise none but vile or infamous professions. One attends to the most urgent; one thinks of rebellions and not invasions. But invasions will soon come; the two peoples unite; they corrupt each other. I should prefer that the laws maintained the roughness of the victorious people than that they kept up the softness of the vanquished people.

Aristodemus, tyrant of Cumae,[10] sought to weaken the courage of the youth. He wanted the boys to let their hair grow long like a girl's, dressing it with flowers, and to wear variously colored robes down to their heels; to have women bring them their parasols, perfumes, and fans when they went to their dancing masters and their music masters; in the bath women gave them their combs and mirrors. This education lasted until the age of twenty. This is suitable only for a petty tyrant, who risks his sovereignty in order to defend his life.

[10] Dion. Hal. [*Ant. Rom.*], bk. 7 [7.9.3–5].

CHAPTER 13
Charles XII

This prince, who used only his own forces, brought on his fall by forming designs that could be executed only by a long war, one which his kingdom could not support.

It was not a state in its decline that he attempted to overthrow, but a rising empire. The war this prince waged against the Muscovites served them as a school. After each defeat, they came closer to victory; and, while losing abroad, they learned to defend themselves at home.

Charles believed himself master of the world in the uninhabited regions of Poland where he roamed and in which Sweden was spread out, as it were, while his principal enemy strengthened itself against him, surrounded him, established itself on the Baltic Sea, and destroyed or captured Livonia.

Sweden was like a river whose waters were cut off at the source while its course was being deflected.

It was not Poltava that ruined Charles; if he had not been destroyed at that place, he would have been destroyed at another. Accidents of fortune are easily rectified; one cannot avert events that continuously arise from the nature of things.[e]

But neither nature nor fortune was ever as strong against him as he himself.

He was not ruled by the actual arrangement of things, but rather by a certain model he had chosen; even this he followed badly. He was not Alexander but he would have been Alexander's best soldier.

Alexander's project succeeded only because it was sensible. The unfavorable results of the Persians' invasions of Greece, the conquests of Agesilaus and the retreat of the Ten Thousand had made known just how superior the Greek manner of doing battle and their sort of weapons were; and it was well known that the Persians were too great to correct themselves.

They could no longer weaken Greece by dividing it; it was then united under a leader for whom there was no better means of hiding its

[e]In 1757 the beginning of this clause was changed from *mais comment parer* to *on ne peut pas parer*. Although in the Masson edition the punctuation has not been changed from a question-mark to a period, we have changed it in the translation.

servitude from it than to dazzle it by the destruction of its eternal enemies and by the expectation of conquering Asia.

As the empire was cultivated by a nation of the most industrious people in the world who plowed their lands on account of religious principle, a nation fertile and abundant in all things, it was very easy for an enemy to subsist there.

By the arrogance of these kings, always humbled in vain by their defeats, one might judge that they would hasten their downfall by always giving battle and that flattery would never allow them to doubt of their greatness.

And not only was the project wise, but it was wisely executed. Alexander, in the rapidity of his actions, even in the heat of his passions, was led by a vein of reason, if I dare use the term, and those who have wanted to make a romance of his story, those whose spirit was more spoiled than his, have been unable to hide it from us. Let us speak about him at length.

CHAPTER 14
Alexander

He left Greece only after securing Macedonia from the neighboring barbarian peoples and completely oppressing the Greeks; he used this oppression only for the execution of his enterprise; he rendered the Lacedaemonians' jealousy powerless; he attacked the maritime provinces; he made his army follow the seashore in order not to be separated from his fleet; he used discipline remarkably well against numbers; he did not lack provisions; and if it is true that victory gave him everything, he also did everything in order to gain victory.

In the beginning of his enterprise, that is, at a time when a defeat could have set him back, he left little to chance; when fortune set him above events, temerity was sometimes one of his means. When he marches against the Triballians and Illyrians before his departure, you see a war like the one Caesar later waged in Gaul.[11] On his way to Greece,[12] it is almost in spite of himself that he captures and destroys

[11] See Arrian, *Anabasis*, bk. 1 [1.1.4–1.4.8].
[12] Ibid. [Arrian, *Anabasis* 1.7–8.]

Thebes; camped near their city, he waits until the Thebans want to make peace; they themselves hasten their ruin. When it is a question of battling the naval forces of the Persians,[13] Parmenion is the more audacious, but Alexander is the wiser. By his industry he maneuvered the Persians away from the seashore and reduced them to abandoning their navy, which was superior. In principle, Tyre was attached to the Persians, who could not do without its commerce and its navy; Alexander destroyed it. He took Egypt, which Darius had left stripped of troops while he was collecting innumerable armies in another universe.

Alexander owed his mastery of the Greek colonies to the crossing of the Granicus; the battle of Issus gave him Tyre and Egypt; the battle of Arbela gave him the whole earth.

After the battle of Issus, he lets Darius flee and concerns himself only with consolidating and ruling his conquests; after the battle of Arbela, he follows Darius so closely[14] that he leaves him no retreat in his empire. Darius enters his towns and provinces only to leave again; Alexander's marches are so rapid that you believe that empire of the universe is the prize for running, as in the Greek games, rather than the prize for victory.

It is thus that he made his conquests; let us see how he preserved them.

He resisted those who wanted him to treat[15] the Greeks as masters and the Persians as slaves; he thought only of uniting the two nations and wiping out the distinctions between the conquerors and the vanquished: after the conquest, he abandoned all the prejudices that had served him in making it; he assumed the mores of the Persians in order not to distress the Persians by making them assume the mores of the Greeks; this is why he showed so much respect for the wife and the mother of Darius and why he was so continent. Who is this conqueror who is mourned by all the peoples he subjected? Who is this usurper whose death moved to tears the family he had removed from the throne? This aspect of his life, historians tell us, can be claimed by no other conqueror.

Nothing strengthens a conquest more than unions by marriage

[13] Ibid. [Arrian, *Anabasis* 1.18.6–9.]

[14] Ibid. [Arrian, *Anabasis*], bk. 3 [3.19–21].

[15] This was Aristotle's counsel. Plutarch, *Moralia, De Alexandri Magni fortuna aut virtute* [1.6; 329b–d].

between two peoples. Alexander took wives from the nation he had vanquished; he wanted the men of his court[16] to do likewise; the rest of the Macedonians followed his example. The Franks and the Burgundians[17] allowed these marriages; in Spain the Visigoths forbade[18] them and later permitted them; the Lombards not only permitted them but even fostered them;[19] when the Romans wanted to weaken Macedonia, they established there that no unions by marriage could be made between the peoples of one province and another.

Alexander, who sought to unite the two peoples, thought of making a large number of Greek colonies in Persia; he built an infinite number of towns and cemented all the parts of this new empire so well that after his death, in the trouble and confusion of the most horrible civil wars, after the Greeks had annihilated themselves, so to speak, none of the Persian provinces rebelled.

In order not to drain Greece and Macedonia, he sent a colony of Jews to Alexandria;[20] it was unimportant to him what mores these peoples had, provided they were faithful to him.

He left to the vanquished peoples not only their mores but also their civil laws and often even the kings and governors he had found there. He put the Macedonians[21] at the head of the troops and people from the invaded country at the head of the government, preferring to run the risk of the unfaithfulness of some individuals (which occured a few times) to a general rebellion. He respected the old traditions and everything that recorded the glory or the vanity of these peoples. The kings of Persia had destroyed the temples of the Greeks, Babylonians, and Egyptians; he rebuilt them;[22] there were few nations at whose altars he did not sacrifice; it seemed he had conquered only to be the monarch of each nation and the first citizen of each town. The Romans conquered all in order to destroy all; he wanted to conquer all in order to preserve all, and in every country he entered, his first ideas, his first designs, were always to do something to increase its prosperity and

[16] See Arrian, *Anabasis*, bk. 7 [7.4.4–8].
[17] See the *Leges Burgundionum*, tit. 12, art. 5 [12.5].
[18] See the *Lex Wisigothorum*, bk. 3, tit. 5, para. 1 [3.1.1]. It abrogates the earlier law, which, it says, had more regard to the difference between nations than to that between conditions.
[19] See the *Leges Langobardorum*, bk. 2, tit. 7, paras. 1 [Liut. 127] and 2 [Loth. 14 (pap)].
[20] The kings of Syria, abandoning the plan of the empire's founders, wanted to oblige the Jews to take on the mores of the Greeks, which jolted their state terribly.
[21] See Arrian, *Anabasis*, bk. 3 and elsewhere [for example, 3.5, 16] and others.
[22] Ibid. [Arrian, *Anabasis*, 3.16.4–5.]

power. He found the first ways for doing this in the greatness of his genius; the second, in his own frugality and his own economy;[23] the third, in his immense prodigality for great things. His hand was closed for private expenditures; it opened for public expenditures. Was it a question of regulating his household? He was a Macedonian. Was it a question of paying soldiers' debts, of letting the Greeks share in his conquest, of making the fortune of each man in his army? He was Alexander.

He did two things that were bad: he burned Persepolis and killed Clitus. He made them famous by his repentance, so that one forgot his criminal actions and remembered his respect for virtue, so that these actions were considered misfortunes rather than things proper to him, so that posterity finds the beauty of his soul at virtually the same time as his ravings and his weaknesses, so that one had to be sorry for him and it was no longer possible to hate him.

I shall compare him to Caesar: when Caesar wanted to imitate the kings of Asia, he drove the Romans to despair over a thing of pure ostentation; when Alexander wanted to imitate the kings of Asia, he did a thing that entered into the plan of his conquest.

[23] See Arrian, *Anabasis*, bk. 7 [7.9.9.]

CHAPTER 15

A new means for preserving the conquest

When a monarch conquers a large state, there is an admirable practice, equally proper for moderating despotism and for preserving the conquest; those who conquered China put it to use.

In order not to drive the vanquished people to despair and not to make the victor more arrogant, in order to keep the government from becoming military and to hold the two peoples to their duty, the Tartar family now reigning in China has established that each body of troops in the provinces would be composed half of Chinese and half of Tartars, so that the jealousy between the two nations will hold them to their duty. The tribunals are likewise half Chinese, half Tartar. This produces many good results: 1. the two nations constrain one another; 2. both keep military and civil power, and one is not wiped out by the other; 3. the conquering nation can spread throughout without weakening and ruining itself; it becomes capable of resisting civil and foreign wars. This is such a sensible institution, that the absence of a like one has led to the ruin of almost all the conquerors on earth.

CHAPTER 16
On a despotic state that conquers

An immense conquest presupposes despotism. In this case, the army that is spread out in the provinces is insufficient. There must always be a specially trustworthy body around the prince, always ready to assail the part of the empire that may waver. This guard should constrain the others and make tremble all those to whom one has been obliged to leave some authority in the empire. Around the emperor of China, a massive body of Tartars always stands ready in case of need. Among the Moguls, among the Turks, and in Japan, there is a body in the prince's pay, independent of the one maintained by the revenue from the lands. These special forces keep the general ones respectful.

CHAPTER 17
Continuation of the same subject

We have said that the states conquered by the despotic monarch should be feudatory. Historians tire themselves praising the generosity of conquerors who have returned the crown to princes whom they have vanquished. Therefore, the Romans, who made kings everywhere in order to have instruments of servitude, were quite generous.[24] Such an action is a necessary act. If the conqueror keeps the conquered state, the governors he sends will not be able to constrain the subjects, nor will he, his governors. He will be obliged to strip his first patrimony of troops in order to safeguard the new one. All the misfortunes of the two states will be shared; the civil war of the one will be the civil war of the other. But if, on the contrary, the conqueror returns the throne to the

[24] "They considered even kings to be instruments of servitude" [L.] [Tacitus, *Agricola* 14].

legitimate prince, he will of necessity have an ally who, with his own forces, will increase those of the conqueror. We have recently seen Shah Nadir conquer the treasures of the Mogul and leave Hindustan to him.

BOOK 11

On the laws that form political liberty in its relation with the constitution

CHAPTER 1

General idea

I distinguish the laws that form political liberty in its relation with the constitution from those that form it in its relation with the citizen. The first are the subject of the present book; I shall discuss the second in the next book.

CHAPTER 2

The various significations given to the word liberty

No word has received more different significations and has struck minds in so many ways as has *liberty*. Some have taken it for the ease of removing the one to whom they had given tyrannical power; some, for the faculty of electing the one whom they were to obey; others, for the right to be armed and to be able to use violence; yet others, for the privilege of being governed only by a man of their own nation, or by their own laws.[1] For a certain people liberty has long been the usage of wearing a long beard.[2] Men have given this name to one form of government and have excluded the others. Those who had tasted republican government put it in this government; those who had enjoyed monarchical government placed it in monarchy.[3] In short, each

[1] Cicero [*Epistolae ad Atticum* 6.1.15] says, "I have copied Scaevola's edict, which permits the Greeks to end their differences among themselves according to their laws; this makes them regard themselves as free peoples."

[2] The Muscovites could not bear Czar Peter's order to cut them off.

[3] The Cappadocians refused the republican state the Romans offered them.

has given the name of *liberty* to the government that was consistent with his customs or his inclinations; and as, in a republic, one does not always have visible and so present the instruments of the ills of which one complains and as the very laws seem to speak more and the executors of the law to speak less, one ordinarily places liberty in republics and excludes it from monarchies. Finally, as in democracies the people seem very nearly to do what they want, liberty has been placed in this sort of government and the power of the people has been confused with the liberty of the people.

CHAPTER 3
What liberty is

It is true that in democracies the people seem to do what they want, but political liberty in no way consists in doing what one wants. In a state, that is, in a society where there are laws, liberty can consist only in having the power to do what one should want to do and in no way being constrained to do what one should not want to do.

One must put oneself in mind of what independence is and what liberty is. Liberty is the right to do everything the laws permit; and if one citizen could do what they forbid, he would no longer have liberty because the others would likewise have this same power.

CHAPTER 4
Continuation of the same subject

Democracy and aristocracy are not free states by their nature. Political liberty is found only in moderate governments. But it is not always in moderate states. It is present only when power is not abused, but it has eternally been observed that any man who has power is led to abuse it; he continues until he finds limits. Who would think it! Even virtue has need of limits.

So that one cannot abuse power, power must check power by the arrangement of things. A constitution can be such that no one will be constrained to do the things the law does not oblige him to do or be kept from doing the things the law permits him to do.

CHAPTER 5

On the purpose of various states

Although all states have the same purpose in general, which is to maintain themselves, yet each state has a purpose that is peculiar to it. Expansion was the purpose of Rome; war, that of Lacedaemonia; religion, that of the Jewish laws; commerce, that of Marseilles; public tranquillity, that of the laws of China;[4] navigation, that of the laws of the Rhodians; natural liberty was the purpose of the police of the savages; in general, the delights of the prince are the purpose of the despotic states; his glory and that of his state, that of monarchies; the independence of each individual is the purpose of the laws of Poland, and what results from this is the oppression of all.[5]

There is also one nation in the world whose constitution has political liberty for its direct purpose. We are going to examine the principles on which this nation founds political liberty. If these principles are good, liberty will appear there as in a mirror.

Not much trouble need be taken to discover political liberty in the constitution. If it can be seen where it is, if it has been found, why seek it?

[4] The natural purpose of a state having no enemies on the outside or believing them checked by barriers.
[5] Drawback of the *liberum veto*.

CHAPTER 6

On the constitution of England

In each state there are three sorts of powers: legislative power, executive power over the things depending on the right of nations, and executive power over the things depending on civil right.

By the first, the prince or the magistrate makes laws for a time or for always and corrects or abrogates those that have been made. By the second, he makes peace or war, sends or receives embassies, establishes security, and prevents invasions. By the third, he punishes crimes or judges disputes between individuals. The last will be called the power of judging, and the former simply the executive power of the state.

Political liberty in a citizen is that tranquillity of spirit which comes from the opinion each one has of his security, and in order for him to have this liberty the government must be such that one citizen cannot fear another citizen.

When legislative power is united with executive power in a single person or in a single body of the magistracy, there is no liberty, because one can fear that the same monarch or senate that makes tyrannical laws will execute them tyrannically.

Nor is there liberty if the power of judging is not separate from legislative power and from executive power. If it were joined to legislative power, the power over the life and liberty of the citizens would be arbitrary, for the judge would be the legislator. If it were joined to executive power, the judge could have the force of an oppressor.

All would be lost if the same man or the same body of principal men, either of nobles, or of the people, exercised these three powers: that of making the laws, that of executing public resolutions, and that of judging the crimes or the disputes of individuals.

In most kingdoms in Europe, the government is moderate because the prince, who has the first two powers, leaves the exercise of the third to his subjects. Among the Turks, where the three powers are united in the person of the sultan, an atrocious despotism reigns.

In the Italian republics, where the three powers are united, there is less liberty than in our monarchies. Thus, in order to maintain itself, the government needs means as violent as in the government of the Turks; witness the state inquisitors[6] and the lion's maw into which an informer can, at any moment, throw his note of accusation.

Observe the possible situation of a citizen in these republics. The body of the magistracy, as executor of the laws, retains all the power it has given itself as legislator. It can plunder the state by using its general wills; and, as it also has the power of judging, it can destroy each citizen by using its particular wills.

[6] In Venice.

There, all power is one; and, although there is none of the external pomp that reveals a despotic prince, it is felt at every moment.

Thus princes who have wanted to make themselves despotic have always begun by uniting in their person all the magistracies, and many kings of Europe have begun by uniting all the great posts of their state.

I do believe that the pure hereditary aristocracy of the Italian republics is not precisely like the despotism of Asia. The multitude of magistrates sometimes softens the magistracy; not all the nobles always concur in the same designs; there various tribunals are formed that temper one another. Thus, in Venice, the *Great Council* has legislation; the *Pregadi*, execution; *Quarantia*, the power of judging. But the ill is that these different tribunals are formed of magistrates taken from the same body; this makes them nearly a single power.

The power of judging should not be given to a permanent senate but should be exercised by persons drawn from the body of the people[7] at certain times of the year in the manner prescribed by law to form a tribunal which lasts only as long as necessity requires.

In this fashion the power of judging, so terrible among men, being attached neither to a certain state nor to a certain profession, becomes, so to speak, invisible and null. Judges are not continually in view; one fears the magistracy, not the magistrates.[a]

In important accusations, the criminal in cooperation with the law must choose the judges, or at least he must be able to challenge so many of them that those who remain are considered to be of his choice.

The two other powers may be given instead to magistrates or to permanent bodies because they are exercised upon no individual, the one being only the general will of the state, and the other, the execution of that general will.

But though tribunals should not be fixed, judgments should be fixed to such a degree that they are never anything but a precise text of the law. If judgments were the individual opinion of a judge, one would live in this society without knowing precisely what engagements one has contracted.

Further, the judges must be of the same condition as the accused, or

[7] As in Athens.

[a] These *juges*, "jurors," as the office is called in English, are judges as they make the judgments.

his peers, so that he does not suppose that he has fallen into the hands of people inclined to do him violence.

If the legislative power leaves to the executive power the right to imprison citizens who can post bail for their conduct, there is no longer any liberty, unless the citizens are arrested in order to respond without delay to an accusation of a crime the law has rendered capital; in this case they are really free because they are subject only to the power of the law.

But if the legislative power believed itself endangered by some secret conspiracy against the state or by some correspondence with its enemies on the outside, it could, for a brief and limited time, permit the executive power to arrest suspected citizens who would lose their liberty for a time only so that it would be preserved forever.

And this is the only means consistent with reason of replacing the tyrannical magistracy of the *ephors* and the *state inquisitors* of Venice, who are also despotic.

As, in a free state, every man, considered to have a free soul, should be governed by himself, the people as a body should have legislative power; but, as this is impossible in large states and is subject to many drawbacks in small ones, the people must have their representatives do all that they themselves cannot do.

One knows the needs of one's own town better than those of other towns, and one judges the ability of one's neighbors better than that of one's other compatriots. Therefore, members of the legislative body must not be drawn from the body of the nation at large; it is proper for the inhabitants of each principal town to choose a representative from it.

The great advantage of representatives is that they are able to discuss public business. The people are not at all appropriate for such discussions; this forms one of the great drawbacks of democracy.

It is not necessary that the representatives, who have been generally instructed by those who have chosen them, be instructed about each matter of business in particular, as is the practice in the Diets of Germany. It is true that, in their way, the word of the deputies would better express the voice of the nation; but it would produce infinite delays and make each deputy the master of all the others, and on the most pressing occasions the whole force of the nation could be checked by a caprice.

Mr. Sidney says properly that when the deputies represent a body of people, as in Holland, they should be accountable to those who have commissioned them; it is another thing when they are deputed by boroughs, as in England.[b]

In choosing a representative, all citizens in the various districts should have the right to vote except those whose estate is so humble that they are deemed to have no will of their own.

A great vice in most ancient republics was that the people had the right to make resolutions for action, resolutions which required some execution, which altogether exceeds the people's capacity. The people should not enter the government except to choose their representatives; this is quite within their reach. For if there are few people who know the precise degree of a man's ability, yet every one is able to know, in general, if the one he chooses sees more clearly than most of the others.

Nor should the representative body be chosen in order to make some resolution for action, a thing it would not do well, but in order to make laws or in order to see if those they have made have been well executed; these are things it can do very well and that only it can do well.

In a state there are always some people who are distinguished by birth, wealth, or honors; but if they were mixed among the people and if they had only one voice like the others, the common liberty would be their enslavement and they would have no interest in defending it, because most of the resolutions would be against them. Therefore, the part they have in legislation should be in proportion to the other advantages they have in the state, which will happen if they form a body that has the right to check the enterprises of the people, as the people have the right to check theirs.

Thus, legislative power will be entrusted both to the body of the nobles and to the body that will be chosen to represent the people, each of which will have assemblies and deliberations apart and have separate views and interests.

Among the three powers of which we have spoken, that of judging is in some fashion, null. There remain only two; and, as they need a power whose regulations temper them, that part of the legislative body composed of the nobles is quite appropriate for producing this effect.

The nobility should be hereditary. In the first place, it is so by its nature; and, besides, it must have a great interest in preserving its

[b] Algernon Sidney, 1622–1683, an English Whig politician and author of *Discourses Concerning Government* (1698), chap. 3, sect. 38.

prerogatives, odious in themselves, and which, in a free state, must always be endangered.

But, as a hereditary power could be induced to follow its particular interests and forget those of the people, in the things about which one has a sovereign interest in corrupting, for instance, in the laws about levying silver coin, it must take part in legislation only through its faculty of vetoing and not through its faculty of enacting.

I call the right to order by oneself, or to correct what has been ordered by another, the *faculty of enacting*. I call the right to render null a resolution taken by another the *faculty of vetoing*, which was the power of the tribunes of Rome. And, although the one who has the faculty of vetoing can also have the right to approve, this approval is no more than a declaration that one does not make use of one's faculty of vetoing, and it derives from that faculty.

The executive power should be in the hands of a monarch, because the part of the government that almost always needs immediate action is better administered by one than by many, whereas what depends on legislative power is often better ordered by many than by one.

If there were no monarch and the executive power were entrusted to a certain number of persons drawn from the legislative body, there would no longer be liberty, because the two powers would be united, the same persons sometimes belonging and always able to belong to both.

If the legislative body were not convened for a considerable time, there would no longer be liberty. For one of two things would happen: either there would no longer be any legislative resolution and the state would fall into anarchy; or these resolutions would be made by the executive power, and it would become absolute.

It would be useless for the legislative body to be convened without interruption. That would inconvenience the representatives and besides would overburden the executive power, which would not think of executing, but of defending its prerogatives and its right to execute.

In addition, if the legislative body were continuously convened, it could happen that one would do nothing but replace the deputies who had died with new deputies; and in this case, if the legislative body were once corrupted, the ill would be without remedy. When various legislative bodies follow each other, the people, holding a poor opinion of the current legislative body, put their hopes, reasonably enough, in the one that will follow; but if the legislative body were always the same, the people, seeing it corrupted, would expect nothing further from its laws; they would become furious or would sink into indolence.

The legislative body should not convene itself. For a body is considered to have a will only when it is convened; and if it were not convened unanimously, one could not identify which part was truly the legislative body, the part that was convened or the one that was not. For if it had the right to prorogue itself, it could happen that it would never prorogue itself; this would be dangerous in the event that it wanted to threaten executive power. Besides, there are some times more suitable than others for convening the legislative body; therefore, it must be the executive power that regulates, in relation to the circumstances it knows, the time of the holding and duration of these assemblies.

If the executive power does not have the right to check the enterprises of the legislative body, the latter will be despotic, for it will wipe out all the other powers, since it will be able to give to itself all the power it can imagine.

But the legislative power must not have the reciprocal faculty of checking the executive power. For, as execution has the limits of its own nature, it is useless to restrict it; besides, executive power is always exercised on immediate things. And the power of the tribunes in Rome was faulty in that it checked not only legislation but even execution; this caused great ills.

But if, in a free state, legislative power should not have the right to check executive power, it has the right and should have the faculty to examine the manner in which the laws it has made have been executed; and this is the advantage of this government over that of Crete and Lacedaemonia, where the *kosmoi* and the *ephors* were not held accountable for their administration.

But, whether or not this examination is made, the legislative body should not have the power to judge the person, and consequently the conduct, of the one who executes. His person should be sacred because, as he is necessary to the state so that the legislative body does not become tyrannical, if he were accused or judged there would no longer be liberty.

In this case, the state would not be a monarchy but an unfree republic. But, as he who executes cannot execute badly without having as ministers wicked counsellors who hate the law although the laws favor them as men, these counsellors can be sought out and punished.

And this is the advantage of this government over that of Cnidus, where the people could never get satisfaction for the injustices that had been done to them, as the law did not permit calling the *amymones*[8] to judgment even after their administration.[9]

Although in general the power of judging should not be joined to any part of the legislative power, this is subject to three exceptions founded on the particular interests of the one who is to be judged.

Important men are always exposed to envy; and if they were judged by the people, they could be endangered and would not enjoy the privilege of the last citizen of a free state, of being judged by his peers. Therefore, nobles must not be called before the ordinary tribunals of the nation but before that part of the legislative body composed of nobles.

It could happen that the law, which is simultaneously clairvoyant and blind, might be too rigorous in certain cases. But the judges of the nation are, as we have said, only the mouth that pronounces the words of the law, inanimate beings who can moderate neither its force nor its rigor. Therefore, the part of the legislative body, which we have just said is a necessary tribunal on another occasion, is also one on this occasion; it is for its supreme authority to moderate the law in favor of the law itself by pronouncing less rigorously than the law.

It could also happen that a citizen, in matters of public business, might violate the rights of the people and commit crimes that the established magistrates could not or would not want to punish. But, in general, the legislative power cannot judge, and even less so in this particular case, where it represents the interested party, the people. Therefore, it can be only the accuser. But, before whom will it make its accusation? Will it bow before the tribunals of law, which are lower than it and are, moreover, composed of those who, being also of the people, would be swept along by the authority of such a great accuser? No: in order to preserve the dignity of the people and the security of the individual, that part of the legislature drawn from the people must make its accusation before the part of the legislature drawn from the nobles, which has neither the same interests nor the same passions.

[8] These were magistrates elected annually by the people. See Stephanus of Byzantium [*Ethnika* 686; 1958 edn].

[9] One could accuse the Roman magistrates after their magistracy. In Dion. Hal. [*Ant. Rom.*], bk. 9 [9.37.2–4], see the affair of the tribune Genutius.

This last is the advantage of this government over most of the ancient republics, where there was the abuse that the people were judge and accuser at the same time.

Executive power, as we have said, should take part in legislation by its faculty of vetoing; otherwise it will soon be stripped of its prerogatives. But if legislative power takes part in execution, executive power will equally be lost.

If the monarch took part in legislation by the faculty of enacting, there would no longer be liberty. But as in spite of this, he must take part in legislation in order to defend himself, he must take part in it by the faculty of vetoing.

The cause of the change in government in Rome was that the senate, which had one part of the executive power, and the magistrates, who had the other, did not have the faculty of vetoing, as the people had.

Here, therefore, is the fundamental constitution of the government of which we are speaking. As its legislative body is composed of two parts, the one will be chained to the other by their reciprocal faculty of vetoing. The two will be bound by the executive power, which will itself be bound by the legislative power.

The form of these three powers should be rest or inaction. But as they are constrained to move by the necessary motion of things, they will be forced to move in concert.

As executive power belongs to the legislative only through its faculty of vetoing, it cannot enter into the discussion of public business. It is not even necessary for it to propose, because, as it can always disapprove of resolutions, it can reject decisions on propositions it would have wanted left unmade.

In some ancient republics, where the people as a body discussed the public business, it was natural for the executive power to propose and discuss with them; otherwise, there would have been a strange confusion in the resolutions.

If the executive power enacts on the raising of public funds without the consent of the legislature, there will no longer be liberty, because the executive power will become the legislator on the most important point of legislation.

If the legislative power enacts, not from year to year, but forever, on the raising of public funds, it runs the risk of losing its liberty, because the executive power will no longer depend upon it; and when one holds such a right forever, it is unimportant whether that right comes from oneself or from another. The same is true if the legislative power enacts, not from year to year, but forever, about the land and sea forces, which it should entrust to the executive power.

So that the one who executes is not able to oppress, the armies entrusted to him must be of the people and have the same spirit as the people, as they were in Rome until the time of Marius. This can be so in only two ways: either those employed in the army must have enough goods to be answerable for their conduct to the other citizens and be enrolled for a year only, as was practiced in Rome; or, if the troops must be a permanent body, whose soldiers come from the meanest parts of the nation, legislative power must be able to disband them as soon as the legislature so desires; the soldiers must live with the citizens, and there must not be a separate camp, a barracks, or a fortified place.

Once the army is established, it should be directly dependent on the executive power, not on the legislative body; and this is in the nature of the thing, as its concern is more with action than with deliberation.

Men's manner of thinking is to make more of courage than of timidity; more of activity than of prudence; more of force than of counsel. The army will always scorn a senate and respect its officers. It will not make much of the orders sent from a body composed of people it believes timid and, therefore, unworthy to command it. Thus, whenever the army depends solely on the legislative body, the government will become military. And if the contrary has ever occured, it is the effect of some extraordinary circumstances; it is because the army there is always separate, because it is composed of several bodies each of which depends upon its particular province, because the capitals are in excellent locations whose situation alone defends them and which have no troops.

Holland is even more secure than Venice; it could flood rebellious troops; it could leave them to die of hunger; since the troops are not in towns that could give them sustenance, their sustenance is precarious.

For if, in the case of an army governed by the legislative body, particular circumstances keep the government from becoming military, one will encounter other drawbacks; one of these two things must happen, either the army must destroy the government, or the government must weaken the army.

And this weakening will have a fatal cause: it will arise from the very weakness of the government.

If one wants to read the admirable work by Tacitus, *On the Mores of the Germans*,[10] one will see that the English have taken their idea of political government from the Germans. This fine system was found in the forests.

Since all human things have an end, the state of which we are speaking will lose its liberty; it will perish. Rome, Lacedaemonia, and Carthage have surely perished. This state will perish when legislative power is more corrupt than executive power.

It is not for me to examine whether at present the English enjoy this liberty or not. It suffices for me to say that it is established by their laws, and I seek no further.

I do not claim hereby to disparage other governments, or to say that this extreme political liberty should humble those who have only a moderate one. How could I say that, I who believe that the excess even of reason is not always desirable and that men almost always accommodate themselves better to middles than to extremities?

Harrington, in his *Oceana*,[c] has also examined the furthest point of liberty to which the constitution of a state can be carried. But of him it can be said that he sought this liberty only after misunderstanding it, and that he built Chalcedon with the coast of Byzantium before his eyes.

[10] "On lesser matters the princes consult, on greater ones, everybody does; yet even when a decision is in the power of the people, it is thoroughly considered by the princes" [L.]. [Tacitus, *Germania*, chap. 11.]

[c] James Harrington, *Commonwealth of Oceana*.

CHAPTER 7
The monarchies that we know

The monarchies we know do not have liberty for their direct purpose as does the one we have just mentioned; they aim only for the glory of the citizens, the state, and the prince. But this glory results in a spirit of liberty that can, in these states, produce equally great things and can perhaps contribute as much to happiness as liberty itself.

The three powers are not distributed and cast on the model of the constitution which we have mentioned; each instance shows a particular distribution of them and each approximates political liberty accordingly; and, if it did not approximate it, the monarchy would degenerate into despotism.

CHAPTER 8

Why the ancients had no clear idea of monarchy

The ancients did not at all know the government founded on a body of nobility and even less the government founded on a legislative body formed of the representatives of a nation. The republics of Greece and Italy were towns in which each had its own government and assembled its own citizens within its walls. Before the Romans had swallowed up all the republics, there were almost no kings anywhere, in Italy, Gaul, Spain, Germany; all of these were small peoples or small republics. Even Africa was subject to a large republic; Asia Minor was occupied by Greek colonies. Therefore, there was no example either of deputies from towns or of assemblies of the estates; one had to go as far as Persia to find the government of one alone.

It is true that there were federal republics; many towns sent deputies to an assembly. But I say that there was no monarchy on this model.

Here is how the plan for the monarchies that we know was formed. The Germanic nations who conquered the Roman Empire were very free, as is known. On the subject one has only to see Tacitus on the *Mores of the Germans*. The conquerors spread out across the country; they lived in the countryside, rarely in the towns. When they were in Germany, the whole nation could be assembled. When they dispersed during the conquest, they could no longer assemble. Nevertheless, the nation had to deliberate on its business as it had done before the conquest; it did so by representatives. Here is the origin of Gothic government among us. It was at first a mixture of aristocracy and monarchy. Its drawback was that the common people were slaves; it was a good government that had within itself the capacity to become better. Giving letters of emancipation became the custom, and soon the civil liberty of the people, the prerogatives of the nobility and of the clergy, and the power of the kings, were in such concert that there has never been, I believe, a government on earth as well tempered as that of each part of Europe during the time that this government continued to exist; and it is remarkable that the corruption of the government of a conquering people should have formed the best kind of government men have been able to devise.

CHAPTER 9

Aristotle's manner of thinking

An awkwardness is clearly seen in Aristotle's treatment of monarchy.[11] He establishes five kinds: he does not distinguish among them by the form of the constitution but by accidental things, like the virtues or the vices of the prince, or by extrinsic things, like the usurpation of the tyranny or succession to it.

Aristotle includes in the list of monarchies both the empire of the Persians and the kingdom of Lacedaemonia. But who does not see that the one was a despotic state and the other a republic?

The ancients, who did not know of the distribution of the three powers in the government of one alone, could not achieve a correct idea of monarchy.

[11] [Aristotle] *Pol.*, bk. 3, chap. 14 [1284b35–1285b33].

CHAPTER 10

The manner of thinking of other political men

In order to temper the government of one alone, Arribas,[12] king of Epirus, could imagine only a republic. The Molossians, not knowing how to restrict this power, made two kings;[13] this weakened the state more than the command: one wanted rivals, and one had enemies.

Two kings were allowed only in Lacedaemonia; they did not form the constitution there but rather were a part of the constitution.

[12] See Justin [*Epitome historiarum Philippicarum*], bk. 17 [17.3.12].
[13] Aristotle, *Pol.*, bk. 5, chap. 9 [1313a24].

CHAPTER 11

On the kings of heroic times among the Greeks

Among the Greeks in heroic times, a kind of monarchy was established that did not continue to exist.[14] Those who had invented the arts, waged war for the people, assembled men who were scattered here and there or given them lands, won the kingdom for themselves and passed it down to their children. They were kings, priests, and judges. This is one of the five kinds of monarchy of which Aristotle speaks,[15] and this is the only one that might arouse the idea of the monarchical constitution. But the plan of this constitution is the opposite of that of our monarchies today.

The three powers were distributed there so that the people had the legislative power,[16] and the king, the executive power and the power of judging; whereas, in the monarchies we know, the prince has the executive and the legislative power, or at least a part of the legislative power, but he does not judge.

In the government of the kings of heroic times, the three powers were badly distributed. These monarchies could not continue to exist; for, as soon as the people could legislate, they could reduce royalty to nothing at the least caprice, as they did everywhere.

Among a free people who have legislative power, among a people enclosed within a town, where everything odious becomes even more odious, the masterwork of legislation is to know where properly to place the power of judging. But it could not be placed worse than in the hands of the one who already had executive power. The monarch became terrible immediately. But at the same time, since he did not legislate, he could not defend himself against legislation; he had too much power and he did not have enough.

It had not yet been discovered that the prince's true function was to establish judges and not to judge. The opposite policy rendered unbearable the government of one alone. All these kings were driven out. The Greeks did not imagine the true distribution of the three powers in the government of one alone, they imagined it only in the

[14] Aristotle, *Pol.*, bk. 3, chap. 14 [1285b2–19].
[15] Ibid. [Aristotle, *Pol.* 1285b2–19].
[16] See Plutarch [*Vit.*], *Theseus* [24, 25.2]. See also Thucydides [*The Peloponnesian War*], bk. 1 [1.13].

government of many, and they called this sort of constitution, *police*.[17d]

[17]See Aristotle, *Pol.*, bk. 4, chap. 8 [1293b30–1294a25].

[d]Here Montesquieu makes a connection between *police* (see note [c], bk. 4; note [a], bk. 12; note [c], bk. 26) and the "polity" of the Greeks.

CHAPTER 12

On the government of the Roman kings and how the three powers were distributed in it

The government of the Roman kings was somewhat related to that of the kings of heroic times among the Greeks. Like them it fell, from its general vice, although in itself and in its particular nature it was very good.

In order to make this government understood, I shall distinguish the government of the first five kings from that of Servius Tullius and from that of Tarquin.

The crown was elective; and under the first five kings, the senate took the greatest part in their election.

After a king died, the senate considered whether one would keep the form of government that had been established. If the senate judged it advisable to keep the form of government, it named a magistrate[18] drawn from its body to elect a king; the senate had to approve the election; the people, to confirm it; the auspices, to guarantee it. If one of these three conditions were missing, there had to be another election.

The constitution was monarchical, aristocratic, and popular, and such was the harmony of power that there was neither jealousy nor dispute in the first reigns. The king commanded the armies and had the stewardship of the sacrifices; he had the power of judging civil[19] and criminal[20] suits; he convoked the senate; he assembled the people; he

[18]Dion. Hal. [*Ant. Rom.*], bk. 2, p. 120 [2.58.3]; bk. 4, pp. 242–243 [4.40.2].

[19]See the discourse by Tanaquil in Livy, decade 1, bk. 1 [1.41, 43]; and the ruling of Servius Tullius in Dion. Hal. [*Ant. Rom.*], bk. 4, p. 229 [4.25.2].

[20]See Dion. Hal. [*Ant. Rom.*], bk. 2, p. 118 [2.56.3; see also 2.14.1], and bk. 3, p. 171 [3.30.1–5].

brought certain matters of public business before them and ruled on others with the senate.[21]

The senate had great authority. The kings often picked senators to judge with them; they brought matters of public business to the people only after these had been deliberated upon in the senate.[22]

The people had the right to elect magistrates,[23] to consent to the new laws, and, when the king permitted, to declare war and to make peace. They did not have the power to judge. When Tullius Hostilius referred the judgment of Horatius to the people, he had particular reasons that are found in Dionysius of Halicarnassus.[24]

The constitution changed under Servius Tullius.[25] The senate had no part in his election; he had himself proclaimed king by the people. He divested himself of civil judgments[26] and kept only criminal judgments for himself; he carried all public business directly to the people; he relieved the people of taxes and put the entire load on the patricians. Thus, to the extent that he weakened the royal power and the authority of the senate, he increased the power of the people.[27]

Tarquin had himself elected neither by the senate nor by the people; he regarded Servius Tullius as a usurper and took the crown as a hereditary right; he exterminated most of the senators; he no longer consulted those who remained and did not even summon them to hear his judgments.[28] His power increased, but what was odious about this power became still more odious: he usurped the power of the people; he made laws without them; he even made some in opposition to them.[29] He would have united the three powers in his person, but the people remembered at a certain moment that they were the legislator, and Tarquin was no longer.

[21] It was by a senatus-consult that Tullius Hostilius was sent to destroy Alba. Dion. Hal. [*Ant. Rom.*], bk. 3, pp. 167 and 172 [3.26.6; 3.31.1–2].

[22] Ibid. [Dion. Hal., *Ant. Rom.*], bk. 4, p. 276 [[275] 4.84.2; see also 4.75.4].

[23] Ibid. [Dion. Hal., *Ant. Rom.*], bk. 2 [2.14.3]. They nevertheless must not have filled all the posts, because Valerius Publicola made the famous law forbidding any citizen to hold any post unless he had obtained it by the suffrage of the people.

[24] [Dion. Hal., *Ant. Rom.*] bk. 3, p. 159 [3.22.4–8].

[25] [Dion. Hal., *Ant. Rom.*] bk. 4 [4.40.1].

[26] "He gave up half the royal power," says Dion. Hal. [*Ant. Rom.*], bk. 4, p. 229 [4.25.1].

[27] People believed that if he had not been prevented by Tarquin, he would have established popular government. Dion. Hal. [*Ant. Rom.*], bk. 4, p. 243 [4.40.3].

[28] Dion. Hal. [*Ant. Rom.*], bk. 4 [4.42.4].

[29] Ibid. [Dion. Hal., *Ant. Rom.*, 4.43–44.]

CHAPTER 13

General reflections on the state of Rome after the expulsion of the kings

One can never leave the Romans; thus it is that even today in their capital one leaves the new palaces to go in search of the ruins; thus it is that the eye that has rested on flower-strewn meadows likes to look at rocks and mountains.

The patrician families had always had great prerogatives. These distinctions, great under the kings, became much more important after the kings were expelled. This caused jealousy among the plebeians, who wanted to bring down the patricians. Disputes struck at the constitution without weakening the government, for, provided the magistracies preserved their authority, it did not matter from which family the magistrates came.

An elective monarchy, as was Rome, necessarily assumes a powerful aristocratic body that sustains it; this failing, it changes immediately into a tyranny or into a popular state. But a popular state does not need family distinctions to maintain itself. This is why the patricians, who were necessary parts of the constitution at the time of the kings, became a superfluous part of it at the time of the consuls; the people were able to bring down the patricians without destroying themselves and to change the constitution without corrupting it.

When Servius Tullius debased the patricians, Rome had to fall from the hands of the kings into those of the people. But when the people brought the patricians down, they did not have to fear falling back into the hands of the kings.

A state can change in two ways: either because its constitution is corrected or because it is corrupted. If the state has preserved its principles and its constitution changes, the latter corrects itself; if the state has lost its principles when its constitution starts to change, the constitution is corrupted.

After the expulsion of the kings, Rome would have been a democracy. The people already had legislative power; their unanimous vote had driven out the kings, and if their will had flagged, the Tarquins could have returned at any moment. To claim that the people had wanted to drive away the kings only to become slaves to a few families would not be reasonable. Therefore the situation required that Rome be a democracy, but nevertheless it was not one. The power of the principal men had yet to be tempered, and the laws had yet to be inclined toward democracy.

States are often more flourishing during the imperceptible shift from one constitution to another than they are under either constitution. At that time all the springs of the government are stretched; all the citizens have claims; one is attacked or flattered; and there is a noble rivalry between those who defend the declining constitution and those who put forward the one that prevails.

CHAPTER 14

How the distribution of the three powers began to change after the expulsion of the kings

Four things principally ran counter to the liberty of Rome. The patricians alone had obtained all the sacred, political, civil and military employments; an exorbitant power had been attached to the consulate; the people were subjected to outrages; finally, they had almost no influence left in the voting. The people corrected these four abuses.

1. They had it established that there would be magistracies to which plebeians could aspire, and they gradually obtained a place for themselves in all of them except that of the Interrex.

2. The consulate was broken up and formed into several magistracies. Praetors were created[30] who were given the power to judge on private suits; quaestors[31] were named in order to have public crimes judged; aediles were established to whom supervision of the police was given; also treasurers[32] were made who were to administer the public monies; finally, by the creation of censors, the consuls were removed from the part of the legislative power that regulates the mores of citizens and the immediate police of the various bodies of the state. The principal prerogatives that remained to the consuls were that they presided over the great assemblies of the people,[33] convened the senate, and commanded the armies.

[30] Livy, decade 1, bk. 6 [6.42.11].

[31] *Quaestores parricidi*: Magistrates to try parricides. Pomponius, Law 2, para. 23 [*Corpus Juris Civilis, Digest* 1.2.23]; *de origine juris et omnium magistratuum et successione prudentum*.

[32] Plutarch [*Vit.*], *Publicola* [12.2].

[33] *Comitiis centuriatis.*

3. The sacred laws established tribunes who could, at any moment, check the enterprises of the patricians and who prevented not only particular wrongs but also general ones.

Finally, the plebeians increased that influence in public decisions. The Roman people were divided in three ways: by centuries, by curiae, and by tribes; and when they voted, they were convened and formed in one of these three ways.

In the first, the patricians, the principal men, the rich people, and the senate, groups that were nearly the same, had almost all the authority; in the second, they had less; in the third, still less.

The division by centuries was a division based on the census and on means, rather than a division by persons. The whole of the people was divided into one hundred and ninety-three centuries,[34] each having one vote. The patricians and the principal men formed the first ninety-eight centuries; the rest of the citizens were spread over the other ninety-five. Therefore the patricians were the masters of the votes in this division.

In the division by curiae,[35] the patricians did not have the same advantages. Yet they had some. The auspices had to be consulted, and the patricians were in control of them; no proposition could be made to the people that had not previously been brought to the senate and approved by a senatus-consult. But in the division by tribes, there was no question of auspices or of senatus-consult, and the patricians were not admitted.

Now, the people kept on seeking to use the division by curiae for those assemblies that were customarily divided by centuries and the division by tribes for those assemblies that were done by curiae, which led to the transfer of public business from the hands of the patricians into those of the plebeians.

Thus, when the plebeians had gained the right to judge patricians, beginning with the affair of Coriolanus,[36] the plebeians wanted to judge them assembled by tribes[37] and not by centuries; and when the new magistracies of tribunes and aediles, which favored the people, were

[34] See on this, Livy, bk. 1 [1.43]; and Dion. Hal. [*Ant. Rom.*], bk. 4 [4.16–22] and bk. 7 [7.59.2–8].

[35] Dion. Hal. [*Ant. Rom.*], bk. 9, p. 598 [9.41.2–4].

[36] Dion. Hal. [*Ant. Rom.*], bk. 7 [7.59.9–10].

[37] Contrary to the former usage, as can be seen in Dion. Hal. [*Ant. Rom.*], bk. 5, p. 320 [5.10.7].

established,[38] the people obtained that they would be assembled by curiae to name them; and when their power was firm, they gained the naming of the tribunes and the aediles in an assembly by tribes.[39]

[38] [Dion. Hal., *Ant. Rom.*] bk. 6, pp. 410 and 411 [6.89.1–2]. [On the aediles, see 6.90.]
[39] [Dion. Hal., *Ant. Rom.*] bk. 9, p. 605 [9.43.4].

CHAPTER 15

How, in the flourishing state of the republic, Rome suddenly lost its liberty

In the heat of the disputes between the patricians and the plebeians, the latter asked for fixed laws to be given so that judgments would no longer be the result of a capricious will or an arbitrary power. After much resistance, the senate acquiesced. Decemvirs were named to compose these laws. It was believed that they had to be granted great power because they had to give laws to parties that were almost incompatible. The naming of all the magistrates was suspended, and in the *comitia* they were elected sole administrators of the republic. They were invested with both the power of the consuls and the power of the tribunes. The former gave them the right to convene the senate; the latter, that of convening the people; but they convoked neither the senate nor the people. Ten men alone in the republic had all the legislative power, all the executive power, all the power of judgment. Rome saw itself subject to a tyranny as cruel as that of Tarquin. When Tarquin exercised his oppressive measures, Rome was indignant at the power he had usurped; when the decemvirs exercised theirs, it was astonished by the power it had given away.

But what was this tyrannical system, produced by people who had gained political and military power only from their knowledge of civil business, and who in the circumstances of that time needed the citizens' cowardice inside so that they would let themselves be governed, and the citizens' courage outside as a defense?

The spectacle of the death of Virginia, sacrificed by her father to modesty and to liberty, made the power of the decemvirs evaporate. Each man was free because each one was offended; everyone became a citizen because everyone was a father. The senate and the people returned to a liberty that had been entrusted to ridiculous tyrants.

The Roman people, more than any other, were moved by spectacles. That of the bloody body of Lucretia brought royalty to an end. The debtor who appeared covered with sores in the square changed the form of the republic. The sight of Virginia drove out the decemvirs. For Manlius to be condemned, the people had to be put where they could not see the Capitol. The bloody robe of Caesar returned Rome to servitude.

CHAPTER 16

On legislative power in the Roman republic

There were no rights to dispute under the decemvirs, but when liberty returned, jealousies could be seen anew; so long as some privileges remained to the patricians, the plebeians took them away.

Little ill would have been done if the plebeians had been satisfied to deprive the patricians of the prerogatives instead of also offending them in their status as citizens.[e] When the people were assembled by curiae or by centuries, they were composed of senators, patricians and plebeians. In the disputation, the plebeians won the point[40] that they alone, without the patricians or the senate, could make laws, which were called plebiscites, and the *comitia* where they were made was called the *comitia* by tribes. Thus, there were cases in which the patricians[41] had no part in legislative power[42] and in which they were subject to the legislative power of another body of the state. It was a frenzy of liberty. The people, in order to establish democracy, ran counter to the very principles of democracy. It seemed that such an exorbitant power should have reduced the authority of the senate to

[40] Dion. Hal. [*Ant. Rom.*], bk. 11, p. 725 [11.45].

[41] By the sacred laws, the plebeians could hold plebiscites alone and without admitting the patricians to their assembly. Dion. Hal. [*Ant. Rom.*], bk. 6, p. 410 [6.89] and bk. 7, p. 430 [7.16.1–2].

[42] By the law made after the expulsion of the decemvirs, patricians were made subject to plebiscites though they had no voice in them. Livy, bk. 3 [3.55.3]; and Dion. Hal. [*Ant. Rom.*], bk. 11, p. 775 [11.45]. And this law was confirmed by that of Publius Philo, dictator in the Roman year 416 [338(339) B.C.]. Livy, bk. 8 [8.12.14–16].

[e] *qualité de citoyen.*

nothing; but Rome had admirable institutions. These were principally two: in the one, the legislative power of the people was regulated; in the other, it was limited.

Every five years the censors formed and created the body of the people, as the consuls had formerly done;[43] they exercised legislation even over the body that had legislative power. "Tiberius Gracchus, censor," says Cicero, "transferred the freedmen to the tribes of the town, not by the force of his eloquence, but by a word and by a gesture, and if he had not, we would no longer have this republic, which we barely sustain today."[f]

On the other hand, the senate had the power to remove the republic from the hands of the people, so to speak, by creating a dictator before whom the sovereign bowed and the most popular laws remained silent.[44]

[43] In the Roman year 312 [442 B.C.], the consuls still took the census, as appears in Dion. Hal. [*Ant. Rom.*], bk. 11 [11.63.2].

[44] Such as those that permitted the ordinances of every magistrate to be appealed to the people.

[f] Cicero, *De oratore* 1.9.38.

CHAPTER 17
On executive power in the same republic

If the people were jealous of their legislative power, they were less so of their executive power. They left it almost entirely to the senate and the consuls, and they reserved to themselves scarcely more than the right to elect magistrates and to confirm the acts of the senate and of the generals.

Rome, whose passion was to command, whose ambition was to subject everything, who had always usurped, who usurped still, continually pursued great matters of public business; its enemies plotted against it, or it plotted against them.

As it was obliged to conduct itself, on the one hand, with heroic courage and, on the other hand, with consummate wisdom, the state of things required that the senate direct public business. The people quarreled with the senate over all the branches of legislative power, because they were jealous of their liberty; they did not quarrel with it over the branches of executive power, because they were jealous of their glory.

The part played by the senate in executive power was so great that Polybius[45] says all foreigners thought that Rome was an aristocracy. The senate disbursed the public funds and farmed out the revenues; it was the arbiter for suits of the allies; it decided on war and peace and directed the consuls in this regard; it fixed the number of Roman and allied troops, distributed the provinces and the armies to the consuls or the praetors, and, when their year of command expired, it could give them to a successor; it decreed triumphs; it received and sent embassies; it named kings, rewarded them, punished them, judged them, and gave or made them lose the title of allies of the Roman people.

The consuls levied the troops that they were to lead to war; they commanded the armies on land or on sea, they marshaled the allies; in the provinces they had all the power of the republic; they made peace with vanquished peoples, and imposed conditions on them or referred them to the senate.

In early times, when the people had some part in the business of war and peace, they exercised their legislative power rather than their executive power. They scarcely did more than confirm what the kings had done and what the consuls or the senate had done after them. The people were so far from being the arbiters of war that we see that the consuls or the senate often made war in spite of the opposition of their tribunes. But in the drunkenness of their prosperity, they increased their executive power.[g] Thus,[46] they themselves created tribunes in the legions who had until then been named by the generals, and some time before the first Punic War they ruled that they alone would have the right to declare war.[47]

[45] [Polybius, *Historiae*] bk. 6 [6.13.8–9].

[46] In the Roman year 444 [310 B.C.], Livy, bk. 9 [9.30.3]. When the war against Perseus appeared perilous, a senatus-consult ordained that this law would be suspended, and the people consented to it. Livy, decade 5, bk. 2 [42.31.5].

[47] They wrested it from the senate, says Johann Freinsheim [*Supplementorum Livianorum*], decade 2, bk. 6 [16.23].

[g] This sentence appears in earlier editions, but not in the Masson edition. We have included it here as it seems to be required for the sense of the paragraph.

CHAPTER 18

On the power of judging in the Roman government

The power of judging was given to the people, to the senate, to the magistrates, and to certain judges. Its distribution must be seen. I begin with matters of civil business.

After the kings, the consuls judged,[48] and the praetors judged after the consuls. Servius Tullius had divested himself of judging civil suits; the consuls did not judge them either except in very rare cases[49] that were called, for this reason, *extraordinary*.[50] They were satisfied to name the judges and to form the tribunals that were to judge. It seems, according to the discourse of Appius Claudius, in Dionysius of Halicarnassus,[51] that as early as the Roman year 259 [495 B.C.] this was regarded as an established custom among the Romans, and tracing it back to Servius Tullius is not going very far back.

Each year, the praetor made a list[52] or table of those he chose to perform the function of judges during the year of his magistracy. A number sufficient for each suit was taken from it. The English practice is quite similar. And, what was very favorable to liberty[53] is that the praetor selected the judges with the consent of both parties.[54] That many objections to judges may be made in England today amounts to approximately this usage.

These judges decided only questions of fact;[55] for example, if a sum had been paid or not, if an action had been committed or not. But

[48] One cannot doubt that before the creation of the praetors, the consuls had had civil judgments. See Livy, decade 1, bk. 2, p. 19 [2.1.7–8]; Dion. Hal. [*Ant. Rom.*], bk. 10, p. 627 [10.1.3], and bk. 10, p. 645 [10.19.1].

[49] The tribunes often judged alone; nothing made them more odious. Dion. Hal. [*Ant. Rom.*], bk. 11, p. 709 [11.39.1].

[50] *Judicia extraordinaria*: a legal investigation not following the normal procedure. See *Institutes*, bk. 4 [*Corpus Juris Civilis, Institutes* 4.15.8; *de interdictis*].

[51] [Dion. Hal., *Ant. Rom.*] bk. 6, p. 360 [6.24.1].

[52] *Album judicum*: a list of judges chosen by the quaestors.

[53] In *Pro Cluentio* [43.120], Cicero says, "Our ancestors did not want a man upon whom the parties had not agreed to be able to be a judge of the reputation of a citizen or of the slightest pecuniary matter."

[54] In the fragments of the Servilian law, the Cornelian law, and others, see the way in which these laws provided the judges in the crimes they proposed to punish. The judges were often selected by choice, sometimes by lot, or, finally, by lot and choice together.

[55] Seneca, *De beneficiis*, bk. 3, chap. 7 *in fine* [3.7.5–7].

because questions of right[56] required a certain ability, these were taken to the tribunal of the centumvirs.[57]

The kings kept for themselves the judgment of criminal suits, and the consuls succeeded them in this. As a consequence of this authority the consul Brutus had his children put to death as well as all who had conspired on behalf of the Tarquins. This power was exorbitant. The consuls, who already held military power, carried its exercise even into the public business of the town, and their proceedings, devoid of the forms of justice, were violent actions rather than judgments.

This brought about the Valerian law, which permitted an appeal to the people of all the ordinances of the consuls that might imperil the life of a citizen. The consuls could no longer pronounce a capital penalty against a Roman citizen except with the will of the people.[58]

One sees in the first conspiracy to reinstate the Tarquins that the consul Brutus judges the guilty; in the second, the senate and the *comitia* are convened to judge.[59]

The laws called *sacred* gave the plebeians the tribunes, who formed a body that at first made immense claims. One does not know which was greater, the cowardly effrontery of the plebeians in asking or the complaisance and readiness of the senate in acquiescing. The Valerian law had permitted appeals to the people, that is, to the people composed of senators, patricians, and plebeians. The plebeians established that appeals would be brought before them. Soon the question was raised as to whether the plebeians could judge a patrician; this was the subject of a debate that arose with the affair of Coriolanus and ended with it. Coriolanus, accused by the tribunes before the people, maintained, contrary to the spirit of the Valerian law, that, being a patrician, he could be judged only by the consuls; the plebeians, contrary to the spirit of the same law, claimed that he was to be judged by them alone, and they judged him.

The Law of the Twelve Tables modified the preceding. It ordered that one could not decide upon the life of a citizen except in the great

[56] See Quintilian [*Institutio oratoria*], bk. 4, p. 54, Paris edn. 1541 [4.2.5].

[57] Law 2, para. 24 [*Corpus Juris Civilis, Digest* 1.2.24]; *de origine juris et omnium magistratuum et successione prudentum*. Magistrates called decemvirs presided at the judgment, and the entire proceeding was under the direction of a praetor.

[58] "Thus it was not permissible for the consuls to pronounce the capital penalty against a Roman citizen without the command of the Roman people" [L.]. See Pomponius, Law 2, para. 16 [*Corpus Juris Civilis, Digest* 1.2.23]; *de origine juris et omnium magistratuum et successione prudentum*.

[59] Dion. Hal. [*Ant. Rom.*], bk. 5, p. 322 [5.10.7].

estates of the people.[60] Thus, the body of plebeians, or what is the same thing, the *comitia* by tribes, no longer judged any but the crimes whose penalty was only a pecuniary fine. There had to be a *law* to inflict a capital penalty; to condemn to a pecuniary penalty, there had only to be a *plebiscite*.

This provision of the Law of the Twelve Tables was very wise. It led to forming an admirable conciliation between the body of the plebeians and the senate. For, as the competence of each to judge depended on the magnitude of the penalty and the nature of the crime, they had to join together.

The Valerian law removed all that remained in Rome of that government which was related to the Greek kings of heroic times. The consuls found themselves without the power to punish crimes. Although all crimes are public, one must distinguish between those of more interest to the citizens among themselves and those of more interest to the state in its relation with a citizen. The first crimes are called private, the second are public. The people themselves judged public crimes, and in regard to private ones, they named through a particular commission a quaestor to pursue each crime. The people often chose one of the magistrates, but sometimes they chose a private man. He was called a *questor of parricide*. This is mentioned in the Law of the Twelve Tables.[61]

The questor named the judge of the question, as he was called, who picked the judges by lot, formed the tribunal, and presided under him at the judgment.[62]

It is well to observe here the part the senate took in naming the questor, so that one may see how the powers were balanced in this regard. Sometimes the senate had a dictator elected to perform the function of the questor;[63] sometimes it ordered the people to be convoked by a tribune so that they would name a questor;[64] finally, the

[60] The *comitia* by centuries. Thus Manlius Capitolinus was judged in these *comitia*. Livy, decade 1, bk. 6, p. 68 [6.20.10].

[61] So Pomponius says in Law 2, *Digest* [*Corpus Juris Civilis*, *Digest* 1.2.23]; *de origine juris et omnium magistratuum et successione prudentum*. [See bk. 11, n. 31.]

[62] See a fragment of Ulpian, who reports of another one in the Cornelian law; it is found in the *Mosaicarum et Romanorum legum collatio*, tit. 1 [1.1.3; 2, 544, *FIRA*]; *de sicariis et homicidiis*.

[63] That occurred chiefly in the crimes committed in Italy, where the senate had a principal *inspection*. See Livy, decade 1, bk. 9 [9.26.6–19], on the conspiracies of Capua.

[64] It was thus in the prosecution resulting from the death of Posthumius, in the Roman year 340 [414 B.C.]. See Livy [4.50.3–5].

people sometimes named a magistrate to report to the senate about a certain crime and to ask it to name a questor, as seen in the judgment of Lucius Scipio[65] in Livy.[66]

In the Roman year 604 [150 B.C.], some of these commissions were made permanent.[67] One gradually divided all criminal matters into various parts, which were called *perpetual questions*. Various praetors were created, and each was given one of these questions. The praetors were given the power to judge the crimes which fell to them for a year, and after that they went to govern their provinces.

In Carthage, the senate of the One Hundred was composed of judges serving for life.[68] But in Rome the praetors served for one year and the judges served even less than a year because they were chosen for each suit. One has seen, in chapter 6 of this Book, how much this provision was favorable to liberty in certain governments.

Judges were drawn from the order of senators until the times of the Gracchi. Tiberius Gracchus ordered that they be drawn from that of knights; this was such a considerable change that the tribune boasted of having by a single rogation cut the sinews of the senatorial order.

It must be observed that the three powers may be well distributed in relation to the liberty of the constitution, though they are not so well distributed in their relation with the liberty of the citizen. In Rome, as the people had the greater part of the legislative power, part of the executive power, and part of the power of judging, they were a great power that had to be counter-balanced by another. The senate certainly had part of the executive power; it had some branch of the legislative power,[69] but this was not enough to counter-balance the people. It had to have part of the power of judging, and it had a part when judges were chosen from among the senators. When the Gracchi deprived the senators of the power of judging,[70] the senate could no longer stand up to the people. Therefore, they ran counter to the liberty of the constitution in order to favor the liberty of the citizen, but the latter was lost along with the former.

[65] This judgment was rendered in the Roman year 567 [187 B.C.].

[66] [Livy] bk. 8 [38.54].

[67] Cicero, *Brutus* [27.106].

[68] This is proven by Livy, bk. 43 [33.46.7], who says that Hannibal made the magistracy annual.

[69] The senatus consults were in force for a year, though they were not confirmed by the people. Dion. Hal. [*Ant. Rom.*], bk. 9, p. 595 [9.37.2], and bk. 11, p. 735 [11.60.5].

[70] In the year 630 [124 B.C.].

Infinite ills resulted. The constitution was changed at a time when, in the heat of civil discords, there was scarcely a constitution. The knights were no longer the middle order uniting the people and the senate, and the chain of the constitution was broken.

There were also some particular reasons that should have kept judging from being transfered to the knights. The Roman constitution was founded on the principle that those who had enough goods to be responsible to the republic for their conduct should be soldiers. The knights, as the richest men, formed the cavalry of the legions. When their status was raised, they refused to serve any longer in this guard; another cavalry had to be levied; Marius admitted all sorts of people into the legions, and the republic was lost.[71]

In addition, the knights were the tax-collectors of the republic; they were rapacious, they heaped misfortune on misfortune and made public needs rise from public needs. Far from giving such people the power of judging, they should continually have been watched by judges. It must be said in praise of the old French laws that the stipulations made for the men of public business were made with the distrust one has for enemies. In Rome, when judgments were transferred to the tax-collectors, virtue, police, laws, magistracy, and magistrates were no longer.

An artless picture of this is found in fragments of Diodorus of Sicily and of Dio. Diodorus[72] says, "Mutius Scaevola wanted to call back the old mores and live from his own means with frugality and integrity. For his predecessors, in league with the tax-collectors who were at that time judging in Rome, had filled the province with all sorts of crimes. But Scaevola meted out justice to the publicans and put into prison those who had been sending others there."

Dio tells us[73] that Publius Rutilius, his lieutenant, who was no less odious to the knights, was accused on his return of having accepted some presents and was condemned to pay a fine. He surrendered his goods at once. His innocence was manifest, for he was found to have many fewer goods than he was accused of having stolen and he showed the titles to the property; he would no longer remain in the town with such people.

[71] *Capite censos plerosque*: most from the poorest citizens. Sallust, *Jurgurtha* [86.2].

[72] Fragment of this author [Diodorus Siculus, *Bibliotheca historica*], bk. 36 [37.5], in the collection of Constantine Porphyrogenitus, *Extracts of Virtues and Vices*.

[73] Fragment of [Cass. Dio] *Historia Romana* [28.97] drawn from the *Extracts of Virtues and Vices*.

Diodorus says further,[74] "The Italians bought troops of slaves in Sicily to plow their fields and care for their herds; they refused them food. These unfortunate men were obliged to rob on the highways, armed with lances and clubs, covered with the skins of beasts and accompanied by big dogs. The whole province was ravaged, and the people of that country could properly call their own only the things within the town walls. There was neither proconsul nor praetor who could or would oppose this disorder or who would dare punish these slaves, because they belonged to the knights who were the judges in Rome."[75] This was one of the causes of the Slave War. I shall say only one word; a profession that neither has nor can have any object but gain, a profession that was always asking and of whom nothing was asked, an insidious and inexorable profession which impoverished wealth and even poverty, should not have been giving judgments in Rome.

[74] Fragment of [Diodorus Siculus, *Bibliotheca historica*] bk. 34 [34/35.2.32, 29–30], in the *Extracts of Virtues and Vices.*

[75] "They [the slaves] belonged to the ones who did the judging in Rome, and it was from among the Equestrian order that lots were cast to choose judges on the cases involving praetors and proconsuls, who, after having administered a province, were called to trial" [L.]. [Diodorus Siculus, *Bibliotheca historica* 34/35.2.32, 30, 31 (3).]

CHAPTER 19

On the government of the Roman provinces

The three powers were distributed in the town in this way, but it was far from being the same in the provinces. Liberty was at the center and tyranny at the extremities.

At the time when Rome dominated only Italy, the peoples were governed as confederates; the laws of each republic were followed. But, when it carried its conquests further, when the senate had no direct view of the provinces, when the magistrates in Rome could no longer govern the empire, then praetors and proconsuls had to be sent. From then on, there was no longer harmony between the three powers. The power of those who were sent brought together that of all the Roman magistrates (what am I saying?):[h] even that of the senate, even that of

[h] Translator's parentheses.

the people![76] These were despotic magistrates, quite suitable for the far-distant places to which they were sent. They exercised the three powers; they were, if I dare use this term, the pashas of the republic.

We have said elsewhere[77] that by the nature of things in a republic the same citizens had civil and military employments. The result is that a conquering republic can scarcely extend its government and control the conquered state in accordance with the form of its constitution. Indeed, since the magistrate it sends to govern has the executive power over both civil and military business, he must also have legislative power, for who else would make the laws? He must also have the power of judging, for who would judge independently of him? Therefore, the governor sent by a republic must have the three powers, as he had in the Roman provinces.

A monarchy can more easily extend its government, because some of the officers it sends to the provinces have executive power in matters of civil business and others, executive power in matters of military business, which does not bring about despotism.

That a Roman citizen could be judged only by the people was a privilege of great consequence for him. Otherwise he would have been subjected to the arbitrary power of a proconsul or a propraetor in the provinces. The town did not feel the tyranny, which was exercised only over the subject nations.

Thus, in the Roman world, as in Lacedaemonia, those who were free were exceedingly free, and those who were slaves were exceedingly enslaved.

While the citizens paid taxes, they were levied with a very great fairness. The levy was in accord with the establishment of Servius Tullius, who had distributed all the citizens into six classes in the order of their wealth and had set their share of the impost in proportion to the share each one had in the government. The result was that some tolerated the high tax because of their great influence, and that others consoled themselves for their small influence with their low tax.

There was another remarkable thing: it is that, since the division of Servius Tullius by classes was the fundamental principle of the constitution, so to speak, it happened that fairness in levying taxes derived from the fundamental principle of this government and could be removed only when it was.

[76] They gave their edicts upon entering the provinces.

[77] Above, in bk. 5, chap. 19. See also bks. 2, 3, 4, and 5.

But while Rome paid taxes painlessly or paid none at all,[78] the provinces were ravaged by the knights, who were the tax-collectors for the republic. We have spoken of their harassments, and all history is full of them.

"All Asia awaits me as its liberator," said Mithridates,[79] "the pillages of the pronconsuls,[80] the exactions[i] of the men of public business,[j] and the calumny of their judgments[81] have aroused such great hatred for the Romans."

This is why the force of the provinces added nothing to the force of the republic and, on the contrary, only weakened it. This is why the provinces regarded the loss of liberty in Rome as the period of the establishment of their own.

[78] After the conquest of Macedonia, the taxing ceased in Rome.

[79] Harangue taken from Trogus Pompeius and related by Justin [*Epitoma historiarum Philippicarum*], bk. 38 [38.7.8].

[80] See [Cicero] *The Orations against Verres* [the entire case].

[81] It is known that it was the tribunal of Varus that made the Germans rebel [see bk. 19, n. 1].

[i] *exécutions* in text.

[j] *gens d'affaires* are not strictly "businessmen" here. *Affaires* usually means "public business."

CHAPTER 20

End of this book

I should like to seek out in all the moderate governments we know the distribution of the three powers and calculate thereupon the degrees of liberty each one of them can enjoy. But one must not always so exhaust a subject that one leaves nothing for the reader to do. It is not a question of making him read but of making him think.

BOOK 12

On the laws that form political liberty in relation to the citizen

CHAPTER I

The idea of this book

It is not enough to treat political liberty in its relation to the constitution; it must be shown in its relation to the citizen.

I have said that, in the former instance, liberty is formed by a certain distribution of the three powers, but in the latter it must be considered with a different idea in view. It consists in security or in one's opinion of one's security.

It can happen that the constitution is free and that the citizen is not. The citizen can be free and the constitution not. In these instances, the constitution will be free by right and not in fact; the citizen will be free in fact and not by right.

Only the disposition of the laws, and especially of the fundamental laws, forms liberty in its relation to the constitution. But, in the relation to the citizen, mores, manners, and received examples can give rise to it and certain civil laws can favor it, as we shall see in the present book.

Further, as in most states liberty is more hampered, countered, or beaten down than is required by their constitutions, it is well to speak of the particular laws that, in each constitution, can aid or run counter to the principle of the liberty of which each government can admit.

CHAPTER 2
On the liberty of the citizen

Philosophical liberty consists in the exercise of one's will or, at least (if all systems must be mentioned), in one's opinion that one exerts one's will. Political liberty consists in security or, at least, in the opinion one has of one's security.

This *security* is never more attacked than by public or private accusations. Therefore, the citizen's liberty depends principally on the goodness of the criminal laws.

Criminal laws were not perfected all at once. In the very places one most sought liberty, one did not always find it. Aristotle[1] tells us that at Cumae, the accuser's relatives could be witnesses. Under the Roman kings, the law was so imperfect that Servius Tullius pronounced sentence against the children of Ancus Martius, accused of having assassinated his father-in-law, the king.[2] Under the first kings of the Franks, Clotaire made a law[3] that an accused man could not be condemned without being heard, which proves that there was an opposite practice in some particular case or among some barbarian people. It was Charondas who introduced judgments against false testimonies.[4] When the innocence of the citizens is not secure, neither is liberty.

The knowledge already acquired in some countries and yet to be acquired in others, concerning the surest rules one can observe in criminal judgments, is of more concern to mankind than anything else in the world.

Liberty can be founded only on the practice of this knowledge, and in a state that had the best possible laws in regard to it, a man against whom proceedings had been brought and who was to be hung the next day would be freer than is a pasha in Turkey.

[1] [Aristotle] *Pol.*, bk. 2 [1269a1–1269a3].
[2] Tarquinius Priscus. See Dion. Hal. [*Ant. Rom.*], bk. 4 [4.5.3].
[3] In the year 560 [*CRF* 8.3].
[4] Aristotle, *Pol.*, bk. 2, chap. 12 [1247b5–8]. He gave his laws at Thurium in the 84th Olympiad [444 B.C.].

CHAPTER 3
Continuation of the same subject

The laws that send a man to his death on the deposition of a single witness are fatal to liberty. Reason requires two, because a witness who affirms and an accused who denies produce a division, and there must be a third for a decision.

The Greeks[5] and the Romans[6] required one additional voice to condemn. Our French laws require two. The Greeks claimed that their usage had been established by the gods,[7] but ours was.

[5]See [Aelius] Aristides, *Oratio in Minervam* [Athena, 37(2).17].
[6]Dion. Hal. [*Ant. Rom.*]., bk. 7 [7.64.6], on the judgment of Coriolanus.
[7]*Minervae calculus*: vote of Minerva.

CHAPTER 4
That liberty is favored by the nature of penalties, and by their proportion

It is the triumph of liberty when criminal laws draw each penalty from the particular nature of the crime. All arbitrariness ends; the penalty does not ensue from the legislator's capriciousness but from the nature of the thing, and man does not do violence to man.

There are four sorts of crimes. Those of the first kind run counter to religion; those of the second, to mores; those of the third, to tranquility; those of the fourth, to the security of the citizens. The penalties inflicted should derive from the nature of each of these kinds.

I include in the class of crimes concerning religion only those that attack it directly, such as all cases of simple sacrilege. For crimes of disturbing the exercise of religion are of the nature of those that run counter to the tranquility or the security of the citizens and should be shifted to these classes.

In order for the penalty against simple sacrilege to be drawn from the nature[8] of the thing, it should consist in the deprivation of all the

[8]St. Louis made such exaggerated laws against those who swore that the Pope felt obliged to caution him about it. This prince moderated his zeal and softened his laws. See his

advantages given by religion: expulsion from the temples; deprivation of the society of the faithful for a time or forever; shunning the presence of the sacrilegious; execration, detestation, and exorcism.

In the things that disturb the tranquility or security of the state, hidden actions are a concern[a] of human justice. But in those that wound the divinity, where there is no public action, there is no criminal matter; it is all between the man and god who knows the measure and the time of his vengeance. For if the magistrate, confusing things, even searches out hidden sacrilege, he brings an inquisition to a kind of action where it is not necessary; he destroys the liberty of citizens by arming against them the zeal of both timid and brash consciences.

The ill came from the idea that the divinity must be avenged. But one must make divinity honored, and one must never avenge it. Indeed, if one were guided by the latter idea, where would punishments end? If men's laws are to avenge an infinite being, they will be ruled by his infinity and not by the weakness, ignorance, and caprice of human nature.

An historian of Provence[9] reports a fact that paints very clearly for us what this idea of avenging the divinity can produce in weak spirits. A Jew, accused of having blasphemed the Holy Virgin, was condemned to be flayed. Masked knights with knives in their hands mounted the scaffold and drove away the executioner in order to avenge the honor of the Holy Virgin themselves . . . I certainly do not want to anticipate the reader's reflections.

The second class is of crimes against the mores: these are the violation of public or individual continence, that is, of the police concerning how one should enjoy the pleasures associated with the use of one's senses and with corporal union. The penalties for these crimes should also be drawn from the nature of the thing. Deprivation of the advantages that society has attached to the purity of mores, fines, shame, the constraint to hide oneself, public infamy, and expulsion from the town and from society; finally, all the penalties within the correctional jurisdiction suffice to repress the temerity of the two sexes.

Ordinances. [*Recueil général des anciennes lois françaises. Capétiens*, 216.2; see also 218.1; 1, 341–342, 346].

[9] Father Bougerel.

[a] *ressort*. We usually translate *ressort* as "spring." See also note [e], bk. 19.

Indeed, these things are founded less on wickedness than on forgetting or despising oneself.

Here it is a question only of crimes that involve mores alone, not of those that also run counter to public security, such as kidnapping and rape, which are of the fourth kind.

The crimes of the third class are those that run counter to the citizens' tranquility, and the penalties for them should be drawn from the nature of the thing and relate to that tranquility, such as deprivation, exile, corrections, and other penalties that restore men's troubled spirits and return them to the established order.

I restrict crimes against tranquility to the things that are a simple breach of police; the ones that, while disturbing tranquility, attack security at the same time, should be put in the fourth class.

The penalties for these last crimes are what are called punishments.[b] They are a kind of retaliation, which causes the society to refuse to give security to a citizen who has deprived or has wanted to deprive another of it. This penalty is derived from the nature of the thing and is drawn from reason and from the sources of good and evil. A citizen deserves death when he has violated security so far as to take or to attempt to take a life. The death penalty is the remedy, as it were, for a sick society. When one violates security with respect to goods there can be reasons for the penalty to be capital; but it would perhaps be preferable, and it would be more natural, if the penalty for crimes committed against the security of goods were punished by the loss of goods. And that ought to be so, if fortunes were common or equal; but as those who have no goods more readily attack the goods of others, the corporal penalty has had to replace the pecuniary penalty.

All that I say is drawn from nature and is quite favorable to the citizen's liberty.

[b] *peines* is translated "penalties," and *supplices*, "punishments."

CHAPTER 5

On certain accusations in particular need of moderation and prudence

Important maxim: one must be very circumspect in the pursuit of magic and of heresy. Accusation of these two crimes can offend liberty in the extreme and be the source of infinite tyrannies if the legislator does not know how to limit it. For, as it does not bear directly on the actions of a citizen, but rather on the idea one has of his character, the accusation becomes dangerous in proportion to the people's ignorance, and from that time, a citizen is always in danger because the best conduct in the world, the purest morality, and the practice of all one's duties do not guarantee one from being suspected of these crimes.

Under Manuel Comnenus, the *protestator*[10] was accused of conspiring against the emperor and of using to this end certain secrets that made men invisible. It is said, in the *Life* of this emperor,[11] that Aaron was caught reading a book of Solomon, and that by reading it legions of demons would appear. Now, by supposing a power in magic that can arm hell and by starting from this, he whom one calls a magician is considered the man in the world most likely to disturb and overthrow society, and one is drawn to punish him immeasurably.

Indignation grows when one includes in magic the power to destroy religion. The history of Constantinople[12] tells us that, when a bishop had the revelation that a miracle had ceased because of the magic of a certain individual, that person and his son were condemned to death. On how many prodigious things did this crime not depend? That it should not be rare for there to be revelations; that this bishop had had one; that it was true; that there had been a miracle; that this miracle had ceased; that there is magic; that magic can overturn religion; that this individual was a magician; finally, that he had done this act of magic.

The emperor Theodore Lascaris attributed his illness to magic. Those who were accused of it had no other recourse but to handle a hot iron without burning themselves. It would have been a good thing,

[10] Nicetas Acominatus [*Historia*], *De Manuele Commeno*, bk. 4 [4.7; pp. 146–147; 1975 edn; 190–192, Bekker].

[11] Nicetas Acominatus [*Historia*], *De Manuele Commeno*, bk. 4 [4.7; pp. 146–147; 1975 edn.; 190–192, Bekker].

[12] [Simocatta] Theophylactus, *Historiarum*, chap. 11 [1.11; pp. 53–57, Bekker edn].

among these Greeks, to be a magician in order to vindicate oneself of the accusation of magic. Such was the excess of their ignorance that, to the most dubious crime in the world, they joined the most dubious proofs.

Under the reign of Philip the Tall, the Jews were run out of France, having been accused of allowing lepers to pollute the wells. This absurd accusation certainly should cast doubt on all accusations founded on public hatred.

I have not said here that heresy must not be punished; I say that one must be very circumspect in punishing it.

CHAPTER 6
On the crime against nature

Please god that I may not diminish the horror that one has for a crime that religion, morality, and policy condemn in turn. It would have to be proscribed if it did no more than give to one sex the weaknesses of the other and prepare for an infamous old age by a shameful youth. What I shall say will leave it all of its stigma and will bear only on the tyranny that can take an unfair advantage of even the horror in which it should be held.

As it is in the nature of this crime to be hidden, legislators have often punished it on the deposition of a child. This opened wide the door to calumny. "Justinian," says Procopius,[13] "published a law against this crime; he made inquiries about those who were guilty of it, not only after the law was made but before. The deposition of a witness, sometimes a child, sometimes a slave, sufficed, especially against the rich and those who were of the faction of the *Greens*."

It is singular that among ourselves three crimes, magic, heresy, and the crime against nature, of which it can be proved that the first does not exist, that the second is susceptible to infinite distinctions, interpretations and limitations, and that the third is often hidden, were all three punished by the penalty of burning.

I shall assert that the crime against nature will not make much progress in a society unless the people are also inclined to it by some

[13] [Procopius] *Anecdota sive Historia arcana* [19.11].

custom, as among the Greeks, where the young people performed all their exercises naked, as among ourselves where education at home is no longer the usage, as among the Asians where some individuals have a large number of wives whom they scorn while others can have none. Do not clear the way for this crime, let it be proscribed by an exact police, as are all the violations of mores, and one will immediately see nature either defend her rights or take them back. Gentle, pleasing, charming, nature has scattered pleasures with a liberal hand; and by overwhelming us with delights, she prepares us with our children through whom we are born again, as it were, for satisfactions greater even than those delights.

CHAPTER 7
On the crime of high treason

The laws of China decide that whoever lacks respect for the emperor should be punished by death. As they do not define what lack of respect is, anything can furnish a pretext for taking the life of whomever one wants and for exterminating whatever family one wants.

Two persons charged with writing the court gazette noted some circumstances about a deed which were found not to be true, and, as lying in a court gazette was said to show lack of respect for the court, they were put to death.[14] When a prince of the blood inadvertently placed a note on a day-book signed with the red paintbrush of the emperor, it was decided that he had shown a lack of respect for the emperor, which brought against this family one of the most terrible persecutions of which history has ever spoken.[15]

Vagueness in the crime of high treason is enough to make government degenerate into despotism. I shall treat the subject at length in the Book "On the composition of the laws."[c]

[14] Father [Jean Baptiste] du Halde [*Description de l'Empire de la Chine*, "De la forme du gouvernement"], vol. 1, p. 43 [2.50 H; 2.43 P; 2.71 L].

[15] Letters of Father Parennin in *Lettres édifiantes et curieuses* [Peking, September 26, 1727; 19, 156–158; 1729 edn].

[c] Book 29.

CHAPTER 8
On the wrong application of the name of crime of sacrilege and high treason

It is also a violent abuse to give the name of crime of high treason to an action which is not one. A law of the emperors[16] pursued as sacrilegious those who called the prince's judgment into question and doubted the merit of those he had chosen for certain employments.[17] The cabinet and the favorites established this crime. Another law declared that those who made an attempt on the prince's ministers and officers were guilty of the crime of treason, as if they had made an attempt on the prince himself.[18] We owe this law to two princes[19] whose weakness is famous in history, two princes who were led by their ministers as flocks are led by shepherds, two princes, slaves in the palace, children in the council, strangers in the armies, who preserved the empire only because they gave it away every day. Several of these favorites conspired against their emperors. They did more: they conspired against the empire, they summoned the barbarians, and when one wanted to check them, the state was so weak that it had to violate their law and run the risk of committing the crime of treason in order to punish them.

Yet the Judge-Advocate for M. de Cinq-Mars[20] relied upon this law when, wanting to prove the latter guilty of the crime of treason for attempting to dismiss Cardinal Richelieu from matters of public business, he said, "By the constitutions of the emperors the crime touching the person of the prince's ministers is counted of the same weight as one affecting the prince's person. A minister serves both his prince and his state; if he is removed, it is as if the former were deprived of an arm[21] and the latter of a part of its power." If servitude herself arrived on earth, she would not speak otherwise.

[16] Gratian, Valentinian, and Theodosius. It is the third one of the *Code* [*Corpus Juris Civilis, Code* 9.29.2(3)]; *de crimine sacrilegii.*

[17] "It is the equivalent of sacrilege to doubt whether he whom the Emperor has chosen shall be worthy" [L.]. Ibid. [*Corpus Juris Civilis, Code* 9.29.2(3); *de crimine sacrilegii*]. This law was a model for Roger's law in the Institutions of Naples, tit. 4 [*Liber Augustalis or The Constitutions of Melfi*, 1231; 1.4].

[18] Law 5 [*Corpus Juris Civilis, Code* 9.8.5]; *ad legem Juliam maiestatis.*

[19] Arcadius and Honorius.

[20] [Claude de Bourdeille, Comte de] Montresor, *Memoirs*, vol. 1 [1, 238–239; 1723 edn].

[21] "For they themselves are a part of our body" [L.]. Same law in the *Code* [*Corpus Juris Civilis, Code* 9.8.5]; *ad legem Juliam maiestatis.*

Another law of Valentinian, Theodosius, and Arcadius[22] declares counterfeiters guilty of the crime of high treason. But does that not confuse ideas about things? Does not giving the name of high treason to another crime diminish the horror of the crime of high treason?

[22] It is Law 9 in the *Codex Theodosianus*; *de falsa moneta* [9.21.9].

CHAPTER 9

Continuation of the same subject

When Paulinus sent word to the Emperor Alexander that "he was preparing to pursue as a traitor a judge who had pronounced against his orders," the emperor answered him that, "in a century like this, indirect crimes of high treason had no place."[23]

When Faustinianus wrote to the same emperor that, having sworn on the life of the prince that he would never pardon his slave, he was obliged to keep his anger alive in order not to make himself guilty of the crime of high treason, the emperor answered him, "Your terror has been empty[24] and you do not know my maxims."

A senatus-consult[25] ordered that anyone who had melted down the rejected statues of the emperor would not be at all guilty of high treason. The emperors Severus and Antoninus wrote to Pontius[26] that one who sold unconsecrated statues of the emperor would not fall under the crime of high treason. The same emperors wrote to Julius Cassianus that one who chanced to throw a rock at a statue of the emperor should not be pursued as a traitor.[27] The Julian law required these sorts of modifications, for it had rendered guilty of treason not only those who melted down the statues of the emperors but those who committed some similar action,[28] making this crime arbitrary. Once

[23] "In my generation, the accusation of high treason for a variety of causes shall cease" [L.]. Law 1, *Code* [*Corpus Juris Civilis, Code* 9.8.1]; *ad legem Juliam maiestatis*.

[24] "You conceive my bent of mind with unsuitable anxiety" [L.]. [*Corpus Juris Civilis, Code* 9.8.2]; *ad legem Juliam maiestatis*.

[25] See Law 4, para. 1, *Digest* [*Corpus Juris Civilis, Digest* 48.4.4.1]; *ad legem Juliam maiestatis*.

[26] See Law 5, para. 1, ibid. [*Corpus Juris Civilis, Digest* 48.4.5.2; *ad legem Juliam maiestatis*].

[27] Ibid., para. 1 [*Corpus Juris Civilis, Digest* 48.4.5.1; *ad legem Juliam maiestatis*].

[28] "Those who might commit some similar thing or another" [L.]. [*Corpus Juris Civilis, Digest* 48.4.6.1]; *ad legem Juliam maiestatis*, Law 6.

many crimes of high treason had been established, one necessarily had to distinguish among these crimes. Thus the jurist Ulpian, after saying that the accusation of the crime of high treason did not cease on the death of the guilty parties, added that this did not extend to all[29] the crimes of high treason as established by the Julian law, but only to the one that included an attempt on the empire or on the emperor's life.

[29] [*Corpus Juris Civilis, Digest* 48.4.11]; *ad legem Juliam maiestatis*, in the last law.

CHAPTER 10

Continuation of the same subject

A law of England, passed under Henry VIII, declared that all those who predicted the king's death were guilty of high treason. This law was very vague. Despotism is so terrible that it even turns against those who exercise it. In the last illness of this king, the doctors never dared to say that he was in danger, and no doubt they acted accordingly.[30]

[30] Gilbert Burnet, *The History of the Reformation of the Church of England* [pt. 1, bk. 3; 1547; 1, 548; 1969 edn].

CHAPTER 11

On thoughts

A certain Marsyas dreamed he cut the throat of Dionysius.[31] Dionysius had him put to death, saying that Marsyas would not have dreamed it at night if he had not thought it during the day. This was a great tyranny; for, even if he had thought it, he had not attempted it.[32] Laws are charged with punishing only external actions.

[31] Plutarch [*Vit.*], *Dion* [9.5].
[32] Thought must be joined to some sort of action.

CHAPTER 12

On indiscreet speech

Nothing makes the crime of high treason more arbitrary than when indiscreet speech becomes its material. Discourse is so subject to interpretation, there is so much difference between indiscretion and malice and so little in the expressions they use, that the law can scarcely subject speech to a capital penalty, unless it declares explicitly which speech is subject to it.[33]

Speech does not form a *corpus delicti*: it remains only an idea. Most frequently it has no meaning in itself but rather in the tone in which it is spoken. Often when repeating the same words, one does not express the same meaning; the meaning depends on the link the words have with other things. Silence sometimes expresses more than any speech. Nothing is so equivocal. How, then, can one make speech a crime of high treason? Wherever this law is established, not only is there no longer liberty, there is not even its shadow.

In the manifesto of the late Czarina against the family Olguruki,[34] one prince of this family is condemned to death for speaking indecently of her person and another for interpreting spitefully her wise arrangements for the empire and for offending her sacred person by disrespectful speech.

I do not intend to diminish the indignation one should have against those who want to stigmatize the glory of their prince, but I do say that if one wants to moderate despotism, punishing with a simple correction will suit these occasions better than an accusation of high treason, which is always terrible, even to the innocent.[35]

Actionable acts are not an everyday occurrence; they may be observed by many people: a false accusation over facts can easily be clarified. The words that are joined to an act take on the nature of that action. Thus a man who goes into the public square to exhort the subjects to revolt becomes guilty of high treason, because the speech is

[33] "It should not be punished as a crime unless it be set down in the letter of the law or established by examples in the law" [L.], says Moestinus in Law 7, para. 3 of the *Digest* [*Corpus Juris Civilis, Digest* 48.4.7.3]; *ad legem Juliam maiestatis*.

[34] In 1740.

[35] "It is in no way easy to interpret the deceits of language" [L.], Modestinus, in Law 7, para. 3 of the *Digest* [*Corpus Juris Civilis, Digest* 48.4.7.3]; *ad legem Juliam maiestatis*.

joined to the act and participates in it. It is not speech that is punished but an act committed in which speech is used. Speech becomes criminal only when it prepares, when it accompanies, or when it follows a criminal act. Everything is turned upside down if speech is made a capital crime instead of being regarded as the sign of a capital crime.

The emperors Theodosius, Arcadius, and Honorius wrote to Ruffinus, the praetorian prefect: "If someone speaks ill of our person or our government, we do not want to punish him;[36] if he has spoken frivolously, he must be scorned; if it is madness, he must be pitied; if it is an insult, he must be pardoned. Thus, looking at the thing as a whole, you will inform us of it so that we may judge speeches by the persons and weigh carefully whether we should subject them to judgment or ignore them."

[36] "If this should proceed from levity, it deserves contempt; if from insanity, it is most deserving of pity; if with intent to injure, it ought to be pardoned" [L.]; a single law in the *Code* [*Corpus Juris Civilis, Code* 9.7.1]; *si quis imperatori maledixerit*.

CHAPTER 13

On writings

Writings contain something more permanent than speech, but when they do not prepare the way for high treason, they are not material to the crime of high treason.

Nevertheless Augustus and Tiberius appended to writings the penalty for this crime:[37] Augustus, when certain things were written against illustrious men and women; Tiberius, because of those he believed written against himself. Nothing was more fatal to Roman liberty. Cremutius Cordus was accused because in his annals he had called Cassius the last of the Romans.[38]

Satirical writings are scarcely known in despotic states, where dejection on the one hand and ignorance on the other produce neither the talent nor the will to write them. In democracy, they are not prevented, for the very reason that they are prohibited in the govern-

[37] Tacitus, *Annales*, bk. 1 [1.72.3–4]. That continued under the subsequent reigns. See the first law of the *Code* [*Corpus Juris Civilis, Code* 9.36.2]; *de famosis libellis*.

[38] Idem, bk. 4 [Tacitus, *Annales*, 4.34].

ment of one alone. As they are usually composed against powerful people, they flatter the spitefulness of the people who govern in a democracy. In a monarchy, they are prohibited, but they have been made an object of police rather than of crime.[d] They can amuse the general spitefulness, console malcontents, reduce envy of those in high positions, give the people the patience to suffer, and make them laugh about their sufferings.

Aristocracy is the government that most proscribes satirical works. Magistrates there are little sovereigns who are not big enough to scorn insults. If in monarchy some barb is thrown against the monarch, he is so high that the barb does not reach him. An aristocratic lord is pierced through and through. Thus, the decemvirs, who formed an aristocracy, punished satirical writings with death.[39]

[39] The Law of Twelve Tables.

[d] See 26.24 and note [c] for Montesquieu's explanation of the meaning of *police*.

CHAPTER 14

The violation of modesty in punishing crimes

Rules of modesty are observed among almost all the nations of the world; it would be absurd to violate them in punishing crimes, when its purpose should always be the reestablishment of order.

Did those in the East, who exposed women to elephants trained for an abominable kind of punishment, want to make the law violate the law?

An old usage of the Romans forbade putting to death girls who were not nubile. Tiberius hit upon the expedient of having them raped by the executioner before sending them to their punishment;[40] a crafty and cruel tyrant, he destroyed mores in order to preserve customs.

When the Japanese magistracy had naked women exposed in public squares and forced them to walk like beasts, it made modesty tremble;[41]

[40] Suetonius [*Vitae duodecim Caesarum*], *Tiberius* [61.5].
[41] *Recueil des voyages qui ont servi à l'éstablissement de la Compagnie des Indes*, vol. 5, pt. 2 [Reyer Gysbertsz, "Histoire d'une persécution"; 5, 425; 1706 edn; 5, 496; 1725 edn].

but when it wanted to compel a mother..., when it wanted to compel a son..., I cannot go on, it made even nature tremble.[42]

[42] Ibid., p. 496 [*Recueil des voyages qui ont servi à l'éstablissement de la Compagnie des Indes* Reyer Gysbertsz, "Histoire d'une persécution"; 5, 425–426; 1706 edn; 5, 496; 1725 edn].

CHAPTER 15

On freeing the slave in order to accuse the master

Augustus established that the slaves of those who had conspired against him would be sold to the public, so that they could make depositions against their masters.[43] Nothing should be neglected that leads to the discovery of a serious crime. Thus, in a state where there are slaves, it is natural for them to be informers, but they cannot be witnesses.

Vindex denounced the conspiracy in support of Tarquin, but he was not a witness against the children of Brutus. To give liberty to one who had rendered such a great service to his homeland was just, but liberty was not given to him so that he would render this service to his homeland.

Thus, the emperor Tacitus ordered that slaves would not be witnesses against their master, even in the crime of high treason,[44] a law that was not put into Justinian's compilation.

[43] Cass. Dio [*Historia Romana*, 55.5.4], in Xiphilinus.
[44] Flavius Vopiscus [*Tacitus*, 27.9.4].

CHAPTER 16

Slander in the crime of high treason

One must be just to the Caesars: they were not the first to imagine the sad laws they made. It was Sulla[45] who taught them that slanderers must not be punished. Soon one went so far as to reward them.[46]

[45] Sulla made a law of high treason, mentioned in Cicero's orations, *Pro Cluentio*, art. 3 [24–25, 94–97, 99]; *In Pisonem*, art. 21 [21.50]; *In Verrem*, 2nd art. 5 [2.1.5.12–13]; *Epistolae ad familiares*, bk. 3, letter 2 [3.11.1–3]. Caesar and Augustus inserted them in the Julian laws; others added to them.

[46] "The one who was the more distinguished informer would achieve more honors; it was as

if he were a sacred personage" [L.]. Tacitus [*Annales* 4.36]. [M. has cited the passage incorrectly and is perhaps quoting from memory.]

CHAPTER 17

On revealing conspiracies

"If thy brother, or thy son, or thy daughter, or the wife of thy bosom, or thy friend, which is as thine own soul, entice thee secretly, saying: 'Let us go to other gods,' thou shalt stone him; thine hand shall be first upon him, and afterwards the hand of all the people." This law of Deuteronomy[47] cannot be a civil law among most of the peoples that we know because it would open the door to all crimes.

The law in many states that ordered that, on penalty of death, one reveal even the conspiracies in which one did not have a hand, is scarcely less harsh. It is very suitable to restrict this law when it is carried into a monarchical government.

It should be applied there in all its severity only to the crime of high treason in the first degree. In such states it is very important not to confuse the different degrees of this crime.

In Japan, where the laws upset all ideas of human reason, the failure to reveal a crime is considered a crime in the most ordinary cases.

An account[48] tells us of two young ladies who were shut up in a box studded with nails until they died; the one, for having had some intrigue of gallantry; the other, for not having revealed it.

[47] [Deuteronomy] chap. 13, vv. 6–9 [M. quotes part of vv. 6 and 9].
[48] *Recueil des voyages qui ont servi à l'éstablissement de la Compagnie des Indes*, bk. 5, pt. 2, p. 423 ["Voiage de Hagenaar aux Indes Orientales"; 5, 347; 1706 edn; 5, 423; 1725 edn].

CHAPTER 18

How dangerous it is in republics to punish excessively the crime of high treason

When a republic has destroyed those who want to upset it, one must hasten to put an end to vengeances, penalties, and even rewards.

One cannot inflict great punishments, and consequently, make great changes, without putting a great power into the hands of a few citizens. It is better then, in this case, to pardon many than to punish many, to exile few than to exile many, to leave men their goods than to multiply confiscations. On the pretext of avenging the republic, one would establish the tyranny of the avengers. It is not a question of destroying the one who dominates but of destroying domination. One must return as quickly as possible to the ordinary pace of government where the laws protect all and are armed against no one.

The Greeks put no limits to the vengeances they wreaked on tyrants or on those they suspected of being tyrants. They put children to death,[49] sometimes five of the closest relatives.[50] They drove out an infinite number of families. Their republics were shaken by this; exile and the return of the exiled were always periods marking a change in the constitution.

The Romans were wiser. When Cassius was condemned for aspiring to tyranny, the question of putting his children to death was raised; his children were not condemned to any penalty. "Those who wanted to change this law at the end of the war with the Marsi and of the civil war and to exclude from public offices the children of those proscribed by Sulla, are certainly criminal," says Dionysius of Halicarnassus.[51]

In the wars of Marius and Sulla one sees the extent to which the souls of the Romans had gradually become depraved. Things were so lamentable that one believed they would not be seen again. But under the Triumvirate one wanted to be more cruel and appear less so; the sophisms that were used by cruelty are distressing to see. The formula for proscriptions is found in Appian.[52] You would say that one has there no other purpose than the good of the republic, so coolly does one speak there, so many advantages does one show, so preferable to others are the means one takes, so secure will the rich be, so tranquil will the common people be, so much does one fear to put the citizen's lives in danger, so much does one want to pacify the soldiers, finally, so happy will one be.[53]

Rome was drowned in blood when Lepidus triumphed over Spain,

[49] Dion. Hal., *Ant. Rom.*, bk. 8 [8.80.3].

[50] "The tyrant being killed, a magistrate shall slay his five closest relatives" [L.] [Cicero] *De inventione*, bk. 2 [2.49.144].

[51] [Dion. Hal. *Ant. Rom.*] bk. 8, p. 547 [8.80.2].

[52] [Appian] *The Civil Wars*, bk. 4 [4.2.11].

[53] "May it be fortunate and auspicious with you!" [L.] [Appian, *The Civil Wars* 4.2.11].

and, by an unexampled absurdity, he ordered the people to rejoice over the triumph, on penalty of proscription.[54]

[54]"Let this day be given over to feasts and sacrifices; those who do otherwise, let them be among the proscribed" [L.]. [Appian, *The Civil Wars* 4.5.31].

CHAPTER 19
How the usage of liberty is suspended in a republic

There are, in the states where one sets the most store by liberty, laws that violate it for a single person in order to keep it for all. Such are what are called *bills of attainder*[55] in England. They are related to those laws of Athens that were enacted against an individual[56] provided they were made by the vote of six thousand citizens. They are related to those laws made in Rome against individual citizens, which were called *privileges*.[57] They were made only in the great estates of the people. But, however the people made them, Cicero wanted them abolished, because the force of the law consists only in its being enacted for everyone.[58] I admit, however, that the usage of the freest peoples that ever lived on earth makes me believe that there are cases where a veil has to be drawn, for a moment, over liberty, as one hides the statues of the gods.

[55]It is not enough, in the tribunals of the kingdom, for there to be a piece of evidence that convinces the judges; this piece of evidence must also be formal, that is, legal; and the law requires there to be two witnesses against the accused; an additional piece of evidence would not suffice. Now if a man, presumed guilty of what is called a high crime, had found a way to keep the witnesses from appearing so that it was impossible to condemn him under the law, one could bring a special bill of attainder against him, that is, make a singular law concerning his person. One proceeds as with any other bill: it must pass the two Houses and the king must give his consent, otherwise there is no *bill*, that is, no judgment. The accused can have his advocates speak against the *bill*, and one can speak for the *bill* in the House.

[56]"A law concerning a single individual ought not to be proposed unless six thousand have considered it" [L.] Andocides, *Orationes, De mysteriis* [87]. This is ostracism.

[57]"Proposed concerning private individuals" [L.]. Cicero, *De legibus*, bk. 3 [3.19.44–45].

[58]"A decree and law over all" [L.]. Cicero, ibid. [*De legibus* 3.19.44].

CHAPTER 20

On laws favorable to the citizen's liberty in the republic

It often happens in popular states that accusations are made in public and any man is permitted to indict whomever he wants. This has brought about the establishment of laws proper to the defense of the innocence of the citizens. In Athens, the accuser who did not get a fifth of the votes for his side paid a fine of a thousand drachmas. Aeschines, who had accused Ctesiphon, was condemned for this.[59] In Rome, the unjust accuser was branded with infamy,[60] and the letter "K" was stamped on his forehead. Guard was kept on the accuser so that he would not be in a position to corrupt the judges or witnesses.[61]

I have already spoken of that Athenian and Roman law that permitted the one indicted to go into exile before the judgment.

[59] See [Flavius] Philostratus, *Vitae sophistarum*, *Aeschines*, bk. 1 [510, Olearius]. See also Plutarch [*Moralia. Vitae decem oratorum* 840d–e] and Photius [*Bibliotheca* 61, "Aeschines"; 20a18–30].

[60] By the Remnian law.

[61] Plutarch [*Moralia*], *De capienda ex inimicis utilitate* [91d–e].

CHAPTER 21

On the cruelty of laws concerning debtors in a republic

One citizen has already gained a great superiority over another citizen by lending silver that the latter had borrowed only to disburse and that, in consequence, he no longer has. What will happen in a republic, if the laws increase this servitude still more?

In Athens and in Rome,[62] it was at first permitted to sell debtors who were not in a position to pay. Solon corrected this usage in Athens;[63] he ordered that no one would be obligated by his person for civil debts. But the decemvirs[64] did not similarly reform the Roman usage, and although they had Solon's regulation before their eyes, they refused to

[62] Many sold their children to pay their debts. Plutarch [*Vit.*], *Solon* [13.3].

[63] Ibid. [Plutarch, *Vit.*, *Solon* 15.3].

[64] In history it appears that this usage was established among the Romans before the Law of Twelve Tables. Livy, decade 1, bk. 2 [2.23–24].

follow it. This is not the only place in the Law of Twelve Tables where one sees that the design of the decemvirs ran counter to the spirit of democracy.

The cruel laws concerning debtors often endangered the Roman republic. A man covered with sores escaped from the house of his creditor and appeared in the square.[65] The people were moved by this spectacle. Other citizens left their prisons when their creditors no longer dared hold them. Promises were made, but they were broken: the people withdrew to the Mons Sacer. The people gained, instead of the abrogation of these laws, a magistrate to defend them. One was moving away from anarchy; one risked falling into tyranny. Manlius, in order to make himself popular, was going to take from the hands of their creditors the citizens who had been reduced to slavery.[66] One prevailed against his designs, but the evil remained. Particular laws facilitated payments by debtors,[67] and in Roman year 428 [328 B.C.], the consuls proposed a law[68] that took away the creditors' right to hold debtors in servitude in their houses.[69] A usurer named Papirius had wanted to corrupt the modesty of a young man named Publius whom he kept in irons. The crime of Sextus gave Rome political liberty; that of Papirius gave it civil liberty.

It was Rome's fate that new crimes confirmed the liberty that old crimes had procured for it. The attempt of Appius on Virginia revived in the people the horror of tyrants inspired in them by Lucretia's misfortune. Thirty-seven years[70] after the crime of the infamous Papirius, a similar crime[71] made the people withdraw to the Janiculum[72] and renewed the force of the law made for the security of debtors.

[65] Dion. Hal., *Ant. Rom.*, bk. 6 [6.26].
[66] Plutarch [*Vit.*], *Furius Camillus* [36.3–4].
[67] See below, bk. 22, chap. 22.
[68] One hundred and twenty years after the Law of Twelve Tables. "For the Roman plebeians, this year was like another beginning of liberty because they ceased to be enslaved for debts" [L.]. Livy, bk. 8 [8.28.1].
[69] "The property of the debtors but not their bodies would be held liable" [L.]. Ibid. [Livy 8.28.9].
[70] In Roman year 465 [289 B.C.].
[71] That of Plautius, who attacked the modesty of Veturius. Valerius Maximus [*Factorum et dictorum memorabilium*], bk. 6, art. 9 [6.1.9]. One should not confuse these two events; they are neither the same persons nor the same times.
[72] See a fragment of Dion. Hal., in [*Ant. Rom.* 16.5 (9)], *Extracts of Virtues and Vices*; Livy, *Epitome*, bk. 11; and Johann Freinsheim [*Supplementorum Livianorum*], bk. 11 [11.25–26].

Subsequently, more creditors were pursued by debtors for violating the laws made against usurers than debtors were pursued for not having paid their debts.

CHAPTER 22
On things that attack liberty in a monarchy

The least useful thing in the world to the prince has often weakened liberty in monarchies: the commissioners sometimes named to judge an individual.

The prince has so little use for commissioners that it is not worthwhile for him to change the order of things for their sake. It is morally certain that he has more of the spirit of integrity and justice than his commissioners, who always believe themselves sufficiently justified by orders, by a hidden interest of the state, by having been chosen, and even by their fears.

Under Henry VIII, when a peer was tried, he was to be judged by commissioners drawn from the House of Lords; with this method one put to death all the peers one wanted.

CHAPTER 23
On spies in a monarchy

Must there be spies in a monarchy? It is not the ordinary practice of good princes. When a man is faithful to the laws, he has satisfied what he owes to the prince. He must at least have his house as an asylum and be secure about the rest of his conduct. Spying would perhaps be tolerable if it could be exercised by honest people, but the necessary infamy of the person can make the thing be judged infamous. A prince should act toward his subjects with candor, frankness, and trust. He who has so many anxieties, suspicions, and fears, is an actor who plays his role awkwardly. When he sees that in general the laws are enforced and respected, he can judge himself secure. The general demeanor speaks to him for the demeanor of all the individuals. Let him have no fear; he cannot believe how readily he is loved. Indeed, why would one not love him? He is the source of almost all the good that is done, and almost all punishing is the responsibility of the laws. He shows himself to the people only with a serene countenance; his very glory is communicated to us and his power sustains us. A proof that one loves him is that one trusts him; and what a minister refuses, one always imagines the prince would have granted. Even during public calamities, one does not accuse his person; one complains that he is unaware of them or that he is importuned by corrupt people: *If only the prince knew*! say the people. These words are a kind of invocation and a proof of their trust in him.

CHAPTER 24
On anonymous letters

The Tartars are obliged to put their name on their arrows, so that the hand from which they come can be known. When Philip of Macedonia was wounded at the siege of a town, one found on the javelin, *Aster gave this mortal blow to Philip*.[73] If those who accuse a man did it with a view to the public good, they would not accuse him before the prince, for he can easily be prejudiced; instead they would go before the magistrates, whose rules are fearsome only to slanderers. For if they do not want to leave the laws between themselves and the accused, it proves that they have cause to fear the laws, and the least penalty that might be inflicted on these men is not to believe them. One can pay attention to them only in cases that cannot tolerate the delays of ordinary justice and when it is a question of the prince's safety. In that instance, one can believe that the accuser has made an effort that loosened his tongue and made him talk. But in other cases one must say with the Emperor Constantius: "We cannot suspect a man who has no accuser although he does not lack enemies."[74]

[73] Plutarch, *Moralia, Parallela Graeca et Romana*, vol. 2, p. 487 [307d #8].
[74] Law 6, *Codex Theodosianus* [9.34.6]; *de famosis libellis*.

CHAPTER 25

On the manner of governing in monarchy

Royal authority is a great spring that should move easily and noiselessly. The Chinese praise one of their emperors who governed, they say, like the heavens, that is, by example.

There are cases when power should act to its full extent; there are cases when it should act within its limits. An administration is sublime if it is well aware what part of power, great or small, should be used in various circumstances.

In our monarchies, all felicity lies in the people's opinion of the gentleness of the government. An unskillful minister always wants to tell you that you are slaves. But, if that were so, he should seek to keep it from being known. He can say or write nothing to you, except that the prince is angry, that he is surprised, that he will restore order. In a certain way, command is easy: the prince must encourage and the laws must menace.[75]

[75] "Nerva [Nerva Traianus] eased the weight of empire." Tacitus [*Agricola* 3].

CHAPTER 26

That, in a monarchy, the prince should be accessible

This will be much better felt by contrasts. "Czar Peter I," says Lord Perry,[76] "has made a new ordinance that forbids presenting him with a request before presenting it twice to his officers. One can, in the case of denial of justice, present it to him the third time, but if he who presents it is wrong, he must lose his life. Since that time, no requests have been addressed to the czar."

[76] [John Perry] *The State of Russia under the Present Czar* (Paris, 1717), p. 173 [pp. 142–143; 1967 edn].

CHAPTER 27

On the mores of the monarch

The mores of the prince contribute as much to liberty as do the laws; like the laws, the prince can make beasts of men and men of beasts. If he loves free souls, he will have subjects; if he loves common souls, he will have slaves. Does he want to know the great art of ruling? Let him bring honor and virtue close to him, let him call forth personal merit. He can sometimes even cast his eyes toward the talented. Let him not fear his rivals, who are called men of merit; he is their equal once he loves them. Let him win the heart, but let him not capture the spirit. Let him make himself popular. He should be flattered by the love of the least of his subjects; they are all men. The people ask so little attention that it is just to grant it to them; the infinite distance between the sovereign and the people keeps them from disturbing him. Let him yield to prayers but be firm against demands, and let him know that his people benefit from his refusals as do his courtiers from his favors.

CHAPTER 28

On the regard monarchs owe their subjects

They must be extremely restrained in their banter. It flatters when it is moderate because it provides the means of becoming familiar, but a caustic banter is much less permissible to them than to the least of their subjects because they are the only ones who always wound mortally.

Even less should they conspicuously insult one of their subjects; they are established to pardon, to punish, never to insult.

When they insult their subjects, they treat them more cruelly than the Turk or the Muscovite treats his. When the latter insult someone, they humble and do not dishonor; but, as for monarchs, they both humble and dishonor.

Such is the prejudice of those of the East that they consider an affront by the prince to be a result of paternal goodness; and such is our way of thinking that we join to the bitter feeling resulting from this affront the despair of being unable to clear ourselves of it.

They should be charmed to have subjects whose honor is dearer to them than life and is no less a motive for faithfulness than for courage.

One can recall misfortunes that have befallen princes as a result of insulting their subjects: the vengeances of Chaerea, of the eunuch Narses, and of the Count Julian; finally, of the Duchess of Montpensier, who, enraged at Henry III for having revealed some one of her secret failings, vexed him for the rest of his life.

CHAPTER 29

On civil laws appropriate for putting a little liberty in despotic government

Though despotic government in its nature is everywhere the same, yet circumstances, a religious opinion, a prejudice, received examples, a turn of mind, manners, mores, can leave considerable differences among them.

It is well for certain ideas to be established in them. Thus in China, the prince is regarded as the father of the people, and, at the beginning of the empire of the Arabs, the prince was their preacher.[77]

It is suitable for there to be some sacred book that acts as a rule, like the Koran for the Arabs, the books of Zoroaster for the Persians, the Veda for the Indians, the classics for the Chinese. The religious code replaces the civil code and fixes what is arbitrary.

It is not bad for judges to consult the ministers of religion in cases that are unclear.[78] Thus in Turkey, the cadis question the mullahs. And, if the case merits death, the particular judge, if there is one, may also suitably seek the advice of the governor, so that the civil power and the ecclesiastic power are further tempered by the political authority.

[77] The caliphs.

[78] [Ebulgazi Bahadir Han, Khan of Khorezm] *Histoire généalogique des Tatars*, pt. 3, p. 277, in the remarks [Bentinck's note, pt. 3, chap. 14; 1, 290; 1726 edn].

CHAPTER 30
Continuation of the same subject

It is despotic rage that has established that the father's disgrace would involve the disgrace of children and wives. The latter are already unfortunate without being criminal; and besides, the prince must leave suppliants between the accused and himself to soften his wrath or enlighten his justice.

In the Maldives,[79] it is a good custom for a lord who is disgraced to pay daily court to the king until he is returned to favor; his presence disarms the prince's wrath.

There are despotic states[80] in which it is thought that speaking to a prince on behalf of a disgraced man is to lack the respect due the prince. These princes seem to make every effort to deprive themselves of the virtue of mercy.

Arcadius and Honorius, in the law[81] of which I have spoken at length,[82] declare that they will not pardon those who dare entreat them on behalf of guilty men.[83] This law was very bad, for it is bad even in despotism.

The Persian custom that permits anyone to leave the kingdom who wants to, is very good; and though the opposite usage had its origin in despotism, where subjects were regarded as slaves[84] and those who left were regarded as fugitive slaves, nevertheless, the Persian practice is very good in despotisms, where fear of the people's fleeing or departing with what they owe checks or moderates the persecution of pashas and extortioners.

[79] See François Pyrard [*Voyages*, pt. 1, chap. 8; 1, 89; 1887–1890 edn].

[80] As today in Persia according to the report of [John] Chardin. This usage is quite old. Procopius says [in *The Persian Wars*, "History of the Wars"; 1.5.7–8], "Cabades was put into the castle of oblivion; there is a law forbidding one to speak of those shut up there or even to mention their names."

[81] Law 5 of the *Code* [*Corpus Juris Civilis, Code* 9.8.5.2]; *ad legem Juliam maiestatis*.

[82] In chapter 8 of this book.

[83] Frederick copied this law from the *Constitutions of Naples*, bk. 1 [*Liber Augustalis or the Constitutions of Melfi* [1231], 1.4].

[84] In monarchies, there is ordinarily a law prohibiting those who have public employments from leaving the kingdom without the permission of the prince. This law must also be established in republics. But in the ones with singular institutions, the prohibition must be generalized so that foreign mores will not be brought in.

BOOK 13

On the relations that the levy of taxes and the size of public revenues have with liberty

CHAPTER I

On the revenues of the state

The revenues of the state are a portion each citizen gives of his goods in order to have the security or the comfortable enjoyment of the rest.

In order to fix these REVENUES well one must consider both the necessities of the state and the necessities of the citizens. One must not take from the real needs of the people for the imaginary needs of the state.

Imaginary needs are the ones sought by the passions and weaknesses of those who govern, the charm of an extraordinary project, the sick envy of vainglory, and a certain impotence of spirit in the face of their fancies. Often those who, with restless spirit, were at the head of public business under a prince have thought that the needs of their small souls were the needs of the state.

There is nothing that wisdom and prudence should regulate more than the portion taken away from the subjects and the portion left to them.

Public revenues must not be measured by what the people can give but by what they should give, and if they are measured by what the people can give, it must at least be by what they can always give.

CHAPTER 2

That it is bad reasoning to say that large taxes are good in themselves

In certain monarchies one has seen that small countries that were exempt from taxes were as poverty-stricken as the places all around them that were overwhelmed by taxes. The principal reason for this is that a small, hemmed-in state cannot have industry, arts, or manufacturing because it is hampered in a thousand ways by the large state which encloses it. The large surrounding state has industry, manufacturing, and the arts, and it makes regulations procuring all advantages for itself. Therefore, the small state necessarily becomes poor, however few imposts are levied there.

Yet it was concluded from the poverty of these little countries that there must be heavy burdens[a] in order to make the people industrious. One would have done better to conclude that there must be none. All the wretched people from the surrounding area withdraw to these places and do nothing; already discouraged by overwhelming work, they make their whole felicity consist in idleness.

The effect of the wealth of a country is to fill all hearts with ambition; the effect of poverty is to bring them to despair. Ambition is excited by work; poverty is consoled by laziness.

Nature is just toward men. She rewards them for their pains; she makes them hard workers because she attaches greater rewards to greater work. But if an arbitrary power removes nature's rewards, the distaste for work recurs and inaction appears to be the only good.

[a] Montesquieu uses the term *charges*, "charges," "burdens," to cover a variety of ways a government imposes on its subjects: posts, taxes, and services.

CHAPTER 3

On taxes in countries where part of the people are slaves to the land

Slavery to the land[b] is sometimes established after a conquest. In this case, the slave who cultivates the land should be the share-cropper of the master. Only the sharing of loss and gain can reconcile those who are destined to work with those who are destined to enjoyment.

[b] *esclavage de la glèbe*. See 30.5, where Montesquieu speaks of "serfdom," *servitude de la glèbe* (notes [a] and [b], bk. 30).

CHAPTER 4

On a republic in a like case

When a republic has reduced a nation to cultivating lands for it, one should not tolerate the citizen's increasing the tax of the slave. It was not permitted in Lacedaemonia; it was thought that the Helots[1] would better cultivate the lands when they knew that their servitude would not increase; it was believed that the masters would be better citizens when they desired only what they were accustomed to having.

[1] Plutarch [*Moralia, Apophthegmata Laconica, Instituta Laconica* 41, 239d–e].

CHAPTER 5

On a monarchy in a like case

In a monarchy, when the nobility has the lands cultivated for its profit by the conquered people, again the ground-rent must not increase.[2] Moreover, it is well for the prince to be satisfied with his domain and with military service. But, if the prince wants to levy taxes in silver on the slaves of his nobility, the lord must stand warrant for the tax,[3] pay it

[2] This is why Charlemagne made his fine institutions about it. See bk. 5 of the Capitularies, art. 303 [*MGH*, LL. II, pt. 2, *Capitularia spuria, Benedicti capitularium*, 1.303].
[3] It is thus practiced in Germany.

for the slaves, and collect it back from them; and if this rule is not followed, the lord and those who levy the revenues for the prince, each in his turn, will harass the slave and will, one after the other, collect from him until he perishes from poverty or flees into the woods.

CHAPTER 6

On a despotic state in a like case

What I have just said is still more indispensable in the despotic state. The lord, who can be stripped of his lands and his slaves at any moment, is not inclined to preserve them.

Peter I, wanting to adopt the practice of Germany and levy his taxes in silver, made a very wise regulation that is still observed in Russia. The gentleman levies an assessment on the peasants and pays it to the czar. If the number of the peasants decreases, he pays the same amount; if the number increases, he pays no more; therefore, it is in his interest not to harass his peasants.

CHAPTER 7

On taxes in countries where slavery to the land is not established

In a state, when all the individuals are citizens and each one there possesses by his domain that which the prince possesses by his empire, imposts can be placed on persons, on lands, or on commodities, on two of these, or on all three together.

In respect to an impost on persons, an unjust proportion would be one that followed strictly the proportion of goods. In Athens, the citizens were divided[4] into four classes. Those who received five hundred measures of liquid or dry fruit from their goods paid one talent to the public; those who received three hundred measures from them, half a talent; those who had two hundred measures paid ten minas, or a sixth of a talent; those of the fourth class gave nothing. The

[4] [Julius] Pollux [*Onomasticon*], bk. 8, chap. 10, art. 130 [8.10.130].

assessment was just although it was not proportional; if it did not follow the proportion of goods, it followed the proportion of needs. It was judged that each one had an equal *physical necessity*, that this physical necessity should not be assessed, that the useful came next, and that it should be assessed, but at less than the superfluous, and that the size of the assessment on the superfluous prevented superfluity.

In the assessment on lands, registers are made for the various classes of lands. But it is very difficult to recognize these differences, and still more difficult to find people without an interest in failing to recognize them. Therefore, there are two kinds of injustice in this case: the injustice of the man and the injustice of the thing itself. But if the assessment is not excessive in general, if the people are left plenty for necessities, the particular injustices will be as nothing. But if, on the contrary, the people are left strictly with what they must have in order to live, the least disproportion will be of the greatest consequence.

If some citizens do not pay enough, there is no great harm; their plenty always reverts to the public; if some individuals pay too much, their ruin turns against the public. If the state matches its fortune to that of individuals, the plenty of the individuals will soon make its fortune increase. Everything depends on the moment. Will the state begin by impoverishing its subjects in order to enrich itself? Or will it wait for its subjects to enrich it at their own pace? Will it have the first advantage or the second? Will it begin by being rich or will it end by being so?

Duties on commodities are the ones the least felt by the people, because no formal request is made for them. They can be so wisely managed that the people will be almost unaware that they pay them. To do this, it is of great consequence that it be the one who sells the commodity who pays the duty. He well knows that he is not paying for himself; and the buyer, who ultimately pays it, confounds it with the price. Some writers have said that Nero removed the duty of one-twenty-fifth on slaves who were sold;[5] yet he did no more than order that the seller would pay it instead of the buyer: this regulation, which left all the impost, appeared to have removed it.

There are two kingdoms in Europe where very high imposts have been put on beverages: in one of them the brewer alone pays the duty;

[5] "The tax on the sale of slaves was remitted, but this remission was more specious than real because it was also ordered that the seller pay it; this simply increased the price for the buyer because it was made part of the price" [L.]. Tacitus, *Annales*, bk. 13 [13.31].

in the other, it is levied alike on all the subjects who drink. In the first, no one feels the severity of the impost; in the second, it is regarded as onerous: in the former, the citizen feels only his liberty in not paying; in the latter, he feels only the necessity that obliges him to pay it.

Furthermore, in order that the citizen pay, his house must be perpetually searched. Nothing is more contrary to liberty, and those who establish these sorts of imposts have not the good fortune of having discovered, in this regard, the best kind of administration.

CHAPTER 8
How the illusion is preserved

In order to make the price of a thing and its duty become confused in the head of the one who pays, there must be some relation between the commodity and the impost, and one must not charge excessive duty on a product of small value. There are countries where the duty is more than seventeen times greater than the value of the commodity. In this way the prince removes the illusion from his subjects; they see that they are led in an unreasonable manner, and this makes them feel every bit of their servitude.

Besides, for the prince to be able to levy a duty so disproportionate to the value of the thing, he must sell the commodity himself and the people must not be able to buy it elsewhere; this is subject to a thousand drawbacks.

As fraud is very lucrative in this case, the natural penalty, the one reason demands, which is confiscation of the commodity, becomes incapable of checking it, especially because the commodity ordinarily has a very low price. Therefore, one must have recourse to extravagant penalties like those inflicted for the greatest crimes. This removes all proportion in penalties. Men whom one could not consider wicked are punished like scoundrels, which is the thing in the world most contrary to the spirit of moderate government.

I add that the more opportunities a people are given to defraud the tax-collector, the more the latter is enriched and the former are impoverished. In order to check fraud, tax-collectors must be given extraordinary means of harassment, and all is lost.

CHAPTER 9

On a bad sort of impost

We shall speak incidentally of an impost established in some states on the various clauses of civil contracts. In order to protect oneself from the tax-collector, one must have a vast knowledge, as these things are subject to subtle examinations. So, the tax-collector, the interpreter of the prince's regulations, exercises an arbitrary power over fortunes. Experience has shown that an impost on the paper on which the contract is to be written would be much better.

CHAPTER 10

That the size of taxes depends on the nature of the government

Taxes should be very light in despotic government. Otherwise, who would want to take the trouble to cultivate the land? Moreover, how can high taxes be paid in a government that does nothing to replace what the subject has given?

Given the stunning power of the prince and the strange weakness of the people, there must be no ambiguity about anything. Taxes should be so easy to collect and so clearly established that they cannot be increased or diminished by those who levy them. A portion of the fruits of the earth, an assessment by head, a tax of some percent on commodities are the only suitable ones.

It is well in despotic government for merchants to have a personal passage of safe-conduct and for usage to make them respected; otherwise, they would be too weak in discussions they might have with the officers of the prince.

CHAPTER 11
On fiscal penalties

A peculiarity of *fiscal penalties* is that, contrary to general practice, they are more severe in Europe than in Asia. In Europe, commodities, sometimes even ships and vehicles, are confiscated; in Asia, one takes neither the one nor the other. This is because in Europe the merchant has judges who can protect him from oppression; in Asia, despotic judges would themselves be the oppressors. What would the merchant do against a pasha who had decided to confiscate his commodities?

This harassment defeats itself and one sees it constrained to be somewhat gentle. In Turkey, only one entry duty is levied; after that, the whole country is open to merchants. False declarations result neither in confiscation nor in increase of duties. In China, packages that belong to people who are not merchants are not opened.[6] Fraud among the Moguls is punished not by confiscation but by the doubling of the duty. The Tartar princes[7] who live in Asian towns levy almost nothing on the commodities that pass through. And, if in Japan the crime of commercial fraud is a capital crime, it is because one has reasons for prohibiting all communication with foreigners and because fraud[8] there is an infringement of the laws made for the security of the state rather than of the laws of commerce.

[6] [Jean Baptiste] du Halde [*Description de l'Empire de la Chine*, "De la police de la Chine"], vol. 2, p. 37 [2, 67 H; 2, 57 P; 2, 97 L].

[7] [Ebulgazi Bahadir Han, Khan of Khorezm] *Histoire généalogique des Tatars*, pt. 3, p. 290 [Bentinck's note, pt. 3, chap. 16; 1, 290; 1726 edn].

[8] As they wanted to have a commerce with foreigners without entering into communication with them, they chose two nations: the Dutch for the commerce with Europe and the Chinese for that with Asia. They keep factors and sailors in a kind of prison and hamper them so much that they lose patience.

CHAPTER 12
The relation of the size of taxes to liberty

GENERAL RULE: One can levy heavier taxes in proportion to the liberty of the subjects and one is forced to moderate them insofar as servitude increases. This has always been and will always be. It is a rule drawn from nature, which does not change; this rule is found in all countries, in England, in Holland, and in all states of decreasing liberty down to Turkey. Switzerland does not seem to conform to this because no taxes are paid there, but the particular reason is known, and it even confirms what I say. In those barren mountains, food is so dear and the country so heavily populated that a Swiss pays four times more to nature than a Turk pays to the sultan.

Dominant peoples such as the Athenians and the Romans can free themselves from every impost because they reign over subject nations. So they do not pay in proportion to their liberty; this is because, in this regard, they are not a people but a monarch.

But the general rule still holds. In moderate states, there is a compensation for heavy taxes; it is liberty. In despotic states,[9] there is an equivalent for liberty; it is the modest taxes.

In certain European monarchies there are provinces[10] that, by the nature of their political government, are in a better position than others. One always imagines that they do not pay enough, because as a result of the goodness of their government, they could pay even more; and it keeps coming to mind to take away the very government that produces the good that is communicated, that spreads afar, and that it would be much better to enjoy.

[9] In Russia, taxes are of medium size; they have been increased since despotism has become more moderate. See [Ebulgazi Bahadir Han, Khan of Khorezm] *Histoire généalogique des Tatars*, pt. 2 [Bentinck's note, pt. 9, chap. 9, "Du règne d'Arap-Mohamet-Chan"; 2, 726; 1726 edn].

[10] The *pays d'Etats*.

CHAPTER 13

In which government taxes are susceptible of increase

Taxes can be increased in most republics because the citizen, who believes he is paying to himself, has the will to pay them and ordinarily has the power to do so as a result of the nature of the government.

In monarchy, taxes can be increased because the moderation of the government can procure wealth there; it is a kind of reward to the prince for his respect of the laws.

In the despotic state they cannot be increased because extreme servitude cannot be increased.

CHAPTER 14

That the nature of taxes is relative to the government

An impost by head is more natural to servitude; the impost on commodities is more natural to liberty because it relates less directly to the person.[c]

It is natural in despotic government for the prince not to pay his militia or the people in his court in silver but to distribute lands to them, and there are, consequently, few taxes levied. For if the prince pays in silver, the most natural tax he can levy is a tax by head. This tax can only be very modest, for, as one cannot make various classes of wealthy tax-payers because of the abuses that would result, given the injustice and the violence of the government, one must necessarily be ruled by the rates that the poorest can pay.

The tax natural to moderate government is the impost on commodities. This impost, really paid by the buyers although advanced by the merchant, is a loan the merchant makes to the buyer; thus, the trader must be regarded as both the general debtor of the state and the creditor of all the individuals. He advances to the state the duty the buyer will eventually pay, and he has paid, for the buyer, the duty he has paid for the commodity. Therefore, it is felt that the more moderate the government, the more the spirit of liberty reigns, and the more secure fortunes are, the easier it is for the merchant to advance substantial duties to the state and to lend them to individuals. In England, a merchant really lends the state fifty to sixty pounds sterling for every barrel of wine he receives. What merchant would dare to do this kind of thing in a country governed like Turkey? And, if he dared to do it, how would he be able to, with a suspect, uncertain, and ruined fortune?

[c]It is clear from this sentence that an "impost," *impot*, is a particular "tax," *tribute*. These may be based on an "assessment," *taxe*.

CHAPTER 15
The abuse of liberty

These great advantages of liberty have caused the abuse of liberty itself. Because moderate government has produced remarkable results, this moderation has been abandoned; because large taxes have been raised, one has wanted to raise excessive ones; and, disregarding the hand of liberty that gave this present, one has turned to servitude, which refuses everything.

Liberty has produced excessive taxes, but the effect of these excessive taxes is to produce servitude in their turn, and the effect of servitude is to produce a decrease in taxes.

The monarchs of Asia make edicts about almost nothing except the exempting each year of some province in their empire;[11] such manifestations of their will are kindnesses. But in Europe, the edicts of the princes cause grief even before they are seen because they always speak of their needs and never of ours.

From an inexcusable listlessness that the ministers in these countries get from their government and often from their climate, the people gain the advantage that they are not constantly overwhelmed with new demands. Expenditures there do not increase because there are no new projects and if by chance there are some, they are projects whose end can be seen and not projects just beginning. Those who govern the state do not harry it because they do not endlessly harry themselves. But for us, it is impossible to have regularity in our finances because we always know that we shall do something, and never what we shall do.

Among ourselves, we no longer consider a great minister to be one who dispenses public revenues wisely, but rather one who is an industrious man and who finds what are called expedients.

[11] This is the usage of the emperors of China.

CHAPTER 16
On the conquests of the Mohammedans

These excessive taxes[12] accounted for the strange ease with which the Mohammedans made their conquests. Instead of that continuous succession of harassments devised by the subtle avarice of the emperors, the peoples saw themselves subjected to a simple tax that was easily paid and was similarly accepted; they obeyed a barbarian nation more happily than the corrupt government under which they had suffered both all the drawbacks of a liberty they no longer had and all the horrors of a present servitude.

[12] See what history says about the greatness, the eccentricity, and even the madness of these taxes. Anastasius devised one for breathing air: "so that whoever inhaled a breath of air paid the penalty" [L.].

CHAPTER 17
On the increase in troops

A new disease has spread across Europe; it has afflicted our princes and made them keep an inordinate number of troops. It redoubles in strength and necessarily becomes contagious; for, as soon as one state increases what it calls its troops, the others suddenly increase theirs, so that nothing is gained thereby but the common ruin. Each monarch keeps ready all the armies he would have if his peoples were in danger of being exterminated; and this state in which all strain against all is called peace.[13] Thus Europe is so ruined that if individuals were in the situation of the three most opulent powers in this part of the world, they would have nothing to live on. We are poor with the wealth and commerce of the whole universe, and soon, as a result of these soldiers, we shall have nothing but soldiers and we shall be like the Tartars.[14]

The great princes, not content to buy troops from smaller ones, seek everywhere to buy alliances, that is, almost always to lose their silver.

[13] It is true that it is this state of effort which principally maintains the balance, because it exhausts the great powers.

[14] For this, one must make use of the new invention of the militia established in almost the whole of Europe and push them to the same excess as the regular troops.

The consequence of such a situation is the permanent increase in taxes; and that which prevents all remedies in the future is that one no longer counts on the revenues, but makes war with one's capital. It is not unheard of for states to mortgage their lands even during peace and to ruin themselves by means they call extraordinary, which are so highly extraordinary that the most deranged son of a family could scarcely imagine them.

CHAPTER 18
On the remission of taxes

The maxim of the great eastern empires, that taxes should be returned to provinces that have suffered, could well be brought to monarchical states. There are many places where this is established, but more are overwhelmed than if it were not established, because, since the prince does not vary his levy, the whole state becomes jointly responsible. To relieve a village whose payments are deficient, one burdens another that pays more; the first is not restored, the second is destroyed. The people grow desperate between the necessity of paying from fear of exactions and the danger of paying from fear of surcharges.

A well-governed state should put in the first item of its expenditures a regular sum for fortuitous cases. In this, the public is like those individuals who ruin themselves by spending exactly the income from their lands.

In regard to the joint responsibility among the inhabitants of a village, this has been said[15] to be reasonable because one could assume a fraudulent plot on their part; but, where has one found that, based on suppositions, a thing that is unjust in itself and ruinous for the state has to be established?

[15] See [Pieter Burman] *Vectigalia populi Romani*, chap. 2, Paris, Briasson, 1740 [chap. 2, "De vectigali ex agris publici"; pp. 12–25; 1734 edn].

CHAPTER 19

What is most suitable for the prince and the people, tax-farming or direct taxes?

Direct taxes[d] are the administration of a good father of a family who levies his revenues himself with economy and order.

With direct taxes, the prince is in charge of hastening or delaying their levy, either according to his needs or according to those of his peoples. With direct taxes, he saves the state the immense profits made by tax-farmers, who impoverish it in infinite ways. With direct taxes, he saves the people from the grievous spectacle of sudden fortunes. With direct taxes, the silver levied passes through few hands; it goes directly to the prince and consequently reverts more promptly to the people. With direct taxes, the prince saves the people from an infinity of bad laws that are ever extorted from him by the importunate avarice of the tax-farmers whose present advantage lies in regulations that are fatal for the future.

Since the one who has silver is always the master of the one without, the tax-farmer is despotic over even the prince; he is not a legislator but he forces him to give laws.

I admit that it is sometimes useful to begin by farming out a newly established duty. There are arts and inventions for warding off frauds that the interest of the tax-farmers suggests to them and that agents could not have devised; but, once the system for the levy is made by the tax-farmer, direct taxes can be successfully established. In England, the administration of the *excise* and of the revenues from the *post office*, such as it is today, was borrowed from that of the tax-farmers.

In republics, the revenues of the state are almost always from direct taxes. The contrary establishment was a great vice of the Roman government.[16] In despotic states, where direct taxes are established, the

[16] Caesar was obliged to take the publicans out of the province of Asia and to establish there another sort of administration, as we learn from Cass. Dio [*Historia Romana* 42.6.3]. And Tacitus tells us [*Annales* 1.76.2] that it was granted to Macedonia and Achaea, provinces which Augustus had left to the Roman people, and which, consequently, were governed on the old plan, to be among those the emperor governed through his officers.

[d] *La régie*, "direct taxes," or the collection of taxes by governmental officials paid to do the task. This contrasts with tax-farming, where the collectors keep some part of the taxes they collect.

peoples are infinitely happier: witness Persia and China.[17] The unhappiest are those where the prince farms out his sea-ports and commercial towns. The history of monarchies is full of the ills caused by tax-collectors.

Nero, indignant at the harassments of the publicans, formed the impossible and magnanimous project of abolishing all imposts. He did not devise direct taxation; he made[18] four ordinances: that the laws made against the publicans, hitherto kept secret, would be published; that they could no longer exact what they had neglected to demand during the year; that a praetor would be established to judge the praetors' claims with no formality; and that the merchants would pay nothing for ships. Those were the halcyon days of this emperor.

[17] See [John] Chardin, *Voyages en Perse et autres lieux de l'Orient*, vol. 6 ["Description du gouvernement politique militaire et civil des Persans", chap. 2; 5, 237; 1811 edn].

[18] Tacitus, *Annales*, bk. 13 [13.51].

CHAPTER 20
On tax-collectors

All is lost when the lucrative profession of tax-collectors, by its wealth, comes to be an honored profession. This can be good in despotic states, where their employment is often a part of the functions of the governors themselves. It is not good in a republic, and a similar thing destroyed the Roman republic. It is no better in a monarchy; nothing is more contrary to the spirit of this government. Disgust infects all the other estates; honor loses all its esteem there; the slow and natural means for distinguishing oneself no longer have an effect, and the principle of the government is stricken.

In times past, one certainly saw scandalous fortunes; it was one of the calamities of the Fifty Years Wars; but at that time this wealth was regarded as ridiculous, and we admire it.

Every profession has some things as its lot. The lot of those who levy taxes is wealth, and the reward for this wealth is wealth itself. Glory and honor are for that nobility which knows, sees, and feels no real good except honor and glory. Respect and esteem are for those ministers and those magistrates who, finding only work upon work, watch day and night over the happiness of the empire.

Part 3

BOOK 14

On the laws in their relation to the nature of the climate

CHAPTER I

The general idea

If it is true that the character[a] of the spirit and the passions of the heart are extremely different in the various climates, *laws* should be relative to the differences in these passions and to the differences in these characters.

[a] *Caractère* can mean mark or sign, trait, or a habitual way of acting and feeling. When Montesquieu uses *caractère*, he seems to mean a form or shape of the spirit, combining these meanings.

CHAPTER 2

How much men differ in the various climates

Cold air[1] contracts the extremities of the body's surface fibers; this increases their spring and favors the return of blood from the extremities of the heart. It shortens these same fibers;[2] therefore, it increases their strength[b] in this way too. Hot air, by contrast, relaxes these extremities of the fibers and lengthens them; therefore, it decreases their strength and their spring.

Therefore, men are more vigorous in cold climates. The action of the heart and the reaction of the extremities of the fibers are in closer

[1] This is even visible: in the cold, one appears thinner.
[2] It is known that it shortens iron.

[b] We translate *force* as both "force" and "strength," as the context is more and less abstract.

accord, the fluids are in a better equilibrium, the blood is pushed harder toward the heart and, reciprocally, the heart has more power. This greater strength should produce many effects: for example, more confidence in oneself, that is, more courage; better knowledge of one's superiority, that is, less desire for vengeance; a higher opinion of one's security, that is, more frankness and fewer suspicions, maneuvers, and tricks. Finally, it should make very different characters. Put a man in a hot, enclosed spot, and he will suffer, for the reasons just stated, a great slackening of heart. If, in the circumstance, one proposes a bold action to him, I believe one will find him little disposed toward it; his present weakness will induce discouragement in his soul; he will fear everything, because he will feel he can do nothing. The peoples in hot countries are timid like old men; those in cold countries are courageous like young men. If we turn our attention to the recent wars,[3] which are the ones we can best observe and in which we can better see certain slight effects that are imperceptible from a distance, we shall certainly feel that the actions of the northern peoples who were sent to southern countries[4] were not as fine as the actions of their compatriots who, fighting in their own climate, enjoyed the whole of their courage.

The strength of the fibers of the northern peoples causes them to draw the thickest juices from their food. Two things result from this: first, that the parts of the chyle, or lymph,[c] being broad surfaced, are more apt to be applied to the fibers and to nourish them; and second, that, being coarse, they are less apt to give a certain subtlety to the nervous juice. Therefore, these people will have large bodies and little vivacity.

The nerves, which end in the tissue of our skin, are made of a sheaf of nerves. Ordinarily, it is not the whole nerve that moves, but an infinitely small part of it. In hot countries, where the tissue of the skin is relaxed, the ends of the nerves are open and exposed to the weakest action of the slightest objects. In cold countries, the tissue of the skin is contracted and the papillae compressed. The little bunches are in a way paralyzed; sensation hardly passes to the brain except when it is extremely strong and is of the entire nerve together. But imagination,

[3] The War of the Spanish Succession.
[4] In Spain, for example.

[c] In the eighteenth century these words referred to various body fluids, without the precise denotations they have in modern physiology.

taste, sensitivity, and vivacity depend on an infinite number of small sensations.

I have observed the place on the surface tissue of a sheep's tongue which appears to the naked eye to be covered with papillae. Through a microscope, I have seen the tiny hairs, or a kind of down, on these papillae; between these papillae were pyramids, forming something like little brushes at the ends. It is very likely that these pyramids are the principal organ of taste.

I had half of the tongue frozen; and, with the naked eye I found the papillae considerably diminished; some of the rows of papillae had even slipped inside their sheaths: I examined the tissue through a microscope; I could no longer see the pyramids. As the tongue thawed, the papillae appeared again to the naked eye, and, under the microscope, the little brushes began to reappear.

This observation confirms what I have said, that, in cold countries, the tufts of nerves are less open; they slip inside their sheaths, where they are protected from the action of external objects. Therefore, sensations are less vivid.

In cold countries, one will have little sensitivity to pleasures; one will have more of it in temperate countries; in hot countries, sensitivity will be extreme. As one distinguishes climates by degrees of latitude, one can also distinguish them by degrees of sensitivity, so to speak. I have seen operas in England and Italy; they are the same plays with the same actors: but the same music produces such different effects in the people of the two nations that it seems inconceivable, the one so calm and the other so transported.

It will be the same for pain; pain is aroused in us by the tearing of some fiber in our body. The author of nature has established that this pain is stronger as the disorder is greater; now it is evident that the large bodies and coarse fibers of the northern peoples are less capable of falling into disorder than the delicate fibers of the peoples of hot countries; therefore, the soul is less sensitive to pain. A Muscovite has to be flayed before he feels anything.

With that delicacy of organs found in hot countries, the soul is sovereignly moved by all that is related to the union of the two sexes; everything leads to this object.

In northern climates, the physical aspect of love has scarcely enough strength to make itself felt; in temperate climates, love, accompanied by a thousand accessories, is made pleasant by things that at first seem to be love but are still not love; in hotter climates, one likes love for itself; it is the sole cause of happiness; it is life.

In southern climates, a delicate, weak, but sensitive machine gives itself up to a love which in a seraglio is constantly aroused and calmed; or else to a love which as it leaves women much more independent is exposed to a thousand troubles. In northern countries, a healthy and well-constituted but heavy machine finds its pleasures in all that can start the spirits in motion again: hunting, travels, war, and wine. You will find in the northern climates peoples who have few vices, enough virtues, and much sincerity and frankness. As you move toward the countries of the south, you will believe you have moved away from morality itself: the liveliest passions will increase crime; each will seek to take from others all the advantages that can favor these same passions. In temperate countries, you will see peoples whose manners, and even their vices and virtues are inconstant; the climate is not sufficiently settled to fix them.

The heat of the climate can be so excessive that the body there will be absolutely without strength. So, prostration will pass even to the spirit; no curiosity, no noble enterprise, no generous sentiment; inclinations will all be passive there; laziness there will be happiness; most chastisements there will be less difficult to bear than the action of the soul, and servitude will be less intolerable than the strength of spirit necessary to guide one's own conduct.

CHAPTER 3
A contradiction in the characters of certain peoples of the South

Indians[5] are by nature without courage; even the children[6] of Europeans born in the Indies lose the courage of the European climate. But how does this accord with their atrocious actions, their barbaric

[5] [Jean Baptiste] Tavernier says, "A hundred European soldiers would have little difficulty routing a thousand Indian soldiers." [*Travels in India*; bk. 2, ch. 9; 1, 391; 1889 edn.]

[6] Even Persians who settle in the Indies take on, in the third generation, the indolence and cowardice of the Indians. See [François] Bernier, *Travels in the Mogul Empire*, vol. 1, p. 282 ["Letter to Colbert concerning Hindustan"; p. 209; 1916 edn].

customs and penitences? Men there suffer unbelievable evils; women burn themselves: this is considerable strength for so much weakness.

Nature, which has given these peoples a weakness that makes them timid, has also given them such a lively imagination that everything strikes them to excess. The same delicacy of organs that makes them fear death serves also to make them dread a thousand things more than death. The same sensitivity makes the Indians both flee all perils and brave them all.

As a good education is more necessary to children than to those of mature spirit, so the peoples of these climates have greater need of a wise legislator than the peoples of our own. The more easily and forcefully one is impressed, the more important it is to be impressed in a suitable manner, to accept no prejudices, and to be led by reason.

In the time of the Romans, the peoples of northern Europe lived without arts, without education, almost without laws, and still, with only the good sense connected with the coarse fibers of these climates, they maintained themselves with remarkable wisdom against the Roman power until they came out of their forests to destroy it.

CHAPTER 4

The cause of the immutability of religion, mores, manners, and laws in the countries of the east

If you join the weakness of organs that makes the peoples of the East receive the strongest impressions in the world to a certain laziness of the spirit, naturally bound with that of the body, which makes that spirit incapable of any action, any effort, any application, you will understand that the soul can no longer alter impressions once it has received them. This is why laws, mores,[7] and manners, even those that seem not to matter, like the fashion in clothing, remain in the East today as they were a thousand years ago.

[7]In a fragment from Nicholas of Damascus, in the collection of Constantine Porphyrogenitus, one sees that it was an ancient custom in the East to send someone to strangle a governor who displeased; this dates from the times of the Medes. [Nicholas of Damascus, *Fragments*, #66.26; *FGrH*; 2A, 366–367.]

CHAPTER 5

That bad legislators are those who have favored the vices of the climate and good ones are those who have opposed them

Indians believe that rest and nothingness are the foundation of all things and the end to which they lead. Therefore, they consider total inaction as the most perfect state and the object of their desires. They give to the sovereign being[8] the title of the unmoving one. The Siamese believe that the supreme felicity[9] consists in not being obliged to animate a machine or to make a body act.

In these countries where excessive heat enervates and overwhelms, rest is so delicious and movement so painful that this system of metaphysics appears natural; and Foë,[10] legislator of the Indies, followed his feelings when he put men in an extremely passive state; but his doctrine, born of idleness of the climate, favoring it in turn, has caused a thousand ills.

The legislators of China were more sensible when, as they considered men not in terms of the peaceful state in which they will one day be but in terms of the action proper to making them fulfill the duties of life, they made their religion, philosophy, and laws all practical. The more the physical causes incline men to rest, the more the moral causes should divert them from it.

[8] Panamanack. See [Athanasius] Kircher [*La Chine illustrée*, pt. 3, chap. 6; p. 215; 1670 edn].

[9] [Simon de] la Loubère, *The Kingdom of Siam*, p. 446 [pt. 3, chap. 22; p. 129; 1969 edn].

[10] Foë wants to reduce the heart to pure emptiness. "We have eyes and ears, but perfection consists in not seeing or hearing; perfection, for those members, the mouth, hands, etc., is to be inactive." This is taken from the "Dialog of a Chinese Philosopher," reported by Father [Jean Baptiste] du Halde [*Description de l'Empire de la Chine*], vol. 3 [3, 59 H; 3, 49 P; 3, 268 L].

CHAPTER 6

On the cultivation of land in hot climates

The cultivation of land is the greatest labor of men. The more their climate inclines them to flee this labor, the more their religion and laws should rouse them to it. Thus, the laws of the Indies, which give the lands to the princes and take away from individuals the spirit of ownership, increase the bad effects of the climate, that is, natural laziness.

CHAPTER 7
On monasticism

Monasticism causes the same evils there; it was born in the hot eastern countries where one is given to action less than to speculation.

In Asia the number of dervishes, or monks, seems to increase with the heat of the climate; the Indies, where it is extremely hot, are full of them; one finds the same difference in Europe.

In order to conquer the laziness that comes from the climate, the laws must seek to take away every means of living without labor, but in southern Europe they do the opposite: they give to those who want to be idle places proper for the speculative life, and attach immense wealth to those places. These people who live in an abundance that is burdensome to them correctly give their excess to the common people: the common people have lost the ownership of goods; the people are repaid for it by the idleness they enjoy and they come to love their very poverty.

CHAPTER 8
A good custom in China

The accounts[11] of China tell us of the ceremony that the emperor performs every year to open the cultivation of the fields.[12] By this public and solemn act one has wanted to rouse[13] the peoples to their plowing.

[11] Father [Jean Baptiste] du Halde, *Description de l'Empire de la Chine*, vol. 2, p. 72 ["De la fertilité des terres"; 2, 70–71 P; 2, 81–84 H; 2, 120–123 L].

[12] A number of the kings in the Indies do the same thing. *The Kingdom of Siam*, by [Simon de] la Loubère, p. 69 [pt. 1, chap. 8; p. 20; 1969 edn].

[13] Ven-ti, third emperor of the fifth dynasty, cultivated the land with his own hands, and had the empress and her women make silk in the palace. [Jean Baptiste du Halde] *Description de l'Empire de la Chine*, ["Ven Ti, 3rd emperor, 5th Dynasty"; 1, 380 P; 1, 350 H; 1, 349 L].

Moreover, each year the emperor is informed of the plowman who has most distinguished himself in his profession; he makes him a mandarin of the eighth order.

Among the ancient Persians,[14] on the eighth day of the month named *Chorem ruz* the kings would lay aside their pomp and eat with the plowmen. These institutions are remarkable for encouraging agriculture.

[14] [Thomas] Hyde, *Historia religionis veterum Persarum in Sad-der* [chap. 19; pp. 253–254; 1700 edn].

CHAPTER 9

A means of encouraging industriousness

I shall show in Book 19 that, ordinarily, lazy nations are arrogant. One could turn effect against cause and destroy laziness by arrogance. In southern Europe, where peoples are so impressed by the point of honor, it would be well to give prizes to the plowmen who had best cultivated their lands and to the workers who had been most industrious. This practice will succeed in every country. In our time it has been used in Ireland to establish one of the largest textile mills in Europe.

CHAPTER 10

On laws related to the sobriety of peoples

In hot countries, perspiration dissipates much of the watery part of the blood;[15] a like liquid must therefore be substituted for it. Water is remarkably useful for this; alcoholic beverages there would coagulate

[15] Mr. Bernier, traveling from Lahore to Kashmir, wrote: "My body is a sieve; scarcely do I swallow a pint of water than I see it come out like a dew from all my members, including my fingertips; I drink ten pints a day and it does me no harm." [François] Bernier, *Travels in the Mogul Empire*, vol. 2, p. 261 ["Journey to Kachemire, Sixth Letter"; p. 388; 1916 edn].

the globules[16] of blood that remain after the dissipation of the watery part.

In cold countries, perspiration releases little of the watery part of the blood; it remains in abundance; therefore one can use spirits there without making the blood coagulate. One is full of humors there; alcoholic beverages, which give motion to the blood, are suitable.

The law of Mohammed that prohibits the drinking of wine is, therefore, a law of the climate of Arabia; thus, before Mohammed, water was the ordinary drink of the Arabs. The law[17] that prohibits the Carthaginians from drinking wine was also a law of the climate; in effect, the climate of these two countries is about the same.

Such a law would not be good in cold countries, where the climate seems to force a certain drunkenness of the nation quite different from drunkenness of the person. Drunkenness is found established around the world in proportion to the cold and dampness of the climate. As you go from the equator to our pole, you will see drunkenness increase with the degree of latitude. As you go from the same equator to the opposite pole, you will find drunkenness to the south,[18] as on our side to the north.

It is natural that excess should be more severely punished where wine is contrary to the climate and consequently to health than in countries where drunkenness has few ill effects for the person, few for the society, and does not make men frenzied, but only dull witted. Thus, the laws[19] that punished a drunken man both for the error committed and for drunkenness were applicable only to drunkenness of the person and not to drunkenness of the nation. A German drinks by custom, a Spaniard by choice.

In hot countries, relaxation of the fibers produces a great perspiration of liquids, but solids dissipate less. The fibers, which have only a very weak action and little spring, are scarcely used; little nutritious juice is needed to repair them; thus, one eats little there.

The differing needs of differing climates have formed differing ways

[16] In the blood there are red globules, fibrous particles, white globules, and the water in which all this swims.

[17] Plato, *Laws*, bk. 2 [674a]; Aristotle, *Oeconomica* [1344a33–34]; Eusebius, *Praeparationes evangelicae*, bk. 12, chap. 17 [12.25.1; 598d].

[18] This is seen among the Hottentots and the peoples at the tip of Chile, who are further to the south.

[19] Like those of Pittacus, according to Aristotle, *Pol.*, bk. 2, chap. 3 [1274b18–23]. He lived in a climate in which drunkenness is not a vice of the nation.

of living, and these differing ways of living have formed the various sorts of laws. If men communicate much with each other in a nation, there must be certain laws; there must be others for a people where there is no communication.

CHAPTER II

On the laws relating to diseases from the climate

Herodotus[20] tells us that the laws of the Jews about leprosy were drawn from the practice of the Egyptians. Indeed, the same diseases required the same cures. These laws, as well as the illness, were unknown to the Greeks and the first Romans. The climate of Egypt and Palestine made these laws necessary, and the ease with which this disease spread should make us feel clearly the wisdom and foresight of such laws.

We ourselves have suffered the effects of disease. The Crusades brought us leprosy; wise rulings were made that prevented it from spreading to the mass of the people.

One sees in the Law of the Lombards[21] that this disease was widespread in Italy before the Crusades and deserved the attention of legislators. Rotharis ordered that a leper driven from his house and kept in a particular spot could not make disposition of his goods, because he was presumed dead from the moment he was taken from his house. In order to prevent any communication with lepers, they were not allowed to have any possessions.[d]

I think that this disease was brought to Italy by the conquests of the Greek emperors, whose armies may have included militia from Palestine or Egypt. Whatever the case, its progress was checked until the time of the Crusades.

It is said that Pompey's soldiers, on returning from Syria, brought back a disease somewhat like leprosy. No regulation made at that time has come down to us, but it is likely that there were some, for this ill was checked until the time of the Lombards.

[20] [Herodotus, *The Persian Wars*] bk. 2. [Herodotus nowhere mentions the Hebrews, but consider 1.138 (9) for Persian customs concerning leprosy; consider also Leviticus 4.22, 30.]

[21] [*Leges Langobardorum*] bk. 2, tit. 1, para. 3 [Roth. 180] and bk. 2, tit. 18, para. 1 [Roth. 176].

[d] *effets civils.*

Two centuries ago, a disease unknown to our fathers traveled from the New World to this one and came to attack human nature at the very source of life and pleasures. Most of the important families of southern Europe were afflicted by a disease that became so common that it was no longer shameful and was merely deadly. It was the thirst for gold that perpetuated this disease; men continued their voyages to America and brought back new leaven of it each time they returned.

For reasons of piety one wanted to let this be the punishment of the crime, but the disaster had entered marriages and had already corrupted childhood itself.

As it is in the wisdom of legislators to keep watch over the health of the citizens, it would have been very sensible to check the spread of the disease by laws made on the plan of the Mosaic laws.

The plague is an evil whose ravages are even more prompt and rapid. Its principal seat is in Egypt, from which it spreads over the universe. In most of the states of Europe very good regulations have been made to prevent its entry, and in our times a remarkable means has been devised to check it; a line of troops is formed around the infected country, which prevents communication of the disease.

The Turks,[22] who have no police on these matters, see Christians in the same town escape the danger and themselves alone perish. They buy the clothing of those stricken by the plague, wear it, and go their way. The doctrine of a rigid destiny ruling all makes the magistrate a tranquil spectator; he thinks that god has already done everything and that he himself has nothing to do.

[22] [Paul] Rycaut, *The History of the Present State of the Ottoman Empire*, p. 284 [bk. 2, chap. 6; p. 46; 1703 edn].

CHAPTER 12

On laws against those who kill themselves[23]

We see in the histories that the Romans did not inflict death on themselves without cause, but the English resolve to kill themselves when one can imagine no reason for their decisions; they kill themselves in the very midst of happiness. Among the Romans, the act was

[23] The act of those who kill themselves is contrary to natural law and to revealed religion.

the consequence of education; it comes from their way of thinking and their customs: among the English, it is the effect of an illness;[24] it comes from the physical state of the machine and is independent of any other cause.

It is likely that there is a failure in the filtering of the nervous juice; the machine, when the forces that give it motion stay inactive, wearies of itself; it is not pain the soul feels but a certain difficulty in existence. Pain is a local ill which inclines us to the desire to see this pain cease; the weight of life is an illness having no particular place, which inclines us to the desire to see this life end.

It is clear that the civil laws of some countries have had reasons to stigmatize the murder of oneself, but in England one can no more punish it than one can punish the effects of madness.

[24] It could well be complicated by scurvy, which, especially in some countries, makes a man eccentric and intolerable to himself. François Pyrard, *Voyages*, pt. 2, chap. 21 [vol. 2, pt. 2; 3, 391; 1887–1889 edn].

CHAPTER 13

Effects resulting from the climate of England

In a nation whose soul is so affected by an illness of climate that it could carry the repugnance for all things to include that of life, one sees that the most suitable government for people to whom everything can be intolerable would be the one in which they could not be allowed to blame any one person for causing their sorrows, and in which, as laws rather than men would govern, the laws themselves must be overthrown in order to change the state.

For if the same nation had also received from the climate a certain characteristic of impatience that did not permit it to tolerate the same things for long, it can be seen that the government of which we have just spoken would still be the most suitable.

The characteristic of impatience is not serious in itself, but it can become very much so when it is joined to courage.

It is different from fickleness, which makes one undertake things without purpose and abandon them likewise. It is nearer to obstinacy because it comes from a feeling of ills which is so lively that it is not weakened even by the habit of tolerating them.

In a free nation, this characteristic would be one apt to frustrate the projects of tyranny,[25] which is always slow and weak in its beginnings, just as it is prompt and lively at its end, which shows at first only a hand extended in aid, and later oppresses with an infinity of arms.

Servitude always begins with drowsiness. But a people who rest in no situation, who constantly pinch themselves to find the painful spots, could scarcely fall asleep.

Politics is a dull rasp which by slowly grinding away gains its end. Now the men of whom we have just spoken could not support the delays, the details and the coolness of negotiations; they would often succeed in them less well than any other nation, and they would lose by their treaties what they had gained by their weapons.

[25] I take this word to mean the design of upsetting the established power, chiefly democracy. This was its meaning for the Greeks and Romans.

CHAPTER 14

Other effects of the climate

Our fathers, the ancient Germans, lived in a climate where the passions were calm. Their laws found in things only what they saw, and they imagined nothing more. And just as these laws judged insults to men by the size of the wounds, they put no greater refinement in the offenses to women. The Law of the Alemanni[26] on this point is quite singular. If one exposes a woman's head, one will pay a fine of six sous; it is the same for exposing a leg up to the knee; double above the knee. The law, it seems, measured the size of the outrages done a woman's person as one measures a geometric figure; the law did not punish the crime of the imagination, it punished that of the eyes. But when a Germanic nation moved to Spain, the climate required quite different laws. The laws of the Visigoths prohibited doctors from bleeding a *freeborn* woman except in the presence of her father or mother, her brother, her son, or her uncle. The imagination of the peoples was fired, that of the legislators was likewise ignited; the law suspected everything in a people capable of suspecting everything.

Therefore, these laws gave an extreme attention to the two sexes.

[26] [*Leges Alamannorum*] chap. 58, paras. 1–2 [A56.1–2; B58.1–2].

But it seems that in their punishing they thought more of gratifying individual vengeance than of exercising public vengeance. Thus, in most cases they reduced the two guilty ones to the servitude of their relatives or of the offended husband. A freeborn woman [27] who had given herself to a married man was put into the power of his wife, to do with as she wanted. These laws required that slaves[28] bind up and present to the husband his wife whom they had caught in adultery; they permitted her children[29] to accuse her, and they permitted torturing her slaves in order to convict her. Thus these laws were more proper for the excessive refinement of a certain point of honor than for the formation of a good police. And one must not be astonished if Count Julian believed an outrage of this kind required the loss of one's country or of one's king. One should not be surprised that the Moors, whose mores were so similar, found it so easy to establish themselves in Spain, to maintain themselves there, and to delay the fall of their empire.

[27] *Lex Wisigothorum*, bk. 3, tit. 4, para. 9 [3.4.9].
[28] Ibid. [*Lex Wisigothorum*], bk. 3, tit. 4, para. 6 [3.4.6].
[29] Ibid. [*Lex Wisigothorum*], bk. 3, tit. 4, para. 13 [3.4.13].

CHAPTER 15

On the differing trust the laws have in people according to the climate

The Japanese people have such an atrocious character that their legislators and magistrates have not been able to place any trust in them; they have set before the eyes of the people only judges, threats, and chastisements; they have subjected them at every step to the inquisition of the police. These laws that establish, in every five heads of families, one as magistrate over the other four, these laws that punish a whole family or a whole neighborhood for a single crime, these laws that find no innocent men where there can be a guilty one, are made so that all men distrust one another, so that each scrutinizes the conduct of the other, and so that each is his own inspector, witness, and judge.

On the other hand, the people of the Indies are gentle,[30] tender, and

[30] See [François] Bernier [*Travels in the Mogul Empire*], vol. 2, p. 140 ["History of the States of the Great Mogul"; p. 99, 1916 edn].

compassionate. Thus, their legislators have put great trust in them. They have established few penalties,[31] and these are not very severe or even strictly executed. They have given nephews to uncles and orphans to guardians, as elsewhere they are given to their fathers; they have regulated inheritance by the recognized merit of the heir. It seems they have thought that each citizen should rely on the natural goodness of the others.

They easily give liberty[32] to their slaves; they marry them; they treat them like their children:[33] happy is the climate that gives birth to candor in mores and produces gentleness in laws!

[31] See *Lettres édifiantes et curieuses*, vol. 14, p. 403 [Lettre du P. Bouchet, Pontichéry, October 2, 1714; 14, 402–404; 1720 edn] for the principal laws or customs of the peoples of India on the peninsula this side of the Ganges.

[32] Vol. 9 of the *Lettres édifiantes et curieuses*, p. 378 [Lettre du P. Bouchet, 9, 37; 1730 edn].

[33] I had thought that the gentleness of slavery in the Indies had made Diodurus say that in this country there was neither master nor slave, but Diodorus attributed to the whole of India what, according to Strabo [*Geographica*], bk. 15 [15.1.54], was proper only to a particular nation.

BOOK 15

How the laws of civil slavery are related with the nature of the climate

CHAPTER I

On civil slavery

Slavery in its proper sense is the establishment of a right which makes one man so much the owner of another man that he is the absolute master of his life and of his goods. It is not good by its nature; it is useful neither to the master nor to the slave: not to the slave, because he can do nothing from virtue; not to the master, because he contracts all sorts of bad habits from his slaves, because he imperceptibly grows accustomed to failing in all the moral virtues, because he grows proud, curt, harsh, angry, voluptuous, and cruel.

In despotic countries, where one is already in political slavery, civil slavery is more bearable than elsewhere. Each one there should be satisfied to have his sustenance and his life. Thus, the condition of the slave is scarcely more burdensome than the condition of the subject.

But in monarchical government, where it is sovereignly important neither to beat down nor to debase human nature, there must be no slaves. In democracy, where everyone is equal, and in aristocracy, where the laws should put their effort into making everyone as equal as the nature of the government can permit, slaves are contrary to the spirit of the constitution; they serve only to give citizens a power and a luxury they should not have.

CHAPTER 2

The origin of the right of slavery according to the Roman jurists[a]

One would never believe that pity established slavery and that in order to do so it went about it in three ways.[1]

The right of nations wanted prisoners to become slaves so that they would not be killed. The civil right of the Romans permitted debtors whose creditors might have mistreated them to sell themselves; and natural right wanted the children of an enslaved father who was no longer able to feed them to be enslaved like their father.

These reasons of the jurists are not sensible. It is false that killing in war is permissible except in the case of necessity; but, when a man has made another man his slave, it cannot be said that he had of necessity to kill him, since he did not do so. The only right that war can give over captives is that they may be imprisoned so that they can no longer do harm. Murdering in cold blood by soldiers after the heat of the action is condemned by all the nations of the world.[2]

2. It is not true that a freeman can sell himself. A sale assumes a price; if the slave sold himself, all his goods would become the property of the master; therefore, the master would give nothing and the slave would receive nothing. He would have some *savings*, one will say, but the savings are attached to the person. If it is not permitted to kill oneself because one will be lost to one's homeland, no more is it permitted to sell oneself. The liberty of each citizen is a part of the public liberty. This status in the popular state is also a part of sovereignty. To sell one's status as a citizen[b] is an act of such extravagance[3] that one cannot suppose a man would do it. If liberty has a price for the one who buys it, it is priceless for the one who sells it. Civil law, which has permitted the division of goods among men, could not have put among those goods some of the men who were to take part in the division. Civil law, which makes restitution in contracts that

[1] [*Corpus Juris Civilis*] *Institutes*, bk. 1 [1.3; *de jure personarum*].

[2] Unless one wants to mention those who eat their prisoners.

[3] I speak of slavery in the strict sense, such as it was among the Romans and as it is established in our colonies.

[a] By the Roman jurists M. means the views expressed in the *corpus juris civilis*.

[b] *qualité de citoyen*.

contain some injury, cannot keep from making restitution for an agreement that contains the most enormous of all injuries.

The third way is birth. This falls along with the other two. For, if a man cannot sell himself, even less can he sell a man who has not been born; if a prisoner of war cannot be reduced to servitude, still less can his children.

What makes the death of a criminal lawful is that the law punishing him was made in his favor. A murderer, for example, has enjoyed the law that condemns him; it has preserved his life at every moment; therefore, he cannot make a claim against it. It is not the same with the slave; the law of slavery has never been useful to him; it is against him in every case, without ever being for him, which is contrary to the fundamental principle of all societies.

One will say that the law has been useful to the slave because the master has nourished him. Therefore, those persons incapable of earning their living must be reduced to servitude. But one does not want such slaves as these. As for children, nature, which has given milk to mothers, has provided for their nourishment, and the remainder of their childhood is so nearly at the age when they have the greatest ability to make themselves useful, that one could not say that he who had nourished them, even though he was their master, had given them anything.

Moreover, slavery is as opposed to civil right as to natural right. What civil law could keep a slave from flight, since he is not in society and, consequently, civil laws are not his concern? He can be restrained only by a family law, that is, by the law of the master.

CHAPTER 3
Another origin of the right of slavery

I would as soon say that the right of slavery comes from the scorn that one nation conceives for another, founded on the difference in customs.

Lopez de Gomara[4] says that "the Spanish found, close to Sainte-

[4] *Bibliothèque anglaise*, vol. 13, pt. 2, art. 3. [Gomara is quoted in a review of Hans Sloane's *A Voyage to the Islands of Madera* [*sic*], *Barbados, Nieves, St. Christopher's, and Jamaica*, pp. 399–440 of the *Bibliothèque*; the Gomara quotation is on pp. 425–426 of the *Bibliothèque*. It can

Marie, baskets in which the inhabitants had put produce; there were crabs, snails, crickets, and grasshoppers. The victors treated this as a crime in the vanquished." The author claims that the right that made the Americans slaves of the Spanish was founded on this, not to mention the fact that they smoked tobacco and that they did not cut their beards in the Spanish fashion.

Knowledge makes men gentle, and reason inclines toward humanity; only prejudices cause these to be renounced.

be found in Francisco Lopez de Gomara, *Historia general de las Indias*, chap. 71, "Santa Marta," 1, 168–171; 1932 edn.]

CHAPTER 4

Another origin of the right of slavery

I would as soon say that religion gives to those who profess it a right to reduce to servitude those who do not profess it, in order to work more easily for its propagation.

It was this way of thinking that encouraged the destroyers of America in their crimes.[5] On this idea they founded the right of making so many peoples slaves; for these brigands, who absolutely wanted to be both brigands and Christians, were very devout.

Louis XIII[6] was extremely pained by the law making slaves of the Negroes in his colonies, but when it had been brought fully to his mind that this was the surest way to convert them, he consented to it.

[5] See the history of the conquest of Mexico by [Antoine de] Solis [y Rivadeneyra] [*History of the Conquest of Mexico by the Spaniards*], and that of Peru, by Garcilaso de la Vega [El Inca, *Royal Commentaries of the Incas and General History of Peru*].

[6] [Jean Baptiste] Labat, *Nouveau voyage aux isles de l'Amérique*, vol. 4, p. 114, 1722 edn [pt. 4, chap. 7, p. 38; 1698 edn].

CHAPTER 5
On the slavery of Negroes

If I had to defend the right we had of making Negroes slaves, here is what I would say:

The peoples of Europe, having exterminated those of America, had to make slaves of those of Africa in order to use them to clear so much land.

Sugar would be too expensive if the plant producing it were not cultivated by slaves.

Those concerned are black from head to toe, and they have such flat noses that it is almost impossible to feel sorry for them.

One cannot get into one's mind that god, who is a very wise being, should have put a soul, above all a good soul, in a body that was entirely black.

It is so natural to think that color constitutes the essence of humanity that the peoples of Asia who make eunuchs continue to deprive blacks of their likeness to us in a more distinctive way.

One can judge the color of the skin by the color of the hair, which, among the Egyptians, who are the best philosophers in the world, was of such great consequence that they had all the red-haired men who fell into their hands put to death.

A proof that Negroes do not have common sense is that they make more of a glass necklace than of one of gold, which is of such great consequence among nations having a police.

It is impossible for us to assume that these people are men because if we assumed they were men one would begin to believe that we ourselves were not Christians.

Petty spirits exaggerate too much the injustice done the Africans. For, if it were as they say, would it not have occurred to the princes of Europe, who make so many useless agreements with one another, to make a general one in favor of mercy and pity?

CHAPTER 6

The true origin of the right of slavery

It is time to seek the true origin of the right of slavery. It should be founded on the nature of things; let us see if there are cases where it does derive from it.

In every despotic government, it is very easy to sell oneself; there political slavery more or less annihilates civil liberty.

Mr. Perry[7] says that the Muscovites sell themselves easily: I know the reason well; it is because their liberty is worth nothing.

In Achim everyone seeks to sell himself. Some of the principal lords have no fewer than a thousand slaves,[8] who are the principal merchants, who also have many slaves under them, and these latter many others; they are inherited and there is a traffic in them. In these states, the freemen, who are too weak to oppose the government, seek to become the slaves of those who tyrannize the government.

Here lies the just origin, the one conforming to reason, of the very gentle right of slavery that one sees in some countries, and it has to be gentle because it is founded on the free choice of a master, a choice a man makes for his own utility and which forms a reciprocal agreement between the two parties.

[7]John Perry, *The State of Russia under the Present Czar* (Paris, 1717). [Perry describes all Russians as slaves to the Czar; perhaps M. has in mind pp. 258–260; 1967 edn.]
[8]William Dampier, *Voyages*, vol. 3 (Amsterdam, 1711) [vol. 2, pt. 1, chap. 7; 2, 67; 1906 edn].

CHAPTER 7

Another origin of the right of slavery

Here is another origin of the right of slavery and even of that cruel slavery seen among men.

There are countries where the heat enervates the body and weakens the courage so much that men come to perform an arduous duty only from fear of chastisement; slavery there runs less counter to reason, and as the master is as cowardly before his prince as his slave is before him, civil slavery there is again accompanied by political slavery.

Aristotle[9] wants to prove that there are slaves by nature, and what he says scarcely proves it. I believe that, if there are any such, they are those whom I have just mentioned.

But, as all men are born equal, one must say that slavery is against nature, although in certain countries it may be founded on a natural reason, and these countries must be distinguished from those in which even natural reasons reject it, as in the countries of Europe where it has so fortunately been abolished.

Plutarch tells us in the life of Numa that there was neither master nor slave in the age of Saturn.[c] In our climates, Christianity has brought back that age.

[9][Aristotle], *Pol.*, bk. 1, chap. 1 [1254a17–1255a2].

[c]See Plutarch, *Comp, Lycurgus and Numa*, 1.5.

CHAPTER 8

Uselessness of slavery among ourselves

Therefore, natural slavery must be limited to certain particular countries of the world. In all the others, it seems to me that everything can be done by freemen, however arduous the work that society requires.

What makes me think this is that before Christianity had abolished civil servitude in Europe, work in the mines was regarded as so arduous that one believed it could be done only by slaves or criminals. But today one knows that men employed there live happily.[10] One has encouraged this profession by small privileges; to an increase in work one has joined an increase in gain, and one has come to make them love their condition more than any other they could have assumed.

There is no work so arduous that one cannot adjust it to the strength of the one who does it, provided that reason and not avarice regulates it. With the convenience of machines invented or applied by art, one can replace the forced labor that elsewhere is done by slaves. The mines of

[10]One can learn what happens in this respect in the mines of the Hartz in lower Saxony and in those of Hungary.

the Turks, in the Province of Timisuara,[d] were richer than those in Hungary, but they did not produce as much because the imagination of the Turks never went beyond the brawn of their slaves.

I do not know if my spirit or my heart dictates this point. Perhaps there is no climate on earth where one could not engage freemen to work. Because the laws were badly made, lazy men appeared; because these men were lazy, they were enslaved.

[d] In present-day Rumania.

CHAPTER 9

On nations among whom civil liberty is generally established

Every day one hears it said that it would be good if there were slaves among us.

But, to judge this, one must not examine whether they would be useful to the small, rich, and voluptuous part of each nation; doubtless they would be useful to it; but, taking another point of view, I do not believe that any one of those who make it up would want to draw lots to know who was to form the part of the nation that would be free and the one that would be enslaved. Those who most speak in favor of slavery would hold it the most in horror, and the poorest of men would likewise find it horrible. Therefore, the cry for slavery is the cry of luxury and voluptuousness, and not that of the love of public felicity. Who can doubt that each man, individually, would not be quite content to be the master of the goods, the honor, and the life of others and that all his passions would not be awakened at once at this idea? Do you want to know whether the desires of each are legitimate in these things? Examine the desires of all.

CHAPTER 10

The various kinds of slavery

There are two sorts of slavery: real and personal. The real one is the one that attaches the slave to the land. Such were the slaves among the Germans, so Tacitus relates.[11] They held no office in the household; they returned a certain quantity of grain, livestock, or cloth to their master; the purpose of their slavery went no further. This kind of servitude is still established in Hungary, Bohemia, and several places in southern Germany.

The concern of personal servitude is service in the household, and it relates more to the person of the master.

Extreme abuses of slavery occur when it is personal and real at the same time. Such was the servitude of the Helots among the Lacedaemonians; they were subjected to all the work outside the household and to all sorts of insults within the household: this *helotism* is contrary to the nature of things. Simple peoples have only real slavery[12] because their women and children do the domestic work. Voluptuous peoples have personal slavery, because luxury requires the service of slaves in the house. Now, *helotism* unites in the same persons the slavery established among voluptuous peoples and the one established among simple peoples.

[11] [Tacitus] *Germania* [25].
[12] Tacitus [*Germania*, 20] says, "You could not distinguish master from slave by the delights of life."

CHAPTER 11

What the laws ought to do in relation to slavery

But whatever the nature of slavery, civil laws must seek to remove, on the one hand, its abuses, and on the other, its dangers.

CHAPTER 12
The abuse of slavery

In the Mohammedan states,[13] one is not only the master of the life and goods of the female slaves, but also of what is called their virtue or their honor. One of the misfortunes of these countries is that the larger part of the nation exists only in order to serve the voluptuousness of the other. This servitude is rewarded by the laziness that such slaves are given to enjoy, which is yet another misfortune for the state.

This laziness makes the seraglios of the East[14] delightful places even for those against whom they are made. People who fear only work can find their happiness in these tranquil places. But one sees that in this way one runs counter even to the spirit in which slavery is established.

Reason wants the power of the master not to extend beyond things that are of service to him; slavery must be for utility and not for voluptuousness. The laws of modesty are a part of natural right and should be felt by all the nations in the world.

For if the law that preserves the modesty of slaves is good in these states where unlimited power mocks everything, how good will it be in monarchies, how good in republican states?

A provision of the law of the Lombards[15] seems good for all governments. "If a master debauches the wife of his slave, both of them will be free." This tempering is admirable for preventing and checking the incontinence of masters without too much severity.

I do not see that the Romans had a good police in this regard. They gave rein to the incontinence of masters; in a way they even deprived their slaves of the right of marriage. The slaves were the meanest part of the nation, but mean as they were, it was good for them to have mores, and further, by denying them marriages, one corrupted the marriages of the citizens.

[13] See [John] Chardin, *Voyages en Perse et autres lieux de l'Orient* ["Voyage de Paris à Ispahan"; 2, 224; 1811 edn].

[14] See [John] Chardin [*Voyages en Perse et autres lieux de l'Orient*], vol. 2, "Description du marché d'Isagour" ["Voyage de Paris à Ispahan"; 1, 345–347; 1811 edn].

[15] [*Leges Langobardorum*] bk. 1, tit. 32, para. 5 [Liut. 140].

CHAPTER 13

The danger of a large number of slaves

Having a large number of slaves has different effects in the various governments. It is not a burden in despotic government; political slavery, established in the body of the state, makes civil slavery little felt. Those who are called freemen are scarcely more free than those without this status; and as these latter, whether eunuchs, freed men, or slaves, have almost all matters of business in their hands, the condition of a freeman and that of a slave are nearly alike. It is almost indifferent whether few or many people there live in slavery.

But in moderate states, it is very important not to have too many slaves. Political liberty makes civil liberty precious, and the one who is deprived of the latter is also deprived of the former. He sees a happy society of which he is not even a part; he finds security established for others and not for himself; he feels that his master's soul can expand, and that his own soul is constantly constrained to sink. Nothing brings the condition of the beasts closer than always to see freemen and not to be one. Such people are the natural enemies of society, and it would be dangerous for them to be numerous.

Therefore, one must not be astonished that in moderate governments the state has been so disturbed by the rebellion of slaves and that this has happened so rarely[16] in despotic states.

[16] The rebellion of the Mamelukes was a particular case: they were a body of militia which usurped the empire.

CHAPTER 14

On armed slaves

It is less dangerous to arm slaves in a monarchy than in republics. There a warrior people, a body of nobility, will sufficiently contain armed slaves. In a republic, men who are citizens will scarcely be able to contain people who, bearing arms, are the equals of the citizens.

The Goths who conquered Spain scattered throughout the country and soon were very weak. They made three noteworthy regulations:

they abolished the former custom that prohibited them from allying themselves with the Romans through marriage;[17] they established that all those freed from the fisc would go to war on pain of being reduced to servitude;[18] they ordered that each Goth would lead to war and arm a tenth of his slaves.[19] This number was not very large by comparison with the number who remained. In addition, these slaves led to war by their master did not make up a separate body; they were in the army and remained, so to speak, in the family.

[17] *Lex Wisigothorum*, bk. 3, tit. 1, para. 1 [3.1.1].
[18] Ibid. [*Lex Wisigothorum*], bk. 5, tit. 7, para. 20 [5.7.20].
[19] Ibid. [*Lex Wisigothorum*], bk. 9, tit. 1, para. 9 [9.2.9].

CHAPTER 15
Continuation of the same subject

When all in the nation are warriors, armed slaves are to be feared even less.

By the law of the Alemanni, a slave who stole something that had been put down[20] was subject to the penalty one would have inflicted on a freeman, but, if he took it by violence,[21] he was obliged only to restore the stolen thing. Among the Alemanni, actions whose principle was courage and strength were not odious. They made use of their slaves in their wars. In most republics, one has always sought to beat down the courage of the slaves; the Alemanni, sure of themselves, thought of increasing the audacity of their own; always armed, they feared nothing from the slaves; these were the instruments of their brigandage or of their glory.

[20] *Leges Alamannorum*, chap. 5, para. 3 [B5.3].
[21] Ibid. [*Leges Alamannorum*], chap. 5, para. 5 [B5.3], *per virtutem*: "by strength."

CHAPTER 16

Precautions to take in moderate governments

In the moderate state, the humanity one has for slaves will be able to prevent the dangers one could fear from there being too many of them. Men grow accustomed to anything, even to servitude, provided the master is not harsher than the servitude. The Athenians treated their slaves with great gentleness; one sees that the slaves did not disturb the state in Athens, whereas they shook it in Lacedaemonia.

One sees that the first Romans were not at all uneasy about their slaves. It was when they had lost every feeling of humanity for them that one saw arise those slave wars that have been compared to the Punic Wars.[22]

Simple nations who are attached to work are ordinarily gentler toward their slaves than those who have renounced work. The first Romans lived, worked, and ate with their slaves; they were gentle and fair to them; the greatest penalty they inflicted on them was to make them walk before their neighbors with a forked stick on their backs. Mores were enough to maintain the fidelity of slaves; they did not have to have laws.

But when Rome expanded, when the slaves of the Romans were no longer companions in their work but instruments of their luxury and arrogance, laws were needed as there were no mores at all. There had even to be terrible laws in order to establish security for these cruel masters who lived among their slaves as if among their enemies.

One made the senatus-consult Silanianium and other laws[23] which established that, when a master was killed, all the slaves under the same roof or within earshot would without distinction be condemned to death. Those who, in this case, gave refuge to a slave to save him were punished as murderers.[24] Even the slave whose master had ordered him to kill him[25] and who obeyed was guilty; the one who had not kept

[22] Florus [*Epitome rerum Romanorum*], bk. 3 [2.7.2], says, "Sicily, more cruelly devastated by the Slave War than by the Punic War."

[23] See all of the article *de senatus consultu Silaniano et Claudiano quorum testamenta ne aperiantur* [*Corpus Juris Civilis, Digest* 29.5].

[24] Law 3, para. 12 [*Corpus Juris Civilis, Digest* 29.5.3.12]; *de senatus consultus Silaniano.*

[25] When Anthony commanded Eros to kill him this was not only a command to kill him but also to kill himself, for, if he had obeyed, he would have been punished as the murderer of his master.

the master from killing himself was punished.[26] If a master were killed while traveling, one put to death[27] those who remained with him and those who had fled. All these laws were applicable even to those whose innocence was proven. Their purpose was to give the slaves a prodigious respect for their master. The laws were not dependent on civil government but on a vice or imperfection in civil government. They were not derived from the fairness of the civil laws because they were contrary to the principles of the civil laws. They were properly founded on the principle of war, except that the enemies were in the bosom of the state. The senatus-consult Silanianium derived from the right of nations, which wants a society, even an imperfect one, to preserve itself.

It is a misfortune in government when the magistracy sees itself thus constrained to make cruel laws. Because obedience has been made difficult, one is obliged to augment the penalty for disobedience or to make faithfulness suspect. A prudent legislator avoids the misfortune of becoming a terrifying legislator. Because the slaves among the Romans could have no trust in the law, the law could have no trust in them.

[26] Law 1, para. 22 [*Corpus Juris Civilis*, *Digest* 29.5.1.22]; *de senatu consultu Silaniano.*
[27] Law 1, para. 31, ibid. [*Corpus Juris Civilis*, *Digest* 29.5.1.31]; *de senatu consultu Silaniano.*

CHAPTER 17

Regulations to make between the master and the slaves

The magistrate should see to it that the slave is nourished and clothed; this should be regulated by law.

The laws should take care that slaves are looked after in sickness and in old age. Claudius[28] ordered that sick slaves who were abandoned by their masters would be free if they escaped. This law secured their liberty; it should also have secured their life.

When the law permits the master to take the life of his slave, it is a right he should exercise as a judge and not as a master; the law must order formalities, which remove the suspicion of a violent action.

In Rome when fathers were no longer permitted to put their children

[28] Xiphilinus, *in Claudio* [Cass. Dio, *Historia Romana*, 60 (61).29.7; Xiph. 142.26–29].

to death, the magistrates imposed[29] the penalty that the father wanted to prescribe. A like usage would be reasonable between master and slaves in countries where masters have the right of life and death.

The law of Moses was very crude.[e] "If someone beats his slave and the slave dies under his hand, he will be punished; but if the slave survives a day or two, he will not be punished because it is his silver."[f] What a people, whose civil law ceased to cling to natural law!

According to a Greek law,[30] slaves treated too roughly by their master could ask to be sold to another. In later times, there was a similar law in Rome.[31] A master incensed with his slave and a slave incensed with his master should be separated.

When a citizen mistreats the slave of another, the latter must be able to go before a judge. The laws of Plato[32] and of most peoples take natural defense away from slaves; therefore, they must be given civil defense.

In Lacedaemonia, slaves could expect no justice for either insults or injuries. The extremity of their unhappiness was that they were the slaves not only of a citizen but also of the public; they belonged to everyone and to one alone. In Rome one considered only the interest of the master[33] in the harm done to a slave. In the application of the Aquilian law, a wound inflicted on a beast and one inflicted on a slave were confounded; attention was paid only to the reduction in their price. In Athens[34] he who had mistreated the slave of another was punished severely, sometimes even by death. The Athenian law, with reason, did not want to add the loss of security to that of liberty.

[29] See law 3 of the *Code* [*Corpus Juris Civilis*, *Code* 8.46.3]; *de patria potestate*, which is by the Emperor Alexander [Severus].

[30] Plutarch [*Moralia*] *De superstitione* [166d].

[31] See the constitution of Antoninus Pius [*Corpus Juris Civilis*], *Institutes*, bk. 1, tit. 7 [1.7; *de lege Fufia caninia sublata*].

[32] [Plato, *Laws*] bk. 9 [865c–d]. [This may not be the clearest interpretation of the Plato passage, but I am convinced this is the one M. had in mind. Consider footnote 26.1 in bk. 26, chap. 3.]

[33] This was also often the spirit of the laws of the peoples who came from Germany, as can be seen in their codes.

[34] Demosthenes, *Orationes*, *Contra Midiam*, p. 610, Frankfurt, 1604 edn [21.47].

[e] The word here is *rude*, meaning both primitive and hard.

[f] Exodus 20.20–21.

CHAPTER 18
On freeing slaves

One certainly feels that when there are many slaves in a republican government, many of them must be freed. The trouble is that, if there are too many slaves, they cannot be contained; if there are too many freed men, they cannot survive and they become a burden to the republic; moreover, the republic can be equally endangered by too many freed men and by too many slaves. Therefore, the laws must keep an eye on these two drawbacks.

The various laws and the senatus-consults made in Rome for and against slaves, sometimes to hamper, sometimes to facilitate, the freeing of slaves, make their uneasiness in this regard easy to see. There were even times when one did not dare make laws. When, under Nero,[35] the senate was asked to permit the patrons to return ungrateful freed men to servitude, the emperor wrote that particular suits were to be judged and nothing general was to be enacted.

I scarcely know how to say which regulations a good republic should make on this matter; it depends too much on circumstances. Here are some reflections.

Slaves must not be freed suddenly in considerable numbers by a general law. One knows that, among the Volscians,[36] when the freed men became masters of the voting, they made an abominable law giving themselves the right to be the first to lie with girls who married freeborn men.

There are various ways to introduce new citizens into the republic imperceptibly. The laws can favor savings and put the slaves in a position to buy their liberty. They can set the term of servitude, as did those of Moses which limited the servitude of Hebrew slaves to six years.[37] It is easy each year to free a certain number of slaves among those who, by their age, health, or industry, will have the means to earn a living. One can even heal the ill at its root; as a great number of slaves are bound to the various employments given them, transferring to the freeborn a part of these employments, for example, commerce or navigation, decreases the number of slaves.

[35] Tacitus, *Annales*, bk. 13 [13.27].
[36] [Johann] Freinsheim, *Supplementorum Livianorum*, decade 2, bk. 5 [15.14].
[37] *Exodus*, chap. 21 [21.2].

When there are many freed men, the civil laws must specify what they owe to their patron, or the contract of emancipation must specify these duties for them.

One feels that their condition should be more favored in the civil state than in the political state because even in popular government, power should not fall into the hands of the common people.

In Rome, where there were so many freed men, the political laws in their regard were admirable. They were given little and excluded from almost nothing. They certainly took part in legislation, but they almost never influenced the resolutions that were taken. They could hold posts and even belong to the priesthood,[38] but this privilege was in a way rendered empty by the disadvantages they had in the elections. They had the right to enter the militia; but to be a soldier one had to be in a certain census. Nothing kept freed men[39] from uniting by marriage with freeborn families, but they were not permitted alliances with senators' families. Finally, their children were freeborn, although they themselves were not.

[38] Tacitus, *Annales*, bk. 3 [13.27].
[39] Harangue of Augustus, in Cass. Dio [*Historia Romana*], bk. 56 [56.7.2].

CHAPTER 19
On freed men and eunuchs

Thus in the government of many, it is often useful for the condition of the freed men to be but slightly below that of the freeborn and for the laws to work to remove their aversion to their condition. But in the government of one alone, while luxury and arbitrary power reign, there is nothing to be done in this regard. The freed men are almost always above the freemen. They dominate in the court of the prince and in the palaces of the important men; and, as they have studied the weaknesses of their master and not his virtues, they make him reign not by his virtues but by his weaknesses. Such men were the freed men in Rome at the time of the emperors.

When the principal slaves are eunuchs, despite the privileges accorded them, they can scarcely be regarded as freed men. For, as they cannot have families, they are bound to a family by their nature, and it is only by a kind of fiction that one can regard them as citizens.

Nevertheless, there are countries where they are given all the magistracies: "In Tonkin,"[40] Dampier says, "all the civil and military mandarins are eunuchs."[41] They have no family, and although they are naturally avaricious, the master or prince profits in the end from their very avarice.

The same Dampier[42] tells us that, in this country, eunuchs cannot do without wives and that they marry. This law permitting them to marry can be founded only, on the one hand, on the consideration one has there for such people, and, on the other, on the scorn one has there for women.

Thus, one entrusts magistracies to these people because they have no family, and yet they are permitted to marry because they have magistracies.

It is then that the remaining senses obstinately want to make up for those that are lost, and the enterprises of despair are a kind of enjoyment. Thus in Milton's work, that spirit, to whom only desires remain, being filled with his degradation, wants to make use even of his powerlessness.[g]

In the history of China, one sees a great number of laws that remove eunuchs from all civil and military employments, but they always return to them. It seems that eunuchs are a necessary ill in the East.

[40] [William Dampier, *Voyages*] vol. 3, p. 91 [vol. 2, pt. 1, chap. 4; 2, 14; 1906 edn].

[41] It was formerly thus in China. The two Mohammedan Arabs who traveled there in the ninth century say "the eunuch" when they want to speak to the governor in a town. [Eusèbe Renaudot, *Anciennes relations des Indes et de la Chine*, pp. 29, 60–61; 1718 edn.]

[42] [William Dampier, *Voyages*] vol. 3, p. 94 [vol. 2, pt. 1, chap. 4; 2, 15, 1906 edn.]

[g] John Milton, *Paradise Lost*.

BOOK 16

How the laws of domestic slavery are related to the nature of the climate

CHAPTER 1

On domestic servitude

Slaves are established for the family rather than in the family. Thus, I shall distinguish their servitude from that in which women are held in some countries and which I shall call domestic servitude proper.

CHAPTER 2

That, in the countries of the South, there is a natural inequality between the sexes

Women are marriageable in hot climates at eight, nine, and ten years of age; thus, childhood and marriage almost always go together there.[1] They are old at twenty: thus reason in women is never found with beauty there. When beauty demands empire, reason refuses it; when reason could achieve it, beauty exists no longer. Women should be held in dependence, for reason cannot procure for them in their old age an empire that beauty did not give them even in youth. Therefore, when reason does not oppose it, it is very simple there for a man to leave his wife to take another and for polygamy to be introduced.

In temperate countries, where women's charms are better

[1] Mohammed wed Cadigha when she was five, and took her to bed at eight. In the hot countries of Arabia and the Indies, girls are nubile at eight and give birth the following year. [Humphrey] Prideaux, *The True Nature of Imposture Fully Displayed in the Life of Mahomet* [p. 30; 1718 edn]. [M. is in error; he should be referring to Ayesha, not Cadigha.] One sees women in the kingdom of Algeria give birth at nine, ten, and eleven years. Laugier de Tassy, *Histoire du royaume d'Alger*, p. 61 [chap. 2, "Des Habitans du Royaume d'Alger. Des Maures"; p. 61; 1720 edn].

preserved, where they become marriageable later, and where they have children at a more advanced age, their husbands' old age more or less follows on their own; and, as they have more reason and knowledge there when they marry, if only because they have lived longer, a kind of equality between the two sexes has naturally been introduced, and consequently the law permitting only a single wife.

In cold countries, the almost necessary use of strong drink establishes intemperance among the men; so women, who have a natural reserve in this respect because they must always defend themselves, again have the advantage of reason over the men.

Nature, which has distinguished men by strength and by reason, has put no term to their power but the term of their strength and their reason. She has given women charms and has wanted their ascendancy to end with these charms, but in hot countries these are found only at the beginning and never through the course of their lives.

Thus, the law permitting only one wife has more relation to the physical aspect of the climate of Europe than to the physical aspect of the climate of Asia. It is one of the reasons why Mohammedanism found it so easy to establish itself in Asia and so difficult to spread into Europe, why Christianity has been maintained in Europe and destroyed in Asia, and why, finally, the Mohammedans make so much progress in China and the Christians so little. Human reasons are always subordinate to that supreme cause that does all that it wants and makes use of whatever it wants.

Certain reasons peculiar to Valentinian[2] made him allow polygamy in the Empire. That law, which was violent for our climates, was removed by Theodosius, Arcadius, and Honorius.[3]

[2] See Jordanes, *Romana* [#307; *MGH* Auct., vol. 5, p. 39] and the ecclesiastical historians.
[3] See law 7 [*Corpus Juris Civilis*] *Code* [1.9.7]; *de Iudaeis et caelicolis*, and *Novellae* 18, chap. 5 [18.5].

CHAPTER 3
That having multiple wives depends greatly on the support for them

Although a large number of wives depends much on the husband's wealth in countries where polygamy has been established, still one cannot say that wealth causes the establishment of polygamy in a state: poverty can have the same effect, as I shall say when speaking of savages.

In powerful nations polygamy is less a luxury than the occasion for a great luxury. In hot climates, one has fewer needs;[4] it costs less to support a wife and children. Therefore, the number of wives one can have is greater there.

[4]In Ceylon a man lives for ten sous a month; people there eat only rice and fish. *Recueil des voyages qui ont servi à l'établissement de la Compagnie des Indes*, vol. 2, pt. 1 ["Divers mémoires touchant les Indes Orientales, premier discours"; 2, 258; 1703 edn; 2, 228; 1725 edn].

CHAPTER 4
On polygamy, its various circumstances

According to calculations made in various places in Europe, more boys are born than girls,[5] whereas accounts from Asia[6] and Africa[7] tell us that more girls are born there than boys. Therefore the law permitting only a single wife in Europe and the one permitting several in Asia and in Africa had a certain relation to the climate.

In the cold climates of Asia, as in Europe, more boys are born than girls. This is, say the Lamas,[8] the reason for the law in cold countries that allows a woman here to have several husbands.[9]

[5]Mr. Arbuthnot finds that in England the number of boys exceeds that of girls; it has been mistakenly concluded that it was the same in all climates.

[6]See [Engelbert] Kaempfer, who reports an enumeration of Meaco, in which one finds 182,072 males and 223,573 females [Engelbert Kaempfer, *The History of Japan together with a description of the Kingdom of Siam, 1690–1692*, bk. 2, chap. 5; 1, 332; 1906 edn].

[7]See [William] Smith, *A New Voyage to Guinea*, pt. 2 [pp. 223–224; 1967 edn], on the country of Ante.

[8][Jean Baptiste] du Halde, vol. 4, p. 46, *Description de l'Empire de la Chine*, ["Observations sur le Thibit," 4, 572 H; 4, 461 P; 4, 443–444 L].

[9]Hasan ibn Yazid, Abu Zaid al Sirafi, one of the two Mohammedan Arabs who went to the

But I do not believe that there are many countries where the disproportion is so great that it requires the introduction of a law permitting several wives or one permitting several husbands. It means only that having many wives or even many husbands is not as far from nature in certain countries as in others.

I admit that if what the accounts tell us were true, that in Bantam[10] there are ten women for every man, it would be a very particular case of polygamy.

In all this I do not justify usages, but I give the reasons for them.

Indies and China in the ninth century, takes this usage for prostitution. This is because nothing else ran so counter to Mohammedan ideas. [Eusèbe Renaudot, *Anciens relations des Indes et de la Chine*, 56–57, 106, 109; 1718 edn.]

[10] *Recueil des voyages qui ont servi à l'établissement de la Compagnie des Indes*, vol. 1 ["Premier voyage des Hollandais aux Indes Orientales," 1, 383; 1702 edn; 1, 347; 1725 edn].

CHAPTER 5

A reason for a law of Malabar

On the coast of Malabar, in the caste of the Nairs,[11] men can have only one wife, whereas a woman can have several husbands. I believe one can discover the origin of this custom. The Nairs are a caste of nobles who are the soldiers of all these nations. In Europe one keeps soldiers from marrying; in Malabar, where the demands of the climate are greater, one has been content to make marriage as slight an encumbrance as possible for them; one wife has been given to several men, which diminishes to that degree the attachment to a family and the cares of a household and leaves these people their military spirit.

[11] François Pyrard, *Voyage*, chap. 27 [vol. 1, chap. 27; 1, 384, 372; 1887–90 edn]. *Lettres édifiantes et curieuses*, 3 and 10 [Lettre du R. P. Tachard, Pondichéry, February 16, 1702; 3, 187–189; 1713 edn, Lettre du P. de la Lane, Pondichéry, January 13, 1709; 10, 22–23; 1732 edn], on the Malleami of the coast of Malabar. This is regarded as an abuse of the military profession and, as Pyrard says, a woman of the Brahmin caste would never have several husbands.

CHAPTER 6

On polygamy in itself

Considering polygamy in general, independent of the circumstances that can make it somewhat tolerable, it is not useful to mankind or to either of the sexes, either to the one which abuses or to the one abused. Nor is it useful to children; and one of its major drawbacks is that the father and mother cannot have the same affection for their children; a father cannot love twenty children as a mother loves two. It is much worse when a woman has several husbands, for then paternal love depends only on the opinion which a father can believe if he wants, or which others can believe, that certain children belong to him.

It is said that the king of Morocco has in his seraglio white women, black women, and yellow women. The unfortunate man scarcely needs a color!

Possessing many wives does not always prevent one from desiring[12] the wife of another; with avarice as with luxury, thirst increases with the acquisition of treasures.

In the time of Justinian many philosophers who had been hampered by Christianity withdrew to the court of Chosroes in Persia.[a] What struck them most, says Agathias,[13] was that the people to whom polygamy was permitted did not even abstain from adultery.

Having multiple wives (who could guess it!)[b] leads to the love that nature disavows; this is because one sort of dissoluteness always entails another. During the revolution in Constantinople, when the sultan Ahmed was deposed, the accounts told that the people, pillaging the house of the kehaya,[c] found not a single woman. They say that it has come to the point that most of the seraglios in Algiers[14] have none.

[12] This is why women in the East are so carefully hidden.

[13] [Agathias] *Historiarum, On the Life and Actions of Justinian*, p. 403 [2.30].

[14] Laugier de Tassy, *Histoire du royaume d'Alger* [chap. 5, "Des Turcs du Royaume d'Alger"; p. 80; 1720 edn].

[a] This refers to Justinian's closing of the schools of Athens, 526 A.D. *ca.*

[b] Translators' parentheses.

[c] A kehaya was a Turkish viceroy, deputy agent, etc., or a local governor, or a village chief.

CHAPTER 7

On equality of treatment in the case of multiple wives

From the law concerning multiple wives follows the law concerning the equality of their treatment. Mohammed, who permits four, wants everything to be equal among them; food, clothing, and conjugal duty. This law is also established in the Maldives,[15] where one can have three wives.

The law of Moses[16] even wants the man, married by his father to a slave, who later marries a free woman, to deny her nothing in clothing, food, or duties. One could give more to the new wife, but the first was not to have less.

[15] François Pyrard, *Voyages*, chap. 12 [bk. 1, chap. 12; 1, 151; 1887–1889 edn].
[16] Exodus, chap. 21, vv. 10–11 [21.10–11].

CHAPTER 8

On the separation of women from men

One consequence of polygamy is that in the rich and voluptuous nations one has a very great number of wives. Their separation from the men and their enclosure follow naturally from their great number. Domestic order requires it to be so; an insolvent debtor seeks to hide from the pursuit of his creditors. There are climates in which the physical aspect has such strength that morality can do practically nothing. Leave a man with a woman; a temptation is a fall, attack is sure, and resistance null. In these countries there must be bolted doors instead of precepts.

One of China's classics considers it a prodigy of virtue for a man to be alone in a distant apartment with a woman and not do violence to her.[17]

[17] "To come upon a treasure of which one makes oneself master, or a beautiful woman alone in an isolated apartment, to hear the voice of one's enemy who will perish if one does not give aid: admirable touchstone." Translation of a Chinese work on morals, in [Jean Baptiste] du Halde, [*Description de l'Empire de la Chine*], vol. 3, p. 151 ["Caractères ou Moeurs des Chinois," 3, 183 H; 3, 151 P].

CHAPTER 9

A link between domestic government and politics

In a republic, the condition of the citizens is limited, equal, gentle, and moderate; the effects of public liberty are felt throughout. Empire over women could not be as well exercised; and, when climate required this empire, the government of one alone was the most suitable. This is one of the reasons it has always been difficult to establish popular government in the East.

On the other hand, the servitude of women is very much in conformity with the genius of despotic government, which likes to abuse everything. Thus in Asia domestic servitude and despotic government have been seen to go hand in hand in every age. In a government in which one requires tranquility above all and in which extreme subordination is called peace, women must be enclosed; their intrigues would be disastrous for the husband. A government that has not the time to examine the conduct of its subjects is suspicious of it simply because it appears and makes itself felt.

Let us assume for a moment that the fickleness of spirit and indiscretions of our women, what pleases and displeases them, their passions, both great and small, were transfered to an Eastern government along with the activity and liberty they have among us: what father of a family could be tranquil for a moment? Suspects everywhere, enemies everywhere; the state would be shaken, one would see rivers of blood flowing.

CHAPTER 10

Principle of morality in the East

In the case of multiple wives the more the family ceases to be a unity, the more the laws should reunite the detached parts to a center, and the more various the interests, the better it is for the laws to return them to one interest.

This is done chiefly by enclosure. Wives should not only be separated from men by their enclosure in the house, but they should also be separated within that same enclosure, so that each one becomes almost a particular family within the family. Women's entire practice of morality, modesty, chastity, discretion, silence, peace, dependency, respect, love derives from this; in sum here their feelings are universally directed to that which is best in the world by its nature, which is one's exclusive attachment to one's family.

By nature women have to perform so many duties proper to them that one cannot separate them enough from everything that could give them other ideas, from everything one treats as amusement and from everything one calls business.

In the various states of the East, the mores are purer as the enclosure of women is stricter. In large states, there are necessarily great lords. The greater their means, the more they are in a position to keep women in a strict enclosure and prevent them from returning to society. This is why women have such admirable mores in the empires of the Turks, Persians, Moguls, China and Japan.

One cannot say the same of the Indies, which have been divided into an infinity of little states by the infinite number of islands and the situation of the terrain, and which are rendered despotic by a great number of causes that I have no time to record here.

There, only the destitute plunder and only the destitute are plundered. Those whom one calls important men have only scant means; those whom one calls rich men have scarcely more than their sustenance. The enclosure of women cannot be strict there; one cannot take such careful precautions to contain them; their mores are inconceivably corrupt.

It is there that one sees the point to which the vices of climate, left in great liberty, can carry disorder. There nature has a strength, and modesty, a weakness that is incomprehensible. In Patani,[18] women's lust[19] is so great that men are constrained to make a kind of rigging to shield themselves from women's enterprises. According to Mr. Smith,[20] things are no better in the little kingdoms of Guinea. It seems

[18] *Recueil des voyages qui ont servi à l'établissement de la Compagnie des Indes*, vol. 2, pt. 2, p. 196 ["Voyage de T. van Neck"; 2, 222; 1703 edn; 2, 192; 1725 edn].

[19] In the Maldives, fathers give their daughters in marriage at the age of ten or eleven because it is a great sin, they say, to let them suffer the need for men. François Pyrard, *Voyages*, chap. 12 [vol. 1, chap. 12; 1, 152; 1887–1890 edn]. In Bantam, as soon as a daughter is thirteen or fourteen, she must be married if she is not to lead a disorderly life. *Recueil des voyages qui ont servi à l'établissement de la Compagnie des Indes*, p. 348 ["Voyage des Hollandais aux Indes," 1, 384; 1702 edn; 1, 348; 1725 edn].

[20] [William Smith] *A New Voyage to Guinea*, pt. 2, p. 192 of the translation [pp. 221–222; 1967 edn]. "When the women," he says, "meet a man, they seize him and threaten to

that in these countries, the two sexes lose everything, including the laws proper to them.

denounce him to their husbands if he disregards them. They slip into a man's bed, awaken him, and if he refuses them, they threaten to have him caught in the act."

CHAPTER 11
On domestic servitude independent of polygamy

In certain places in the East, it is not only multiple wives that require their enclosure; it is the climate. Those who read of the horrors, crimes, perfidies, atrocities, poisons, and murders caused by the liberty of women in Goa and in the establishments of the Portuguese in the Indies where religion permits only one wife, and who will compare these to the innocence and purity of the mores of wives in Turkey, in Persia, among the Moguls, in China, and in Japan, will see that it is often as necessary to separate women from men when there is only one wife as when there are many.

It is climate that should decide these things. What would be the use of enclosing wives in our northern countries, where their mores are naturally good, where all their passions are calm, scarcely active, and scarcely refined, where love has such a regulated empire over the heart that the slightest police is sufficient to lead them?

One is fortunate to live in these climates that allow communication between people, where the sex with the most charms seems to adorn society and where women, keeping themselves for the pleasures of one man, yet serve for the diversion of all.

CHAPTER 12
On natural modesty

All nations are equally agreed in attaching scorn to the incontinence of women; this is because nature has spoken to all nations. She has established defense, she has established attack; and, having put desires into both sides, she has placed temerity in the one and shame in the other. She has given individuals long periods of time to preserve themselves and only brief moments for their perpetuation.

Therefore, it is not true that incontinence follows the laws of nature; on the contrary, it violates them. It is modesty and discretion that follow these laws.

Besides, it is in the nature of intelligent beings to feel their imperfections; therefore, nature has given us modesty, that is, shame for our imperfections.

Therefore, when the physical power of certain climates violates the natural law of the two sexes and that of intelligent beings, it is for the legislator to make civil laws which forcefully oppose the nature of the climate and reestablish the primitive laws.

CHAPTER 13
On jealousy

Among peoples one must distinguish between jealousy that comes from passion and jealousy from custom, mores, or laws. The former is an ardent fever that devours; the latter, cold, but sometimes terrible, can be joined to indifference and scorn.

The first, which is abuse of love, is born of love itself. The other depends solely on the mores, the national manners, the laws of the country, the morality, and sometimes even the religion.[21]

Jealousy is almost always the result of the physical force of the climate, and it is the remedy for this physical force.

[21] Mohammed recommended to his disciples that they keep their wives safe; a certain Iman said the same thing on dying, and Confucius too preached this doctrine. [John Chardin, *Voyages*, "Description du Gouvernment", chap. 12, "Du Palais des femmes du Roi"; 6, 9–10; 1811 edn.]

CHAPTER 14
On household government in the East

One changes wives in the East so frequently that the domestic government cannot be theirs. Therefore, the eunuchs are put in charge of it; they are given all the keys, and they arrange the business of the house. "In Persia," says M. Chardin, "wives are given their clothing as it would be given to children."[d] Thus that concern which seems to suit them so well, that concern which everywhere else is the first of their concerns, is not theirs.

[d] John Chardin, *Voyages*, "Description du Gouvernement," chap. 12, "Du palais des femmes du roi;" 6,30; 1811 edn.

CHAPTER 15

On divorce and repudiation

A difference between divorce and repudiation is that divorce occurs by mutual consent on the occasion of a mutual incompatibility, whereas repudiation is done by the will and for the advantage of one of the two parties, independently of the will and the advantage of the other.

It is sometimes so necessary for wives to repudiate their husbands and always so trying for them to do it, that it is a hard law that gives this right to men without giving it to their wives. A husband is the master of the house; he has a thousand ways to hold his wives to their duty or to return them to it, and it seems that, in his hands, repudiation is only a new abuse of his power. But a wife who repudiates her husband exercises only a sad remedy. It is always a great misfortune for her to be constrained to go and look for a second husband when she has lost most of her charms while married to another. One of the advantages of youthful charm in wives is that, at an advanced age, a husband is inclined to kindness by the memory of his pleasures.

Therefore, it is a general rule that in all countries where the law grants men the faculty of repudiation, it should also grant it to wives. Further, in the climates where wives live in domestic slavery, it seems that the law should permit wives repudiation and husbands divorce only.

When wives are in a seraglio, the husband cannot repudiate one of them because of the incompatibility of mores; it is the husband's fault if the mores are incompatible.

Repudiation by reason of barrenness can occur only in the case of a single wife;[22] when one has several wives, this reason is not of any importance for the husband.

[22] This does not mean that repudiation by reason of barrenness is permitted in Christianity.

The law of the Maldives[23] allows one to take back a wife one has repudiated. The law of Mexico[24] prohibited them from coming back together on penalty of death. The law of Mexico was more sensible than the law of the Maldives; even at the time of dissolving a marriage, the Mexican law thought about its eternity; whereas the law of the Maldives seems to trifle equally with marriage and repudiation.

The Mexican law granted divorce only. This was an additional reason not to allow people to reunite who had voluntarily separated. Repudiation seems rather to stem from a quickness of spirit and some passion of the soul; divorce seems to be a matter of counsel.

Ordinarily divorce has great political utility, and as for its civil utility, it is established for the husband and the wife and is not always favorable to the children.

[23] François Pyrard, *Voyages* [vol. 1, chap. 12; 1, 153; 1887–1890 edn]. She is taken rather than another because there are fewer expenses in this case.

[24] [Antoine de] Solis [y Rivadeneyra], *History of the Conquest [of Mexico by the Spaniards]*, p. 499 [bk. 3, chap. 17; 345–355; 1973 edn].

CHAPTER 16

On repudiation and divorce among the Romans

Romulus allowed the husband to repudiate his wife if she had committed adultery, prepared poison, or tampered with the keys. He did not give wives the right to repudiate their husbands. Plutarch[25] calls this a very harsh law.

As the law in Athens[26] gave the wife as well as the husband the faculty of repudiating, and as one sees that the wives had obtained this right among the earliest Romans in spite of the law of Romulus, it is clear that this institution was one of those brought from Athens by the Roman deputies and that it was put into the Law of Twelve Tables.

Cicero[27] says that the causes of repudiation came from the Law of Twelve Tables. Therefore, one cannot doubt that this law had increased the number of causes for repudiation established by Romulus.

[25] [Plutarch, *Vit.*] *Romulus* [22.3].

[26] It was one of Solon's laws.

[27] [Cicero] *Philippicae* 2 [2.28.69]. "He has ordered his actress to take up her own property [this constituted divorce]; he based his case on the Twelve Tables" [L.].

The faculty of divorce was also a provision, or at least a consequence of the Law of Twelve Tables. For as soon as the wife or the husband separately had the right of repudiation, they would all the more be able to separate by agreement and by a mutual will.

The law did not require one to give any causes for divorce.[28] This is because, by the nature of the thing, there must be causes for repudiation and not for divorce; for when the law establishes causes that can dissolve a marriage, mutual incompatibility is the strongest of all.

Dionysius of Halicarnassus,[29] Valerius Maximus,[30] and Aulus Gellius[31] report a fact that does not seem probable to me; they say that, although in Rome one had the faculty of repudiating one's wife, there was such respect for the auspices that in 520 years[32] no one had used this right until Carvilius Ruga repudiated his wife as a consequence of her barrenness. But simply knowing the nature of the human spirit is to feel what a prodigy it would be if the law that had given the whole people such a right was used by no one. Coriolanus, on going into exile, counseled his wife to marry a happier man than himself.[33] We have just seen that the Law of Twelve Tables and the mores of the Romans greatly extended the law of Romulus. Why would there be these extensions if one had never used the faculty of repudiating? Moreover, if the citizens had such respect for the auspices that they never repudiated their wives, why would the Roman legislators have had less? How did the law constantly corrupt the mores?

By comparing two passages in Plutarch, one will see the element of marvel in the fact in question disappear. The royal law[34] permitted the husband to repudiate in the three cases mentioned. "And it wanted," says Plutarch,[35] "anyone who repudiated in the other cases to be obliged to give half his goods to his wife and to dedicate the other half to Ceres." Therefore, one could repudiate in any case by submitting to

[28] Justinian changed this. [*Corpus Juris Civilis*] *Novellae* 117, chap. 10 [117.10].

[29] [Dion. Hal., *Ant. Rom.*] bk. 2 [2.25.7].

[30] [Valerius Maximus, *Factorum et dictorum memorabilium*], bk. 2, chap. 4 [2.1.4].

[31] [Aulus Gellius, *Noctium Atticarum*], bk. 4, chap. 3 [4.3].

[32] According to Dion. Hal. [*Ant. Rom.*, 2.25.7] and Valerius Maximus [2.14]; and 523 [231 B.C.] according to Aulus Gellius [*Noctium Atticarum* 4.3.2]; M. has confused his sources: Aulus Gellius and Dionysius of Halicarnassus agree on the date of 231 B.C., Valerius dates the event at 604 B.C.

[33] See the discourse of Veturia, in Dion. Hal. [*Ant. Rom.*], bk. 8 [8.41.4].

[34] Plutarch [*Vit.*], *Romulus* [22.3].

[35] Ibid. [Plutarch, *Vit.*, *Romulus* 22.3.]

the penalty. No one did it before Carvilius Ruga,[36] "who," as Plutarch goes on to say,[37] "repudiated his wife for barrenness 230 years after Romulus;" that is, he repudiated her 71 years before the Law of Twelve Tables, which extended the power to repudiate as well as the causes for repudiation.

The authors to whom I have referred say that Carvilius Ruga loved his wife but that because of her barrenness the censors made him take an oath that he would repudiate her so that he could give children to the republic and that this made him odious to the people. The genius of the Roman people must be known in order to reveal the true cause of the hatred they conceived for Carvilius. Carvilius did not fall into disgrace with the people for repudiating his wife; that is a thing that did not disturb them. But Carvilius had sworn an oath to the censors that, given the barrenness of his wife, he would repudiate her in order to give children to the republic. The people saw that this was a yoke that the censors were going to put on them. I shall show later in this work[38] the repugnance they always had for such regulations. But where could such a contradiction between these authors have begun? Here Plutarch has examined a fact and the others have told of a marvel.

[36] In fact, sterility is not indicated as a cause in the law of Romulus. It seems likely that it was not subject to the penalty of confiscation, as it followed the order of the censors.
[37] In [Plutarch, *Vit.*] *The Comparison of Theseus and Romulus* [6.3].
[38] In bk. 23, chap. 21 [below].

BOOK 17

How the laws of political servitude are related to the nature of the climate

CHAPTER 1

On political servitude

Political servitude depends no less on the nature of the climate than do civil and domestic servitude, as will be shown.

CHAPTER 2

Differences between peoples in relation to courage

We have already said that great heat enervates the strength and courage of men and that there is in cold climates a certain strength of body and spirit that makes men capable of long, arduous, great, and daring actions. This is noticeable not only from nation to nation but even from one part of the same country to another. The peoples of northern China[1] are more courageous than those of the south; the peoples of southern Korea[2] are not as courageous as those of the north.

Therefore, one must not be surprised that the cowardice of the peoples of hot climates has almost always made them slaves and that the courage of the peoples of cold climates has kept them free. This is an effect that derives from its natural cause.

This is also found to be true in America; the despotic empires of Mexico and Peru were near the equator, and almost all the small free peoples were and still are toward the poles.

[1] [Jean Baptiste] du Halde [*Description de l'Empire de la Chine*, "Province de Pe Tcheli"], vol. 1, p. 112 [1, 133–134 H; 1, 112 P; 1, 111 L].

[2] So say the Chinese books. Ibid. [Jean Baptiste du Halde, *Description de l'Empire de la Chine*, "Histoire de la Corée"], vol. 4, p. 448 [4, 557 H; 4, 448 P; 4, 423 L].

CHAPTER 3
On the climate of Asia

Accounts tell us[3]

> that the north of Asia, that vast continent extending from about the fortieth parallel to the pole and from the border of Muscovy to the Eastern Ocean, has a very cold climate; that this immense terrain is divided from west to east by a chain of mountains that puts Siberia to the north and Greater Tartary to the south; that the climate of Siberia is so cold that, although the Russians have settlements along the Irtysh, they cultivate nothing there; that nothing grows in this country but a few small fir trees and shrubs; that the natives of the country are divided into destitute tribes like those of Canada; that the reason for this cold is, on the one hand, the elevation of the terrain, and on the other, that as one goes from south to north the mountains level out and the north wind blows everywhere unobstructed; and that, when this wind that makes Novaya Zemlya uninhabitable blows in Siberia, it makes it a wasteland. In Europe, on the other hand, the mountains of Norway and Lapland are admirable bulwarks shielding the countries of the north from this wind; that thus in Stockholm, which is at about 59 degrees latitude, the terrain can produce fruits, grains, and plants; and that around Abo, which is at 61 degrees north, just as at the 63rd and 64th degree, there are silver mines and the terrain is quite fertile.

We see further in the accounts

> that Greater Tartary, which is to the south of Siberia, is also very cold; that the country is not cultivated; that only pastures for herds are found there; that as in Iceland some bushes but not trees grow there; that close to China and the Moguls there are some countries where a kind of millet grows, but where neither wheat nor rice can ripen; that there are scarcely any spots in Chinese Tartary, at the 43rd, 44th, and 45th parallel, where it does not freeze seven or eight months a year; so that it is as cold as Iceland although it should be warmer than the south of France; that there are no

[3] See the *Receuil de Voyages au Nord*, vol. 8 ["Les moeurs et usages des Ostiackes," 8, 389–392; 1727 edn]; [Ebulgazi Bahadir Han, Khan of Khorezm] *Histoire généalogique des Tatars* [Bentinck's note, pt. 2, chap. 12, "De la tribu des Moguls," 1, 127–129; 1726 edn]; and Father [Jean Baptiste] du Halde, *Description de l'Empire de la Chine*, vol. 4 ["Voiage du Père Gerbillon en Tartarie"; 4, 103–528 H; 4, 87–422 P; 4, 214–380 L].

> towns, except four or five near the Eastern Ocean and some that the Chinese have built close to China for political reasons; that in the remainder of Greater Tartary there are only a few located in the Boucharies, Turkistan, and Charizme; that the reason for this extreme cold is found in the nature of the terrain, which is nitrous, full of saltpeter, and sandy, as well as in its elevation. Father Verbiest had found that a certain spot eighty leagues north of the Great Wall, toward the source of the Kavamhuram, that rose three thousand geometric feet above the coast of the ocean near Peking; that this elevation[4] is the cause for the fact that, although almost all the great rivers of Asia have their source in the countryside, it nevertheless lacks water, so it can be inhabited only near the rivers and lakes.

These facts stated, I reason thus: Asia has no temperate zone, properly so called, and the places situated in a very cold climate there are immediately adjacent to those that are in a very warm climate, that is, Turkey, Persia, the Mogul Empire, China, Korea, and Japan.

In Europe, on the other hand, the temperate zone is very broad, although the climates within it are very different from each other, as there is no relation between the climate of Spain and Italy and that of Norway and Sweden. But as the climate there grows colder gradually as one goes from south to north approximately in proportion to the latitude of each country, it happens that there each country is very like its neighbor, that there is not a notable difference between them, and that, as I have just said, the temperate zone is very broad.

From this, it follows that in Asia the strong and weak nations face each other; the brave and active warrior peoples are immediately adjacent to effeminate, lazy and timid peoples; therefore, one must be the conquered and the other the conqueror. In Europe, on the other hand, strong nations face the strong; those that are adjacent have almost the same amount of courage. This is the major reason for the weakness of Asia and the strength of Europe, for the liberty of Europe and the servitude of Asia: a cause that I think has never before been observed. This is why liberty never increases in Asia, whereas in Europe it increases or decreases according to the circumstances.

Although the Muscovite nobility was reduced to servitude by one of its princes, one will always see there marks of impatience that the southern climates do not produce. Did we not see aristocratic govern-

[4]Tartary is, then, a kind of high plateau.

ment established there briefly? Although another kingdom in the north has lost its laws, one can trust to the climate that it has not lost them irrevocably.

CHAPTER 4
A consequence of this

What we have just said agrees with the events of history. Asia has been subjugated thirteen times; eleven times by the peoples of the North, twice by those of the South. In the distant past, the Scythians conquered it three times, then the Medes and the Persians once each; then the Greeks, the Arabs, the Moguls, the Turks, the Tartars, the Persians, and the Afghans. I speak only of upper Asia and I say nothing of the invasions made in the southern part, which has continually suffered great revolutions.

In Europe, on the other hand, we know of only four great changes since the establishment of the Greek and Phoenician colonies: the first, caused by the Roman conquests; the second, by the inundations of the barbarians who destroyed these same Romans; the third, by the victories of Charlemagne; and the last, by the Norman invasions. And, upon examining these closely, one will find that, by these very changes, force was spread generally throughout all the parts of Europe. One knows the difficulty the Romans found in conquering Europe and the ease with which they invaded Asia. One knows the pains the northern peoples had to take to overthrow the Roman Empire, the wars and works of Charlemagne, the various enterprises of the Normans. The destroyers were constantly destroyed.

CHAPTER 5

That, when the peoples of northern Asia and those of northern Europe conquered, the effects of their conquests were not the same

The peoples of northern Europe have conquered as free men; the peoples of northern Asia have conquered as slaves and have been victorious only for a master.

The reason is that the Tartar people, Asia's natural conquerors, have become slaves themselves. They constantly conquer southern Asia, they form empires; but the part of the conquering nation that remains in this country is subject to a great master, who is despotic in the south, who also wants to be so in the north and who, with arbitrary power over the conquered subjects, claims it also over the conquering subjects. This can be seen today in that vast country called Chinese Tartary, which the emperor governs almost as despotically as China itself and which he extends every day by his conquests.

One can also see in the history of China that the emperors[5] sent colonies of Chinese into Tartary. These Chinese became Tartars and mortal enemies of China, but that did not keep them from carrying the spirit of Chinese government into Tartary.

Often a part of the Tartar nation that conquered was itself driven out, and it went back to its deserts with a spirit of servitude acquired in the climate of slavery. The history of China furnishes us with great examples, as does our ancient history.[6]

This is why the genius of the Tartar or Getae nation has always been similar to that of the empires of Asia. The peoples in the latter are governed by the cudgel; the Tartar peoples, by the lash. The spirit of Europe has always been contrary to these mores; and what the peoples of Asia have always called punishment, the peoples of Europe have always called gross offence.[7]

[5] As did Ven-ti [actually Vou-ti], fifth emperor of the fifth dynasty. [Father Jean Baptiste du Halde, *Description de l'Empire de la Chine*, "Fastes de la monarchie chinoise"; 1, 354 H; 1, 384 P; 1, 352 L].

[6] The Scythians conquered Asia three times and were driven out three times. Justin, bk. 2 [*Epitoma historiarum Philippicarum* 2.3].

[7] This is not at all contrary to what I shall say in bk. 28, chap. 20, on the manner of thinking of the German peoples concerning the staff. Whatever instrument it was, they always regarded as an affront the arbitrary power to beat and the action of beating.

When the Tartars destroyed the Greek empire, they established servitude and despotism in the conquered countries; when the Goths conquered the Roman empire, they founded monarchy and liberty everywhere.

I do not know if the famous Rudbeck, who in his *Atlantica*[a] has so praised Scandinavia, has mentioned the great prerogative that should put the nations inhabiting it above all the peoples of the world: it is that they have been the source of European liberty, that is, of almost all of it that there is today among men.

The Goth Jordanes has called northern Europe the manufactory of the human species.[8] I shall rather call it the manufactory of the instruments that break the chains forged in the south. It is there that are formed the valiant nations who go out of their own countries to destroy tyrants and slaves and to teach men that, as nature has made them equal, reason can make them dependent only for the sake of their happiness.

[8] [Jordanes, *Getica*, chap. 4]: "the workshop for the human race" [L.].

[a] Olof Rudbeck, *Atlantica*.

CHAPTER 6

An additional physical cause for the servitude of Asia and the liberty of Europe

In Asia one has always seen great empires; in Europe they were never able to continue to exist. This is because the Asia we know has broader plains; it is cut into larger parts by seas; and, as it is more to the south, its streams dry up more easily, its mountains are less covered with snow, and its smaller rivers[9] form slighter barriers.

Therefore, power should always be despotic in Asia. For if servitude there were not extreme, there would immediately be a division that the nature of the country cannot endure.

In Europe, the natural divisions form many medium-sized states in which the government of laws is not incompatible with the maintenance of the state; on the other hand, they are so favorable to this that without

[9] Waters are lost or evaporate before they converge or after they converge.

laws this state falls into decadence and becomes inferior to all the others.

This is what has formed a genius for liberty, which makes it very difficult to subjugate each part and to put it under a foreign force other than by laws and by what is useful to its commerce.

By contrast in Asia there reigns a spirit of servitude that has never left it, and in all the histories of this country it is not possible to find a single trait marking a free soul; one will never see there anything but the heroism of servitude.

CHAPTER 7
On Africa and on America

This is what I can say about Asia and Europe. Africa has a climate like that of southern Asia, and it has the same servitude. America,[10] destroyed and newly repopulated by the nations of Europe and Africa, can scarcely demonstrate its own genius today, but what we know of its former history is quite in conformity with our principles.

[10]The little barbarian peoples of America are called *Indios bravos* by the Spanish; they are much more difficult to subject than the great empires of Mexico and Peru.

CHAPTER 8
On the capital of the empire

One of the consequences of what we have just said is that it is important to a very great prince to choose well the seat of his empire. He who puts it in the south will run the risk of losing the north, and he who puts it in the north will easily preserve the south. I do not speak of particular cases: as mechanics has its frictions which often change or check its theoretical effects, politics, too, has its frictions.

BOOK 18

On the laws in their relation with the nature of the terrain[a]

CHAPTER I

How the nature of the terrain influences the laws

The goodness of a country's lands establishes dependence there naturally. The people in the countryside, who are the great part of the people, are not very careful of their liberty; they are too busy and too full of their individual matters of business. A countryside bursting with goods fears pillage, it fears an army. "Who is it that forms the good party?" Cicero asked Atticus.[1] "Is it the people in commerce and in the countryside? Not unless we imagine that the people for whom all governments are equal provided they are tranquil oppose monarchy."

Thus, government by one alone appears more frequently in fertile countries and government by many in the countries that are not, which is sometimes a compensation for them.

The barrenness of the Attic terrain established popular government there, and the fertility of the Lacedaemonian terrain, aristocratic government. For, in those days in Greece, one did not want government by one alone; now, aristocratic government is more closely related to the government by one alone.

Plutarch tells us[2] that "when the sedition of Cylon had been pacified in Athens, the town fell back into its former dissensions and was divided into as many parties as there were sorts of territories in the country of Attica. The people in the mountains wanted popular government at any cost; those of the plains demanded government by

[1] [Cicero, *Epistolae ad Atticum*] bk. 7 [7.7].
[2] [Plutarch, *Vit.*] *Solon* [13.1].

[a] "Terrain," *terrein*, includes the quality of the soil as well as the configuration of the land – flat, hilly, etc.

the principal men; those near the sea were for a government mixing the two."

CHAPTER 2

Continuation of the same subject

The fertile countries have plains where one can dispute nothing with the stronger man: therefore, one submits to him; and, when one has submitted to him, the spirit of liberty cannot return; the goods of the countryside are a guarantee of faithfulness. But in mountainous countries, one can preserve what one has, and one has little to preserve. Liberty, that is, the government they enjoy, is the only good worth defending. Therefore, it reigns more frequently in mountainous and difficult countries than in those which nature seems to have favored more.

The mountain people preserve a more moderate government because they are not as greatly exposed to conquest. They defend themselves easily, they are attacked with difficulty; ammunition and provisions are brought together and transported against them at great expense, as the country provides neither. Therefore, it is more difficult to wage war against them, more dangerous to undertake it, and there is less occasion for all the laws one makes for the people's security.

CHAPTER 3

Which countries are the most cultivated

Countries are not cultivated in proportion to their fertility, but in proportion to their liberty, and if one divides the earth in thought, one will be astonished to see that most of the time the most fertile parts are deserted and that great peoples are in those where the terrain seems to refuse everything.

It is natural for a people to leave a bad country in search of a better and not for them to leave a good country in search of a worse. Therefore, most invasions occur in countries nature had made to be happy, and as nothing is nearer to devastation than invasion, the best countries most often lose their population, whereas the wretched countries of the north continue to be inhabited because they are almost uninhabitable.

Historians' accounts of the crossing of the Danube by the Scandinavian peoples show that it was not a conquest but only a migration into deserted lands.

Therefore these happy climates had been depopulated by other migrations, and we do not know what tragic things occurred.

"Many records show," says Aristotle,[3] "that Sardinia is a Greek colony. It was formerly rich, and Aristaeus, whose love for agriculture has been so vaunted, gave it laws. But, it has fallen into ruin since then for, when the Carthaginians made themselves masters of it, they destroyed everything that could make it fit to nourish men and prohibited cultivating the land on penalty of death." Sardinia had not recovered in Aristotle's time, nor has it to this day.

The most temperate parts of Persia, Turkey, Muscovy, and Poland have not been able to recover after the devastations of the greater and lesser Tartars.

[3] Or the one who wrote the book [Aristotle, *De mirabilibus auscultationibus* 838b12–29, #100].

CHAPTER 4

Other effects of the fertility and barrenness of a country

The barrenness of the land makes men industrious, sober, inured to work, courageous, and fit for war; they must procure for themselves what the terrain refuses them. The fertility of a country gives, along with ease, softness and a certain love for the preservation of life.

It has been observed that the troops of Germany levied in places where the peasants are rich, as in Saxony, are not as good as the others. Military laws can provide for this drawback by a more severe discipline.

CHAPTER 5
On island peoples

Island peoples are more inclined to liberty than continental peoples. Islands are usually small;[4] one part of the people cannot as easily be employed to oppress the other; the sea separates them from great empires, and tyranny cannot reach them; conquerors are checked by the sea; islanders are not overrun by conquest, and they preserve their laws more easily.

[4] Japan is an exception to this because of its size and its servitude.

CHAPTER 6
On countries formed by the industriousness of men

Countries which have been made inhabitable by the industry of men and which need that same industry in order to exist call for moderate government. There are three principal ones: the two fine provinces of Kiangsu and Chekiang in China, Egypt, and Holland.

The former emperors of China were not conquerors. The first thing that they did to enlarge their country was the one that most demonstrated their wisdom. The finest provinces in the empire were seen to rise from under the water; they were made by men. The indescribable fertility of these two provinces has given Europe its ideas of the felicity of that vast region. But the continuous care necessary to protect such an important part of the empire from destruction required the mores of a wise people rather than those of a voluptuous people, the legitimate power of a monarch rather than the tyrannical power of a despot. Power had to be moderate there, as it was in times past in Egypt. Power had to be moderate there as it is in Holland, which nature made so that attention would be paid to her and that she would not be abandoned to indifference or caprice.

Thus, in spite of the climate of China, where one is by nature inclined to servile obedience, in spite of the horrors that attend an excessively large empire, the first legislators of China were obliged to make very good laws, and the government was often obliged to observe them.

CHAPTER 7

On the works of men

Men, by their care and their good laws, have made the earth more fit to be their home. We see rivers flowing where there were lakes and marshes; it is a good that nature did not make, but which is maintained by nature. When the Persians[5] were the masters of Asia, they permitted those who diverted the water from its source to a place that had not yet been watered to enjoy it for five generations, and, as many streams flow from the Taurus mountains, they spared no expense in getting water from there. Today, one finds it in one's fields and gardens without knowing where it comes from.

Thus, just as destructive nations do evil things that last longer than themselves, there are industrious nations that do good things that do not end with themselves.

[5] Polybius [*Historiae*], bk. 10 [10.28.3–4].

CHAPTER 8

General relation of the laws

The laws are very closely related to the way that various peoples procure their subsistence. There must be a more extensive code of laws for a people attached to commerce and the sea than for a people satisfied to cultivate their lands. There must be a greater one for the latter than for a people who live by their herds. There must be a greater one for these last than for a people who live by hunting.

CHAPTER 9

On the American terrain

There are so many savage nations in America because the land by itself produces much fruit with which to nourish them. If the women cultivate a bit of the earth around their huts, corn grows immediately.

Hunting and fishing complete their abundance. Moreover, grazing animals, like cattle, buffalo, etc., succeed better there than carnivorous beasts. The latter have had dominion in Africa from time immemorial.

I believe one would not have all these advantages in Europe if the earth were left uncultivated; there would be scarcely anything but forests of oak and of other unproductive trees.

CHAPTER 10

On the number of men in relation to their way of procuring subsistence

The number of men in nations that do not cultivate the land is found in the following proportions. As production on an uncultivated terrain is to production on a cultivated terrain, so the number of savages in one country is to the number of plowmen in another, and as for the people who cultivate the land and also cultivate the arts, this follows proportions that would require many details.

They can scarcely form a large nation. If they are herdsmen, they need a large country so that any number of them can continue to exist; if they are hunters, they are still fewer in number and they form, in order to obtain a livelihood, a smaller nation.

Their country is ordinarily full of forests, and as men have not dug canals for water, it is filled with marshes where each band camps and forms a small nation.

CHAPTER 11

On savage peoples and barbarian peoples

One difference between savage peoples and barbarian peoples is that the former are small scattered nations which, for certain particular reasons, cannot unite, whereas barbarians are ordinarily small nations that can unite together. The former are usually hunting peoples; the latter, pastoral peoples. This is clearly seen in northern Asia. The peoples of Siberia could not live together in a body because they could not feed themselves; the Tartars can live together in a body for some time because their herds can be brought together for that time. All the hordes can, therefore, unite, and this occurs when one leader has subjected many others; after which they must either separate or they must set out to make some great conquest of an empire to the south.

CHAPTER 12

On the right of nations among peoples who do not cultivate the land

As these peoples do not live on a limited and circumscribed terrain, they will have many things to quarrel about; they will dispute over uncultivated land, as our citizens dispute over inheritances. Thus, they will find frequent occasions for war in their hunting, and their fishing, and in providing food for their livestock, and carrying away slaves; and, lacking a territory, they will have so many things to regulate by the right of nations that they will have few to decide by civil right.

CHAPTER 13

On civil laws among peoples who do not cultivate the land

It is the division of lands that principally swells the civil code. In nations that have not been divided there will be very few civil laws.

One can call the institutions of these peoples *mores* rather than *laws*.

In such nations the old men, who remember things past, have great authority; one cannot be distinguished by one's goods there, but by arms and by counsel.

These peoples wander and scatter over the pastures or in the forests. Marriage will not be as secure as among ourselves, where it is fixed by the home and where the wife is attached to a house; they can more easily, therefore, change wives, have several of them, and sometimes mingle indifferently like beasts.

Pastoral peoples cannot be separated from their herds, which provide their subsistence, nor can they be separated from their wives, who take care of them. All this should, therefore, go together; the more so because, as they ordinarily live in great plains where few strongholds are built, their wives, children, and herds would become the prey of their enemies.

Their laws will regulate the division of the spoils and will, like our Salic laws, pay particular attention to theft.

CHAPTER 14

On the political state of peoples who do not cultivate the land

These peoples enjoy a great liberty: for, as they do not cultivate the land, they are not attached to it; they are wanderers, vagabonds; and if a leader wanted to take their liberty from them, they would immediately go and seek it with another leader or withdraw into the woods to live there with their family. Among these peoples, the liberty of the man is so great that it necessarily brings with it the liberty of the citizen.

CHAPTER 15

On peoples who know the use of money

When Aristippus was shipwrecked, he swam until he reached a nearby shore; he saw geometric figures traced in the sand; he rejoiced, judging that he had arrived among a Greek people and not among a barbarian people.

If you are alone and happen to come by accident to the land of an unknown people and if you see a coin, reckon that you have arrived in a nation with a police.

The cultivation of the land requires the use of money. Cultivation assumes many arts and much knowledge, and one always sees arts, knowledge, and needs keeping pace together. All this leads to the establishment of a sign for value.

Storms and fires led us to discover that the earth contained metals.[6] When they were once separated from the earth, it was easy to use them.

[6]Diodorus [Siculus] [*Bibliotheca historica* 5.35.3] tells us that shepherds found the gold [silver, according to Diodorus] of the Pyrenees in this way.

CHAPTER 16

On civil laws among peoples who do not know the use of money

When a people do not use money, one finds among them scarcely any other injustices but those stemming from violence; and weak people, by uniting, defend themselves from violence. Among them, therefore, there are scarcely any arrangements that are not political. But among a people who have established the use of money, one is subject to the injustices that come from trickery, and these injustices can be exercised in a thousand ways. Therefore, one is forced to have good civil laws there; these arise along with the new means and the various ways of being wicked.

In countries where there is no money, the plunderer carries away only things, and things are never alike. In countries where there is money, the plunderer carries away signs, and signs are always alike. In the former countries nothing can be hidden, because the plunderer always carries with him proofs for his conviction; it is not the same in the latter countries.

CHAPTER 17

On political laws among people who do not use money

What most secures the liberty of peoples who do not cultivate the land is that money is unknown to them. The fruits of hunting, fishing, or herding cannot be brought together in great enough quantity or be protected well enough for one man to be in a position to corrupt all the others; whereas, when one has signs for wealth, these signs can be amassed and distributed to whomever one wants.

Among peoples without money, each man has few needs and satisfies them easily and equally. Equality, therefore, is forced; thus, their leaders are not despotic.

CHAPTER 18

The force of superstition

If what the accounts tell us is true, the constitution of a people of Louisiana called the Natchez is an exception. Their leader[7] controls the disposition of the goods of all his subjects and makes them work according to his fancy; they cannot refuse him their heads; he is like the Grand Signior.[b] When an heir presumptive is born, he is given all the suckling children to serve him during his life. You would say he is the great Sesostris. This leader is treated in his hut with the ceremonies one would give to an emperor in Japan or China.

The prejudices of superstition are greater than all other prejudices, and its reasons greater than all other reasons. Thus, although savage peoples do not know despotism naturally, these people know it. They worship the sun, and if their leader had not imagined that he was the brother of the sun, they would have found in him only a poor wretch like themselves.

[7] *Lettres édifiantes et curieuses*, 20 [Lettre du P. Le Petit, la Nouvelle-Orléans, July 12, 1730; vol. 20, 106–113; 1731 edn].

[b] The Turkish emperor.

CHAPTER 19

On the liberty of the Arabs and the servitude of the Tartars

The Arabs and Tartars are pastoral peoples. The Arabs belong to the general case we have mentioned and are free; whereas the Tartars (the most singular people on earth) are in political slavery.[8] I have already[9] given some reasons for this last fact: here are some others.

They have no towns, they have no forests, they have few marshes; their rivers are almost always frozen; they live in an immense plain; they have pastures and herds and consequently goods; but they have no place of retreat or defense. As soon as a khan is vanquished, his head is

[8] When a khan is proclaimed, all the people shout, "May his word serve him as a sword!"
[9] Bk. 17, chap. 5 [above].

cut off,[10] so are his children's, and all his subjects belong to the vanquisher. They are not condemned to a civil slavery; they would be burdensome to a simple nation which has no land to cultivate and no need of domestic service. Therefore, they increase the nation. But one conceives that political slavery instead of civil slavery has had to appear.

Indeed, in a country where the various hordes are continually at war and constantly conquer one another, where the political body of each vanquished horde is always destroyed by the death of the leader, the nation in general can scarcely be free, for there is not a single part of it that must not have been subjugated a great many times.

Vanquished peoples can preserve some liberty, when, by the strength of their situation, they are in a position to make treaties after their defeat. But the Tartars, always defenseless, once vanquished have never been able to make conditions.

I have said in Chapter 2 that the inhabitants of cultivated plains were scarcely free; circumstances put the Tartars, who live in a wasteland, in the same situation.

[10] Thus one must not be astonished if Mir Vais [actually Mir Vais' son Mir Mahaud], after making himself master of Ispahan, had all the princes of the blood killed.

CHAPTER 20

On the right of nations among the Tartars

The Tartars appear gentle and humane to each other, and they are very cruel conquerors; they put to the sword the inhabitants of the towns they take; they believe themselves merciful when they sell or distribute the inhabitants to their soldiers. They have destroyed Asia from the Indies to the Mediterranean; the whole country that forms eastern Persia has become deserted on account of them.

Here is what seems to me to have produced such a right of nations. These peoples had no towns at all; all their wars were waged quickly and impetuously. When they expected to vanquish, they fought; they joined the stronger army when they did not expect to win. With such customs, they found that it was contrary to their right of nations for a town that could not resist them to check them: they did not consider a town as an assembly of inhabitants, but as a place apt to escape their power. They had no art for besieging towns, and they exposed themselves greatly when they did so; they took blood revenge for all the blood they had spilled.

CHAPTER 21

Civil law of the Tartars

Father du Halde says that, among the Tartars, it is always the last male child who inherits, because as the older ones gradually reach a position to lead the pastoral life, they leave their house with a certain quantity of livestock given them by their father and go to build a new dwelling. Therefore, the last of the males remaining in the house with his father is his natural heir.

I have heard it said that a similar custom was observed in some small districts in England, and it is still found in Brittany in the Duchy of Rohan, where it applies to commoners. No doubt it is a pastoral law that came from some lesser Breton people or was brought by some Germanic people. It is known from Caesar and Tacitus that these latter cultivated the land but little.

CHAPTER 22

On a civil law of the Germanic peoples

I shall explain here how a particular text from Salic Law, the text usually called the Salic Law, concerns the institutions of a people who did not cultivate the land, or at least cultivated it but little.

When a man leaves children, the Salic Law[11] wants the males to inherit the Salic land in preference to the daughters.

In order to know what these Salic lands were, one must discover what property was and what the use of the land was among the Franks before they left Germany.

M. Eckhart has nicely proven that the word Salic comes from the word *sala*, which means house, and thus that the Salic land was the land

[11] [*Lex Salica*] tit. 62 [D93; S34].

around the house.[c] I shall go further and examine what were the house and the land around the house among the Germans.

"They do not live in towns," says Tacitus,[12] "and they cannot tolerate their houses touching one another; each leaves around his house a small parcel of ground or a space which is enclosed and shut in." Tacitus spoke correctly. For, many laws in the barbarian codes[13] have different provisions for those who knocked down this enclosure, and for those who entered the house itself.

We know from Tacitus and Caesar that the lands the Germans cultivated were given to them for only a year, and then became public again. The Germans had no patrimony other than the house and a bit of land within the enclosure around the house.[14] This particular patrimony belonged to the males. Indeed, why would it have belonged to the daughters? They entered other houses.

Therefore, the Salic land was that enclosure appended to the German's house; it was the only property he had. After the conquest the Franks acquired new properties, which continued to be called Salic lands.

When the Franks lived in Germany, their goods were slaves, herds, horses, arms, etc. The house and the small portion of land adjoining it were naturally given to the male children who were to live there. But, when the Franks had acquired extensive lands after the conquest, it was found harsh that the daughters and their children could not have a share. A usage was introduced which permitted the father to recall his daughter and his daughter's children. The law was silenced, and these sorts of recalls must have been common because formulas were made for them.[15]

Among all these formulas, I find a singular one.[16] A grandfather

[12] [Tacitus] *Germania* [16]: "It is well known that the peoples of Germany have no cities, nor do they even permit their houses to be joined one to another. They live separate and scattered where a fountain, a field, or a glade has attracted them. They do not establish their villages in our fashion with the buildings being connected and joined together; instead, each home is surrounded by an open space" [L.].

[13] *Leges Alamannorum*, chap. 10 [A9; B10] and *Lex Baiwariorum*, tit. 10, paras. 1–2 [11.1–2].

[14] This enclosure is called *curtis* in the charters.

[15] See Marculf [*Marculfi formulae*], bk. 2, form. 10 and 12 [2.10, 12]; *Appendice de Marculfe*, form. 49 [*Cartae Senonicae*, 45]; and the old formulas, known as "Sirmondi's," form. 22 [*Formulae Turonenses vulgo Sirmondicae dictae* 22].

[16] *Formulae Salicae Lindenbrogianae*, form. 55 [12].

[c] Johann Georg von Eckhart, *Leges Francorum Salicae et Ripuariae*, pp. 20, 42, 44, 56; 1720 edn.

recalls his grandchildren to inherit with his sons and daughters. What had the Salic Law become? It must have been no longer observed, even at that time, or the continual usage of recalling daughters must have qualified them to inherit in the most ordinary case.

As the Salic Law did not have as its purpose a preference for one sex over another, it had still less that of perpetuating a family, a name, or a transfer of land; none of this entered the heads of the Germans. It was a purely economic law which gave the house and the land around it to the males who were to live in it and for whom consequently it was best suited.

One need only transcribe here the article, *On Alloidal Lands* in the Salic Law, that famous text so talked about and so little read:

1. "If a man dies without children, his father or his mother will inherit from him. 2. If he has neither father nor mother, his brother or sister will inherit from him. 3. If he has neither brother nor sister, his mother's sister will inherit from him. 4. If his mother has no sister, his father's sister will inherit from him. 5. If his father has no sister, the nearest relative on the male side will inherit. 6. No portion[17] of the Salic land will pass to the females, but it will belong to the males, that is, the male children will inherit from their father."

It is clear that the first five articles concern the inheritance of one who dies without children; and the sixth, the inheritance of one who has children.

When a man died without children, the law wanted one sex to be preferred over the other only in certain cases. In the first two degrees of inheritance, the advantages of males and females were the same; in the third and fourth, women were preferred; males were preferred in the fifth.

I find the seeds of these eccentricities in Tacitus. "The children of sisters,"[18] he says, "are cherished by their uncle as by their own father. There are some people who consider this bond as closer and even holier; they prefer it when they take hostages." This is why our first

[17]"No portion of the Salic lands will pass as inheritance to women, but it will be acquired by the male sex, that is, the sons shall succeed to the inheritance" [L.]. [*Pactus legis Salicae*], tit. 62, para. 6 [59.6].

[18]"The sons of sisters are held in the same honor by uncles as by the father. Indeed, some judge this blood tie as more sacred and binding, and demand them more often when taking hostages, thinking to have a firmer and more extensive hold upon their spirits and household" [L.]. [Tacitus] *Germania* [20].

historians[19] tell us so much about the love of the Frankish kings for their sister and their sister's children. For if the children of sisters were regarded in the brother's house as his own, it was natural for the children to regard their aunt as their own mother.

The mother's sister was preferred to the father's sister; this is explained by other texts of the Salic law; when a woman was a widow,[20] she came under the guardianship of her husband's relatives; the law preferred the female relatives to the male relatives for this guardianship. Indeed, a woman who entered a family and joined those persons of her sex was closer to the female relatives than to the male relatives. Moreover, when one man had killed another man[21] and could not satisfy the pecuniary penalty he incurred, the law permitted him to cede his goods, and his relatives had to make up what was lacking. After his father, mother, and brother, it was the mother's sister who paid, as if this bond had something more tender about it; now, the kinship that gives burdens had likewise to give advantages.

The Salic Law wanted the closest male relative after the father's sister to have the inheritance, but if he were a relative beyond the fifth degree, he would not inherit it. Thus, a woman of the fifth degree would have inherited in preference to a man of the sixth; and this is seen in the law of the Ripuarian Franks,[22] a faithful interpreter of the Salic Law in the article concerning allodial lands, where it follows step by step the same article of that law.

If the father left children, the Salic Law wanted the daughters to be excluded from the inheritance of the Salic land and wanted this to belong to the male children.

It would be easy for me to prove that the Salic law did not exclude daughters from the Salic land without distinction, but rather only in the case where brothers would exclude them. This is seen in the Salic law itself, which, after saying that the women would possess nothing of the Salic land and that only men would, interprets and restrains itself; "that is," it says, "the son will inherit the father's legacy."

[19] See in Gregory of Tours [*Historia ecclesiastica*] bk. 8, chaps. 18 and 20, and bk. 9, chaps, 16 and 20 [8.18.28; 9.16.20], Guntram's fury at the ill treatment done Ingunda, his niece, by Lenvigilda, and how Childebert, his brother, made war to avenge her.

[20] *Lex Salica*, tit. 47 [D79; S24].

[21] *Lex Salica*, tit. 61, para. 1 [D100; S17].

[22] "And then in succession up to the fifth degree, whoever is closer will succeed to the inheritance" [L.]. [*Lex Ribuaria*] tit. 56, para. 6 [57.3].

2. The text of the Salic law is clarified by the law of the Ripuarian Franks, which has also an article[23] on alloidal lands quite in conformity with the Salic Law.

3. The laws of these barbarian peoples, who all come from Germany, interpret each other; the more so because they all have nearly the same spirit. The law of the Saxons[24] wants the father and mother to leave their inheritance to their son and not to their daughter, but if there are only daughters, it wants them to have the entire inheritance.

4. We have two old formulas,[25] which propose the case in which, in accord with the Salic Law, daughters are excluded by the males: this is when they compete with their brother.

5. Another formula[26] proves that the daughter inherited in preference to the grandson; therefore, she was excluded only by the son.

6. If the daughters had been generally excluded from the inheritance of lands by the Salic Law, it would be impossible to explain the histories, formulas, and charters, which continually speak of the lands and goods of women under the Merovingians.[d]

It has been mistakenly said[27] that the Salic lands were fiefs. 1. This article is entitled, *On Alloidal Lands*. 2. In the beginning fiefs were not hereditary. 3. If the Salic lands had been fiefs, how could Marculf have treated as impious the custom which excluded women from inheriting them, for even males did not inherit fiefs? 4. The charters that are cited to prove that the Salic lands were fiefs prove only that they were free lands.[e] 5. Fiefs were established only after the conquest, and Salic usages existed before the Franks left Germany. 6. It was not the Salic Law that, by limiting the inheritance of women, formed the establishment of fiefs, but rather the establishment of fiefs that put limits on both the inheritance of women and the provisions of the Salic Law.

[23] [*Lex Ribuaria*] tit. 56 [57].

[24] [*Leges Saxonum*] tit. 7, para. 1 [41]. "The father and mother being dead, they shall leave the inheritance to the son, not the daughter" [L.]; para. 4 [44] "They being dead having no sons but leaving only a daughter, the entire inheritance belongs to her" [L.].

[25] In Marculf, bk. 2, form. 12 [*Marculfi Formulae* 2.12], and the *Appendice de Marculfe*, form. 49 [*Cartae Senonicae* 45].

[26] In *Formulae Salicae Lindenbrogianae*, form. 55 [12].

[27] Du Cange, Pithou, etc.

[d] Montesquieu calls the ruling families of France the "First," "Second," and "Third Race." We refer to them as the Merovingians, Carolingians, and Capetians. See also note [j], bk. 23.

[e] *terres franches*. Occasionally Montesquieu uses *franc*, meaning "free"; the instances are marked in these notes.

After what we have just said, one would not believe that the personal inheritance by males of the crown of France could come from the Salic Law. It is, however, indubitable that it comes from there. I can prove this by the various codes of the barbarian peoples. The Salic law[28] and the law of the Burgundians[29] did not give daughters the right to inherit land with their brothers, nor did they inherit the crown. The law of the Visigoths,[30] on the other hand, permitted daughters[31] to inherit land with their brothers; women were qualified to inherit the crown. Among these peoples, the provisions of the civil law forced the political law.[32]

This was not the only case among the Franks where the political law gave way to the civil law. By the provision of the Salic Law, all brothers inherited the land equally, and this was also the provision of the law of the Burgundians. Thus, in the Frankish monarchy and in that of the Burgundians, all the brothers inherited the crown, if we except a few cases of violence, murder and usurpation among the Burgundians.

[28] [*Lex Salica*] tit. 62 [D93; S34].

[29] [*Leges Burgundionum*] tit. 1, para. 3; tit. 14, para. 1; tit. 51 [1.3; 14.1; 51].

[30] [*Lex Wisigothorum*] bk. 4, tit. 2, para. 1 [4.2.1].

[31] The German nations, says Tacitus, had some usages in common; they also had some particular ones. [*Germania* 27.]

[32] Among the Ostrogoths, the crown passed twice from women to men: once through Amalasuntha, in the person of Athalaric, and once through Amalafrede, in the person of Theodohad. It is not that, among them, women could not reign for themselves: Amalasuntha, after the death of Athalaric, reigned, and reigned even after the election of Theodohad and concurrently with him. See the letters of Amalasuntha and those of Theodohad, in Cassiodorus [*Variae*], bk. 10.

CHAPTER 23

On the long hair of the Frankish kings

Peoples who do not cultivate the land do not have even the idea of luxury. The admirable simplicity of the Germanic peoples must be seen in Tacitus; art did not fashion their ornaments, they found them in nature. If the family of their leader was to be marked by some sign, it was again in nature that they had to seek it; the kings of the Franks, Burgundians, and Visigoths wore their long hair as a diadem.

CHAPTER 24

On the marriages of the Frankish kings

I have mentioned earlier that, among peoples who do not cultivate the land, marriages were much less fixed and one ordinarily took several wives. "The Germans were almost alone[33] among the barbarians to be content with a single wife, if one excepts,"[34] says Tacitus, "some persons who, not because of their dissoluteness, but because of their nobility, had many."

This explains why the Merovingian kings had such a great number of wives. These marriages were less an evidence of incontinence than an attribute of rank; it would have wounded them in a tender spot to make them lose such a prerogative.[35] This explains why the example of the kings was not followed by their subjects.

33 "Almost alone among the barbarians they are content with one wife" [L.]. [Tacitus] *Germania* [18].

34 "Except for a very few who are sought for numerous marriages, not on account of lust, but rather for their nobility" [L.]. Ibid. [Tacitus, *Germania*, 18].

35 See Fredegarius' *Chronicon* for *anno* 628 [chap. 58].

CHAPTER 25

Childeric

"Marriages among the Germans are severe;"[36] says Tacitus, "vices are not subject to ridicule there; to corrupt or to be corrupted is not called a usage or a way of life; in so numerous a nation there are few examples[37] of the violation of conjugal faith."

This explains the expulsion of Childeric; he offended the strict mores that conquest had not had time to change.

36 "A severe code for marriage . . . No one laughs at vice; no one says it is the spirit of the times to corrupt and be corrupted" [L.]. [Tacitus] *Germania* [18, 19].

37 "Among such a numerous people, adultery is very rare" [L.]. Ibid. [Tacitus, *Germania*, 19].

CHAPTER 26

On the coming of age of the Frankish kings

Barbarian peoples who do not cultivate the land have no territory properly so-called and are, as we have said, governed by the right of nations rather than by civil right. Therefore, they are almost always armed. Thus Tacitus says that "the Germans engaged in no public or particular matters of business without being armed.[38] They expressed their view by a sign they made with their weapons.[39] As soon as they could carry weapons they were presented to the assembly;[40] a javelin was put in their hands;[41] from this time on they had left behind their childhood;[42] they had been a part of the family, they became part of the republic."

"Eagles," said the king of the Ostrogoths,[43] "stop giving food to their little ones as soon as their feathers and claws are formed; these little ones no longer need the help of others when they themselves go in search of prey. It would be shameful if our youth who are in our armies were presumed to be too weak to control their own goods or regulate the conduct of their lives. Among the Goths it is virtue that sets the coming of age."

Childebert II was fifteen years old[44] when Guntram, his uncle, declared him of age and capable of governing by himself. One sees in the law of the Ripuarian Franks that this age of fifteen years, the ability to carry arms, and the time of one's coming of age go together. "If a Ripuarian has died or has been killed," it is said there,[45] "and he has left a son, the son cannot go in pursuit, or be pursued in judgment,

[38] "They act upon no business, public or private, unless they are armed" [L.]. Tacitus, *Germania* [13].

[39] "If the opinions are displeasing, they are spurned; if pleasing, they shake their spears" [L.]. Ibid. [Tacitus, *Germania*, 11].

[40] "It is not the custom for one to take up arms before the state has approved his competence" [L.]. [Tacitus, *Germania*, 13].

[41] "Then, in the council itself, either some prince or his father, or kinsman, equips the youth with a shield and spear" [L.]. [Tacitus, *Germania*, 13.]

[42] "These [arms] are what the toga is to us, the first honor of youth; before, he is part of the household; afterward, part of the republic" [L.] [Tacitus, *Germania*, 13].

[43] Theodoric, in Cassiodorus [*Variae*], bk. 1, letter 38 [1.38].

[44] He was scarcely more than five, says Gregory of Tours [*Historia ecclesiastica francorum*], bk. 5, chap. 1 [5.1], when he succeeded to his father in 575; that is, he was five. Guntram declared him of age in 585; then he was fifteen.

[45] [*Lex Ribuaria*] tit. 81 [84].

unless he is fully fifteen years old; at that time he will answer for himself or choose a champion." The spirit had to be sufficiently formed for one to be able to defend oneself in a judgment, and the body, for one to be able to defend oneself in combat. Among the Burgundians,[46] who also had the usage of combat in judicial actions, the coming of age was also set at fifteen years.

Agathias tells us that the weapons of the Franks were light; therefore, they could come of age at fifteen. Later, weapons were heavier; they were already so in the time of Charlemagne, as is apparent in our capitularies and romances. Those who had fiefs,[47] and who consequently had to do military service, came of age only when they were twenty-one.[48]

[46] [*Leges Burgundionum*] tit. 87 [87.1].
[47] There was no change for common men [*roturiers*].
[48] St. Louis came of age only then. This was changed by an edict of Charles V, in 1374. [*Recueil general des anciennes lois françaises*, #546; 5, 415–424; 1824 edn.]

CHAPTER 27

Continuation of the same subject

It has been seen that among the Germans one did not go to the assembly before reaching one's majority; one was part of the family and not part of the republic. This caused the children of Clodomir, King of Orleans and conqueror of Burgundy, not to be declared kings because they could not be presented to the asembly at their tender age. They were not yet kings, but they were to become kings when they were able to carry weapons; and, meanwhile Clotilda, their grandmother, governed the state.[49] Their uncles Clotaire and Childebert slaughtered them and divided their kingdom. Because of this example later princes who were wards were declared king immediately after the death of their fathers. Thus, Duke Gondovald saved Childebert II from the cruelty of Chilperic and had him declared king[50] at the age of five.

[49] It appears in Gregory of Tours, *Historia ecclesiastica Francorum*, bk. 3 [3.17], that she chose two men from Burgundy, which had been conquered by Clodomir, to be put on the throne at Tours, which was also in Clodomir's kingdom.
[50] Gregory of Tours [*Historia ecclesiastica Francorum*], bk. 5, chap. 1 [5.1]: "Although scarcely five years old, he began to rule on Christmas Day" [L.].

But, even with this change, one followed the first spirit of the nation, and acts were not passed in the name of kings who were wards. Thus, among the Franks there was a double administration, the one concerning the person of the king who was a ward and the other concerning the kingdom; and in the fiefs there was a difference between guardianship and bailiffry.

CHAPTER 28

On adoption among the Germans

As, among the Germans, one came of age on receiving weapons, one was adopted by the same sign. Thus, Guntram, wanting to declare his nephew Childebert of age and also to adopt him, told him, "I put[51] this javelin in your hands as a sign that I have given you my kingdom." And, turning to the assembly, "You see that my son Childebert has become a man; obey him." When Theodoric, king of the Ostrogoths, wanted to adopt the king of the Heruli, he wrote to him:[52]

> it is a fine thing we have, that we can adopt by weapons, for courageous men are the only ones who are worthy of becoming our children. There is such a force in this act that the one who is the object of it will always prefer to die than to suffer something shameful. Thus, by the custom of nations, and because you are a man, we adopt you by these shields, these swords, and these horses that we are sending you.

[51] See Gregory of Tours [*Historia ecclesiastica Francorum*], bk. 7, chap. 23 [7.33].
[52] In Cassiodorus [*Variae*] bk. 4, letter 2 [4.2].

CHAPTER 29

The bloodthirsty spirit of the Frankish kings

Clovis was not the only prince among the Franks who undertook expeditions into Gaul; many of his relatives had led certain tribes there, and as he had greater success and could give important establishments to those who had followed him, the Franks flocked to him from all the tribes and the other leaders found themselves too weak to resist him. He formed the design of exterminating all those of his house and succeeded at it.[53] He feared, said Gregory of Tours,[54] that the Franks might take another leader. His children and his successors followed this practice as much as they could: the brother, the uncle, the nephew (what can I say?),[f] the son, the father, were seen constantly conspiring against the rest of the family. The law constantly divided the monarchy; fear, ambition, and cruelty wanted to reunite it.

[53]Gregory of Tours [*Historia ecclesiastica Francorum*], bk. 2 [2.42].
[54]Ibid. [Gregory of Tours, *Historia ecclesiastica Francorum* 2.42].

[f]Translators' parentheses.

CHAPTER 30

On the national assemblies among the Franks

It has been mentioned earlier that peoples who do not cultivate the land enjoyed a great liberty. This was the case for the Germans. Tacitus says that they gave their kings or leaders only a very moderate power,[55] and Caesar says[56] that they had no common magistrate during peacetime but that in each village the princes rendered justice among their own. Thus, in Germany the Franks had no king, as Gregory of Tours[57] proves nicely.

"Princes,"[58] says Tacitus, "deliberate on small things, the entire nation on large things, in such a way, however, that the matters that are within the cognizance of the people are also carried to the princes." This usage was preserved after the conquest, as is seen in all the records.[59]

[55]"The kings have neither unlimited nor unbounded power [. . .]. Moreover, neither to punish, to put in bonds, nor to flog, etc." [L.]. [Tacitus] *Germania* [chap. 7].
[56]"During peacetime there is no common magistrate; instead, the princes of the region and cantons give justice among their own people" [L.]. [Gaius Julius Caesar] *De bello Gallico*, bk. 6 [6.23].
[57][Gregory of Tours, *Historia ecclesiastica Francorum*] bk. 2 [2.9].
[58]"On lesser issues, only the princes consult, on greater ones, everyone; but even when it is a decision within the power of the people, first it is thoroughly considered by the princes" [L.] [Tacitus] *Germania* [chap. 11].
[59]"Law is made by the consensus of the people and the constitution of the king" [L.]. Capitularies of Charles the Bald, *anno* 864, art. 6 [*CRF*, 273.6].

Tacitus[60] says that capital crimes could be brought before the assembly. It was the same after the conquest, and the great vassals were judged there as well.

[60] "In their council it is permitted to consider the accusation of a capital crime" [L.] [Tacitus] *Germania* [12].

CHAPTER 31

On the authority of the clergy under the Merovingians

Among barbarian peoples, priests ordinarily have power because they have both the authority, which religion should give them, and the power which superstition gives among such peoples. Thus, we see in Tacitus that the priests were highly esteemed among the Germans and that their presence introduced a police[61] into the assembly of the people. They were permitted only[62] to chastise, to bind, and to strike, which they did, not by order of the prince, or to inflict a penalty, but as by divine inspiration, ever present in those who wage war.

One must not be surprised if, from the beginning of the reign of the Merovingians, bishops are seen to be arbiters[63] of judgments, if they are seen appearing in the national assemblies, if they greatly influence the resolution of the kings, and if they are given so many goods.

[61] "Silence is commanded by the priests who have the right to keep order" [L.]. [Tacitus] *Germania* [11].

[62] "The kings have neither unlimited nor unbounded power [. . .]. Moreover, it is only permitted to priests to punish, to put in bonds, or to flog; and this is done, not as if it were a penalty, or as an order from the leader, but by the command of God, as it were, whom they believe to be present in the warrior" [L.]. Ibid. [Tacitus, *Germania*, 7.]

[63] See *Chlotharii regis constitutio generalis, anno* 560, art. 6 [*CRF*, 8.6].

BOOK 19

On the laws in their relation with the principles forming the general spirit, the mores, and the manners of a nation

CHAPTER I

On the subject of this book

This material is very extensive. In this crowd of ideas that present themselves in my spirit, I shall be more attentive to the order of things than to the things themselves. I must push things away, break through, and bring my subject to light.

CHAPTER 2

How much it is necessary for spirits to be prepared for the best laws

Nothing appeared more intolerable to the Germans[1] than the tribunal of Varus. The one that Justinian set up among the Laxians[2] in order to try the murderer of their king seemed to them a horrible and barbarous thing. Mithridates,[3] inveighing against the Romans, reproached them above all for the formal procedures[4] of their justice. The Parthians could not tolerate this king who, having been raised in Rome, made himself affable[5] and accessible to everyone. Even liberty has appeared

[1] They cut out lawyers' tongues and said, "Viper, stop hissing." Tacitus. [Not Tacitus but Florus, *Epitome rerum Romanorum* 2.30.37; 4.12.37.]

[2] Agathias [*Historiarum*], bk. 4 [4.1–10].

[3] Justin [*Epitoma historiarum Philippicarum*], bk. 38 [38.4–7].

[4] *Calumnias litium*: "false in litigation." Ibid. [Justin, *Epitoma historiarum Philippicarum* 38.7.8].

[5] Tacitus [*Annales* 2.2], "The ease with which he could be approached, his affability, were virtues unknown to the Parthians and instead they seemed to be new vices" [L.].

intolerable to peoples who were not accustomed to enjoying it. Thus is pure air sometimes harmful to those who have lived in swampy countries.

When in Pegu, a Venetian named Balbi was brought to the king.[6] When the latter learned that there was no king in Venice, he laughed so much that he began to cough and could scarcely talk to his courtiers. What legislator could propose popular government to such peoples?

[6] He described it in 1596. *Recueil des voyages qui ont servi à l'établissement de la Compagnie des Indes*, vol. 3, pt. 1, p. 33. ["Relation du second voiage d'Etienne van der Hage," 3, 30; 1705 edn; 3, 28; 1725 edn.]

CHAPTER 3
On tyranny

There are two sorts of tyranny: a real one, which consists in the violence of the government, and one of opinion, which is felt when those who govern establish things that run counter to a nation's way of thinking.

Dio says that Augustus wanted to be called Romulus, but that, on learning that the people feared that he wanted to make himself king, he changed his design. The first Romans did not want a king because they could not suffer his power; the Romans of the time of Augustus did not want a king in order not to suffer his manners. For, although Caesar, the triumvirs, and Augustus were real kings, they had preserved an appearance of equality and in their private lives they seemed opposed to the kingly pomp of that time; and, when the Romans did not want a king, this meant that they wanted to keep their own manners and not take on those of African and Eastern peoples.

Dio[7] tells us that the Roman people were very angry with Augustus because of certain laws he had made which were too harsh, but that their discontent ceased as soon as he brought back the actor Pylades, who had been driven out of the town by the factions.[a] Such a people felt tyranny more vividly when a buffoon was driven out than when all their laws were taken from them.

[7] [Cass. Dio, *Historia Romana*] bk. 54, p. 532 [53.16.7, on Romulus; 54.17.4–5, on Pylades].

[a] These factions were based on the allegiances of the fans of the circus.

CHAPTER 4
What the general spirit is

Many things govern men: climate, religion, laws, the maxims of the government, examples of past things, mores, and manners; a general spirit is formed as a result.

To the extent that, in each nation, one of these causes acts more forcefully, the others yield to it. Nature and climate almost alone dominate savages; manners govern the Chinese; laws tyrannize Japan; in former times mores set the tone in Lacedaemonia; in Rome it was set by the maxims of government and the ancient mores.

CHAPTER 5
How careful one must be not to change the general spirit of a nation

If there were in the world a nation which had a sociable humor, an openness of heart; a joy in life, a taste, an ease in communicating its thoughts; which was lively, pleasant, playful, sometimes imprudent, often indiscreet; and which had with all that, courage, generosity, frankness, and a certain point of honor, one should avoid disturbing its manners by laws, in order not to disturb its virtues. If the character is generally good, what difference do a few faults make?

One could constrain its women, make laws to correct their mores, and limit their luxury, but who knows whether one would not lose a certain taste that would be the source of the nation's wealth and a politeness that attracts foreigners to it?

The legislator is to follow the spirit of the nation when doing so is not contrary to the principles of the government, for we do nothing better than what we do freely and by following our natural genius.

If one gives a pedantic spirit to a nation naturally full of gaiety, the state will gain nothing, either at home or abroad. Let it do frivolous things seriously and serious things gaily.

CHAPTER 6
That one must not correct everything

May we be left as we are, said a gentleman of a nation closely resembling the one of which we have just given an idea. Nature repairs everything. It has given us a vivacity capable of offending and one apt to make us inconsiderate; this same vivacity is corrected by the politeness it brings us, by inspiring us with a taste for the world and above all for commerce with women.

May we be left as we are. Our discretions joined to our harmlessness make unsuitable such laws as would curb our sociable humor.

CHAPTER 7
On the Athenians and Lacedaemonians

The Athenians, continued this gentleman, were a people who had some relation with our own. They put gaiety in their public business; a joke from the rostrum pleased them as much as one in the theater. The vivacity they put into counsels was carried over into their execution. The character of the Lacedaemonians was grave, serious, dry, taciturn. One would have made no better use of an Athenian by boring him than of a Lacedaemonian by amusing him.

CHAPTER 8
Some effects of the sociable humor

The more communicative peoples are, the more easily they change their manners, because each man is more a spectacle for another; one sees the singularities of individuals better. The climate that makes a nation like to communicate also makes it like to change, and what makes a nation like to change also makes its taste take form.

The society of women spoils mores and forms taste; the desire to please more than others establishes ornamentation, and the desire to please more than oneself establishes fashions. Fashions are an important subject; as one allows one's spirit to become frivolous, one constantly increases the branches of commerce.[8]

[8] See [Bernard Mandeville] *The Fable of the Bees* [1, 250–254; 1732 edn; remark T, 1, 225–228; 1924 edn].

CHAPTER 9
On the vanity and the arrogance of nations

Vanity is as good a spring for a government as arrogance is a dangerous one. To show this, one has only to imagine[b] to oneself, on the one hand, the innumerable goods resulting from vanity: luxury, industry, the arts, fashions, politeness, and taste, and, on the other hand, the infinite evils born of the arrogance of certain nations: laziness, poverty, the abandonment of everything, and the destruction of the nations that chance has let fall into their hands as well as their own nation. Laziness[9] is the effect of arrogance; work follows from vanity: the arrogance of a Spaniard will incline him not to work; the vanity of a Frenchman will incline him to try to work better than the others.

Every lazy nation is grave; for those who do not work regard themselves as sovereigns of those who work.

Examine all the nations and you will see that in most of them gravity, arrogance, and laziness go hand in hand.

The people of Achim[10] are proud and lazy: those who have no slaves rent one, if only to walk a hundred steps and carry two pints of rice; they would believe themselves dishonored if they carried it themselves.

In many places on earth people let their fingernails grow in order to indicate that they do not work.

[9] The peoples who follow the Khan of Malacamber, those of Carnataca and Coromandel, are proud and lazy; they consume little because they are miserably poor; whereas the Moguls and the peoples of Hindustan concern themselves with and enjoy the comforts of life, like Europeans. *Recueil des voyages qui ont servi à l'établissement de la Compagnie des Indes*, vol. 1, p. 54 ["Avis sur le Commerce des Indes Orientales"; 1, LIV; 1725 edn].

[10] See [William] Dampier [*Voyages*], vol. 3 [vol. 2, pt. 1, chap. 7; 2, 56 and 62; 1906 edn].

[b] *se représenter.*

Women in the Indies[11] believe it is shameful for them to learn to read; this is the business, they say, of the slaves who sing hymns in the pagodas. In one caste, they do not spin; in another they make only baskets and mats, and should not even mill the rice; in others, they must not fetch water. Arrogance there has established its rules and sees that they are followed. It is unnecessary to say that moral qualities have different effects according to the other qualities united with them; thus arrogance joined to a vast ambition, to the greatness of ideas, etc. produced among the Romans the effects which are known to all.[c]

[11] *Lettres édifiantes et curieuses*, vol. 12, p. 80 [Lettre du P. de Bourzes, Madura, September 21, 1713; 12, 79–80; 1741 edn].

[c] See the discussion of honor, 3.5–8.

CHAPTER 10

On the character of the Spanish and that of the Chinese

The various characters of the nations are mixtures of virtues and vices, of good and bad qualities. The happy mixtures are those that result in great goods, and one often would not expect them; some result in great evils, and one would not expect them either.

The good faith of the Spaniards has been famous in all times. Justin[12] tells us of their faithfulness in guarding deposits; they have often suffered death to keep them secret. The faithfulness they had of old they still have today. All the nations that trade in Cadiz entrust their fortunes to the Spanish; they have never repented of it. But this admirable quality joined to their laziness forms a mixture whose effects are pernicious to them; before their very eyes the peoples of Europe carry on all the commerce of their monarchy.

The mixture that forms the Chinese character contrasts with the mixture that forms the Spanish character. The precariousness of their lives[13] makes them so prodigiously active and so excessively desirous of gain that no commercial nation can trust them.[14] This acknowledged

[12] [Justin, *Epitoma historiarum Philippicarum*] bk. 43 [44.2.3].
[13] Because of the nature of the climate and the terrain.
[14] Father [Jean Baptiste] du Halde [*Description de l'Empire de la Chine*], vol. 2 ["Du commerce du Chinois"; 2, 205 H; 2, 170–172 P].

unfaithfulness has preserved Japanese commerce for the Chinese; no European trader has dared undertake it in their name, however easy this might have been for their maritime provinces in the north.

CHAPTER 11
Reflection

I have not said this to diminish in any way the infinite distance there is between vices and virtues: God forbid! I have only wanted to make it understood that not all political vices are moral vices and that not all moral vices are political vices, and those who make laws that run counter to the general spirit should not be ignorant of this.

CHAPTER 12
On manners and mores in the despotic state

It is a maxim of capital importance that the mores and manners of a despotic state must never be changed; nothing would be more promptly followed by a revolution. For, in these states, there are no laws, so to speak; there are only mores and manners, and if you overturn them, you overturn everything.

Laws are established, mores are inspired; the latter depend more on the general spirit, the former depend more on a particular institution; now, it is as dangerous, if not more so, to overturn the general spirit as to change a particular institution.

One is less communicative in countries where each man, whether a superior or an inferior, exercises and suffers an arbitrary power, than in those in which liberty reigns in all conditions. Therefore, one changes manners and mores less in them; manners that are more fixed are closer to laws: thus, a prince or a legislator must run counter to mores there less than in any other country in the world.

Women are ordinarily enclosed there and have no tone to give. In other countries where they live with men, their desire to please and one's desire to please them too prompt one to change manners continually. The two sexes spoil each other; each loses its distinctive and essential quality; arbitrariness is put into what was absolute, and manners change every day.

CHAPTER 13

On manners among the Chinese

But in China manners are indestructible. Not only are the women completely separated from the men there, but one teaches manners as well as mores in the schools. A lettered person is known[15] by his fashion of bowing graciously. These things, once given as precepts by grave scholars, are fixed as principles of morality and no longer change.

[15] So says Father [Jean Baptiste] du Halde [*Description de l'Empire de la Chine*, "Extrait d'un livre Chinois intitulé l'Arte de rendre le peuple heureux en établissant des Ecoles publiques"; 2, 310–319 H; 2, 259–266 P; 2, 297–304 L.].

CHAPTER 14

What are the natural means of changing the mores and manners of a nation

We have said that the laws were the particular and precise institutions of the legislator and the mores and manners, the institutions of the nation in general. From this it follows that when one wants to change the mores and manners, one must not change them by the laws, as this would appear to be too tyrannical; it would be better to change them by other mores and other manners.

Thus, when a prince wants to make great changes in his nation, he must reform by laws what is established by laws and change by manners what is established by manners, and it is a very bad policy to change by laws what should be changed by manners.

The law that obliged the Muscovites to shorten their beards and their clothing and the violence of Peter I in trimming up to the knees the long robes of those who entered the towns were both tyrannical. The means for preventing crimes are penalties; the means for changing manners are examples.

The ease and promptness with which this nation has become orderly[d] has shown that this prince had too low an opinion of it and that these peoples were not beasts as he said. The violent means he employed were useless; he would have accomplished his purpose as well by gentleness.

He himself saw how easy it was to make changes. The women had been enclosed and in a way enslaved; he called them to court, he had them dress in the German way, and he sent them fabrics. They immediately appreciated a way of life that so flattered their taste, their vanity, and their passions, and they made the men appreciate it.

What made the change easier was that the mores of that time were foreign to the climate and had been carried there by the mixture of nations and by conquests. Peter found it easier than he had expected to give the mores and manners of Europe to a European nation. The empire of climate is the first of all empires. Therefore, he did not need laws to change the mores and manners of his nation; it would have been sufficient for him to inspire other mores and other manners.

In general, peoples are very attached to their customs; taking their customs from them violently makes them unhappy: therefore, one must not change their customs, but engage the peoples to change them themselves.

Every penalty that does not derive from necessity is tyrannical. The law is not a pure act of power; things indifferent by their nature are not within its scope.[e]

[d] *. . . cette nation s'est policée.*

[e] *ressort*. See note [a], bk. 12.

CHAPTER 15

Influence of domestic government on political government

This change in the mores of women will no doubt affect the government of Muscovy very much. Everything is closely linked together: the despotism of the prince is naturally united with the servitude of women; the liberty of women, with the spirit of monarchy.

CHAPTER 16
How some legislators have confused the principles that govern men

Mores and manners are usages that laws have not established, or that they have not been able, or have not wanted, to establish.

The difference between laws and mores is that, while laws regulate the actions of the citizen, mores regulate the actions of the man. The difference between mores and manners is that the first are more concerned with internal, and the latter external, conduct.

Sometimes in a state these things are confused with one another.[16] Lycurgus made a single code for the laws, the mores and the manners, and the legislators of China did the same.

One must not be astonished if the legislators of Lacedaemonia and those of China confused laws, mores, and manners; this is because mores represent laws, and manners represent mores.

The principal object of the Chinese legislators was to have their people live in tranquility. They wanted men to have much respect for each other; they wanted each one to feel at every instant that he owed much to the others; they wanted every citizen to depend, in some respect, on another citizen. Therefore, they extended the rules of civility to a great many people.

Thus, among the Chinese peoples, one sees villagers[17] observe between themselves ceremonies like those of people of a higher condition; this is a very proper means of inspiring gentleness, of maintaining peace and good order among the people, and of removing all the vices that come from a harsh spirit. Indeed, is not freeing oneself from the rules of civility the way one seeks to put oneself more at ease with one's faults?

Civility is preferable, in this regard, to politeness. Politeness flatters the vices of others, and civility keeps us from displaying our own; it is a barrier that men put between themselves in order to keep from being corrupted.

Lycurgus, whose institutions were harsh, did not have civility as an

[16] Moses made a single code of laws and religion. The first Romans mixed together the old customs and the laws.

[17] See Father [Jean Baptiste] du Halde [*Description de l'Empire de la Chine*, "De la morale du Chinois"; 3, 157 H; 3, 129–130 P].

object when he formed manners; he had in view the bellicose spirit he wanted to give his people. Always correcting or being corrected, always instructing and being instructed, as simple as they were rigid, these people practiced virtues for each other, rather than showing them regard.

CHAPTER 17

A property peculiar to the government of China

The legislators of China did more:[18] they confused religion, laws, mores, and manners; all was morality, all was virtue. The precepts concerning these four points were what one called rites. It was in the exact observation of these rites that the Chinese government triumphed. One passed all of one's youth learning them, all of one's life practicing them. The scholars taught them; the magistrates preached them. And, as these rites encompassed all the minor activities of life, China was well governed when a way was found to make them be observed exactly.

Two things made it possible to engrave these rites easily in the hearts and spirits of the Chinese: the one, their extremely complicated manner of writing which kept their spirits solely occupied with these rites for a great part of their lives[19] because one had to learn to read from the books and for the sake of the books that contained them, the other, that as the precepts of rites are in no way spiritual but are simply rules of common practice, it is easier to convince and to stamp spirits with them than with something intellectual.

Those princes who, instead of governing by the rites, governed by the force of punishments, wanted to have punishments do what is not in their power, which is to give mores. Punishments will cast out of society a citizen who, having lost his mores, violates the laws, but if everyone loses his mores, will punishments reestablish them? Punishments will indeed check many consequences of the general evil, but they will not correct this evil. Thus, when one abandoned the principles of Chinese government, when morality was lost there, the state fell into anarchy and one saw revolutions.

[18] See the classic books of which Father du Halde has given us such a fine selection. [*Description de l'Empire de la Chine*, 2, 340–458 H; 2, 284–383 P.]

[19] This is what established emulation, flight from laziness, and high esteem for knowledge.

CHAPTER 18

Consequence of the preceding chapter

The result of this is that conquest does not make China lose its laws. As manners, mores, laws, and religion are but the same thing there, one cannot change all of that at once. And, as either the vanquisher or the vanquished must change, in China it has always had to be the vanquisher; for, as the mores of the vanquishers are not their manners, nor their manners, their laws, nor their laws, their religion, it has been easier for the vanquishers to bend slowly to the vanquished people than for the vanquished people to bend to the vanquishers.

A very sad thing also follows from this; it is almost impossible for Christianity ever to be established in China.[20] The vows of virginity, the assembly of women in churches, their necessary communication with the ministers of religion, their participation in the sacraments, the auricular confession, extreme unction, marriage to a single woman, all this overthrows the mores and manners of the country and strikes against the religion and the laws at the same time.

The Christian religion, by the establishment of charity, by a public worship, and by participation in the same sacraments, seems to require that everything be united; the rites of the Chinese seem to order that everything be separate.

And, as one has seen that such separation[21] is generally linked to the spirit of despotism, one will find in this a reason why monarchical government, indeed any moderate government, makes a better alliance[22] with the Christian religion.

[20] See the reasons given by the Chinese magistrates in the decrees they made to proscribe the Christian religion. *Lettres édifiantes et curieuses*, vol. 17 [Lettre du P. de Mailla, Peking, October 16, 1724; 17, 167–170; 1726 edn].

[21] See bk. 4, chap. 3, and bk. 19, chap. 12 [above].

[22] See below, bk. 24, chap. 3.

CHAPTER 19

How this union of religion, laws, mores, and manners was made among the Chinese

The Chinese legislators had the tranquility of the empire as the principal object of government. Subordination seemed to them the most appropriate means of maintaining it. As part of this idea they believed they should inspire respect for the fathers, and they brought together all their forces to do so. They established an infinity of rites and ceremonies in order to honor fathers during their life and after death. It was impossible to give so much honor to the dead fathers without being drawn to honor the living ones. Ceremonies for dead fathers were more related to religion, and those for living fathers more related to the laws, mores, and manners; but these were only parts of a single code, and this code was very far-reaching.

Respect for fathers necessarily involved everything that represented fathers, old men, teachers, magistrates, the emperor. Respect for fathers implies that a love be returned to children and, as a consequence, implies the return of love from the elders to the young people, from the magistrates to those who were subject to them, from the emperor to his subjects. All this formed the rites, and these rites formed the general spirit of the nation.

One can feel the relation that China's fundamental constitution can have with things that are seemingly indifferent to it. This empire is formed on the idea of family government. If you diminish paternal authority or if you even withdraw the ceremonies that express one's respect for it, you weaken the respect for magistrates, who are regarded as fathers; magistrates will no longer have the same care for the peoples whom they should consider as their children; the relation of love between the prince and his subjects will also be gradually lost. Omit one of these practices, and you shake the state. It is quite indifferent in itself whether a daughter-in-law gets up every morning to perform such and such duties for a mother-in-law; but if one notes that these external practices constantly call one back to a feeling, which it is necessary to impress on all hearts, and which comes from all hearts to form the spirit that governs the empire, one will see that it is necessary for a certain particular action to be performed.

CHAPTER 20

Explanation of a paradox about the Chinese

It is strange that the Chinese, whose life is entirely directed by rites, are nevertheless the most unscrupulous people on earth. This appears chiefly in commerce, which has never been able to inspire in them the good faith natural to it. The buyer should carry his own scale[23] as each merchant has three of them, a heavy one for buying, a light one for selling, and an accurate one for those who are on their guard. I believe I can explain this contradiction.

Chinese legislators have had two objects: they have wanted the people to be both submissive and tranquil, and hardworking and industrious. Because of the nature of the climate and the terrain, their life is precarious; one secures one's life there only by dint of industry and work.

When everyone obeys and everyone works, the state is in a fortunate situation. Necessity and perhaps the nature of the climate have given all the Chinese an unthinkable avidity for gain, and the laws have not dreamed of checking it. Everything has been prohibited if it is a question of acquisition by violence; everything has been permitted if it is a matter of obtaining by artifice or by industry. Therefore, let us not compare the morality of China with that of Europe. Everyone in China has had to be attentive to what was useful to him; if the rascal has watched over his interests, he who is duped has had to think of his own. In Lacedaemonia, stealing was permitted; in China, deceit is permitted.

[23] *Recueil de voyages au nord*, vol. 8, p. 363, Lange, *Journal* for 1721 and 1722 [8, 363; 1727 edn].

CHAPTER 21

How laws should be relative to the mores and the manners

Only singular institutions thus confuse laws, mores, and manners, things that are naturally separate; but, even though they are separate, they are still closely related.

Solon was asked if the laws he had given to the Athenians were the best; "I have given them the best laws they could endure," he replied: this is a fine speech that should be heard by all legislators. When the divine wisdom said to the Jewish people, "I have given you precepts that are not good," this meant that the precepts were only relatively good, which sponges away all the difficulties one can propose about the Mosaic laws.

CHAPTER 22
Continuation of the same subject

When a people have good mores, laws become simple. Plato says[24] that Rhadamanthus, who governed an extremely religious people, dispatched all trials speedily by having only an oath sworn on each count. But, Plato also says,[25] when a people are not religious, one can use the oath only on the occasions when those who swear it, such as the judge and witnesses, are without interest.

[24] [Plato] *Laws*, bk. 12 [948b–d].

[25] Ibid. [Plato, *Laws*, 948c–d].

CHAPTER 23
How the laws follow mores

At the time when the mores of the Romans were pure, there was no specific law against embezzlement. When this crime began to appear, it was deemed so infamous that to be condemned to restore what one had taken[26] was regarded as a great penalty: witness the judgment against L. Scipio.[27]

[26] *In simplum*: "the simple value."

[27] Livy, bk. 38 [38.60].

CHAPTER 24

Continuation of the same subject

The laws that give guardianship to the mother are more attentive to the preservation of the person[f] of the ward; those that give it to the closest heir are more attentive to the preservation of the goods. Among peoples whose mores are corrupt, it is preferable to give the guardianship to the mother. Among those whose laws should trust the mores of the citizens, one gives the guardianship to the heir of the goods, or to the mother, and sometimes to both of them.

If one reflects on the Roman laws, one will find that their spirit conforms to what I say. At the time when the Law of the Twelve Tables was made, mores in Rome were admirable. One gave the guardianship to the closest relative of the ward, thinking that he who could have the advantage of the inheritance should have the charge of the guardianship. It was not believed that the life of a ward was in danger although it was put in the hands of one to whom the ward's death could be useful. But, when mores changed in Rome, legislators were also seen to change their way of thinking. "If, in appointing guardians for the ward," says Gaius[28] and Justinian,[29] "the testator fears that the person appointed will plot against the ward, he can leave the vulgar substitution[30] open and put the wardship in a part of the will that can be disclosed only after a certain time." These fears and precautions were unknown to the first Romans.

[28] [Gaius] *Institutes*, bk. 2, tit. 6, para. 2; Ozel compilation, Leyden, 1658 [2.6.2].

[29] [*Corpus Juris Civilis*] *Institutes*, bk. 2, para. 3 [2.3]; *de pupillari substitutione*.

[30] The vulgar substitution is: "if so and so does not take the inheritance, I appoint instead of him . . ." etc.; the substitution of a guardian [pupillary] is: "If a certain one dies before [the ward's] puberty, I appoint instead of him . . ." etc.

[f] "Person" is distinguished here from estate, title, etc.

CHAPTER 25
Continuation of the same subject

Roman law gave people the liberty to give gifts to one another before marriage; after marriage it no longer permitted them. This was founded on the mores of the Romans, who were drawn to marriage only by frugality, simplicity, and modesty, but who might be seduced by domestic cares, by kindness, and by the happiness of a complete life.

The law of the Visigoths[31] wanted the husband to be kept from giving more than a tenth of his goods to the one he was to marry and to be kept from giving her anything during the first year of his marriage. This comes, in addition, from the mores of the country. The legislators wanted to check that Spanish boastfulness which is drawn only to excessive liberalities dramatically displayed.

The Romans, by their laws, checked some of the defects of the most durable empire in the world, that of virtue; the Spanish, by their laws, wanted to halt the worst effects of the most fragile tyranny in the world, that of beauty.

[31] [*Lex Wisigothorum*] bk. 3, tit. 1, para. 5 [3.1.5].

CHAPTER 26
Continuation of the same subject

The law of Theodosius and Valentinian[32] took the causes for repudiation from the earlier mores[33] and manners of the Romans. It put among those causes the actions of a husband[34] who chastised his wife in the manner unworthy of a freeborn person. This cause was omitted from later laws;[35] this is because the mores had changed in this regard; the usages of the East had taken the place of those of Europe. The first eunuch of the empress, wife of Justinian II, threatened her, history

[32] Law 8 of the *Code* [*Corpus Juris Civilis, Code* 5.17.8]; *de repudiis et judicio de moribus sublato.*
[33] And from the law of the Twelve Tables. See Cicero, *Philippicae* [2.28.69].
[34] "If he be proven to have used whips, a thing unsuitable for any freeborn person" [L.] [*Corpus Juris Civilis, Code* 5.17.8.2; *de repudiis et judicio de moribus sublato.*]
[35] In [*Corpus Juris Civilis*] *Novellae* 117, chap. 14 [117.14].

says, with the chastisement used to punish children in schools. Only established mores or mores seeking to establish themselves could make such a thing imaginable.

We have seen how laws follow mores; let us now see how mores follow laws.

CHAPTER 27

How laws can contribute to forming the mores, manners, and character of a nation

The customs of a slave people are a part of their servitude; those of a free people are a part of their liberty.

I have spoken in Book 11[36] of a free people, and I have given the principles of their constitution; let us see the effects that had to follow, the character that was formed from it, and the manners that result from it.

I do not say that the climate has not in large part produced the laws, the mores, and the manners of this nation, but I say that the mores and the manners of this nation should be closely related to its laws.

Since in this state there would be two visible powers, legislative power and executive power, and as each citizen would have his own will and would value his independence according to his taste, most people would have more affection for one of these powers than for the other, as the multitude is ordinarily not fair or sensible enough to have equal affection for both of them.

And, as the executive power, which has all the posts at its disposal, could furnish great expectations but not fears, all those who would obtain something from it would be inclined to move to that side, and it could be attacked by all those who could expect nothing from it.

As all the passions are free there, hatred, envy, jealousy, and the ardor for enriching and distinguishing oneself would appear to their full extent, and if this were otherwise, the state would be like a man who, laid low by disease, has no passions because he has no strength.

The hatred between the two parties would endure because it would always be powerless.

[36] [Bk. 11] chap. 6 [above].

As these parties are made up of free men, if one party gained too much, the effect of liberty would be to lower it while the citizens would come and raise the other party like hands rescuing the body.

As each individual, always independent, would largely follow his own caprices and his fantasies, he would often change parties; he would abandon one and leave all his friends in order to bind himself to another in which he would find all his enemies; and often, in this nation, he could forget both the laws of friendship and those of hatred.

The monarch would be in the same situation as the individuals; and, against the ordinary maxims of prudence, he would often be obliged to put his trust in those who had most run counter to him and to disgrace those who had best served him, doing by necessity what other princes do by choice.

One is afraid of seeing the escape of a good that one feels, that one scarcely knows, and that can be hidden from us; and fear always enlarges objects. The people would be uneasy about their situation and would believe themselves in danger even at the safest moments.

As those who would most sharply oppose executive power would be unable to admit the interested motives of their opposition, they would increase even more the terrors of the people, who would never know precisely whether or not they were in danger. But even this would help them avoid the real perils to which they might sometimes be exposed.

But, as the legislative body has the trust of the people and is more enlightened than they, it could make them revise the bad impressions they had been given and calm these emotions.

This is the great advantage such a government would have over the ancient democracies, in which the people had an immediate power; for, when the orators agitated them, these agitations always had their effect.

Thus, if the terrors impressed on a people had no certain object, they would produce only empty clamors and insults and would even have the good effect of stretching all the springs of the government and making all the citizens attentive. But, if those terrors arose on the occasion of the overthrow of fundamental laws, they would be insidious, lamentable, and heinous, and would produce catastrophes.

One would soon see an awful calm, during which everything would unite together against the power that violated the laws.

If, in the case where uneasiness has no certain object, some foreign power threatened the state and put its fortune or glory in danger, at that time everything would unite in favor of executive power, as small interests would cede to greater ones.

For, if disputes were formed on the occasion of the violation of the fundamental laws and a foreign power appeared, there would be a revolution that would not change the form of the government or its constitution, as revolutions formed by liberty are but a confirmation of liberty.

A free nation can have a liberator; a subjugated nation can have only another oppressor.

For any man who has enough strength to drive out the one who is already the absolute master in a state has enough strength to become one himself.

Because, in order to enjoy liberty, each must be able to say what he thinks and because, in order to preserve it, each must still be able to say what he thinks, a citizen in this state would say and write everything that the laws had not expressly prohibited him from saying or writing.

This nation, always heated, could more easily be led by its passions than by reason, which never produces great effects on the spirits of men, and it would be easy for those who governed it to make it undertake enterprises against its true interests.

This nation would love its liberty prodigiously because this liberty would be true; and it could happen that, in order to defend that liberty, the nation might sacrifice its goods, its ease, and its interests, and might burden itself with harsher imposts than even the most absolute prince would dare make his subjects bear.

But, as this nation would know with certainty that it was necessary to submit to them, as it would pay them in the well-founded expectation of not having to pay more, the burdens would be heavier than the feeling of these burdens, whereas there are states in which the feeling is infinitely worse than the ill.

This nation would have secure credit because it would borrow from itself and would pay to itself. It could happen that it would undertake something beyond the forces natural to it and would assert against its enemies an immense fictional wealth that the trust and the nature of its government would make real.

In order to preserve its liberty, it would borrow from its subjects, and its subjects, who would see that its credit would be lost if it were conquered, would have a further motive to make efforts to defend its liberty.

If this nation inhabited an island, it would not be a conquering nation because overseas conquests would weaken it. It would be even less a conqueror if the terrain of this island were good, because it would not need war to enrich itself. And, as no citizen would depend on another citizen, each would make more of his liberty than of the glory of a few citizens, or of a single one.

There, one would regard military men as people whose occupation can be useful and often dangerous, as people whose services are arduous for the nation itself, and there civil status would be more highly esteemed.

This nation, made comfortable by peace and liberty, freed from destructive prejudices, would be inclined to become commercial. If it had some one of the primary[g] commodities used to make things that owe their high price to the hand of the worker, it could set up establishments apt to procure for itself the full enjoyment of this gift of heaven.

If this nation were situated toward the north and had many superfluous products, as it would also lack a great many commodities denied by its climate, it would have a necessary, but large, commerce with the peoples of the South; and, choosing which states it would favor with an advantageous commerce, it would make reciprocally useful treaties with the nation it had chosen.

In a state where, on the one hand, opulence was extreme, and, on the other, imposts were excessive, with a limited fortune one could scarcely live without ingenuity. On the pretext of travel or health, many people would go into exile and seek abundance even in the countries of servitude.

A commercial nation has a prodigious number of small, particular interests; therefore, it can offend and be offended in an infinity of ways. This nation would become sovereignly jealous and would find more distress in the prosperity of others than enjoyment in its own.

And its laws, otherwise gentle and easy, might be so rigid in regard to the commerce and navigation carried on with it that it would seem to negotiate only with enemies.

If this nation sent colonies abroad, it would do so to extend its commerce more than its domination.

[g] *primitive.* See note [a], bk. 1.

As one likes to establish elsewhere what is established at home, it would give the form of its own government to the people of its colonies; and as this government would carry prosperity with it, one would see the formation of great peoples, even in the forests to which it had sent inhabitants.

It could be that it had formerly subjugated a neighboring nation which, by its situation, the goodness of its ports, and the nature of its wealth, made the first jealous; thus, although it had given that nation its own laws, the great dependence in which the nation was held was such that the citizens there would be free and the state itself would be enslaved.

The conquered state would have a very good civil government, but it would be crushed by the right of nations; the laws imposed upon it from one nation to another would be such that its prosperity would be only precarious and only a deposit for a master.

The dominant nation, inhabiting a big island and being in possession of a great commerce, would have all sorts of facilities for forces upon the seas; and as the preservation of its liberty would require it to have neither strongholds, nor fortresses, nor land armies, it would need an army on the sea to protect itself from invasions; and its navy would be superior to that of all other powers, which, needing to employ their finances for a land war, would no longer have enough for a sea war.

A naval empire has always given the peoples who have possessed it a natural pride, because, feeling themselves able to insult others everywhere, they believe that their power is as boundless as the ocean.

This nation could have a great influence on the business of its neighbors. For, as it would not employ its power making conquests, one would seek its friendship more, and one would fear its hatred more than the changeableness of its government and its internal agitation would seem to permit.

Thus, it would be the fate of the executive power to be almost always uneasy at home and respected abroad.

If it happened that this nation became on some occasions the center of negotiations in Europe, it would bring to them a little more integrity and good faith than the other nations because, as its ministers would often be obliged to justify their conduct to a popular council, their negotiations could not be secret and they would be forced in this respect to be people of somewhat greater honesty.

In addition, as they would in some way be answerable for the events to which an indirect course could give rise, the surest thing for them would be to take the straightest road.

If at certain times the nobles had an immoderate power in the nation and the monarch had found the way to debase them while raising up the people, the point of extreme servitude would be between the moment of the debasement of the important men and the one when the people began to feel their power.

It could be that this nation, having formerly been subject to an arbitrary power, would, on many occasions, have preserved that style so that one would often see the form of an absolute government over the foundation of a free government.

With regard to religion, as in this state each citizen would have his own will and would consequently be led by his own enlightenment or his fantasies, what would happen is either that everyone would be very indifferent to all sorts of religion of whatever kind, in which case everyone would tend to embrace the dominant religion, or that one would be zealous for religion in general, in which case sects would multiply.

It would not be impossible for there to be in this nation people who had no religion and who would not for all that want to be obliged to change the one they would have had if they had had one, for they would immediately feel that life and goods are no more theirs than their way of thinking and that he who can rob them of the one can more easily take away the other.

If, among the different religions, there were one whose establishment had been attempted by means of slavery, it would be odious there because, as we judge things by what we associate with them or see as dependent upon them, such a religion would never come to mind together with the idea of liberty.

The laws against those who would profess this religion would not be bloodthirsty, for liberty does not imagine these sorts of penalties, but they would be so repressive that they would do all the evil that can be done in cold blood.

It could happen in a thousand ways that the clergy would have so little credit that the other citizens would have more. Thus, instead of being separate, they would prefer to bear the same burden as the lay people and, in that regard, make up only one body, but still seeking to be respected by the people, they would distinguish themselves by a more retired life, a more reserved conduct, and purer motives.

This clergy, unable to protect religion or to be protected by it, lacking force to constrain, would seek to persuade; very fine works would come from their pens, written to prove the revelation and the providence of the great being.

It could happen that one would frustrate their assemblies and would not want to permit the clergy to correct even their abuses and that, in a frenzy of liberty, one would rather leave their reform imperfect than suffer them to be the reformers.

The high positions that are a part of the fundamental constitution would be more fixed than elsewhere, but, on the other hand, the important men in this country of liberty would be closer to the people; therefore, ranks would be more separate and persons more confused.

As those who govern would have a power that revives, so to speak, and is remade daily, they would have more regard for those who are useful to them than for those who divert them; thus, one would see there few courtiers, flatterers, and fawners, and finally, all those kinds of people who take advantage of the very emptiness of spirit of the important men.

Men would scarcely be judged there by frivolous talents or attributes, but by real qualities, and of these there are only two, wealth and personal merit.

There would be a solid luxury, founded not on the refinement of vanity, but on that of real needs, and one would scarcely seek in things any but the pleasures nature had put there.

One would enjoy a great superfluity there, but nevertheless frivolous things would be proscribed; thus, because many men would have more goods than occasions for expenditure, they would employ them eccentrically, and in this nation there would be more wit than taste.

As one would always be busy with one's own interests, one would not have the politeness that is founded on idleness, and one would really have no time for it.

The epoch of Roman politeness is the same as that of the establishment of arbitrary power. Absolute government produces idleness, and idleness gives birth to politeness.

The more people there are in a nation who need to deal with each other and not cause displeasure, the more politeness there is. But we should be distinguished from barbarous peoples more by the politeness of mores than by that of manners.

In a nation where each man in his own way would take part in the administration of the state, the women should scarcely live among men. Therefore, women would be modest, that is, timid; this timidity would be their virtue, whereas the men, lacking gallantry, would throw themselves into a debauchery that would leave them their liberty as well as their leisure.

As the laws there would not be made for one individual more than another, each would regard himself as the monarch; the men in this nation would be confederates more than fellow citizens.

If the climate had given a restless spirit and a broad view to many people in a country where the constitution gave everyone a part in the government along with political interests, one would talk much about politics; one would see people who spent their lives calculating about events, which, given the nature of things and the caprice of fortune (that is of men),[h] are scarcely subject to calculation.

In a free nation it often does not matter whether individuals reason well or badly; it suffices that they reason; from that comes the liberty that protects them from the effects of these same reasonings.

Similarly, in a despotic government, it is equally pernicious whether one reasons well or badly; it suffices that one reason to run counter to the principle of the government.

The many people who would not worry about pleasing anyone would abandon themselves to their own humor. The majority who are witty would be tormented by that very wit;[i] having disdain or disgust for everything, they would be unhappy while having so many grounds not to be so.

As no citizen would fear another citizen, this nation would be proud, for the pride of kings is founded only on their independence.

Free nations are haughty; others can more easily be vain.

But these men who are so proud, living mostly alone with themselves, would often find themselves among unfamiliar people; they would be timid, and one would see in them, most of the time, a strange mixture of bashfulness and pride.

The character of the nation would appear above all in the works of the mind in which one would see a withdrawn people, each of whom thought alone.

[h] Translators' parentheses.

[i] Here *esprit* is translated "wit", although the reader needs to keep in mind Montesquieu's more general notion of "spirit," that is, of directed activity.

Society teaches us to feel the ridiculous; retirement makes us more apt to feel vices. Their satirical writings would be scathing, and one would see many Juvenals among them before finding a Horace.

In extremely absolute monarchies, historians betray the truth because they do not have the liberty to tell it; in extremely free states, they betray truth because of their very liberty for, as it always produces divisions, each one becomes as much the slave of the prejudices of his faction as he would be of a despot.

Their poets would more often have an original bluntness of invention than a certain delicacy of taste; one would find there something closer to Michelangelo's strength than to Raphael's grace.

Part 4

BOOK 20

On the laws in their relation to commerce, considered in its nature and its distinctions

That which great Atlas taught.
VIRGIL, *Aeneid* [1.741]

Invocation to the Muses[a]

Virgins of the Pierian Mount,[1] do you hear the name I give you? Inspire me. I have run a long course. I am crushed by pain, fatigue, and worry. Give my spirit the calm and the gentleness that now flee from me. You are never as divine as when you lead to wisdom and truth through pleasure.

But if you do not want to soften the harshness of my labors, conceal the labor itself. Make it so that I meditate though I appear to feel. Make it so that one is instructed though I do not teach and that, when I announce useful things, one believes that I knew nothing and that you told me everything.

When the waters of your spring come forth from your beloved rock, they rise into the air not to fall back again but to flow over the meadow; they are your delight because they are the delight of the shepherds.

Charming Muses, if you cast me but a single glance, everyone will read my works, and what was not intended as an amusement will be a pleasure.

Divine Muses, I sense that you inspire me, not just what is sung in Tempe with the pipes or what is repeated at Delos on the lyre. You also want me to make reason speak. It is the noblest, the most perfect, the most exquisite of our senses.

[1] "Speak on, O ye Pierian maidens, if it be proper for me to call you maidens" [L.]. Juvenal, *Satires* (4.35–36).]

---

[a] We have placed the "Invocation to the Muses" at the beginning of Book 20, as Montesquieu originally intended.

CHAPTER I

On commerce

The following material would require more extensive treatment, but the nature of this work does not permit it. I should like to glide on a tranquil river; I am dragged along by a torrent.

Commerce cures destructive prejudices, and it is an almost general rule that everywhere there are gentle mores,[b] there is commerce and that everywhere there is commerce, there are gentle mores.

Therefore, one should not be surprised if our mores are less fierce than they were formerly. Commerce has spread knowledge of the mores of all nations everywhere; they have been compared to each other, and good things have resulted from this.

One can say that the laws of commerce perfect mores for the same reason that these same laws ruin mores. Commerce corrupts pure mores,[2] and this was the subject of Plato's complaints; it polishes and softens barbarous mores, as we see every day.

[2] Caesar says of the Gauls that the proximity and commerce of Marseilles had spoiled them so that they, who had formerly always vanquished the Germans, had become inferior to them. [Gaius Julius Caesar] *De bello Gallico*, bk. 6 [6.24].

[b] Although *doux* can be translated as "soft," "gentle," with its less pejorative and more descriptive tone, is most appropriate to Montesquieu's meaning.

CHAPTER 2

On the spirit of commerce

The natural effect of commerce is to lead to peace. Two nations that trade with each other become reciprocally dependent; if one has an interest in buying, the other has an interest in selling, and all unions are founded on mutual needs.

But, if the spirit of commerce unites nations, it does not unite individuals in the same way. We see that in countries[3] where one is affected only by the spirit of commerce, there is traffic in all human

[3] Holland.

activities and all moral virtues; the smallest things, those required by humanity, are done or given for money.

The spirit of commerce produces in men a certain feeling for exact justice, opposed on the one hand to banditry and on the other to those moral virtues that make it so that one does not always discuss one's own interests alone and that one can neglect them for those of others.

By contrast, total absence of commerce produces the banditry that Aristotle puts among the ways of acquiring. Its spirit is not contrary to certain moral virtues; for example, hospitality, so rare among commercial countries, is notable among bandit peoples.

It is a sacrilege among the Germans, says Tacitus, to close one's house to any man whether known or unknown. Anyone who has offered hospitality to a stranger will point him to another house where there is similar hospitality,[4] and he will be received there with the same humanity. But, after the Germans had founded kingdoms, hospitality became burdensome to them. This is shown by two laws in the code of the Burgundians:[5] the one imposes a penalty on any barbarian who would point a stranger to the house of a Roman and the other rules that anyone who receives a stranger will be compensated by the inhabitants, each according to his share.

[4] "The one who was just now the host directs the guest to another host" [L.]. [Tacitus] *Germania* [21]. See also [Gaius Julius] Caesar, *De bello Gallico*, bk. 6 [6.23.9].
[5] [*Leges Burgundionum*] tit. 38 [38.7].

CHAPTER 3
On the poverty of peoples

There are two sorts of poor peoples: some are made so by the harshness of the government, and these people are capable of almost no virtue because their poverty is a part of their servitude; the others are poor only because they have disdained or because they did not know the comforts of life, and these last can do great things because this poverty is a part of their liberty.

CHAPTER 4
On commerce in the various governments

Commerce is related to the constitution. In government by one alone, it is ordinarily founded on luxury, and though it is also founded on real needs, its principal object is to procure for the nation engaging in it all that serves its arrogance, its delights, and its fancies. In government by many, it is more often founded on economy. Traders, eyeing all the nations of the earth, take to one what they bring from another. This is how the republics of Tyre, Carthage, Marseilles, Florence, Venice, and Holland engaged in commerce.

This kind of traffic concerns the government of many by its nature and monarchical government on occasion. For, as it is founded only on the practice of gaining little and even of gaining less than any other nation and of being compensated only by gaining continually, it is scarcely possible for it to be done by a people among whom luxury is established who spend much and who see only great objects.

In keeping with these ideas, Cicero said so well:[6] "I do not like a people to be both the rulers and the clerks of the universe." Indeed, one would have to assume that each individual in this state and even the whole state always had a head full of both great projects and small ones, which is contradictory.

Yet the greatest enterprises are also undertaken in those states which subsist by economic commerce, and they show a daring not to be found in monarchies: here is the reason for it.

One commerce leads to another, the small to the middling, the middling to the great, and he who earlier desired to gain little arrives at a position where he has no less of a desire to gain a great deal.

Moreover, the great enterprises of the traders are always necessarily mixed with public business. But, public business is for the most part as suspect to the merchants in monarchies as it appears safe to them in republican states. Therefore, great commercial enterprises are not for monarchies, but for the government by many.

In short, one's belief that one's prosperity is more certain in these states makes one undertake everything, and because one believes that what one has acquired is secure, one dares to expose it in order to

[6] "I do not wish the same people to be both the ruler and customs officer for the world" [L.] [Cicero, *De republica* 4.7].

acquire more; only the means for acquisition are at risk; now, men expect much of their fortune.

I do not mean that any monarchies are totally excluded from economic commerce, but they are less inclined to it by its nature; I do not mean that the republics we know are entirely without the commerce of luxury, but it is less related to their constitution.

As for the despotic state, it is useless to talk about it. General rule: in a nation that is in servitude, one works more to preserve than to acquire; in a free nation, one works more to acquire than to preserve.

CHAPTER 5

On peoples who have engaged in economic commerce

Marseilles, a necessary retreat in the midst of a stormy sea, Marseilles, where all the winds, the shoals, and the coastline order ships to put in, was frequented by sea-faring people. The barrenness[7] of its territory made its citizens decide on economic commerce. They had to be hardworking in order to replace that which nature refused them; just, in order to live among the barbarian nations that were to make their prosperity; moderate, in order for their government always to be tranquil; finally, of frugal mores, in order to live always by a commerce that they would the more surely preserve the less it was advantageous to them.

It has been seen everywhere that violence and harassment have brought forth economic commerce among men who are constrained to hide in marshes, on islands, on the shoals, and even among dangerous reefs. Thus were Tyre, Venice, and the Dutch towns founded; fugitives found security there. They had to live; they drew their livelihood from the whole universe.

[7]Justin [*Epitoma historiarum Philippicarum*], bk. 43, chap. 3 [43.3.5].

CHAPTER 6

Some effects of a great navigation

It sometimes happens that a nation that engages in economic commerce, needing the commodities of one country to serve as a basis for procuring the commodities of another, is satisfied to gain very little and sometimes nothing on the former, in the expectation or the certainty of gaining much on the latter. Thus, when Holland almost alone traded from the south of Europe to the north, the French wines, which it carried to the north, in a way served it only as a base for its commerce in the north.

It is known that in Holland certain kinds of commodities imported from a distance often sell for no more than they cost where they come from. Here is the reason given: a captain who needs ballast in his ship will take on marble; he needs wood for packing his cargo, he will buy it; and provided he loses nothing on it, he will believe he has done well. Thus, Holland also has its quarries and its forests.

Not only can a commerce that produces nothing be useful, but so can even a disadvantageous commerce. I have heard that in Holland whale-hunting generally speaking almost never returns what it costs; but those who have been employed in building the ship, those who have provided the rigging, the gear, and the provisions, are also those who take the principal interest in the hunt. Even if they lose on the hunt, they have come out ahead on the equipage. This commerce is a kind of lottery, and each one is seduced by the hope of a lucky number. Everyone loves to play, and the most sober[c] people willingly enter the play when it does not have the appearance of gambling, with all its irregularities, its violence, its dissipation, the loss of time, and even of life.

[c] *les plus sages*. (See note [b], bk. 1 and note [b], bk. 5.)

CHAPTER 7

The spirit of England concerning commerce

Almost none of England's tariffs with other nations are regular; tariffs change, so to speak, with each parliament, as it lifts or imposes particular duties. England has also wanted to preserve its independence in this matter. Sovereignly jealous of the commerce that is done there, it binds itself with few treaties and depends only on its laws.

Other nations have made commercial interests give way to political interests: England has always made its political interests give way to the interests of its commerce.

This is the people in the world who have best known how to take advantage of each of these three great things at the same time: religion, commerce, and liberty.

CHAPTER 8

How economic commerce has sometimes been hampered

In certain monarchies, laws have been made which serve to lower the states that engage in economic commerce. They have been forbidden to supply commodities other than those produced in their country; they have been permitted to trade only with ships built in their own country.

The state imposing these laws must be able to engage in the commerce easily itself; otherwise, it would do itself at least an equal wrong. It is better to deal with a nation that requires little and that the needs of commerce render somewhat dependent; with a nation that knows where to place all superfluous commodities due to the breadth of its views or its business; that is rich and can itself take many products; that will pay promptly for them; that has, so to speak, necessities for being faithful; that is peaceful on principle; that seeks to gain, and not to conquer: it is better, I say, to deal with this nation than with others that are ever rivals and would not offer all these advantages.

CHAPTER 9

On exclusion in commerce

The true maxim is to exclude no nation from one's commerce without great reasons. The Japanese trade with only two nations, the Chinese and the Dutch. The Chinese[8] earn a thousand percent on sugar and

[8] Father [Jean Baptiste] du Halde [*Description de l'Empire de la Chine*], vol. 2, pp. 170 ["Du commerce du Chinois," 2, 205–206 H; 2, 170 P; 2, 297 L.].

sometimes as much on return commodities. The Dutch make about the same profit. Any nation that is guided by the maxims of the Japanese will necessarily be deceived. It is competition that puts a just price on goods and establishes the true relations between them.

Still less should a state subject itself to selling its commodity to but a single nation on the pretext that it will take all of it at a certain price. For their grain, the Poles made this bargain with the town of Danzig; many kings of the Indies have similar contracts with the Dutch for spices.[9] These agreements are appropriate only for a poor nation, which willingly abandons the expectation of becoming rich, provided it has secured its sustenance, or for nations whose servitude consists in renouncing the use of the things nature has given them or in using these things to engage in a disadvantageous commerce.

[9] This was first established by the Portuguese. François Pyrard, *Voyages*, pt. 2, chap. 15 [vol. 2, pt. 1, chap. 15; 2, 204–205; 1887–1890 edn].

CHAPTER 10

Establishment proper to economic commerce

In states that engage in economic commerce, one has fortunately established banks, which, by means of their credit, have formed new signs of values. But it would be wrong to introduce them into states that carry on a commerce of luxury. To put them into countries governed by one alone is to assume silver on one side and power on the other: that is, on the one side, the faculty of having everything without any power, and, on the other, power with the faculty of having nothing at all. In such a government, there has never been anyone but the prince who has obtained or has been able to obtain a treasury, and wherever there is a treasury, as soon as it is excessive, it immediately becomes the prince's.

For the same reason, trading companies that associate for the sake of a certain commerce are rarely suited to the government by one alone. The nature of these companies is to give to individual wealth the force of public wealth. But in these states this force can be found only in the hands of the prince. I would go further: trading companies do not always suit states where there is economic commerce; and, if the business is not so large as to be beyond the reach of individuals, it is better not to hamper the liberty of commerce by exclusive privileges.

CHAPTER II

Continuation of the same subject

In states that engage in economic commerce, one can establish a free[d] port. The economy of the state, which always follows the frugality of individuals, gives its economic commerce a soul, so to speak. What it loses in taxes by the establishment considered here is offset by what it can draw from the republic in wealth made by industriousness. But in monarchical government such establishments would be contrary to reason; their only effect would be to relieve luxury of the weight of imposts. It would deprive itself of the sole good this luxury can procure and of the only bridle that, in such a constitution, it can have.

[d] *franc.*

CHAPTER 12

On the liberty of commerce

Liberty of commerce is not a faculty granted to traders to do what they want; this would instead be the servitude of commerce. That which hampers those who engage in commerce does not, for all that, hamper commerce. It is in countries of liberty that the trader finds innumerable obstacles; the laws never thwart him less than in countries of servitude.

England prohibits the export of its wool; it wants coal brought to the capital by sea; it does not permit the export of horses unless they are gelded; the ships[10] from its colonies that trade in Europe are to anchor in England. It hampers the trader, but it does so in favor of commerce.

[10] Navigation Act of 1660 [*The Statutes of the Realm*, 12 Car., vol. 2, chap. 18; 5, 246–250; 1963 edn; consider the Act of Interregnum, October 9, 1651]. It was only in wartime that those [merchants] of Boston and Philadelphia sent the vessels carrying their goods directly to the Mediterranean.

CHAPTER 13

What destroys that liberty

Where there is commerce there are customs houses. The object of commerce is to export and import commodities in favor of the state, and the object of the customs houses is a certain duty[e] on that same exporting, also in favor of the state. Therefore, the state must be neutral between its customs houses and its commerce and must arrange that these two things never thwart one another; then one enjoys the liberty of commerce there.

The farming of the customs[f] destroys commerce by its injustices and harassments and by the excess of what it imposes, but independently of that it also destroys it further by the difficulties to which it gives rise and the formalities it requires. In England, where customs are imposed directly,[g] there is a singular ease in trade: a word in writing accomplishes the greatest business; the merchant does not have to waste an infinite time and have specified agents in order to conclude all the difficulties brought up by the tax-farmers or to submit to them.

[e] *droit.*
[f] *la finance* here means the work of the *financiers*, tax-farmers, in regard to customs. See note [b], bk. 3.
[g] *régie.* See 13.19 (note [d], bk. 13).

CHAPTER 14

On the laws of commerce that entail the confiscation of commodities

The Magna Carta of England forbids in the event of war the seizure and confiscation of the commodities of foreign traders, except as a reprisal. It is a fine thing for the English nation to have made this one of the articles of its liberty.

In the war Spain waged against the English in 1740, a law was made[11] that punished with death those who introduced English commodities

[11] Published at Cadiz in March 1740. [See Jean Rousset de Missy, *Les Procès entre l'Espagne et Grande-Bretagne*, vol. 13, Supplement of the *Recueil historique*, Declaration of War, November 28, 1739; p. 252; 1756 edn.]

into the Spanish states;[h] it imposed this same penalty on those who carried Spanish commodities to the English states. Such an ordinance can find, I believe, no other model than the laws of Japan. It runs counter to our mores, to the spirit of commerce, and to the harmony that should prevail in proportioning penalties; it confuses all ideas, making a state crime of what is only a violation of the police.

[h] Here *états*, "states," are what we today would call the Spanish colonies.

CHAPTER 15
On corporal constraint

Solon[12] ordered that there would no longer be corporal obligations for civil debts in Athens. He drew this law from Egypt;[13] Bocchoris had made it, and Sesostris had revived it.

This law is good for ordinary civil business,[14] but we are right not to observe it in commercial business. For as traders are obliged to entrust great sums for often quite short periods of time, to give them and take them back again, the debtor must fulfill his engagements at the appointed time; this assumes corporal constraint.

In business deriving from ordinary civil contracts, the law should not provide for corporal constraint because it makes more of the liberty of one citizen than of the convenience of another. But, in agreements that derive from commerce, the law should make more of public convenience than of the liberty of a citizen; this does not prevent the restrictions and limitations that humanity and a good police can require.

[12] Plutarch [*Moralia*], *De vitando aere alieno* [828f].

[13] Diodorus Siculus [*Bibliotheca historica*], bk. 1, pt. 2, chap. 3 [1.79].

[14] Those Greek legislators were blameworthy who had forbidden taking a man's weapons and cart as securities but had permitted taking the man himself. Diodorus Siculus [*Bibliotheca historica*], bk. 1, pt. 2, chap. 3 [1.79.5].

CHAPTER 16

A fine law

The law of Geneva that excludes from magistracies and even from entry to the Great Council the children of those who have lived or who have died insolvent, unless the children discharge their father's debts, is a very good one. It has the effect of building up trust in traders, in magistrates, and in the city itself. Here again, confidence in an individual has the force of public confidence.

CHAPTER 17

A law of Rhodes

The Rhodians went further. Sextus Empiricus[15] says that there a son could not be excused from paying his father's debts by renouncing his inheritance. This law of Rhodes was given to a republic founded on commerce: now, I believe that reasons drawn from commerce itself should have set this limitation, that the debts contracted by the father after his son had begun to carry on the commerce would not affect the goods acquired by the son. A merchant should always know his obligations and conduct himself at every moment in accordance with the state of his fortune.

[15] [Sextus Empiricus, *Pyrrhoeia*] *Hippotiposes*, bk. 1, chap. 14 [1.149].

CHAPTER 18

On judges for commerce

Xenophon, in his book, *Ways and Means*,[i] wanted one to reward those prefects of commerce who dispatched proceedings most quickly. He felt the need for our commercial jurisdiction.[j]

Commercial business is only slightly susceptible to formalities. The

[i] Xenophon, *Ways and Means* 3.3.

[j] *jurisdiction consulaire.*

actions of one day have to be followed the next day by others of the same nature. Therefore, they must be decided every day. It is otherwise in the actions of life that have much influence on the future, but which happen rarely. One usually marries only once; one does not make bequests or testaments every day; one comes of age only once.

Plato[16] says that, in a town where there is no maritime commerce, half the number of civil laws are needed, and this is very true. Commerce brings into a country different sorts of peoples, a great number of agreements, kinds of goods, and ways of acquisition.

Thus, in a commercial town there are fewer judges and more laws.

[16] [Plato] *Laws*, bk. 8 [842c–d].

CHAPTER 19

That the prince should not engage in commerce

Theophilus,[17] on seeing a ship which carried commodities for his wife Theodora, had it burned. "I am the emperor," he told her, "and you make me a shipmaster. How can the poor people earn a living if we too ply their trade?" He could have added: who will restrain us if we make monopolies? Who will require us to fulfill our engagements? The courtiers will want to do our commerce; they will be more avid and more unjust than we. The people have trust in our justice; they have none in our opulence; the many imposts that make their misery[k] are certain proofs of our own.

[17] [Johannes] Zonaras [*Epitome historiarum* 25.25.41–42].

[k] Here *misère* means both "misery" and "poverty".

CHAPTER 20

Continuation of the same subject

When the Portuguese and Castilians dominated the East Indies, commerce had such rich branches that their princes did not fail to seize them. This ruined their establishments in those parts.

The viceroy of Goa granted exclusive privileges to individuals. One has no trust in such people; commerce is interrupted by the perpetual change of those to whom it is entrusted; no one manages this commerce or is concerned that one leaves only ruins to one's heir; the profit stays in the hands of individuals and is not spread out enough.

CHAPTER 21

On commerce by the nobility in a monarchy

It is against the spirit of commerce for the nobility to engage in it in a monarchy. "That would be pernicious for the towns," say the emperors Honorius and Theodosius,[18] "and would take away the ease with which merchants and plebeians buy and sell."

It is against the spirit of monarchy for the nobility to engage in commerce. The usage that permitted commerce to the nobility in England is one of the things that most contributed to weakening monarchical government there.

[18] Law "Nobiliores," *Code* [*Corpus Juris Civilis*, *Code* 4.63.3] *de commerciis et mercatoribus*, and the last law of *de rescindenda venditione* [*Corpus Juris Civilis*, *Code* 4.44].

CHAPTER 22

A particular reflection

People who are struck by what is practiced in some states think there should be laws in France engaging the nobles to carry on commerce. This would be the way to destroy the nobility, without being of any utility to commerce. The practice of this country is very wise; traders are not nobles, but they may become nobles. They can have the expectation of becoming noble without the drawback of being nobles. They have no surer way of quitting their profession than to do it well or to do it successfully: something usually linked to prosperity.

The laws ordering each man to stay in his profession and to pass it down to his children are and can be useful only in despotic states,[19] where none can or should be rivals.

[19] Indeed, they are often established that way.

Let it not be said that each man will follow his profession better when he cannot leave it for another. I say that a profession will be better pursued when those who have excelled in it can expect to attain another.

When nobility can be acquired with silver, it greatly encourages traders to put themselves in a position to attain it. I am not examining whether it is good thus to give the prize of virtue to wealth; there are governments in which this can be quite useful.

In France, that estate of the robe lying between the great nobility and the people, which, without having the brilliance of the former, has all its privileges; that estate which leaves individuals at mid-level while the body, the depository of the laws, is glorified; that estate in which one has no way to distinguish oneself but by prosperity and virtue; an honorable profession, but one which always lets a more distinguished one be seen: that altogether warlike nobility, who think that, whatever degree of wealth one has, one's fortune is yet to be made but that it is shameful to increase one's goods if one does not begin by dissipating them; that part of the nation who always serve with their capital goods; who, when they are ruined, give their place to others who will serve with their capital again; who go to war so that no one will dare to say they did not go; who expect honors when they cannot expect wealth, and when they do not get wealth, console themselves because they have acquired honor: all these things have necessarily contributed to the greatness of the kingdom. And if, over the past two or three centuries, the kingdom has endlessly increased its power, this must be attributed to the goodness of its laws and not to fortune, which does not have this sort of consistency.[l]

[l] *ces sortes de constance*. See note [b], bk. 1.

CHAPTER 23

Those nations for whom it is disadvantageous to engage in commerce

Wealth consists in land or in movable effects; the land of each country is usually possessed by its inhabitants. Most states have laws that discourage foreigners from acquiring their lands; only the presence of the master can increase their value; therefore, this kind of wealth belongs to each state particularly. But movable effects, such as silver, notes, letters of exchange, shares in companies, ships, and all commodities, belong to the whole world, which, in this regard comprises but a single state of which all societies are members; the people that possess the most of such movable effects in the universe are the richest. Some states have an immense number of them; they acquire them by their produce, by the labor of their workers, by their industry, by their discoveries, even by chance. The avarice of nations disputes the movables of the whole universe. There may be a state so unhappy that it will be deprived of the movable effects of other countries and also even of almost all its own; the owners of its land will be but the colonists of foreigners. This state will lack everything and will be able to acquire nothing; it would be far better for it to have commerce with no nation in the world; in these circumstances commerce has led to poverty.

A country which always sends out fewer commodities or less produce than it receives puts itself in equilibrium by impoverishing itself; it will receive ever less, until, in extreme poverty, it receives nothing.

In commercial countries, silver that has suddenly vanished comes back because the states that received it owe it; in the states of which we speak, silver never comes back because those who have taken it owe nothing.

Poland will serve here as our example. It has almost none of the things we call the movable effects of the universe except the grain of its fields. A few lords possess whole provinces; they oppress the plowman in order to have a greater quantity of grain to send to foreigners and procure for themselves the things their luxury demands. If Poland had commerce with no nation, its people would be happier. Its important men, who would have only their grain, would give it to their peasants for them to live on; excessively large domains would be burdensome to them, they would divide them among their peasants; as everyone would have skins or wools from his herds, there would no longer be an immense expense in making clothing; the important men, who always love luxury and who would be able to find it only in their own country, would encourage the poor in their work. I say that this nation would flourish more, unless it became barbarous; something that the laws could prevent.

Now let us consider Japan. The excessive quantity of what it can accept produces the excess of what it can send out: things will be in equilibrium as if imports and exports were moderate, and besides, this kind of inflation[m] will produce a thousand advantages for the state; there will be more consumption, more things on which the arts can be exercised, more men employed, more means of acquiring power. In cases in which one needs prompt aid, a state that is so filled can give it more quickly than another. It is hard when a country does not have superfluous things, but it is the nature of commerce to make superfluous things useful and useful ones necessary. Therefore, the state will be able to give the necessary things to a greater number of its subjects.

Let us say, therefore, that it is not the nations who need nothing that lose by carrying on commerce; it is those who need everything. It is not the peoples who have enough among themselves but those who have nothing at home who find it advantageous to trade with no one.

[m] *enflure*, "inflation," means blown up like a balloon.

BOOK 21

On laws in their relation to commerce, considered in the revolutions it has had in the world

CHAPTER I

Some general considerations

Though commerce is subject to great revolutions, it can happen that certain physical causes such as the quality of the terrain or of the climate fix its nature forever.

Today we engage in commerce with the Indies only through the silver we send there. The Romans[1] took about fifty million sesterces there every year. Just as with our silver today, this silver was converted into commodities that they brought back to the West. All peoples who have traded with the Indies have always taken metals there and brought back commodities.

Nature herself produces this effect. The Indians have their arts, which are adapted to their manner of living. Our luxury cannot be theirs, nor our needs their needs. Their climate requires and permits them to have almost nothing that comes from us. They generally go naked; the land has furnished them suitably with the clothes they have; and their religion, which has such empire over them, makes repugnant to them the things that serve as food for us. Therefore, they need only our metals, which are the signs of value and for which they give the commodities that their frugality and the nature of their land procure for them in great abundance. The ancient authors who mentioned the Indies depict them[2] as we see them today in respect to police, manners, and mores. The Indies have been, the Indies will be, what they are at

[1] Pliny the Elder [*Naturalis historia*], bk. 6, chap. 23 [6.26.101].

[2] See Pliny the Elder [*Naturalis historia*], bk. 6, chap. 19 [6.22.66]; and Strabo [*Geographica*], bk. 15 [15.1.39–73].

present, and in all times those who deal with the Indies will take silver there and bring back none.

CHAPTER 2

On the peoples of Africa

Most of the peoples on the coasts of Africa are savages or barbarians. I believe that this comes largely from there being some uninhabitable countries that separate those small countries which can be inhabited. They are without industry; they have no arts; they have precious metals in abundance which they take immediately from the hand of nature. Therefore, all peoples with a police are in a position to trade advantageously with them; they can make them have a high regard for things of no value and receive a very high price for them.

CHAPTER 3

That the needs of the peoples of the South are different from those of the peoples of the North

There is a kind of balance in Europe between the nations of the South and those of the North. The first have all sorts of the comforts of life and few needs; the second have many needs and few of the comforts of life. To the former, nature had given much, and they ask but little of it; to the others nature gives little, and they ask much of it. Equilibrium is maintained by the laziness it has given to the southern nations and by the industry and activity it has given to those of the north. The latter are obliged to work much; if they did not, they would lack everything and become barbarians. What has naturalized servitude among the southern peoples is that, as they can easily do without wealth, they can do even better without liberty. But the northern peoples need liberty, which procures for them more of the means of satisfying all the needs nature has given them. The northern peoples are, therefore, in a forced state unless they are either free or barbarians; almost all the southern peoples are, in some fashion, in a violent state unless they are slaves.

CHAPTER 4

The principal difference between the commerce of the ancients and that of today

From time to time the world meets with situations that change commerce. Today the commerce of Europe is principally carried on from north to south. However, the difference in climates makes people have a great need for each other's commodities. For example, the beverages of the South carried to the North form a kind of commerce scarcely pursued by the ancients. Thus the capacity of ships formerly measured by hogsheads of grain is measured today by casks of liquor.

As the ancient commerce that is known to us was from one Mediterranean port to another, it was almost entirely in the South. But, as peoples of the same climate have almost the same things, they do not need commerce with one another as much as do peoples of differing climates. Therefore, commerce in Europe was less extensive formerly than it is at present.

This is not in contradiction with what I have said about our commerce in the Indies; the difference in climates is so extreme that there is no relation between their needs and ours.

CHAPTER 5

Other differences

Commerce, sometimes destroyed by conquerors, sometimes hampered by monarchs, wanders across the earth, flees from where it is oppressed, and remains where it is left to breathe: it reigns today where one used to see only deserted places, seas, and rocks; there where it used to reign are now only deserted places.

Today upon seeing Colchis, which is no more than a vast forest where the people, who are fewer every day, defend their liberty only in order to sell themselves one by one to the Turks and Persians, one would never say that this region had been at the time of the Romans full of towns whose commerce called all the nations of the world to it. No record of this is to be found in the country; there are traces of it only in Pliny[3] and Strabo.[4]

The history of commerce is that of communication among peoples. Its greatest events are formed by their various destructions and certain ebbs and flows of population and of devastations.

[3] [Pliny the Elder, *Naturalis historia*] bk. 6 [6.4.11–5.18].
[4] [Strabo, *Geographica*] bk. 2 [11.2.18].

CHAPTER 6

On the commerce of the ancients

The immense treasures of Semiramis,[5] which could not have been acquired in a day, make us think that the Assyrians themselves had pillaged other wealthy nations, as other nations later pillaged them.

The effect of commerce is wealth; the consequence of wealth, luxury; that of luxury, the perfection of the arts. The arts, carried to the point at which they were found in the time of Semiramis,[6] indicate to us that a great commerce was already established.

There was a great commerce of luxury in the empires of Asia. The history of luxury would be a fine part of the history of commerce; the luxury of the Persians was that of the Medes, as that of the Medes was that of the Assyrians.

Great changes have occurred in Asia. The northeastern parts of Persia, Hyrcania, Margiana, Bactria, etc., were formerly full of flourishing towns[7] which exist no more, and the north of this empire,[8] that is the isthmus separating the Caspian Sea from the Black Sea, was covered with towns and nations which are no more.

Eratosthenes[9] and Aristobulus found in Patrocles[10] that the com-

[5] Diodorus Siculus [*Bibliotheca historica*], bk. 2 [2.7–12].
[6] Ibid. [Diodorus Siculus, *Bibliotheca historica* 2.7–9].
[7] See Pliny the Elder [*Naturalis historia*], bk. 6, chap. 16 [6.17.46–49]; and Strabo [*Geographica*], bk. 11 [11.1.1– 11.8.1].
[8] Ibid. [Strabo, *Geographica* 11.8.2.]
[9] Ibid. [Strabo, *Geographica* 11.7.3.]
[10] As appears in Strabo's account Patrocles' authority is considerable. [*Geographica*], bk. 2 [11.7.3].

modities of the Indies went down the Oxus into the Black Sea.[a] Marcus Varro[11] tells us that at the time of Pompey during the war against Mithridates it was learned that it took seven days to go from the Indies to Bactria and thus to the river Icarus, which flows into the Oxus; that in this way the commodities of the Indies could cross the Caspian Sea to enter the mouth of the Cyrus; that from this river there was only a five-day journey overland to the Phasis, which flowed into the Black Sea. No doubt the great empires of the Assyrians, the Medes, and the Persians communicated with the most remote parts of the East and the West by way of the nations that populated these various countries.

This communication no longer exists. All these countries have been laid waste by the Tartars,[12] and this destructive nation still lives there and infects them. The Oxus no longer runs to the Caspian Sea; the Tartars have diverted it for particular reasons;[13] it disappears into arid sands.

The Jaxartes, which once formed a barrier between the nations with a police and the barbarian nations, has been similarly diverted[14] by Tartars and no longer flows to the sea.

Seleucus Nicator formed the project[15] of joining the Black Sea to the Caspian Sea. This design, which would have made the commerce of that time very easy, vanished with his death.[16] One does not know whether he could have carried it out in the isthmus that separates the two seas. This country is very little known today; it is depopulated and filled with forests. Water is not lacking there, for an infinity of rivers descends from the Caucasus mountains, but the Caucasus, which forms the north of the isthmus and whose arms[17] reach to the south,

[11] In Pliny the Elder [*Naturalis historia*], bk. 6, chap. 17 [6.19.51–52]. See also Strabo [*Geographica*], bk. 11 [11.2.17], for the route of merchandise from Phasis to Cyrus.

[12] Many changes must have occurred in this country since the time of Ptolemy, who describes so many rivers flowing into the eastern part of the Caspian Sea. The map of the Czar shows only the river of Astrabat in that part, and Bathalsi's shows nothing. [The "Map of the Czar" was a map of the Caspian region made by J. G. Homann under the direction of Karl van Verden and was published in Leipzig in the early eighteenth century (1720). Bathalsi is Basil Battazi or Vatace, a Greek cartographer who prepared a map of central Asia (*ca.* 1732).]

[13] See Jenkinson's account in the *Recueil de voyages au nord*, vol. 4 [Voyage d'Antoine Jenkinson; 4, 487; 1732 edn].

[14] I believe Lake Aral was formed from this.

[15] Claudius Caesar, in Pliny the Elder [*Naturalis historia*], bk. 6, chap. 2 [6.12.31].

[16] He was killed by Ptolemy Keraunos.

[17] See Strabo [*Geographica*], bk. 11 [11.14.4].

[a] The Hircanian Sea (the Caspian Sea), according to Strabo.

would have been a great obstacle, especially in those times when the art of making locks did not yet exist.

One might believe that Seleucus wanted to join the two seas at the very place where Czar Peter I has since done it, that is, on that spit of land where the Tanais is close to the Volga, but the north of the Caspian Sea had not yet been discovered.

While there was a commerce of luxury among the empires of Asia, the Tyrians engaged in an economic commerce around the whole world. Bochart has used the first book of his *Canaan*[b] to enumerate the colonies they sent to all the countries along the sea coast; they went beyond the Pillars of Hercules and set up establishments[18] on the coasts of the ocean.

In those times, navigators were obliged to follow the coast, which was their compass, so to speak. Their voyages were long and arduous. The laborious voyage of Ulysses was a fertile subject for the finest poem in the world, after the one which is the first of all.

The little knowledge most people had about those who were far away from them favored the nations that engaged in economic commerce. They put what obscurities they wanted into their trading; they had all the advantages of intelligent nations over ignorant peoples.

Egypt, removed by its religion and mores from any communication with foreigners, did scarcely any commerce abroad; it enjoyed a fertile terrain and extreme abundance. It was the Japan of those times; it was sufficient to itself.

The Egyptians were so little jealous of external commerce that they left that of the Red Sea to all the small nations that had ports there. They permitted the Idumaeans, the Jews, and the Syrians to have fleets there. For this navigation Solomon[19] employed the Tyrians, who knew these seas.

Josephus[20] says that his nation, occupied exclusively with agriculture, knew the sea but little; thus the Jews traded on the Red Sea only occasionally. They conquered the Idumaean towns of Elath and Ezion-geber, which gave them this commerce; they lost these two towns and this commerce as well.

[18] They founded Tartessos and settled at Cadiz.
[19] I Kings, chap. 9 [I Kings 9.26]; II Chronicles, chap. 8 [2.8.17].
[20] [Josephus] *Contra Appian* [1.12.60–68].

[b] Samuel Bochart, *Geographia sacra seu Phaleg et Canaan* (1692).

It was not the same for the Phoenicians; they did not engage in a commerce of luxury; they did not trade as a result of conquest; their frugality, their ability, their industry, their perils, and their hardships made them necessary to all the nations in the world.

The nations neighboring on the Red Sea traded only on this sea and on that of Africa. The universal astonishment at Alexander's discovery of the Indian Ocean is sufficient proof of this. We have said[21] that precious metals are still carried to the Indies and that none are brought back;[22] the Jewish fleets which brought back gold and silver through the Red Sea were returning from Africa and not from the Indies.

I say further: this voyage was made along the eastern coast of Africa, and the state of sailing at that time is sufficient proof that one did not go to very distant places.

I know that the fleets of Solomon and of Jehoshaphat returned only in the third year, but I do not see that the length of the voyage proves the greatness of the distance.

Pliny and Strabo tell us that the route traversed in twenty days by a ship made of rushes in the Indies or the Red Sea could be covered in seven days by a Greek or Roman ship.[23] Using this proportion, a voyage of about one year for the Greek or Roman fleet was a voyage of about three years for Solomon's fleets.

Two ships of unequal speeds do not make their voyages in times proportional to their speeds; slowness often produces an even greater slowness. When it is a question of following the coasts and when one is constantly in a different situation, when one must wait for a good wind in order to leave a gulf and have another in order to set out, a ship that is a good sailor profits from all the favorable weather, while the other one remains in a difficult spot and waits several days for another change.

This slowness of the Indians ships, which, in an equal time, could go but a third of the distance covered by the Greek and Roman ships, can be explained by what we see today in our sailing. The Indian ships made of rushes drew less water than the Greek and Roman vessels made of wood joined with iron.

One can compare the Indian ships to those of some nations today

[21] In chapter 1 of this book [that is, 21.1, above].

[22] The proportion established in Europe between gold and silver can sometimes permit one to profit by taking gold from the Indies for silver; but it amounts to little.

[23] See Pliny the Elder [*Naturalis historia*], bk. 6, ch. 22 [6.24.82]; and Strabo [*Geographica*], bk. 15 [15.1.14–15].

whose ports are not very deep, such as those of Venice and even Italy generally,[24] the Baltic Sea, and the province of Holland.[25] Their ships, which have to go in and out of these ports, are built with round, broad bottoms, whereas the ships of nations that have good ports have hulls formed to lie deep in the water. This mechanism makes the latter ships sail closer to the wind and the former sail almost only when they have the wind to the stern. A ship that lies deeper in the water sails in the same direction in almost any wind; this comes from the resistance that the boat, pushed by the wind, finds in the water, which gives it a point of support, and from the long form of the vessel, which presents its side to the wind while, because of the shape of the rudder, one turns the prow in the direction one proposes; in this way one can go very close to the wind, that is, nearly in the direction from which the wind comes. But when the ship is round and broad-bottomed and consequently does not sink deep into the water, there is no point of support; the wind pushes the vessel, which can neither resist nor go scarcely anywhere but where the wind blows. From this it follows that vessels constructed with a round bottom are slower in their voyages: (1) they lose much time waiting for the wind, especially if they are often obliged to change directions; (2) they go more slowly because, not having a point of support, they cannot carry as many sails as the others. For if, at a time when sailing has much improved, at a time when the arts are communicated, at a time when one corrects with art both the defect of nature and the defects of art itself, one feels these differences, what must it have been for the sailing of the ancients?

I cannot leave this subject. The Indian ships were small, and those of the Greeks and Romans, if one excepts those machines made for ostentation, were smaller than ours. The smaller the ship, the more it is endangered by bad weather. A tempest that can sink a ship would only make it roll if it were larger. The relation between a large body and its surface is smaller than that of a small body and its surface; from which it follows that a small ship has a smaller ratio, that is, a greater difference between the surface of the ship and the weight or load it can carry than a large one has. One knows that in an almost general practice, a ship takes cargo equal to half the weight of the water it could contain. Let us assume that a ship could hold eight hundred tons of water: its load would be four hundred tons; that of a ship which could hold only four

[24] Italy has almost nothing but roads, but Sicily has very good ports.
[25] I say the province of Holland, for the ports of the province of Zeeland are quite deep.

hundred tons of water would be two hundred tons. Thus, the size of the first ship to the weight it would carry would be as 8 is to 4; and that of the second, as 4 is to 2. Let us assume that the surface of the large one is to the surface of the small one, as 8 is to 6; the surface[26] of the latter to its weight will be as 6 is to 2; while the surface of the former to its weight will be only as 8 is to 4; and with the winds and the waves acting only on the surface of each, the large vessel with its weight will resist their impetus better than the small one.

[26] That is, to compare sizes of the same kind: the action or pressure of the water on the boat will be to the resistance of the same boat as . . . etc.

CHAPTER 7
On the commerce of the Greeks

The first Greeks were all pirates. Minos, who had empire on the sea, was perhaps only a more successful bandit; his empire was limited to the environs of his island. But when the Greeks became a great people, the Athenians gained a true empire on the sea because this commercial and victorious nation gave laws to the most powerful monarch[27] at that time and crushed the maritime forces of Syria, of the island of Cyprus, and of Phoenicia.

I must speak of Athens' empire on the sea. "Athens," says Xenophon,[28]

> has empire on the sea, but as Attica is on the land, enemies ravage it when it makes expeditions to distant places. The principal men permit their lands to be destroyed and put their goods securely on some island; the populace, which has no lands, lives without worry. But if the Athenians lived on an island and had also empire on the sea, they would have the power to harm others and no one would be able to harm them, so long as they remained masters of the sea.

You might say that Xenophon intended to speak of England.

Athens, filled with projects for glory, Athens, which increased jealousy instead of increasing in influence, more attentive to extending its maritime empire than to using it, with a political government such

[27] The King of Persia.
[28] [Xenophon, "The Old Oligarch"] *The Constitution of Athens* [2.14–16].

that the common people distributed the public revenues to themselves while the rich were oppressed, did not engage in the great commerce promised it by the work of its mines, the multitude of its slaves, the number of its sailors, its authority over the Greek towns, and, more than all that, the fine institutions of Solon. Its trading was limited almost entirely to Greece and the Black Sea, from which it drew its sustenance.

Corinth was admirably well situated; it separated two seas, opened and shut the Peloponnesus, and opened and shut Greece. It was a town of the greatest importance in a time when the Greek people were a world, and the Greek towns, nations. It did a greater commerce than Athens. It had one port to receive commodities from Asia; it had another to receive those from Italy; for, as there were great difficulties in going around Cape Malea, where opposing winds[29] meet causing shipwrecks, one preferred to go to Corinth where vessels could even be carried overland from one sea to another. In no other town were works of art carried so far. Religion completed the corruption of what its opulence had left of its mores. It erected a temple to Venus, to whom more than a thousand courtesans were dedicated. From this seminary graduated most of the celebrated beauties whose history Athenaeus dared to write.

It seems that in the time of Homer, the opulence of Greece was in Rhodes, Corinth, and Orchomenus. "Jupiter," he says,[30] "loved the Rhodians and gave them great wealth." He attached the epithet of wealthy to Corinth.[31] Similarly, when he wants to speak of towns having much gold, he cites Orchomenus,[32] which he adds to Thebes in Egypt. Rhodes and Corinth preserved their power and Orchomenus did not. The location of Orchomenus close to the Hellespont, Propontis, and the Black Sea naturally makes one think that it drew its wealth from commerce on the coasts of these seas, which occasioned the story of the golden fleece; and, indeed, the name of Minyan is given to Orchomenus[33] and also to the Argonauts.[c] But later, as these seas became

[29] See Strabo [*Geographica*], bk. 8 [8.6.20].
[30] [Homer] *Iliad*, bk. 2 [2.667–669].
[31] Ibid. [Homer, *Iliad* 2.570].
[32] Ibid. [Homer, *Iliad*], bk. 1, l. 381 [9.381]. See Strabo [*Geographica*], bk. 9, p. 414; 1620 edn [9.2.40].
[33] Strabo [*Geographica*], bk. 9, p. 414 [9.2.40].

[c] Apollonius Rhodius, *Argonautica* 2.1186.

better known, as the Greeks established a great number of colonists there, as these colonies dealt with the barbarian peoples, as they communicated with their mother country, Orchomenus began to decline, and it disappeared into the crowd of other Greek towns.

Before Homer the Greeks had traded almost only with each other and with some barbarian peoples, but they extended their domination gradually as they formed new peoples. Greece was a great peninsula whose capes seemed to have made the seas roll back and the gulfs open on all sides as if to receive them. If one looks at Greece, one will see, in a rather compact country, a very extensive coastline. Innumerable colonies lay in a wide circle around it; and in them the Greeks saw, so to speak, everyone who was not a barbarian. Did they penetrate Sicily and Italy? They formed nations there. Did they sail toward the Black Sea, toward the coasts of Asia Minor, toward those of Africa? They did the same. Their towns became prosperous the closer they were to the new peoples. And, remarkably, innumerable islands stood as if to make a wall around Greece.

What causes for Greek prosperity were the games it gave, so to speak, to the universe; the temples to which all the kings sent offerings; the festivals where people gather from all parts; the oracles, which attracted all human curiosity; finally, taste and the arts, which were brought to a point that whoever believes they have been surpassed will forever be in ignorance of them?[d]

[d] This sentence ends in a question mark in the text.

CHAPTER 8

On Alexander. His conquest

Four events occurred under Alexander that produced a great revolution in commerce: the capture of Tyre, the conquest of Egypt, that of the Indies, and the discovery of the sea to the south of that country.

The empire of the Persians reached as far as the Indus.[34] Long before Alexander, Darius[35] had sent out sailors who descended this

[34] Strabo [*Geographica*], bk. 15 [15.2.1].
[35] Herodotus [*The Persian Wars*] in Melpomene [4.44].

river and went as far as the Red Sea.[e] How, therefore, could the Greeks have been the first to bring commerce to the Indies from the South? How had the Persians not done this before? Of what use to them were the seas that were so close to them, the seas that bathed the shores of their empire? It is true that Alexander conquered the Indies, but must one conquer a country in order to trade with it? I shall examine this.

Ariana,[36] which stretched from the Persian Gulf to the Indus and from the Southern Sea to the mountains of the Paropamisus, was certainly dependent in some way on the Persian empire, but its southern part was arid, burned, uncultivated, and barbarian. Tradition says[37] that armies of Semiramis and of Cyrus had perished in these deserts, and Alexander, who had his fleet follow him, did not fail to lose a large part of his army. The Persians left the whole coast in the power of the Icthyophagi,[38] the Oreitae, and other barbarian peoples. Further, the Persians were not sailors, and their religion itself barred them from any idea of maritime commerce.[39] The voyage that Darius had them make down the Indus and the Indian Sea was the fancy of a prince who wants to show his power rather than the orderly project of a monarch who wants to use it. This had no consequences, either for commerce, or for sailing, and if one departed from ignorance, it was only to return to it shortly.

There is more: it was accepted,[40] before Alexander's expedition, that the southern part of the Indies was uninhabitable;[41] this followed from a tradition that Semiramis[42] had brought back only twenty men and Cyrus only seven.

Alexander entered from the north. His design was to march to the

[36] Strabo [*Geographica*], bk. 15 [15.2.1].
[37] Ibid. [Strabo, *Geographica* 15.2.5].
[38] Pliny the Elder [*Naturalis historia*], bk. 6, chap. 23 [6.26.97]; Strabo [*Geographica*], bk. 15 [15.2.2].
[39] In order not to defile the elements, they did not navigate on the rivers. [Thomas] Hyde, *Historia religionis veterum Persarum in Sad-der* [chap. 6; p. 139; 1700 edn]. Still today they have no maritime commerce and they call those who sail the seas atheists.
[40] Strabo [*Geographica*], bk. 15 [15.1.5 and 15.2.5].
[41] Herodotus [*The Persian Wars*] in Melpomene [4.44] says that Darius conquered the Indies. This can be understood only of Ariana; even so, it was only an imagined conquest.
[42] Strabo [*Geographica*], bk. 15 [15.1.5 and 15.2.5].

[e] Known today as the Persian Gulf. Montesquieu often uses the place names used in his references.

east, but, upon finding the southern part full of great nations, towns, and rivers, he attempted to conquer it and did so.

At that time he formed the design of uniting the Indies with the west by a maritime commerce, as he had united them by the colonies he had established on the land.

He had a fleet built on the Hydaspes, descended this river, entered the Indus, and sailed to its mouth. He left his army and his fleet at Patala, went himself with some vessels to reconnoiter that sea, marked the places where he wanted ports, harbors, and arsenals constructed. On returning to Patala, he left his fleet and took the land route in order to help the fleet and receive help from it. The fleet followed the coast from the mouth of the Indus, along the shore of the countries of the Oreitae, of the Icthyophagi, of Caramania, and of Persia. He had wells dug and towns built; he prohibited the Ichthyophagi[43] from living on fish; he wanted the shores of this sea to be inhabited by civilized nations. Nearchus and Onescicritus kept a journal of this voyage, which took ten months. They arrived at Susa; they found Alexander there, feasting his army.

This conqueror had founded Alexandria with a view to securing Egypt for himself; this was a key for opening it in the very place where the kings, his predecessors, had locked it;[44] and he did not dream of commerce, the thought of which could come to him only with the discovery of the Indian Sea.

It appears that even after this discovery he had no new views about Alexandria. He certainly had, in general, the project of establishing a commerce between the Indies and the western part of his empire, but he had too little information to be able to form the project of carrying this commerce through Egypt. He had seen the Indus; he had seen the Nile, but he did not know about the Arabian Seas that are between the two. He had scarcely arrived in the Indies when he had new fleets built

[43] This cannot be understood of all the Ichthyophagi [the Fish-Eaters] who inhabited a coast of ten thousand furlongs. How could Alexander have provided them their subsistence? How would he have made himself obeyed? Here it can be a question only of a few specific peoples. Nearchus, in the book [Arrian] *Indica* [28], says that at the extremity of this coast, near Persia, he had found some peoples whose diet was less dependent on fish. I would believe that this order of Alexander's concerned this region or some other one even closer to Persia.

[44] Alexandria was founded near a beach called Rhacotes. Ancient kings kept a garrison there to protect the entrance of the country from foreigners and chiefly from the Greeks, who were, as is known, great pirates. See Pliny the Elder [*Naturalis historia*], bk. 6, chap. 10 [5.11.62–63]; and Strabo [*Geographica*], bk. 18 [17.1.6].

and set sail[45] on the Eulaeus, the Tigris, the Euphrates, and the sea; he removed the cataracts the Persians had put in these rivers; he discovered that the Persian Gulf was a gulf of the ocean. As he set out to explore this sea[46] in the same way he had explored that of the Indies, as he had a port for a thousand vessels and arsenals built in Babylon, as he sent five hundred talents to Phoenicia and Syria in order to attract pilots whom he wanted to settle in the colonies that he built along the coasts, and finally, as he did immense work on the Euphrates and the other Assyrian rivers, one cannot doubt that his design was to engage in commerce with the Indies through Babylon and the Persian Gulf.

Some people, assuming that Alexander wanted to conquer Arabia,[47] have said that he had formed the design of putting the seat of his empire there; but, how could he have chosen a place unknown to him?[48] Besides, it was the most out-of-the-way country in the world; he would have been separated from his empire. The caliphs, who conquered faraway lands, left Arabia immediately in order to establish themselves elsewhere.

[45] Arrian, *Anabasis*, bk. 7 [7.7].
[46] Ibid. [Arrian, *Anabasis* 7.7].
[47] Strabo [*Geographica*], at the end of bk. 16 [16.4.27].
[48] Seeing Babylon flooded, he considered Arabia, which is nearby, an island. Aristobulus in Strabo [*Geographica*], bk. 16 [16.1.11].

CHAPTER 9

On the commerce of the Greek kings after Alexander

When Alexander conquered Egypt, the Red Sea was almost unknown, and nothing was known of that part of the ocean that joins this sea and bathes the coast of Africa on one side and that of Arabia on the other; it was even believed later that it was impossible to go around the Arabian peninsula. Those who had tried to go around from each side had abandoned their enterprise. It was said:[49] "How would it be possible to sail south from the coasts of Arabia, as almost the whole army of Cambyses perished crossing Arabia from the north, and the army that Ptolemy, son of Lagus, sent to help Seleucus Nicator in Babylon

[49] See the book [Arrian] *Indica* [43.4–5].

suffered unbelievable ills and could march only at night because of the heat?"

The Persians had no shipping of any sort. When they conquered Egypt, they brought with them the same spirit they had at home, and their indifference to sailing was so extreme that the Greek kings found them ignorant not only of the ocean voyages made by the Tyrians, the Idumaeans, and the Jews, but also even of those on the Red Sea. I believe that the destruction of the first Tyre by Nebuchadnezzar, and that of several small nations and towns near the Red Sea, caused the loss of the knowledge that had been acquired.

Egypt did not reach to the Red Sea in the time of the Persians; it included[50] only that long narrow strip of land covered by the Nile during its floods and enclosed on each side by mountain chains. Therefore, the Red Sea had to be discovered a second time, and the ocean a second time, too, and this discovery awaited the curiosity of the Greek kings.

The Nile was explored; elephants were hunted in the countries between the Nile and the sea; the shores of this sea were discovered by land; and as this discovery was made under the Greeks, the names are Greek, and the temples are dedicated[51] to Greek divinities.

The Greeks of Egypt were able to engage in a very extensive commerce: they were the masters of the Ports of the Red Sea; Tyre, the rival of every commercial nation, was no longer; the Greeks of Egypt were not hampered by that country's ancient superstitions;[52] Egypt had become the center of the universe.

In the Indies, the kings of Syria left the commerce of the south to the kings of Egypt and pursued only that of the north through the Oxus and the Caspian Sea. It was believed at that time that this sea was a part of the northern ocean,[53] and that Alexander, some time before his death, had had a fleet built[54] in order to discover if it connected with the ocean by the Black Sea or by some other eastern sea toward the Indies. After him, Seleucus and Antiochus paid particular attention to its exploration; they stationed fleets there.[55] What Seleucus explored was called

[50] Strabo, bk. 16 [*Geographica* 16.4.20].

[51] Ibid. [Strabo, *Geographica* 16.4.5–19.]

[52] They gave them a horror of foreigners.

[53] Pliny the Elder [*Naturalis historia*], bk. 2, chap. 68 [2.67.168] and bk. 6, chaps. 9 and 12 [6.10.28; 6.14.33]; Strabo [*Geographica*], bk. 11 [11.1.5; 11.6.1]; Arrian, *Anabasis*, bk. 3, p. 74 [3.30.7] and bk. 5, p. 104 [5.5.4].

[54] Arrian, *Anabasis*, bk. 7 [7.16.1–2].

[55] Pliny the Elder [*Naturalis historia*], bk. 2, chap. 64 [2.67.168].

the Sea of Seleucus; what Antiochus discovered was called the Sea of Antiochus. While attending to projects they could undertake along this coast, they neglected the southern seas, either because the Ptolemies had already gained empire of them with their fleets on the Red Sea, or because they had discovered an unconquerable aversion among the Persians to seafaring. The southern coast of Persia did not furnish sailors; they were seen there only at the end of Alexander's life. But the kings of Egypt, masters of the island of Cyprus, of Phoenicia, and of a large number of places on the coast of Asia Minor, had all sorts of ways of undertaking maritime enterprises. They did not have to constrain the genius of their subjects; they had only to follow it.

One can scarcely understand the ancients' obstinacy in believing that the Caspian Sea was a part of the ocean. The expeditions of Alexander, of the kings of Syria, of the Parthians and the Romans could not alter their thinking; this is because one retracts one's errors as slowly as one can. At first only the southern part of the Caspian Sea was known; it was taken for the ocean; as one moved north along its shores, one still believed that it was the ocean extending inland; by following the coasts one explored to the east only as far as the Jaxartes, and to the west, only to the farthest points of Albania.[f] The sea to the north was muddy[56] and consequently little suited to navigation. The result of all this was that one always saw only the ocean.

Alexander's army had gone east only as far as the Hyphasis, which is the last of the rivers that flow into the Indus. Thus, the first commerce the Greeks had with the Indies was with a very small part of that country. Seleucus Nicator went as far as the Ganges,[57] and this led to the discovery of the sea into which that river flows, that is, the Gulf of Bengal. Today lands are discovered by sea voyages; formerly, seas were discovered by the conquest of lands.

Strabo,[58] in spite of the testimony of Apollodorus, appears to doubt that the Greek kings of Bactria[59] went further than Seleucus and Alexander. If it is true that they did not go further east than Seleucus,

[56] See the Map of the Czar [see translators' note at 21.n.12].

[57] Pliny the Elder [*Naturalis historia*], bk. 6, chap. 17 [6.21.63].

[58] [Strabo, *Geographica*] bk. 15 [15.1.3].

[59] When the Macedonians of Bactria, of the Indies, and of Ariana separated from the kingdom of Syria, they formed a great state.

---

[f] This Albania is on the west coast of the Caspian Sea, north of the Kura River and south of the Caucasus Mountains.

they went further south; they discovered[60] Siger and the ports of Malabar, which occasioned the navigation of which I am about to speak.

Pliny[61] tells us that three successive routes were taken to the Indies. First, one went from the headland of Siagre to the Island of Patala, which is at the mouth of the Indus; it will be remembered that this was the route taken by Alexander's fleet. Then a shorter and more secure route[62] was found from this same headland to Sigerus. This Sigerus can only be the kingdom of Sigerus that Strabo mentions,[63] which was discovered by the Greek kings of Bactria. Pliny could say that this route was shorter only because it took less time, for Sigerus had to be further than the Indus, as it was discovered by the kings of Bactria. Therefore, this route must have avoided certain coasts, and certain winds must have been advantageous. Finally, the merchants took a third route; they went to Cane or to Cella, ports situated at the mouth of the Red Sea, from which by a west wind they came to Muziris, the first trading town in the Indies, and from there to other ports. One sees that instead of going from the mouth of the Red Sea to Siagre along the coast of Arabia Felix to the northeast, they went directly from west to east, from one side to the other, by means of the monsoon whose changes had been discovered while navigating these latitudes. The ancients left the coasts only when they took advantage of the monsoons[64] or the trade winds, which were a kind of compass for them.

Pliny says[65] that they left for the Indies in the middle of the summer and returned toward the end of December and the beginning of January. This corresponds exactly with the journals of our navigators. In the part of the Indian Sea that lies between the peninsula of Africa and the one of this side of the Ganges, there are two monsoons: the first, during which winds go from west to east, begins in August and September; the second, when the winds go from east to west, begins in January. Thus, we leave Africa for Malabar at the time the fleet of Ptolemy left, and we return at the same time.

[60] Apollonius [Apollodorus] of Artemita, in Strabo [*Geographica*], bk. 11 [11.11.1].
[61] [Pliny the Elder, *Naturalis historia*] bk. 6, chap. 23 [6.26.96–101, 104–105].
[62] Pliny the Elder [*Naturalis historia*], bk. 6, chap. 23 [6.26.101].
[63] [Strabo, *Geographica*] bk. 11 [11.11.1]: "the kingdom of Sigerdis" [L.].
[64] The monsoons blow for a part of the year in one direction and for a part of the year in the other; the tradewinds blow in the same direction the year around.
[65] [Pliny the Elder, *Naturalis historia*] bk. 6, chap. 23 [6.26.106].

Alexander's fleet took seven months to go from Patala to Susa. It left in the month of July, that is, at a time when no ship today dares put out to return from the Indies. Between the first and the second monsoon, there is a period when the winds vary and when a north wind, mixed with the ordinary winds, causes terrible storms, especially along the coasts. This lasts through the months of June, July, and August. Alexander's fleet, leaving Patala in the month of July, endured many storms, and the voyage was long because the fleet sailed against the monsoon.

Pliny says that they left for the Indies at the end of the summer; thus they used the interval between the monsoons to travel from Alexandria to the Red Sea.

See, I beg you, how navigation gradually improved. It took two and a half years for Darius to descend the Indus and reach the Red Sea.[66] Alexander's fleet[67] descended the Indus and arrived at Susa ten months later, having sailed three months on the Indus and seven on the Indian Sea. Later, the trip from the Malabar coast to the Red Sea was made in forty days.[68]

Strabo, who explains their ignorance of the countries between the Hyphasis and the Ganges, says that among the navigators who went from Egypt to the Indies few went as far as the Ganges. Indeed, one sees that their fleets did not go there; they went with the monsoons, from west to east, from the mouth of the Red Sea to the Malabar coast. They stopped at the trading towns and did not go around the peninsula, which lies this side of the Ganges, by Cape Comorin and the Coromandel coast. The plan of navigation of the kings of Egypt and of the Romans was to return in the same year.[69]

Thus, the commerce of the Greeks and Romans in the Indies was far less extensive than ours; yet we know of immense countries that they did not know; we engage in commerce with all the Indian nations and even do their commerce and navigation for them.

But they engaged in commerce with greater ease than we do, and if today we traded only on the coast of Gujarat and Malabar, and if, without seeking the Southern Islands, we were satisfied with the commodities the islanders would bring us, the Egyptian route would

[66] Herodotus [*The Persian Wars*], in Melpomene [4.44].
[67] Pliny the Elder [*Naturalis historia*], bk. 6, chap. 23 [6.23.96–100].
[68] Ibid. [Pliny the Elder, *Naturalis historia* 6.26.104].
[69] Ibid. [Pliny the Elder, *Naturalis historia* 6.26.106].

have to be preferred to that of the Cape of Good Hope. Strabo says[70] that trade with the peoples of Taprobane[g] was done in this way.

[70][Strabo, *Geographica*] bk. 15 [15.1.14–15].

[g]Sri Lanka.

CHAPTER 10

On sailing around Africa

We learn from history that before the discovery of the compass, there were four attempts to sail around Africa. The Phoenicians, who were sent first by Necho,[71] and then by Eudoxus,[72] fleeing the anger of Ptolemy-Lathyrus, set out from the Red Sea and succeeded. Sataspes,[73] under Xerxes, and Hanno, who was sent by the Carthaginians, went by way of the Pillars of Hercules and failed.

The main problem in sailing around Africa was to discover and weather the Cape of Good Hope. But, if one set out from the Red Sea, this Cape was nearer by half than if one went by way of the Mediterranean. The coast from the Red Sea to the Cape is safer than[74] the one from the Cape to the Pillars of Hercules. For those who set out from the Pillars of Hercules to discover the Cape, the compass had to be invented, so that they could leave the coast of Africa and sail into the vast ocean,[75] either going towards the island of Saint Helena or towards the coast of Brazil. Therefore, it was quite possible for them to have gone from the Red Sea to the Mediterranean without ever going from the Mediterranean to the Red Sea.

Thus, without making this great circuit, from which one could never return, it was more natural to engage in commerce with east Africa by

[71]Herodotus [*The Persian Wars*], bk. 4 [4.42].

[72]Pliny the Elder [*Naturalis historia*], bk. 2, chap. 67 [2.67.167–170]; Pomponius Mela [*De situ orbis*], bk. 3, chap. 9 [3.9.20].

[73]Herodotus [*The Persian Wars*], in Melpomene [4.43].

[74]Join to this what I say about Hanno's navigation in chap. 11 of this book.

[75]A north-east wind is found in the Atlantic ocean in October, November, December, and January. One crosses the line and, to avoid the general east wind, one directs one's route to the south, or else one enters the torrid zone where the wind blows from the west to the east.

way of the Red Sea and with the west coast by way of the Pillars of Hercules.

In the Red Sea the Greek kings of Egypt first discovered the part of the African coast that stretches from the bottom of the gulf where the city of Heroum is situated to Deidre, that is, to the straits called Bab el Mandeb. From there to the Cape of Aromatum at the entrance to the Red Sea,[76] the coast had not been explored by sailors, and this is clear in what Artemidorus[77] tells us, that the places along this coast were known but the distances unknown; this came from the fact that one had explored these ports one by one over land routes, without going from one port to another.

Nothing was known beyond the promontory where the coast of the ocean begins, as we learn[78] from Eratosthenes and Artemidorus.

Such was the knowledge about the coasts of Africa in the time of Strabo, that is, in the time of Augustus. But, after Augustus, the Romans discovered Cape Raptum and Cape Prassum, which Strabo does not mention because they were not yet known. These two names are Roman.

Ptolemy, the geographer, lived under Hadrian and Antoninus Pius; and the author of the *Periplus* of the Erythraien Sea, whoever he was, lived somewhat later. However, the former sets the limits of known Africa[79] at Cape Prassum, which is about fourteen degrees south latitude, and the author of the *Periplus*[80] sets them at Cape Raptum, which is about ten degrees south latitude. It appears that the latter took for the limit a place habitually reached, and Ptolemy a place one no longer went.

What confirms me in this idea is that the peoples around the Prassum were cannibals.[81] Ptolemy, who tells us of a great number of places between the port of Aromatus and Cape Raptum,[82] leaves the space from the Rhaptum to the Prassum completely empty. The great profits from navigation to the Indies must have led to the neglect of

[76] The gulf to which we give this name today was called the Gulf of Arabia by the ancients: they called the part of the ocean that borders on this gulf the Red Sea.

[77] Strabo [*Geographica*], bk. 15 [16.4.5–19].

[78] Strabo [*Geographica*], bk. 16 [16.4.4–5]. Artemidorus followed the known coast to the place called *Austricornu*; the Eratosthenes, to that called *ad Cinnamomiferam*.

[79] [Claudius Ptolemy, *Geographica*] bk. 1, chap. 7 and bk. 4, chap. 9 [1.7 and 4.7]; map 4 of Africa.

[80] This *Periplus* has been attributed to Arrian.

[81] [Claudius Ptolemy, *Geographica*], bk. 4, chap. 9 [4.8(9)].

[82] [Claudius Ptolemy, *Geographica*] bk. 4, chaps. 7 and 8 [4.7, 8(9)].

African navigation. Finally, the Romans did not navigate regularly on this coast; they had discovered these ports by land and by ships driven there in storms; and just as today one knows the coasts of Africa rather well and the interior very poorly,[83] the ancients knew the interior rather well, and the coasts very poorly.

I have said that the Phoenicians, sent by Necho and Eudoxus under Ptolemy Lathyrus, had sailed around Africa; these two voyages must have been thought to be fables at the time of Ptolemy, the geographer, because he puts[84] below the Sinus Magnus, which is, I believe, the Gulf of Siam, an unknown land which extends from Asia and Africa to border upon Cape Prassum, making only a lake of the Indian Sea. The ancients, who explored the Indies from the north and advanced eastward, put this unknown land to the south.

[83] Note with what exactitude Strabo and Ptolemy describe the various parts of Africa. This knowledge came from the many wars that the Carthaginians and the Romans, the two most powerful nations in the world, had with the peoples of Africa and from the alliances they contracted and their commerce with these lands.

[84] [Claudius Ptolemy, *Geographica*] bk. 7, chap. 3 [7.3].

CHAPTER II
Carthage and Marseilles

Carthage had a singular right of nations; it had all the foreigners who dealt with Sardinia and beyond it to the Pillars of Hercules drowned:[85] its political right was no less extraordinary; it prohibited the Sardinians from cultivating their land on penalty of death. It increased its power by its wealth, and subsequently its wealth by its power. Master of the coasts of Africa washed by the Mediterranean, it also reached to the shores of the Ocean. Hanno, by order of the Senate of Carthage, distributed thirty thousand Carthaginians between the Pillars of Hercules and Cerne. He says that this place is as far from the Pillars of Hercules as the Pillars are from Carthage. This positioning is worthy of note; it shows that Hanno limited his establishments to twenty-five degrees north latitude, that is, two or three degrees south of the Canary Islands.

Hanno, from Cerne, made another voyage whose purpose was to

[85] Eratosthenes, in Strabo [*Geographica*], bk. 17, p. 802 [17.1.19].

make discoveries further to the south. He gained almost no knowledge of the continent. He sailed along the coast for twenty-six days and was obliged to return for lack of food. It appears that the Carthaginians made no use of this enterprise of Hanno. Scylax[86] says that the sea is not navigable beyond Cerne[87] because it is shallow, full of silt and sea plants; actually, they are thick in this section of the ocean.[88] The Carthaginian merchants of whom Scylax speaks may have found obstacles that Hanno, with sixty ships of fifty oars each, had surmounted. Difficulties are relative, and moreover, one should not confuse an enterprise whose object is boldness and fearlessness with one that is the result of ordinary conduct.

Hanno's account is a fine bit of antiquity: the man who performed it wrote about it; he puts no ostentation in his narrations. The great captains write with simplicity about their actions because their glory comes more from what they have done than from what they have said.

His subject is like his style. He does not tend to the marvelous; all that he says of the climate, the terrain, the mores, and the manners of the inhabitants relates to what one sees today on the coast of Africa; it seems to be the journal of one of our own sailors.

Hanno observed from his fleet that during the day a vast silence reigned over the continent, that during the night one heard the sounds of various musical instruments, and that one saw fires everywhere, some large and some small.[89] Our accounts confirm this; it has been found that the savages stay in the forests in the daytime in order to avoid the heat of the sun, that at night they make large fires to keep away the wild beasts, and that they passionately love dancing and musical instruments.

Hanno describes a volcano displaying the phenomena Vesuvius shows today, and his account of two hairy women, who preferred to be killed than to follow the Carthaginians and whose skins he took

[86] See his *Periplus*, in the section on Carthage [Scylax Caryandensis, *Periplus*, "Carthage," #112, *Geographi Gracei minores*, 1, 93–94].

[87] See Herodotus [*The Persian Wars*], Melpomene [4.43], about the obstacles Sataspes encountered.

[88] See the maps and accounts in the first volume of the *Recueil des Voyages qui ont servi à l'établissement de la Compagnie des Indes*, pt. 1, p. 201 ["Relation du premier voiage des Hollandais", 1, 206; 1702 edn; 1, 201; 1725 edn]. This plant covers the surface of the sea so that one can scarcely see the water, and vessels can cross it only with a fresh wind.

[89] Pliny the Elder [*Naturalis historia* 5.1.7], speaking of Mount Atlas, tells us the same thing: "At night it flashes with numerous fires, the playing of flutes and tambourines resounds, by day no one is seen" [L.].

to Carthage, is not, in spite of what has been said, altogether unlikely.

This account is all the more precious because it is a Punic record; and because it is a Punic record, it has been regarded as a legend. For, the Romans preserved their hatred of the Carthaginians even after destroying them. But it was only their victory that determined whether one would say *Punic faith* or *Roman faith*.

Some moderns[90] have continued this prejudice. What has become, they ask, of the towns Hanno describes to us and of which, even in the time of Pliny, there remained no vestige? It would have been a marvel if they had remained. Was it Corinth or Athens that Hanno was going to build on these shores? He left Carthaginian families at locations suitable for commerce and quickly made them secure from the savage men and wild beasts. The calamities of the Carthaginians put an end to navigation around Africa; these families surely must have perished or become savage. I say further: if the ruins of these towns still remained, who would have gone to discover them in the woods and marshes? One finds, however, in Scylax and Polybius, that the Carthaginians had great establishments on these shores. Here are the vestiges of the towns of Hanno; there are no others because there are hardly any others of Carthage itself.

The Carthaginians were on the path to wealth, and if they had gone to four degrees north latitude and fifteen degrees longitude,[h] they would have discovered the Gold Coast and the neighboring coasts. They would have engaged in a commerce there of an importance quite different from that of the present, when America seems to have depreciated the wealth of all the other countries; they would have found treasures that could not have been taken away by the Romans.

Surprising things have been said about the wealth of Spain. If one believes Aristotle,[91] the Phoenicians who landed at Tartessus found so much silver there that their ships could not hold it, and they had their most common utensils made of this metal. The Carthaginians, according to the report of Diodorus,[92] found so much gold and silver in the

[90] [Henry] Dodwell: see his treatise on the Periplus of Hanno. [Not Hanno, but *Dissertation de Arriani Nearcho*, p. 251; 1798 edn.]

[91] [Aristotle] *De mirabilibus auscultationibus* [844a18–23, #135].

[92] [Diodorus Siculus, *Bibliotheca historica*] bk. 6 [5.35.4].

[h] Montesquieu's map placed 0 degrees longitude at Dakar, about 14 degrees west of Greenwich. This location would now be about 1 degree west longitude.

Pyrenees that they put it on the anchors of their ships. One must not rely on these popular accounts; here are some precise facts.

One sees in a fragment of Polybius, cited by Strabo,[93] that the silver mines, which were at the source of the Baetis[i] where forty thousand men were employed, gave the Roman people twenty-five thousand drachmas a day; this is about five million livres a year at fifty francs a mark. The mountains where these mines were found were called the Silver Mountains,[94] which shows that it was the Potosi of those times. Today the mines of Hanover do not have a quarter of the workers that were employed in those of Spain, and they produce more; but as the Romans had almost only copper mines and few silver mines and the Greeks knew only of the very poor mines in Attica, they must have been astonished by the abundance of the Spanish mines.

In the War of the Spanish Succession, a man called the Marquis of Rhodes, of whom it was said that he had been ruined by gold mines and made wealthy by poorhouses,[95] proposed to the court of France to open the mines in the Pyrenees. He cited the Tyrians, the Carthaginians, and the Romans: he was permitted to search; he sought, he dug everywhere; he continued to cite them, and he found nothing.

The Carthaginians, masters of the commerce in gold and silver, also wanted to be masters of the commerce in lead and tin. These metals were conveyed over land from the ports of Gaul on the ocean to those of the Mediterranean. The Carthaginians wanted to receive them themselves; they sent Himilco to form[96] establishments on the Cassiterides Islands, which are believed to be the Scilly Islands.

These voyages from Baetica to England have made some people think that the Carthaginians had compasses, but it is clear that they followed the coasts. I need no other proof than the comments by Himilco, who took four months to go from the mouth of the Baetis to England; in addition, the famous story[97] of that Carthaginian pilot who, on seeing a Roman vessel approach, ran aground in order not to let him know the route to England[98] shows that these vessels were very near the coasts when they met.

[93] [Strabo, *Geographica*] bk. 3 [3.2.10].

[94] Mons Argentarius.

[95] He had had charge of infirmaries somewhere.

[96] See [Rufus] Festus Avienus [*Carmina, Orae maritimae* 4.259–264].

[97] Strabo [*Geographica*], bk. 3 [3.5.11] toward the end.

[98] He was rewarded for it by the Senate of Carthage.

[i] the Gaudalquivir.

The ancients may have made sea voyages which would suggest that they had compasses, although they had none. If a pilot was far from the coasts and there was a quiet time during his voyage, if at night he could see the North Star and in the daytime the rising and setting of the sun, it is clear that he could have guided himself as one does today by a compass; but this would be a fortuitous event and not a regular voyage.

One can see in the treaty which ended the First Punic War that Carthage was principally concerned with preserving its empire of the sea, and Rome, with keeping that of the land. Hanno[99] declared in the negotiation with the Romans that he would not even suffer them to wash their hands in the seas of Sicily; they were not permitted to navigate beyond the *promontorium pulchrum*:[j] they were prohibited[100] from trading in Sicily,[101] Sardinia, and Africa, except in Carthage; this exception shows that no advantageous commerce awaited them there.

In earliest times there were great wars between Carthage and Marseilles[102] over fishing grounds. After the peace they both engaged in economic commerce. Marseilles was the more jealous because, while equaling its rival in industry, it had become inferior in power; this is the reason for its great faithfulness to the Romans. The war the Romans waged against the Carthaginians in Spain was a source of wealth for Marseilles, which served as their storehouse. The ruin of Carthage and Corinth increased further the glory of Marseilles; and, if it had not been for the civil wars in which one had blindly to choose a party, it would have been happy under the protection of the Romans, who were not jealous of its commerce.

[99] Livy. Johann Freinsheim, *Supplementorum Livianorum*, decade 2, bk. 6 [16.20].
[100] Polybius [*Historiae*], bk. 3 [3.23–27].
[101] In the part subject to the Carthaginians.
[102] Justin [*Epitoma historiarum Philippicarum*], bk. 43, chap. 5 [43.5.2].

[j] *beau promontoire*. Montesquieu has translated this and other Latin terms into French, although they are often left in Latin in English texts.

CHAPTER 12

The island of Delos. Mithridates

When Corinth was destroyed by the Romans, the merchants withdrew to Delos. Because of religion and the people's veneration, this island was regarded as a secure place;[103] moreover, it was very well situated for commerce with Italy and Asia, which had become more important after the destruction of Africa and the weakening of Greece.

As we have said, the Greeks sent colonies to the Propontis and the Black Sea from the earliest times; these colonies preserved their laws and their liberty under the Persians. Alexander, who moved only against the barbarians, did not attack them.[104] It does not even seem that the kings of Pontus, who occupied many of them, took away their political government.[105]

The power of these kings increased as soon as they had subdued these colonies.[106] Mithridates was in a position to buy troops everywhere, to repair his losses continually,[107] to have workers, vessels, and machines of war, to procure allies for himself, to corrupt those of the Romans and even the Romans, to hire as mercenaries[108] the barbarians of Asia and Europe, to wage war for a long time, and consequently to discipline his troops; he was able to arm them, to instruct them in the military art of the Romans,[109] and to form units of considerable size from the deserters; finally, he was able to sustain great losses and suffer great setbacks without being ruined; and he would not have been ruined if the voluptuous and barbaric king had not

[103] See Strabo [*Geographica*], bk. 10 [10.5.4].

[104] He strengthened the liberty of the town of Amisus, an Athenian colony, which had enjoyed a popular state even under Persian kings. Lucullus, who took Sinope and Amisus, returned their liberty to them and recalled the inhabitants who had fled in their ships.

[105] See what Appian writes about the Phanagoreans, the Amisians, and the Sinopians in his book [*Roman History*], *The War with Mithridates* (12.78,83,113,120).

[106] See Appian on the immense treasures Mithridates used in his wars, those he had hidden, those he so often lost through the treason of his people, and those found after his death. [Appian, *Roman History*, *The War with Mithridates* 12.69,85,87,112,115.]

[107] At one time he lost 170,000 men, and new armies reappeared instantly. [Appian, *Roman History*, *The War with Mithridates* 12.112.]

[108] See Appian [*Roman History*], *The War with Mithridates* [12.69].

[109] Ibid. [Appian, *Roman History*, *The War with Mithridates* 12.68.]

women of the theater, and the daughters of a man who keeps a house of prostitution or of one who has been condemned to fight in the arena: this came down from the ancient Roman institutions.

I know well that people, filled with two ideas, the one that commerce is the most useful thing in the world to a state, and the other, that the Romans had the best police in the world, have believed that the Romans greatly encouraged and honored commerce; but the truth is that they rarely thought about it.

CHAPTER 15

The commerce of the Romans with the barbarians

The Romans made a vast empire of Europe, Asia and Africa; the weakness of the peoples and the tyranny of the command united all the parts of this immense body. Then, Roman policy was to be separate from all the nations that had not yet been subjected; fear of giving them the art of conquering led the Romans to neglect the art of enriching themselves. They made laws to halt all commerce with barbarians. "Let no one," say Valens and Gratian,[117] "send wine, oil, or other liquors to barbarians, even for them to taste." "Let no one carry gold to them and see that even what they have of it is cleverly taken away," added Gratian, Valentinian, and Theodosius.[118] The transport of iron was prohibited on penalty of death.[119]

Domitian, a timid prince, had the grape vines uprooted in Gaul[120] from the fear, doubtless, that the wine might attract the barbarians, as it had formerly attracted them to Italy. Probus and Julian, who never feared the barbarians, replanted the vines.

I know very well that, when the empire became weak, the barbarians obliged the Romans to establish trading centers[121] and engage in

[117] Law *ad Barbaricum*, *Code* [*Corpus Juris Civilis*, *Code* 4.41.1]; *quae res exportari non debeant.*

[118] Law 2, *Code* [*Corpus Juris Civilis*, *Code* 4.63.2]; *de commerciis et mercatoribus.*

[119] Law 2 [*Corpus Juris Civilis*, *Code* 4.41.2]; *quae res exportari non debeant.*

[120] Procopius, *Persian Wars*, bk. 1. [This does not appear to be in Procopius. The story about Domitian comes from Suetonius, *Vitae duodecim Caesarum*, *Domitian* 14.2 and 7.2; on Probus, see *Augustan History*, Vopiscus, *Probus* 28.18.8. On the topic of vineyards, there is interesting information in Cicero, *De republica* 3.9.16, but this passage was not known to M.]

[121] See [M.'s] *Considerations on the Causes of the Greatness of the Romans and their Decline*, Paris, 1755 edn [chap. 19, p. 182, n. 12; 1965 edn].

commerce with them. But this proves that commerce was not a part of the Roman spirit.

CHAPTER 16

On the commerce of the Romans with Arabia and the Indies

Trade with Arabia Felix and trade with the Indies were the two branches, and almost all the branches, of their external commerce. The Arabs had great wealth; they drew it from their sea and forests, and, as they bought little and sold much, they drew[122] to themselves the gold and silver of their neighbors. Augustus[123] knew their opulence and resolved to have them either for friends or for enemies. He sent Aelius Gallus from Egypt to Arabia. Gallus found the peoples idle, quiet, and unwarlike. He fought battles, staged sieges, and lost only seven soldiers, but the perfidy of his guides, the marching, the climate, along with hunger, thirst, sickness, and ill-chosen measures made him lose his army.

One had, therefore, to be content to trade with the Arabs as other peoples had, that is, to bring them gold and silver for their commodities. Commerce continues with them in the same manner today; the caravan of Aleppo and the royal vessel of Suez take immense sums there.[124]

Nature destined the Arabs to commerce; she had not destined them for war; but, when these tranquil peoples found themselves between the Parthians and the Romans, they became the auxiliaries of both. Aelius Gallus had found them a commercial people, Mohammed found them warriors; he gave them enthusiasm, and they became conquerors.

The Romans did considerable commerce in the Indies. Strabo[125] learned in Egypt that the Romans employed one hundred and twenty ships in that commerce; it was still sustained only by their silver. They

[122] Pliny the Elder [*Naturalis historia*], bk. 7, chap. 28 [6.32.162]; and Strabo [*Geographica*], bk. 16 [16.4.22].

[123] Ibid. [Pliny the Elder, *Naturalis historia* 6.32.162, and Strabo, *Geographica* 16.4.22].

[124] The caravans of Aleppo and Suez take two million of our money there and an equal sum is smuggled in; the royal vessel of Suez also takes two million there.

[125] [Strabo, *Geographica*] bk. 2, p. 81 [2.5.12].

sent fifty million sesterces there every year. Pliny[126] says that the commodities they brought back were sold in Rome at a hundred times their cost. I believe he speaks too generally; if this profit is made once, everyone will want to make it, and, from then on, no one will make it.

One can enquire whether it was to the Romans' advantage to engage in commerce with Arabia and the Indies. They had to send their silver there, and they did not have, as we do, the resource of America, which replaces what we send. I am persuaded that one of the reasons for the increase in the numerary value of their monies,[l] that is, for the establishment of copper or nickel coinage, was the scarcity of silver caused by its continual transport to the Indies. For if the goods of this country were sold in Rome at a hundred times their cost, the profit of the Romans was made from Romans themselves and did not enrich the empire.

One will be able to say, on the other hand, that this commerce procured a great navigation for the Romans, that is, a great power; that new commodities increased internal commerce, favored the arts, supported industry; that the number of citizens increased in proportion to the new means for making a living; that this new commerce produced luxury, which we have proved to be as favorable to the government of one alone as it is fatal to that of many; that this establishment dated from the fall of their republic; that the luxury of Rome was necessary; and that a town that attracted all the wealth of the universe had to pay for that wealth with her luxury.

Strabo[127] says that the Romans' commerce with the Indies was even more considerable than that of the kings of Egypt; and it is singular that the Romans, who knew little about commerce, paid more attention to commerce with the Indies than did the kings of Egypt, who had it, so to speak, under their noses. This must be explained.

After the death of Alexander, the kings of Egypt established a maritime commerce with the Indies; and the kings of Syria, who held the easternmost provinces of the empire and consequently the Indies, maintained the commerce by both land and river we have mentioned in

[126] [Pliny the Elder, *Naturalis historia*] bk. 6, chap. 23 [6.26.101].

[127] He says in bk. 12 that the Romans used 120 ships there; and in bk. 17, that the Greek kings sent scarcely twenty. [Strabo, *Geographica* 2.5.12 and 17.1.13.]

[l] More units of the money were required for each unit of silver.

Chapter 6, which was made easier by the establishment of Macedonian colonies: the result was that Europe communicated with the Indies both by way of Egypt and by way of the kingdom of Syria. The dismemberment of the kingdom of Syria, from which the kingdom of Bactria was formed, did no harm to this commerce. Marinus, the Tyrian, who is cited by Ptolemy,[128] speaks of the discoveries made in the Indies by some Macedonian merchants. Discoveries not made by the expeditions of the kings were made by these merchants. We see in Ptolemy[129] that they went from the Stone Tower[130] to Sera; and their discovery of a market town so distant, situated in the eastern and northern part of China, was a kind of wonder. Thus, under the kings of Syria and of Bactria, commodities from southern India passed by way of the Indus, the Oxus, and the Caspian Sea, to the west; and those of the more easterly and northerly regions were carried from Sera, the Stone Tower, and other market towns to the Euphrates. These merchants followed a route that lay along forty degrees north latitude, through the countries situated in western China, which had more of a police then than today because the Tartars had not yet tainted them.

Now, while the empire of Syria was expanding its commerce so greatly over land, Egypt did not much increase its maritime commerce.

The Parthians appeared and founded their empire; and, when Egypt fell under Roman power, this empire was at its full force and at its full extent.

The Romans and the Parthians were two rival powers, who fought, not to know which of them should reign, but which should exist. Uninhabited areas formed between the two empires; one always went armed between the empires; for from there being commerce, there was not even communication. Ambition, jealousy, religion, hatred, and mores completed the separation. Thus commerce between the west and the east, which had followed several routes, now followed only one; and as Alexandria had become the only market town, it grew.

I shall say but a word about internal commerce. Its principal branch was in the grains that were ordered for the sustenance of the Roman people; this was more a concern of the police than an object for

128 [Claudius Ptolemy, *Geographica*] bk. 1, chap. 2 [1.11].

129 [Claudius Ptolemy, *Geographica*] bk. 6, chap. 13 [6.13].

130 Our best maps place the Stone Tower at 100 longitude and at about 40 latitude. [These measurements refer to the map in this text. The Stone Tower was a fortification mentioned by ancient geographers that stood on the Bactrian frontier. See bk. 21, n.[h].]

commerce. In these circumstances sailors received certain privileges[131] because the health of the empire depended on their vigilance.

[131]Suetonius [*Vitae duodecim Caesarum*], *Claudius* [18–19]. Law 7, *Codex Theodosianus* [13.5.7]; *de navicularis*.

CHAPTER 17

On commerce after the destruction of the Romans in the West

The Roman empire was invaded, and one of the effects of the general calamity was the destruction of commerce. The barbarians regarded it at first as only an object for their banditry, and when they established themselves, they honored it no more than they did agriculture and the other professions of the vanquished people.

Soon there was almost no more commerce in Europe; the nobility, who reigned everywhere, did not trouble themselves with it.

The law of the Visigoths[132] permitted individuals to occupy half the bed on the great rivers, provided the other half remained free for nets and boats; there must not have been much commerce in the countries they conquered.

At that time the senseless rights of escheatage and shipwreck were established; men thought that, as foreigners were not united with them by any communication of the civil right, they did not owe them, on the one hand, justice of any sort or, on the other, pity of any sort.

Given the narrow bounds within which the northern peoples lived, everything was foreign to them; given their poverty, everything was an object of wealth to them. Established before their conquests on the shores of a confined sea full of reefs, they drew profit from the reefs themselves.

But the Romans, who made laws for the whole universe, had made very humane ones concerning shipwrecks;[133] they restrained in that regard the banditry of those who inhabited the coasts, and furthermore, they restrained their rapacious fisc.[134]

[132][*Lex Wisigothorum*] bk. 8, tit. 4, para. 9 [8.4.29].

[133]The entire title [*Corpus Juris Civilis, Digest* 47.9]; *de incendio ruina naufragio rate nave expugnata*; *Code* [*Corpus Juris Civilis, Code* 11.6]; *de naufragiis*, and Law 3 [*Corpus Juris Civilis, Digest* 48.8.1.3]; *ad legem Corneliam de sicariis et veneficis*.

[134]Law 1 [*Corpus Juris Civilis*], *Code* [11.6(5).1]; *de naufragiis*.

CHAPTER 18

A particular regulation

A law of the Visigoths,[135] however, had a provision favorable to commerce: it ordered that the merchants who came from across the sea would be judged by the laws and the judges of their own nation when differences sprang up among them. This was founded on the usage established among all these combinations of peoples, that each man should live under his own law, something I shall discuss later at length.[m]

[135] [*Lex Wisigothorum*] bk. 11, tit. 3, para. 2 [11.3.2].

[m] See Book 28.

CHAPTER 19

On commerce after the weakening of the Romans in the East

The Mohammedans appeared, conquered, and were divided. Egypt had its own sovereign. It continued to engage in commerce with the Indies. Master of the goods of that country, it attracted the wealth of all the others. Its sultans were the most powerful princes of those times; one can see in history how, with a constant and well-managed force, they checked the ardor, fire, and impetuosity of the crusaders.

CHAPTER 20

How commerce in Europe penetrated barbarism

When the philosophy of Aristotle was brought to the West, the shrewd minds, who are the great minds in times of ignorance, found it very agreeable. The schoolmen were infatuated with it and took from this philosopher[136] many explanations on lending at interest, whereas its very natural source was the gospel; they condemned it without distinc-

[136] See Aristotle, *Pol.*, bk. 1, chaps. 9, 10 [1256b40–1258b8].

tion and in every case. Thus, commerce, which was the profession only of mean people, also became that of dishonest people; for, whenever one prohibits a thing that is naturally permitted or necessary, one only makes dishonest the people who do it.

Commerce passed to a nation then covered with infamy, and soon it was no longer distinguished from the most horrible usuries, from monopolies, from the levy of subsidies, and from all the dishonest means of acquiring silver.

The Jews,[137] who were made wealthy by their exactions, were pillaged with the same tyranny by the princes, a thing that consoled the people and did not relieve them.

What happened in England will give an idea of what was done in other countries. When King John[138] imprisoned the Jews in order to have their goods, there were few who did not have at least an eye put out; thus did this king conduct his chamber of justice. A Jew who had had seven teeth pulled out, one each day, gave ten thousand silver marks on the eighth. From Aaron, a Jew of York, Henry III got fourteen thousand silver marks and ten thousand for the queen. In those times, one did violently what is done in Poland today with some measure. As the kings were not able to search into the pockets of their subjects because of their privileges, they tortured the Jews, who were not regarded as citizens.

Finally, the custom was introduced of confiscating the goods of the Jews who embraced Christianity. We know of this outlandish custom from the law abrogating it.[139] The reasons given for it have been very empty; it has been said that one wanted to test them and make nothing remain of their enslavement to the devil. But, it is clear that this confiscation was a kind of right of amortization[140] of the taxes which the

[137] See in [Pierre de Marca] *Marca Hispanica*, the constitutions of Aragon of the years 1228 [chap. 507, pp. 1415–1416; see also pp. 522–528; 1688 edn] and 1231 [chap. 511, 1233, p. 1427; 1688 edn]; in [Nicolas] Brussel [*Nouvel examen de l'usage général des fiefs en France pendant le XIe, le XIIe, le XIIIe et le XIVe siècle*], the agreement of 1206 reached between the king, the countess of Champagne, and Guy de Dampierre. [Actually 1200, vol. 2, *Chartres, lettres-patentes, traités*; xxii–xxiii; 1727 edn.]

[138] [John] Stow, in his *Survey of London*, bk. 3, p. 54 ["Coleman Street Ward"; 1, 279–280; 1908 edn; pp. 250–251; 1929 edn].

[139] Edict given at Baville, April 4, 1392. [Actually Abbeville, April 25, 1393. *Recueil général des anciennes lois franaises*, #181; 6, 728–729.]

[140] In France, the Jews were serfs subject to mortmain and the lords inherited from them. [Nicolas] Brussel reports an agreement of 1206 between the king and Thibaut, Count of Champagne, by which it was agreed that the Jews of the one would not lend in the land of

prince or the lords levied on the Jews and which they were denied when the latter embraced Christianity. In those times, men were regarded as lands. And, I shall note in passing how much one has toyed with that nation from one century to another. Their goods were confiscated when they wanted to be Christians, and soon afterwards they were burned when they did not want to be Christians.

Nevertheless, one saw commerce leave this seat of harassment and despair. The Jews, proscribed by each country in turn, found the means for saving their effects. In that way, they managed to fix their refuges forever; a prince who wanted very much to be rid of them would not, for all that, be in a humor to rid himself of their silver.

They invented letters of exchange,[141] and in this way commerce was able to avoid violence and maintain itself everywhere, for the richest trader had only invisible goods, which could be sent everywhere and leave no trace anywhere.

Theologians were obliged to curb their principles, and commerce, which had been violently linked to bad faith, returned, so to speak, to the bosom of integrity.

Thus, to the speculations of the schoolmen we owe all the misfortunes[142] that accompanied the destruction of commerce; and to the avarice of princes we owe the establishment of a device that puts it, in a way, out of their power.

Since that time princes have had to govern themselves more wisely than they themselves would have thought, for it turned out that great acts of authority were so clumsy that experience itself has made known that only goodness of government brings prosperity.

One has begun to be cured of Machiavellianism, and one will continue to be cured of it. There must be more moderation in councils. What were formerly called *coups d'état* would at present, apart from their horror, be only imprudences.

And, happily, men are in a situation such that, though their passions

the other. [Nicolas Brussel, *Nouvel examen de l'usage général des fiefs en France pendant le XIe, le XIIe, le XIIIe et le XIVe siècles.* Actually 1200, vol. 2, *Chartes, lettres-patentes, traités*; xxii–xxiii; 1727 edn.]

[141] It is known that under Philip Augustus and Philip the Tall, the Jews, driven out of France took refuge in Lombardy and that there they gave the foreign traders and travelers secret letters for those to whom they had entrusted their effects in France, with which their debts were paid.

[142] See, in the Corpus of the Law, *Novellae Leonis 83*, which revokes the law of Basil, his father. The law of Basil is in [Konstantin] Hermenopoulus [*Manuale legum sive Hexabiblos*] under "Leon," bk. 3, tit. 7, para. 27 [3.7.24].

inspire in them the thought of being wicked, they nevertheless have an interest in not being so.

CHAPTER 21

The discovery of two new worlds: the state of Europe in this regard

The compass opened the universe, so to speak. Discovery was made of Asia and Africa of which only some coasts had been known, and of America, which had been completely unknown.

The Portuguese, sailing the Atlantic Ocean, discovered the southern tip of Africa; they saw a vast sea; it carried them to the East Indies. Their perils on this sea and the discovery of Mozambique, Melinde, and Calicut were sung by de Camoens,[n] in whose poetry one feels something of the charms of the *Odyssey* and the magnificence of the *Aeneid*.

Until then the Venetians had engaged in commerce with the Indies through the countries of the Turks and had pursued it in the midst of insults and outrages. By the discovery of the Cape of Good Hope and by other discoveries made soon after, Italy was no longer at the center of the commercial world; it was in a corner of the universe, so to speak, and it remains there today. As the commerce of the Levant itself depends today on that done by the great nations in the two Indies, Italy engages in it now only in a secondary way.

The Portuguese dealt in the Indies as conquerors; the laws[143] hampering commerce that the Dutch impose at present on the commerce of the petty Indian princes were established by the Portuguese before them.

The House of Austria had a prodigious fortune. Charles inherited Burgundy together with Castile and Aragon; he succeeded to an empire; and, in order to procure for him a new kind of greatness, the universe expanded and a new world obedient to him appeared.

Christopher Columbus discovered America, and, though Spain sent

[143] See the account of François Pyrard [*Voyage*], pt. 2, chap. 15 [vol. 2, pt. 1, chap. 15; 2, 204–205; 1887–1890 edn].

[n] Luis Vaz de Camoens.

no more forces there than a minor European prince could have sent, it brought into subjection two great empires and other great states.

While the Spanish were discovering and conquering in the west, the Portuguese were extending their conquests and discoveries to the east: these two nations met; they had recourse to Pope Alexander VI, who made the famous line of demarcation and thus gave judgment on a great lawsuit.

But the other nations of Europe did not let them enjoy this division in quiet; the Dutch drove the Portuguese out of much of the East Indies, and various nations set up establishments in America.

At first, the Spanish considered the newly discovered lands as objects of conquest; peoples more refined than they saw them as objects of commerce and as such directed their attention to them. Many peoples acted so wisely that they granted empire to trading companies who, governing these distant states only for trade, made a great secondary power without encumbering the principal state.

The colonies formed there are in a kind of dependence of which there are very few examples among the ancient colonies, because those of today belong either to the state itself or to some commercial company established in that state.

The purpose of these colonies is to engage in commerce under better conditions than one has with neighboring peoples with whom all advantages are reciprocal. It has been established that only the mother country can trade with the colony, and this was done with very good reason, for the goal of the establishment was to extend commerce, not to found a town or a new empire.

Thus, in Europe it remains a fundamental law that any commerce with a foreign colony is regarded as a pure monopoly enforceable by the laws of the country; and one must not judge this by the laws and examples of ancient peoples,[144] which are hardly applicable.

It is acknowledged that the commerce established between mother countries does not include permission to trade in the colonies, where it continues to be prohibited to them.

The disadvantage to the colonies, which lose the liberty of commerce, is visibly compensated by the protection of the mother country,[145] which defends them by her arms or maintains them by her laws.

[144] Except the Carthaginians, as seen in the treaty ending the First Punic War.

[145] In the language of the ancients, the mother country [metropolis] is the state that has founded the colony.

What follows from this is a third law of Europe, that, when foreign commerce is prohibited with the colony, one can navigate its seas only when this is established by treaties.

Nations, which are to the entire universe what individuals are to a state, govern themselves as do the latter by natural right and by laws they have made for themselves. A people can give up the sea to another, as it can give up land. The Carthaginians required[146] the Romans to navigate no further than certain limits, just as the Greeks had required the king of Persia to stay as far away from the sea coast[147] as a horse could run a race.

The extreme distance of our colonies is not a drawback for their security; yet if the mother country is far away for their defense, the nations that are rivals of the mother country are no less far away for their conquest.

In addition, this distance makes those who go there to establish themselves unable to take up the way of life of such a different climate; they are obliged to get all the comforts of life from the country from which they have come. The Carthaginians,[148] in order to make the Sardinians and the Corsicans more dependent, prohibited them from planting, sowing, or doing anything of the like on penalty of death; they sent them their food from Africa. We have come to the same point without making such harsh laws. Our colonies in the Antilles are admirable; they have objects of commerce that we do not and cannot have; they lack that which is the object of our commerce.

The consequence of the discovery of America was to link Asia and Africa to Europe. America furnished Europe with the material for its commerce in that vast part of Asia called the East Indies.

Silver, that metal so useful to commerce as a sign, was also the basis for the greatest commerce of the universe as a commodity. Finally, voyages to Africa became necessary; they furnished men to work the mines and lands of America.

Europe has reached such a high degree of power that nothing in history is comparable to it, if one considers the immensity of expenditures, the size of military engagements, the number of troops,

[146] Polybius [*Historiae*], bk. 3 [3.22–24].

[147] The king of Persia was obliged by treaty to sail no war vessel beyond the Cyanean rocks and the Chelidonian Islands. In Plutarch [*Vit.*], *Cimon* [13.4].

[148] Aristotle, *De mirabilibus auscultationibus* [838b26–29, #100]; Livy, decade 2 bk. 7 [in Johann Freinsheim, *Supplementorum Livianorum* 17.15].

and their continuous upkeep, even when they are the most useless and are only for ostentation.

Father du Halde[149] says that the internal commerce of China is greater than that of all Europe. This might be, if our external commerce did not increase our internal commerce. Europe carries on the commerce and navigation of the other three parts of the world, just as France, England, and Holland carry on nearly all the navigation and commerce of Europe.

[149] [Jean Baptiste du Halde, *Description de la Chine*] bk. 2, p. 170 ["Du commerce des Chinois"; 2, 204 H; 2, 169 P; 2, 296 L].

CHAPTER 22

On the health that Spain drew from America

If Europe[150] has found so many advantages in commerce with America, it would be natural to believe that Spain would have gained even greater ones. It drew from the newly discovered world so prodigious a quantity of gold and silver that there was no possible comparison with what there had previously been.

But (what one would never have suspected), poverty made it fail almost everywhere. Philip II, who succeeded Charles, was obliged to declare bankruptcy, as everyone knows, and scarcely any prince has even suffered more than he from the grumbling, the insolence, and the rebelliousness of his invariably poorly paid troops.

After this time, the Spanish monarchy went into an uninterrupted decline. This was because there was an internal and physical vice in the nature of this wealth, which made it hollow, and this vice increased daily.

Gold and silver are a wealth of fiction or of sign. These signs are very durable and almost indestructible by their nature. The more they increase, the more they lose of their worth, because they represent fewer things.

When they conquered Mexico and Peru, the Spanish abandoned natural wealth in order to have a wealth of sign, which gradually

[150] This appeared more than twenty years ago, in a small manuscript work of the author, and has been almost entirely incorporated into this one.

became debased. Gold and silver were very scarce in Europe; and Spain, suddenly mistress of a great quantity of these metals, conceived expectations she had never had before. The wealth found in the conquered countries was not, however, in proportion to that of their mines. The Indians hid part of it, and moreover these peoples, who used gold and silver only for the magnificence of temples of their gods and palaces of their kings, did not search for it with the same avarice as we; finally, they did not have the secret of extracting metals from all their mines, but only from those where fire separated the metal, as they did not know how to use mercury and perhaps were even unfamiliar with it.

Nevertheless, soon there was double the silver in Europe; this was evident when the price of everything purchasable doubled.

The Spanish worked the mines, excavated the mountains, and invented machines to draw the waters, break ore and separate it; and, as they mocked the lives of the Indians, they worked them mercilessly. There was soon double the silver in Europe, and the profit diminished by half for Spain, which had each year only the same quantity of a metal which had become half as precious.

As the time doubled, silver doubled again, and the profit again decreased by half.

The profit decreased by more than half; here is how.

In order to take gold from the mines, in order to give it the required preparation and carry it to France, there had to be some expense. I assume that it was as 1 is to 64; when silver had doubled once, and was consequently half as precious, the expense was as 2 is to 64. Thus, the fleets that carried the same quantity of gold to Spain carried what really was valued at half as much and cost twice as much.

If one follows things from one doubling to the next, one will see how the cause of the powerlessness of Spanish wealth progressed.

The mines of the Indies have been worked for some two hundred years. I assume that the quantity of silver at present in the commercial world is to that which there was before the discovery as 32 is to 1, that is, it has doubled five times in two hundred more years, and the same quantity will be to what there was before the discovery as 64 is to 1, that is, it will double again. Now, at present fifty quintals[151] of gold ore gives four, five, and six ounces of gold, and when it only gives two, the miner

[151] See [Amédée F.] Frézier, *Relation du voyage de la mer du Sud, du Chili, du Pérou, et du Brésil* ["Minières d'or de Tiltil"; 1, 185–190; 1717 edn].

covers only his costs. In two hundred years, if it gives only four, the miner will still make only his costs. Therefore, there will be little profit in mining gold. The same reasoning follows for silver, except that working silver mines is a little more advantageous than gold mines.

Now, if one discovers mines so abundant that they give more profit, the more abundant they are, the sooner the profit will end.

The Portuguese have found so much gold[152] in Brazil that soon the Spaniards' profit must necessarily diminish markedly, and their own also.

I have more than once heard deplored the blindness of the Council of Francis I for refusing Christopher Columbus' proposal to go to the Indies. In truth one did, perhaps imprudently, a very wise thing. Spain acted like the foolish king who asked that everything he touched turn into gold and who was obliged to go back to the gods and beg that they put an end to his destitution.

The companies and banks that many nations established completed the debasement of gold and silver in their status as signs, for by new fictions, they so increased the signs for produce that gold and silver performed that office only in part and became less precious.

Thus public credit replaced mines and diminished still further the profit the Spanish drew from theirs.

It is true that Dutch commerce with the Indies gave some price to the Spanish commodities for, as the Dutch carried silver to barter for the commodities of the East, in Europe they relieved the Spanish of part of the produce, which was over-abundant.

And this commerce, which seems to concern Spain only indirectly, is advantageous to Spain as well as to those nations that engage in it themselves.

By all that has just been said, one can judge the ordinances of the Council of Spain, which prohibited the use of gold and silver for gilding and other superfluities; this is as if the states of Holland made a decree prohibiting the consumption of cinnamon.

My reasoning does not apply to all mines; those of Germany and Hungary, from which one gets little more than costs, are very useful.

[152] According to Lord Anson, Europe receives from Brazil every year two million sterling of gold that is found in the sand at the foot of the mountains or in riverbeds. When I wrote the short book I have mentioned in the first note of this chapter, the proceeds from Brazil were far from being as important as they are today. [George Anson, *A Voyage Round the World in the Years MDCCXL, I, II, III, IV*, pp. 59–64; 1974 edn.]

They are found in the principal state; they employ several thousand men who consume the over-abundant produce; the mines are properly a manufactory[o] of the country.

The German and Hungarian mines make cultivating the land worthwhile, and working those of Mexico and Peru destroys that cultivation.

The Indies and Spain are two powers under the same master, but the Indies are the principal one, and Spain is only secondary. In vain policy wants to reduce the principal one to a secondary one; the Indies continue to attract Spain to themselves.

Of the fifty million in commodities which go to the Indies every year, Spain furnishes only two and a half million; therefore, the Indies engage in a commerce worth fifty million, and Spain in one worth two and a half million.

An accidental tax that does not depend on the industry of the nation, the number of its inhabitants, or the cultivation of its lands is a bad kind of wealth. The king of Spain, who receives great sums from his customs houses in Cadiz, is, in this regard, only a very wealthy individual in a very poor state. Everything goes from foreigners to him with his subjects taking almost no part in it; this commerce is independent of the good and bad fortune of his kingdom.

If some of the provinces in Castile gave him a sum like that of the customs houses in Cadiz, his power would be very much greater: his wealth would be only the result of the country's wealth; these provinces would enliven all the others; and all together they would be in a better position to support their respective burdens; instead of a great treasury, one would have a great people.

[o]See 23.14 (note [d], bk. 23). We have used this eighteenth-century English word in order for Montesquieu's economics not to appear even more modern than it is.

CHAPTER 23

A problem

It is not for me to pronounce on the question of whether it would be more worth while for Spain, if it cannot engage in that commerce by itself, to open the Indies to foreigners. I shall say only that it is suitable for it to put the fewest obstacles in the way of commerce that its policy can permit. When the commodities that the various nations carry to the Indies are expensive there, the Indies give many of their commodities, which are gold and silver, for a few of the foreign commodities; the opposite happens when the latter have a low price. It would perhaps be useful for these nations to work against each other so that the commodities they carry to the Indies would always be inexpensive. These are principles that must be examined without, however, separating them from other considerations: the security of the Indies, the usefulness of a single customs house, the dangers of great change, and the drawbacks that one foresees and which are often less dangerous than those one cannot foresee.

BOOK 22
On laws in their relation to the use of money

CHAPTER I
The reason for the use of money

Peoples who have little in the way of commodities for commerce, such as savages, and peoples with a police who have only two or three kinds, trade by exchange. Thus the Moorish caravans that go to Timbuktu in the heart of Africa to barter salt for gold need no money. The Moor puts his salt in a pile; the Negro, his gold dust in another; if there is not enough gold, the Moor takes back some of his salt or the Negro adds to his gold, until the parties agree.

But when a people deals in a large number of commodities, there must necessarily be money, because a metal that is easy to transport saves much of the cost one would be obliged to incur if one always proceeded by exchange.

As all nations have reciprocal needs, it often happens that one of them wants a very large number of the other's commodities and the latter very few of the former's; whereas, with regard to another nation, the situation is reversed. But when nations have money and proceed by sale and purchase, the ones that take more commodities settle their accounts, or pay the excess, with silver; and there is the difference that, in the case of purchase, commerce is done in proportion to the needs of the nation that requires the most and, in exchange, commerce is done only to the extent of the needs of the nation that requires the least; if this were not so, the latter would find it impossible to settle its accounts.

CHAPTER 2
On the nature of money

Money is a sign representing the value of all commodities. Some metal is chosen, so that the sign will be durable,[1] will be little worn by use, and can be divided many times without being destroyed. A precious metal is chosen so that the sign can be carried easily. A metal is an altogether appropriate common measure because it can easily be reduced to the same grade. Each state stamps it, so that the form reflects the grade and the weight and so that both may be known simply by looking at it.

Before using metals, the Athenians used oxen,[2] and the Romans sheep, but one ox is not the same as another in the way one piece of metal can be the same as another.

As silver is the sign of the values of commodities, paper is a sign of the value of silver, and when the paper is good, it represents silver so well that there is no difference in its effect.

Just as silver is the sign of a thing and represents it, each thing is a sign of silver and represents it; and a state is prosperous insofar as, on the one hand, the silver indeed represents all things, and on the other, all things indeed represent silver, and they are signs of one another; that is, their relative value is such that one can have the first as soon as one has the other. This happens only in a moderate government, but it does not always happen in a moderate government; for example, if the laws favor an unjust debtor, the things belonging to him do not represent silver and are not a sign of it. With regard to despotic government, it would be a marvel if things there represented their sign; tyranny and distrust make everyone bury his silver;[3] therefore, things there do not represent silver at all.

Legislators have sometimes used such art that things have not only represented silver by their nature but they have become money like silver itself. Caesar[4] as dictator permitted debtors to give lands in

[1] Salt, used in Abyssinia, has the shortcoming of constantly wasting away.

[2] Herodotus [*The Persian Wars*] in Clio [1.94], tells us that the Lydians discovered the art of minting money; the Greeks took it from them; the ancient ox was stamped on the money of Athens. I have seen one of these coins in the Earl of Pembroke's collection.

[3] It is an old usage in Algiers for each father of a family to have a buried treasure. Laugier de Tassy, *Histoire du royaume d'Alger* [chap. 8, "Des Mœurs et des Coutumes des Algériens"; p. 117; 1720 edn].

[4] See Julius Caesar, *De bello Civili*, bk. 3 [3.1].

payment to their creditors at the price they fetched before the civil war. Tiberius[5] ordered that those who wanted silver could have it from the public treasury by pledging lands worth double the amount. Under Caesar, lands were the money that paid all debts; under Tiberius, ten thousand sesterces of land became the money in common use, like five thousand sesterces of silver.

In England the Magna Carta prohibits seizing the lands or the income of a debtor when his movable or personal goods are sufficient for the payment and when he offers to give them; henceforth, all the goods of an Englishman represented silver.

The Germans' laws gave an appraisal in silver for the satisfactions for wrongs one had committed and the penalties for crimes. But as there was very little silver in the country, the laws reappraised the silver in produce or livestock. This occurs in the law of the Saxons, with certain differences for the various peoples according to their ease and comfort. At first[6] the law declared the value of a sou in livestock; the sou of two tremises corresponded to an ox of twelve months or a sheep with its lamb; that of three tremises was worth an ox of sixteen months. Among these peoples, money became livestock, commodities, or produce, and these things became silver.

Not only is silver a sign of things, it is also a sign of silver and represents silver, as we shall see in the chapter on exchange.

[5] Tacitus [*Annales*], bk. 6 [6.17].
[6] *Leges Saxonum*, chap. 18 [66].

CHAPTER 3
On ideal monies

There are real monies and ideal monies. Peoples with a police, almost all of whom use ideal monies, do so only because they have converted their real monies into ideal ones. At first, their real monies have a certain weight and a certain grade of some metal. But soon bad faith or need makes them withdraw part of the metal from each piece of money, leaving it with the same name; for example, from a coin weighing a livre, one takes away half the silver and it is still called a livre; the coin that was a twentieth part of the livre of silver is still called a sou, although it is no longer the twentieth part of that livre.[a] So, the livre is an ideal livre and the sou an ideal sou, and the same for the other subdivisions, and this can reach the point at which what is called a livre will be no more than a very small portion of a livre, which renders it still more ideal. It can even happen that a coin worth precisely a livre or a coin worth a sou is no longer made; so, the livre and the sou will be purely ideal monies. One will give to each coin the denomination of as many livres and as many sous as one likes; the variation can be continual, because it is as easy to give another name to a thing as it is difficult to change the thing itself.

In order to remove the source of abuses, it is very good, in every country where one wants commerce to flourish, for there to be a law that orders one to use real monies and to perform no operation that might render them ideal.

Nothing should be as exempt from variation as that which is the common measure of everything.

Trade itself is very uncertain, and it is a great ill to add a new uncertainty to the one founded on the nature of the thing.

[a] The livre, or pound, was a measure of weight as well as a unit of the currency.

CHAPTER 4
On the quantity of gold and silver

When nations with a police are masters of the world, the quantities of gold and silver increase every day, because the nations either mine them at home or go abroad to find them where they are. On the other hand, they diminish when barbarian nations gain the advantage. One knows how scarce these metals were when the Goths and Vandals, from one side, and the Saracens and Tartars, from the other, had invaded everywhere.

CHAPTER 5

Continuation of the same subject

The silver mined in America, transported to Europe, and sent from there to the east, has favored European navigation; it is an additional commodity that Europe receives in barter with America and that it sends to the Indies for barter. Therefore, a greater quantity of gold and silver is favorable when one considers these metals as commodities; it is not favorable when one regards them as a sign, because their abundance runs counter to their status as a sign, which is founded largely on scarcity.

Before the First Punic War, the proportion of copper to silver was 960 to 1;[7] today it is about 73½ to 1.[8] If the proportion were as it was formerly, silver would all the better fulfill its function as a sign.

[7] See below, chap. 12.
[8] Assuming silver at 49 pounds a mark and copper at twenty sous a pound.

CHAPTER 6

For what reason the price of usury diminished by half on the discovery of the Indies

Garcilaso de la Vega, El Inca,[9] says that incomes in Spain, which were at ten percent, fell to five percent after the conquest of the Indies. This had to be so. A great quantity of silver was suddenly brought to Europe; soon fewer persons needed silver; the price of everything increased and that of silver diminished; the proportion was, therefore, disrupted; all the old debts were annulled. One recalls the time of the System,[10b] when everything had great value except silver. After the conquest of the Indies, those who had silver were obliged to lower the price or the rental, that is, the interest, on their merchandise.

[9] [Garcilaso de la Vega, El Inca] *Royal Commentaries of the Incas and General History of Peru* [p. 2, bk. 1, chaps. 6; 2, 644–645; 1966 edn].
[10] This is what [John] Law's plan was called in France.

---

[b] See 22.10 (note [e], bk. 22) for Montesquieu's explanation of the System under John Law, 1671–1729.

Since that time, loans have not been made at their former rate because the quantity of silver has increased every year in Europe. Further, as the public funds of some few states, founded on the wealth that commerce has procured for them, gave a very modest interest, the contracts of individuals had to be regulated by that. Finally, as the exchange has made it uncommonly easy for men to carry silver from one country to another, silver could not be scarce in one place without flooding in from those places where it was plentiful.

CHAPTER 7

How the price of things is fixed when wealth in signs varies

Silver is the price[c] of commodities or produce. But how can this price be fixed? That is, by what portion of silver will each thing be represented?

If one compares the mass of silver and gold in the world to the total of the commodities there are, it is certain that each kind of produce or commodity can be compared to a certain portion of the entire quantity of gold or silver. As the total of one is to the total of the other, the part of the one will be to the part of the other. Let us assume that there is only a single product or commodity in the world, or that there is only one that is purchased and that it is divisible like silver; a part of that commodity will correspond to a part of the quantity of silver; half of the total of one to half of the total of the other; the tenth, the hundredth, and thousandth of the one to the tenth, the hundredth, and the thousandth of the other. But as what forms property among men is not all in commerce at the same time and because metals or monies, which are the sign of it, are not all there at the same time either, prices will be fixed in a compound ratio of the total of things in commerce with the total of the signs that are also there; and as the things not in commerce today can be there tomorrow, and as the signs not there today can likewise return there, the establishment of the price of things always depends fundamentally on the ratio of the total of things to the total of signs.

Thus the prince or magistrate can no more assess the value of

[c]Here Montesquieu begins to use "price" as it is used today in economics, where it is the result of a market, an exchange, not the worth of a thing.

commodities than he can establish by an ordinance that the relation of one to ten is equal to that of one to twenty. Julian caused a horrible famine when he lowered the price of produce at Antioch.[11]

[11] Socrates, *Historia ecclesiastica*, bk. 2 [3.17].

CHAPTER 8

Continuation of the same subject

The blacks on the coast of Africa have a sign of values without money; it is a purely ideal sign, founded on the degree of esteem they have in mind for each commodity in proportion to their need for it. A certain product or commodity is worth three macutes; another, six macutes; another, ten macutes; it is as if they simply said three, six, and ten. The price is formed by the comparison they make of all the commodities with each other; so, there is nothing that is only money, but each kind of commodity is money for the other.

Let us for a moment bring that way of evaluating things here and join it to our own: all the commodities and produce in the world or even all the commodities or produce of one state in particular considered separately from all the others will be worth a certain number of macutes; and, dividing the silver of this state into as many parts as there are macutes, each of these divided parts of silver will be the sign of a macute.

If one assumes that the quantity of silver in a state doubles, there will have to be twice as much silver for each macute, but if, by doubling silver, you also double the macutes, the proportion will remain as it was before either one of them doubled.

If, since the discovery of the Indies, gold and silver have increased in Europe in the ratio of one to twenty, the price of produce and commodities should have risen in the proportion of one to twenty; but if, on the other hand, the number of commodities has increased as one to two, the price of these commodities and products will have had to rise, on the one hand, in the ratio of one to twenty, and fall at the ratio of one to two, and will consequently be in the ratio of one to ten.

The quantity of commodities and produce grows with an increase in commerce; the increase in commerce, with the increase in the silver that follows it and with new communication to new lands and new seas, which give us new produce and new commodities.

CHAPTER 9
On the relative scarcity of gold and silver

In addition to the positive abundance and scarcity of gold and silver, there is also a relative abundance and scarcity of one of these metals to the other.

Avaricious men hoard gold and silver, because, as they do not want to consume, they love signs that cannot be destroyed. They would rather hoard gold than silver, because they fear losing it and they can better hide the one with the smaller volume. Therefore, gold disappears when silver is common because everyone has some to hide; it reappears when silver is scarce because one is obliged to remove it from its niches.

It is, therefore, a rule: gold is common when silver is scarce, and gold is scarce when silver is common. One senses the difference between relative abundance and scarcity and real abundance and scarcity, about which I shall speak at length.

CHAPTER 10
On the exchange

The relative abundance and scarcity of the monies of various countries forms what is called the exchange.[d]

The exchange fixes the present and temporary value of monies.

Silver, as a metal, has a value like all other commodities; and it also has a value that comes from its capacity to become the sign of other commodities; and if it were only a simple commodity, it must not be doubted that it would lose much of its price.

Silver, as a money, has a value that the prince can fix in some respects and cannot fix in other respects.

[d] In this chapter, and generally in Montesquieu, there is no distinction between the exchange as a process and the institution or place where that process ordinarily takes place. This occasionally makes the language somewhat difficult.

The prince establishes a proportion between a quantity of silver as a metal and the same quantity as money; (2) he fixes the proportion between the various metals used as money; (3) he establishes the weight and grade of each coin; finally, he gives to each coin that ideal value I have mentioned. I shall call the value of money in these four relations, *positive value*, because it can be fixed by a law.

The money of each state has, in addition, a *relative value*, in the sense that it is compared with the money of other countries; it is this relative value that the exchange establishes; it depends largely on the positive value; it is fixed by the most general esteem of the traders and cannot be fixed by the ordinance of the prince, because it varies endlessly and depends on a thousand circumstances.

In order to fix the relative value, the various nations will regulate themselves for the most part by the nation that has the most silver. If it has as much silver as all the others together, each will certainly have to measure itself by that one; this will make the others regulate themselves against one another more or less as they have measured themselves against the principal nation.

In the present state of the universe, Holland[12] is the nation to which we refer. Let us examine the exchange in relation to that country.

In Holland there is a coin called a florin; the florin is worth twenty sous or forty half-sous or groschen. In order to simplify the idea, let us imagine there were no florins in Holland and that there were only groschen there; a man with a thousand florins will have forty thousand groschen, and so forth: now, the exchange with Holland consists in knowing how many groschen each coin of the other country is worth, and as one usually counts by ecus of three livres in France, the exchange will ask how many groschen an ecu of three livres is worth. If the exchange is at fifty-four, the ecu of three livres will be worth fifty-four groschen; if it is at sixty, it will be worth sixty groschen; if silver is scarce in France, the ecu of three livres will be worth more groschen; if it is abundant, it will be worth fewer groschen.

This scarcity or abundance, causing an alteration in the exchange, is not real scarcity or abundance, it is a relative scarcity or abundance: for example, when France has more need to have funds in Holland than the Dutch need them in France, silver is called common in France and scarce in Holland, and vice versa.

[12] The Dutch regulate the exchange for almost all of Europe by a kind of deliberation among themselves, in accordance with their interests.

Let us assume that the exchange with Holland is at fifty-four. If France and Holland made up only one town, one would do what one does when making change for an ecu; the Frenchman would take three livres from his pocket, and the Dutchman would take fifty-four groschen from his own. But as there is a distance between Paris and Amsterdam, the one who gives me for my ecu of three livres the fifty-four groschen one has in Holland must give me a letter of exchange for fifty-four groschen against Holland. Here it is no longer a question of fifty-four groschen, but of a letter for fifty-four groschen. Thus, in order to judge[13] the scarcity or abundance of silver, one must know if there are in France more letters of fifty-four groschen destined for France than there are ecus destined for Holland. If there are many letters offered by the Dutch and few ecus offered by the French, silver is scarce in France and common in Holland, and the exchange must rise and one must give me more than fifty-four groschen for my ecu, otherwise, I would not relinquish it, and vice versa.

One sees that the various operations of the exchange form an account of receipts and expenses that must always be brought into balance and that a state that owes repays others no more through the exchange than an individual pays his debt by changing his silver.

I assume that there are only three states in the world, France, Spain, and Holland; that various individuals in Spain owe to France the value of a hundred thousand marks of silver and that various individuals in France owe one hundred and ten thousand marks to Spain; and that some circumstance makes everyone, in Spain and in France, suddenly want to have his silver back: what would be the operations of the exchange? It would repay the two nations reciprocally in the amount of one hundred thousand marks; but France would continue to owe ten thousand marks to Spain, and the Spanish would still have letters against France for ten thousand marks, and France would have none at all against Spain.

Now, if Holland's situation with France were reversed, and if, in order to bring the account into balance, it owed France ten thousand marks, France could pay Spain in two ways: either by giving its creditors in Spain letters payable by its debtors in Holland in the amount of ten thousand marks, or else by sending ten thousand marks of silver specie to Spain.

[13] There is much silver in a place when there is more silver than paper; there is little, when there is more paper than silver.

From this it follows that when a state needs to remit a sum of silver to another country, it is by the nature of the thing indifferent whether silver should be sent there or letters of exchange should be given. The better way of paying depends solely on the immediate circumstances; one will have to see what, at that time, will give more groschen in Holland, silver carried in specie[14] or a letter payable in Holland for the same amount.

When the same grade and the same weight of silver in France give me the same weight and the same grade of silver in Holland, the exchange is said to be at par. In the present state of monies,[15] par is about fifty-four groschen per ecu: if the exchange is above fifty-four groschen, it is said to be high; when it is below, it is said to be low.

In order to know whether the state loses or gains in a certain situation of exchange, it must be considered as debtor, as creditor, as seller, and as buyer. When the exchange is lower than par, the state loses as debtor and gains as creditor; it loses as buyer and gains as seller. It is easily seen that it loses as debtor: for example, when France owes Holland a certain number of groschen, the fewer groschen its ecu is worth, the more ecus it will need to pay its debt; whereas, if France is creditor for a certain number of groschen, the fewer groschen each ecu is worth the more ecus it will receive. The state also loses as buyer, for the same number of groschen is still needed in order to buy the same quantity of commodities and when the exchange drops, each French ecu gives fewer groschen. For the same reason, the state gains as seller: I sell my commodity in Holland for the same number of groschen that I sold it for before; I shall then have more ecus in France when I procure one ecu with fifty groschen than when I have to have fifty-four in order to have that same ecu; the reverse of all this will occur in the other state. If Holland owes a certain number of ecus, it will gain; and if it is owed, it will lose; if it sells, it will lose; if it buys, it will gain.

Something more must be said about this: when exchange is below par, for example, if it is at fifty instead of fifty-four, what should happen is that France, sending fifty-four thousand ecus to Holland by exchange, would buy commodities for only fifty thousand, and that on the other hand, Holland, sending the value of fifty thousand ecus to France, would buy commodities for fifty-four thousand; this would make a difference of eight fifty-fourths, that is, of more than a seventh

[14] With the expenses of carriage and insurance deducted.
[15] In 1744.

lost for France, so that one would have to send to Holland a seventh more in silver or commodities than one did when the exchange was at par, and with the ill continuing to exist because such a debt would lower the exchange still further, France would in the end be ruined. It seems, I say, that this should happen, and yet it does not, because of the principle I have already established elsewhere,[16] which is that states tend to bring themselves into balance and liberate themselves; thus they borrow only in proportion to what they can pay and buy only as much as they sell. And, taking the above example, if the exchange falls in France from fifty-four to fifty, the Dutchman, who bought commodities from France for a thousand ecus and who paid fifty-four thousand groschen for them, would not pay more than fifty thousand for them if the Frenchman wanted to agree to it: but the French commodity will gradually rise in price; the profit will be divided between the Frenchman and the Dutchman, for a trader readily divides his profit when he can gain: therefore, the profit will be spread between the Frenchman and the Dutchman. In the same way, the Frenchman, who bought Dutch commodities for fifty-four thousand groschen and paid for them with a thousand ecus when the exchange was at fifty-four, would be obliged to add four fifty-fourths more in French ecus in order to buy the same commodities: but the French merchant, who will feel the loss he would suffer, will want to give less for the Dutch commodity; the loss will then be spread between the French merchant and the Dutch merchant; the state will imperceptibly bring itself into balance, and the lowering of the exchange will not have all the drawbacks one might have feared.

When the exchange is lower than par, the trader can, without decreasing his fortune, remit his funds to foreign countries because, on retrieving them, he regains what he has lost, but a prince who sends to foreign countries only a silver that is never to return always loses.

When traders do a great deal of business in a country, the exchange infallibly rises. This occurs because one undertakes many engagements and buys more commodities, and one draws on the foreign country in order to pay them.

If a prince amasses a great quantity of silver in his state, silver there may be scarce really and common relatively; for example, if at the same time that state had to pay for many commodities in the foreign country, the exchange would be lowered though silver was scarce.

[16] See bk. 20, ch. 21 [above].

The exchange everywhere always tends to bring itself into a certain proportion, and this is in the very nature of the thing itself. If the exchange from Ireland to England is lower than par and if that from England to Holland is also lower than par, that from Ireland to Holland will be even lower; that is, in a ratio compounded of that from Ireland to England and that from England to Holland; for a Dutchman, who can have his funds sent indirectly from Ireland by way of England, will not want to pay dearer to make them come directly. I say that it should be thus, but it does not occur exactly thus; there are always circumstances that make things vary, and in the difference of the profit made by drawing them from one place or another lies the art or peculiar cleverness of bankers, which is not the issue here.

When a state raises its money; for example, when it calls six livres or two ecus what it formerly called only three livres or one ecu, this new denomination, which adds nothing real to the ecus, should not procure a single groschen more by the exchange. One should get, for the two new ecus, only the same quantity of groschen that one received for the old one, and if this is not the case, it is not the result of the rate set for the money itself, but rather of its newness and its suddenness. The exchange is concerned with business that has already begun and corrects itself only after a certain time.

When a state, instead of simply raising its money by a law, makes a new recoinage in order to turn a strong money into a weaker one, it happens that there are two sorts of money during the time of the operation: the strong, which is the old one, and the weak, which is the new one; and as the strong one is depreciated by proclamation and is accepted only at the mint, and as letters of exchange, consequently, have to be paid in the new specie, it seems that the exchange should regulate itself by the new specie. If, for example, the weakening in France were by half and if the old ecu of three livres gave sixty groschen in Holland, the new ecu should give only thirty groschen. On the other hand, it seems that the exchange should regulate itself by the value of the old specie, because the banker who has some silver and who takes letters is obliged to carry old specie to the mint in order to have new specie on which he loses. Therefore, the exchange will be between the value of the new specie and that of the old. The value of the old specie falls, so to speak, both because new specie is already used in commerce and because the banker cannot hold strictly to either, as it is in his interest to take the old silver quickly from his till in order to put it to work and as he is even forced to do so to make his payments; on the other hand, the value of the new specie rises, so to speak, because the banker with the new specie is in circumstances which allow him, as we shall show, to procure old specie to his great advantage. Therefore, the exchange will set itself, as I have said above, between the new specie and the old. So, the bankers profit by sending the old specie out of the state, because they gain for themselves in this way the same advantage they would have by an exchange regulated on the old specie, that is, many groschen in Holland, and also because the exchange they return to is regulated between the new specie and the old specie, that is, it is lower; this procures many ecus in France.

I assume that three livres of the old specie make, by the present exchange, forty-five groschen, and that by carrying this same ecu to Holland one would have sixty; but with a letter of forty-five groschen, one will procure an ecu of three livres in France, which, carried in old specie in Holland, will still get sixty groschen; therefore, all the old specie will leave the state that makes the recoinage, and the profit will go to the bankers.

In order to remedy this, one will be forced to perform a new operation. The state which does the recoinage will itself send a great quantity in old specie to the nation that regulated the exchange, and procuring a credit for itself there, it will make the exchange rise to the point that one will have very nearly as many groschen by the exchange of an ecu of three livres as one would have had by sending an ecu of three livres in old coins out of the country. I say *very nearly* because, when the profit is modest, one will not be tempted to send coins out because of the expense of carrying it and the risks of confiscation.

It is well to give a clear idea of this. Mr. Bernard, or any other banker the state wants to use, offers his letters to Holland at one, two, or three groschen higher than the immediate exchange; he has a supply in foreign countries of the old specie that he has continually sent out; therefore, he has made the exchange rise to the point mentioned above: still, by giving his letters, he collects all the new specie and forces the other bankers, who have payments to make, to take their old specie to the mint, and moreover, as he had imperceptibly taken all the silver, he constrains the other bankers, in their turn, to give him letters at a very high rate of exchange; the profit at the end indemnifies him in large part for the loss at the beginning.

One senses that, during this entire operation, the state has to suffer a violent crisis. Silver will become very scarce there: (1) because most of it must be depreciated by proclamation; (2) because part of it will have to be carried into foreign countries; (3) because everyone will keep it under lock, as no one will want to leave to the prince a profit one hopes to have oneself. It is dangerous to do it slowly; it is dangerous to do it quickly. If the gain expected is immoderate, the drawbacks increase accordingly.

It has been seen above that, when the exchange was lower than the specie, there was profit in sending silver out; for the same reason, when it is higher than the specie, there is profit in bringing it back again.

But there is a case in which one finds profit in having the specie leave the country although the exchange is at par; it is when one sends it into foreign countries to have it marked again or recoined. When it returns, one makes a profit on the money whether one uses it in the country or takes letters for foreign countries.

If it happened that, in a state, one made a company having a very considerable number of shares and made the value of the first purchase rise twenty or twenty-five times within a few months, and that this same state had established a bank whose notes were to serve the function of money, and that the numerical value of these notes was prodigiously high in order to correspond to the prodigiously high numerical value of the shares (this is Mr. Law's System),[e] it would follow from the nature of the thing that these shares and notes would be destroyed in the same way they had been established. One could not have made the shares suddenly rise to twenty or twenty-five times their original value without giving many people the means of procuring immense wealth on paper; each one would seek to secure his fortune, and as the exchange provides the easiest route for changing its nature or for sending it where one wants, one could continually remit a part of one's effects to the nation that regulated the exchange. A plan of continually remitting it to foreign countries would make the exchange fall. Let us assume that, at the time of the System, with respect to the grade and the weight of the silver money, the rate of exchange was at forty groschen per ecu; when innumerable pieces of paper had become money, one wanted to give no more than thirty-nine groschen per ecu, then no more than thirty-eight, thirty-seven, etc. This went so far that one gave no more than eight groschen, and finally there was no longer an exchange.

[e]Here Montesquieu offers his account of John Law's System.

The exchange in this case should have regulated the proportion of silver to paper in France. I assume that, by the weight and grade of the silver, the ecu of three livres of silver was worth forty groschen and that when the exchange was done in paper, the ecu of three livres in paper was worth only eight groschen; the difference was four-fifths. Therefore, the ecu of three livres in paper was worth four-fifths less than the ecu of three livres in silver.

CHAPTER II

On the operations the Romans performed on monies

Whatever acts of authority have been performed on monies in our time in France in two consecutive ministries, the Romans performed even greater ones, not at the time of the corrupt republic or at that of the republic which was only anarchy, but when, having the full force of the institution, as much by its wisdom as by its courage, after vanquishing the towns of Italy, it disputed empire with the Carthaginians.

I am very glad to pursue this matter somewhat further, so that an example will not be made of something that is not one.

In the First Punic War[17] the as, which was supposed to be of twelve ounces of copper, weighed only two, and in the Second Punic War, it weighed only one. This retrenching corresponds to what we today call expansion of the currency; to remove half the silver from an ecu of six livres in order to make two ecus, or to make it worth twelve livres, is precisely the same thing.

There remains no record of the way the Romans performed their operation in the First Punic War, but what they did in the Second points to a remarkable wisdom. The republic was not in a position to pay its debts; the as weighed two ounces of copper; and the denarius, valued at ten ases, weighed twenty ounces of copper. The republic made the as of one ounce of copper;[18] it gained half on its creditors; it paid a denarius with these ten ounces of copper. This operation gave the state a great jolt: it should have been as small as possible; the operation contained an injustice: it should have been as small as possible; its object was the liberation of the republic from its citizens: it

[17] Pliny the Elder, *Naturalis historiae*, bk. 33, art. 13 [33.13.44–35].
[18] Ibid. [Pliny the Elder, *Naturalis historiae* 33.13.44].

could not, therefore, have been the liberation of the citizens from themselves: this brought about a second operation, and one ordered that the denarius, which had until then been only ten ases, would contain sixteen. It resulted from this double operation that, while the creditors of the republic lost half,[19] those of the individuals lost only a fifth;[20] commodities increased only a fifth; the real change in the money was only a fifth; the other consequences can be seen.

Therefore, the Romans conducted themselves better than we, who in our operations have included both public fortunes and individual fortunes. That is not all: one will see that they performed them in circumstances more favorable than ours.

[19] They received ten ounces of copper for twenty.
[20] They received sixteen ounces of copper for twenty.

CHAPTER 12

The circumstances in which the Romans performed their operations on money

Long ago there was very little silver or gold in Italy; this country has few if any gold or silver mines: when Rome was taken by the Gauls, there were only a thousand pounds of gold there.[21] Still, the Romans sacked several powerful towns and carried their wealth home. For a long time they used only copper money; it was only after the peace of Pyrrhus that they had enough silver to make money of it:[22] they made denarii with this metal, which were valued at ten ases[23] or ten pounds of copper. Therefore, the proportion of silver to copper was as 1 to 960, for, as the Roman denarius was valued at ten ases or ten pounds of copper, it was valued at 120 ounces of copper and, as the same denarius was valued at an eighth of an ounce of silver,[24] this gives the proportion we have just mentioned.[f]

[21] Pliny the Elder, [*Naturalis historiae*] bk. 33, art. 5 [33.5.14].
[22] [Johann] Freinsheim [*Supplementorum Livianorum*], decade 2, bk. 5 [15.6].
[23] Ibid. [Freinsheim, *Supplementorum Livianorum*, 15.6]. They also struck halves called "quinaires," and quarters called "sesterces."
[24] [Guillaume Budé, *De Asse et partibus eius*, bk. 1; 2, 3; 1969 edn.] According to Budé, an eighth; according to others, a seventh.

[f] There were twelve ounces in the Roman pound or livre.

When Rome became the master of this part of Italy, with Greece and Sicily as her closest neighbours, little by little it found itself between two rich peoples, the Greeks and the Carthaginians; its silver increased at home; and, as the proportion of 1 to 960 between silver and copper could no longer be sustained, Rome performed various operations on the monies, of which we know nothing. We know only that at the beginning of the Second Punic War, the Roman denarius was valued at only twenty ounces of copper[25] and that thus the proportion between silver and copper was only 1 to 160. The reduction was quite considerable, for the republic gained five-sixths on all the copper money, but one had done only what the nature of thing required and had reestablished the proportion between the metals that served as money.

The peace that ended the First Punic War had left the Romans masters of Sicily. They soon entered Sardinia; they began to know Spain: the stock of silver continued to increase in Spain; an operation was performed reducing the silver denarius from twenty ounces to sixteen,[26] and it had the effect of putting silver and copper back in proportion; this proportion was 1 to 160; it had been 1 to 128.

Study the Romans: their superiority will never be more evident than in the choice of the circumstances in which they did good and evil things.

[25] Pliny the Elder, *Naturalis historiae*, bk. 33, art. 13 [33.13.45].
[26] Ibid. [Pliny the Elder, *Naturalis historiae*, 33.13.45.]

CHAPTER 13

Operations on the monies at the time of the emperors

In the operations performed on the monies during the republic, one proceeded by way of retrenchment; the state disclosed its needs to the people and did not try to seduce them. Under the emperors, one proceeded by alloying metals: these princes, reduced to despair by their very liberalities, were obliged to tamper with the monies, an indirect path which decreased the ill but appeared not to touch it; one took back part of the gift and hid one's hand, and, without speaking of decrease in pay or largess, these were diminished.

One can still see in some collections[27] what are called plated metals, which have only a sheath of silver covering the copper. This money is discussed in a fragment of Dio's book 77.[28]

Didius Julianus began the weakening. One finds that the money of Caracalla was more than half alloy;[29] that of Alexander Severus two-thirds;[30] the weakening continued; and under Galienus, one saw only silvered copper.[31]

One can feel that these violent operations could not occur in our time; a prince would deceive himself and would deceive no one else. The exchange has taught the banker to compare all the monies of the world and set them at their just value; the grade of monies can no longer be kept secret. If a prince begins to alloy precious metal with copper, everyone continues to do so and does it for him; strong specie leave first and return to him weakened. If, like the Roman emperors, he weakened silver without weakening gold, he would see the gold suddenly disappear and he would be reduced to his bad silver. The exchange, as I have said in the preceding book,[32] has curtailed the great acts of authority, or at least the success of the great acts of authority.

[27] See Father [Louis] Jobert, *The Knowledge of Medals* (Paris, 1739), p. 59 [chaps. 2, 8, pp. 13–14, 93–94; 1715 edn].
[28] *Extract of Virtues and Vices* [Cass Dio, *Historia Romana* 77 (78.14.3–4; Exc. Val. 378; Xiph. 333.18–20)].
[29] See [Louis] Savot [*Discours sur les medailles antiques*], pt. 2, chap. 12 [p. 95, 1627 edn], and the *Journal des Sçavans*, July 28, 1681 [340–342] concerning a discovery of 50,000 medals.
[30] Ibid. [Louis Savot, *Discours sur les medailles antiques*, pp. 95–96; 1627 edn.]
[31] Ibid. [Louis Savot, *Discours sur les medailles antiques*, p. 97; 1627 edn.]
[32] [Bk. 21] chap. 16 [above].

CHAPTER 14
How exchange hampers despotic states

Muscovy has tried to leave its despotism; it cannot. The establishment of commerce requires the establishment of the exchange, and the operations of the exchange contradict all Muscovy's laws.

In 1745, the Czarina[g] made an ordinance driving the Jews out because they had sent to foreign countries the silver of those who had been exiled to Siberia and that of the foreigners who were in her

[g] Elizabeth.

service. The subjects of the empire, like slaves, were unable to leave or to send out their goods without permission. The exchange, which gives the means of transfering silver from one country to another, contradicts, therefore, the laws of Muscovy.

Commerce itself is in contradiction to these laws. The people comprise only slaves attached to the land and slaves called ecclesiastics or gentlemen because they are the lords of these slaves; there remains, therefore, scarcely anyone for the third estate, which is formed of workers and merchants.

CHAPTER 15
Usage of several countries of Italy

In some Italian countries laws were made to prevent subjects from selling land in order to transfer their silver to foreign countries. These laws could be good ones, when the wealth of each state was so much its own that there were many difficulties in sending it to another. But since, by the use of the exchange, wealth somehow does not belong to any state in particular and since it is so easily transfered from one country to another, it is a bad law that does not allow one to dispose of one's lands for one's business when one can dispose of one's silver. This law is bad because it gives the advantage to movable effects over land, because it makes foreigners dislike coming to establish themselves in the country, and finally, because one can evade it.

CHAPTER 16
On the aid the state can draw from bankers

Bankers are made in order to change silver and not to lend it. If the prince uses them only to change his silver, as his affairs are always extensive, the slightest profit he gives the bankers for their remittance becomes considerable, and, if large profits are asked of the prince, he can be sure that it is due to a fault in administration. When, on the other hand, bankers are used for making advances of silver, their art consists in procuring large profits from it for themselves, without anyone's being able to accuse them of usury.

CHAPTER 17
On public debts

Some people have thought that it was good for a state to owe itself; they have thought that this multiplied wealth by increasing circulation.

I believe there has been a confusion between a circulating paper that represents money or a circulating paper that is the sign of the profits a company has made or will make in commerce, and a paper that represents a debt. The first two are very advantageous to the state; the third cannot be advantageous, and all that one can expect of it is that it should be a good guarantee for individuals against the nation's debt, that is, that it will procure payment of the debt. But here are the drawbacks that result.

If foreigners possess much paper that represents a debt, they draw, every year, from the nation, a considerable sum in interest.

2. In a nation thus perpetually indebted, the exchange should be very low.

3. The impost levied for the payment of the interest on the debt injures manufactures by making workmanship dearer.

4. One takes the true revenues of the state from those who are active and industrious to transfer them to idle people, that is, one gives the comforts of working to those who do not work, and the difficulties of working to those who work.

These are the drawbacks; I know of no advantages. Ten persons have a thousand ecus each in revenue from land or industry; this makes, at five percent, a capital of 200 thousand ecus for the nation. If these ten persons used half their revenue, that is five thousand ecus, to pay interest on 100 thousand ecus that they have borrowed from others, this still makes only 200 thousand ecus for the state; it is, in the language of algebra, 200,000 ecus − 100,000 ecus + 100,000 ecus = 200,000 ecus.

What can lead one into error is that a paper representing the debt of a nation is a sign of wealth, for only a rich state could sustain such a paper without falling into decadence; so that it does not fall, the state must have great wealth from elsewhere. One says that there is no harm in it because there are resources against this ill, and one says that the ill is a good because the resources are greater than the ill.

CHAPTER 18

On the payment of public debts

There must be a proportion between the state as creditor and the state as debtor. The state can be a creditor infinitely, but it can be a debtor only to certain degree, and when it goes beyond it, the status of creditor vanishes. If this state also has a credit that has not been jeopardized, it can do what has been so happily practiced in a European state;[33] that is, it can procure a great quantity of specie and offer reimbursement to all individuals, unless they want to reduce the interest. Indeed, just as it is individuals who fix the rate of interest when the state borrows, it is for the state to fix it when the state wants to pay.

It is not enough to reduce interest, but the benefit of the reduction must form a fund for amortization[h] to pay a part of the capital every year; an operation the happier as its success increases every day.

When the credit of the state is not complete, there is a further reason to seek to form a fund for amortization because this fund, once established, soon restores confidence.

If the state is a republic, whose government by its nature undertakes projects that take a long time, the capital of the fund for amortization can be small; in a monarchy, this capital must be larger.

2. The regulations should be such that all the citizens of the state bear the weight of establishing this fund, because they all bear the weight of establishing the debt; the creditor of the state pays himself with the sums he contributes.

3. There are four classes of people who pay the debts of the state: the owners of lands, those who practice their industry through trade, the plowmen and artisans, and the state pensioners or individuals. Of these

[33] England.

[h] See 21.20 (p. 388). This term, *fonds d'amortissement*, can also be translated as "sinking fund" and it is related to *mortmain* in 30.11 (p. 629).

four classes, the last, in a case of necessity, would seem to have to be the least carefully managed because it is an entirely passive class in the state, whereas this same state is sustained by the active force of the other three. But, as one cannot burden it more without destroying public confidence, of which the state in general and these three classes in particular have a sovereign need, as a certain number of citizens cannot lack public faith without all appearing to lack it, as the class of creditors is always the most exposed to the projects of the ministers and is always under their eyes and hands, the state must accord it a singular protection, and the indebted part must never have the slightest advantage over the crediting part.

CHAPTER 19
On lending at interest

Silver is the sign of values. It is clear that he who needs this sign should rent it, as he does everything he needs. The whole difference is that other things can either be rented or bought, whereas silver, which is the price of things, is rented and not bought.[34]

To lend one's silver without interest is a very good act, but one senses that this can be only a religious counsel and not a civil law.

In order for commerce to proceed well, silver must have a price, but this price must be small. If it is too high, the trader, who sees that it would cost him more in interest than he could gain in his commerce, undertakes nothing; if silver has no price, no one lends it, and the trader still undertakes nothing.

I am mistaken when I say that no one lends it. The business of society must always go forward; usury is established, bringing with it the disorder that has been experienced at all times.

The law of Mohammed confuses usury with the loan at interest.[i] Usury increases in Mohammedan countries in proportion to the severity of the prohibition; the lender indemnifies himself for his peril in infringing the law.

[34]This does not include cases in which gold and silver are considered as merchandise.

[i]Montesquieu's use of "interest" and "usury" needs to be followed here. Usury seems to be what one pays beyond interest for danger in lending.

In these countries of the East, most men have nothing that is secure; there is almost no relation between the present possession of a sum and the expectation of having it back after lending it; therefore, usury increases in proportion to the peril of insolvency.

CHAPTER 20

On maritime usuries

The amount of maritime usury is founded on two things: the peril of the sea, which makes one risk lending his silver only in order to have much more, and the readiness commerce gives the borrower to effect much business of great consequence, whereas, since usury on land is founded on neither of these two reasons, it is either proscribed by legislators, or, more sensibly, kept within just bounds.

CHAPTER 21

On the loan by contract and on usury among the Romans

In addition to the loan made for commerce, there is another kind of loan made by civil contract, which results in interest or usury.

As, among the Romans, the people increased their power every day, the magistrates sought to flatter them and have them make the laws that would be the most pleasant for them. They withdrew their capital; they lowered the interest; they forbade its being taken; they removed physical constraint; finally, the question of the abolition of debts was brought up every time a tribune wanted to make himself popular.

These continual changes, both by laws and by plebiscites, naturalized usury in Rome, as the creditors who saw in the people their debtor, their legislator, and their judge no longer had trust in contracts. The creditors were not tempted to lend money to the people except at great profits, as to discredited debtors, especially because, as laws came only from time to time, the people's complaints were continual and always intimidated the creditors. This caused all honest means of borrowing and lending to be abolished in Rome, and a frightful usury, which was repeatedly crushed only to rise again, became established.[35] The evil came from the fact that things had not been well managed. Extreme laws for good give rise to extreme evil. The people had to pay for the loan of the silver and for the danger of legal penalties.

[35] Tacitus, *Annales*, bk. 6 [6.16].

CHAPTER 22

Continuation of the same subject

The first Romans had no laws to regulate the rate of usury.[36] In the ensuing embroilments between plebeians and patricians, even during the sedition of the Mons Sacer,[37] on the one side, only good faith was alleged, and, on the other, only the harshness of contracts.

Individual agreements were, therefore, followed, and I believe that they were ordinarily at 12 percent per year. My reason is that in the old language of the Romans, interest at 6 percent was called half of usury, interest at 3 percent, quarter of usury;[38] the total of usury was, therefore, interest at 12 percent.

But if one asks how such high rates of usury could have become established among a people who were almost without commerce, I shall say that this people, who were very often obliged to go to war without pay, very often needed to borrow and that, as their expeditions were constantly successful, they often found it easy to pay. And this is easily sensed in the narrative of the embroilment that arose in this regard; there was no argument with the avarice of those who lent money, but it was said that those who complained would have been able to pay it if their conduct had not been irregular.[39]

Laws were made, therefore, that affected only the immediate situation: an ordinance was made, for example, that those who enrolled for a war that had to be fought would not be pursued by their creditors,

[36] Usury and interest meant the same thing to the Romans.

[37] See Dion. Hal. [*Ant. Rom.*], who has described it so well [6.45–48].

[38] *Usurae semisses, trientes, quadrantes*. For this, see the various titles of the *Digest* and the *Code de usuris*, and especially law 17, with its note [*Corpus Juris Civilis*, *Code* 4.32; *Digest* 22.1, esp. 17]; *de usuris et fructibus et causis et omnibus accessionibus et mora.*

[39] See Appius' speech on this subject, in Dion. Hal. [*Ant. Rom.* 5.66].

that those who were in irons would be set free, that the most indigent would be taken to the colonies; sometimes the public treasury was opened. The people were pacified as their present ills were relieved, and as they asked for nothing for the future, the senate was careful not to provide it.

At the time when the senate defended so consistently the cause of usury, the Romans' love of poverty, of frugality, and of mediocrity in fortunes was at its peak; but the constitution was such that the principal citizens bore all the burdens of the state and the common people paid nothing. How could the former be deprived of the right to pursue their debtors, and be asked to fulfill their posts and to fund the pressing needs of the republic?

Tacitus says[40] that the Law of the Twelve Tables fixed interest at 1 percent per year. It is clear that he was mistaken and that he took for a law of the Twelve Tables another law I shall mention. If the Law of the Twelve Tables had ruled that, how was it that one did not use its authority in the disputes that arose after that time between creditors and debtors? One finds no vestige of this law about lending at interest, and, however little one may know about Roman history, one will see that such a law could not have been the work of the decemvirs.

The Licinian law,[41] made eighty-five years after the Law of the Twelve Tables, was one of those short-lived laws we have mentioned. It ordered one to withdraw from the capital what had been paid as interest and to discharge the remainder in three equal payments.

In Roman year 398 [356 B.C.], the tribunes Duilius and Maenius had a law passed that reduced interest to 1 percent per year.[42] It is this law that Tacitus[43] confuses with the Law of the Twelve Tables, and it is the first one the Romans made to fix the rate of interest. Ten years later,[44] this usury was reduced by half;[45] subsequently it was entirely removed,[46] and if we are to believe some of the authors Livy had read,

[40] [Tacitus] *Annales*, bk. 6 [6.16].
[41] Roman year 388 [366 B.C.]. Livy, bk. 6 [6.35.4].
[42] *Unciaria usura*. Livy, bk. 7 [7.16.1]. See the *Defense of the Spirit of the Laws*, art. "Usury" [2.1151–1160; Pleiade edn, 1951; "Usure," vol. 1, pt. 2, 474–485; Masson edn, 1950].
[43] [Tacitus] *Annales*, bk. 6 [6.16].
[44] Under the consulate of L. Manlius Torquatus and C. Plautius, according to Livy, bk. 7 [7.27.3]; and it is the law spoken of by Tacitus, *Annales*, bk. 6 [6.16].
[45] *Semiunciaria usura*: interest at $\frac{1}{24}$ or 4.2%.
[46] As reported by Tacitus, *Annales*, bk. 6 [6.16].

this occurred during the consulate of C. Marcius Rutilius and Q. Servillius,[47] in Roman year 413 [341 B.C.].

This law followed in the path of all laws in which the legislator has carried things to excess; a way was found to avoid it. Many others had to be made to strengthen, correct, and temper it. Sometimes one departed from laws to follow usages,[48] sometimes one departed from usages to follow laws; but, in this case, usage easily prevailed. When a man borrows, he finds an obstacle in the very law that is made in his favor; that law has against it both the one it aids and the one it condemns. As the lender Sempronius Asellus permitted debtors to act according to the laws,[49] he was killed by creditors[50] for having wanted to recall the memory of a rigidity they could no longer bear.

I leave the town to glance briefly at the provinces.

I have said elsewhere[51] that the Roman provinces were devastated by a despotic and harsh government. That is not all; they were further devastated by frightful usuries.

Cicero says[52] that the people of Salamis wanted to borrow silver from Rome and that they could not because of the Gabinian law. I must explore this law.

When loans at interest had been prohibited in Rome, all sorts of ways were devised to avoid the law.[53] And, as the allies[54] and those of the Latin nations were not subject to the Roman civil law, an ally or Latin, who lent his name and appeared to be the creditor, was used. Therefore, the law had only made the creditors submit to a formality, and the people were not relieved.

The people complained of this fraud, and Marcus Sempronius, tribune of the people, by the authority of the senate, had a plebiscite passed[55] that stipulated that, in the matter of loans, laws prohibiting

[47] The law about it was made at the prosecution of M. Genucius, tribune of the people. Livy, bk. 7 at the end [7.42].

[48] "The taking of interest was accepted, as it was an old custom" [L.]. Appian [*Roman History*], *The Civil Wars*, bk. 1 [1.6.54].

[49] "He permitted them to take it to court" [L.]. Appian [*Roman History*], *The Civil Wars*, bk. 1 [1.6.54]; and Livy, *Epitome*, bk. 64 [*Epitome* 74; see also Johann Freinsheim, *Supplementorum Livianorum* 74.41–42].

[50] Roman year 663 [91 B.C.].

[51] Bk. 11, chap. 19 [above].

[52] [Cicero] *Epistolae ad Atticum*, bk. 5, letter 21 [5.21].

[53] Livy [35.7.2].

[54] Ibid. [Livy 35.7.2.]

[55] Roman year 561 [193 B.C.]. See Livy [35.7.4–5].

usurious loans between one Roman citizen and another would apply equally to those between a citizen and an ally or a Latin.

At that time, those called allies were the peoples of Italy proper, which extended to the Arno and the Rubicon and was not governed as were Roman provinces.

Tacitus says[56] that there were always new evasions of the laws checking usuries. When one could no longer lend or borrow under the name of an ally, it was easy to bring in a man from the provinces who lent his name.

There had to be a new law against these abuses, and when Gabinius[57] made the famous law whose purpose was to check corruption in voting, he naturally thought that the best way to accomplish it was to discourage borrowing; these two things were naturally bound together, for usury always increased at the time of the elections[58] because silver was needed in order to win votes. One clearly sees that the Gabinian law had extended the senatus-consult Sempronian to the provincial people, as the people of Salamis could not borrow silver in Rome because of this law. Brutus, using borrowed names, lent it to them[59] at 4 percent per month[60] and obtained for that two senatus-consults, in the first of which it was said that the loan would not be considered as evading the law and that the governor of Cilicia would judge in accordance with the agreements stipulated in the note of the people of Salamis.[61]

The Gabinian law prohibited loans with interest between the people of the provinces and Roman citizens, and since the latter had, at that time, all the silver in the world in their hands, they had to be tempted by high rates of usury so that in the eyes of the avaricious the danger of losing the debt would disappear. And, as in Rome there were powerful people who intimidated the magistrates and silenced the laws, they were bolder in lending and bolder in requiring high rates of usury. Because of this, the provinces were ravaged one by one by those who had credit in Rome, and as each governor made his edict on entering

56 [Tacitus] *Annales*, bk. 6 [6.16].
57 Roman year 615 [139 B.C.].
58 See Cicero, *Epistolae ad Atticum*, bk. 4, letters 15 and 16 [4.9, 16].
59 Cicero, *Epistolae ad Atticum*, bk. 6, letter 1 [6.1].
60 Pompey, who had lent six hundred talents to King Ariobarsanus, had himself paid thirty-three Attic talents every thirty days. Cicero, *Att.*, bk. 3, letter 21; bk. 6, letter 1 [5.21; 6.1].
61 "So that neither the people of Salamis nor those who gave it [the loan] should be cheated" [L.]. Ibid. [Cicero, *Epistolae ad Atticum* 5.21.]

his province,[62] setting the rate of usury that suited him, avarice assisted legislation, and legislation assisted avarice.

Business must go forward, and a state is lost if everything falls into inaction. There were occasions when the towns, the corporate bodies, the societies of towns, and individuals all borrowed, and the need to borrow was only too great, whether to pay for the ravages of the armies, for the rapaciousness of the magistrates, for the extortions of men of business, or for the bad usages that were continually established; one had never been as rich or as poor. The senate, which had executive power, gave by necessity and often by favor permission to borrow from the citizens and thereupon made senatus-consults. But even these senatus-consults were brought into discredit by the law; these senatus-consults[63] gave rise to the people's demand for new Tables, which, by increasing the danger of the loss of capital, increased usury further. I shall continue to repeat: moderation governs men, not excesses.

He who pays later, says Ulpian,[64] pays less. The legislators were led by this principle after the destruction of the Roman republic.

[62] Cicero's edict fixed it at 1 percent per month, adding the usury on the usury at the end of the year. With regard to the tax farmers of the Republic, he engaged them to give respite to their debtors: if they did not pay at the fixed time, he awarded the usury stated on the bond. Cicero, *Epistolae ad Atticum*, bk. 6, letter 1 [6.1].

[63] See what Lucceius says [Cicero] *Epistolae ad Atticum*, bk. 5, letter 21 [5.21]. There was even a general senatusconsult, which fixed usury at 1 per cent per month. See the same letter.

[64] Law 12 [*Corpus Juris Civilis, Digest* 50.12]; *de verborum significatione.*

BOOK 23
On laws in their relation to the number of inhabitants

CHAPTER I

On men and animals in relation to the multiplication of their species

Venus, life-giver

. . . .

For soon as the year has bared her springtime face,
and bars are down for the breeze of growth and birth,
in heaven the birds first mark your passage, Lady,
and you; your power pulses in their hearts.
Then wild beasts, too, leap over rich, lush lands
and swim swift streams; so prisoned by your charms
they follow lustily where you lead them on.
Last, over sea and hill and greedy river,
through leaf-clad homes of birds, through fresh green fields,
in every creature you sink love's tingling dart,
luring them lustily to create their kind.
Since you, and only you, rule the world of nature,
and nothing, without you, comes forth to the coasts
of holy light, or makes for joy and love . . .[1a]

The fertility of female animals is virtually consistent.[b] But in the human species, the way of thinking, character, passions, fantasies, caprices, the idea of preserving one's beauty, the encumbrance of pregnancy, that of a too numerous family, disturb propagation in a thousand ways.

[1] Translation of the beginning of Lucretius by le Sieur d'Hesnaut [Lucretius, *De rerum natura* 1.2, 6–20].

[a] Lucretius, *The Nature of Things*, tr. Frank O. Copley (W. W. Norton, New York, 1977) p. 1. We have chosen to use another's translation of this poetry, as did Montesquieu.

[b] *constant.* See note [c], bk. 1.

CHAPTER 2
On marriages

The natural obligation of the father to nourish his children has established marriage, which declares the one who should fulfill this obligation. The peoples[2] of whom Pomponius Mela[3] speaks fixed it by resemblance alone.

Among well-policed peoples, the father is the one whom the laws in the ceremony of marriage declare to be such[4] because they find in him the person they seek.

Among animals this obligation is such that the mother can usually meet it. The obligation is much broader among men: their children partake of reason, but it comes to them by degrees; it is not enough to nourish them, they must also be guided; even when they can sustain their lives, they cannot govern themselves.

Illicit unions contribute little to the propagation of the species. In them the father, whose natural obligation is to nourish and raise the children, is not fixed, and the mother, on whom the obligation falls, meets thousands of obstacles: in shame, in remorse, in the constraints her sex imposes, in the rigor of the laws, and she generally lacks means of support.

Women who have submitted to public prostitution cannot have the comforts required to raise their children. Even the care required for the education of their children is incompatible with their condition, and they are so corrupt that the law cannot trust them.

It follows from all of this that public continence is joined naturally to the propagation of the species.

[2] The Garamantes.
[3] [Pomponius Mela, *De situ orbis*] bk. 1, chap. 3 [1.7.45].
[4] "The father is he whom the marriage indicates" [L.]. [*Corpus Juris Civilis, Digest* 2.4.5; *de in jus vocando*].

CHAPTER 3
On the condition of children

Reason dictates that children follow the condition of the father when there is a marriage, and when there is no father, they can only be the concern of the mother.[5]

[5] This is why, among nations with slaves, the child almost always follows the condition of the mother.

CHAPTER 4
On families

It is accepted almost everywhere that the wife passes into the family of the husband. The contrary is established without any difficulty in Formosa,[6] where the husband goes to form the wife's family.

Independently of its first motives, this law which fixes the family in a succession of persons of the same sex contributes much to the propagation of the human species. The family is a sort of property; a man who has children of the sex that does not perpetuate it is never content until he has those of the sex that does.

Names, which give men the idea of a thing that seemingly should not perish, are very appropriate for inspiring in each family the desire to extend its duration. Among some peoples, names distinguish families; among others, they distinguish only persons, which is not as good.

[6] Father [Jean Baptiste] du Halde, [*Description de l'Empire de la Chine*, "Tai ovan ou l'isle de Formose"], vol. 1, p. 156 [1, 182 H; 1, 165 P; 1, 178–179 L].

CHAPTER 5
On various orders of legitimate wives

Sometimes laws and religion have established many sorts of civil unions, for example among the Mohammedans, where there are several orders of wives whose children are recognized by their birth in a household, by civil contracts, or even by the slavery of the mother and their subsequent recognition by the father.

It would be contrary to reason for the law to stigmatize in the children what it has approved in the father; therefore, all these children should inherit, unless some particular reason opposes it, as in Japan, where only the children of a wife given by the emperor may inherit. Policy requires that the goods the emperor gives not be excessively divided because they include a service, as did our fiefs in former times.

There are countries in which a legitimate wife enjoys within the household nearly the same honors that the single wife has in our climate; there the children of concubines are taken to belong to the first wife: it is established thus in China. Filial respect,[7] the ceremony of strict mourning, are due not to the natural mother, but to the mother given by the law.

With the help of such a fiction,[8] there are no longer bastard children, and in the countries where this fiction has no place, one surely sees that the law that makes legitimate the children of concubines is a forced law, for the largest part of the nation would be stigmatized by the law. Nor is there a question in these countries of children born of adultery. The separation of women, the enclosure, the eunuchs, the locks, render the thing so difficult that the law judges it impossible; besides, the same sword would exterminate the mother and the child.

[7] Father [Jean Baptiste] du Halde [*Description de l'Empire de la Chine*, "Des cérémonies"], vol. 2, p. 124 [2, 143 H; 2, 124 P; 2, 207 L].

[8] Wives are distinguished as great and small, that is, legitimate or not; but there is not a like distinction of the children. "This is the great doctrine of the empire," it is said in a Chinese work on morality translated by the same Father [Jean Baptiste du Halde, *Description de l'Empire de la Chine*, "Morale des Chinois"], p. 140 [3, 169 H; 3, 140 P].

CHAPTER 6

On bastards in various governments

Therefore, one finds scarcely any bastards in the countries where polygamy is permitted; these are found in those where the law establishes a single wife. Concubinage has had to be stigmatized in these countries; therefore the children born of it have had also to be stigmatized.

In republics, where it is necessary for mores to be pure, bastards should be still more odious than they are in monarchies.

In Rome, the provisions made against them were perhaps too harsh; but, as the ancient institutions made it necessary for all citizens to marry, and moreover, as marriages were softened by permission to repudiate or to divorce, only a very great corruption of mores could have brought about concubinage.

It must be remarked that, because of the esteem accorded citizenship[c] in democracies, where it carried with it sovereign power, laws were often made about the position of bastards that had less relation to the thing itself and to the honesty of marriage than to the particular constitution of the republic. Thus the people sometimes accepted bastards as citizens[9] in order to increase their power against the important men. Thus in Athens the people subtracted the bastards from the number of citizens in order to have a greater portion of the grain sent them by the king of Egypt. Finally, Aristotle[10] teaches us that in many towns, where there were not enough citizens, bastards inherited, and that when there were enough of them, they did not inherit.

[9]See Aristotle, *Pol.*, bk. 6, chap. 4 [1319b8–10].
[10]Ibid. [Aristotle, *Pol.*], bk. 3, chap. 3 [1278a28–34].

[c]*qualité de citoyen.*

CHAPTER 7
On the fathers' consent to marriage

The consent of fathers is founded on their power, that is, on their right of property; it is also founded on their love, on their reason, and on the uncertainty of the reason of their children, whose age keeps them in a state of ignorance and whose passions keep them in a state of drunkenness.

In the small republics or in the singular institutions of which we have spoken, there can be laws assigning magistrates to inspect marriages between the children of citizens, a thing nature had already assigned to fathers. The love of the public good can be such that it equals or surpasses any other love. This is why Plato wanted magistrates to regulate marriages; this is why the Lacedaemonian magistrates directed them.

But in ordinary institutions, it is for the fathers to marry their children; their prudence in this regard will always be greater than any other prudence. Nature gives fathers a desire to procure heirs for their children, which they scarcely feel for themselves; in the various degrees of primogeniture, they see themselves gradually advancing toward the future. But what would happen if harassment and avarice went to the point of usurping the authority of fathers? Let us listen to Thomas Gage[11] on the conduct of the Spanish in the Indies.

"In order to increase the number of people who pay tribute, all Indians who are fifteen years old must marry, and the age of marriage of Indians has been ruled to be fourteen years for males and thirteen for girls. This is founded on a canon that says that craftiness can replace age." He saw one of these enumerations made; it was a shameful thing, he said. Thus, in the action that should be the freest in the world, the Indians are still slaves.

[11] Thomas Gage, *Travels in the New World*, p. 171 [chap. 19, p. 345: 1699 edn; chap. 15, pp. 241–242; 1958 edn].

CHAPTER 8

Continuation of the same subject

In England, daughters often abuse the law in order to marry according to their fancy without consulting their parents. I do not know whether this usage might not be better tolerated there than elsewhere because, as the laws have not established a monastic celibacy, girls have no other state to take than that of marriage and cannot refuse it. On the other hand, in France monasticism is established, daughters always have the recourse of celibacy, and the law ordering them to await the consent of their fathers could be more suitable there. The usage in Italy and Spain would be the least reasonable in respect to this idea; monasticism is established there, and one can marry without the fathers' consent.

CHAPTER 9

On girls

Girls, who are led to pleasure and liberty only by marriage, whose spirit dares not think, whose heart dares not feel, whose eyes dare not see, whose ears dare not hear, who are introduced only to show themselves dull-witted, and who are condemned without respite to trifles and to precepts are quite drawn to marriage; it is the boys who must be encouraged.

CHAPTER 10

What induces one to marry

Wherever there is a place for two persons to live comfortably, a marriage is made. Nature very much inclines to this when she is not checked by the difficulty of sustenance.

Nascent peoples multiply and increase greatly. Among them it would be a great discomfort to live in celibacy; it is not a discomfort to have many children. The contrary occurs when the nation is formed.

CHAPTER 11

On the harshness of the government

People who have absolutely nothing, like beggars, have many children. This is because their case is like that of nascent peoples; it costs nothing for the father to give his art to his children, who even at birth have the instruments of that art. These people, in a rich or superstitious country, multiply because they do not bear the burdens of the society but are themselves the burdens of society. But people who are poor only because they live under a harsh government, who regard their fields less as the foundation of their sustenance than as a pretext for harassments; these people, I say, have few children. They cannot even nourish themselves; how could they dream of sharing? They cannot take care of themselves when they are ill; how could they raise creatures who are in that continuous illness which is childhood?

It is ease of speaking and inability to examine that have caused it to be said that the poorer the subjects, the larger their families; that the more one is burdened with imposts, the more one puts oneself in a position to pay them: two sophisms that have always ruined and will forever ruin monarchies.

The harshness of the government can go as far as destroying natural feelings by natural feelings themselves; did not the women in America make themselves miscarry in order for their children not to have such cruel masters?[12]

[12]Thomas Gage, *Travels in the New World*, p. 58 [chap. 13, p. 175; 1699 edn; omitted from 1958 edn].

CHAPTER 12

On the number of girls and boys in different countries

I have already said that in Europe a few more boys than girls are born;[13] it has been observed that in Japan a few more girls than boys were born.[14] All things being equal, there will be more fertile women in Japan than in Europe, and consequently more people.

Some accounts say that in Bantam there are ten girls for each boy;[15] such a disproportion, which would make the number of families there to the number of families in other climates be as one is to five-and-a-half, would be excessive. Indeed, families there could be larger, but there are few people sufficiently well-off to be able to take care of such a large family.

[13]In bk. 16, chap. 4 [above].

[14]See [Engelbert] Kaempfer [*The History of Japan Together with a Description of the Kingdom of Siam, 1690–1692*, bk. 2, chap. 5; 1, 331–332; 1906 edn], who reports an enumeration in Meaco.

[15]*Recueil des voyages qui ont servi à l'établissement de la Compagnie des Indes*, vol. 1, p. 347 ["Relation du premier voyage des Hollandais aux Indes Orientales"; 1, 383; 1702 edn; 1, 342; 1725 edn].

CHAPTER 13
On seaports

In seaports, where men are exposed to a thousand dangers and go to live or die in distant climates, there are fewer men than women; nevertheless, more children are seen there than elsewhere, which is a result of the ease of gaining sustenance. Perhaps, too, the oily parts of fish can supply the matter that serves for procreation. This would be one of the causes of the infinite number of people there are in Japan[16] and in China,[17] where they live almost exclusively on fish.[18] If this were so, certain monastic rules that oblige one to live on fish would be contrary to the spirit of the legislator himself.

[16] Japan is composed of islands, there is much shoreline, and the sea is filled with fish.
[17] China is full of streams.
[18] See Father [Jean Baptiste] du Halde [*Description de l'Empire de la Chine*], vol. 2, p. 139, 142, etc. ["De l'abondance qui règne à la Chine"; 2, 164–169 H; 2, 139–142 P; 2, 238–245 L].

CHAPTER 14
On the products of the land that require more or fewer men

The countries that are in pasture are little populated because few people find occupation there; lands in grain occupy more men, and vineyards infinitely more.

In England, there have often been complaints that the increase in pasturelands has led to a decrease in inhabitants,[19] and it is observed in France that the great quantity of its vineyards is one of the great causes for the multitude of men.

Countries with coal mines to supply material for fuel have an advantage over the others since they do not have to have any forests and all the lands can be cultivated.

[19] Most owners of land-holdings, says [Gilbert] Burnet, finding greater profit in the sale of their wool than of their wheat, enclosed their possessions; the commons, who were dying of hunger, rose up; an agrarian law was proposed; the young king even wrote on the matter; proclamations were made against those who had enclosed their lands. *Abrégé de l'histoire de la réformation de l'église de l'Angleterre*, pp. 44 and 83 [*History of the Reformation of the Church of England*, vol. 2, pt. 2, bk. 1 (1549); pp. 207–208, 247; 1969 edn (reprint of the 1865 edn)].

In places where rice is grown there must be many projects to control the water; therefore, many of their people can be occupied. Furthermore, less land is needed there to provide the sustenance of a family than in those countries that produce other grains; finally, the land that elsewhere is used for feeding animals serves immediately there for the sustenance of men; the work that animals do elsewhere is done there by men; and the cultivation of the land becomes for men an immense manufactory.[d]

[d]See 21.22 (note [o], bk. 21).

CHAPTER 15

On the number of inhabitants in relation to the arts

When there is an agrarian law and the lands are equally divided, the country can be heavily populated although there are few arts, because each citizen finds that working his land provides him precisely enough to feed himself and because all the citizens together consume all the fruit of the country; it was thus in some ancient republics.

But in our states today, the land is unequally distributed; it produces more fruit than those who cultivate it can consume; and if one neglects the arts and attaches oneself only to agriculture, the country cannot be populated. As those who cultivate or supervise cultivation have fruit remaining, nothing commits them to work the following year; the fruit would not be consumed by idle people, for idle people would not have the wherewithal to buy them. Therefore, the arts must be established in order for the fruit to be consumed by plowmen and artisans. In a word, these states need many people to grow more than is necessary for themselves; for that, they must be given the desire to have the superfluous, but only artisans can give that.

Those machines whose purpose is to simplify the craft are not always useful. If a work is at a medium price, suitable to both the one who purchases it and the other worker who makes it, machines that would simplify its manufacture, that is, that would decrease the number of workers, would be pernicious; and if water-mills were not established everywhere, I would not believe them to be as useful as is said because they have put an infinity of hands to rest, they have deprived many people of the use of water, and they have made many lands lose their fertility.

CHAPTER 16

On the views of the legislator concerning the propagation of the species

Regulations concerning the number of inhabitants depend greatly on circumstances. There are countries where nature has done everything; the legislator, therefore, has nothing to do. What good is it for the laws to encourage propagation when the fertility of the climate gives enough people? Sometimes the climate is more favorable than the terrain; the people multiply and famines destroy them: this is the situation in China; thus a father there sells his daughters and exposes his children. The same causes bring about the same effects in Tonkin,[20] and one must not, like the Arab travelers who appear in Renaudot's account, seek to explain it by the opinion on metempsychosis.[21]

For the same reasons, the religion of the island of Formosa[22] does not permit women to have children before they are thirty-five years old; before this age, the priestess crushes their womb and makes them miscarry.

[20] [William] Dampier, *Voyages*, vol. 2, p. 41 [vol. 2, pt. 1, chap. 3; 1, 588; 1906 edn].

[21] [Eusèbe Renaudot, *Anciennes relations des Indes et de la Chine*] p. 167 [pp. 165–167; 1718 edn].

[22] See the *Recueil des voyages qui ont servi à l'établissement de la Compagnie des Indes*, vol. 5, pt. 1, pp. 182 and 188. ["Relation de l'état de l'isle Formose, écrite par George Candidus"; 5, 96–97; 1706 edn; 5, 185–186; 1725 edn.]

CHAPTER 17

On Greece and the number of its inhabitants

This effect, which depends on physical causes in certain eastern countries, was produced in Greece by the nature of the government. The Greeks were a great nation made up of towns, each having its government and its laws. They conquered no more than the towns of

Switzerland, Holland, and Germany, do today; in each republic, the legislator had had for his purposes the happiness of the citizens at home and a power abroad that was not inferior to that of the neighboring towns.[23] With a small territory and a great felicity, it was easy for the number of citizens to increase and become a burden; thus, they constantly made colonies;[24] they were mercenaries like the Swiss of today; nothing was neglected that could prevent the excessive multiplication of children.

There were among them republics whose constitution was singular. Subject peoples were obliged to supply sustenance to the citizens: the Lacedaemonians were fed by the Helots; the Cretans by the Periokoi; the Thessalians by the Penestai. There had to be only a certain number of free men there so that the slaves would be in a position to furnish their sustenance. We say today that the number of regular troops must be limited; Lacedaemonia was an army kept up by peasants; therefore, this army had to be limited; if not, the free men who had all the advantages of the society would have multiplied without number, and the plowmen would have been overwhelmed.

The Greek political men were thus particularly attached to regulating the number of citizens. Plato[25] fixes it at five thousand forty, and he wants propagation to be checked or encouraged according to need, by honors, by shame, and by the warnings of the old men; he even wants the number of marriages to be regulated[26] in such a way that the people replace themselves without overburdening the republic.

If the law of the country, says Aristotle,[27] prohibits the exposing of infants, the number of children each man is to beget has to be limited. To someone who has more children than the number specified by the law, he counsels[28] causing the woman to miscarry before the fetus has life.

The vile means employed by the Cretans to prevent having too many children is reported by Aristotle, and I have felt modesty frightened when I wanted to report it.[e]

[23] In valor, discipline, and military exercises.
[24] The Gauls, who were in the same situation, did the same thing.
[25] [Plato] in his *Laws*, bk. 5 [737e].
[26] [Plato] *Republic*, bk. 5 [460a].
[27] [Aristotle] *Politics*, bk. 7, chap. 16 [1335b21–23].
[28] Ibid. [Aristotle, *Politics* 1335b23–25.]

---

[e] Aristotle, *Politics* 1272a24–26.

There are places, Aristotle goes on to say,[29] where the law makes citizens of foreigners, bastards, or those who are born only of a citizen mother, but as soon as they have enough people they no longer do it. The savages of Canada burn their prisoners, but when they have empty huts to give, they recognize their prisoners as a part of their nation.

Sir William Petty[f] has assumed in his calculations that a man in England is worth what he would be sold for in Algiers.[30] This can be good only for England: there are countries in which a man is worth nothing; there are some in which he is worth less than nothing.

[29] [Aristotle] *Politics*, bk. 3, chap. 3 [1278a28–34].
[30] Sixty pounds sterling.

[f] Sir William Petty, *Economic Writings*, "An essay in Political Arithmetic;" 512, 1986 edn.

CHAPTER 18

On the state of peoples before the Romans

Italy, Sicily, Asia Minor, Spain, Gaul, and Germany, like Greece, were full of small peoples and glutted with inhabitants; in them there was no need to make laws to increase the numbers.

CHAPTER 19

Depopulation of the universe

All these small republics were swallowed up by a great one, and the universe was gradually seen to lose population; one has only to look at Italy and Greece before and after the Roman victories.

"I shall be asked," says Livy,[31] "where the Volscians were able to find enough soldiers to wage war after having been vanquished so often. There had to have been an infinity of people in these regions, which today would be uninhabited except for some soldiers and Roman slaves."

[31] [Livy] bk. 6 [6.12.2–5].

"The oracles have ceased," says Plutarch,[32] "because the places where they spoke have been destroyed; in Greece today one would find scarcely three thousand soldiers."

"I shall not describe," says Strabo,[33] "Epirus and the neighboring places, because these countries are entirely uninhabited. This depopulation, which began long ago, continues every day, so that Roman soldiers camp in abandoned houses." He finds the cause of this in Polybius, who says that Aemilius Paullus destroyed seventy towns in Epirus after his victory and returned home with a hundred and fifty thousand slaves.

[32] [Plutarch] *Moralia, De defectu oracularum* [413f–414a].
[33] [Strabo, *Geographica*] bk. 7, p. 496 [7.7.3].

CHAPTER 20

That it was necessary for the Romans to make laws for the propagation of the species

The Romans, by destroying all the peoples, destroyed themselves; constantly active, striving, and violent, they wore themselves out, just as a weapon that is always in use wears out.

I shall not speak here of their attentiveness to replacing the citizens they lost,[34] of the associations[g] they made, of the rights to citizenship[h] they gave, or of that immense nursery of citizens they found in their slaves. I shall say what they did to replace not the loss of citizens, but that of men, and as they were the people in the world who best knew how to fit their laws to their projects, to examine what they did in this regard is not a matter of indifference.

[34] I took up this subject in the *Consideration on the Causes of the Greatness of the Romans and their Decline* [chap. 13; p. 124; 1968 edn].

[g] The allies in Italy were called the *socii*.
[h] *droits de cité.*

CHAPTER 21

On Roman laws concerning the propagation of the species

The old laws of Rome sought to induce the citizens to marry. The senate and the people often made regulations about this, as Augustus says in the speech reported by Dio.[35]

Dionysius of Halicarnassus[36] cannot believe that after the death of three hundred and five Fabians wiped out by the Veiians, there remained of this family[i] but a single child, because the old law that ordered each citizen to marry and raise all his children was still in force.[37]

Independently of the laws, the censors kept an eye on marriage, and according to the needs of the republic, they engaged people to it both by shame and by penalties.[38]

The mores, which had begun to be corrupted, contributed much to the citizens' distaste for marriage, which is only trouble for those who are no longer sensitive to the pleasures of innocence. This is the spirit of the speech[39] that Metellus Numidicus made to the people during his censorship. "If it were possible not to have wives, we would be delivered from this evil, but as nature has established that one can scarcely live happily with them, or continue to exist without them, there must be more regard for our preservation than for fleeting satisfactions."

The corruption of mores destroyed the censorship, itself established to destroy the corruption of mores; but when this corruption becomes general, censorship no longer has force.[40]

Civil discords, triumvirates, and proscriptions weakened Rome more than any war that it had yet waged; few citizens remained,[41] and

[35] [Cass. Dio, *Historia Romana*] bk. 56 [56.6.4].
[36] [Dion. Hal., *Ant. Rom.*] bk. 2 [9.22.1–3].
[37] In the Roman year 277 [477 B.C.].
[38] See, for what they did in this regard, Livy, bk. 45 [45.15], *Epitome*, bk. 59 [See also Johann Freinsheim, *Supplementorum Livianiorum* 59.53]; Aulus Gellius [*NA*], bk. 1, chap. 6 [1.6]; Valerius Maximus [*Factorum et dictorum memorabilium*], bk. 2, chap. 19 [2.9].
[39] It appears in Aulus Gellius [*Noctium Atticum*], bk. 1, chap. 6 [1.6.2].
[40] See what I have said in bk. 5, chap. 19 [above].
[41] After the civil war, Caesar, having had the census taken, found only 150,000 heads of families. Livy, in the *Epitome* of Florus, twelfth decade [Livy, *Epitome*, bk. 115].

[i] Here Montesquieu uses the same word, *race*, that is used for the families that ruled France, making it clear that it means a tribe, or extended family. See note [d], bk. 18.

most of them were not married. In order to remedy this last ill, Caesar and Augustus reestablished the censorship and even wanted to be censors.[42] They made various regulations: Caesar rewarded those who had many children;[43] he forbade women under forty-five and who had neither husbands nor children to wear precious stones or to use litters,[44] an excellent method of attacking celibacy through vanity. The laws of Augustus were more pressing;[45] he imposed[46] new penalties on those who were not married and increased the rewards for those who were and for those who had children. Tacitus calls them the Julian laws;[47] it is likely that the old regulations made by the senate, the people, and the censors were recast into them.

The Augustan law met with a thousand obstacles, and thirty-four years after it had been made,[48] the Roman knights asked him to revoke it. He had those who were married put on one side and those who were not, on the other; these last appeared in greater number, which astonished and confused the citizens. Augustus, with the gravity of the censors of old, spoke to them thus:[49]

> While diseases and wars take so many citizens from us, what will become of the town if marriages are no longer contracted? The city does not consist in houses, porticoes, public squares; it is men who make the city. You will not see men emerge from the earth to take care of your business, as in legend. It is not to live alone that you remain celibate; each one of you has companions at his table and in his bed, and you seek only peace for your profligacy. Will you cite the example of the Vestal Virgins? If you were not to observe the laws of modesty, you would have, therefore, to be punished as they are. You are equally bad citizens whether everyone imitates your example or no one follows it. My only purpose is the perpetuation of the republic. I have increased the penalties for those who have not obeyed, and, with regard to rewards, they are such that I do not

[42] See Cass. Dio [*Historia Romana*], bk. 43 [43.25.2 and 44.5.3] and Xiphilinus, *In August.* [Cass. Dio, *Historia Romana* 52.42.1–6].

[43] Cass. Dio [*Historia Romana*], bk. 43 [43.25.2]; Suetonius, *Vitae duodecim Caesarum*, *Julius*, chap. 20 [20.3]; Appian [*Roman History*], *The Civil Wars*, bk. 2 [2.2.10].

[44] Eusebius Pamphilii, *Chronicon bipartitum* [183rd Olympiad, p. 238].

[45] Cass. Dio [*Historia Romana*], bk. 54 [54.16.1–2].

[46] In Roman year 736 [18 B.C.].

[47] *Julias rogationes*: "The Julian proposal [statutes]," [Tacitus] *Annales*, bk. 3 [3.25].

[48] In Roman year 762 [A.D. 9]. Cass. Dio [*Historia Romana*], bk. 56 [56.1.2].

[49] I have shortened this speech, which is of a wearisome length; it is reported in Cass. Dio [*Historia Romana*], bk. 56 [56.2–9].

> know whether virtue has ever had greater ones; if lesser ones lead a thousand people to risk their lives, would not these of mine get you to promise to take a wife and nourish children?

He gave this law, which he named Julia, for himself, and Papia Poppaea, for those who were consuls for a part of that year.[50] The size of the ill appeared even in their election: Dio[51] tells us that they were not married and that they had no children.

The Augustan law promptly became a code of laws and a systematic body of all the regulations that could be made on this subject. The Julian laws were recast into them[52] and were given more force; they have so many aspects, they influence so many things, that they form the finest part of the Roman civil laws.

Scattered bits of them are to be found in the precious fragments of Ulpian,[53] in the laws of the *Digest* drawn from the authors who have written on the Papian laws, in the historians and other authors who have cited them, in the Theodosian code, in the fathers who censored them, doubtless with a commendable zeal for things of the next life, but with very little knowledge of the business of this one.

These laws had several articles, of which thirty-five are known.[54] But, proceeding to my subject as directly as possible, I shall begin with the article that Aulus Gellius[55] tells us was the seventh, and which concerns the honors and rewards granted by the law.

The Romans, who came for the most part from the Latin towns, which were Lacedaemonian colonies,[56] and who had even drawn a part of their laws from these towns,[57] had, like the Lacedaemonians, the respect for old age that gives it all honors and all precedence. When the republic lacked citizens, marriage and the number of children were granted the prerogatives that had been given to age;[58] some were attached to marriage alone, independently of the children who could be

[50] Marcus Pappius Mutilus and Quintus Poppaeus Secundus. Cass. Dio [*Historia Romana*], bk. 56 [56.10.3].

[51] Cass. Dio [*Historia Romana*], bk. 56 [56.10.3].

[52] Article 14 of the *Fragmenta* [14] of Ulpian clearly distinguished the Julian law from the Papian law.

[53] Jacques Godefroy has compiled them [*Fragmenta legis Juliae et Papiae*, 1617 edn].

[54] The thirty-fifth is cited in law 19 [*Corpus Juris Civilis*, *Digest* 23.2.19]; *de ritu nuptiarum*.

[55] [Aulus Gellius, *NA*] bk. 2, chap. 15 [2.15.4–8].

[56] Dion. Hal. [*Ant. Rom.* 2.49.4–5].

[57] The Roman deputies who were sent in search of the Greek laws went to Athens and into the towns of Italy.

[58] Aulus Gellius [*NA*], bk. 2, chap. 15 [2.15].

born of it: this was called the right of husbands. Others were given to those citizens with children; greater ones to those with three children. These three things must not be confused: some of these privileges married people could always enjoy, for example, a particular seat in the theater;[59] some they enjoyed only when the people who had children, or when those who had more than they, did not take them away.

These privileges were very extensive; the married people who had the greatest number of children were always preferred, both in the pursuit of honors and in the exercise of these same honors.[60] The consul who had the most children took the fasces first;[61] he had the choice of provinces;[62] the senator who had the most children was the first inscribed in the catalog of senators; he gave his opinion first in the senate.[63] One could attain magistracies before the required age because each child counted for one additional year.[64] If one had three children in Rome, one was exempt from all personal charges.[65]Free women who had three children and freed women who had four came out of that perpetual wardship[66] in which the old Roman laws kept them.[67]

But if there were rewards, there also were penalties.[68] Those who were not married could receive nothing from the testaments of those who were not relatives,[69] and those who were married but without children received only half.[70] The Romans, according to Plutarch,[71] married in order to be heirs, not in order to have heirs.

The benefits a husband and a wife could give to each other by testament was limited by the law. They could give each other every-

[59] Suetonius, *Vitae duodecim Caesarum, Augustus*, chap. 44 [44.2].

[60] Tacitus [*Annales*], bk. 2 [2.51]: "The law demanded that the number of the candidate's children be the overriding concern" [L.].

[61] Aulus Gellius [*Noctium Atticum*], bk. 2, chap. 15 [2.15.4].

[62] Tacitus, *Annales*, bk. 15 [15.19].

[63] See law 6, para. 5 [*Corpus Juris Civilis, Digest* 50.2.6.5]; *de decurionibus et filiis eorum*.

[64] See law 2 [*Corpus Juris Civilis, Digest* 4.4.2]; *de minoribus viginti quinque annis*.

[65] Law 1, para. 3, and law 2, para. 1 [*Corpus Juris Civilis, Digest* 50.5.1.3; 50.5.2.1]; *de vacatione et excusatione munerum*.

[66] Ulpian, *Fragmenta*, tit. 29, para. 3 [29.3].

[67] Plutarch [*Vit.*], *Numa* [10.3].

[68] See Ulpian, *Fragmenta*, tits. 14–18 [14–18], which are a fine selection of the old Roman jurisprudence.

[69] Sozomen [*Historia ecclesiastica*], bk. 1, chap. 9 [1.9]. One received from his relatives. Ulpian, *Fragmenta*, tit. 16, para. 1 [16.1].

[70] Sozomen [*Historia ecclesiastica*], bk. 1, chap. 9 [1.9] and the single law, in the *Codex Theodosianus* [8.16]; *de infirmandis poenis caelibatus et orbitatis*.

[71] [Plutarch] *Moralia, De amore prolis* [493e].

thing[72] if they had children by each other; if they had none, they could receive a tenth of the inheritance because of the marriage; and if they had children from another marriage, they could give each other as many tenths as they had children.

If a husband absented himself[73] from his wife for a cause other than the business of the republic, he could not be her heir.

The law gave a surviving husband or wife two years to remarry,[74] and a year and a half in the case of divorce. Fathers who did not want to marry their children or give dowries to their daughters were constrained to do so by magistrates.[75]

One could not have an engagement when the marriage was to be more than two years away,[76] and, as one could not marry a girl before twelve years of age, one could not become engaged to her before she was ten years of age. The law did not want one to be able to enjoy uselessly,[77] and on the pretext of an engagement, the privileges of married people.

A man of sixty years was prohibited from marrying a woman of fifty.[78] As one had given great privileges to married people, the law did not want useless marriages. For the same reason, the senatus-consult Calvisianus declared irregular the marriage of a woman of more than fifty years with a man of less than sixty[79] so that a woman of more than fifty could not marry without incurring the penalties of these laws. Tiberius increased the severity of the Papian law[80] and prohibited a man of sixty from marrying a woman who was under fifty, so a man of

[72] See this in more detail in Ulpian, *Fragmenta*, tits. 15 and 16 [15, 16].

[73] Ulpian, *Fragmenta*, tit. 16, para. 1 [16.1a].

[74] Ulpian, *Fragmenta*, tit. 14 [14]. It appears that the first Julian laws gave three years. The Speech of Augustus in Cass. Dio [*Historia Romana*], bk. 56 [56.7.3]; Suetonius, *Vitae duodecim Caesarum, Augustus*, chap. 34 [34]. Other Julian laws granted only one year; finally, the Papian law gave two. Ulpian, *Fragmenta*, tit. 14 [14]. These laws were not pleasing to the people, and Augustus tempered them or made them more strict in accordance with the people's disposition to tolerate them.

[75] It was the thirty-fifth heading of the Papian law. Law 19 [*Corpus Juris Civilis, Digest* 23.2.19]; *de ritu nuptiarum*.

[76] See Cass. Dio [*Historia Romana*], bk. 54 [54.16.7], year 736 [18 B.C.]; Suetonius, *Vitae duodecim Caesarum, Octavian* [Augustus], chap. 34 [34.1].

[77] See Cass. Dio [*Historia Romana*], bk. 54 [54.16.7] and also in Cass. Dio, "The Speech of Augustus," bk. 56 [56.1–10].

[78] Ulpian, *Fragmenta*, tit. 16 [16.1] and law 26 in the *Code* [*Corpus Juris Civilis, Code* 5.4.27]; *de nuptiis*.

[79] Ulpian, *Fragmenta*, tit. 16, para. 3 [16.4].

[80] See Suetonius, *Vitae duodecim Caesarum, Claudius*, chap. 23 [23.1].

sixty could not marry in any case without incurring the penalty, but Claudius repealed what had been done under Tiberius in this regard.[81]

All these provisions were more in conformity with the climate of Italy than with that of the north, where a man of sixty is still strong and women of fifty are not generally barren.

In order for one not to be uselessly limited in the choice one could make, Augustus permitted all freemen who were not senators[82] to marry freed women.[83] The Papian law prohibited senators from marrying women who had been freed, or who had appeared in the theater;[84] and at the time of Ulpian freed men were prohibited from marrying women who had led a dissolute life, who had appeared in the theater, or who had been condemned by a public judgment.[85]Some senatus-consults had to have established this. In the time of the republic, few of these sorts of laws were made, because the censors corrected in this regard the disorders that arose, or kept them from arising.

As Constantine had made a law[86] which included in the prohibition of the Papian law not only senators but also those who had a considerable rank in the state, not to mention those who were of an inferior condition, this formed the right of that time; only freemen included in the law of Constantine[87] were forbidden such marriages. Justinian also repealed the law of Constantine and permitted all sorts of persons to contract these marriages; it is in this way that we have acquired such a sorry liberty.

It is clear that the penalties imposed on those who married contrary to the prohibition of the law were the same as the ones imposed on those who did not marry at all. These marriages gave them no civil advantages;[88] the dowry[89] was null and void after the death of the wife.[90]

As Augustus had awarded to the public treasury the inheritances and

[81] See Suetonius, *Vitae duodecim Caesarum, Claudius*, chap. 23 [23.1] and Ulpian, *Fragmenta*, tit. 16, para. 3 [16.4].

[82] Cass. Dio [*Historia Romana*], bk. 54 [54.16.2]; Ulpian, *Fragmenta*, tit. 13 [13.1].

[83] "The Speech of Augustus," in Cass. Dio. [*Historia Romana*], bk. 56 [56.7.2].

[84] Ulpian, *Fragmenta*, chap. 13 [13]; and law 44 [*Corpus Juris Civilis, Digest* 23.2.44]; *de ritu nuptiarum*.

[85] See Ulpian, *Fragmenta*, tits. 13 and 16 [13.1–2; 16.2].

[86] See law 1 of the *Code* [*Corpus Juris Civilis, Code* 5.27.1]; *de naturalibus liberis*.

[87] *Novellae* 117 [*Corpus Juris Civilis, Novellae* 117].

[88] Law 37, para. 7 [*Corpus Juris Civilis, Digest* 38.37.7]; *de operis libertorum*; Ulpian, *Fragmenta*, tit. 16, para. 2 [16.2].

[89] [Ulpian] *Fragmenta*, ibid. [16.2.4].

[90] See bk. 26, chap. 13 below.

legacies of those the laws declared disqualified from making them,[91] these laws appeared to be fiscal rather than political or civil. The distaste one already had for a seemingly oppressive burden was increased by that of seeing onself continually prey to the avidity of the fisc. The results were that under Tiberius one was obliged to modify these laws,[92] that Nero decreased the rewards given those who informed for the fisc,[93] that Trajan checked their banditry,[94] that Severus modified these laws,[95] and that the jurists regarded them as odious and abandoned this rigor in their decisions.

Besides, the emperors weakened these laws by giving away as privileges the rights of husbands, of children, and of three children.[96] They did more: they relieved individuals from the penalties of these laws.[97] But it seemed that relief should not have been permitted from rules established for public utility.

It had been reasonable to grant the right of those with children to the Vestals, whom religion necessarily kept virginal;[98] similarly one gave the privilege of married men to soldiers[99] because they could not marry. It was the custom to exempt the emperors from the annoyance of certain civil laws: thus, Augustus was exempt from the annoyance of the law that limited the faculty of freeing,[100] and from the one that set bounds to the faculty of making testaments.[101] All these were only particular cases; but subsequently relief was given readily, and the rule became only an exception.

Sects of philosophy had already introduced into the empire a spirit of

91 Except in certain cases. See Ulpian, *Fragmenta*, tit. 18 [18] and the single law of the *Code* [*Corpus Juris Civilis*, *Code* 6.51.1]; *de caducis tollendis*.

92 "The proposal to relax the lex Papia Poppaea" [L.]. Tacitus, *Annales*, bk. 3, p. 117 [3.25].

93 He reduced them to one-fourth. Suetonius, *Vitae duodecim Caesarum*, *Nero*, chap. 10 [10.1].

94 See Pliny the Younger, *Panegyricus* [36.1–2].

95 Severus postponed the time for the provisions of the Papian law to age 25 for males and age 20 for girls, as one sees by comparing Ulpian, *Fragmenta*, tit. 16 [16.1] with what Tertullian says, *Apologeticus*, chap. 4 [4.8].

96 Publius Scipio, censor, in his speech to the people on mores, complains of the abuse that had already appeared, that an adopted son was assured the same privilege as a natural one. Aulus Gellius [*Noctium Atticum*], bk. 5, chap. 19 [5.19.16].

97 See law 31 [*Corpus Juris Civilis*, *Digest* 23.2.31]; *de ritu nuptiarum*.

98 Augustus, by the Papian law, gave them the same privilege as mothers had; see Cass. Dio [*Historia Romana*], bk. 56 [56.10.2–3]. Numa had given them the privilege to have no overseer, the same as women who had three children. Plutarch [*Vit.*], *Numa* [10.3].

99 Claudius granted it to them. Cass. Dio [*Historia Romana*], bk. 60 [60.24.3].

100 Law "apud eum" [*Corpus Juris Civilis*, *Digest* 40.1.14]; *de manumissionibus*, para. 1.

101 Cass. Dio [*Historia Romana*], bk. 55 [56.32.1].

distance from public business which could not have reached this point at the time of the republic, when everyone was busy with the arts of war and peace.[102] From it came an idea of perfection attached to all that leads to a speculative life; from it came distance from the cares and encumbrance of a family. The Christian religion, succeeding philosophy, fixed, so to speak, ideas for which the former had only cleared the way.

Christianity gave its character to jurisprudence, for empire always has some relation to priesthood. This can be seen in the Theodosian code, which is but a compilation of the ordinances of the Christian emperors.

One of the eulogists of Constantine said to that emperor: "Your laws were made only to correct vices and to regulate mores; you have removed the artifice of the old laws which seemed to have no other view than that of setting traps for simplicity."[103]

It is certain that Constantine's changes were based either on ideas related to the establishment of Christianity, or on ideas drawn from its perfection. From this first purpose came those laws that gave such authority to the bishops that they were the foundation of ecclesiastical jurisdiction; from it came those laws that weakened paternal authority, by removing from the father the ownership of the children's goods.[104] In order to spread a new religion, one must take away the extreme dependence of children, who are always less concerned with what is established.

The laws made with Christian perfection as their object were chiefly those by which he removed the penalties of the Papian laws[105] and exempted from them both those who were not married and those who, being married, had no children.

"These laws were established," says an ecclesiastical historian,[106] "as if the multiplication of mankind could be a result of our cares, instead of seeing that this number grows larger or smaller according to the order of providence."

The principles of religion have greatly influenced the propagation of

[102] See in Cicero, *De Officiis* [1.43.153–155] his ideas about this spirit of speculation.

[103] Nazarius, *Panegyricus Constantinii, anno* 321 [38.4].

[104] See laws 1, 2, and 3 in the *Code* [*Codex Theodosianus* 8.18.1–3]; *de maternis bonis et materni generis et cretione sublata*, and the single law in the same *Code* [*Codex Theodosianus* 8.19.1]; *de bonis quae filiis familias ex matrimonio adquiruntur.*

[105] Single law, *Codex Theodosianus* [8.16]; *de infirmandis poenis caelibatus et orbitatis.*

[106] Sozomen, p. 27 [*Historia ecclesiastica* 1.9].

the human species; sometimes they have encouraged it, as among the Jews, the Mohammedans, the Ghebers,[j] and the Chinese; sometimes they have run counter to it, as they did among the Romans who became Christians.

One continued to preach continence everywhere, that is, that virtue which is more perfect, because, by its nature, it must be practiced by very few people.

Constantine did not remove the decimal laws, which gave greater extent to the gifts a husband and wife could make to each other in proportion to the number of their children; Theodosius the young repealed these laws.[107]

Justinian declared valid all the marriages that the Papian laws had prohibited.[108] These laws wanted one to remarry; Justinian granted advantages to those who would not remarry.[109]

By the old laws, the natural faculty that each one has to marry and have children could not be taken away; thus, when one received a legacy on condition that one did not marry,[110] when a patron made his freed man swear that he would not marry and that he would not have children,[111] the Papian law annulled both this condition and this oath.[112] Therefore, the provisos, *upon remaining widowed*, that we have established contradict the old right and descend from the constitutions of the emperors, which were based on ideas of perfection.

There is no law containing an express repeal of the privileges and honors the pagan Romans had granted for marriages and for some number of children, but where celibacy was preeminent, marriage could no longer be honored, and as one could oblige the tax-collectors to renounce so much profit when penalties were abolished, one senses that it was easier yet to remove the rewards.

The same reason of spirituality that permitted celibacy soon imposed the necessity of that celibacy. God forbid that I should speak here against the celibacy that religion has adopted, but who could be silent

[107] Laws 2 and 3 *Codex Theodosianus* [8.17.2–3]; *de jure liberorum.*
[108] Law "Sancimus" in the *Code* [*Corpus Juris Civilis, Code* 5.4.27]; *de nuptiis.*
[109] [*Corpus Juris Civilis*] *Novellae* 127, chap. 3; 118, chap. 5 [127.3; 118.5].
[110] Law 54 [*Corpus Juris Civilis, Digest* 35.1.64]; *de conditionibus et demonstrationibus.*
[111] Law 5, para. 4 [*Corpus Juris Civilis, Digest* 37.14.6.3]; *de jure patronatus.*
[112] Paul the Jurist, in his *Sentiarum*, bk. 3, tit. 12, para. 15 [3.4a.2].

[j] The Ghebers (Gabars) are a small group of Zoroastrians in Iran. See also *Persian Letters*, 67.

about the one formed by libertinage, the one where the two sexes corrupting one another even by natural feelings themselves, flee a union that should make them better in order to live in one that makes them ever worse?

It is a rule drawn from nature that the more one decreases the number of marriages that can be made, the more one corrupts those that are made; the fewer married people there are, the less fidelity there is in marriages, just as when there are more robbers, there are more robberies.

CHAPTER 22

On the exposure of children

The first Romans had a quite good police concerning the exposure of children. Romulus, says Dionysius of Halicarnassus, imposed on all citizens the necessity of raising all male children and the oldest daughter.[113] If the children were deformed and monstrous, he permitted them to be exposed, after they had been shown to five of the closest neighbors.

Romulus did not permit killing any child under three years;[114] in that way he reconciled the law which gave fathers the right of life and death over their children and the one that prohibited their being exposed.

One also finds in Dionysius of Halicarnassus that the law which ordered citizens to marry and raise all their children was in force in Roman year 277 [477 B.C.];[115] one sees that usage had restrained the law of Romulus that permitted exposing younger daughters.

We know what the Law of Twelve Tables of Roman year 301 [453 B.C.] enacted about exposing children only from a passage in Cicero,[116] who, while speaking of the tribunate of the people, says that it was suffocated immediately after its birth like the monstrous child in the Law of Twelve Tables; therefore, children who were not monstrous were kept, and the Law of Twelve Tables changed nothing of the former institutions.

[113] [Dion. Hal.] *Ant. Rom.*, bk. 2 [2.15.2].
[114] Ibid. [Dion. Hal., *Ant. Rom.* 2.15.2].
[115] [Dion. Hal., *Ant. Rom.*] bk. 9 [9.22.2].
[116] [Cicero] *De legibus*, bk. 3 [3.8.19].

"The Germans," says Tacitus,[117] "do not expose their children, and good mores have more force among them than have good laws elsewhere." Therefore, among the Romans there were laws against this practice, and they were no longer followed. No Roman law can be found that permits exposing children;[118] it was doubtless an abuse introduced in later times when luxury took away comfort, when wealth that was shared was called poverty, when a father believed he had lost what he gave to his family, and when he made a distinction between this family and his property.

[117] [Tacitus] *Germania* [19].

[118] There is no article on this in the *Digest*; the article of the *Code* says nothing about it [*Code* 8.51 (52)], nor do the *Novellae*.

CHAPTER 23

On the state of the universe after the destruction of the Romans

The regulations made by the Romans to increase the number of their citizens had their effect while their republic, in the full force of its institution, had only to recover from the losses due to its courage, its audacity, its firmness, its love for glory, even its virtue. But soon the wisest laws could not reestablish what a dying republic, a general anarchy, a military government, a harsh empire, a haughty despotism, a weak monarchy, and an inane, idiotic, and superstitious court had by turns beaten down; one would have said that they had conquered the world only to weaken it and to deliver it defenseless to the barbarians. The nations of the Goths, the Getae, the Saracens, and the Tartars each in turn bore down on them; soon the barbarian peoples had only barbarian peoples to destroy. Thus in legendary times after floods and storms, armed men came out of the ground who did away with each other.

CHAPTER 24

Changes that occurred in Europe in relation to the number of inhabitants

In the state Europe was in at that time, one would not have believed that it could reestablish itself; above all when, under Charlemagne, it formed only one vast empire. But the nature of the government of that time divided Europe into an infinity of small sovereignties. And, as a lord lived in his village or in his town, as he was not great, rich, powerful (what shall I say?),[k] as he was kept secure only by the number of his inhabitants, each one strove with a singular attentiveness to make his little country flourish; this succeeded so well that, in spite of the irregularities of the government, the lack of knowledge that has since been gained about commerce, and the great number of wars and quarrels which constantly arose, there were in most of the regions of Europe more people than there are today.

I do not have time to treat this matter in depth, but I shall cite the prodigious armies of crusaders made up of all kinds of men. Mr. Pufendorf says that under Charles IX there were twenty million men in France.[119]

It is the perpetual unions of many small states that produced this decrease. Formerly, each village in France was a capital; there is only one large one today: each part of the state was a center of power; today everything relates to one center, and this center is, so to speak, the state itself.

[119] [Samuel Pufendorf] *Introduction à l'histoire général et politique de l'univers*, chap. 5, "De la France" [p. 433; 1700 Lat. edn; bk. 1, chap. 4; pp. 443–444; 1743 Fr. edn].

[k] These parentheses are not in the text.

CHAPTER 25

Continuation of the same subject

It is true that Europe has for two centuries greatly increased its navigation; this has both gained and lost inhabitants. Holland sends a great number of sailors to the Indies every year, of which only two-thirds return; the remainder perish or settle in the Indies; nearly the same thing should happen in other nations that engage in this commerce.

One must not judge Europe as if it were a single state, which alone sends its fleets there. Such a state would increase in people because all the neighboring nations would come to take part in this navigation; sailors would arrive from every direction. Europe, separated from the rest of the world by religion,[120] by vast seas, and by deserts, does not replenish itself in this way.

[120] Mohammedan countries almost entirely surround it.

CHAPTER 26
Consequences

From all this one must conclude that Europe today is an instance of the case in which laws are needed to favor the propagation of the human species; thus, just as the Greek political men always tells us that the republic is tormented by having a large number of citizens, today political men tell us only of the means proper for increasing it.

CHAPTER 27
On the law made in France to encourage the propagation of the species

Louis XIV ordered certain pensions for those who had ten children and larger ones for those who had twelve;[121] but it was not a question of rewarding prodigies. In order to give a certain general spirit that would lead to the propagation of the species, general rewards or general penalties had to be established as among the Romans.

[121] Edict of 1666 favoring marriages [*Recueil général des anciennes lois françaises*, November 1666, #493; 18, 90].

CHAPTER 28

How one can remedy depopulation

When a state is depopulated by particular accidents, wars, plagues, or famines, there are resources. The remaining men can preserve the spirit of work and industry; they can seek to undo their misfortunes and to become more industrious by their calamity itself. An almost incurable ill is seen when depopulation is of long standing because of an internal vice and a bad government. Men there have perished from an imperceptible and habitual illness; born in languor and poverty, in the violence or the prejudices of the government, they have seen themselves destroyed often without sensing the causes of their destruction. Those countries desolated by despotism or by the excessive advantages of the clergy over the laity are great examples of this.

In order to reestablish a country thus depopulated one would wait in vain for the help of children who might be born. Time has run out; the men, in their isolation, lack courage and industry. With enough lands to nourish a people, one can scarcely nourish a family. In these countries, the common people have no share even in their poverty, that is to say, in the fallow lands with which the countries are filled. The clergy, the prince, the towns, the important men, and some principal citizens have gradually become owners of the whole region; it is uncultivated, but the ruined families have left their pastures to them, and the working man has nothing.

In this situation, one would have to do throughout the empire what the Romans did in a part of theirs, that is, practice in the shortage of inhabitants what they observed in their plenty, distribute the lands to all of the families who have nothing, provide for them the means of clearing them and cultivating them. This distribution should be made until the last man gets a share, so that not a moment for work is lost.

CHAPTER 29
On poorhouses

A man is not poor because he has nothing, but because he does not work. The one who has no goods and who works is as comfortable as the one who has a hundred ecus of revenue without working. Whoever has nothing and has a craft is no poorer than he who has ten arpents of land of his own and who has to work them to continue to exist. The worker who has given his art to his children for an inheritance has left them a good which multiplies in proportion to their number. It is not the same for the one who has ten arpents of land to live on and divides them among his children.

In commercial countries where many people have only their art, the state is often obliged to provide for the needs of the old, the sick, and the orphaned. A state with a good police draws upon the arts themselves for this sustenance; it gives some the work of which they are capable, and it teaches others to work, which already makes work.

A few alms given to a naked man in the streets does not fulfill the obligations of the state, which owes all the citizens an assured sustenance, nourishment, suitable clothing, and a kind of life which is not contrary to health.

Aurangzeb,[122] of whom one asked why he did not build poorhouses, says: "I shall make my empire so rich that it will not need poorhouses." He should rather have said: I shall begin by making my empire rich, and I shall build poorhouses.

The wealth of a state presupposes much industry. When there are such a great number of branches of commerce, it is not possible for some branch not to suffer and, consequently, for its workers not to be in some temporary necessity.

It is then that the state needs to bring help promptly, whether to keep the people from suffering or to avoid their rebellion; it is in this situation that there must be poorhouses or some equivalent regulation which can prevent that distress.

But when a nation is poor, individual poverty derives from general distress and is, so to speak, the general distress. All the poorhouses in the world could not cure that individual poverty; on the other hand, the

[122] See [John] Chardin, *Voyages en Perse*, vol. 8 ["Description particulière de la ville d'Ispahan"; 7, 392; 1811 edn].

spirit of laziness that poorhouses inspire increases general poverty, and consequently that of the individual.

When Henry VIII wanted to reform the Church of England, he destroyed the monks,[123] a nation in itself lazy and one that maintained the laziness of others, because, as they practiced hospitality, an infinity of idle people, gentlemen and bourgeois spent their lives running from monastery to monastery. He also took away the poorhouses where the common people found their sustenance, as the gentlemen found theirs in the monasteries. After these changes, the spirit of commerce and industry became established in England.

In Rome, poorhouses make it so that everyone lives well except those who work, those who are industrious, those who cultivate the arts, those who have land, those who engage in commerce.

I have said that wealthy nations needed poorhouses because fortune was subject to a thousand accidents, but one feels that short-term help would be preferable to perpetual establishments. The ill is temporary; help must be of the same nature and applicable to the particular accident.

[123] See [Gilbert] Burnet, *The History of the reformation of the Church of England* [pt. 1, bk. 3 (1536); 1, 357; 1969 edn].

Part 5

BOOK 24

On the laws in their relation to the religion established in each country, examined in respect to its practices and within itself

CHAPTER I

On religions in general

Just as one can judge among shadows those that are the least dark, and among abysses, those that are the least deep, so among the false religions can one seek the ones that are the most in conformity with the good of society, the ones that, though they do not have the effect of leading men to the felicities of the next life, can most contribute to their happiness in this one.

Therefore, I shall examine the various religions of the world only in relation to the good to be drawn from them in the civil state, whether I speak of the one whose roots are in heaven or of those whose roots are in the earth.

As in this work I am not a theologian but one who writes about politics, there may be things that would be wholly true only in a human way of thinking, for they have not been at all considered in relation to the more sublime truths.

With regard to the true religion, the slightest fairness will show that I have never claimed to make its interests cede to political interests, but to unite them both; now, in order to unite them, they must be known.

The Christian religion, which orders men to love one another, no doubt wants the best political laws and the best civil laws for each people, because those laws are, after it, the greatest good men can give and receive.

CHAPTER 2

Bayle's paradox

M. Bayle claims to have proven that it is better to be an atheist than a idolater;[1] that is, in other terms, it is less dangerous to have no religion at all than to have a bad one. "I should prefer," he says, "for one to say of me that I do not exist, than for one to say that I am a wicked man." This is only a sophistry, founded on the fact that it is of no use to mankind for one to believe that a certain man exists, while it is quite useful for one to believe that god is. From the idea that he is not follows the idea of our independence or, if we cannot have this idea, that of our rebellion. To say that religion gives no motive for restraint because it does not always restrain is to say that the civil laws are not a motive for restraint either. It is to reason incorrectly against religion to collect in a large work a long enumeration of the evils it has produced, without also making one of the good things it has done. If I wanted to recount all the evils that civil laws, monarchy, and republican government have produced in the world, I would say frightful things. Even if it were useless for subjects to have a religion, it would not be useless for princes to have one and to whiten with foam the only bridle that can hold those who fear no human laws.

A prince who loves and fears religion is a lion who yields to the hand that caresses him or to the voice that pacifies him; the one who fears and hates religion is like the wild beasts who gnaw the chain that keeps them from throwing themselves on passers-by; he who has no religion at all is that terrible animal that feels its liberty only when it claws and devours.

It is not a question of knowing whether it would be better for a certain man or a certain people to be without religion than to abuse the one that they have, but of knowing which is the lesser evil, that one sometimes abuse religion or that there be none among men.

In order to diminish the horror of atheism, one accuses idolatry too much. It is not true that, when the ancients raised altars to some vice, it meant that they loved the vice; on the contrary, it meant that they hated it. When the Lacedaemonians raised a chapel to Fear, it did not mean that this bellicose nation begged fear to take possession of the hearts of

[1] [Pierre Bayle] *Pensées diverses à l'occasion d'une comète*. [Consider *Pensées diverses*, chap. 145 and *Continuation des Pensées diverses*, chap. 144.]

the Lacedaemonians in battle. There were divinities who were asked not to inspire crime and others who were asked to turn it away.

CHAPTER 3

That moderate government is better suited to the Christian religion, and despotic government to Mohammedanism

The Christian religion is remote from pure despotism; the gentleness so recommended in the gospel stands opposed to the despotic fury with which a prince would mete out his own justice and exercise his cruelties.

As this religion forbids having more than one wife, princes here are less confined, less separated from their subjects, and consequently more human; they are more disposed to give laws to themselves and more capable of feeling that they cannot do everything.

Whereas Mohammedan princes constantly kill or are killed, among Christians religion makes princes less timid and consequently less cruel. The prince counts on his subjects, and the subjects on the prince. Remarkably, the Christian religion, which seems to have no other object than the felicity of the other life, is also our happiness in this one!

In spite of the size of the Ethiopian empire and the vice of its climate, the Christian religion has kept despotism from being established there and has carried the mores and laws of Europe to the middle of Africa.

The crown prince of Ethiopia enjoys a principality and gives his subjects an example of love and obedience. Not far from there, one sees Mohammedanism enclose the children of the king of Sannar; at the king's death, the council sends them off to be slaughtered in favor of the one who mounts the throne.[2]

Let us envisage, on the other hand, the continual massacres of the kings and leaders of the Greeks and Romans, and on the other, the destruction of peoples and towns by Tamerlane and Genghis Khan, the very leaders who ravaged Asia, and we shall see that we owe to Christianity both a certain political right in government and a certain

[2] Poncet, "Relation abrégée du voyage que M. Charles Jacques Poncet, Médecin français, fit en Ethiopie en 1698, 1699, et 1700," in *Lettres édifiantes et curieuses*, vol. 4 [4, 290–291; 1700 edn].

right of nations in war, for which human nature can never be sufficiently grateful.

This right of nations, among ourselves, has the result that victory leaves to the vanquished these great things: life, liberty, laws, goods, and always religion, when one does not blind oneself.

One can say that the peoples of Europe today are no more disunited than were the peoples and the armies, or the armies themselves, in the Roman Empire when it became despotic and military; on the one hand, the armies waged war with one another, and, on the other, they were allowed to take the spoils of the towns and to divide or confiscate the lands.

CHAPTER 4

Consequences of the character of the Christian religion and of that of the Mohammedan religion

From the character of the Christian religion and that of the Mohammedan religion, one should, without further examination, embrace the one and reject the other, for it is much more evident to us that a religion should soften the mores of men than it is that a religion is true.

It is a misfortune for human nature when religion is given by a conqueror. The Mohammedan religion, which speaks only with a sword, continues to act on men with the destructive spirit that founded it.

The history of Sabaco,[3] one of the pastoral kings, is remarkable. The god of Thebes appeared to him in a dream and ordered him to put to death all the princes of Egypt. He judged that the gods were no longer pleased for him to reign because they ordered him to do things so contrary to their usual will, and he withdrew into Ethiopia.

[3] See Diodorus Siculus, bk. 2 [*Bibliotheca historica* 1.65.5–8].

CHAPTER 5

That the Catholic religion better suits a monarchy and that the Protestant religion is better adapted to a republic

When a religion is born and is formed in a state, it usually follows the plan of the government in which it is established, for the men who accept it and those who make it accepted entertain scarcely any ideas about the police other than those of the state in which they were born.

When, two centuries ago, the Christian religion suffered the unfortunate division that divided it into Catholic and Protestant, the peoples of the north embraced the Protestant religion and those of the south kept the Catholic.

This is because the peoples of the north have and will always have a spirit of independence and liberty that the peoples of the south do not, and because a religion that has no visible leader is better suited to the independence fostered by the climate than is the religion that has one.

In the very countries in which the Protestant religion was established, revolutions were made on the plan of the political state. As the great princes were on his side, Luther could scarcely have given them a taste for ecclesiastical authority without outward preeminence, and as the people who lived in republics and the obscure townsmen[a] of the monarchies were on his side, Calvin could easily avoid establishing preeminences and dignities.

Each of these two religions could believe itself the most perfect: Calvinism considering itself more in conformity with what Jesus had said, and Lutheranism, with what the Apostles had done.

[a] *bourgeois.*

CHAPTER 6

Another of Bayle's paradoxes

Bayle, after insulting all religion, stigmatizes the Christian religion; he dares propose that a state formed by true Chistians would not continue to exist. Why not? They would be citizens infinitely enlightened about their duties and having a very great zeal to perform them; they would sense the rights of natural defense; the more they believed they owed to the religion, the more they would think they owed to the homeland. The principles of Christianity, engraved in their hearts, would be infinitely stronger than the false honor of monarchies, the human virtues of republics, or that servile fear of despotic states.

It is astounding that one can impute to this great man a misunderstanding of the spirit of his own religion, an inability to distinguish the orders for the establishment of Christianity from Christianity itself, and the precepts of the gospel from their counsels. When the legislator, instead of giving laws, has given counsels, it is because he has seen that his counsels, if they were ordained like laws, would be contrary to the spirit of the laws.

CHAPTER 7

On the laws of perfection in religion

Human laws made to speak to the spirit should give precepts and no counsels at all; religion, made to speak to the heart, should give many counsels and few precepts.

When, for example, it gives rules, not for the good but for the better, not for what is good but for what is perfect, it is suitable for these to be counsels and not laws, for perfection does not concern men or things universally. Moreover, if these are laws, there will have to be an infinity of others so that the first ones will be observed. Celibacy was a counsel of Christianity; when it was made into a law for a certain order of people, new laws had to be made every day in order to bring men to observe the first one.[4] The legislator tired himself, he tired the society, making men execute by precept what those who love perfection would have executed by counsel.

[4] See the *Bibliothèque des auteurs ecclésiastiques*, vol. 5, by [Louis Ellies] Dupin [5, 114–115, 129; 1691 edn].

CHAPTER 8

On the agreement of the laws of morality with those of religion

In a country where one has the misfortune of having a religion not given by god, it is always necessary for it to be in agreement with morality, because religion, even a false one, is the best warrant men can have of the integrity of men.

The principal points of the religion of the people of Pegu are not to kill, not to steal, to avoid immodesty, to cause no displeasure to one's fellow man, and instead, to do him all the good one can.[5] Further, they believe that one will be saved in any religion whatever; this makes these peoples, though they are proud and poor, show gentleness and compassion to unfortunates.

[5] *Recueil des voyages qui ont servi à l'établissement de la Compagnie des Indes*, vol. 3, pt. 1, p. 63 ["Relation du second voyage d'Etienne van der Hagen"; 3, 63; 1725 edn].

CHAPTER 9

On the Essenes

The Essenes[6] took an oath to observe justice toward men, to do no harm to anyone even in order to obey, to hate unjust men, to keep faith with everyone, to command with modesty, always to take the side of the truth, and to flee all illicit gain.

[6] [Humphrey] Prideaux, *The Old and New Testament Connected in the History of the Jews* [bk. 5, ann. 107 B.C.; 2, 326; 1831 edn. Prideaux is quoting Josephus, *De bello judaico* 2.12].

CHAPTER 10

On the Stoic sect

The various sects of philosophy among the ancients could be considered as kinds of religion. There has never been one whose principles were more worthy of men and more appropriate for forming good men than that of the Stoics, and, if I could for a moment cease to think that I am a Christian, I would not be able to keep myself from numbering the destruction of Zeno's sect among the misfortunes of human kind.

It exaggerated only those things in which there is greatness: scorn for pleasures and pains.

It alone knew how to make citizens; it alone made great men; it alone made great emperors.

Let us momentarily lay aside the revealed truths; seek in all of nature and you will find no greater object than the Antonines; Julian even, Julian (a vote thus wrenched from me will not make me an accomplice to his apostasy); no, since him there has been no prince more worthy of governing men.

While the Stoics considered wealth, human greatness, suffering, sorrows, and pleasures to be vain things, they were occupied only in working for men's happiness and in exercising the duties of society; it seemed that they regarded the sacred spirit which they believed to be within themselves as a kind of favorable providence watching over mankind.

Born for society, they all believed that their destiny was to work for it; it was the less burdensome as their rewards were all within themselves; as, happy in their philosophy alone, it seemed that only the happiness of others could increase their own.

CHAPTER II
On contemplation

Men, being made to preserve, feed and clothe themselves, and to do all the things done in society, religion should not give them an overly contemplative life.[7]

Mohammedans become speculative by habit; they pray five times a day, and each time they must do something that makes them turn their backs on all that belongs to this world: this forms them for speculation. Add to this the indifference toward all things given by the dogma of an inflexible destiny.

If, moreover, other causes concur to inspire their detachment, as

[7] This is the defect in the doctrine of Foë and of Laockium.

when the harshness of the government or of the laws concerning the ownership of land gives a spirit of uncertainty, all is lost.

The religion of the Ghebers formerly caused the kingdom of Persia to flourish; it corrected the bad effects of despotism: today the Mohammedan religion destroys that same empire.

CHAPTER 12
On penances

It is well for penances to be joined with the idea of work, not with the idea of idleness; with the idea of the good, not with the idea of the extraordinary; with the idea of frugality, not with the idea of avarice.

CHAPTER 13
On inexpiable crimes

From a passage in the books of the pontiffs reported by Cicero,[8] it seems that among the Romans there were inexpiable crimes,[9] and it is on this that Sozomen bases the account that so nicely poisons the motives of Constantine's conversion, and on this that Julian bases his bitter mockery of that conversion in his *Caesars*.[b]

The pagan religion, which prohibited only some glaring crimes, which checked the hand and abandoned the heart, could have inexpiable crimes; but a religion that envelops all the passions, that is no more jealous of acts than of desires and thoughts, that attaches us not by some few chains, but by innumerable threads, that leaves human injustice behind to begin another justice, that is made in order to lead constantly from repentance to love and from love to repentance, that puts a great mediator between the judge and the criminal, a great judge between the just man and the mediator: such a religion should not have

[8] [Cicero] *De legibus*, bk. 2 [2.22].

[9] "A profanation which cannot be expiated will be deemed to be committed impiously; that which can be expiated will be expiated by the public priest" [L.] [Cicero, *De legibus* 2.22].

[b] Julianus Apostata, emperor of Rome, A.D. 331–363, *Caesares* 336.

inexpiable crimes. But, though it gives fears and expectations to all, it makes them feel sufficiently that if there is no crime that is inexpiable by its nature, yet a whole life can be so; that it would be very dangerous to harry mercy constantly with new crimes and new expiations; that, troubled over old debts, never settled with the lord, we should fear contracting new ones, overfilling the cup and reaching the point at which paternal goodness ends.

CHAPTER 14
How the force of religion bears on that of the civil laws

As religion and the civil laws should aim principally to make good citizens of men, one sees that when either of these departs from this end, the other should aim more toward it; the less repressive religion is, the more the civil laws should repress.

Thus, in Japan, as the dominant religion has almost no dogmas and proposes neither paradise nor hell, the laws, in order to supplement it, have been made with an extraordinary severity and have been executed with an extraordinary punctiliousness.

When religion establishes the dogma of the necessity of human actions, the penalties of the laws should be more severe and the police more vigilant so that men, who without them would let themselves go, will base their decisions on these other motives; but if the religion establishes the dogma of liberty, it is something else again.

From laziness of the soul arises the Mohammedan dogma of predestination, and from this dogma of predestination is born laziness of the soul. One has said, it is decreed by god, so one must rest. In such a case, the laws should arouse men made drowsy by the religion.

When religion condemns things that civil laws should permit, there is the danger that civil laws will permit on their side what the religion should condemn, as one of the things always indicates a defect in the harmony and precision of ideas, which spreads to the other.

Thus the Tartars of Genghis Khan, for whom it was a sin and even a capital crime to put a knife into the fire, to lean on a whip, to beat a horse with his bridle, or to break one bone with another, believed there was no sin in violating faith, ravishing the goods of others, injuring a man, or killing him.[10] In a word, laws that cause what is indifferent to be regarded as necessary have the drawback of causing what is necessary to be considered as indifferent.

The Formosans believe in a kind of hell,[11] but it is for punishing those who have failed to go naked in certain seasons, who have worn clothing of linen and not of silk, who have gathered oysters, and who have acted without consulting the songs of birds; thus they do not regard drunkenness and licentiousness with women as a sin; they even believe that the debauchery of their children is pleasing to the gods.

When religion justifies an accidental thing, it uselessly loses the greatest spring there is among men. It is believed among the Indians that the waters of the Ganges have a sanctifying virtue;[12] those who die on its banks are reputed to be exempt from the penalties of the other life and supposed to live in a region of delights; urns full of the ashes of the dead are sent from the most distant places to be thrown into the Ganges. What does it matter if one lives virtuously, or not? One will have oneself thrown into the Ganges.

The idea of a place of reward necessarily brings with it the idea of a region of penalties, and when one hopes for the former without fearing the latter, civil laws no longer have any force. Men who believe in the certainty of rewards in the next life will escape the legislator; they will have too much scorn for death. How can one constrain by the laws a man who believes himself sure that the greatest penalty the magistrates can inflict on him will end in a moment only to begin his happiness?

[10] See the account by Jean Du Plan Carpin, sent to Tartary by Pope Innocent IV in 1246 [*Recueil de voyages au Nord*, "Relation du voyage de Jean du Plan Carpin"; 7, 339–340; 1725 edn].

[11] *Recueil des voyages qui ont servi à l'établissement de la Compagnie des Indes*, vol. 5, pt. 1, p. 192 ["Relation de l'état de l'îsle Formose, écrite par George Candidus"; 5, 103–105; 1706 edn; 5, 192; 1725 edn].

[12] *Lettres édifiantes et curieuses*, vol. 15 [Lettre de P. Bouchet, Pondichéry, April 1719; 15, 13; 1722 edn].

CHAPTER 15

How the civil laws sometimes correct false religions

Respect for ancient things and simplicity or superstition have sometimes established mysteries or ceremonies that could run counter to modesty, and examples of this have not been rare in the world. Aristotle says that in this case the law permits fathers of families to go to the temple to celebrate these mysteries in the place of their wives and children.[13] A remarkable civil law, that preserves the mores from religion!

Augustus forbade young people of both sexes to attend any nighttime ceremony unless they were accompanied by an older relative,[14] and when he reestablished the Lupercalian festival, he did not want the young people to run about naked.[15]

[13] [Aristotle] *Pol.*, bk. 7, chap. 17 [1336b17–19].
[14] Suetonius, *Vitae duodecim Caesarem, Augustus*, chap. 31 [31.4].
[15] Ibid. [Suetonius, *Vitae duodecim Caesarem, Augustus* 31.4.]

CHAPTER 16

How the laws of religion correct the defects of the political constitution

On the other hand, religion can sustain the political state when the laws are powerless.

Thus, when the state is often agitated by civil wars, religion will do much if it establishes that some part of the state always remain at peace. Among the Greeks, the Eleans, as priests of Apollo, enjoyed an eternal peace. In Japan, the town of Meaco,[c] a holy town, is always left in peace;[16] religion maintains this regulation; and that empire, which seems to be alone on the earth, which has and wants to have no

[16] *Recueil des voyages qui ont servi à l'établissement de la Compagnie des Indes*, vol. 4, pt. 1, p. 127 ["Voyage de l'Amiral Pierre Willemsz, voyage au Japon"; 4, 133; 1705 edn; 4, 126; 1725 edn].

[c] Kyoto.

recourse to foreigners, always has within itself a commerce that war does not ruin.

In the states where wars are not waged by a common deliberation and where the laws have not kept for themselves any means of terminating or preventing them, religion establishes times of peace or truce, so that the people can do the things, such as harvesting and similar work, without which the state could not continue to exist.

Every year for four months, all hostilities would cease between the Arab tribes;[17] the slightest disturbance would have been an impiety. When each lord in France waged war or made peace, religion provided truces which were to occur at certain seasons.

[17] See [Humphrey] Prideaux, *The True Nature of Imposture Fully Displayed in the Life of Mohamet*, p. 64 [p. 67; 1718 Eng. edn].

CHAPTER 17
Continuation of the same subject

When there are many grounds for hatred in a state, religion must give many means for reconciliation. The Arabs, a bandit people, often did harm or injustice to one another. Mohammed made this law:[18] "If someone forgives the shedding of his brother's blood,[19] he will be able to pursue the malefactor for damages and interest, but any one who harms the wicked man after receiving satisfaction from him will suffer grievous torments on judgment day."

Among the Germans, hatreds and enmities were inherited from one's near relations, but these were not eternal. Homicide was expiated by giving a certain quantity of livestock, and the whole family received satisfaction; a very useful thing, says Tacitus,[20] because enmities are more dangerous among a free people. I believe indeed that the ministers of religion, who had so much influence among them, took part in these reconciliations.

Among the Malayans, where reconciliation is not established, he who has killed someone, sure of being murdered by the friends or

[18] In the Koran, bk. 1, "The Cow" [2.178].
[19] By renouncing the law of retaliation. [Cf. bk. 6, chap. 19.]
[20] [Tacitus] *Germania* [21].

relatives of the dead man, gives himself up to his fury, wounding and killing everything he meets.[21]

[21] *Recueil des voyages qui ont servi à l'établissement de la Compagnie des Indes*, vol. 7, p. 303 ["Relation du premier voyage des Hollandais"; 1, 391–392; 1705 edn; 1, 354; 1725 edn]. See also Comte Claude de Forbin, *Mémoires* [1686; 74, 368–389; 1829 edn], and what he says about the Macassars.

CHAPTER 18

How the laws of religion have the effect of civil laws

The first Greeks were small, often scattered, peoples, pirates on the sea, unjust on land, without a police and without laws. The fine actions of Hercules and Theseus make clear the condition of this nascent people. What could religion do to give a horror of murder other than what it did? It established that a man killed by violence was instantly angry with the murderer, that he inspired distress and terror in the murderer and wanted him to give up those places he had frequented;[22] one could neither touch the criminal nor converse with him without being tainted or being disqualified from making a testament;[23d] the town had to be protected from the presence of the murderer and had to be purified.[24]

[22] Plato, *Laws*, bk. 9 [865 d–e].
[23] See the tragedy [Sophocles] *Oedipus at Colonus* [e.g. 443–444].
[24] Plato, *Laws*, bk. 9 [865d–866b].

[d] See 5.5 (note [c], bk. 5).

CHAPTER 19

That it is less the truth or falsity of a dogma that makes it useful or pernicious to men in the civil state than the use or abuse made of it

The truest and most saintly dogmas can have very bad consequences when they are not bound with the principles of society, and, on the other hand, the falsest dogmas can have remarkable consequences when they are made to relate to those same principles.

The religion of Confucius denies the immortality of the soul,[25] and the sect of Zeno did not believe in it. Who would say it? From their bad principles these two sects drew consequences that were not just, but were admirable for society. The religion of Tao and Foë[e] believes in the immortality of the soul, but from such a saintly dogma they have drawn frightful consequences.

Almost everywhere in the world, and in all times, the opinion that the soul is immortal, wrongly taken, has engaged women, slaves, subjects, and friends to kill themselves in order to go to the next world and serve the object of their respect or their love. Thus it was in the West Indies; thus it was among the Danes;[26] and so is it still today in Japan,[27] Makasar,[28][f] and in many other places on earth.

These customs emanate directly less from the dogma of the immortality of the soul than from that of the resurrection of the body; a consequence has been drawn from this that after his death an individual would have the same needs, the same feelings, and the same passions as before. From this point of view, the dogma of the immortality of the soul affects men prodigiously, because the idea of a simple change of abode can more nearly be grasped by our minds and is more flattering to our hearts than the idea of a new mode.

It is not enough for a religion to establish a dogma; it must also direct it. This is what the Christian religion has done remarkably well with regard to the dogmas we have mentioned; it makes us hope for a state that we believe in, not a state that we feel or that we know; everything, including the resurrection of the body, leads us to spiritual ideas.

[25] A Chinese philosopher argues thus against the doctrine of Foë: "It is said in a book of this sect that our body is our house and the soul, the immortal host living in it; but if the body of our parents is only a dwelling, it is natural to consider it with the same disdain that one has for a pile of mud and dirt. Does this not intend to uproot from the heart the virtue of loving one's parents? This also leads to neglecting the care of the body and refusing to it the compassion and affection so necessary for its preservation; thus the disciples of Foë kill themselves by the thousands." "Dialogue d'un philosophe Chinois," in the collection by Father [Jean Baptiste] du Halde [*Description de l'Empire de la Chine*], vol. 3, p. 52 [3, 61–62 H; 3, 51 P; 3, 271 L].

[26] See Thomas Bartholin, *Antiquitatum Danicarum de causis contemptae a Danis adhuc gentilibus mortis* [1689].

[27] Account of Japan, in the *Recueil des voyages qui ont servi à l'établissement de la Compagnie des Indes* ["Relation de l'état de l'isle Formose, écrite par George Candidus"; 5, 103–105, 1706 edn; 5, 192; 1725 edn].

[28] [Comte Claude de] Forbin, *Mémoires* [1686; 74, 381–382; 1829 edn].

---

[e] Foë is a form of Chinese Buddhism.

[f] Usung Pandang.

CHAPTER 20

Continuation of the same subject

The sacred books of the ancient Persians said: "If you want to be a saint, instruct your children, because all the good acts they do will be attributed to you."[29] They counseled early marriage because the children would be like a bridge on Judgment Day and because those who had no children could not cross. These dogmas were false, but they were very useful.

[29] [Thomas] Hyde [*Historia religionis veterum Persarum, Sad-der*, Porta 55, p. 465; 1700 edn].

CHAPTER 21

On metempsychosis

The dogma of the immortality of the soul is divided into three branches: that of pure immortality, that of simple change of abode, and that of metempsychosis; that is, the system of the Christians, the system of the Scythians, and the system of the Indians. I have just spoken of the first two, and I shall say of the third that, as it has been well and badly directed, it has both good and bad effects in the Indies; as it gives men a certain horror of spilling blood, there are very few murders in the Indies, and though one almost never punishes with death, everyone there is tranquil.

On the other hand, wives burn themselves when their husbands die; only innocent people suffer violent death there.

CHAPTER 22

How dangerous it is for religion to inspire horror for indifferent things

A certain honor established by religious prejudices in the Indies makes the various castes hold one another in horror. This honor is founded solely on religion; these distinctions by family do not form civil distinctions: there are Indians who would believe themselves dishonored if they ate with their king.

These sorts of distinctions are bound to a certain aversion for other men, an aversion quite different from the feelings that should arise from differences in rank and which among ourselves include love for one's inferiors.

The laws of religion will avoid inspiring any scorn other than scorn for vice and especially will avoid moving men away from love and pity for men.

The Mohammedan religion and the Indian religion comprise an infinite number of peoples: the Indians hate the Mohammedans because they eat cows; the Mohammedans detest the Indians because they eat pigs.

CHAPTER 23
On festivals

When a religion orders that work come to an end, it should have more regard for the needs of men than for the greatness of the being that it honors.

In Athens[30] the excessive number of festivals was a great problem. Frequently, business could not be conducted among this dominating people to whom all the Greek towns brought their differences.

When Constantine established that one would rest on Sunday, he made this ordinance for the towns[31] and not for the peoples of the countryside; he felt that useful work was in the towns and necessary work in the country.

For the same reason, in the countries that maintain themselves by commerce, the number of festivals should be relative to that same commerce. Protestant countries and Catholic countries are situated in such a way that one needs to work more in the former than in the latter;[32] therefore, the suppression of festivals suited Protestant countries better than Catholic countries.

[30] Xenophon, "The Old Oligarch," *The Constitution of Athens* [3.1–2].

[31] Law 3, *Code* [*Corpus Juris Civilis*, *Code* 3.12.3]; *de feriis*. This law was doubtless made only for the pagans.

[32] There are more Catholics in the South and Protestants in the North.

Dampier observes[33] that the people's diversions vary greatly according to the climate. As hot climates produce a quantity of delicate fruits, the barbarians, who find what is necessary instantly, spend more time amusing themselves; the Indians of the cold countries do not have so much leisure; they must continually fish and hunt; therefore, they have fewer dances, less music, and fewer festivals, and a religion that would become established among these peoples should show regard for this when instituting festivals.

[33] [William Dampier] *Voyages*, vol. 2 [bk. 1, chap. 19; 1, 521–522; 1906 edn].

CHAPTER 24

On local religious laws

There are many local laws in the various religions. And when Montezuma persisted in saying that the religion of the Spaniards was good for their country and that of Mexico for his own, he was not saying an absurd thing, because, indeed, legislators could not have kept from having regard for what nature had established before them.

The opinion of metempsychosis is made for the climate of the Indies. Excessive heat scorches[34] the whole countryside; one can feed only very little livestock; one is always in danger of having little stock for plowing; the livestock reproduce poorly;[35] they are subject to many diseases: therefore, a law of religion that preserves them is very suitable to the police of this country.

While the meadows are scorched, rice and vegetables are grown successfully because water can be diverted to them; therefore, a law of religion that permits only this food is very useful to the men of these climates.

The flesh of cattle[36] there is tasteless, and the milk and butter they get from them is part of their sustenance; therefore, the law that forbids eating and killing cows is not unreasonable in the Indies.

[34] [François] Bernier, *Travels in the Mogul Empire*, vol. 2, p. 137 ["The Gentiles of Hindoustan"; p. 326; 1916 edn].

[35] *Lettres édifiantes et curieuses*, vol. 12, p. 95 [Lettres du P. du Bourzes, Madure, September 21, 1713; 12, 93–94; 1741 edn].

[36] [François] Bernier, *Travels in the Mogul Empire*, vol. 2, p. 137 ["The Gentiles of Hindoustan"; pp. 326–327; 1916 edn].

There was an innumerable multitude of people in Athens; the territory was barren; it was a religious maxim that those who offered certain little presents to the god honored them more than those who sacrificed oxen.[37]

[37] Euripides, in Athenaeus Naucratia [*Deipnosophistae*], bk. 2, p. 40 [40d].

CHAPTER 25

The drawback in transferring a religion from one country to another

It follows that there are often many drawbacks in transferring a religion from one country to another.[38]

M. de Boulainvilliers says,[39] "Pigs must be very scarce in Arabia, where there are almost no woods and almost no appropriate feed for these animals; besides, the saltiness of their food and water makes the people very susceptible to skin diseases." The local law that forbids eating pork could not be good for other countries,[40] where pigs are an almost universal food and, in a way, necessary.

I shall make a reflection here. Santorio has observed that when one eats pork it transpires little and that this food even greatly prevents the transpiration of other foods; he has found that the decrease was as much as a third;[41] one knows, besides, that the lack of transpiration forms or sharpens diseases of the skin: therefore, eating pork should be forbidden in climates where one is subject to these diseases, as in Palestine, Arabia, Egypt, and Libya.

[38] The Christian religion is not spoken of here because, as was said in bk. 24, chap. 1 at the end, the Christian religion is the first good.

[39] [Comte de Boulainvilliers] *La Vie de Mahamed* [bk. 1; pp. 161–162; 1731 edn].

[40] As in China.

[41] [Santorio Santorio] *De medicine statica aphorismi*, sect. 3, aphorism 23 [3. 23; p. 220; 1784 edn].

CHAPTER 26

Continuation of the same subject

M. Chardin says[42] that there is no navigable river in Persia except the river Kura, which is at the border of the empire. Therefore, the old law of the Ghebers, which prohibited navigation on rivers, was no drawback in their country, but it would have wrecked commerce in some other country.

The continual application of lotions is a common usage in hot climates. This makes the Mohammedan law and the Indian religion order that application. To pray to god in running water[43] is a very meritorious act in the Indies, but how are these things to be executed in other climates?

When a religion founded on a climate runs counter to the climate of another country, it has not been able to establish itself there, and when it has been introduced there, it has been driven out. In human terms, it seems that climate has prescribed limits to the Christian religion and to the Mohammedan religion.

It follows that it is almost always suitable for a religion to have particular dogmas and a general worship. In the laws that concern the practices of worship, there must be few details, for example mortification but not some certain mortification. Christianity is full of common sense; abstinence comes from divine right, but a particular abstinence comes from the right of the police and can be changed.

[42] [John Chardin], *Voyages en Perse et autres lieux de l'Orient*, vol. 2 ["Voyage de Paris à Ispahan"; 2, 30; 1811 edn].

[43] [François] Bernier, *Travels in the Mogul Empire*, vol. 2, ["The Gentiles of Hindoustan"; pp. 327–328; 1916 edn].

BOOK 25

On the laws in their relation with the establishment of the religion of each country, and of its external police

CHAPTER I

On the feeling for religion

The pious man and the atheist always speak of religion; the one speaks of what he loves and the other of what he fears.

CHAPTER 2

On the motive for attachment to the various religions

The various religions of the world do not give to those who profess them equal motives for attachment to them; this depends largely on how they fit into men's way of thinking and feeling.

We are exceedingly drawn to idolatory, and nevertheless we are not strongly attached to idolatrous religions; we are scarcely inclined to spiritual ideas, and nevertheless we are very attached to religions that have us worship a spiritual being. It is a happy feeling that comes, in part, from the satisfaction we find in ourselves for having been intelligent enough to have chosen a religion that withdraws divinity from the humiliation in which others had placed it. We regard idolatory as the religion of coarse peoples, and a religion whose object is a spiritual being, as that of enlightened peoples.

When we can join to the idea of a supreme spiritual being, which forms the dogma, the sensible ideas that enter into the worship, this gives us great attachment to the religion because the motives we have just mentioned are joined to our natural penchant for things that can be felt. Thus, Catholics, who have more of this sort of worship than Protestants, are more invincibly attached to their religion than Protestants are to theirs and more zealous of its propagation.

When the people of Ephesus learned that the Fathers at the Council had decided that one could call the Virgin the *Mother of God*, they were overjoyed; they kissed the hands of the bishops; they embraced their knees; acclamations rang out everywhere.[1]

When an intellectual religion also gives us the idea of a choice made by the divinity, and of a distinction between those who profess it and those who do not profess it, this attaches us greatly to the religion. The Mohammedans would not be such good Muslims if there were not, on the one hand, idolatrous peoples who make them think they are avengers of the unity of god and, on the other, Christians, to make them believe that they are the object of his preferences.

A religion burdened with many practices[2] attaches people to it more strongly than another one that has fewer; one is attached to the things that continually occupy one: witness the tenacious obstinacy of the Mohammedans and the Jews, and the ease of changing religions for barbarian and savage peoples, who, wholly occupied with hunting or warring, scarcely burden themselves with religious practices.[3]

Men are exceedingly drawn to hope[a] and to fear, and a religion that had neither hell nor paradise would scarcely please them. This is proved by the ease with which foreign religions have been established in Japan and the zeal and love with which they have been received.[4]

In order for a religion to attach men to it, it must have pure morality.

[1] St. Cyril [Bishop of Alexandria], *Epistolae*. [The relevant letter, perhaps, is "Epistola 24. Cyrilli ad Clerum Populumque Alexandrinum"; Migne PG 77, 137–138.]

[2] This is not contradictory to what I have said in the next to last chapter of the preceding book [24.25]; here I speak of the motives of attachment to a religion and there of the means of making it more widespread.

[3] This can be seen everywhere around the earth. For the Turks, see *Nouveau mémoire des Missions de la compagnie de Jesus dans le Levant* [e.g., "La Conversation et le martyre d'une jeune infidèle"; 4, 195–204; 1724 edn, and 8, 137–213; 1745 edn]; for the Moors of Batavia, *Recueil des voyages qui ont servi à l'établissement de la Compagnie des Indes*, vol. 3, pt. 1, p. 201 [2. "Voyage de P. van Caerden"; 3, 660–661; 1705 edn; 3, 626; 1725 edn]; and for the black Mohammedans, Father [Jean Baptiste] Labat [*Nouvelle Relation de l'Afrique*, vol. 1, chap. 20; p. 251; 1728 edn].

[4] The Christian religion and the religions of the Indies; these have a hell and a paradise, whereas the religion of the Shintos has none.

[a] Here the translation of *espérer* as "hope" rather than "expectation" seems to be required by the context. (See note [a], Preface.)

Men, rascals when taken one by one, are very honest as a whole; they love morality; and if I were not considering such a serious subject, I would say that this is remarkably clear in the theaters: one is sure to please people by the feelings that morality professes, and one is sure to offend them by those that it disapproves.

When the externals of worship are very magnificent, we are flattered and we become very attached to the religion. Wealth in the temples and the clergy affects us greatly. Thus, the very poverty of peoples is a motive attaching them to that religion, which has served as a pretext for those who have caused their poverty.

CHAPTER 3
On temples

Almost all the peoples with a police live in houses. From this has naturally come the idea of building a house for god where they can worship him and go to seek him in their fears or their hopes.

Indeed, nothing consoles men more than a place where they find the divinity more present and where all together they give voice to their weakness and their misery.

But this very natural idea comes only to peoples who cultivate land, and one will not see temples built by those who have no houses themselves.

This is why Genghis Khan showed such great scorn for mosques.[5] This prince[6] interrogated the Mohammedans; he approved all their dogmas, except the one on the necessity of going to Mecca; he could not understand that one could not worship god everywhere. As the Tartars did not live in houses, they did not know of temples.

Peoples who have no temples have little attachment to their religion: this is why the Tartars have always been so tolerant,[7] why the barbarian

[5] Entering the mosque of Buchara, he picked up the Koran and threw it under his horses' hooves. [Ebulgazi Bahadir Han, Khan of Khorezm] *Histoire des Mongols et des Tatares*, pt. 3, p. 273 [pt. 3, chap. 14; "De l'éxpedition de Zinghis–Chan"; p. 263; 1726 edn; p. 110; 1970 edn].

[6] Ibid. [Ebulgazi Bahadir Han, Khan of Khorezm, *Histoire des Mongols et des Tatares*], p. 342 [pt. 3, chap. 19; "De retour de Zinghis-Chan"; p. 335; 1726 edn; p. 139; 1970 edn].

[7] This turn of mind has been transmitted as far as the Japanese, who were originally the Tartars, as is easily proved.

peoples who conquered the Roman empire did not hesitate for a moment to embrace Christianity, why the savages of America are so little attached to their own religion, and why, since our missionaries have had them build churches, they have so much zeal for ours.

As the divinity is the refuge of the unfortunate and as no people are more fortunate than criminals, one has been led naturally to think of temples as an asylum for criminals, and this idea seemed even more natural among the Greeks, where murderers, driven from their town and the presence of men, seemed to have no houses other than the temples and no protectors other than the gods.

At first, this concerned only those who unintentionally committed murder, but when great criminals were included in the refuge, one fell into a glaring contradiction; if the criminals had offended men, there is even greater reason for them to have offended the gods.

These asylums multiplied in Greece: the temples, Tacitus says,[8] were filled with insolvent debtors and wicked slaves; it was difficult for the magistrates to carry out the police; the people protected men's crimes just as they did the god's ceremonies; the Senate was obliged to close a great number of temples.

The laws of Moses were very wise. Those who murdered involuntarily were innocent, but they had to be removed from the sight of the relatives of the deceased; therefore, Moses established an asylum for them.[9] The greatest criminals did not merit any asylum; they had none.[10] The Jews had only a portable tabernacle, which changed its place continually; this excluded the idea of asylum. It is true that they were to have a temple, but the criminals, who would have come there from everywhere, could have disturbed the divine service. If the murderers had been driven out of the country, as they were by the Greeks, it would have been feared that they would worship foreign gods. All these considerations led to the establishment of towns of asylum where one had to remain until the death of the high priest.[b]

[8] [Tacitus] *Annales*, bk. 2 [3.60].
[9] Numbers, chap. 35 [35.14].
[10] Ibid. [Numbers 35.16–21].

[b] *souverain pontife.*

CHAPTER 4
On the ministers of religion

The first men, says Porphyry, sacrificed only plants. For such a simple worship, each man could be a pontiff within his family.[c]

The natural desire to please the divinity multiplied ceremonies; this caused men, who were engaged in agriculture, to be unable to execute them all and to observe all the details.

Particular places were dedicated to the gods; there had to be ministers to take care of them, just as each citizen takes care of his house and his domestic business. Thus, peoples without priests are usually barbarians. Such were the Pedalians in other times;[11] such are still the Wolgusky.[12]

Those who were dedicated to the divinity had to be honored, above all among peoples who had formed for themselves a certain idea of the bodily purity necessary for approaching the places that were the most pleasing to the gods and dependent on certain practices.

As worship of the gods required continual attention, most peoples were inclined to make the clergy a separate body. Thus, among the Egyptians, the Jews, and the Persians,[13] certain families, who were perpetuated and who performed the services, were dedicated to the divinity. There were even religions in which one thought not merely of withdrawing ecclesiastics from business, but even of relieving them of the encumbrance of a family, and this is the practice of the principal branch of Christian law.

I shall not speak here of the consequences of the law of celibacy; one senses that it could become harmful in proportion as the body of the clergy became too large and, consequently, that of the laity not large enough.

By the nature of human understanding, we love in religion everything that presumes an effort, just as on the subject of morality, we love in theory all that has the character of severity. Celibacy has been more

[11] Lilio Giraldi [*De deis gentium*], p. 726 [p. 726, Basel, 1548 edn, reprinted 1976; p. 527; 1696 edn]. [Giraldi is quoting Stobaeus.]

[12] Peoples of Siberia. See the account of Everard Isbrands-Ides, in the *Recueil de voyages au Nord*, vol. 8 ["Voyage de Moscou à Chine"; chap. 2; pp. 8, 13; 1727 edn].

[13] See [Thomas] Hyde [*De religione veterum Persarum*, chap. 28, p. 349; 1700 edn].

[c] Porphyry, *De abstinentia* 2.5.2.

pleasing to the peoples whom it seemed to suit the least and for whom it could have the most grievous results. In the countries of southern Europe, where by the nature of the climate the law of celibacy is the most difficult to observe, it has been retained; in those of the north, where the passions are less lively, it has been proscribed. Furthermore, in countries that have few inhabitants, it has been admitted; in those that have many, one has rejected it. One senses that all these reflections are only about the too great extension of celibacy and not about celibacy itself.

CHAPTER 5
On the limits that the laws should set on the wealth of the clergy

Particular families can perish; thus, their goods do not have a perpetual destination. The clergy is a family which cannot perish; therefore, goods are attached to it forever and cannot pass out of it.

Particular families can increase; therefore, their goods must also be able to grow. The clergy is a family which should not increase; therefore, its goods should be limited.

We have retained the provisions in Leviticus for the goods of the clergy, except those regarding the limits on those goods; indeed, among ourselves, the boundary beyond which a religious community is no longer to acquire will always be unknown.

These endless acquisitions seem so unreasonable to the peoples that anyone who would want to speak in their favor would be regarded as imbecilic.

Civil laws sometimes find obstacles to changing established abuses because these abuses are linked to things the laws should respect; in this case, an indirect provision is more indicative of a good spirit in the legislator than another that would strike against the thing itself. Instead of prohibiting acquisitions to the clergy, one must seek to make them distasteful, to leave the right and remove the fact.

In some countries of Europe, attention to the rights of the lords has caused the establishment in their favor of a right of indemnity over the landed property that people have acquired by mortmain. The interest of the prince has made him require a right of amortization in this same case. In Castile, where there is no similar right, the clergy has invaded everything; in Aragon, where there is some right of amortization, it has acquired less; in France, where this right and that of indemnity are established, it has acquired still less, and one can say that the prosperity of this state is due in part to the exercise of these two rights. Increase these rights and check mortmain, if possible.

Render sacred and inviolable the ancient and necessary domain of the clergy; let the domain be fixed and eternal like the clergy, but take new domains from their hands.

Permit the rule to be violated when the rule has become an abuse; suffer the abuse when it reverts to the rule.

In Rome one still remembers a report sent there at the time of several contentions with the clergy. This maxim was put in it: "The clergy should help pay for the burdens of the state, whatever the Old Testament may say about it." One concludes from this that the author of the report understood the language of the maletolt[d] better than that of religion.

[d]The *maltôte* was a tax levied by Philip the Fair; the term came to mean abusive taxation.

CHAPTER 6
On monasteries

The least bit of common sense shows that those bodies that are to be perpetual should not sell their lands for life, or borrow for life, unless one wants them to become the heirs of all those who have no relatives and of all those who do not want to have any; the monastics gamble with the people, but they hold the bank themselves.

CHAPTER 7
On the luxury of superstition

"It is impious toward the gods," Plato says,[14] "to deny their existence, or to grant it but to hold that they do not take a hand in the things here below, or finally to think that they are easily appeased by sacrifices: three equally pernicious opinions." Plato says there all of the most sensible things that natural enlightenment has ever said on the subject of religion.

Magnificence in the externals of worship is closely related to the constitution of the state. In good republics not only has the luxury of vanity been repressed, but also that of superstition; religion has made laws limiting expenditures. Among them number some laws of Solon, some laws of Plato on funerals that Cicero has adopted, and, finally, some laws of Numa about sacrifices.[15]

"Birds," says Cicero, "and paintings made in a single day are very divine gifts."[e] "We offer common things," said a Spartan, "so that we have the means for honoring the gods every day."[f]

The care men should take in worshiping the divinity is very different from the magnificence of that worship. Let us not offer him our treasures if we do not want to display to him our esteem for the things that he wants us to distrust.

"What are the gods to think of the gifts of the impious," Plato says admirably, "for a good man would blush to receive presents from a dishonest man?"

Religion must not, with gifts as the pretext, exact from the peoples what the necessities of the state have left over for them, and, as Plato says,[16] chaste and pious men should offer gifts that resemble themselves.

Nor should religion encourage expenditures for funerals. What is

[14] [Plato[*Laws*, bk. 10 [885b].
[15] "Let no one sprinkle wine upon the funeral pyre" [L.]. Law of the Twelve Tables. [Actually *Leges regiae*, *Numa* 7; its source is Pliny, *Historia Naturalis* 14.14.88. A very similar law to this one appears in Table x of the Twelve Tables (x.6b), but M.'s quotation is from *Numa*.]
[16] [Plato] *Laws*, bk. 3 [716e–717a].

[e] Cicero, *De legibus* 2.18.45.
[f] Plato, *Laws* 956b, 959.

more natural than to remove the difference of fortunes for a thing and at a time that equalizes all fortunes?

CHAPTER 8
On the pontificate

When a religion has many ministers, it is natural for them to have a leader and for the pontificate to be established in it. In monarchy, where one cannot too much separate the orders of the state and where one should not bring together all the powers in the same head, it is good for the pontificate to be separated from the empire. The same necessity is not encountered in despotic government, whose nature is to unite all powers in the same person. But, in this case, it could happen that the prince would regard the religion as he does his laws themselves and as effects of his will. In order to prevent this, there must be records of the religion, for example, sacred books that fix and establish it. The king of Persia is the leader of the religion, but the Koran regulates the religion; the emperor of China is the sovereign pontiff, but there are books, which are in everyone's hands and to which he should himself conform. In vain did an emperor want to abolish them; they triumphed over tyranny.

CHAPTER 9
On toleration in religious matters

Here we are political men and not theologians, and even for theologians there is much difference between tolerating and approving a religion.

When the laws of a state have believed they should allow many religions, they must also oblige them to tolerate each other. The principle is that every religion which is repressed becomes repressive itself; for as soon as, by some chance, it can shake off oppression, it attacks the religion which repressed it, not as a religion, but as a tyranny.

Therefore, it is useful for the laws to require of these various religions not only that they not disturb the state, but also that they not disturb each other. A citizen does not satisfy the laws by contenting himself with not agitating the body of the state; he must also not disturb any citizen whatsoever.

CHAPTER 10

Continuation of the same subject

As there are scarcely any but intolerant religions that are greatly zealous to establish themselves elsewhere, for a religion that can tolerate others scarcely thinks of its propagation, it will be a very good civil law, when the state is satisfied with the established religion, not to allow the establishment of another.[17]

Here, therefore, is the fundamental principle for political laws in religious matters. When one is the master of the state's accepting a new religion, or not accepting it, it must not be established; when it is established, it must be tolerated.

[17] I do not speak of the Christian religion in this chapter because, as I have said elsewhere, the Christian religion is the first good. See the end of chap. 1 of the preceding book and the *Defense of the Spirit of the Laws*, pt. 2.

CHAPTER 11

On changing religion

A prince who undertakes to destroy or to change the dominant religion in his state is greatly exposed. If his government is despotic, he runs a greater risk of seeing a revolution than he would by any tyranny whatever, which is never a new thing in these sorts of states. The revolution results from the fact that a state does not change religion, mores, and manners in an instant, or as soon as the prince publishes the ordinance establishing a new religion.

In addition, the former religion is linked with the constitution of the state, and the new one is not attached to it; the first is in accord with the climate and the new one often resists it. Furthermore, the citizens find their laws distasteful; they scorn the government already established; suspicions of both religions are substituted for a firm belief in one; in a word, one gives the state, at least for some time, bad citizens and bad believers.

CHAPTER 12
On penal laws

Penal laws must be avoided in the matter of religion. They impress fear, it is true, but as religion also has its penal laws which inspire fear, the one is canceled out by the other. Between these two different fears, souls become atrocious.

Religion has such great threats, it has such great promises, that when they are present to our spirits, no matter what the magistrate does to constrain us to abandon it, it seems that we are left with nothing when religion is taken away, and that nothing is taken from us when religion is left to us.

Therefore, one does not succeed in detaching the soul from religion by filling it with this great object, by bringing it closer to the moment when it should find religion of greater importance; a more certain way to attack religion is by favor, by the comforts of life, by the hope of fortune, not by what reminds one of it, but by what makes one forget it; not by what makes one indignant, but by what leads one to indifference when other passions act on our souls and when those that religion inspires are silent. General rule: in the matter of changing religion, invitations are stronger than penalties.

The character of the human spirit has appeared in even the order of the penalties that one has used. Remember the persecutions in Japan;[18] one is more revolted by cruel punishments than by the long penalties that weary more than they frighten, that are more difficult to overcome because they seem less difficult.

In a word, history teaches us well enough that the penal laws have never had any effect other than destruction.

[18] See the *Recueil des voyages qui ont servi à l'établissement de la Compagnie des Indes*, vol. 5, pt. 1, p. 192 ["Histoire d'une persécution qui a été faite aux Chrétiens Romains au Japon"; 5, 395–428; 1706 edn; 5, 468–499; 1725 edn].

CHAPTER 13

Very humble remonstrance to the inquisitors of Spain and Portugal

An eighteen-year-old Jewess, burned in Lisbon at the last auto-da-fe, occasioned this small work, and I believe it is the most useless that has ever been written. When it is a question of proving such clear things, one is sure not to convince.

The author declares that, although he is a Jew, he respects the Christian religion and that he loves it enough to take away from princes who will not be Christians a plausible pretext for persecuting it.

"You complain," he says to the inquisitors, "that the emperor of Japan had all the Christians in his states burned by a slow fire, but he will answer: We treat you, you who do not believe as we do, as you yourselves treat those who do not believe as you do; you can complain only of your weakness, which keeps you from exterminating us and which makes it so that we exterminate you.

"But it has to be admitted that you are much more cruel than this emperor. You kill us, we who believe no more than what you believe because we do not believe everything that you believe. We follow a religion that you yourself know to have been formerly cherished by god; we think that god loves it still, and you think that he does not love it any longer, and because you judge it thus, you have afflicted with iron and fire those who are in the quite pardonable error of believing that god still loves that which he loved.[19]

"If you are cruel in our regard, you are even more so in regard to our children; you have them burned because they follow the suggestions instilled in them by those whom the natural law and the laws of all the peoples teach them to respect like gods.

"You deprive yourselves of the advantage over the Mohammedans given you by the manner in which their religion was established. When they flaunt the number of their faithful, you say to them that only force has acquired that number for them and that they have extended their religion by iron; therefore, why establish yours by fire?

"When you want to make us come to you, we use as our objection

[19]The source for the Jews' blindness is in their failure to sense that the economy of the Gospel is within the order of God's designs, and that thus it follows from his immutability itself.

that source in whose descent you take pride. You reply that though your religion is new, it is divine, and your proof is that it has grown by the persecution of the pagans and by the blood of your martyrs; but today you take the role of the Diocletians, and you make us take yours.

"We entreat you, not by the powerful god we both serve, but by the Christ that you tell us took on the human condition in order to give you examples you could follow; we entreat you to act with us as he himself would act if he were still on earth. You want us to be Christians, and you do not want to be Christian yourselves.

"But if you do not want to be Christians, at least be men; treat us as you would if, having only the feeble lights of justice that nature gives us, you had no religion to guide you and no revelation to enlighten you.

"If heaven has loved you enough to show you the truth, it has done you a great favor, but is it for the children who receive their father's inheritance to hate those who did not receive it?

"For if you have this truth, do not hide it from us by the way in which you propose it. The character of truth is in its triumph over hearts and spirits and not in this powerlessness you avow when you want to make it accepted by punishments.

"If you are reasonable, you should not have us killed because we do not want to deceive you. If your Christ is the son of god, we hope he will reward us for not having wanted to profane his mysteries, and we believe that the god we both serve will not punish us for having suffered death for a religion he formerly gave us because we believe that he still gives it to us.

"You live in a century when natural enlightenment is more alive than it has ever been, when philosophy has enlightened spirits, when the morality of your gospel has been better known, when the respective rights of men over each other, the empire that one conscience has over another conscience, are better established. Therefore, if you do not give up your old prejudices, which, if you do not take care, are your passions, it must be admitted that you are incorrigible, incapable of all enlightenment and of all instruction; and a nation is very unhappy that gives authority to men like you.

"Do you want us to tell you our thought naively? You regard us as your enemies rather than as enemies of your religion for, if you loved your religion, you would not let it be corrupted by gross ignorance.

"We must warn you of one thing; it is that, if someone in the future ever dares to say that the peoples of Europe had a police in the century in which we live, you will be cited to prove that they were barbarians, and the idea one will have about you will be such that it will stigmatize your century and bring hatred on all your contemporaries."

CHAPTER 14
Why the Christian religion is so odious in Japan

I have spoken of the atrocious character of the souls of the Japanese.[20] The magistrates regarded the firmness inspired by Christianity as very dangerous when it was a question of renouncing the faith; one thought one saw audacity increase. The law of Japan severely punished the slightest disobedience: one was ordered to renounce the Christian religion; not to renounce it was to disobey; one was chastised for this crime, and the continuation of disobedience seemed to merit another chastisement.

Among the Japanese, punishing is regarded as vengeance for an insult done the prince. Our martyrs' songs of gladness seemed to be an attack on him: martyrdom intimidated the magistrates; to their spirit it denoted rebellion; they did everything to keep one from it. It was then that souls grew fierce and one saw a horrible combat between the tribunals that condemned and the accused who suffered, between the civil laws and those of religion.

[20] Bk. 6, chap. 24 [above].

CHAPTER 15
On the propagation of religion

All the eastern peoples, except the Mohammedans, believe all religions are indistinguishable in themselves. It is only as a change in government that they fear the establishment of another religion. Among the Japanese, where there are several sects and where the state has for a long time had an ecclesiastical leader, one never debates about religion.[21] It is the same among the Siamese.[22] The Kalmucks do more; they make it a matter of conscience to allow all sorts of religions.[23] In Calicut, it is a maxim of state that every religion is good.[24]

But it does not result from this that a religion brought from a distant country, totally different in climate, laws, mores, and manners, has all the success that its holiness ought to promise it. This is chiefly true in the great despotic empires: at first foreigners are tolerated because no attention is paid to what does not appear to harm the power of the prince; there one is extremely ignorant of everything. A European can make himself agreeable by having certain bits of knowledge; this is good at the beginning. But, as soon as one has some success, or some debate occurs, or people who can have some interest are alerted, because this state by its nature requires tranquility above all and because the slightest disturbance can overturn it, the new religion and those who announce it are instantly proscribed; when debates break out among those who preach, one begins to find distasteful a religion in which those who propose it are not in agreement.

[21] See [Engelbert] Kaempfer [*The History of Japan Together with a Description of the Kingdom of Japan, 1690–1692*, bk. 3, chap. 1; 2, 1; 1906 edn].

[22] Comte [Claude de] Forbin, *Mémoires* [1688; 74, 431–432; 1829 edn].

[23] [Ebulgazi Bahadir Han, Khan of Khorezm] *Histoire généalogique des Tatars*, pt. 5 [pt. 5, chap. 5, "Des princes de la posterité de Zagatai Chan"; Bentinck's note, 2, 409; 1726 edn].

[24] François Pyrard, *Voyages*, chap. 27 [vol. 1, chap. 27; 1, 404–405; 1887–1890 edn].

BOOK 26

On the laws in the relation they should have with the order of things upon which they are to enact

CHAPTER I

The idea of this book

Men are governed by various sorts of laws: by natural right; by divine right, which is that of religion; by ecclesiastical right, otherwise called canonical, which is that of the police of religion; by the right of nations, which can be considered as the civil right of the universe in the sense that each people is a citizen of it; by the general political right, whose object is the human wisdom that has founded all societies; by the particular political right, which concerns each society; by the right of conquest founded on the fact that one people wanted, was able, or had to do violence to another people; by the civil right of each society, which allows a citizen to defend his goods and his life against every other citizen; finally, by domestic right, which comes from the fact that a society is divided into various families needing a particular government.

Therefore, there are different orders of laws, and the sublimity of human reason consists in knowing well to which of these orders principally relate the things on which one should enact and in not putting confusion into the principles that should govern men.

CHAPTER 2

On divine laws and human laws

One should not enact by divine laws that which should be enacted by human laws, or regulate by human laws that which should be regulated by divine laws.

These two sorts of laws differ as to their origin, as to their object, and as to their nature.

Everyone readily agrees that human laws are of a different nature from that of the laws of religion, and this is a great principle, but this principle itelf is subject to others which must be sought.

1. The nature of human laws is to be subject to all the accidents that occur and to vary as men's wills change, whereas the nature of the laws of religion is never to vary. Human laws enact about the good; religion, about the best. The good can have another object because there are several goods, but the best is one alone and can, therefore, never change. One can certainly change laws because they are thought to be good only, but the institutions of religion are always presumed to be the best.

2. There are states in which the laws are nothing, or nothing but a capricious and transitory will of the sovereign. If, in these states, the laws of religion were of the same nature as human laws, the laws of religion would also be nothing; however, it is necessary in society for something to be fixed, and religion is that fixed thing.

3. The principal force of religion comes from its being believed; the force of human laws come from their being feared. Antiquity is suitable to religion because often the more distant things are from us the more we believe them, for we have in our heads no secondary ideas drawn from those times that can contradict them. Human laws, on the other hand, gain advantage from their novelty, which shows the legislator's particular and present attentiveness to their observation.

CHAPTER 3
On civil laws that are contrary to natural law

"If a slave," says Plato, "defends himself and kills a free man, he should be treated as a parricide."[1] This is a civil law that punishes natural defense.

Under Henry VIII, the law that condemned a man who had not been confronted by witnesses was contrary to natural defense; indeed, in order to condemn, the witnesses must know that the man against whom they make a deposition is the one whom they accuse, and the accused man must be able to say, "I am not the man of whom you speak."

A law passed during the same reign condemned every girl who, having had illicit commerce with someone, did not declare this to the king before marrying the man; this violated the natural defense of modesty; it is as unreasonable to require a girl to make this declaration as to ask a man not to seek to defend his life.

A law of Henry II, which condemns a girl whose child had died to death unless she had declared her pregnancy before a magistrate, is no less contrary to natural defense. It would have been enough to oblige her to inform one of her closest relatives, who would see to the preservation of the child.

In this punishment of her natural modesty, could she make any other confession? Education has strengthened in her the idea of preserving that modesty, and at such times she can scarcely retain an idea concerning the loss of life.

Much has been said of a law in England that let a seven-year-old girl choose her husband.[2] This law was outrageous in two ways; it had regard neither for the time set by nature for the maturation of the spirit nor for the time it sets for the maturation of the body.

Among the Romans, a father could oblige his daughter to repudiate her husband, although he himself had consented to the marriage.[3] But it is against nature for divorce to be put into the hands of a third party.

If divorce is in conformity with nature, it is so only when consent is

[1] [Plato] *Laws*, bk. 9 [869d].

[2] [Pierre] Bayle, in his *Critique de l'histoire du calvinisme*, speaks of this law, p. 293. [It is actually in *Nouvelles lettres de l'auteur de la Critique*, Lettre 8; 2.214–215; 1964 edn].

[3] See law 5 of the *Code* [*Corpus Juris Civilis*, *Code* 5.17.5]; *de repudiis et judicio de moribus sublato.*

given by the two parties, or at least one of them; and when neither the one nor the other consents to it, divorce is a monster. Finally, the faculty of divorce can be given only to those who bear the discomforts of the marriage and who sense the moment when it is in their interest to make them cease.

CHAPTER 4
Continuation of the same subject

Gundobad, king of Burgundy, wanted the wife or the son of one who had stolen to be reduced to slavery if they did not reveal the crime.[4] This law was against nature. How could a wife be her husband's accuser? How could a son be his father's? In order to avenge a criminal action, he ordered one that was yet more criminal.

The law of Reccesuinth permitted the children of the adulterous wife, or those of her husband, to accuse her and to torture the house slaves.[5] This was an iniquitous law that, in order to preserve the mores, overturned nature, in which the mores have their origin.

In our theaters we watch with pleasure when a young hero shows as much horror on discovering his step-mother's crime as he had for the crime itself; in his surprise, accused, judged, condemned, banished, and covered with infamy, he scarcely dares do more than make a few reflections on the abominable blood from which Phaedra is descended; he abandons what he holds most dear, his most tender object, all that speaks to his heart, all that can arouse his indignation, to give himself up to the vengeance of the gods, a vengeance he has not deserved. The accents of nature cause this pleasure; it is the sweetest of all voices.

[4] *Leges Burgundionum*, tit. 41 [47.1–2].
[5] In the *Lex Wisigothorum*, bk. 3, tit. 4, para. 13 [3.4.13].

CHAPTER 5

A case in which one can judge by the principles of civil right by modifying the principles of natural law

An Athenian law obliged children to feed their fathers if they had fallen into indigence;[6] it excepted those who were born of a courtesan, those whose father had exposed their modesty to infamous dealings,[7] and those to whom he had not given a trade to earn their living.[8]

The law considered that, in the first case, as it was uncertain who the father was, he had rendered his natural obligation precarious; that, in the second, he had stigmatized the life which he had given and that he had done the greatest evil he could do to his children by taking away their character; that, in the third case, he had made their life, which they found difficult to sustain, unbearable. The law envisaged the father and son simply as two citizens; it enacted only from political and civil points of view; it considered that, in a good republic, mores were necessary above all else. I believe that Solon's law was good in the first two cases, the one in which nature leaves the son in ignorance of his father, and the one in which nature seems even to order the son to disown him, but one cannot approve of it in the third case, where the father had violated only a civil regulation.

[6]On pain of infamy; another, on pain of prison.
[7]Plutarch [*Vit.*], *Solon* [22.4].
[8]Plutarch [*Vit.*], *Solon* [22.4]; and Galen, *Protreptikos logos, Paraphrastae Menodoti, Adhortatio ad artes addiscendas*, chap. 8 [1, 15; 1821 Kuehn edn].

CHAPTER 6

That the order of inheritance depends on principles of political or civil right, and not on principles of natural right

The Voconian law did not permit one to appoint a woman heir, not even one's only daughter. "There never was," says Saint Augustine,[9] "a more unjust law." A formula of Marculf[10] terms impious that custom

[9][St. Augustine] *The City of God*, bk. 3 [3.21].
[10][*Marculfi formulae*] bk. 2, chap. 12 [2.12].

which deprives daughters of their father's inheritance. Justinian calls[11] the right of inheritance for males to the detriment of daughters barbarous. These ideas come from regarding the right of children to inherit from their fathers to be a consequence of natural law, which it is not.

Natural law orders fathers to feed their children, but it does not oblige them to make them their heirs. The division of goods, laws concerning this division, inheritances after the death of the one who made this division, all this can only be regulated by the society and, consequently, by political and civil laws.

It is true that the political or civil order often asks that the children inherit from their fathers, but it does not always require it.

The laws about our fiefs might have had reasons for giving everything to the eldest male, or the closest relative among the males, and for giving nothing to the daughters; and the laws of the Lombards[12] might have had reasons for allowing sisters, natural children, other relatives, and, in their absence, the fisc, to rank equally with daughters.

The rule in some dynasties in China was that the Emperor's brothers would succeed to the throne and that his children would not. If one wanted the prince to have a certain amount of experience, if minorities were feared, if it were necessary to keep eunuchs from putting children successively on the throne, such an order of inheritance could well be established, and when certain writers[13] have called these brothers usurpers, they have judged according to ideas taken from the laws of their own countries.

According to custom in Numidia,[14] Oezalces the brother of Gala inherited the kingdom, and not Masinissa, his son. And still today,[15] among the Arabs of Barbary, where each village has a leader, the uncle or some other relative is chosen to inherit according to this old custom.

There are purely elective monarchies; and as soon as it is clear that the order of inheritance should derive from political or civil laws, it is for them to decide in which cases reason wants this inheritance to be

[11] [*Corpus Juris Civilis*] *Novellae* 21 [21, Preface].

[12] [*Leges Langobardorum*] bk. 2, tit. 14, paras. 6–8 [Roth. 158–160].

[13] Father [Jean Baptiste] du Halde [*Description de l'Empire de la Chine*], second dynasty ["Tsou Sin, twelfth Emperor"; 1, 299 H; 1, 313–334 P; 1, 304 L].

[14] Livy, decade 3, bk. 9 [29.29].

[15] See [Thomas] Shaw, *Travels or Observations Relating to Several Parts of Barbary and the Levant*, vol. 1, p. 402 ["Physical and Miscellaneous Observations"; chap. 4, "Of the Government, Forces and Revenues of the Algerines [*sic*]"; p. 310; 1738 edn].

passed down to the children and in which cases the inheritance must be given to others.

In countries where polygamy is established, the prince has many children; their number is larger in some countries than in others. There are some states[16] in which the upkeep of the king's children by the people would be impossible; there, one has been able to establish that the king's children do not inherit, but rather his sister's children.

A prodigious number of children would expose the state to horrible civil wars. The order of inheritance that gives the crown to the sister's children, who are no more numerous than would be the children of a prince having a single wife, provides against these drawbacks.

There are nations where reasons of state or some religious maxim have demanded that a certain family should always reign; in the Indies,[17] such is the jealousy of one's caste and the fear of not descending from it; it has been thought that, in order always to have princes of royal blood, the king's oldest sister's children always had to be chosen.

General maxim: feeding one's children is an obligation of natural right; giving them one's inheritance is an obligation of civil or political right. From this derive the different provisions concerning bastards in the different countries of the world; they follow the civil or political laws of each country.

[16] See the *Recueil des voyages qui ont servi à l'établissement de la Compagnie des Indes*, vol. 4, pt. 1, p. 114 ["Voyage de P. van den Broeck, Description du royaume de Lowango"; 4, 339–340; 1705 edn; 4, 319–320; 1725 edn]; and [William] Smith, *A New Voyage to Guinea*, pt. 2, p. 150 [pp. 200–206; 1967 edn] on the kingdom of Whyday.

[17] See *Lettres édifiantes et curieuses*, vol. 14 [Lettre du P. Bouchet, Pondichéry, October 2, 1714; 14, 382–389; 1720 edn] and *Recueil des voyages qui ont servi à l'établissement de la Compagnie des Indes*, vol. 3, pt. 2, p. 644 ["II. Voyage de Paul van Caerden aux Indes Orientales"; 3, 679; 1705 edn; 3, 644; 1725 edn].

CHAPTER 7

That one must not decide by the precepts of religion when those of natural law are in question

The Abyssinians have a harsh fast of fifty days, which so weakens them that they cannot act for a long time; the Turks do not fail to attack them after this fast.[18] To favor natural defense religion ought to put some limits on these practices.

The Jews were ordered to observe the Sabbath, but it was dull-witted of this nation not to defend itself[19] when its enemies chose that day to attack.

Cambyses, laying siege to Pelusium, put in his front rank a large number of animals that the Egyptians held sacred; the soldiers of the garrison dared not shoot. Who can fail to see that natural defense is of a higher order than all precepts?

[18] *Recueil des voyages qui ont servi à l'établissement de la Compagnie des Indes*, vol. 4, pt. 1, pp. 35 and 103 ["Voyage de l'amiral Pierre Willemsz Verhoeven" (1607); 4, 36; 1705 edn; 4, 34; 1725 edn].

[19] As they did when Pompey besieged the temple. See Cass. Dio [*Historia Romana*], bk. 37 [37.16].

CHAPTER 8

That things ruled by the principles of civil right must not be ruled by the principles of what is called canonical right

According to the civil right of the Romans,[20] he who removes a private thing from a sacred site is punished only for the crime of robbery; according to canonical right,[21] he is punished for the crime of sacrilege. Canonical right pays attention to the place; civil right, to the thing. But to pay attention to the place alone is to fail to reflect either on the nature and definition of robbery or on the nature and definition of sacrilege.

[20] Law 5 [*Corpus Juris Civilis, Digest*, 48.13.6(5)]; *ad legem Juliam peculatus et de sacrilegis et de residuis.*

[21] [*Corpus Juris Canonici, Decretum Magistri Gratiani*] *Quisquis inventus* [chap. 21], canon XVII, quaestione 4; [Jacques] Cujas, *Observationum et emendationum libri* [chap. 28], bk. 13, chap. 19, tit. 3 [1, 270; 1868 edn].

As the husband can ask for separation because of the wife's infidelity, the wife could formerly ask for separation because of the infidelity of the husband.[22] This usage, contrary to the provision of the Roman laws,[23] was introduced in the courts of the church,[24] where one only attended to the maxims of canonical right; and, indeed, considering marriage only according to purely spiritual ideas and to its relation to the things of the next life, the violation is the same. But the political and civil laws of almost all peoples have, with reason, distinguished between these two things. They have required a degree of restraint and of continence from women that they do not require from men, because the violation of modesty presupposes in women a renunciation of all virtues, because a woman in violating the laws of marriage leaves her state of natural dependency, because nature has marked the infidelity of women by certain signs; besides, the bastard children of a wife belong necessarily to the husband and are the husband's burden, whereas the bastard children of a husband neither belong to his wife nor are her burden.

[22] Beaumanoir, *Coutumes de Beauvaisis*, chap. 18 [#583].
[23] Law 1, *Code* [*Corpus Juris Civilis*, *Code* 9.9.1]; *ad legem Juliam de adulteriis et de stupro*.
[24] In France none of these things is known today.

CHAPTER 9

The things that should be ruled by the principles of civil right can rarely be ruled by principles of the laws of religion

Religious laws are more sublime; civil laws are more extensive.

The laws of perfection, drawn from religion, have for their object the goodness of the man who observes them, more than that of the society in which they are observed; civil laws, on the other hand, have for their purpose the moral goodness of men in general, more than that of individuals.

Thus, however respectable may be the ideas which spring immediately from religion, they should not always serve as principles for civil laws, because civil laws have another principle, which is the general good of society.

In the Roman repulic, regulations were made in order to preserve the mores of women; these were political institutions. When the monarchy was established, they made civil laws about them, and they made them on the principles of the civil government. When the Christian religion arose, the new laws that were made had less relation to the general goodness of the mores than to the sanctity of marriage; there was less regard for the union of the two sexes in the civil state than in a spiritual state.

At first, according to the Roman law[25] the husband who took his wife back to his house after she had been condemned for adultery was punished as an accomplice of her debauchery. In another spirit, Justinian[26] ordered that the husband could take her away from the convent within two years.

When a woman whose husband was at war no longer received word of him, she could, in earlier times, easily remarry, because the power to divorce was in her hands. The law of Constantine[27] wanted her to wait four years, after which she could send the document for the divorce to the commander; and, therefore, if her husband came back, he could not accuse her of adultery. But Justinian[28] established that, however long it had been since the husband's departure, she could not remarry unless she proved the death of her husband by the deposition and oath of his commander. Justinian had in view the indissolubility of marriage, but one could say that he had it too much in view. He asked for a positive proof, when a negative proof sufficed; he required a very difficult thing, an account of the fate of a man far way, and exposed many accidents; he assumed a crime, that is, the desertion of the husband, when it was very natural to assume his death. His law ran counter to public good by leaving a woman unmarried; it ran counter to particular interest by exposing her to a thousand dangers.

The law of Justinian[29] that put among the causes of divorce the consent of the husband and the wife to enter a monastery was entirely removed from the principles of the civil laws. It is natural for the origin of the causes of divorce to be in certain difficulties that one could not have foreseen before marriage, but the desire to stay chaste could have

[25] Law 11, last para. [*Corpus Juris Civilis, Digest* 48.5.11 (13)]; *ad legem Juliam de adulteriis coercendis*.

[26] [*Corpus Juris Civilis*] *Novellae* 134, chap. 10 [134.10].

[27] Law 7, *Code* [*Corpus Juris Civilis, Code* 5.17.7]; *de repudiis et judicio de moribus sublato.*

[28] *Authentica. Hodie quantiscumque* [*Corpus Juris Civilis, Novellae* 117, chap. 11; *Code* 5.17.7]; *de repudiis et judicio de moribus sublato.* [See *Code* 5.17.7, Scott's Eng. translation.]

[29] *Authentica. Quod Hodie, Code* [*Corpus Juris Civilis, Novellae* 117, chap. 11; *Code* 5.17.9]; *de repudiis et judicio de moribus sublato.* [See *Code* 5.17.7, Scott's Eng. translation.]

been envisaged because it is in ourselves. This law favors inconstancy in a state which is permanent by its nature; it runs counter to the fundamental principle of divorce which suffers the dissolution of one marriage only in the expectation of another; finally, even following along religious ideas, it succeeds only in giving victims, but not a sacrifice to god.

CHAPTER 10

In what case one must follow the civil law that permits and not the religious law that forbids

When a religion that forbids polygamy comes into a country in which it is permitted, one does not believe, speaking politically only, that the law of the country should permit a man with several wives to embrace this religion, unless the magistrate or the husband compensates the wives while returning them in some way to their civil state. Failing this, their condition would be deplorable; they would have but obeyed the laws and would find themselves deprived of the greatest advantages of society.

CHAPTER 11

That human tribunals must not be ruled by the maxims of the tribunals that regard the next life

The tribunal of the Inquisition, formed by Christian monks along the idea of the tribunal of penance, is contrary to all good police. It has met with a general protest everywhere, and it would have given way to its contradictions, if those who wanted to establish it had not taken advantage of those very contradictions.

This tribunal is unbearable in all governments. In monarchy, it can make only informers and traitors; in republics, it can form only dishonest people; in the despotic state, it is as destructive as the state.

CHAPTER 12

Continuation of the same subject

One of the abuses of this tribunal is that, when two persons are accused of the same crime, the one who denies it is condemned to death and the one who confesses it avoids punishment. This is drawn from monastic ideas in which the one who denies appears to be unrepentant and damned and the one who confesses seems to be repentant and saved. But such a distinction cannot be the concern of human tribunals; human justice, which sees only acts, has only one pact with men, that of innocence; divine justice, which sees thoughts, has two pacts, that of innocence and that of repentance.

CHAPTER 13

In which case the laws of religion must be followed in regard to marriages, and in which case the civil laws must be followed

It has happened, in all countries and all times, that religion has occupied itself with marriages. From the moment certain things were regarded as impure or illicit and were nevertheless necessary, religion has had to be called up in order to legitimate them in the one case and condemn them in others.

On the other hand, as of all human acts marriage is the one that is of the most interest to society, it has certainly had to be ruled by civil laws.

All that regards the character of marriage, its form, the way it is contracted, its fruitfulness, and all that has made every people understand that marriage is the object of a particular benediction which, as it was not always attached to it, depended on certain higher favors; all the above belongs to the spring of religion.

The consequences of this union relative to goods, to reciprocal advantages, to all that is relative to the new family, the one from which it has come, and the one that will be born; all this concerns the civil laws.

As one of the great objects of marriage is to remove all the uncertainties of illegitimate unions, religion impresses its character on it, and the civil laws join theirs to it so that it will have all the authenticity possible. Thus, beyond the conditions demanded by religion for the marriage to be valid, civil laws can exact still others.

What makes civil laws have this power is that these characteristics are ones that are added, not ones that are in conflict. The law of religion wants certain ceremonies, and the civil laws want the consent of the fathers; in this way they ask something more, but they ask nothing that is contrary to it.

It follows that it is for the law of religion to decide whether or not the bond will be indissoluble; for if the laws of religion had established an indissoluble bond and the civil laws had ruled that it could be broken, these two things would be contradictory.

Sometimes the characteristics impressed on marriage by civil laws are not of an absolute necessity; such are the ones that are established by laws that, instead of annulling the marriage, have been satisfied to punish those who contracted it.

Among the Romans, the Papian laws declared the marriages they prohibited unjust and only subjected them to penalties,[30] and the senatus-consult rendered on the discourse of the emperor Marcus Antoninus declared them null; there was no longer a marriage, a wife, a dowry, or a husband.[31] Civil law determines according to circumstances; sometimes it is more attentive to rectifying the ill, sometimes to preventing it.

[30] See what I have said above, in the book "On the Laws in their Relation to the Number of Inhabitants" [bk. 23], chap. 21.

[31] See law 16 [*Corpus Juris Civilis, Digest* 23.2.16]; *de ritu nuptiarum*, and law 3, para. 1, also in the *Digest* [*Corpus Juris Civilis, Digest* 24.1.3.1]; *de donationibus inter virum et uxorem.*

CHAPTER 14

In which cases of marriages between relatives must one be ruled by the laws of nature, and in which cases should one be ruled by civil laws

In the matter of prohibiting marriage between relatives, it is a very delicate thing to set clearly the point at which the laws of nature cease and where the civil laws begin. For this, principles must be established.

The marriage of a son with his mother confuses the state of things: the son owes an unlimited respect to his mother, the wife owes an unlimited respect to her husband; the marriage of a mother to her son would overturn the natural state of each of them.

There is more: nature has set the time earlier for women to have children; it has set it later for men; and, for the same reason, the woman ceases earlier to have this faculty and the man later. If marriage between mother and son were permitted, it would almost always happen that, when the husband was able to take part in the aims of nature, the wife could no longer.

Marriage between father and daughter is, like the preceding one, repugnant to nature, but it is less repugnant because it does not have these two obstacles. Thus, the Tartars, who can marry their daughters,[32] never marry their mothers, as we see in the accounts.[33]

It has always been natural for fathers to watch over the modesty of their children. As fathers are charged with the care of settling them in life, they have had to preserve in them both the most perfect body and the least corrupt soul; all that can better inspire desires and all that most properly produces tenderness. Fathers, ever occupied in preserving the mores of their children, should be at a distance that is natural from everything that could corrupt them. One will say that marriage is not a corruption, but before marriage one must speak, one must make oneself loved, one must seduce; it is this seduction that should have inspired horror.

Therefore, there has had to be an insurmountable barrier between those who should educate and those who should be educated, and any sort of corruption, even for legitimate cause, has had to be avoided. Why do fathers so carefully deprive of the company and intimacy of their daughters those who are to marry them?

The horror of incest between brother and sister must have come from the same source. That fathers and mothers wanted to preserve the purity of the mores of their children and their houses is enough for them to have inspired their children with a horror of everything that could incline them to the union of the two sexes.

The prohibition on marriage between first cousins has the same origins. In earliest times, that is, in holy times, in the ages when luxury

[32] This law is quite ancient among them. Attila, says Priscus in his *De legationibus*, stops in a certain place to wed Esca, his daughter; "a thing permitted," he says, "by the law of the Scythians," p. 22 [Priscus, *Fragments*, 55c; p. 183, CSHB].

[33] [Ebulgazi Bahadir Han, Khan of Khorezm] *Histoire généalogique des Tatars*, pt. 3, p. 256 [pt. 2, chap. 2, "De la naissance du regne d'Ogus-Chan"; 1, 36–37; 1726 edn].

was unknown, all the children stayed in the house[34] and settled there; this was because a large family needed only a small house. The children of two brothers, or first cousins, were regarded and regarded one another as brothers.[35] Therefore, the distance in regard to marriage was the same for first cousins as for brothers and sisters.[36]

These causes are so strong and so natural that they have acted almost everywhere on earth, independent of any communication. It was not the Romans who taught the Formosans[37] that marriage with their relatives in the fourth degree was incestuous; it was not the Romans who told this to the Arabs;[38] they did not teach it in the Maldives.[39]

But if certain peoples have not rejected marriages between fathers and their children, between sisters and brothers, it has been seen in the first book that intelligent beings do not always follow their laws. Who would have thought that religious ideas have often made men fall into these errors! If the Assyrians and the Persians married their mothers, the former did so out of a religious respect for Semiramis, and the latter because the religion of Zoroaster gave preference to these marriages.[40] If Egyptians married their sisters, this was still another frenzy of the Egyptian religion, which consecrated these marriages in honor of Isis. As the spirit of religion is to lead us to exert effort to perform great and difficult things, a thing must not be judged natural for having been consecrated by a false religion.

The principle that marriages between fathers and children, brothers and sisters, are forbidden in order to preserve a natural modesty in the house will help us discover which marriages are forbidden by natural law, and which can be forbidden only by civil law.

As children live, or are supposed to live in the house of their father

[34] Thus it was among the first Romans.

[35] Indeed, among the Romans, they had the same name; first cousins were called "brothers."

[36] In earliest times in Rome cousins were kept from marrying until the people made a law permitting it; the people wanted to favor an extremely popular man, one who had married his first cousin. Plutarch [*Moralia*], *Quaestiones Romanae* [265d–e; question 6].

[37] *Recueil des voyages qui ont servi à l'établissement de la Compagnie des Indes*, vol. 5, pt. 1 [Voyage de Seyger van Rechteren; "Relation de l'état de l'île de Formose," (écrite par George Candidus); 5, 98, 1706 edn; 5, 187; 1725 edn].

[38] *Koran*, "On Women" [4.23].

[39] See François Pyrard [*Voyages*, vol. 1, chap. 12; 1, 152; 1887–1890 edn].

[40] They were regarded as more honorable. See Philo Judaeus, *De specialibus legibus*, Paris, 1640, p. 778 [3.13 (chap. 3)].

and consequently the son-in-law with the mother-in-law, the father-in-law with the daughter-in-law or with the daughter of his wife, marriage between them is forbidden by the law of nature. In this case, the image has the same effect as the reality, because it has the same cause; the civil law neither can nor should permit these marriages.

There are peoples among whom, as I have said, first cousins are regarded as brothers because they usually live in the same house; there are some among whom this usage is hardly known. Among these former peoples, marriage between first cousins should be regarded as contrary to nature; among the latter, not.

But laws of nature cannot be local laws. Thus, whether these marriages are forbidden or permitted, they are permitted or forbidden by a civil law according to the circumstances.

The usage in which the brother-in-law and the sister-in-law live in the same house is not necessary. Therefore, marriage between them is not forbidden in order to preserve modesty in the house, and the law that permits or forbids it is not the law of nature, but a civil law which is regulated according to the circumstances and depends on usages in each country; these are cases in which the laws depend on mores and manners.

Civil laws prohibit marriages when, by the received usages of a certain country, they are in the same circumstances as those that are prohibited by the laws of nature, and they permit them when this is not the case. The prohibition made by the laws of nature is invariable because it depends on an unvarying thing; the father, the mother, and the children necessarily live in the same house. But the prohibitions of the civil laws are accidental because they depend on an accidental circumstance; that first cousins, and others, live in the same house is an accident.

This explains how the laws of Moses, of the Egyptians, and of several other peoples[41] permit marriages between brother-in-law and sister-in-law, whereas these same marriages are prohibited in other nations.

In the Indies, there is a quite natural reason for admitting these sorts of marriages. The uncle there is regarded as a father, and he is obliged to support and establish his nephews as if they were his own children; this comes from the character of his people, which is good and full of

[41] See law 8 of the *Code* [*Corpus Juris Civilis*, *Code* 5.5.8]; *de incestis et inutilibus nuptiis.*

humanity. This law or this usage has produced an additional one: if a husband has lost his wife, he does not fail to marry her sister,[42] and this is very natural, for the new wife becomes the mother of her sister's children and there is no unjust stepmother.

[42] *Lettres édifiantes et curieuses*, vol. 14, p. 403 [Lettre du P. Bouchet, Pondichéry, October 2, 1714; 14, 403; 1720 edn].

CHAPTER 15

That things that depend on principles of civil right must not be ruled by principles of political right

As men have renounced their natural dependence to live under political laws, so have they renounced the natural community of goods to live under civil laws.

These first laws acquire liberty for them; the second, property. What should be decided by the laws of property should not be decided by the laws of liberty which, as we have said, is the empire of the city alone. It is a fallacy to say that the good of the individual should yield to the public good; this occurs only when it is a question of the empire of the city, that is, of the liberty of the citizen; it does not occur when it is a question of the ownership of goods because it is always in the public good for each one to preserve invariably the property given him by the civil laws.

Cicero held that the agrarian laws were deadly because the city was established only in order for each one to preserve his goods.

Let us propose as a maxim that, when it is a question of the public good, it is never in the public good for an individual to be deprived of his goods, or even for the least part of them to be taken from him by a political law or regulation. In this case, it is necessary to observe strictly the civil law which is the *palladium* of property.

Thus, when the public needs an individual's land, one must never act according to the strictness of political law; but this is when the civil law, which, with a mother's eyes, considers each individual as the whole city, should triumph.

If the political magistrate wants to build some public edifice, some new road, he must pay compensation; in this regard the public is like an individual who deals with another individual. It is quite enough that the public can constrain a citizen to sell it his inheritance and that it takes away from him his great privilege under civil law, that he cannot be forced to alienate his goods.

After the peoples who destroyed the Romans had abused even their conquests, the spirit of liberty called them back to that of fairness; they exercised the most barbarous rights with moderation; and if anyone doubts it, he has only to read the remarkable work by Beaumanoir, who wrote about jurisprudence in the twelfth century.

In his time, highways were repaired as they are today. He says that, when a highway could not be restored, another was built as close as possible to the old one but that the property-owners were compensated at the expense of those who got some benefit from the road.[43] In those days the determination was made according to the civil law; today it is made according to the political law.

[43] The lord named some men of experience and wisdom, *des prud'hommes*, to impose the levy on the peasant; gentlemen were constrained by the count to make their contribution; the churchmen by the bishop. Beaumanoir [*Coutumes de Beauvaisis*], chap. 22 [#734].

CHAPTER 16

That one must not decide by the rules of civil right when it is a matter to be decided by those of political right

The basis for resolving all questions will be seen if one does not confuse the rules that derive from the property of the city with those that arise from the liberty of the city.

Is the domain of a state alienable or is it not? This question should be decided by political law and not by civil law. It should not be decided by civil law because it is as necessary for there to be a domain for the sustenance of the state as it is for there to be civil laws in the state that regulate the disposition of goods.

Therefore, if one alienates the domain, the state will be forced to make a new fund for another domain. But this expedient also overturns political government because, by the nature of the thing, the subject will pay ever more for each domain that is established and the sovereign will reap ever less; in a word, domain is necessary and alienation is not.

The order of succession, in monarchies, is founded on the good of the state, which requires that this order be fixed to avoid the misfortunes that I have said have to occur in despotisms where everything is uncertain because everything there is arbitrary.

The order of succession in the reigning family is established not for its sake, but because it is in the interest of the state for there to be a reigning family. The law which regulates the inheritance of individuals is a civil law, which has for its purpose the interest of individuals; that which regulates succession to monarchy is a political law, which has for its purpose the good and the preservation of the state.

It follows that, when the political law has established an order of succession in a state and this order ends, it is absurd to lay a claim to the succession by virtue of the civil law of whatever people it may be. A particular society does not make laws for another society. The civil laws of the Romans are no more applicable than any other civil laws; they did not employ them themselves when they judged the kings, and the maxims by which they judged the kings are so abominable that they must not be revived.

It also follows that, when the political law makes a certain family renounce the succession, it is absurd to want to use restitutions drawn from the civil law. Restitutions are within the law and can be good against those who live within the law, but they are not good for those who have been established for the sake of the law and who live for the sake of the law.

It is ridiculous to claim to decide the rights of kingdoms, nations, and the universe by the same maxims used to decide among individuals a right concerning a drain pipe, if I may use Cicero's expression.[44]

[44] [Cicero] *De legibus*, bk. 1 [1.4.14].

CHAPTER 17

Continuation of the same subject

Ostracism should be examined by rules of political law and not by the rules of civil law; far from being able to stigmatize popular government, this usage is, on the contrary, quite apt for proving its gentleness; we would have sensed this if, in spite of exile's always being a penalty among ourselves, we had been able to separate the idea of ostracism from that of being punished.

Aristotle tells us[45] that everyone agrees that this practice has something human and popular about it. If, in the times and places one exercised this judgment, it was not found odious, is it for us, who see things from such a distance, to think otherwise than did the accusers, the judges, and even the accused?

And, if one pays attention to the fact that this judgment of the people filled with glory the one against whom it was rendered, that, when it had been abused in Athens by being used against a man without merit,[46] its use ceased at that moment,[47] one will surely see that one has had a false idea of it and that it was a remarkable law which prevented the bad effects of a citizen's glory by heaping a new glory on him.

[45] [Aristotle, *Politics*] *Republic*, bk. 3, chap. 13 [1284a17–22]. [M. usually cites this work as *Politique*; here he uses *République*.]
[46] Hyperbolus. See Plutarch [*Vit.*], *Aristides* [7.3–4].
[47] It was contrary to the spirit of the legislator.

CHAPTER 18

That one must examine whether laws that appear to be contradictory are of the same order

In Rome the husband was permitted to lend his wife to another. Plutarch tells us this explicitly;[48] it is known that Cato lent his wife to Hortensius,[49] and Cato was not a man to violate the laws of his country.

On the other hand, a husband who suffered the debauchery of his wife, who did not give her over to judgment, or who took her back after the condemnation, was punished.[50] These laws appear contradictory and are not. The law permitting a Roman to lend his wife is manifestly a Lacedaemonian institution, established to give the republic children of a certain breeding,[a] if I dare use this term; the purpose of the other was

[48] Plutarch [*Vit.*], *Comp. Lycurgus & Numa* [3.1].
[49] Plutarch [*Vit.*], *Cato the Younger* [25.4–5]. This occurred in our time, says Strabo [*Geographica*], bk. 11 [11.9.1].
[50] Law 11 [*Corpus Juris Civilis*, *Digest* 48.5.11(13)]; *ad legem Juliam de adulteriis coercindis*.

[a] *bonne espèce*.

to preserve the mores. The first was a political law; the second, a civil law.

CHAPTER 19

That things that should be decided by domestic laws must not be decided by the civil laws

The Law of the Visigoths wanted slaves to be obligated to tie up the man and woman they surprised in adultery[51] and to present them to the husband and the judge: a terrible law which put in the hands of these mean persons the care of public, domestic, and individual vengeance!

This law would be good only in the seraglios of the east, where the slave in charge of the enclosure has broken his trust as soon as the women break theirs. He checks criminals, less to have them judged than to have himself judged and to see whether one might lose one's suspicion that he was negligent in a search into the circumstances of the act.

But in countries where women are not under guard, it is senseless for civil law to subject those who govern the house to the inquisition of their slaves.

That inquisition could be at the very most, in certain cases, a particular domestic law and never a civil law.

[51] *Lex Wisigothorum*, bk. 3, tit. 4, para. 6 [3.4.6].

CHAPTER 20

That things that belong to the right of nations must not be decided by the principles of civil laws

Liberty consists principally in not being forced to do a thing that the law does not order, and one is in this state only because one is governed by civil laws; therefore, we are free because we live under civil laws.

It follows that princes, who do not live under civil laws among themselves, are not free; they are governed by force, and they can continually force or be forced. From this it follows that the treaties they have made by force are as obligatory as those they may have made willingly. When we, who live under civil laws, are constrained to make some contract not required by law, we can, with the favor of the law, recover from the violence; but a prince, who is always in this state of forcing or being forced, cannot complain of a treaty that violence has had him make. It is as if he complained of his natural state; it is as if he wanted to be a prince in regard to other princes and wanted the other princes to be citizens in regard to him; that is, as if he wanted to run counter to the nature of things.

CHAPTER 21

That things that belong to the right of nations must not be decided by political laws

Political laws require that every man be subject to the criminal and civil tribunals of the country in which he lives and to the animadversion of the sovereignty.

The right of nations has wanted princes to send ambassadors to each other, and reason, drawn from the nature of the thing, has not permitted these ambassadors to depend on the sovereign to whom they are sent or on his tribunals. They speak for the prince who sends them, and that speech should be free. No obstacle should prevent them from acting. They can often displease because they speak for an independent man. One might impute crimes to them, if they could be punished for crimes; one might assume they had debts, if they could be seized for debts. A prince who has a natural pride would speak through the mouth of a man who would have everything to fear. Therefore, with regard to ambassadors the reasons drawn from the right of nations must be followed, and not those derived from political right. For if they abuse their status as a representative,[b] this is stopped by sending them home; one can even accuse them before their master, who becomes in this way their judge or their accomplice.

[b] *leur être représentatif.*

CHAPTER 22

The unhappy lot of the Inca Atahualpa

The principles we have just established were cruelly violated by the Spanish. The Inca Atahualpa could be judged only by the right of nations;[52] they judged him by political and civil laws. They accused him of having put some of his subjects to death, of having had several wives, etc. And the height of stupidity was that they did not condemn him by the political and civil laws of his country, but by the political and civil laws of their own.

[52] See Garcilaso de la Vega, El Inca [*Royal Commentaries of the Incas and General History of Peru*], p. 108 [pt. 2, bk. 1, chap. 37; 2, 713–714; 1966 edn].

CHAPTER 23

That when, by some circumstances, the political law destroys the state, decisions must be made by the political law that preserves it, which sometimes becomes a right of nations

When the political law, which has established in the state a certain order of succession, becomes destructive of the political body for which it was made, there must be no doubt that another political law can change that order; and far from that same law being in opposition to the first, it will be at bottom entirely in conformity with it, because both will depend on this principle: THE WELL-BEING OF THE PEOPLE IS THE SUPREME LAW.

I have said that a great state[53] that became secondary to another would be weakened and even weaken the principal one. It is known that the state has an interest in having its leader at home, that public revenues should be well administered, and that its money should not go out to enrich another country. It is important for the one who should govern not to be imbued with foreign maxims; they suit less than those already established; moreover, men care prodigiously for their laws and

[53] See above, bk. 5, chap. 14; bk. 8, chaps. 16, 17, 18, 19 and 20; bk. 9, chaps. 4, 5, 6 and 7; bk. 10, chaps. 9 and 10.

their customs; these make the felicity of every nation; it is rare for them to be changed without great upsets and a great shedding of blood, as is shown in the histories of all countries.

It follows that, if a great state has for heir the possessor of a great state, the former can quite well exclude him because it is useful to both states to change the order of succession. Thus, the Russian law made at the beginning of the reign of Elizabeth quite prudently ruled out any heir who possessed another monarchy; thus, the Portuguese law rejects any foreigner who would be called to the crown by the right of blood.

But, if a nation can exclude, it has, with even stronger reason, the right to require renunciation of the throne. If it fears that a certain marriage will have consequences that can make it lose its independence or divide it, this nation will be quite able to require those contracting the marriage and their offspring to renounce all the rights they would have over the nation; both the one who renounces and those in favor of whom one renounces will be the less able to complain, as the state could have made a law to exclude them.

CHAPTER 24

That the regulations of a police are of another order than the other civil laws

There are criminals whom the magistrate punishes; there are others whom he corrects; the former are subject to the power of the law, the others to its authority; the former are withdrawn from society, one obliges the latter to live according to the rules of society.

In the exercise of the police it is the magistrate who punishes rather than the law; in the judgments of crimes it is the law that punishes rather than the magistrate. Matters of police are things of every instant, which usually amount to but little; scarcely any formalities are needed. The actions of the police are quick and the police is exerted over things that recur every day; therefore, major punishments are not proper to it. It is perpetually busy with details; therefore, great examples do not fit it. It has regulations rather than laws. The people who belong to it are constantly under the eyes of the magistrates; therefore, it is the fault of the magistrate if they fall into excess. Thus, one must not confuse great violations of the laws with the simple violation of the police; these things are of different orders.[c]

From this it follows that one has not conformed to the nature of things in that Italian republic[54] where bearing firearms is punished as a capital crime and where it is no more dangerous to make bad use of them than to bear arms.

It also follows that the much-praised action of the emperor who had a baker impaled whom he had caught engaging in fraud is the act of a sultan who knows how to be just only by carrying justice itself to excess.

[54] Venice.

[c] Here Montesquieu offers a description of the *police*.

CHAPTER 25

That one must not follow the general provisions of the civil right when it is a question of things that should be subjected to particular rules drawn from their own nature

Is it a good law that all the civil obligations incurred among sailors on a boat in the course of a voyage should be null? François Pyrard tells us that in his time this was not observed by the Portuguese, but that it was by the French.[55] People who are together for only a short while, who have no needs because the prince provides for them, who can have but one purpose, which is that of their voyage, who are no longer in society but are citizens of the ship, should not contract obligations that have been introduced only to support the burdens of civil society.

It is in this same spirit that the law of the Rhodians, made for a time when one still sailed along the coasts, wanted those who remained in the vessel during a storm to have the ship and the cargo and those who abandoned it to have nothing.

[55] [François Pyrard, *Voyages*] chap. 14, pt. 12 [vol. 2, pt. 1, chap. 14; 2, 188; 1887–1890 edn].

Part 6

BOOK 27

ONLY CHAPTER

On the origin and revolutions of the Roman laws on inheritance

This material concerns establishments of a very remote antiquity, and, in order to probe it deeply, permit me to seek in the first Roman laws something I think no one has seen there before.

It is known that Romulus divided the lands of his small state among its citizens;[1] it seems to me that the Roman laws on inheritance derive from this.

The law dividing the lands required that the goods of one family should not pass to another; it followed that there were only two orders of heirs established by the law:[2] the children and all the descendants who lived under the power of the father, who were called the *sui heredes*, and, in their absence, the closest relatives on the male side, who were called *agnati*.

It also followed that the relatives on the women's side, called *cognati*, should not inherit; they would have transferred the goods to another family, and it was established thus.

It also followed that the children should not inherit from their mother, nor the mother from her children; this would have moved the goods of one family to another family. Thus, both are seen to be ruled out by the Law of the Twelve Tables;[3] it called for agnates to inherit only, and the son and the mother were not agnates of each other.

But it made no difference whether the *suus heres*, or if there were

[1] Dion. Hal. [*Ant. Rom*], bk. 2, chap. 3 [2.7.2–4]. Plutarch [*Vit.*], *Comp. Lycurgus and Numa* [2.6].

[2] "If anyone should die intestate and there are no family heirs, the nearest male agnate shall have the estate" [L.]. Fragment of the Law of the Twelve Tables, Ulpian, last title [Table v, Ulpian, *Fragmenta* 29.1].

[3] See Ulpian, *Fragmenta*, tit. 26, para. 8 [26.8]; tit. 3 *Institutes* [*Corpus Juris Civilis*, *Institutes* 3.3]; *de senatus consulto Tertulliano.*

none, the closest agnate, was male or female because, as the relatives on the mother's side did not inherit though a woman who inherited might marry, the goods always returned to the family they had left. This is why no distinction between male and female heirs was made in the Law of the Twelve Tables.[4]

The result was that though the grandchildren by the son inherited from the grandfather, the grandchildren by the daughter did not inherit, for, to keep the goods from passing to another family, agnates were preferred. Thus, the daughter inherited from her father, but not her children.[5]

Thus, among the first Romans, women inherited when this agreed with the law on the division of lands, and they did not inherit when this could run counter to that law.

Such were the inheritance laws among the first Romans, and, as they had a natural dependence on the constitution and were derived from the division of lands, one surely sees that they did not have a foreign origin and were not among those laws brought back by the deputies sent to the Greek towns.

Dionysius of Halicarnassus[6] tells us that when Servius Tullius found that the laws of Romulus and Numa on the division of lands had been abolished, he reestablished them and made new laws in order to give new weight to the old ones. Thus, one cannot doubt that the laws just mentioned, made as a consequence of this division, were the work of these three Roman legislators.

Since the order of inheritance was established as a consequence of a political law, a citizen was not to disturb it by the will of an individual; that is, in the early Roman times, he was not to be permitted to make a testament.[a] However, it would have been harsh for him to be deprived in his last moments of any commerce in good deeds.

A means was found of reconciling the laws in this regard with the wills of individuals. One was permitted to dispose of one's goods in an assembly of the people, and each testament was, in a way, an act of legislative power.

[4]Paul the Jurist, *Sententiarum*, bk. 4, tit. 8, para. 3 [4.8.3].

[5]*Institutes*, bk. 3, tit. 1, para. 15 [*Corpus Juris Civilis, Institutes* 3.1.15; *de hereditatibus quae ab intestato deferuntur*].

[6][Dion. Hal. *Ant. Rom.*], bk. 4, p. 276 [4.10.3].

[a]See also 5.5 (note [b], bk. 5) for the distinction between "will" and "testament".

The Law of Twelve Tables permitted the one who made his testament to choose as heir the citizen he wanted. The reason that the Roman laws so severely restricted the number of those who could inherit *ab intestato*[b] was the law on the division of lands, and the reason they so broadly extended the faculty of making a testament was that if the father could sell his children,[7] he could with better reason deprive them of his goods. Therefore, these were different effects because they derived from different principles; and this is the spirit of the Roman laws in this regard.

The old laws of Athens did not permit citizens to make a testament. Solon permitted it,[8] except to those who had children, and the Roman legislators, imbued with the idea of paternal power, permitted a citizen to make a testament even to the prejudice of his children. It must be admitted that the old Athenian laws were more consistent than the Roman laws. The indefinite permission to make testaments, granted among the Romans, gradually ruined the political provision on the sharing of lands; more than anything else it introduced the ominous difference between wealth and poverty; many shares were brought together in the same person; some citizens had too much, an infinity of others had nothing. Thus, the people, continually deprived of their share, constantly asked for a new distribution of lands. They asked for it at the time when frugality, parsimony, and poverty were the distinctive character of the Romans, and again at the time when their luxury was carried to excess.

As a testament was, properly speaking, a law made in the assembly of the people, those who were in the army were deprived of the faculty of making testaments. The people gave soldiers the power to make[9] before some of their companions the provisions they would have made before the assembly.[10]

The people held their great assemblies only twice a year; moreover,

[7]Dionysius of Halicarnassus proves, by a law of Numa, that the law that permitted the father to sell his son three times was a law of Romulus, not of the decemvirs [Dion. Hal. [*Ant. Rom.*], bk. 2 [2.27].

[8]See Plutarch [*Vit.*], *Solon* [21.2].

[9]This testament, called *in procinctu*, was different from the one that was called military, which was established only by the constitutions of the emperors. Law 1 [*Corpus Juris Civilis*, *Digest* 29.1]; *de testamento militis*; this was a way to cajole the soldiers.

[10]This testament was not written and had no formalities, "without balances or tablets" [L.] as Cicero says, *De Oratore*, bk. 1 [1.53.228].

[b]"intestate," without a will.

the number of people as well as the amount of business had increased: it was judged suitable to permit all the citizens to make their testaments before certain Roman citizens over the age of puberty[11] who represented the body of the people; in the presence of five citizens,[12] the heir bought his family, that is his inheritance,[13] from the one making the testament, and another citizen carried scales to weigh its price, as the Romans did not yet have money.[14]

It appears likely that these five citizens represented the five classes of the people and that the sixth, composed of people who had nothing, was not counted.

It must not be said, along with Justinian, that these sales were imaginary; they became so, but in the beginning they were not. Most later laws regulating testaments originate from the reality of these sales; the proof of it can be found in the fragments of Ulpian.[15] The deaf, the mute, and the prodigal could not make testaments: the deaf because he could not hear the speech of the buyer of the family, the mute because he could not pronounce the terms of the nomination, the prodigal because, as all management of business was forbidden to him, he could not sell his family. I omit other examples.

As testaments were made in the assembly of the people, they were acts of political right more than of civil right, of public right more than of private right; it followed that a father could not permit his son, who was in his power, to make a testament.

Among most peoples, testaments are subject to no greater formalities than ordinary contracts; because both the one and the other are only expressions of the will of the one who contracts, both belong equally to private right. But, among the Romans, where testaments derived from public right, there were greater formalities than for other acts,[16] and this still exists today in those countries of France that are under Roman right.

[11] *Institutes*, bk. 2, tit. 10, para. 1 [*Corpus Juris Civilis*, *Institutes* 2.10.1; *de testamenta ordinandis*]; Aulus Gellius [*NA*], bk. 15, chap. 27 [15.27.3]. This kind of testament is called *per aes et libram* [the scales were touched by a piece of bronze].

[12] Ulpian [*Fragmenta*], tit. 10, para. 2 [20.2].

[13] Theophilos, *Institutes* [*Paraphrasis Graeca Institutionum Caesarearum*], bk. 2, tit. 10 [2.10.1].

[14] They had it only from the time of the war of Pyrrhus. Livy, speaking of the siege of Veii, says in bk. 4 [4.60.6] "there was not yet coined silver" [L.].

[15] [Ulpian, *Fragmenta*] tit. 20, para. 13 [20.3].

[16] *Institutes*, bk. 2, tit. 10, para. 1 [*Corpus Juris Civilis*, *Institutes* 2.10.1; *de testamenta ordinandis*].

As testaments were, as I have said, a law of the people, they were to be made with the force of command and in language called *direct* and *imperative*. From this was formed a rule that one could neither give nor transfer one's inheritance except in the language of command,[17] from which it followed that one might well, in certain cases, make a substitution[18] and order that the inheritance should pass to another heir, but that one could not make a trust,[19] that is, give a charge in the form of an entreaty that someone release all or a part of the inheritance from his care.

When the father neither appointed as heir nor disinherited his son, the testament was annulled, but it was valid though he neither disinherited nor appointed his daughter. I see the reason for this. When he neither appointed as heir nor disinherited his son, he wronged his grandson who would have inherited from his father *ab intestato* but in neither appointing nor disinheriting his daughter, he did no wrong to the children of his daughter, who would not have inherited *ab intestato* from their mother[20] because they were neither *sui heredes* nor agnates.

The laws of the first Romans concerning inheritances thought only to observe the spirit of the division of lands; they did not sufficiently restrict the wealth of women and thereby left a door open to luxury, which is always inseparable from this wealth. Between the Second and the Third Punic Wars, the ill began to make itself felt; the Voconian law was made.[21] And, as very great considerations caused it to be made, as only a few records of it remain to us, and as no one has spoken of it up to now except in a very confused manner, I shall clarify it.

Cicero has preserved for us one fragment from it that forbids appointing a woman as heir, whether or not she was married.[22]

The *Epitome* of Livy, where this law is mentioned, says nothing

[17] "Let Titius be my heir." [*Corpus Juris Civilis, Institutes* 2.16].

[18] Common, guardian, and exemplary.

[19] Augustus, for particular reasons, began to authorize trusts. *Institutes*, bk. 2, tit. 23, para. 1 [*Corpus Juris Civilis, Institutes* 2.23.1; *de fedeicommissariis hereditatibus*].

[20] "According to the Law of the Twelve Tables the inheritance of an intestate person does not pertain to the children of the mother since women cannot have heirs" [L.]. Ulpian, *Fragmenta*, tit. 26, para. 7 [26.7].

[21] Quintus Voconius, tribune of the people, proposed it. See Cicero, *In Verrem* [2.1.42.107]. In Livy, *Epitome*, bk. 41, one must read "Voconius" instead of "Volumnius." [This emendation, originally made by Sigonius, has wide acceptance; see also Johann Freinsheim, *Supplementorum Livianorum* 41.34].

[22] "It confirmed . . . that no one might make a girl or a woman an heir" [L.]. Cicero, *In Verrem* [2.1.42.107].

further about it.[23] It seems, according to Cicero[24] and Saint Augustine,[25] that any daughter and even the only daughter were included in the prohibition.

Cato the Elder contributed with all his power to the passage of this law.[26] Aulus Gellius cites a fragment of the speech he gave on this occasion.[27] By preventing women from inheriting he wanted to preclude the cause of luxury, as by defending the Oppian law he wanted to check luxury itself.

In the *Institutes* of Justinian[28] and of Theophilus[29] mention is made of an article of the Voconian law, which restricted the faculty of making legacies. On reading these authors, one could not help but think that this article was made to keep the inheritance from being so drained by legacies that the heir would refuse to accept it. But this was not the spirit of the Voconian Law. We have just seen that its purpose was to keep women from receiving any inheritance. The article of this law which puts limits to the faculty of making legacies shared in this purpose, for, if one had been able to make as many legacies as one wanted, women would have been able to receive as a legacy what they could not obtain as an inheritance.

The Voconian law was made to prevent women from having excessively great wealth. Therefore, they were to be deprived of considerable inheritances, not those which could not support luxury. The law fixed a certain sum which was to be given to the women it deprived of the inheritance. Cicero,[30] who informs us of this fact, does not tell us what this sum was, but Dio says that it was a hundred thousand sesterces.[31]

The Voconian law was made to regulate wealth and not to regulate poverty; thus Cicero tells us[32] that it was enacted only for those who were enrolled in the census.

[23] "He supported a law that no one could make a woman his heir" [L.]. [Livy, *Epitome*] bk. 41.

[24] Cicero, *In Verrem* [2.1.41.107].

[25] [St. Augustine] *The City of God*, bk. 3 [3.21].

[26] Livy, *Epitome*, bk. 41.

[27] [Aulus Gellius, *NA*] bk. 17, chap. 6 [17.6].

[28] *Institutes*, bk. 2, tit. 22 [*Corpus Juris Civilis*, *Institutes* 2.22; *de lege falcidia*].

[29] [Theophilos] bk. 2, tit. 22 [*Paraphrasis Graeca Institutionum Caesarearum* 2.22. Preface].

[30] "No one advised him to give Fadia more than she could obtain under the Voconian Law" [L.]. [Cicero] *De finibus bonorum et malorum*, bk. 2 [2.17.55].

[31] "It became possible to appeal to the Voconian Law, which had prohibited women to inherit more than 100,000 sesterces" [L.] [Cass. Dio, *Historia Romana*] bk. 56 [56.10.2].

[32] "Who was registered" [L.]. [Cicero] *In Verrem* 2.1.41.107].

This furnished a pretext for evading the law. It is known that the Romans were very fond of forms, and we have said above that the spirit of the republic was to follow the letter of the law. There were fathers who did not have themselves enrolled in the census so that they would be able to leave their inheritances to their daughters, and the praetors judged the Voconian law had not been violated because the letter of it had not been violated.

A certain Annius Asellus had appointed his daughter as his sole heir. He could do it, says Cicero; the Voconian law did not stop him because he was not in the census.[33] Verres, as praetor, deprived the daughter of the inheritance; Cicero asserts that Verres must have been corrupted because, if not, he would not have reversed an order that the other praetors had followed.

Who, therefore, were these citizens who were not in the census that comprised all citizens? But, according to the institution of Servius Tullius reported by Dionysius of Halicarnassus,[34] any citizen who did not have himself enrolled in the census was made a slave; Cicero himself says that such a man lost his liberty;[35] Zonarus says the same thing.[c] Therefore, there must have been some difference between not being in the census in the spirit of the Voconian law and not being in the census according to the spirit of the institutions of Servius Tullius.

Those who were not enrolled in the first five classes, where one's placement depended on the amount of one's goods,[36] were not in the census according to the spirit of the Voconian law; those who were not enrolled in one of the six classes, or who were not put by the censors among those who were called *aerarii*, were not in the census according to the institutions of Servius Tullius. Such was the force of nature that, in order to evade the Voconian law, some fathers consented to suffer the shame of mingling in the sixth class with the proletarians and those who were taxed by head, or perhaps even of being included in the tables of the Caerites.[37]

We have said that Roman jurisprudence did not admit trusts. The

[33] "Who was not registered" [L.]. Ibid. [Cicero, *In Verrem* 2.1.43.111.]

[34] [Dion. Hal., *Ant. Rom.*] bk. 4 [4.9.8].

[35] In [Cicero] *Pro Caecina* [34.99].

[36] These first five classes were so considerable that sometimes writers report only five.

[37] *In Caeritum tabulas referri; aerarii fieri*: to be degraded to a citizen of the lowest class. [Consider Horace, *Epistles* 1.6.62–63; and Asconius, *Diuin. Caecl.*, 3.8.]

[c] Zonaras, *Annales* 7.20 (72a).

expectation of evading the Voconian law introduced them; one appointed an heir able to receive the inheritance under the law, and one asked him to release it to a person the law had excluded. This new arrangement had a variety of effects. Some handed over the inheritance, and the action of Sextus Peducaeus was remarkable.[38] He was given a great inheritance; he alone in all the world knew that he had been asked to release it; he sought out the widow of the testator and gave her all of her husband's goods.

Others kept the inheritance for themselves, and the example of Publius Sextilius Rufus was still remembered because Cicero used it in his debates against the Epicureans.[39] "In my youth," he says, "I was requested by Sextilius to go with him to his friends' house to learn from them if he should release the inheritance of Quintus Fadius Gallus to Fadia, his daughter. He assembled several young people along with some very august personages, and none was of the opinion that he should give more to Fadia than what she should have under the Voconian law. Sextilius had a great inheritance thereby, but he would not have kept a sestertius of it if he had preferred what was just and honest to what was useful." "I can believe," he added, "that you would have given over the inheritance; I can even believe that Epicurus would have given it over, but you would not have followed your principles." Here I shall make some reflections.

It is a misfortune of the human condition that legislators are obliged to make laws that oppose even natural feelings; such was the Voconian law. This is because the statutes of legislators regard the society more than the citizen, and the citizen more than the man. The law sacrificed both the citizen and the man and thought only of the republic. A man requested his friend to release his inheritance to his daughter: the law scorned the sentiments of nature in the testator; it scorned filial piety in the daughter; it had no regard for the one who was charged with releasing the inheritance, who was in terrible circumstances. Did he release it? He was a bad citizen. Did he keep it? He was a dishonest man.[d] Only people who were naturally good thought of evading the law; one could choose only honest people to evade it, for it is always a triumph to overcome avarice and voluptuousness and only honest

[38] Cicero, *De finibus bonorum et malorum*, bk. 2 [2.18.58].
[39] Ibid. [Cicero, *De finibus bonorum et malorum* 2.17.55].

[d] These four short sentences are one sentence in the French text.

people achieve these sorts of triumphs. Perhaps it would even be severe to regard them in this respect as bad citizens. It is not impossible that the legislator had fulfilled a great part of his purpose when his law was such that it forced only honest people to evade it.

At the time the Voconian law was made, the mores preserved something of their old purity. Sometimes the public conscience became interested in favor of the law, and people were made to swear that they would observe it[40] so that integrity waged war, so to speak, against integrity. But in later times, the mores were corrupted to the point that it took less force to elude the Voconian law with respect to trusts than the law could call upon for its own observation.

An infinite number of citizens perished in the civil wars. Rome, under Augustus, was almost uninhabited; it had to be repopulated. The Papian laws were made, from which nothing was omitted that could encourage the citizens to marry and have children.[41] One of the principal ways was to increase the expectation of inheriting in those who favored the aims of the law and to diminish such expectations in those who resisted them, and, as the Voconian law had disqualified women from inheriting, the Papian law ended this prohibition in certain cases.

Wives,[42] especially those who had children, were able to receive legacies on the strength of the testaments of their husbands; they could, when they had children, receive legacies on the strength of the testament of foreigners: all this is against the provisions of the Voconian law, and it is remarkable that the spirit of this law was not entirely abandoned. For example, the Papian law[43] permitted a man with a child[44] to receive the whole inheritance from the testament of a foreigner; it granted the same favor to the wife only when she had three children.[45]

It must be observed that the Papian law made women with three

[40] Sextilius said that he had sworn to observe it. Cicero, *De finibus bonorum et malorum*, bk. 2 [2.17.55].

[41] See what I have said in bk. 23, chap. 21 [above].

[42] See Ulpian, *Fragmenta*, tits. 15 and 16 [15, 16].

[43] The same difference is found in many provisions of the Papian law. See Ulpian, *Fragmenta*, last tit., paras. 4 and 5, and the same at the same tit., para. 6. [29.4–6].

[44] "A little son or daughter was born to you because of me [. . .] You have the rights of parents, you may be appointed an heir because of me" [L.]. Juvenal, *Satire* 9 [9.83,87].

[45] See Law 9, *Codex Theodosianus* [9.42.9.1]; *de bonis proscriptorum seu damnatorum*; and Cass. Dio [*Historia Romana*], bk. 55 [55.2.5–7]; see Ulpian, *Fragmenta*, last tit., para. 6, and tit. 29, para. 3 [29.6, 3].

children qualified to inherit only on the strength of the testament of foreigners and that, in regard to inheritances from relatives, it left the old laws and the Voconian law in their full force.[46] But this did not last.

Rome, spoiled by the wealth of all the nations, changed its mores; it was no longer a question of checking the luxury of women. Aulus Gellius,[47] who lived under Hadrian, tells us that in his time the Voconian law was almost erased; it was covered over by the opulence of the city. Thus, we find in the *Sentences* of Paul,[48] who lived under Pescennius Niger, and in the *Fragments* of Ulpian,[49] who lived at the time of Alexander Severus, that the sisters on the father's side could inherit and that the prohibition of the Voconian law applied only to more distant relatives.

The old Roman law had begun to appear harsh. The praetors were no longer affected except by reasonings of fairness, moderation, and propriety.

We have seen that, by the old Roman laws, mothers had no part in their children's inheritance. The Voconian law was a new reason to exclude them from it. But the emperor Claudius gave the mother the children's inheritance as a consolation for losing them; the senatus consult Tertullianum, made under Hadrian,[50] granted it to her when she had three children, if she were free-born; or when she had four, if she had been freed. It is clear that this senatus consult was only an extension of the Papian law, which had in the same cases granted women inheritances conferred on them by foreigners. Finally, Justinian[51] granted them inheritances independently of the number of children they had.

The same causes which had restrained the law keeping women from inheriting had little by little overthrown the one which had hampered inheritance through relatives on the woman's side. These laws were very much in conformity with the spirit of a good republic, where one should make it so that this sex cannot avail itself, for the sake of luxury, either of its wealth or of the expectation of wealth. By contrast, as the

[46] Ulpian, *Fragmenta*, tit. 16, para. 1 [16.1]; Sozomen [*Historia ecclesiastica*], bk. 1, chap. 19 [1.9].
[47] Aulus Gellius [*NA*], bk. 20, chap. 1 [20.1.23].
[48] [Paul the Jurist, *Sententiarum*] bk. 4, tit. 8, para. 3 [4.8.3].
[49] [Ulpian, *Fragmenta*] tit. 26, para. 6 [26.6].
[50] That is, the Emperor Pius, who took the name Hadrian by adoption.
[51] Law 2, *Code* [*Corpus Juris Civilis*, *Code* 8.59(58).2]; *de jure liberorum*; *Institutes*, bk. 3, tit. 3, para. 4 [*Corpus Juris Civilis*, *Institutes* 3.3.4]; *de Senatus consulto Tertulliano*.

luxury of a monarchy renders marriage burdensome and costly, one must be invited to it, both by the wealth that women can offer and by the expectation of inheritances they can receive. Thus, when the monarchy was established in Rome, the whole system of inheritances was changed. The praetors summoned the relatives on the women's side in the absence of relatives on the men's side; whereas, according to the old laws, relatives on the women's side were never summoned. The senatus consult Orfitianum summoned children to the inheritance of their mother, and the emperors Valentinian, Theodosius, and Arcadius[52] summoned the grandchildren by the daughter to the inheritance of the grandfather. Finally, the emperor Justinian removed the slightest trace of the old right about inheritances; he established three orders of heirs: descendants, ascendants, and collaterals, without any distinction between male and female, or between relatives on the woman's side and relatives on the man's side, and he abrogated all those that remained.[53] He believed he followed nature itself, when he set aside what he called the encumbrances of the old jurisprudence.

[52] Law 9, *Code* [*Corpus Juris Civilis*, *Code* 6.55.9]; *de suis et legitimis liberis et ex filia nepotibus ab intestato venientibus*.

[53] Law 12, *Code*, ibid. [*Corpus Juris Civilis*, *Code* 6.55.9; *de suis et legitimis liberis et ex filia nepotibus ab intestato venientibus*]; and *Novellae* 118 and 127 [*Corpus Juris Civilis*, *Novellae* 118, 127].

BOOK 28

On the origin and revolutions of the civil laws among the French

My imagination brings me to speak of forms changing into new bodies . . .

OVID, *Metam.* [1.1–2]

CHAPTER I

On the different character of the laws of the German peoples

When the Franks left their country, they had the Salic laws drawn up by the sages of their nation.[1] When the tribe of the Ripuarian Franks under Clovis joined[2] that of the Salian Franks, it preserved its usages, and Theodoric[3] King of Austrasia had them written down. He also collected the usages of the Bavarians and Alemanni,[4] which were dependencies of his kingdom. For as Germany was weakened by the departure of so many people, the Franks, after conquering what lay in front of them, took a step backward and brought their domination into the forests of their fathers. It is likely that the code of the Thuringians was given by this same Theodoric,[5] for the Thuringians were also his subjects. As the Frisians were subjected by Charles Martel and Pepin, their law is no earlier than these princes.[6] Charlemagne, who was the first to overcome the Saxons, gave them the law that we have. One has

[1] See the "Prologue" of the *Lex Salica* [pp. 2–9, 198; 1959 edn]. [Gottfried W. F. von] Leibniz, in his *De origine Francorum* [#29, p. 259; 1720 edn], says that this law was made before the reign of Clovis; but this cannot have been before the Franks had left Germany; at that time they did not understand Latin.

[2] See Gregory of Tours [*Historia ecclesiastica Francorum* 2.40].

[3] See the "Prologue" of the *Lex Baiuwariorum* [pp. 201–202] and that of the *Lex Salica* [pp. 2–9, 198; 1958 edn].

[4] Ibid. [*Lex Baiuwariorum*, pp. 201–202].

[5] *Lex Angliorum Werinorum hoc est* [*Lex*] *Thuringorum*.

[6] They did not know how to write.

only to read these last two codes to see that they come from the hands of conquerors. When the Visigoths, Burgundians, and Lombards founded kingdoms, they had their laws written, not in order to make the conquered peoples follow their usages, but in order to follow them themselves.

In the Salic and Ripuarian laws and in those of the Alemanni, Bavarians, Thuringians, and Frisians, there is an admirable simplicity; they show an original roughness and a spirit that was not at all weakened by a different spirit. They changed little because these peoples, with the exception of the Franks, stayed in Germany. The Franks even founded a great part of their empire there; thus their laws were entirely German. It was not the same for the laws of the Visigoths, Lombards, and Burgundians; their laws lost much of their character because these people, who remained in their new dwelling-places, lost much of their character.

The kingdom of the Burgundians did not last long enough for the laws of the conquering people to be greatly changed. Gundobad and Sigismund, who collected their usages, were almost the last of their kings. The laws of the Lombards were augmented rather than changed. Those of Rotharis were followed by those of Grimoald, Liutprand, Ratchis, and Aistulf, but they did not take a new form. It was not the same for the laws of the Visigoths;[7] their kings recast the laws and had them recast by the clergy.

The Merovingian kings indeed removed from the Salic and Ripuarian laws what absolutely could not be in accord with Christianity, but they left in them their whole foundation.[8] One cannot say this for the laws of the Visigoths.

The laws of the Burgundians and especially those of the Visigoths approved corporal penalties. These were not accepted by the Salic and Ripuarian laws;[9] these laws better preserved their character.

The Burgundians and Visigoths, whose provinces were quite

[7] Euric gave them, Leuvigilde corrected them. See the *Chronicles* of Isidorus [Isidorus, *Historia Gotharum Wandalorum Sueborum*, 504 "Spanish era" (A.D. 466), #35; 606 "Spanish era" (A.D. 568), #51]. Chindasuinth and Recessuinth reformed them. Egiga had the code that we now have made and gave the commission for it to the bishops; however, the laws of Chindasuinth and Recessuinth were preserved, as appears in the sixteenth Council of Toledo.

[8] See the "Preface" of the *Lex Baiuwariorum* [p. 202].

[9] Only a few of them are found in the decree of Childebert [*Decretio Childeberti regis. circa 595*, *CRF* 7.9,14].

vulnerable, sought to reconcile the original inhabitants to them and to give the inhabitants the most impartial civil laws,[10] but the Frankish kings, sure of their power, were not so considerate.[11]

The Saxons, who lived under the empire of the Franks, were of an indomitable humor and persisted in rebelling. In their laws one finds[12] the harshnesses of the conqueror, which one does not see in the codes of laws of the other barbarians.

There the spirit of the laws of the Germans is seen in the pecuniary penalties and that of the conqueror in the corporal penalties.

The crimes they commit in their country are punished corporally; and the spirit of the Germanic laws is followed only in the punishment of those committed outside their territory.

In the laws it is declared that, for their crimes, they will never have peace and will be refused asylum even in the churches.

Bishops had an immense authority in the court of the Visigoth kings; the most important business was decided in councils. We owe to the codes of the Visigoths all the maxims, all the principles and all the views of the present-day Inquisitors, for the monks have only copied against the Jews laws formerly made by the bishops.

Further, the laws of Gundobad for the Burgundians appear quite judicious; those of Rotharis and other Lombard princes are even more so. But the laws of the Visigoths, those of Reccesuinth, Chindasuinth, and Egiga, are childish, awkward, and inane; they do not attain their end; they are rhetorical and empty of sense, fundamentally frivolous, and gigantic in their style.

[10]See the "Prologue" of the *Leges Burgundionum*, and the law code itself, especially tit. 12, art. 5 [12.5], and tit. 38 [38.5, 7, 11]. See also Gregory of Tours [*Historia ecclesiastica Francorum*], bk. 2, chap. 33 [2.33], and the Code of the Visigoths.

[11]See [bk. 28] chap. 3 below.

[12]See [*Leges Saxonum*] chap. 2, paras. 8 and 9 [21–22] and chap. 4, paras. 2 and 7 [30, 35].

CHAPTER 2

That the laws of the barbarians were all personal

A peculiar characteristic of these laws of the barbarians is that they were not attached to a certain territory; the Frank was judged by the law of the Franks, the Alemanni by the law of the Alemanni, the

Burgundian by the law of the Burgundians, the Roman by the Roman law, and one was so far from even dreaming in those times of putting uniformity into the laws of the conquering peoples that one did not even think of making oneself the legislator of the vanquished people.

I find the origin of this in the mores of the Germanic peoples. These nations were divided by marshes, lakes, and forests; one can see in Caesar,[13] that they even liked their separation. The fright the Romans gave them made them band together; each man, in this mixture of nations, had to be judged by the usages and customs of his own nation. All these peoples, taken individually, were free and independent, and, when they were mixed together, they remained independent: the homeland was in common and the republic particular; the territory was the same and the nations various. Therefore, there was a spirit of personal laws among these peoples before they left their homes, and they took it with them in their conquests.

One finds this usage established in the formulas of Marculf,[14] in the codes of laws of the barbarians, especially in the law of the Ripuarians,[15] in the decrees of the Merovingian kings,[16] from which were derived the capitularies made on that subject under the Carolingians.[17] Children followed the law of their fathers,[18] wives that of their husbands;[19] widows returned to their own law,[20] and freed men took that of their patron.[21] This is not all: each man could take on the law that he wanted; the constitution[a] of Lothair I required that this choice be made public.[22]

[13] [Gaius Julius Caesar] *De bello Gallico*, bk. 6 [6.23].
[14] [*Marculfi formularum*] bk. 1, form. 8.
[15] [*Lex Ribuaria*] chap. 31 [35].
[16] That of Clotaire of the year 560 in the edition of the Capitularies of Baluze, vol. 1, art. 4, ibid., *in fine* [*Chlotharii regis constituto generalis, circa 560, CRF* 8.4, 13].
[17] Capitularies added to the *Leges Langobardum*, bk. 1, tit. 25, chap. 71 [Kar. 48 (pap.)]; bk. 2, tit. 41, chap. 7 [Lud. 1 (pap.)]; bk. 2, tit. 56, chaps. 1 and 2 [Kar. 143 (pap.); Pip. 27 (pap.)].
[18] Ibid., bk. 2, tit. 5 [*Leges Langobardorum*, Liut. 153; see also gloss on Liut. 152 (153) (pap.)].
[19] Ibid., bk. 2, tit. 7, chap. 1 [*Leges Langobardorum*; Liut. 127].
[20] Ibid., chap. 2 [*Leges Langobardorum*; Loth. 14 (pap.)].
[21] Ibid., bk. 2, tit. 35, chap. 2 [*Leges Langobardorum*; Roth. 226].
[22] In the *Leges Langobardorum*, bk. 2, tit. 57 [Loth. 38 (37) (pap.)].

[a] Here "constitution" and "decree" appear in the same paragraph and seem synonymous; this usage is customary for the time, in contrast to Montesquieu's use of *la constitution* in Book 11.

CHAPTER 3

The chief difference between the Salic laws and the laws of the Visigoths and the Burgundians

I have said[23] that the law of the Burgundians and those of the Visigoths were impartial, but the Salic law was not; it established the most distressing distinctions between the Franks and the Romans. When one killed a Frank, a barbarian, or a man living under the Salic law,[24] one paid his relatives a settlement[b] of two hundred sous; only a hundred was paid when one had killed a property-holding Roman;[25] and only forty-five, when a Roman tributary was killed; the settlement for the murder of a Frank, vassal of the king,[26] was six hundred sous, and that for the murder of a Roman, guest-friend[27] of the king,[28] only three hundred. Thus the law put a cruel difference between the Frankish lord and the Roman lord, and between the Frank and the Roman who were of middling condition.

This is not all: if a group assembled[29] to assault a Frank in his house and killed him, the Salic law ordered a settlement of six hundred sous, but if one had assaulted a Roman or a freed man,[30] only half that settlement was paid. By the same law,[31] if a Roman put a Frank in chains, he owed thirty sous in settlement, but, if a Frank put a Roman in chains, he owed only fifteen sous. A Frank despoiled by a Roman received sixty-two and a half sous in settlement, and a Roman despoiled by a Frank received one of but thirty. All this must have been crushing to the Romans.

[23] In chap. 1 of this book.

[24] *Lex Salica*, tit. 44, para. 1 [D69.1; S11.1].

[25] "Who has property in the region where he abides" [L.]. *Lex Salica*, tit. 44, para. 15; see also para. 7 [D69.7–8; S11.7–8].

[26] "He who is under the protection of the king" [L.]. Ibid., tit. 44, para. 4 [*Lex Salica* D69.4; S11.4].

[27] "A Roman who was a drinking companion with the king" [L.]. Ibid., para. 6 [*Lex Salica* D69.6; S11.6].

[28] The principal Romans were attached to the court, as one can see in the records of the lives of many bishops who were brought up there. Almost no one but Romans knew how to write.

[29] Ibid. [*Lex Salica*], tit. 45 [D70.1; S12.1].

[30] *Lidus*, whose condition was better than that of the serf. *Leges Alamannorum*, chap. 95 [A92.2; B95.2].

[31] [*Lex Salica*] tit. 35, paras. 3–4 [S19.3–4].

[b] *composition.*

A famous writer[32] nevertheless forms a system of the *Establishment of the Franks in Gaul*, on the assumption that they were the best of friends of the Romans. Were the Franks, therefore, the best friends of the Romans, they who caused them, they who received from them, appalling evils?[33] Were the Franks friends of the Romans, they who, after having subjected them by their arms, oppressed them in cold blood by their laws? They were friends of the Romans like the Tartars who conquered China were friends of the Chinese.

If some Catholic bishops wanted to use the Franks to destroy the Arian kings, does it follow that they desired to live under barbarian peoples? Can one conclude from this that the Franks had special regard for the Romans? I would draw quite different consequences from this: the surer the Franks were of the Romans, the less carefully they treated them.

But the Abbé Dubos drew from the wrong sources for an historian, from poets and orators; one must not found systems on works of ostentation.

[32] The Abbé Dubos.

[33] Witness the expedition of Arbogast in Gregory of Tours, *Historia ecclesiastica Francorum*, bk. 2 [2.9].

CHAPTER 4

How the Roman right was lost in the land under the domain of the Franks and was preserved in the land under the domain of the Goths and Burgundians

The things I have said will shed light on others, which have been quite obscure until now.

The country today called France was governed, under the Merovingians, by Roman law, that is, the Theodosian code, and by the various laws of the barbarians who lived in it.[34]

In the country under the domain of the Franks, the Salic law had been established for the Franks, and the Theodosian code[35] for the Romans. In the country under the domain of the Visigoths, a compilation of the Theodosian code, made by order of Alaric,[36] ruled disputes

[34] The Franks, Visigoths, and Burgundians.

[35] It was completed in [A.D.] 438.

[36] In the twentieth year of the reign of this prince, and published two years later by Anian, as appears in the "Preface" of that code [*Lex Wisigothorum*].

between Romans; the customs of the nation, which Euric caused to be written down,[37] decided those of the Visigoths. But why did the Salic laws acquire a nearly general authority in the countries of the Franks? And why was Roman right gradually lost there, while in the domain of the Visigoths, Roman right spread and had general authority?

I say that the usage of Roman right was lost among the Franks because there were great advantages for a Frank,[38] a barbarian, or a man living under Salic law; everyone gave up Roman right in order to live under Salic law. Only the ecclesiastics kept it,[39] because they had no interest in changing. The difference in conditions and ranks consisted only in the amounts of the settlements, as I shall show elsewhere. Now, separate laws[40] gave them settlements as favorable as those the Franks had; therefore, they kept Roman right. It was without prejudice to them, and, moreover, it suited them because it was the work of the Christian emperors.

On the other hand, in the patrimony of the Visigoths, as the Visigoth law[41] gave no civil advantage to the Visigoths over the Romans, the Romans had no reason to quit living under their law and live under another; therefore, they kept their laws and did not take those of the Visigoths.

This is increasingly confirmed the further one pursues the matter. The law of Gundobad was very impartial and was no more favorable to the Burgundians than to the Romans. In the prologue of this law it appears that the law was made for the Burgundians and that it was also made to regulate such business as might arise between Romans and

[37] In 504 of the *Spanish Era* [A.D. 466]; Isidorus of Seville, *Historia Gothorum Wandalorum Sueborum* [#35].

[38] "Frank or barbarian, or a man who lives by the Salic law" [L.], *Lex Salica*, tit. 445, para. 1 [D69.1; S11.1].

[39] "According to Roman law, under which the church lives," as it is said in the *Lex Ribuaria*, tit. 58, para. 1 [61.1]. Also see the innumerable authorities on the subject reported by [Charles] du Cange [*Glossarium mediae et infimae latinitatis*] for the words "Lex Romana" [5.81–82; 1954 edn].

[40] See the capitularies added to the *Lex Salica* in [Friedrich] Lindenbrog [*Leges Francorum Salicae et Ripuarium*, pp. 141–204; 1720 edn] at the end of this law, and the diverse codes of laws of the barbarians on the privileges of the ecclesiastics in this regard [*Capitularia regum Francorum*, 39, 135, 142, esp. 142.7]. See also the letter from Charlemagne to his son Pepin, King of Italy, in 807, in the Baluze edition, Vol. 1, p. 452 [461] [*Epistola Imperatoris ad Pippinum filium*, 103], in which it is said that an ecclesiastic is to receive a triple settlement; and the collection of capitularies in vol. 1 of the Baluze edition, bk. 5, art 302 [336] [*Capitularia spuria. Benedictae levitae* 1, 336.]

[41] See that law [*Lex Wisigothorum*, e.g., 3.1.1–10; 1.8–9, 16].

Burgundians, and in the latter case the tribunal was made up of equal numbers from each nation. This was necessary for particular reasons drawn from the political arrangement in those times.[42] Roman right continued to exist in Burgundy in order to regulate disputes that Romans might have among themselves. The Romans had no reason to abandon their law, as they did in the country of the Franks, particularly since the Salic law was not established in Burgundy, as is shown by the famous letter written by Agobard to Louis the Pious.

Agobard[43] asked this prince to establish Salic law in Burgundy; therefore, it had not been established there. Thus Roman right continued to exist and still exists in so many provinces which were formerly dependencies of this kingdom.

Roman right and Gothic law were likewise maintained in the country of the establishment of the Goths; Salic law was never accepted there. When Pepin and Charles Martel drove out the Saracens, the towns and provinces that submitted to these princes[44] asked to preserve their laws, and this was granted; a thing which, in spite of the usage of those times when all the laws were personal, soon made Roman right regarded as a real and territorial law in those countries.

This is proven by the edict of Charles the Bald, given at Pistes in 864, which distinguishes the countries in which one judged by Roman right from those in which one did not judge by it.[45]

The Edict of Pistes proves two things: first, that there were countries in which one judged according to Roman law and others in which one did not at all judge according to this law; second, that those countries in which one judged by Roman law were precisely those in which it is still

[42] I shall speak of it in another place, bk. 30, chaps. 6, 7, 8 and 9.

[43] Agobard, *Opera* [*Liber adversus legem Gundobadi*, chap. 7; Migne PL 104, 117; *MGH* Epp. 5, 3.7].

[44] See Gervais de Tilburi, in the collection by Duchesne, vol. 3, p. 366. "A treaty was made with the Franks, that they might live in accord with ancestral customs, that is, by the laws of their Gothic homeland. And thus the province of Narbonne was subjected by Pepin" [L.]. [Andre Duchesne, *Historiae Francorum scriptores*, 3, 366; 1636–1649 edn; also in Leibniz, *Scriptores rerum Brunsvicensium*, 1, 881–1004; 1707–1711 edn.] And a chronicle for the year 759, reported by [Guillaume de] Catel, *Mémoires de l'histoire de Languedoc* [bk. 3, p. 598; 1633 edn]. And the anonymous author ["Astronomous"] of the *Vita Hludowici Imperatoris* [chap. 59. 838], concerning the demand made by the peoples of Septimania in the assembly *in Carisiaco*; in the Duchesne collection, vol. 2, p. 316.

[45] "In that land where judgments are determined according to Roman law, a case will be judged according to that law; in those [not determined by Roman law, it will be by monetary penalties]" [L.]. Art. 16 [*Capitularia regum Francorum* 273.16]. See also art. 20 [*Capitularia regum Francorum* 273. 20].

followed today, as can be seen in this same edict:[46] thus the distinction between those countries in France under custom and those governed by written right[c] was already established at the time of the Edict of Pistes.

I have said that, in the beginnings of the monarchy, all laws were personal; thus, when the Edict of Pistes distinguishes between countries of Roman right and those without it, this means that, in the countries that were not those of Roman right, so many people had chosen to live under some one of the laws of the barbarian peoples, that there were almost none in those parts who chose to live under Roman law and that, in the countries of Roman law, few people chose to live under the laws of the barbarians.

I well know that I say new things here, but if they are true, they are quite old. What does it matter after all, whether it is I, the Valois, or the Bignons, who have said them?

[46] See arts. 12 and 16 in the *Edictum Pistensem* [864] [*Capitularia regum Francorum*, 273. 12, 16], *in Cavilono, in Narbona*, etc.

[c] *pays de la France coutumière et de la France régie par le droit écrit.*

CHAPTER 5

Continuation of the same subject

The law of Gundobad continued to exist for a long time among the Burgundians concurrently with Roman law: there it was still used at the time of Louis the Pious; the letter of Agobard leaves no doubt about it. Likewise, though the Edict of Pistes calls the country that had been occupied by the Visigoths the country of Roman law, the law of the Visigoths still continued to exist there, which is proven by the Synod of Troyes, held under Louis the Stammerer in 878, that is, fourteen years after the Edict of Pistes.

Subsequently, the Gothic and Burgundian laws perished even in their own countries from general causes[47] that brought about the disappearance of the personal laws of the barbarian peoples everywhere.

[47] See below, chaps. 9, 10, and 11.

CHAPTER 6

How Roman right was preserved in the domain of the Lombards

Everything bows before my principles. The law of the Lombards was impartial, and the Romans had no interest in turning to it from their own. The motive that prompted the Romans under the Franks to choose Salic law was not present in Italy; Roman right was maintained there along with the law of the Lombards.

It even happened that the latter ceded to Roman right; it ceased to be the law of the dominant nation, and, though it continued to be that of the principal nobility, most of the towns set themselves up as republics, and their nobility fell or was exterminated.[48] The citizens of the new republics were not inclined to take a law that established the usage of judicial combat and whose institutions clung to the customs and usages of chivalry. As the clergy, so powerful in Italy at the time, lived almost entirely under Roman law, the number of those who followed the law of the Lombards had to grow even smaller.

Moreover, the law of the Lombards had not the majesty of Roman right, which reminded Italy of the idea of its domination of the whole world; nor was their law as extensive. Only the law of the Lombards and Roman law could be used to supplement statutes in the towns that had been set up as republics; now, which could better supplement them, the law of the Lombards, which was enacted only for certain cases, or Roman law, which included them all?

[48] See what Machiavelli says of the destruction of the old Florentine nobility [*History of Florence*, bk. 3; 1, 3, 4].

CHAPTER 7

How Roman right was lost in Spain

Things went otherwise in Spain. The law of the Visigoths triumphed and Roman law was lost. Chindasuinth[49] and Reccesuinth[50] proscribed

[49] He began his reign in 642.

[50] "We want to be tormented no longer either by foreign laws or by Roman ones" [L.]. *Lex Wisigothorum*, bk. 2, tit. 1, paras. 9 and 10 [2.1.7–8].

the Roman laws and did not even permit them to be cited in the tribunals. Reccesuinth was also the author of the law that lifted the prohibition on marriage between Goths and Romans.[51] It is clear that these two laws had the same spirit; this king wanted to remove the principal causes for the separation of Goths and Romans. Now, it was thought that nothing separated them more than forbidding marriage to be contracted between them and permitting them to live under different laws.

But, though the kings of the Visigoths proscribed Roman right, it continued to exist in the domains they possessed in southern Gaul. These countries, far from the center of the monarchy, were very independent.[52] One sees in the history of Wamba, who ascended the throne in 672, that the natives of the country gained the upper hand;[53] thus Roman law had more authority there, and Gothic law less. Spanish laws suited neither their manners nor their present situation. Perhaps the people even clung to Roman law because they attached to it the idea of their liberty. There is more: the laws of Chindasuinth and Recessuinth contained frightful provisions against the Jews, but these Jews were powerful in southern Gaul. The author of the history of King Wamba calls these provinces the brothel of the Jews. When the Saracens entered these provinces, they had been summoned; now, who could have summoned them there but the Jews or the Romans? The Goths were the first to be oppressed because they were the dominant nation. One sees in Procopius[54] that, in their calamities, they withdrew from Narbonne Gaul to Spain. In this misfortune they doubtless took refuge in those parts of Spain that still defended themselves, and the

[51] "Matrimony shall be permitted between a Gothic man and a Roman woman and with a Roman man and a Gothic woman" [L.]. *Lex Wisigothorum*, bk. 3, tit. 1, chap. 1.

[52] See in Cassiodorus the deference shown to them by Theodoric, King of the Ostrogoths, the most highly reputed prince of his time: bk. 4, letters 19 and 26 [*Variae* 4.19, 26; consider 4.17 as well].

[53] The rebellion of these provinces was widespread, as appears in the judgment that was a consequence of the event. Paulus and his adherents were Romans; they were even favored by the bishops. Wamba did not dare put to death the seditious men he had conquered. The author of the *Historia Wambae* calls Narbonnensian Gaul the nursery of perfidy. [Saint Julianus of Toledo, *Historia Wambae*; see esp. 22.5. Corpus Christianorum, Series Latina, vol. 115 *MGH* SS. Rer. Mer. 5. 486–535; 1910. Migne PL 96, 759–808].

[54] "The Goths who survived the slaughter went out from Gaul with their wives and children; they were received in Spain by Theudis, who was now a manifest tyrant" [L.] [Procopius] *The Gothic War*, bk. 1, chap. 13 [5.13.13].

number of those who lived under the law of the Visigoths in southern Gaul was much reduced.

CHAPTER 8

A false capitulary

Did not that wretched compiler, Deacon Benedict, change the Visigothic law forbidding the use of Roman right into a capitulary[55] later attributed to Charlemagne? He made of that particular law a general law, as if he wanted to exterminate Roman right throughout the universe.

[55] *Capitularium*, Baluze edn, vol. 1, bk. 6, chap. 343; p. 981 [*Capitularia spuria. Benedictae levitae* 2.343].

CHAPTER 9

How the codes of laws of the barbarians and the capitularies were lost

The Salic, Ripuarian, Burgundian, and Visigothic laws ceased little by little to be used among the French; this is how it happened.

As fiefs had become hereditary and under-fiefs were extended, many usages were introduced to which these laws no longer applied. Indeed their spirit, which was to regulate most business with fines, was retained. But, as values had doubtless changed, fines also changed, and one sees many charters[56] in which the lords set the fines that had to be paid in their tribunals. Thus one followed the spirit of the law without following the law itself.

Besides, as France was divided into an infinity of small lordships, which recognized feudal dependency rather than political dependency,

[56] Mr. Thaumassière has collected a number of them. See, for example, chapters 61, 66 and others. [Gaspard Thaumas de la Thaumassière, *Les Anciennes et Nouvelles Coutumes locales de Berry, et celles de Lorris commentées*, pt. 1, chap. 61, pp. 86–89, chap. 66, pp. 97–102; 1629 edn].

it would have been very difficult for a single law to have authority: indeed, one could not have seen to its enforcement. The usage of sending special officers into the provinces[57] to keep an eye on the administration of justice and on political business had almost vanished; it even appears in the charters that, when new fiefs were established, the kings gave up the right of sending them. Thus, when almost everything had become fiefs, there was no longer any employment for the officers; there was no longer a law held in common because there was no one to enforce it.

Therefore, the Salic, Burgundian, and Visigothic laws were seriously neglected at the end of the reign of the Carolingians, and at the beginning of that of the Capetians, they were almost never mentioned.

Under the Merovingians and Carolingians one often assembled the nation, that is, the lords and bishops; it was not yet a question of the commons. In these assemblies one sought to regulate the clergy, a body which was formed, so to speak, under the conquerors and which had established its prerogatives. The laws made in these assemblies are those we call capitularies. Four things happened: laws of fiefs were established, and a great part of the goods of the church was governed by the laws of the fiefs; the ecclesiastics were further separated, and they neglected laws for reform[58] when they were not the sole reformers; the canons of the synods[59] and the decretals of the popes were collected; and the clergy accepted these laws as coming from a purer source. After the great fiefs had been set up, the kings, as I have said, no longer sent deputies into the provinces to see to the enforcement of the laws they issued; thus under the Capetians there was no longer talk of capitularies.

[57] *Missi dominici*: "Royal commissioner."

[58] "Let not the bishops, on the pretense that they have the authority to make canons, oppose this constitution or neglect it," says Charles the Bald in the capitulary of 844, art. 8 [*Apud Tolosam Civitatem, Capitularia regum Francorum* 255.8]. It seems he already foresaw their downfall.

[59] An infinite number of papal decretals were inserted in the collections of canons; there had been very few in the old collection. Dionysius Exiguus put many in his; but that of Isidoros Mercator was filled with true and false decretals. The old collection was in use in France until Charlemagne. This prince received from the hands of Pope Adrian I the collection of Dionysius Exiguus, and had it accepted. The collection of Isidoros Mercator appeared in France at about the time of the reign of Charlemagne; the people embraced it; it was followed by what is called "the corpus of canon right."

CHAPTER 10

Continuation of the same subject

A number of capitularies were added to the law of the Lombards, the Salic laws, and the law of the Bavarians. The reason for this has been sought; it must be taken from the thing itself. The capitularies were of several kinds. Some related to political government, others to economic government, most to ecclesiastical government, a few to civil government. Those of the last kind were added to the civil law, that is, to the personal laws of each nation; this is why it is said in the capitularies that nothing in them was stipulated against Roman law.[60] Indeed, those concerning economic, ecclesiastical, or political government did not relate to this law, and those concerning civil government related only to the laws of the barbarian peoples, which were explained, corrected, enlarged, and diminished. But adding capitularies to the personal laws caused the neglect, I believe, of the body of capitularies. In times of ignorance, the summary of a work often brings about the decline of the work itself.

[60] See the *Edictum Pistensem* [864], art. 20 [*Capitularia regum Francorum* 273.20].

CHAPTER 11

Other causes for the downfall of the law codes of the barbarians, of the Roman right, and of the capitularies

When the Germanic nations conquered the Roman Empire, they found writing in use there, and in imitation of the Romans they drew up all their usages in writing[61] and arranged them into codes. The unfortunate reigns following the reign of Charlemagne, the incursions of the Normans, and the intestine wars plunged the victorious nations back into the shadows they had left; reading and writing were forgotten. This caused written barbarian laws, Roman right, and capitularies to be

[61] This is noted expressly in some of the prologues of these codes. One can even see in the laws of the Saxons and Frisians different provisions for various districts. Some particular provisions required by the circumstances were added to these usages: such were the harsh laws against the Saxons.

forgotten in France and Germany. The use of writing was better preserved in Italy, where the popes and Greek emperors reigned and where there were flourishing towns and almost the only commerce of the time. The proximity of Italy caused Roman right to be better preserved in the regions of Gaul formerly subjected to the Goths and the Burgundians, the more so because there this right was a territorial law and a kind of privilege. It is likely that ignorance of writing caused the decline of Visigothic laws in Spain. And, with the fall of so many laws, customs were formed everywhere.

Personal laws declined. Settlements and what were called *freda*[62] were more regulated by custom than by the text of these laws. Thus, just as in the establishment of the monarchy German usages passed into written laws, some centuries later written laws returned to unwritten usages.

[62] I shall speak of this elsewhere [bk. 30, chap. 14].

CHAPTER 12

On local customs; the revolution of the laws of the barbarian peoples and that of the Roman right

Many records show us that there were already local customs under the Merovingians and Carolingians. In them, *local custom*,[63] the *old usage*,[64] *custom*,[65] *laws and customs*[66] are mentioned. Some authors have believed that what were called customs were the laws of the barbarian peoples and that what was called law was Roman right. I shall prove that this cannot be so. King Pepin ordered that wherever there was no law, custom would be followed, but that custom would not be preferred to law.[67] Now, to say that Roman right had preference over the codes of laws of the barbarians is to go against all the old records and chiefly against those codes of laws of the barbarians that continually say the opposite.

Far from these customs being the laws of barbarian peoples, these

[63] *Marculfi Formulae*, "Preface" [p. 37, *MGH* edn].
[64] *Leges Langobardorum*, bk. 2, tit. 58, para. 3 [Pip. 43; E codd. 7–9 (pap.)].
[65] *Leges Langobardorum*, bk. 2, tit. 41, para. 6 [Pip. 33 (pap.)].
[66] *Vita S. Liudgeri* [e.g., *anno* 776, bk. 1.17; *MGH*, SS. 2, p. 409].
[67] *Leges Langobardorum*, bk. 2, art. 41, para. 6 [Pip. 33 (pap.)].

very laws, being personal laws, introduced customs. Salic law, for example, was a personal law, but in places inhabited generally or almost generally by Salian Franks, the Salic law, personal though it was, became a territorial law in relation to these Salian Franks, and it was personal only for the Franks living elsewhere. Now, if some Burgundians, Alemanni, or even Romans had often had business in a place where Salic law was territorial, that business would have been decided by the laws of these peoples; and a great number of judgments in conformity with some of these laws had to have introduced new usages into the country. And this explains Pepin's constitution very well. It was natural for these usages to affect the local Franks in cases that were not decided by Salic law, but it was not natural for them to be able to prevail over Salic law.

Thus there was in each place a dominant law, and accepted usages served to supplement the dominant law when they did not run counter to it.

It could even happen that they served as supplements to a law that was not territorial; and to continue this same example, if, in a place where Salic law was territorial, a Burgundian was judged by the law of the Burgundians and if the case was not to be found in the text of that law, there must be no doubt that it was judged by following the local custom.

In the time of King Pepin, the customs that had been formed had less force than the laws, but soon the customs destroyed the laws; and as new regulations are always remedies pointing to a present ill, one can believe that in Pepin's time customs had already begun to be preferred to laws.

What I have said explains how from the earliest times Roman right began to become a territorial law, as can be seen in the Edict of Pistes, and how Gothic law did not cease being used there, as shown by the Synod of Troyes that I have mentioned.[68] Roman law had become the general personal law; and Gothic law, the particular personal law; consequently, Roman law was the territorial law. But how did it happen that ignorance made the personal laws of the barbarian peoples decline everywhere, whereas Roman right continued to exist as territorial law in the Visigothic and Burgundian provinces? I reply that even Roman law had about the same fate as other personal laws; if not, we would still

[68] See chap. 5 above.

have the Theodosian Code in the provinces where Roman law was territorial, whereas we find the law of Justinian in them. About all that remained in these provinces were the name, the country of Roman or of written right, the love the peoples have for their law, particularly when they regard it as a privilege, and some provisions of Roman right that men still remembered. But this was enough to result in the acceptance, as written law, of the compilation of Justinian when it appeared in the provinces that were the domain of the Goths and the Burgundians, whereas it was accepted only as written reasoning in the former domain of the Franks.

CHAPTER 13

The difference between the Salic law, or the law of the Salian Franks, and the law of the Ripuarian Franks and of other barbarian peoples

The Salic law did not admit the use of the negative proof; that is, under Salic law, the one who made a declaration or an accusation had to prove it, and it was not enough for the accused to deny it: this conforms to the laws of almost all the nations of the world.

The law of the Ripuarian Franks had an entirely different spirit;[69] it was satisfied with negative proofs, and the one against whom a declaration or accusation was made could, in most cases, vindicate himself[d] by swearing along with a certain number of witnesses that he had not done what was imputed to him. The number of witnesses who had to swear[70] increased with the importance of the thing; sometimes it was as high as seventy-two.[71] The laws of the Alemanni, Bavarians, Thuringians, and those of the Frisians, Saxons, Lombards, and Burgundians, were made on the same plan as those of the Ripuarians.

I have said that the Salic law did not admit negative proofs. There

[69] This relates to what Tacitus says [*Germania* 27; see bk. 18, n. 31], that the German peoples had some common usages and some particular usages.
[70] *Lex Ribuaria*, tits. 6, 7, 8 and others [6, 7, 8].
[71] Ibid. [*Lex Ribuaria*] tits. 11, 12, 17 [11, 12, 18].

[d] *se justifier.*

was, however, one case in which it admitted them,[72] but in this case it did not admit them alone and without concurrent positive proofs. The complainant had his witnesses heard in order to establish his declaration;[73] the accused had his witnesses heard to vindicate himself; and the judge sought the truth in both sets of testimony.[74] This practice was quite different from that of the Ripuarian and other barbarian laws, where an accused man vindicated himself by swearing that he was not guilty and by having his relative swear that he had told the truth. These laws could be suitable only to a people with a certain simplicity and natural candor. The legislators even had to anticipate their abuse, as will shortly be seen.

[72] It is the one in which an antrustion, that is, a vassal of the king, in whom one assumes a greater frankness, was accused: see the *Pactus legis Salicae*, tit. 76 [73].
[73] See the *Pactus Legis Salicae*, tit. 76 [73].
[74] As it is still practiced today in England.

CHAPTER 14
Another difference

Salic law did not permit proof by single combat; the law of the Ripuarians,[75] and almost all those of the barbarian peoples, accepted it.[76] It appears to me that the law of combat was a natural consequence of, and remedy for, the law that established negative proofs. When one made a declaration and saw that it was going to be unjustly evaded by an oath, what could a warrior do who saw himself about to be confuted[77] but ask satisfaction for the injury done him and for the perjury itself? Salic law, which did not admit the usage of negative proof, did not need proof by combat and did not accept it, but the law of the Ripuarians[78] and that of the other barbarian peoples who admitted the use of negative proofs[79] were forced to establish proof by combat.

[75] [*Lex Ribuaria*] tit. 32 [36.4]; tit. 57, para. 2 [60.2]; tit. 59, para. 4 [62.4].
[76] See the following note.
[77] This spirit indeed appears in the *Lex Ribuaria*, tit. 59, para. 4 [62.4], and tit. 67, para. 5 [69.5]; and the *Capitulae quae in lege Ribuaria mittenda sunt*, 803, art. 22 [12] [*Capitularia regum Francorum* 41.4].
[78] See that law [*Lex Ribuaria* 62.4; 69.5].
[79] The law of the Frisians, Lombards, Bavarians, Saxons, Thuringians, and Burgundians.

I beg that one read the two famous provisions of Gundobad,[80] King of Burgundy, on this subject; one will see that they are drawn from the nature of the thing. According to the language of the barbarian laws, the oath had to be removed from the hands of a man who wanted to abuse it.

Among the Lombards, the law of Rotharis admitted cases in which the one who had defended himself by an oath was not also to undergo the hardship of combat. This usage spread;[81] we shall later see what evils resulted from it and how people had to return to the former practice.

[80] In the *Leges Burgundionum*, tit. 8, paras. 1–2 [8.1, 2] concerning criminal affairs; and tit. 45 [45], which also concerns civil affairs. Also see the law of the Thuringians [*Lex Angliorum et Werinorum hoc est Thurginorum*], tit. 1, para. 31 [2–3]; tit. 7, para. 6 [32], and tit. 8 [35–42, 44]; *Leges Alamannorum*, tit. 89 [A86, B89]. *Lex Baiuwariorum*, tit. 8, chap. 2, para. 6 [9.2]; chap. 3, para. 1 [9.3]; and tit. 9, chap. 4, para. 4 [10.4]; *Lex Frisonum*, tit. 2, para. 3 [2.3]; tit. 14, para. 4[14.4]; *Leges Langobardorum*, bk. 1, tit. 32, para. 3 [Roth. 213]; tit. 35, para. 1 [Kar. 45 (pap.)]; bk. 2, tit. 35, para. 2 [Roth. 235]. [1.35.2 seems more appropriate; Kar. 46 (pap.).]

[81] See below, chap. 18 at the end.

CHAPTER 15
Reflection

I do not say that, in the changes made in the code of laws of the barbarians, in the provisions that were added to it, or in the body of the capitularies, some text cannot be found in which, in fact, proof by combat is not a consequence of negative proof. Particular circumstances could, over the course of several centuries, cause certain particular laws to be established. I am speaking of the general spirit of the German laws, their nature, and their origin; I am speaking of the old usages of these peoples indicated or established by these laws, and this is the only question addressed here.

CHAPTER 16

On the proof by boiling water established by Salic law

Salic law admitted the usage of proof by boiling water,[82] and as this ordeal was quite cruel, the law was tempered in order to soften its strictness.[83] It permitted, upon the consent of the other party, relief to the one whose citation required him to endure the proof by boiling water. The accuser, by means of a certain sum fixed by law, could be satisfied by the oath of several witnesses, who declared that the accused had not committed the crime, and this was a particular case of the Salic law in which negative proof was admitted.

This proof was an agreement allowed by the law but not ordered by it. The law gave a certain compensation to the accuser who wanted to permit the accused to defend himself by a negative proof; the accuser was free to rely on the oath of the accused, as he was free to forgive the injury or the fault.

The law offered a tempering,[84] so that before the judgment, both parties, the one in fear of a terrible ordeal, the other with a view to a small present compensation, might terminate their disputes and end their hatreds. One feels that once this negative proof was given, there did not have to be another and that thus the practice of combat could not be a consequence of this particular provision of Salic law.

[82] And some others of the laws of the barbarians also.
[83] [*Lex Salica*] tit. 56 [D89; S31].
[84] Ibid. [*Lex Salica*], tit. 56 [D89; S31].

CHAPTER 17

The way of thinking of our fathers

One will be astonished to see that our fathers thus made the honor, fortune, and life of the citizens depend on things that belonged less to the province[e] of reason than to that of chance, that they constantly used proofs that did not prove and that were linked neither to innocence nor to the crime.

[e] *ressort*. See note [a], bk. 12 and note [e], bk. 19.

The Germans, who had never been subjugated,[85] enjoyed an extreme independence. Families waged war on one another over murders, robberies, and insults.[86] This custom was modified by putting these wars under regulations; they were waged by order of the magistrate and under his eyes,[87] which was preferable to a general license to do harm to each other.

As the Turks today in their civil wars regard first victory as a judgment of god who decides; so in their individual business the German peoples took the outcome of combat as a mandate of providence, ever mindful to punish the criminal or the usurper.

Tacitus says that among the Germans when one nation wanted to begin war with another, they sought to capture someone who could do battle with one of their own and that the success of the war was judged by the outcome of this battle. Peoples who believed that single combat would settle public business could well have thought that it could also rule on disputes between individuals.

Gundobad,[88] King of Burgundy, was, of all kings, the one who most gave authority to the usage of combat. This prince explains his law in the law itself: "It is," he said, "so that our subjects will no longer take oaths concerning obscure deeds and will not perjure themselves concerning certain deeds." Thus, whereas the ecclesiastics declared impious the law permitting combat,[89] the law of the Burgundians regarded as sacrilegious the one establishing the oath.

Proof by single combat had a certain reason founded in experience. In a nation concerned uniquely with war, cowardice presumes other vices; it proves that one has resisted the education one has been given and that one has not been sensitive to the honor or been led by the principles that have governed other men; it shows that one does not fear their scorn and that one cares not at all for their esteem: if one were well born, one ordinarily would not lack the deftness that should be joined with force, or the force that should accompany courage, for by

[85] This is seen in what Tacitus says: "The same characteristics in each one" [L.] [*Germania* 4].

[86] [Caius] Velleius Paterculus [*Historiae Romanae ad M. Minucium Consulem*], bk. 2, chap. 118 [2.118.1] says that the Germans decided all affairs by combat.

[87] See the barbarian law; and, for more modern times, Beaumanoir, *Coûtumes de Beauvaisis* [see chaps. 61, 62].

[88] *Leges Burgundionum*, chap. 45 [45].

[89] See [Saint] Agobard, *Opera, Liber adversus legem Gundobadi* [e.g., chap. 8; Migne PL 104, p. 118; *MGH* 3.8].

esteeming honor, one will have exercised all one's life in those things without which it cannot be obtained. Moreover, in a warrior nation, where force, courage, and prowess are honored, the truly odious crimes are those that arise from cheating, shrewdness, and deceit, that is, from cowardice.

As for proof by fire, after the accused had put his hand on a hot iron, or in boiling water, the hand was wrapped in a sack that was then sealed; three days later, if no sign of burning appeared, one was declared innocent. Who does not see that, among a people practiced in handling arms, their coarse and callous skin would not sufficiently receive the impression of the hot iron or the boiling water to appear there three days later? And, if it appeared, it was a sign that the one undergoing the ordeal was effeminate. Our peasants, with their calloused hands, handle hot iron at will. And, as for the women, the hands of those who worked could resist the hot iron. The ladies had no lack of champions to defend them,[90] and in a nation where there was no luxury there was scarcely any middle state.

By the law of the Thuringians,[91] a woman accused of adultery was condemned to the ordeal by boiling water only when no one presented himself as her champion, and the law of the Ripuarians admitted this ordeal only when no witnesses were found to vindicate the accused.[92] But a woman whom none of her relatives wanted to defend, or a man who could bring forward no witness to his probity, was, by this alone, already convicted.

Therefore, I say that in the circumstances of the times when proof by combat and proof by hot iron and boiling water were the usages, there was such an agreement between these laws and the mores that the laws less produced injustice than they were unjust, that the effects were more innocent than the causes, that they more ran counter to fairness than they violated rights, that they were more unreasonable than tyrannical.

[90] See Beaumanoir, *Coûtumes de Beauvaisis*, chap. 61 [chap. 63, #1795–1796]. See also the *Lex Angliorum et Werinorum hoc est Thuringorum*, tit. 14 [55], in which proof by boiling water is only subsidiary.

[91] [*Lex Angliorum et Werinorum hoc est Thuringorum*], tit. 14 [55].

[92] [*Lex Ribuaria*] chap. 31, para. 5 [35.5].

CHAPTER 18

How proof by combat was extended

One could conclude from the letter of Agobard to Louis the Pious that proof by combat was not in use among the Franks, for he asks that suits in Burgundy be judged by the law of the Franks after once again showing that prince the abuses of the law of Gundobad.[93] But since judicial combat was in use in France, at that time, as one also knows, the conclusion is awkward. This is explained by what I have said: the law of the Salian Franks did not admit this proof and that of the Ripuarian Franks accepted it.[94]

But in spite of the clamor of the ecclesiastics, the use of judicial combat spread daily in France, and I shall shortly prove that they themselves largely gave rise to it.

The law of the Lombards furnishes us this proof. "A detestable custom was introduced long ago (so it is said in the preamble of the constitution of Otto II);[f] this is, that if the charter of some inheritance be attacked as false, he who presented the charter swore on the Gospels that it was true, and without any preliminary judgment he made himself the owner of the inheritance; thus, perjurers were sure to acquire."[95] When Emperor Otto I was crowned in Rome,[96] at the time that Pope John XII was holding a council, there was an outcry among all the lords of Italy for the Emperor to make a law to correct this shameful abuse.[97] The Pope and the Emperor judged that the business had to be remanded to the council that was to be held shortly in Ravenna.[98] There, the lords made the same declarations and redoubled their outcries, but on the pretext of the absence of certain persons the suit was once again postponed. When Otto II and Conrad,[99] king of

[93] "If it please our lord that it be changed to the law of the Franks" [L.]. [Saint Agobard, *Opera*, *Liber adversus legem Gundobadi*, chap. 7; Migne PL 104, p. 117; *MGH* 3.7].

[94] See that law, tit. 59, para. 4, and tit. 67, para. 5 [*Lex Ribuaria*, 62.4; 69.5].

[95] *Leges Langobardorum*, bk. 2, tit. 55, chap. 34 [Otto 1 Pref. (pap.)].

[96] In 962.

[97] "It is proclaimed by the Princes of Italy that the Holy Emperor in changing that law would destroy a shameful crime" [L.]. *Leges Langobardorum*, bk. 2, tit. 55, chap. 34 [Otto, 1 Pref. (pap.)].

[98] It was held in 967, in the presence of Pope John XIII, and Emperor Otto I.

[99] The uncle of Otto II, son of Rodolphus, and King of Transjurian Burgundy.

[f] The close of this parenthesis is not in the text.

Burgundy, arrived in Italy, they conferred in Verona[100] with the lords of Italy;[101] and on their reiterated insistence the Emperor, by unanimous consent, made a law saying that a suit would be decided by combat when there were contested inheritances, and when one of the parties wanted to use a charter that the other claimed to be false, that the same rule would be observed when it was a question of fiefs, that the churches would be subject to the same law, and that their battle would be done by champions. One can see that the nobility asked for proof by combat because of the drawback of the proof introduced by the churches; that, in spite of the outcry of the nobility, in spite of the abuse which itself cried out, and in spite of the authority of Otto, who came to Italy in order to speak and act as master, the clergy held firm in two synods; that, as the collaboration of the nobility and the princes forced the ecclesiastics to concede, the use of judicial combat should be regarded as a privilege of the nobility, as a rampart against injustice, and as security for its property; and that, from this time on, the practice should spread. And this happened at a time when emperors were great and popes were weak, at a time when the Ottos came to Italy to reestablish the rank of the empire.

I shall make a reflection that will confirm what I have said above, that the establishment of negative proofs brought in its train the jurisprudence of combat. The abuse complained of to the Ottos was that a man to whom one had objected that his charter was false defended himself with a negative proof by declaring on the Gospels that it was not false. What was done to correct the abuse of a law that had been so mutilated? The use of combat was reestablished.

I have hastened to speak of the constitution of Otto II in order to give a clear idea of the contentions in those times between the clergy and the laymen. Before this there had been a constitution of Lothair I[102] who, on the same complaints and the same contentions, wanting to secure the ownership of goods, had ordered that the notary would swear that his charter was not false, and if he were dead, the witnesses who had signed it would be made to swear to it; but the ill still remained; there had to be recourse to the remedy I have just mentioned.

[100] In 988.

[101] "Thus, from all sides they bombarded the ears of the emperor" [L.], *Leges Langobardorum*, bk. 2, tit. 55, chap. 34 [Otto 1 (pref) (pap.)].

[102] In the *Leges Langobardorum*, bk. 2, tit. 55, para. 33 [Loth. 56]. In the text used by Muratori, it is attributed to Emperor Widonis.

I find that before this time in the general assemblies held by Charlemagne the nation represented to him that in this state of things it was quite difficult for the accuser or the accused not to commit perjury, and that it was better to reestablish judicial combat,[103] which is what he did.

The use of judicial combat spread among the Burgundians, and the use of the oath was limited there. Theodoric, King of Italy, abolished single combat among the Ostrogoths;[104] the laws of Chindasuinth and Reccesuinth apparently wanted to remove even the idea of it. But these laws were so little accepted in Narbonne that there combat was regarded as a prerogative of the Goths.[105]

The Lombards, who conquered Italy after the destruction of the Ostrogoths by the Greeks, brought the use of combat into that country, but their first laws restricted it.[106] Charlemagne,[107] Louis the Pious, and the Ottos made various general constitutions that are found inserted in the laws of the Lombards and added to the Salic laws, which extended duelling first into criminal suits and later into civil suits. One did not know what to do. The negative proof by an oath had drawbacks, and that by combat had them also; one changed as one was more struck by those of the former or by those of the latter.

On the one hand, the ecclesiastics took pleasure in seeing that in all secular business one had recourse to the churches and altars,[108] and, on the other, a proud nobility liked to maintain its rights by the sword.

I do not say that it was the clergy who introduced this usage of which the nobility complained. This custom derived from the spirit of the laws of the barbarians and from the establishment of negative proofs. But as

[103] In the *Leges Langobardorum*, bk. 2, tit. 55, para. 23 [Kar. 65 (pap.)].

[104] See Cassiodorus [*Variae*], bk. 3, letters 23, 24 [3.23, 24].

[105] "In that palace [. . .] Bera, Count of Barcinoninia, was sought out by a certain man called Sunila, and was accused by him of being faithless; he fought him on horseback in accordance with their own law, for they both were Goths; and he was victorious" [L.]. Anonymous, "Astronomous," *Vita Hludowici Imperatoris* [chap. 33, *anno* 820.]

[106] See in the *Leges Langobardorum*, bk. 1, tit. 4 [Liut. 71]; tit. 9, para. 23 [Liut. 118]; bk. 2, tit. 35, paras. 4–5 [Grim. 2–4]; and tit. 55, paras. 1–3 [Roth, 164–166]; and para. 15 [Liut. 61].

[107] Ibid. [*Leges Langobardorum*], bk. 2, tit. 55, para. 23 [Kar. 65 (pap.)].

[108] The judicial oath was sworn at that time in churches; and in Merovingian times there was a chapel in the king's palace expressly for the affairs that were judged there. See the *Marculfi Formulae*, bk. 1, chap. 38 [1.38]; *Lex Ribuaria*, tit. 59, para. 4 [62.4]; tit. 65, para. 5 [69.5]; Gregory of Tours, *Historia ecclesiastica Francorum* [e.g., 5.14; 8.6]; the capitulary for the year 803 added to the Salic law *the Capitularia quae in lege Salica mittenda sunt, 803* [*Capitularia Regum Francorum* 39.3].

this practice of procuring immunity for so many criminals caused it to be thought that the sanctity of the churches had to be used to stun the guilty and to make those who committed perjury blanch, the ecclesiastics supported that usage and the practice joined to it, for they were in all else opposed to negative proof. We see in Beaumanoir[109] that these proofs were never admitted in the ecclesiastic tribunals, which doubtless contributed greatly to their decline and to the weakening of the provision of the codes of laws of the barbarians in this regard.

This will also give a sense of the bond between the use of negative proofs and that of judicial combat of which I have spoken at such length. The lay tribunals admired the one and the other, and the clerical tribunals rejected both.

In the choice of proof by combat, the nation followed its genius for war, for at the same time that one established combat as a judgment of god, one abolished the proofs by the cross, cold water, and boiling water, which had been also regarded as judgments of god.

Charlemagne ordered that, if some difference arose among his children, it should be terminated by a judgment of the cross. Louis the Pious limited this judgment to ecclesiastical business;[110] his son Lothair abolished it in every case; he likewise abolished the proof by cold water.[111]

I do not say that, in a time when so few usages were universally received, these proofs were not brought up again in some churches, the more so because a charter of Philip Augustus mentions them,[112] but I say that they were little used. Beaumanoir, who lived in the time of Saint Louis and a little time after, enumerating the different kinds of proofs, speaks of judicial combat, but not at all of the others.[113]

[109] [Beaumanoir, *Coûtumes de Beauvaisis*] chap. 39, p. 212 [#1191].

[110] His constitutions can be found inserted in the *Leges Langobardorum* and following the Salic laws.

[111] In the constitution inserted in the *Leges Langobardorum*, bk. 2, tit. 55, para. 31 [Loth 56].

[112] Of the year 1200. [*Recueil général des anciennes lois françaises, Capetians*, #99; 1, 190–193.]

[113] [Beaumanoir] *Coûtumes de Beauvaisis*, chap. 39 [#1145–1156].

CHAPTER 19

A new reason for the eclipse of Salic laws, Roman laws, and the capitularies

I have already given the reasons for the loss of the authority of Salic laws, Roman laws, and the capitularies; I shall add that the great extension of the proof by combat was the principal cause of it.

Salic laws, which did not admit that usage, more or less declined; Roman laws, which did not admit it either, likewise perished. One thought only of giving form to the law of judicial combat and of making a good jurisprudence from it. The provisions of the capitularies likewise became useless. Thus many laws lost their authority, and no one can point to the moment when they lost it; they were forgotten, and one finds no others that took their place.

Such a nation had no need of written laws, and its written laws were quite easily eclipsed.

Was there some dispute between two parties? Combat was ordered. For that there did not have to be much competence.

All civil and criminal actions come down to deeds. It is over these deeds that one fought, and it was not only the ground of the suit that was judged by combat, but also the circumstances and the interlocutory judgments, according to Beaumanoir,[114] who gives examples of them.

I find that in the beginning of the reign of the Capetians, jurisprudence was entirely in the proceedings; all was governed by the point of honor. If one had not obeyed the judge, the judge would pursue the offense. At Bourges,[115] if the provost had summoned someone and he did not come, the former would say, "I sent for you; you scorned to come; give me satisfaction for your scorn," and they fought. Louis the Fat reformed this custom.[116]

Judicial combat was in use in Orleans in all the claims concerning debts.[117] Louis the Young declared that this custom would apply only

[114] [Beaumanoir, *Coûtumes de Beauvaisis*] chap. 61, pp. 309–310 [#1718–1725].

[115] Charter of Louis le Gros, 1145 [actually Louis-le-Jeune (Louis VII), *Recueil général des anciennes lois françaises*, #39; 1, 148 – no text – see Laurière, *Ordonnances de rois de France de la troisième race*, 1, 9–11; 1723 edn].

[116] Ibid. [Louis-le-Jeune (Louis VII), *Recueil Général des Anciennes Lois Françaises*, #39; 1, 148 – no text – see Laurière, *Ordonnances de rois de France de la troisième race*, 1, 9–11; 1723 edn.]

[117] Charter of Louis-le-Jeune, 1168 [*Recueil général des anciennes lois françaises*, #54; 1, 162 –

when the claim exceeded five sous. This ordinance was a local law, for in the time of Saint Louis,[118] it was enough that the value be more than twelve deniers. Beaumanoir had heard a lord of the law told that, formerly, in France, there had been, in suits, the bad custom of hiring for a certain time a champion to fight.[119] The use of judicial combat had to have been prodigiously extensive at that time.

– no text – see Laurière, *Ordonnances de rois de France de la troisième race*, 1, 15–17; 1723 edn].

[118] See Beaumanoir [*Coûtumes de Beauvaisis*], chap. 63, p. 325 [#1818].

[119] See [Beaumanoir] *Coûtumes de Beauvaisis*, chap. 38, p. 203 [#1137].

CHAPTER 20
The origin of the point of honor

One finds enigmas in the codes of laws of the barbarians. The law of the Frisians gives only a half-sou in settlement to the one who has been hit with a staff,[120] and for the slightest wound, it gives more. Under Salic law, if one freeborn man hit another three times, he paid three sous; if he drew blood, he was punished as if he had wounded him with a sword, and he paid fifteen sous: the penalty was measured by the size of the wounds. The law of the Lombards established different settlements for one, two, three, or four blows.[121] Today a single blow is worth the same as a hundred thousand.

The constitution of Charlemagne, inserted into the law of the Lombards, wants those to whom duelling is permitted to fight with a staff.[122] Perhaps this was a way of getting around the clergy; as the usage of combat extended, perhaps, one wanted to make it less bloody. The capitulary of Louis the Pious[123] gives the choice of fighting with a staff or with arms. Later only serfs fought with a staff.[124]

Already I see arising and forming the specific articles of our point of honor. The accuser began by declaring before the judge that a certain

[120] *Lex Frisionum. Additio sapientum. Wulemarus*, tit. 5 [5 (4)].

[121] [*Leges Langobardorum*], bk. 1, tit. 6, para. 3 [Roth. 43].

[122] [*Leges Langobardorum*] bk. 2, tit. 5 [55], para. 23 [Kar. 65 (pap.)].

[123] Added to the Salic law, in the year 819 *Capitula addita ad legem Salica 819* [*Capitularia Regum Francorum* 136.10].

[124] See Beaumanoir [*Coûtumes de Beauvaisis*], chap. 64, p. 323 [#1829].

person had committed a certain act, and the accused would reply that the accuser had lied about it;[125] at this, the judge would order the duel. The maxim became established that when one was accused of lying, there had to be combat.

When a man had declared that he would fight, he could not later renounce the declaration; and if he did, he was condemned to a penalty.[126] From this followed the rule that, when a man was committed by his word, honor did not permit him to retract it.

Gentlemen fought each other on horseback with arms;[127] villeins fought one another on foot and with a staff.[128] From this it followed that a staff was the instrument of flagrant insult[129] because a man who was beaten with one had been treated like a villein.

Only villeins fought with the face exposed;[130] they were thus the only ones who could be hit in the face. A slap became an insult that had to be cleansed with blood, because a man who had received it had been treated as a villein.

The German peoples were no less sensitive than we ourselves about the point of honor; indeed they were more so. Thus the most distant relatives had a lively concern about insults, and all their codes are founded on this. The law of the Lombards wants the one who goes with his people to beat a man who is not on his guard in order to cover him with shame and ridicule to pay half the settlement that he would have owed if he had killed him[131] and to pay three-quarters of the same settlement if he binds him up for this same motive.[132]

Let us say, therefore, that our fathers were extremely sensitive to affronts, but that affronts of a special kind such as receiving blows from a certain instrument on a certain part of the body in a certain way were not yet known to them. All of this was included in the affront of being

[125] Ibid. [Beaumanoir, *Coûtumes de Beauvaisis*, chap. 64, p. 329 [#1839.]

[126] See Beaumanoir [*Coûtumes de Beauvaisis*], chap. 3, pp. 25 and 329 [#109, #1836–1838].

[127] See for the weapons of the combatants Beaumanoir [*Coûtumes de Beauvaisis*], chap. 61, p. 308 [#1714], chap. 64, p. 328 [#1830].

[128] Ibid. [Beaumanoir, *Coûtumes de Beauvaisis*], chap. 64, p. 328 [#1830]; see also the charters of Saint Aubin of Anjou, reported by [Auguste] Galland [*Du franc-aleu et origine des droits seigneuriaux, avec les lois données au pays d'Albigeois*], p. 263 [chap. 17, p. 295; 1637 edn].

[129] Among the Romans, it was not an infamy to be struck by a staff [*Corpus Juris Civilis, Digest* 3.2.22] *de his qui notantur infamia.*

[130] They had only the shield and the staff. Beaumanoir [*Coûtumes de Beauvaisis*], chap. 64, p. 328 [#1830].

[131] [*Leges Langobardorum*] bk. 1, tit. 6, para. 1 [Roth. 41].

[132] Ibid. [*Leges Langobardorum*], tit. 9, para. 2 [Roth. 42].

beaten, and, in this case, the flagrancy of the outrage was measured by the magnitude of the violation.

CHAPTER 21

New reflection on the point of honor among the Germans

"Among the Germans," says Tacitus,[133] "it was a great infamy to leave one's buckler behind in combat, and several killed themselves after this misfortune." Thus the old Salic law gives fifteen sous in settlement to the one to whom it was said as an insult that he had left his buckler behind.[134]

When Charlemagne corrected the Salic law,[135] he established only three sous in settlement for this case. One cannot suspect this prince of wanting to weaken military discipline; it is clear that this change came from a change in arms and many usages owe their origin to this change in arms.

[133] [Tacitus] *Germania* [6].
[134] In the *Pactus legis Salicae* [30.6].
[135] We have the earlier law, and the one which this prince corrected.

CHAPTER 22

On the mores relative to combat

Our connection with women is founded on the happiness attached to the pleasures of the senses, on the charm of loving and being loved, and also on the desire to please them because they are quite enlightened judges of a part of the things that constitute personal merit. This general desire to please produces a gallantry which is not love, but the delicate, flimsy, and perpetual illusion of love.

According to the different circumstances of each nation and each century, love is inclined more to one of these three things than to the other two. Now I say that at the time of our combats, the spirit of gallantry must have been in force.

I find, in the law of the Lombards,[136] that, if one of the two champions carried magical herbs, the judge had him put them away and made him swear that he had no others. This law can have been founded only on common opinion; fear, which has been said to have invented so many things, causes such illusions to be imagined. Because, in single combat, the champions were fully armed and heavy weapons, both offensive and defensive, of a certain quality and a certain strength gave infinite advantages, the opinion that certain combatants had magical weapons had to have moved many people.

From this was born the marvelous system of chivalry. All spirits were open to these ideas. In the romances one saw knights-errant, necromancers, fairies, winged or intelligent horses, invisible or invulnerable men, magicians concerned with the birth or education of great personages, and enchanted or disenchanted palaces; in our world one saw a new world, and the ordinary course of nature was left only for common men.

Knights-errant, always armed, in a part of the world full of castles, fortresses, and brigands, found honor by punishing injustice and defending weakness. From this too came a gallantry founded on the idea in our romances of love joined with that of strength and protection.

Thus gallantry was born when one imagined extraordinary men who, upon seeing virtue joined to beauty and weakness in the same person, were led to expose themselves to danger for her sake and to please her in all the ordinary actions of life.

Our romances of chivalry flattered this desire to please and gave to a part of Europe that spirit of gallantry that one can say was little known to the ancients.

The prodigious luxury of Rome when it was immense flattered the idea of the pleasures of the senses. A certain idea of tranquility in the Greek countryside caused the Greeks to describe the feelings of love.[137] The idea of knights-errant, protectors of the virtue and beauty of women, led to the idea of gallantry.

This spirit was perpetuated by the usage of tournaments, which, bringing together the rights of valor and love, again gave great importance to gallantry.

[136] [*Leges Langobardorum*] bk. 2, tit. 55, para. 11 [Roth 368].

[137] One can see the Greek romances as told in the Middle Ages.

CHAPTER 23
On the jurisprudence of judicial combat

One will perhaps be curious to see the monstrous usage of judicial combat reduced to principles and to find the body of so singular a jurisprudence. Men who are fundamentally reasonable place even their prejudices under rules. Nothing was more contrary to common sense than judicial combat, but once this point was granted, it was executed with a certain prudence.

In order to grasp the jurisprudence of those times, one must read attentively the regulations of Saint Louis, who made such great changes in the judicial order. Defontaines was a contemporary of that prince; Beaumanoir wrote after him;[138] the others have lived since his time. Therefore, we must seek the former practice in the corrections that were made in it.

[138] In 1283.

CHAPTER 24
Regulations established in judicial combat

When there were several accusers,[139] they had to agree in order for the suit to be prosecuted by a single one, and if they could not concur, the one before whom the plea was brought named one of them to prosecute the quarrel.

When a gentleman challenged[g] a villein,[140] he had to present himself on foot with shield and staff, and if he came on horseback and armed as a gentleman, his horse and arms were taken from him; he was left only his shirt and was obliged to fight the villein in this state.

[139] Beaumanoir [*Coûtumes de Beauvaisis*], chap. 6, pp. 40–41 [#213–215].
[140] Ibid. [Beaumanoir, *Coûtumes de Beauvaisis*], chap. 64, p. 328 [#1829–1830].

[g] In the remainder of this chapter Montesquieu traces the development of the practice of appealing the judgments of a court from the feudal usage of judicial combat. In French, the verb *appeler* embraces both "challenge" and "appeal," and has thus been translated as the context requires, although there is no lexical distinction in Montesquieu's text.

Before the combat, justice required three bans to be proclaimed.[141] With the one, the relatives of the parties were ordered to withdraw; with the other, the people were warned to keep silent; with the third, aiding one of the parties was forbidden under heavy penalties, even death, if by this aid one of the combatants had been vanquished.

The men charged with justice guarded the enclosure,[142] and in case the parties spoke of peace, careful attention was paid to the actual position of each at that moment, so that they could be returned to the same places if peace was not made.[143]

When gages were received for a crime or for false judgment, peace could not be made without the consent of the lord, and when one of the parties was vanquished, there could no longer be peace except by the vow of the count;[144] this is related to our letters of pardon.

But, if the crime were capital and if the lord, corrupted by presents, consented to peace, he paid a fine of sixty pounds, and his right to have the malefactor punished devolved on the count.[145]

There were many people who were not in a position to offer or accept combat. They were permitted to take a champion when cause was shown, and the champion had his hand cut off if he lost, so that he would have the greatest interest in defending his party.[146]

When in the last century laws were made making duels capital crimes, perhaps it would have been enough to remove from one of the combatants his capacity to fight by the loss of a hand, as there is usually nothing sadder for a man than to survive the loss of his character.

When in a capital crime[147] combat was waged by champions, the parties were put where they could not see the battle; each was bound with the cord that was to serve for his punishment if his champion were beaten.

The one who was overcome in combat did not always lose the

[141] Beaumanoir [*Coûtumes de Beauvaisis*], ibid., p. 330 [#1842].
[142] Ibid. [Beaumanoir, *Coûtumes de Beauvaisis* #1843].
[143] Ibid. [Beaumanoir, *Coûtumes de Beauvaisis* #1844].
[144] The important vassals had particular rights.
[145] Beaumanoir [*Coûtumes de Beauvaisis*], chap. 64, p. 330 [#1847–1848] says "He would lose his justice." These words, in the writers of those times, do not have a generalized meaning, but one restricted to the law-suit in question: [Pierre] de Fontaines [*Le Conseil*], chap. 21, art. 29 [chap. 21, para. 22, pp. 247–248; 1846 edn].
[146] This usage, which can be found in the capitularies, still existed at the time of Beaumanoir; see [*Coûtumes de Beauvaisis*] chap. 61, p. 315 [#1764].
[147] Beaumanoir [*Coûtumes de Beauvaisis*], chap. 64, p. 330 [#1841].

contested thing. If, for example, one fought about an interlocutory judgment, one lost only the interlocutory judgment.[148]

[148] Ibid. [Beaumanoir, *Coûtumes de Beauvaisis*], chap. 61, p. 309 [#1712].

CHAPTER 25

On the limits put to the usage of judicial combat

When battle gages had been received for a civil suit of small importance, the lord obliged the parties to take them back.

If a deed were well known,[149] for example, if a man had been killed in the middle of the market place, neither proof by witnesses nor proof by combat was ordered; the judge based his pronouncement on public knowledge of the deed.

When, in the lord's court, one had often judged in the same way and the usage thus was known,[150] the lord refused to let the parties engage in combat, so that customs would not be changed by conflicting outcomes of combat.

One could ask for combat only for oneself or for someone of one's lineage or for one's leige-lord.[151]

When the accused was absolved,[152] another relative could not demand combat; otherwise suits would never have ended.

If relatives were seeking to avenge the death of a man who then happened to reappear, it could no longer be a matter for combat; it was the same case if, because of a manifest absence, the deed were found to be impossible.[153]

If a man who was killed[154] had, before dying, exonerated the accused and named another, one did not proceed to combat, but if he named no one, his declaration was regarded only as a pardon for his death; the

[149] Beaumanoir [*Coûtumes de Beauvaisis*], chap. 61, p. 308 [#1710]. Ibid., chap. 43, p. 239 [#1812].

[150] Ibid. [Beaumanoir, *Coûtumes de Beauvaisis*], chap. 61, p. 314 [#1758]; see also [Pierre] de Fontaines [*Le Conseil*], chap. 22, art. 24 [chap. 22, para. 31, pp. 311–312; 1846 edn].

[151] Beaumanoir [*Coûtumes de Beauvaisis*], chap. 63, p. 322, #1797].

[152] Ibid. [Beaumanoir, *Coûtumes de Beauvaisis*, #1798].

[153] Ibid. [Beaumanoir, *Coûtumes de Beauvaisis*, #1803–1804].

[154] Ibid. [Beaumanoir, *Coûtumes de Beauvaisis*], p. 323 [#1807].

prosecution continued, and among gentlemen war could even be waged.

When there was such a war and one of the relatives gave or accepted battle gages, the right to make war ceased; the parties were considered to want to follow the ordinary course of justice, and the party that continued the war was condemned to make good the damages.

Thus the advantage of the practice of judicial combat was that it could change a general quarrel into an individual quarrel, return strength to the tribunals, and restore to the civil state those who had been governed until then only by the right of nations.

As an infinity of wise things are pursued in a very foolish way, there are also foolish things conducted in a very wise way.

When a man who was challenged for a crime[155] showed clearly that it was the challenger himself who had committed it, there were not battle gages, for no guilty man would fail to prefer uncertain combat to certain punishment.

There was no combat in suits that were decided by arbiters or by ecclesiastical courts;[156] nor was there any when women's dowries were in question.

Women, says Beaumanoir, *cannot fight*. If a woman challenged someone without naming her champion, battle gages were not accepted. A woman had also to be authorized by her baron,[157] that is, her husband, in order to challenge, but she could be challenged without this authority.

If the challenger or the one who was challenged was under fifteen years of age,[158] there was no combat. One could, however, order it in the business of wards when the guardian or the one with the bailiffry wanted to run the risk of this procedure.

It seems to me that these were the cases in which a serf was permitted to engage in combat. He fought against another serf; he fought against a free person, and even against a gentleman, if he were challenged; but if the serf challenged the free person,[159] the latter could refuse combat; and the serf's lord even had the right to withdraw him from the court.

[155] Ibid. Beaumanoir [*Coûtumes de Beauvaisis*], chap. 63, p. 324 [#1812].

[156] Ibid. [Beaumanoir, *Coûtumes de Beauvaisis*], p. 325 [#1818].

[157] Ibid. [Beaumanoir, *Coûtumes de Beauvaisis*, #1796].

[158] Beaumanoir [*Coûtumes de Beauvaisis*], p. 323 [#1810]. See also what I have said bk. 18 [above].

[159] Ibid. [Beaumanoir, *Coûtumes de Beauvaisis*], chap. 63, p. 322 [#1799].

The serf could, by a charter of the lord[160] or by usage, engage in combat with all free persons,[h] and the church claimed this same right for its serfs[161] as a mark of respect for itself.[162]

160 [Pierre] de Fontaines [*Le Conseil*], chap. 22, art. 7 [chap. 22, para. 16, pp. 298–299; 1846 edn].
161 "They have the liberty to engage in combat and to give evidence" [L.]. Charter of Louis le Gros, 1118 [*Recueil général des anciennes lois françaises. Capétiens*, #28, 1, 135].
162 Ibid. [Charter of Louis le Gros, 1118, *Recueil général des anciennes lois françaises. Capétiens*, #28, 1, 135].

h *personnes franches*.

CHAPTER 26

On judicial combat between one of the parties and one of the witnesses

Beaumanoir[163] says that a man who saw that one witness was going to submit a deposition against him could avoid the second witness by telling the judges[i] that the opposing party had produced a false and libelous witness,[164] and if the witness wanted to sustain the quarrel, he gave battle gages. It was no longer a question of a hearing for, if the witness were defeated, it would be decided that the other party lost his suit.[j]

The second witness could not be allowed to swear, for if he pronounced his testimony the business would end with the deposition of the two witnesses. But, by checking the second, the deposition of the first became useless.

As the second witness was thus rejected, the other party could not have others heard, and he lost his suit, but in case there were no battle gages[165] one could produce other witnesses.

163 [Beaumanoir, *Coûtumes de Beauvaisis*] chap. 61, p. 315 [#1762–1765].
164 "They must be asked, before they take any oath, for whom they want to testify; for the accusation of false testimony rests on this" [O.F.]. Beaumanoir [*Coûtumes de Beauvaisis*], chap. 39, p. 218 [#1222]. [M.'s text differs slightly from the modern edition; the exact meaning of the Old French is uncertain to us.]
165 Beaumanoir [*Coûtumes de Beauvaisis*], chap. 61, p. 316 [#1766–1768].

i *juges*. See 11.6 (note [a], bk. 11).
j Here Montesquieu begins to use the more precise word for a law-suit, *procès*; see note [c], bk. 2.

Beaumanoir says that the witness could tell the other party before making his deposition: "I do not wish to fight for your quarrel or to enter a plea of my own, but if you want to protect me, I shall willingly tell the truth."[166] The other party would be obliged to combat for the witness, and if he were defeated, he did not lose his cause,[167] but the witness was rejected.

I believe this was a modification of the old custom; what makes me think this is that the usage of challenging witnesses was established without any restrictions in the law of the Bavarians[168] and in that of the Burgundians.[169]

I have already spoken of the constitution of Gundobad, against which Agobard[170] and Saint Avitus[171] so expostulated. "When the accused," says this prince, "presents witnesses to swear that he did not commit this crime, the accuser can challenge one of the witnesses to engage in combat, for it is very just for the one who has offered to swear and who has declared that he knew the truth to make no difficulty over engaging in combat to maintain it." This king left the witnesses no subterfuge for avoiding combat.

166 Beaumanoir [*Coûtumes de Beauvaisis*], chap. 6, pp. 39–40 [#212].

167 But if the combat were done by means of champions, the conquered champion had his hand cut off.

168 [*Lex Baiuwariorum*] tit. 16, para. 2 [17.2].

169 [*Leges Burgundionum*] tit. 45 [45].

170 Letter to Louis the Pious [Saint Agobard, *Liber adversus legem Gundobadi*, Migne PL 104; *MGH* 3].

171 *The Life of Saint Avit* [*Acta sanctorum, De s. Avito Episcopo Viennensi in Gallia*; Februarii, tomus primus. 4, 669–670; 1863 edn].

CHAPTER 27

On judicial combat between a party and one of the lord's peers. Challenge of false judgment

As the nature of the decision by combat was to terminate the business forever and was not compatible with a new judgment and new prosecutions,[172] appeal as established by Roman laws and canonical

172 "For at court, where one goes to sustain the challenge to the gages, if battle is done, the quarrel is ended, so that there is no cause for further challenges" [O.F.]. Beaumanoir [*Coûtumes de Beauvaisis*], chap. 2, p. 22 [#93].

laws, that is, appeal to a higher tribunal to rectify the judgment of the other, was unknown in France.

A warrior nation that was governed solely by the point of honor did not know this form of procedure and, even following the same spirit, took measures against judges[k] that it could have used against the parties.[173]

In this nation, the appeal was a challenge to armed combat,[l] which had to end in blood, and not that invitation to a written quarrel known only later.

Thus Saint Louis said in his *Establishments*[174] that appeal is felonious and iniquitous. Thus Beaumanoir tells us that, if a man wanted to complain of some offense committed against him by his lord,[175] he had to denounce the lord and leave his fief; after which he challenged him before his overlord and offered battle gages. The lord likewise renounced the homage if he challenged his man before the count.

To challenge one's lord for false judgment was to say that his judgment had been falsely and wickedly rendered; now, to put forward such words against one's lord was to commit a kind of felony.

Thus, instead of making a challenge for false judgment against the lord who established and regulated the tribunal, one challenged the peers who formed the tribunal itself; one thus avoided a felony; one insulted only one's peers, to whom one could always give satisfaction for the insult.

One exposed oneself greatly by declaring false the judgment of the peers.[176] If one waited for the judgment to be made and pronounced, one was obliged to enter into combat with all the peers when they offered to make good their judgment.[177] If one made the challenge before all the judges had given their opinion, one had to enter into combat with all those who agreed with the same opinion.[178] To avoid this danger, one begged the lord to order each peer to give his opinion

[173] Ibid. [Beaumanoir, *Coûtumes de Beauvaisis*], chap. 61, p. 312 [#1752] and chap. 67, p. 338 [#1894].

[174] [*Les Etablissements de Saint Louis*] bk. 2, chap. 15 [2.16, p. 383; 1881 edn].

[175] Beaumanoir [*Coûtumes de Beauvaisis*], chap. 61, pp. 310–311 [#1735–1740]; and chap. 67, p. 337 [#1888].

[176] Beaumanoir [*Coûtumes de Beauvaisis*], chap. 61, p. 313 [#1755].

[177] Ibid. [Beaumanoir, *Coûtumes de Beauvaisis*, chap. 61], p. 314 [#1752–1755].

[178] Who has agreed on the judgment.

---

[k] *juges*. See note [a], bk. 11.

[l] Here Montesquieu clearly defines the sense of *appel* as "challenge."

aloud, and when the first had pronounced and the second was about to do the same, one said that he was false, wicked, and libelous, and then it was only against him that one had to fight.[179]

Defontaines[180] wanted one to let three judges pronounce before declaring them false,[181] and he does not say that all three had to be fought and even less that there were cases in which one had to enter into combat with all those who had declared their opinion. These differences come from the fact that in those times scarcely any usages were precisely the same. Beaumanoir gave an account of what happened in the county of Clermont; Defontaines, of what was practiced in Vermandois.

When one of the peers or men with fiefs had declared that he would support the judgment,[182] the judge had the battle gages given and also took a surety from the challenger that he would support his challenge. But the peer who was challenged did not give sureties because he was the lord's man and had to defend the challenge or pay the lord a fine of sixty pounds.

If the one who challenged did not prove that the judgment was wrong, he paid the lord a fine of sixty pounds,[183] the same fine to the peer whom he had challenged,[184] and as much to each one of those who had openly consented to the judgment.

When a man strongly suspected of a crime meriting death was seized and condemned, he could not challenge for false judgment,[185] for he would have challenged in any case, either to prolong his life or to make peace.

If someone said that the judgment was false and wrong[186] and did not offer to prove it so, that is, to enter into combat, he was condemned for his vile words to a fine of ten sous if he were a gentleman and to five sous if he were a serf.

[179] Beaumanoir [*Coûtumes de Beauvaisis*], chap. 61, p. 314 [#1755].

[180] [Pierre de Fontaines, *Le Conseil*] chap. 22, arts. 1, 10, and 11 [chap. 22, para. 1, 17, 18; pp. 285–286, 299–300; 1846 edn]. He says only that each one was paid a fine.

[181] To appeal against false judgment.

[182] Beaumanoir [*Coûtumes de Beauvaisis*], chap. 61, p. 314 [#1755].

[183] Idem. Ibid. [Pierre] de Fontaines [*Le Conseil*], chap. 22, art. 9 [chap. 22, para. 16, pp. 298–299; 1846 edn].

[184] [Pierre] de Fontaines, ibid. [*Le Conseil*, chap. 22, para. 16, pp. 298–299; 1846 edn].

[185] Beaumanoir [*Coûtumes de Beauvaisis*], chap. 61, p. 316 [#1769]; and [Pierre] de Fontaines [*Le Conseil*], chap. 22, art. 21 [chap. 22, para. 28, pp. 308–309; 1846 edn].

[186] Beaumanoir [*Coûtumes de Beauvaisis*], chap. 61, p. 314 [#1759].

Judges or peers who were defeated[187] were to lose neither their lives nor their limbs, but a challenger who was defeated was punished with death when the business involved a capital offense.[188]

This way of challenging the men with fiefs for false judgment avoided a challenge to the lord himself. But if the lord had no peers[189] or not enough of them, he could at his own expense borrow peers from his overlord,[190] but these peers were not obliged to swear if they did not want to; they could declare that they had come only to give counsel, and in this particular case,[191] as the lord judged and pronounced the judgment himself, if one challenged him for false judgment, it was for him to sustain the challenge.

If the lord were so poor[192] that he was not in a position to take the peers of his overlord, or if he neglected to ask him for them, or if the latter refused to give them to him, as the lord could not judge alone and no one was obliged to plead before a tribunal where a judgment could not be made, the business was carried to the court of the overlord.

I believe that this was one of the great causes of the separation of the justice from the fief, from which the rule of French jurists was formed: *the fief is one thing; the justice is another*. For as an infinity of men with fiefs had no men under them, they were not in a position to hold their own court; all the business was carried to the court of their overlord; they lost the right of justice because they had neither the power nor the will to claim it.

All the judges who had taken part in the judgment[193] had to be present when it was rendered so that they could attend and say "aye" to the one who, wanting to declare the judgment false, asked them if they

[187] [Pierre] de Fontaines [*Le Conseil*], chap. 22, art. 7 [chap. 22, para. 14, pp. 295–297; 1846 edn].

[188] See [Pierre] de Fontaines [*Le Conseil*], chap. 21, arts. 11 and 12 and following [chap. 22, paras. 14–15, p. 288; 1846 edn], who distinguishes among the cases in which the one who declared another false lost his life, the contested object, or only the interlocutory judgment.

[189] Beaumanoir [*Coûtumes de Beauvaisis*], chap. 62, p. 322 [#1793]. [Pierre] de Fontaines [*Le Conseil*], chap. 22, art. 3 [chap. 21, para. 10, pp. 232–237; 1846 edn].

[190] The count was not obliged to lend them. Beaumanoir [*Coûtumes de Beauvaisis*], chap. 67, p. 337 [#1884].

[191] None can render judgment in his court, says Beaumanoir [*Coûtumes de Beauvaisis*], chap. 67, pp. 336–337 [#1883, 1884, 1888].

[192] Ibid. [Beaumanoir, *Coûtumes de Beauvaisis*], chap. 62, p. 322 [#1793].

[193] [Pierre] de Fontaines [*Le Conseil*], chap. 21, arts. 27–28 [chap. 21, paras. 20–21; pp. 246–267; 1846 edn].

concurred, for, Defontaines says,[194] "it is a business of courtesy and loyalty and from it there is neither flight nor postponement." I believe that this way of thinking gave rise to the usage still followed today in England that all the jurors must be of one opinion in order to condemn a man to death.

Therefore, one had to declare oneself in favor of the opinion of the greater party, and if there were a division, one pronounced, in the case of crime, for the accused; in a case of debts, for the debtor; in a case of inheritance, for the defendant.

A peer, says Defontaines,[195] could not say that he would not judge if there were only four,[196] or if they were all not there, or if the wisest were not there; it was as if he had said, in the fray, that he would not help his lord because he had only a part of his men with him. But it was for the lord to do honor to his court and pick his most valiant and wisest men. I mention this in order to give a sense of the duty of the vassals to enter into combat and to judge; this duty was even such that to judge was to enter into combat.

A lord who pleaded before his court against his vassal[197] and who was condemned there could challenge one of his men for false judgment. But, because of the respect the latter owed to his lord for fealty given and because of the benevolence the lord owed his vassal for fealty received, a distinction was made; either the lord said in general that the judgment was false and wrong,[198] or he imputed a personal breach of trust to his man.[199] In the first case he offended his own court, and in a way himself, and there could be no battle gages; in the second case there were gages because he attacked the honor of his vassal, and the one of the two who was defeated lost his life and goods in order to keep the public peace.

This distinction, necessary in this particular case, was extended. Beaumanoir says that, when the one who challenged for false judgment

[194] Ibid. [Pierre de Fontaines, *Le Conseil*], art. 28 [chap. 21, para. 21; pp. 246–247; 1846 edn].

[195] [Pierre de Fontaines, *Le Conseil*] chap. 21, art. 37 [chap. 21, para. 30; pp. 257–258; 1846 edn].

[196] One had to have at least this number: [Pierre] de Fontaines [*Le Conseil*], chap. 21, art. 36 [chap. 21, para. 29; pp. 255–256; 1846 edn].

[197] See Beaumanoir [*Coûtumes de Beauvaisis*], chap. 77, p. 337 [#1888].

[198] "Which judgment is false and bad." Ibid. [Beaumanoir, *Coûtumes de Beauvaisis*], chap. 67, p. 337 [#1888].

[199] "You have made a false and bad judgment like the bad man you are, either to scheme or to keep a promise" [O.F.]. Beaumanoir [*Coûtumes de Beauvaisis*], chap. 67, p. 337 [#1888].

used personal imputation to attack one of the men, there was a battle, but that if he attacked only the judgment, the peer who was challenged was free to have the business judged by battle or by right.[200] But, as the spirit that reigned in the time of Beaumanoir restricted the usage of judicial combat, and as the liberty given to the challenged peer to defend the judgment by combat or not is contrary equally to the ideas of honor established at that time and to the engagement one had to one's lord to defend his court, I believe that Beaumanoir's distinction was new to jurisprudence among the French.

I do not say that all challenges for false judgment were decided by battle; this challenge was like all the others. One is reminded of the exceptions I have mentioned in Chapter 25. Here, it was the tribunal of the overlord which had to see if the battle gages had to be taken back or not.

One could not declare false the judgments made in the king's court for, as the king had no equal, no one could challenge him and, as the king had no superior, no one could appeal from his court.

This fundamental law, which was necessary as a political law, further lessened, as a civil law, the abuses of judicial practice of that time. When a lord feared that someone might declare false the judgment of his court[201] or saw that someone was presenting himself in order to do so, if it were a privilege in that justice[m] that it not be declared false, he could ask for the men of the king's court, whose judgment could not be declared false; and King Philip, says Defontaines,[202] sent his whole council to judge a business in the court of the abbot of Corbie.

But if the lord could not have the king's judges, he could put his court into the king's court if he were directly answerable to him; and if there were intermediate lords, he addressed himself to his overlord, going from lord to lord up to the king.

Thus, although at that time there was neither the practice nor even the idea of the appeals of today, one had recourse to the king, who was ever the source from which all the rivers flowed and the sea to which they returned.

[200] Ibid. [Beaumanoir, *Coûtumes de Beauvaisis*, chap. 67], pp. 337–338 [#1889].
[201] [Pierre] de Fontaines [*Le Conseil*], chap. 22, art. 14 [chap. 22, para. 21, pp. 301–302; 1846 edn].
[202] Ibid. [Pierre de Fontaines, *Le Conseil*, chap. 22, para. 21, pp. 301–302; 1846 edn.]

[m] On this privilege, *bien de la justice*, see 28.29.

CHAPTER 28

On the challenge for default of right

One challenged for default of right when, in the court of a lord, one postponed, avoided, or refused to render justice to the parties.

Under the Carolingians, though there were several officers under a count, their persons, but not their jurisdictions, were subordinate. These officers, in their day-courts, assizes, and placita, judged in the last resort as the count himself. The whole difference was in the division of the jurisdiction; for example, the count could condemn to death and make judgments concerning liberty and the restitution of goods,[203] and the centenarius could not.

For the same reason major cases were reserved to the king;[204] they were the ones that directly involved the political order. Such were the disputes between bishops, abbots, counts, and other important men, whom the king judged along with his great vassals.[205]

Some authors have said that one appealed from the count to the king's deputy or *missus dominicus*, but this has no foundation. The count and the *missus* had jurisdictions equal to and independent of one another;[206] the whole difference lay in the fact that the *missus* held his sittings four months of the year and the count the other eight.[207]

If someone,[208] condemned in assizes,[209] asked to be rejudged and then lost again, he paid a fine of fifteen sous or was slapped fifteen times by the judges who had decided the business.

When the counts or the deputies of the king did not feel strong enough to reduce the important men to reason, they made them give a pledge that they would present themselves before the tribunal of the king;[210] this was in order to judge the business and not to rejudge it. I

[203] *Capitulare tertium anni, 812*, art. 3, Baluze edn, p. 497 [*Capitularia regum Francorum* 80.4], and of Charles the Bald [Charlemagne] added to the *Leges Langobardorum*, bk. 2, art. 3 [2.52.3; Kar. 43 (48) (pap.)].

[204] *Capitulare tertium anni, 812*, art. 2 [*Capitularia regum Francorum* 80.2].

[205] *Cum fidelibus* [*Capitulare Wormatiense, 829*]; capitulary of Louis the Pious, Baluze edn, p. 667 [*Capitularia regum Francorum* 192.6].

[206] See the capitulary of Charles the Bald [Charlemagne] added to the *Leges Langobardorum*, bk. 2, art. 3 [2.52.3; Kar. 43 (48) (pap.)].

[207] *Capitulare tertium anni, 812*, art. 8 [*Capitularia regum Francorum* 80.8].

[208] Capitulary added to the *Leges Langobardorum*, bk. 2, tit. 59 [Kar. 90 (pap.)].

[209] *Placitum*.

[210] This appears in the formulas, the charters, and the capitularies.

find in the capitulary of Metz[211] that the challenge for false judgment at the court of the king was established and that all other sorts of challenges were proscribed and punished.

If one did not acquiesce[212] in the judgment of the echevins[213] and did not lodge a complaint, one was put in prison until one had acquiesced; and if one lodged a complaint, one was led under safe conduct to the king and the business was argued before his court.

It could scarcely be a question of a challenge for default of right. For, at that time, it was far from customary to complain that counts and other people who had the right to hold assizes were not strict in holding their court; on the other hand, the complaint was that they were too strict,[214] and everything is full of ordinances that forbid counts and other officers of justice to hold more than three assizes a year. One had less to correct their negligence than to check their activity.

But when innumerable little lordships were formed and different degrees of vassalage were established, the negligence of certain vassals in holding their court gave rise to these kinds of challenges,[215] the more so because considerable fines fell on the overlord.

As the usage of judicial combat spread further, there were places, cases, and times when it was hard to assemble the peers, and when, consequently, one neglected to render justice. The challenge for default of right was introduced, and these sorts of challenges have often been remarkable points in our history because most of the wars of those times were motivated by the violation of political right, as the wars of the present time usually have the right of nations as their cause or pretext.

Beaumanoir says[216] that there never was a battle in the case of default of right; here are the reasons for this. One could not challenge the lord himself to combat because of the respect due his person; one could not challenge the peers of the lord because the matter was evident and one

[211] *Capitulare Metense, 757*, arts. 9 and 10, Baluze edition, p. 180 [*Capitularia regum Francorum* 13.6–7]; and the *Capitulare synodi Verensis, 755*, art. 29, Baluze edn, p. 175 [*Capitularia regum Francorum* 13.7]. These two capitularies were made under King Pepin.

[212] [*Capitulare secundum anni, 805*, art. 11, Baluze edition, p. 423 [*Capitularia regum Francorum* 44.8] and the law of Lothar in the *Leges Langobardorum*, bk. 2, tit. 52, art. 23 [Loth. 62 (pap.)].

[213] Officers under the count: *scabini*.

[214] See the *Leges Langobardorum*, bk. 2, tit. 52, art. 22 [Loth. 61 (pap.)].

[215] From the time of Philip Augustus, one sees appeals for default of right.

[216] [Beaumanoir, *Coûtumes de Beauvaisis*] chap. 61, p. 315 [#1761].

had only to count the days of recess or other delays: there was no judgment and one could declare false only a judgment. In the end, the wrong to the peers offended the lord as much as the party, and combat waged between a lord and his peers was not in order.

But before the tribunal of the overlord, as one proved default by means of witnesses, one could challenge the witnesses to combat,[217] and in this way one offended neither the lord nor his tribunal.

In cases where the default arose on the side of the men or peers of the lord who had deferred rendering justice or had avoided passing judgment after a period of delays had passed, the peers of the lord were challenged for default of right before the lord, and if they lost, they paid a fine to their lord.[218] He could bring no aid to his men, but on the contrary, he seized their fiefs until each of them had paid him a fine of sixty pounds.

2. When the default arose on the side of the lord, which happened when there were not enough men in his court to pass the judgment or when he had not assembled his men or had put someone in his place to assemble them, one claimed the default before the overlord; but, because of the respect due the lord, one brought a citation against the party[219] and not against the lord.

The lord asked for his court before the tribunal of the overlord, and if he won the default, the business was remanded to him and he was paid a fine of sixty pounds,[220] but if the default were proven, the penalty against him was to lose the judgment of the thing contested; the substance was judged in the tribunal of the overlord.[221] Indeed, one had claimed default only for that result.

3. If one pleaded in one's lord's court against him,[222] which happened only over business concerning the fief, after allowing all the

[217] Beaumanoir, ibid. [*Coûtumes de Beauvaisis*, #1761].

[218] [Pierre] de Fontaines [*Le Conseil*], chap. 21, art. 24 [chap. 21, para. 17, pp. 241–242; 1846 edn].

[219] Ibid. [Pierre de Fontaines, *Le Conseil*], chap. 21, art. 32 [chap. 21, para. 25, pp. 249–251; 1846 edn].

[220] Beaumanoir [*Coûtumes de Beauvaisis*], chap. 61, p. 312 [#1745].

[221] [Pierre] de Fontaines [*Le Conseil*], chap. 21, arts. 1, 29 [chap. 21, para. 22; pp. 247–248; 1846 edn].

[222] In the reign of Louis VIII, the Sire de Nèle pleaded against Jeanne, Countess of Flanders; he demanded that she be judged within forty days; and summoned her subsequently for default of right in the king's court. She responded that she would have him judged by his peers in Flanders. The king's court pronounced that he would not be sent there, and that the countess would be summoned.

delays to pass, the lord himself was summoned before good people,[223] and he was summoned by the sovereign whose permission was required. Peers did not cite him because peers could not cite their lord, but they could bring a citation on behalf of their lord.[224]

Sometimes the challenge for default of right was followed by a challenge for false judgment[225] when the lord had had the judgment rendered despite the default.

The vassal who failed in his challenge to his lord for default of right[226] was condemned to pay the lord a fine according to his will.

The people of Ghent had challenged the Count of Flanders before the King for default of right,[227] claiming he had delayed rendering them a judgment in his court. It happened that he had delayed less than was the custom of the country. The people of Ghent were remanded to him; their goods to the value of sixty thousand pounds were seized. They returned to the king's court to have the fine moderated; it was decided that the count could take this fine, and even more, if he so willed. Beaumanoir was present at these judgments.

4. With regard to the business that the lord could have against the vassal by reason of the person or the honor of the vassal, or of goods not belonging to the fief, there was no question of challenge for default of right, for one did not judge in the court of the lord but in the court of the one on whom he was dependent, for men, says Defontaines,[228] did not have the right to pass judgment on the person of their lord.

I have tried to give a clear idea of these things which are so confused and obscure in the authors of those times that, in truth, drawing them out of their chaos is to discover them.

[223] [Pierre] de Fontaines [*Le Conseil*], chap. 21, art. 34 [chap. 21, para. 27; pp. 253–254; 1846 edn].

[224] Ibid. [Pierre de Fontaines, *Le Conseil*, chap. 21], art. 9 [chap. 22, para. 3; pp. 287–288; 1846 edn].

[225] Beaumanoir [*Coûtumes de Beauvaisis*], chap. 61, p. 311 [#1739].

[226] Ibid. [Beaumanoir, *Coûtumes de Beauvaisis*, chap. 61], p. 312 [#1740]. But one who was neither a man nor a tenant of the lord paid him only a fine of sixty pounds; ibid. [#1742].

[227] Ibid. [Beaumanoir, *Coûtumes de Beauvaisis*, chap. 61], p. 318 [#1779].

[228] [Pierre de Fontaines *Le Conseil*], chap. 21, art. 35 [chap. 21, para. 28; pp. 254–255; 1846 edn].

CHAPTER 29

The age of the reign of Saint Louis

Saint Louis abolished judicial combat in the tribunals of his domains, as appears in the ordinance he made on that subject[229] and in the *Establishments*.[230]

But he did not remove it from the courts of his barons,[231] except in the case of challenge for false judgment.

One could not declare false the court of one's lord[232] without asking for judicial combat against the judges who had pronounced the judgment. But Saint Louis introduced the usage of declaring judgments false without combat,[233] a change that was a kind of revolution.

He stated that one could not declare judgments false that were rendered in the lordships of his domains because this was a crime of felony.[234] Indeed, if this was a kind of crime of felony against the lord, it was one, for stronger reasons, against the king. But he wanted one to be able to ask for redress for judgments rendered in his courts,[235] not because they were falsely or wickedly rendered but because they produced a certain prejudice.[236] He wanted one instead to be constrained to declare false the judgments of the baronial courts if one wanted to lodge a complaint about them.[237]

According to the *Establishments*, one could not declare false the judgments of the courts in the domains of the king, as has just been said. Redress had to be requested before the same tribunal, and in case the bailiff did not want to make the requisite redress, the king permitted making an appeal to his court,[238] or rather, interpreting the *Establishments* themselves, presenting him with a formal request or supplication.[239]

[229] In 1260. [*Recueil général des anciennes lois françaises. Capétiens.* #189; 1, 283–290.]
[230] [*Les Etablissements de Saint Louis*], bk. 1, chap. 2 [1.3]; 7 [1.9]; bk. 2, chap. 10, 11 [2.12, 14].
[231] As appears everywhere in *Les Etablissements*; and Beaumanoir [*Coûtumes de Beauvaisis*], chap. 61, p. 309 [#1722].
[232] That is, appeal for false judgment.
[233] *Les Etablissements de Saint Louis*, bk. 1, chap. 6 [1.7–8]; bk. 2, chap. 15 [2.16].
[234] Ibid. [*Les Etablissements de Saint Louis*], bk. 2, chap. 15 [2.16].
[235] Ibid. [*Les Etablissements de Saint Louis*], bk. 1, chap. 78 [1.85]; bk. 2, chap. 15 [2.16].
[236] *Les Etablissements de Saint Louis*, bk. 1, chap. 78 [1.85].
[237] Ibid. [*Les Etablissements de Saint Louis*], bk. 2, chap. 15 [2.16].
[238] Ibid. [*Les Etablissements de Saint Louis*], bk. 1, chap. 78 [1.85].
[239] Ibid. [*Les Etablissements de Saint Louis*], bk. 2, chap. 15 [2.16].

With regard to the judgments of the courts of the lords, Saint Louis, by permitting them to be declared false, wanted the business to be carried to the tribunal of the king or the overlord,[240] to be decided there not by combat[241] but by witnesses, following a form of procedure for which he gave rules.[242]

Thus, whether one could make the declaration of falseness, as in the lords' courts, or not, as in the courts of his domains, he established that one could challenge without running the risk of combat.

Defontaines[243] reports to us the first two examples he saw in which one had proceeded thus without judicial combat: the first, in a business judged at the court of Saint Quentin, which was in the domain of the king, and the second, in the court of Ponthieu, where the count, who was present, opposed the old jurisprudence; but these two matters of business were judged according to right.

Perhaps one will ask why, for the courts of his barons, Saint Louis ordered a way of proceeding different from the one he established in the tribunals of his domains: here is the reason. Saint Louis, enacting for the courts of his domains, was not hampered in his aims, but he had to manage carefully those lords who formerly enjoyed the prerogative that business could never be removed from their courts unless one exposed oneself to the dangers of a declaration of falseness. Saint Louis retained the usage of the declaration of falseness, but he wanted it to be possible to declare falseness without combat; that is, so that the change would be felt less, he removed the thing and let the terms continue to exist.

This was not universally accepted in the courts of the lords. Beaumanoir[244] says that in his time there were two ways of judging, the one following the *Establishment of the King* and the other following the former practice, that the lords had the right to follow either of these practices, but that when one of them was chosen for a suit, it was no longer possible to return to the other. He adds that the Count of

[240] But if one did not declare the judgments false and wanted to appeal, one was not admitted. *Les Etablissements de Saint Louis*, bk. 2, chap. 15. "The lord would have recourse to his court in the making of right" [O.F.] [2.16; p. 386; 1881 edn].

[241] Ibid. [*Les Etablissements de Saint Louis*], bk. 1, chap. 6 [1.7–8] and chap. 67 [1.74]; bk. 2, chap. 15 [2.16] and Beaumanoir [*Coûtumes de Beauvaisis*], chap. 11, p. 58 [#322].

[242] *Les Etablissements de Saint Louis*, bk. 1, chaps. 1–3 [1.1–4].

[243] [Pierre de Fontaines, *Le Conseil*] chap. 22, arts. 16 and 17 [chap. 22, paras. 23–24; pp. 303–305; 1846 edn].

[244] [Beaumanoir, *Coûtumes de Beauvaisis*] chap. 61, p. 309 [#1723].

Clermont followed the new practice,[245] whereas his vassals clung to the old one, but that he could reestablish the old one when he wanted, for otherwise he would have had less authority than his vassals.

One must know that France was then divided[246] into the countries of the domain of the king and what were called the countries of the barons, or baronies; and, if I may use the terms of the *Establishments* of Saint Louis, into the countries of obedience to the king and the countries beyond obedience to the king. When kings made ordinances for the countries in their domains, they employed only their authority, but when they made them concerning the countries of their barons also, such ordinances were made together with them, or sealed, or subscribed to, by them;[247] otherwise, the barons could accept them or not, accordingly as they appeared to them to suit the good of the places over which they were the lords, or not. The under-vassals were on the same terms with the great vassals. Now, the *Establishments* were not given with the consent of the lords, though they were enacted on things of great importance to them; thus they were accepted only by those who believed it advantageous to accept them. Robert, son of Saint Louis, admitted them in his county of Clermont, and his vassals did not believe it suitable for them to be practiced in their lands.

[245] Ibid. [Beaumanoir, *Coûtumes de Beauvaisis*, chap. 61; #1723].

[246] See Beaumanoir [*Coûtumes de Beauvaisis*], [Pierre] de Fontaines [*Le Conseil*]; and *Les Etablissements de Saint Louis*, bk. 2, chaps. 10, 11, 15 [2.11, 12, 16] and others.

[247] See the ordinances made at the beginning of the Capetien reign, in the collection of Laurière, especially those of Philip Augustus about ecclesiastical jurisdiction [*Recueil général des anciennes lois françaises, Capétiens*, #80; 1, 177–182] and those of Louis VIII about the Jews [*Recueil général des anciennes lois françaises, Capétiens*, #152; 1, 243–244]; the charters reported by [Nicolas] Brussel [*Nouvel examen de l'usage general des fiefs en France*, xxxiv–xxxvi, 1727 edn]: of special note is that of Saint Louis about the lease and repurchase of lands [*Recueil général des anciennes lois françaises, Capétiens*, #153; 1, 244–246] and the age when girls can inherit a fief, vol. 2, bk. 3, p. 35 [*Recueil général des anciennes lois françaises, Capétiens*, #161, esp. 161.9; 1, 149–151] and ibid., the ordinance of Philip Augustus, p. 7 [Brussels, *Nouvel examen du l'usage general des fiefs en France*, vii–xi; 1727 edn; [*Recueil général des anciennes lois françaises, Capétiens*, #96; 1, 188; and #112; 1, 206].

CHAPTER 30

Observations on challenges

One realizes that challenges, which were provocations to combat, had to be made on the spot. "If he leaves the court without challenging," says Beaumanoir,[248] "he loses his challenge and upholds the judgment as good." This continued even after the usage of judicial combat had been restricted.[249]

[248] [Beaumanoir, *Coûtumes de Beauvaisis*], chap. 63, p. 327 [#1826]; ibid., chap. 61, p. 312 [#1744].

[249] See [*Les Etablissements de Saint Louis*] bk. 2, chap. 15 [2.16]; the ordinance of Charles VII, of 1453 [Laurière, 14, 282; *Recueil général des anciennes lois françaises*, #213, art. 18; 9, 212].

CHAPTER 31

Continuation of the same subject

The villein could not declare the judgments of his lord's court false; we learn this from Defontaines,[250] and it is confirmed by the *Establishments*.[251] "Thus," Defontaines goes on to say,[252] "there is between you, lord, and your villein no other judge but god."

It was the usage of judicial combat that excluded villeins from being able to declare their lord's court false, and this is so true that those villeins who by charter or by usage[253] had the right to combat also had the right to declare the judgments of their lord's court false, even when the men who judged were knights,[254] and Defontaines suggests

[250] [Pierre de Fontaines, *Le Conseil*], chap. 21, arts. 21–22 [chap. 21, paras. 14, 15; p. 240; 1846 edn].

[251] [*Les Etablissements de Saint Louis*] bk. 1, chap. 136 [1.142].

[252] [Pierre de Fontaines, *Le Conseil*], chap. 2, art. 8 [chap. 21, #8, p. 225; 1846 edn].

[253] [Pierre] de Fontaines [*Le Conseil*], chap. 22, art. 7 [chap. 22, para. 14, pp. 295–296; 1846 edn]. This article and the twenty-first article of chap. 22 [chap. 22, para. 28, pp. 308–309; 1846 edn] by the same author have until now been very badly explained. De Fontaines does not set the lord's judgment in opposition to that of the knight's, for they were the same; but he sets the ordinary villein in opposition to the villein who had the privilege of combat.

[254] Knights can always be counted among the judges. [Pierre] de Fontaines [*Le Conseil*], chap. 21, art. 48 [chap. 21, para. 41; p. 263; 1846 edn].

expedients to prevent the scandal of a villein who, by declaring the judgment false, would go into combat with a knight.[255]

As the practice of judicial combat began to be abolished and the usage of the new appeals began to be introduced, it was thought unreasonable for free persons[n] to have a remedy against the injustice of their lord's court and for the villeins to have none, and the *parlement* accepted their appeals as those of free persons.[o]

[255] [Pierre de Fontaines, *Le Conseil*], chap. 22, art. 14 [chap. 22, para. 21; pp. 301–302; 1846 edn].

[n] *personnes franches.* [o] *personnes franches.*

CHAPTER 32

Continuation of the same subject

When the judgments of one's lord's court were declared false, he came in person before the overlord to defend the judgment of his court. Likewise,[256] in the case of challenge for default of right, the party cited before the overlord took his lord with him, so that if the default were not proven the lord could recover his court.

Subsequently, as what had been only two particular cases became general for all business as a result of the introduction of all sorts of appeals, it seemed extraordinary for the lord to be obliged to spend his life in tribunals other than his own and in business other than his own. Philip of Valois ordered the bailiffs alone be cited.[257] And, when the usage of appeals became still more frequent, the parties had to defend the appeal; what the judge once had done, the party now did.[258]

I have said[259] that, in the challenge for default of right, the lord lost only the right to have the business judged in his court. But, if the lord himself were attacked as a party,[260] which became frequent,[261] he paid

[256] [Pierre] de Fontaines [*Le Conseil*], chap. 21, art. 33 [chap. 21, para. 26; pp. 251–253; 1846 edn].

[257] In 1332. [*Recueil général des anciennes lois françaises*, *Valois*, #15; 4, 369–371].

[258] See the state of things in the time of [Jean] Boutillier, who lived in 1402. *Le Grand Coustumier*] *La Somme rural*, bk. 1, pp. 19, 20 [tit. 3, "Des jurisdictions," notes of L. Charondas le Caron, pp. 19–20; 1621 edn].

[259] Above, chap. 30.

[260] Beaumanoir [*Coûtumes de Beauvaisis*], chap. 61, pp. 312 and 318 [#1742–1745, #1776].

[261] Ibid. [Beaumanoir, *Coûtumes de Beauvaisis*, #1742–1745, #1776].

the king or the overlord before whom one had challenged, a fine of sixty pounds. From this came the usage, when appeals were universally accepted, of paying the fine to the lord when the sentence of one's judge was reversed: a usage that continued to exist for a long time, that was confirmed by the ordinance of Roussillon, and whose absurdity ruined it.

CHAPTER 33

Continuation of the same subject

In the practice of judicial combat, the one who declared the judgment of the court false and who challenged one of the judges could lose his trial by combat,[262] but could not win it. Indeed, the party who had a judgment in his favor was not to be deprived of it by what others did. Therefore, the one who declared a judgment false and had won still fought against the other party, not in order to know whether the judgment was good or bad, as this judgment was no longer at issue, having been abolished by the combat, but in order to decide if the claim were legitimate or not; and it is on this new point that one engaged in combat. Our way of pronouncing decisions must have come from this: *The court annuls the appeal; the court annuls the appeal and that for which the appeal was brought.* Indeed, when the one who had challenged for false judgment lost, the judgment was annulled; when he won, the judgment was annulled, and also the challenge: one had to proceed to a new judgment.

This is so true that, when the business was judged by inquests, this way of pronouncing did not apply. M. de La Roche Flavin[263] tells us that when it was first created this form could not be used by the chamber of inquests.

[262] [Pierre] de Fontaines [*Le Conseil*], chap. 21, art. 14 [chap. 22, para. 8, p. 290; 1846 edn].
[263] [Bernard de La Roche Flavin] *Des parlements de France*, bk. 1, chap. 16 [bk. 1, chap. 16, no. 1; "De la Grand Chambre"; p. 32; 1621 edn].

CHAPTER 34
How proceedings became secret

Duels had introduced a form for public proceedings; the attack and the defense were equally known. "Witnesses," says Beaumanoir,[264] "should give their testimony before everyone."

Boutillier's commentator[p] says he had learned from the former practitioners and from some old hand-written trials that formerly in France criminal trials were held publicly in a form scarcely different from the public judgments of the Romans. This was bound up with the ignorance of writing, common in those times. The usage of writing arrests ideas and can establish secrecy, but when one does not have this usage, only public knowledge of the proceedings can fix these same ideas.

And, as there could be uncertainty about what was judged by men or pleaded before them,[265] one could recall the memory of it every time one held court by that which was called the proceedings *of record*,[266] and, in this case, one was not permitted to challenge the witnesses to combat, for the business would never have come to an end.

Later, a form of secret proceedings was introduced. All had been public; interrogations, investigations, verification, confrontation, and conclusions by the public party, all became hidden, and this is the usage today. The first form of procedures suited the government of that time as the new one was proper to the government that was later established.

Boutillier's commentator dates the time of the change to the ordinance of 1539. I believe that it happened gradually and that it passed from lordship to lordship, as the lords gave up the former practice of judging and the one drawn from the *Establishments* of Saint Louis was improved. Indeed, Beaumanoir says that witnesses were heard publicly in cases in which one could give battle gages;[267] in others, they were heard in secret and their depositions were taken in

[264] [Beaumanoir, *Coûtumes de Beauvaisis*] chap. 61, p. 315 [#1761–1762].

[265] As Beaumanoir says [*Coûtumes de Beauvaisis*], chap. 39, p. 209 [#1150].

[266] One took witnesses for what had already occurred, and for what had already been said or ordered by justice.

[267] [Beaumanoir, *Coûtumes de Beauvaisis*] chap. 39, p. 218 [#1222].

[p] Louis Charondas le Caron.

writing. Proceedings thus became secret when there were no longer battle gages.

CHAPTER 35
On costs

Formerly in France no one was condemned to pay the costs in lay courts.[268] The losing party was punished enough by the fines payable to the lord and his peers. The result of proceeding by judicial combat was that, in crimes, the party who was defeated and lost his life and goods was punished as much as he could be; and in other cases of judicial combat, fines were sometimes fixed, sometimes dependent on the will of the lord, which made the outcomes of trials much feared. It was the same in business that was decided only by combat. As it was the lord who had the principal profits, it was also he who paid the principal costs, either to assemble his peers or to put them in a position to proceed to judgment. Moreover, as business was concluded right there and almost always instantly and without the infinite pieces of writing one later saw, it was not necessary to award costs to the parties.

The usage of appeal led naturally to the usage of awarding costs. Thus Defontaines says[269] that when one appealed by written law, that is, when the new laws of Saint Louis were introduced, costs were awarded but that in the ordinary usage, which did not permit appeal without a declaration of falsity, there were none awarded and one obtained only a fine and the possession for a year and a day of the contested thing if the business were remanded to the lord.

But when the new opportunities for appealing increased the number of appeals;[270] when, by the frequent usage of appeals from one tribunal to another, the parties were constantly removed from the place where they lived; when the new art of proceedings multiplied and made the

[268] [Pierre] de Fontaines, *Le Conseil*, chap. 22, arts. 3 and 8 [chap. 21, para. 10; pp. 232–237; chap. 22, para. 15, pp. 297–298; 1846 edn]; Beaumanoir [*Coûtumes de Beauvaisis*], chap. 33 [#989]; *Les Etablissements de Saint Louis*, bk. 1, chap. 90 [1.96].

[269] [Pierre de Fontaines, *Le Conseil*], chap. 22, art. 8 [chap. 22, para. 15; pp. 297–298; 1846 edn].

[270] "At present, when one is so often inclined to appeal," says [Jean] Boutillier, *Le Grand Coustumier, La Somme rural*, bk. 1, tit. 3, p. 16 [tit. 3, "Des jurisdictions," p. 16; 1621 edn].

trials eternal; when the science of evading the most just claims had been refined; when a plaintiff knew how to flee simply to have himself followed; when the claim was ruinous and the defense easy; when reasons were lost in volumes of words and writings; when justice was full of underlings who would not render justice; when bad faith found counsel where it did not find support; the pleaders surely had to be checked by the fear of costs. They had to pay them for the decision and for the means they had used to evade it. Charles the Fair made a general ordinance on this subject.[271]

[271] In 1324 [*Recueil général des anciennes lois françaises, Capetiens*, #622; 3, 314–316].

CHAPTER 36

On the party for the public[q]

As, by the Salic and the Ripuarian laws and by the other laws of the barbarian peoples, the penalties for crimes were pecuniary, they did not have then, as we have now, a party for the public charged with the prosecution of crimes. Indeed, everything was reduced to reparations for damages; every prosecution was, in a way, civil, and each individual could prosecute it. On the other hand, Roman right had popular forms for the prosecution of crimes, which could not fit in with the services of a party for the public.

The usage of judicial combats was no less contrary to this idea, for who would have wanted to be the party for the public and make himself the champion of all against all?

I find, in a collection of formulas added by M. Muratori to the laws of the Lombards, that there was, under the Carolingians, an *attorney* for the public.[272] But if one reads the whole collection of these formulas, one will see that these officers were entirely different from what today we call the public party, our general prosecutors, or our prosecutors for the king or lords. The former were agents of the public for political and domestic management rather than for civil management. Indeed, one

[272] *Advocatus de parte publica.*

[q] *partie publique.* Here Montesquieu shows the development of what we now call the public prosecutor.

sees in these formulas that they were not charged with the prosecution of crimes or business concerning minors, churches, or the state of persons.

I have said that the usage of judicial combat was contrary to the establishment of a party for the public. I find, however, in one of these formulas, an attorney for the party for the public who has the liberty to enter into combat. This formula, made for the constitution of Henry I, has been placed by M. Muratori after that constitution.[273] This constitution says that "if someone kills his father, brother, nephew, or some other of his relatives, he will lose that inheritance, which will pass to other relatives, and that his own will belong to the fisc." Now in order to prosecute for this inheritance that devolved on the fisc, the attorney for the party for the public, who was upholding its rights, had the liberty to combat; this case fell under the general rule.

We see in the formulas the attorney for the party for the public acting against one who had caught a robber and had failed to take him to the count;[274] against one who had caused an uprising or an assembly against the count;[275] against one who had saved the life of a man given him by the count to be killed;[276] against the attorney for some churches, who had been ordered by the count to present that count with a robber and who had not obeyed;[277] against one who had disclosed the king's secret to foreigners;[278] against one who went armed in pursuit of the emperor's deputy;[279] against one who had scorned the emperor's letters[280] and was prosecuted by the attorney of the emperor himself; against one who had refused to accept the prince's money:[281] finally, this attorney claimed the things the law awarded to the fisc.[282]

But in the prosecution of crimes one sees no attorney for the public party, even when duels are fought,[283] even when towns are burned,[284]

[273] See this constitution and this formula in [Ludovico Muratori], *Rerum scriptores Italicarum*, vol. 2 [vol. 1, part 2], p. 175 [*Leges Langobardorum*, Hein. 1.2 (pap.)].

[274] [Ludovico] Muratori, *Rerum scriptores Italicarum*, p. 104, on Law 88 of Charlemagne, bk. 1, tit. 26, para. 78 [*Leges Langobardorum*, Kar. 86 (pap.)].

[275] Another formula, ibid., p. 87 [*Leges Langobardorum*, Rach. 10 and 6 (pap.)].

[276] Ibid., p. 104 [*Leges Langobardorum*, Kar. 85 (87) (pap.)].

[277] Ibid., p. 95 [*Leges Langobardorum*, Kar. 9 (pap.)].

[278] Ibid., p. 88 [*Leges Langobardorum*, Rach. 12 and 8 (pap.)].

[279] Ibid., p. 98 [*Leges Langobardorum*, Kar. 29 (pap.)].

[280] Ibid., p. 132 [*Leges Langobardorum*, Lud. 22 (pap.)].

[281] Ibid., p. 132 [*Leges Langobardorum*, Lud. 24 (pap.)].

[282] Ibid., p. 137 [*Leges Langobardorum*, Loth. 4 (pap.)].

[283] Ibid., p. 147 [*Leges Langobardorum*, Loth 79 (pap.)].

[284] Ibid. [*Leges Langobardorum*, Loth. 81 (pap.)].

even when the judge is killed in his tribunal,[285] even when it is a question of the condition of persons,[286] of their liberty and their servitude.[287]

These formulas are made not only for the laws of the Lombards, but for the added capitularies; thus there is no doubt that on this matter they give us the practice of the Carolingians.

It is clear that these attorneys for the party for the public were to vanish with the Carolingians, like the deputies of the king in the provinces, for the reason that there was no longer a general law or general fisc and that there was no longer a count in the provinces to hold audiences and consequently no more of those kinds of officers who principal function was to maintain the authority of the count.

The usage of combat, which became more frequent under the Capetians, did not permit the establishment of a party for the public. Thus when Boutillier, in his *Somme Rurale*, speaks of the officers of justice, he cites only bailiffs, men with fiefs, and sergeants. See the *Establishments*[288] and Beaumanoir[289] on the manner of prosecuting at that time.

I find in the laws of James II, King of Majorca,[290] the creation of the post of the king's prosecutor with the functions of ours today.[291] It is clear that the king's prosecutors came into being only after the judicial form had changed among ourselves.

[285] Ibid., p. 168 [*Leges Langobardorum*, Wid. 9 (pap.)].

[286] Ibid., p. 134 [*Leges Langobardorum*, Lud. 36 (38) (pap.)].

[287] Ibid., p. 107 [*Leges Langobardorum*, Kar. 106 (107) (pap.)].

[288] [*Les Etablissements de Saint Louis*] bk. 1, chap. 1 [1.1]; bk. 2, chaps. 11 and 13 [2.12, 14].

[289] [Beaumanoir, *Coûtumes de Beauvaisis*] chaps. 1 and 61.

[290] See these laws in the *Acta sanctorum*, for the month of June, vol. 3, p. 26 [Jacob II regis Majoricarum, "Ad leges palatinas," "De procuratore fiscali," #94; in Junii, vol. 3, pp. xxv–xxvi; 1701 edn; in Junii, vol. 4, p. xxiii; 1868 edn].

[291] [*Acta sanctorum*, in Junii, vol. 3, Jacob II regis Majoricarum, "Ad leges palatinas," "De procuratore fiscali," #94; 3, p. xxvi; 1701 edn; in Junii, vol. 4, p. xxiii; 1868 edn]: "This one is to be in constant attendance at our holy court; he is appointed to prosecute the actions and law suits brought forward at our court" [L.].

CHAPTER 37

How the Establishments *of Saint Louis were eclipsed*

The fate of the *Establishments* was to be born, to age, and to die within a short span of time.

I shall make some observations about this. The code we have under the name of the *Establishments* of Saint Louis was never made to serve as law for the whole kingdom, though this is said in the preface to the code. This compilation is a general code that enacts over all civil business, arrangements concerning goods made by testament or between living persons, dowries and privileges of women,[r] profits and prerogatives of fiefs, the business of the police, and so forth. Now, at a time when each town, borough, or village had its own custom, to give a general body of civil laws was to want to reverse in a moment all the particular laws under which men had lived everywhere in the kingdom. To make a general custom of all the particular customs would be rash, even in these times when princes find only obedience everywhere. For, if it is true that one must not alter things when the resulting drawbacks equal the advantages, so much less must one alter them when the advantages are small and the drawbacks immense. Now, if one attends to the state of the kingdom at that time, when everyone grew heady with the idea of his own sovereignty and his power, one surely sees that to undertake to change the accepted laws and usages everywhere was something that could not enter the minds of those who governed.

What I have just said also proves that the code of the *Establishments* was not confirmed in *parlements* by the barons and the men of law in the kingdom, as is said in a manuscript from the town hall of Amiens, cited by M. Ducange.[292] One sees in other manuscripts that this code was given by Saint Louis in 1270 before he left for Tunis; this fact is no truer than the other, for Saint Louis left in 1269 as M. Ducange has observed, when he concludes that this code was published in his absence. But I say that this cannot be. Why would Saint Louis do something when he was absent that would have sown troubles and which would have produced not changes, but revolutions? Such an enterprise, more than any other, needed to be followed closely and was

[292] Preface to *Les Etablissements de Saint Louis* [2, 473–474; 1881 edn].

---

[r] Benefits over and above the established share, *preciput*.

not the work of a weak regency or even one composed of lords who had an interest in seeing that the thing did not succeed. These were Matthew, Abbot of Saint Denis; Simon de Clermont, Count of Nesle; and, in the case of death, Philip, Bishop of Evreus, and Jean, Count of Ponthieu. One has already seen[293] that the Count of Ponthieu opposed the execution of a new judicial order where he was lord.

I say, in the third place, that it is quite likely that the code we have is something other than the *Establishments* of Saint Louis on the judicial order. This code cites the *Establishments*; therefore, it is a work about the *Establishments* and not the *Establishments*. In addition, Beaumanoir, who often speaks of the *Establishments* of Saint Louis, cites only particular *Establishments* of this prince and not this compilation of *Establishments*. Defontaines, who wrote during the reign of this prince,[294] speaks of the first two times that the *Establishments* on the judicial order were executed as of something in the distant past. Therefore, the *Establishments* of Saint Louis were prior to the compilation of which I speak; if one takes it in a strict sense and accepts those inaccurate prologues put at the beginning of this work by some ignorant men, it must have appeared only in the last year of the life of Saint Louis, or even after the death of that prince.

[293] [See above, bk. 28] chap. 29.
[294] See above [bk. 28] chap. 29.

CHAPTER 38
Continuation of the same subject

What, therefore, is this compilation that we have under the name of the *Establishments* of Saint Louis? What is this obscure, confused, and ambiguous code where one constantly mixes French jurisprudence with Roman law; in which one speaks as a legislator and reveals a jurist; where one finds a whole body of jurisprudence covering all situations, all the points of civil right? One must place oneself in those times.

As Saint Louis saw the abuses of the jurisprudence of his time, he sought to make the peoples disgusted with it; he made several regulations for the tribunals of his domains and for those of his barons, and he had such success that Beaumanoir, who wrote shortly after the death of this prince,[295] tells us that the way of judging established by Saint Louis was practiced in a great number of the lords' courts.

Thus, this prince accomplished his purpose, though his rules for the lords' tribunals were not made as a general law for the kingdom, but as an example that each one could follow and would even have an interest in following. He took away the worse by making the better felt. When one saw in his tribunals, and in those of the lords, a more natural, more reasonable way of proceeding, a way more in conformity with morality, religion, public tranquility, and the security of persons and goods, it was taken up and the other was abandoned.

To invite when one must not constrain, to lead when one must not command, is the supreme skill. Reason has a natural empire; it has even a tyrannical empire: one resists it, but this resistance is its triumph; yet a little time and one is forced to come back to it.

Saint Louis, in order to create distaste for French jurisprudence, had the books of Roman right translated so that men of the law of that time would know them. Defontaines, who is the first to write on our practice,[296] made great use of these Roman laws; his work is more or less a combination of old French jurisprudence, the laws or *Establishments* of Saint Louis, and Roman law. Beaumanoir made little use of Roman law, but he reconciled the old French jurisprudence with the regulations of Saint Louis.

In the spirit of these two works, and above all that of Defontaines, some bailiff, I believe, made the work of jurisprudence that we call the *Establishments*. In the title of that work it says that it was made according to the usage of Paris and Orleans, and of the baronial court, and in the prologue, that it is a treatise on the usages of the entire kingdom, of Anjou, and of the baronial court. It can be seen that this work was made for Paris, Orleans, and Anjou, as the works of Beaumanoir and Defontaines were made for the countries of Clermont and Vermandois; and, as it appears from Beaumanoir that many of the laws of Saint Louis had found their way into the baronial courts, the compiler says, with some reason, that his work also concerned the baronial courts.[297]

[295] [Beaumanoir, *Coûtumes de Beauvaisis*] chap. 61, p. 309 [#1722].

[296] He himself says in his "Prologue": "None before me has taken up this subject" [O.F.]. [Pierre de Fontaines, *Le Conseil*, "Prologue"; chap. 1, para. 3, p. 5; 1846 edn].

[297] Nothing is more vague than the title and the "Prologue." First there are the usages of Paris and of Orleans, and of the baronial court; then, there are the usages of all the lay courts of

It is clear that the one who made this work compiled the customs of these countries with the laws and the *Establishments* of Saint Louis. This work is valuable because it contains the old customs of Anjou, the *Establishments* of Saint Louis as they were then practiced, and finally the part of the old French jurisprudence which was still practiced there.

The difference between this work and those of Defontaines and Beaumanoir is that in it one speaks in terms of command, as legislators do, and this could be because it was a compilation of written customs and laws.

There was an internal vice in this compilation: it formed an amphibious code, in which were mixed French jurisprudence and Roman law; things were brought together that had never been related and that were often contradictory.

I know, indeed, that French tribunals of men or peers, judgments without appeal to another tribunal, and the way of pronouncing with these words: *I condemn* or *I absolve*[298] conformed to the popular judgments of the Romans. But that old jurisprudence was little used; what was used was rather the one that was introduced later by the emperors, which was employed everywhere in this compilation to regulate, limit, correct, and extend French jurisprudence.

the kingdom and of the precincts of the provost; then, there are the usages of the whole kingdom, of Anjou, and of the baronial court.

[298] *Les Etablissements de Saint Louis*, bk. 2, chap. 15 [2.16].

CHAPTER 39

Continuation of the same subject

The judicial forms introduced by Saint Louis ceased to be used. This prince had in view less the thing itself, that is, the best way of judging, than the best way of replacing the former practice of judging. The first object was to evoke a dislike for the old jurisprudence, and the second to form a new one. But once the drawbacks of the new one had appeared, another was soon seen to supplant it.

Thus the laws of Saint Louis did not so much change French jurisprudence as they gave new means for changing it; they opened new tribunals, or rather ways to get to them, and when one could easily attain the one that had a general authority, judgments which formerly affected only the usages of a particular lord came to form a universal jurisprudence. By the force of the *Establishments*, the point was reached where there were general decisions, which had been entirely lacking in the kingdom; when the building was constructed, the scaffolding was left to fall.

Thus the laws made by Saint Louis had effects that could never have been expected of a masterpiece of legislation. Sometimes many centuries must pass to prepare for changes; events ripen, and then there are revolutions.

The *parlement* judged in the last resort on almost all the business of the kingdom. It had formerly judged only those between dukes, counts, bishops, abbots,[299] or between the king and his vassals[300] in their relation to the political order rather than to the civil order. Later, one was obliged to make it a sitting *parlement* and keep it permanently assembled; finally, many were created so that there would be enough of them for all the business.

Scarcely had the *parlement* become a fixed body than one began to compile its decisions. Jean de Monluc, during the reign of Philip the Fair, made the collection today called the *Olim Registry*.[301]

[299] See [Jean] Du Tillet [*Recueil des rois de France: leur couronne et maison*, "Des Princes du sang de France," 1, 316] on the court of peers. See also [Bernard de] La Roche Flavin, bk. 1, chap. 3 [*Des parlements de France*, bk. 1, chap. 3; "Description des anciens parlements de France," p. 3; 1621 edn]. Guillaume Budé and Paolo Emili.

[300] The other affairs were decided by ordinary tribunals.

[301] See the excellent work by President [Charles Jean François] Hénault [*Nouvel abrégé chronologique de l'histoire de France*], for the year 1313 [1313/1314, pp. 101–102; 1836 edn].

CHAPTER 40

How the judicial forms were taken from the decretals

But how does it happen that when the established judicial forms were abandoned, those of canonical right, rather than those of Roman right, were taken up? It was because the clerical tribunals, which followed the forms of canonical right, were always in view and because no tribunal following those of Roman right was known. In addition, the limits of ecclesiastical and secular jurisdiction were little known at that time: no distinctions[302] were made in the people who appeared before the two courts;[303] nor were there any in the matters about which one pleaded. It seems[304] that the lay jurisdiction kept for itself, privately from the other, only the judging of feudal matters and crimes committed by the laity in cases that did not run counter to religion.[305] For if one had to go to lay justice in the case of agreements and contracts, the parties could voluntarily proceed to clerical tribunals, which, as they did not have the right to oblige lay justice to execute the sentence, constrained one to obey by way of excommunication.[306] In these circumstances, when one wanted to change practices in the lay tribunals, those of the clerics were taken because they were known and that of Roman right was not chosen because it was not known, for in matters of practice one knows only what one practices.

[302] Beaumanoir [*Coûtumes de Beauvaisis*], chap. 11, p. 58 [#315].
[303] Widows, crusaders, those who held church goods, because of these goods. Ibid. [Beaumanoir, *Coûtumes de Beauvaisis*, #318, #319].
[304] See the whole of chapter 11 in Beaumanoir [*Coûtumes de Beauvaisis*, #311–360].
[305] The clerical tribunals, on the pretext that an oath was taken, had even taken over some of these, as can be seen by the famous Concordat between Philip Augustus, the clergy and the barons, which can be found in the ordinances of Laurière [*Recueil général des anciennes lois françaises*, #104, 1.194–199].
[306] Beaumanoir [*Coûtumes de Beauvaisis*], chap. 11, p. 60 [#322, #323].

CHAPTER 41

The ebb and flow of ecclesiastical jurisdiction and lay jurisdiction

With civil power in the hands of an infinite number of lords, it had been easy for ecclesiastical jurisdiction to give itself more scope daily; but, as ecclesiastical jurisdiction weakened the jurisdiction of the lords and thus contributed to give force to royal jurisdiction, royal jurisdiction gradually restricted ecclesiastical jurisdiction, and the latter retreated before the former. The *parlement*, which had taken, for its form of procedure, everything good and useful from that of the clerical tribunals, soon saw only its abuses; and, as royal jurisdiction became stronger daily, it was increasingly in a position to correct these same abuses. Indeed, they were intolerable; and, without enumerating them, I shall refer to Beaumanoir, Boutillier, and the ordinances of our kings.[307] I shall speak only of the ones which most directly concerned the public fortune. We know these abuses by the decisions that reformed them. Dense ignorance had introduced them; a kind of light appeared, and they existed no longer. One can judge, by the silence of the clergy, that they themselves were in the forefront of the correction; a thing which, given the nature of the human spirit, deserves praise. Any man who died without giving a part of his goods to the church, which was called dying unshriven,[s] was deprived of communion and Christian burial. If someone died without a testament, the relatives had to get the bishop to join with them in naming arbiters to fix what the dead man should have given if he had made a testament. On the wedding night and the two following ones, newlyweds could not sleep together without buying permission; those certainly were the three nights that had to be chosen, for not much silver would have been given for the others. The *parlement* corrected all that. One finds in the *Glossaire du droit français* by Ragueau[308] the decision he rendered against the bishop of Amiens.[309]

I return to the beginning of my chapter. When in a century or a government one sees the various bodies of the state seek to increase their authority and to get certain advantages over each other, one would often be mistaken if their enterprises were considered a sure mark of their corruption. By a misfortune attached to the human condition, great men who are moderate are rare; and, as it is always easier to follow one's strength than to check it, perhaps, in the class of superior people, it is easier to find extremely virtuous people than extremely wise men.[t]

The soul takes such delight in dominating other souls; even those who love the good love themselves so much that no one is so unfortunate as to distrust his good intentions; and, in truth, our actions depend on so many things that it is a thousand times easier to do good than to do it well.

[307] See [Jean] Boutillier, *Le Grand Coustumier, La Somme rural* [bk. 1], tit. 9, "those who cannot petition in lay court" [pp. 42–43; 1621 edn]; and Beaumanoir [*Coûtumes de Beauvaisis*], chap. 11, p. 56 [#311]; the rulings by Philip Augustus on this subject, and the settlement Philip Augustus made between the clerics, the king, and the barons [*Recueil général des anciennes lois françaises*, #104].

[308] At the word, "Executeurs testamentaires" [François Ragueau, *Glossaire du droit français*, pp. 435–444; 1704 edn].

[309] Of March 19, 1409.

[s] *deconfés*.

[t] The wisdom here implied by *sage* is closest to what we call "prudence."

CHAPTER 42

Rebirth of Roman right and its result. Changes in the tribunals

When the *Digest* of Justinian was discovered around the year 1137, Roman right appeared to be reborn. Schools were established in Italy to teach it, the *Code* of Justinian and the *Novellae* had already been found. I have already said that this right gained such favor that it caused the eclipse of the law of the Lombards.

Italian scholars brought the right of Justinian into France, where only the *Code* of Theodosius had been known,[310] because the laws of Justinian were not made until after the establishment of the barbarians in Gaul.[311] This right met with some opposition, but it was maintained in spite of excommunications by the popes, who protected their own canons.[312] Saint Louis sought to give it a standing by having translations made of the works of Justinian, which we still have in manuscript in our libraries, and I have already said that much use was made of them in the *Establishments*. Philip the Fair had the laws of Justinian taught solely as written reasoning in the countries of France governed by custom,[313] and they were adopted as law in the countries where Roman right was the law.

I have said earlier that the manner of proceeding by judicial combat required very little competence in those who judged; business was decided in each place according to the usage of each place and according to certain simple customs that were accepted by tradition. There were in the time of Beaumanoir two different manners of rendering justice:[314] in some places peers judged, in others bailiffs judged;[315] when the first form was followed, peers judged according to

[310] The Justinian Code was followed in Italy; this is why Pope John VIII speaks of this code in the constitution he gave after the Synod of Troyes, not because it was known in France, but because he knew it himself; and his constitution was general.

[311] The code of this emperor was published about 530.

[312] [*Corpus Iuris Canonici*] *Decretalium collectiones. Super specula. Sane de privilegiis*, bk. 5 [5.33.28].

[313] By a charter of 1312 in favor of the University of Orleans, reported by Du Tillet [*Recueil général des anciennes lois françaises*, #452; 3, 22].

[314] [Beaumanoir] *Coûtumes de Beauvaisis*, chap. 1 [#23], "De l'office des baillis."

[315] In the commons, bourgeois were judged by other bourgeois, as men of the fief judged one another. See [Gaspard Thaumas de] la Thaumassière [*Les anciennes et nouvelles coûtumes locales de Berry, et celles de Lorris commentées*], chap. 19 [pt. 1, chap. 19; p. 22; 1629 edn].

the usage of their jurisdiction; in the second, chivalrous men[u] or old men indicated the same usage to the bailiff.[316] None of this required literacy, ability or study. But when the obscure code of the *Establishments* and other works of jurisprudence appeared, when Roman right was translated, when it began to be taught in the schools, when a certain art of procedure and a certain art of jurisprudence began to be formed, when practitioners and jurists appeared, peers and chivalrous men were no longer in a position to judge; peers began to withdraw from the tribunals of the lord; lords were little inclined to convoke them, the more so because judgments, instead of being a striking action, pleasing to the nobility, and interesting to warriors, had become only a practice that they neither knew nor wanted to know. The practice of judging by peers became less used;[317] that of judging by bailiffs spread. Bailiffs had not previously judged;[318] they gave instruction and pronounced the judgment of the chivalrous men, but when these men were no longer in a position to judge, the bailiffs themselves judged.

This happened more easily as they had the practice of the church judges before their eyes; canonical right and the new civil right worked together to abolish the peers.

Thus was lost the usage, consistently observed in the monarchy, that a judge never judged alone, as is seen in the Salic laws, in the

[316] Thus all requests began with these words, "Your honor, it is the usage in your jurisdiction, etc." [O.F.], as appears in the formula reported in [Jean] Boutillier, *Le Grand Coustumier, Le Somme rural*, bk. 1, tit. 21 [tit. 21, "Apres ensuit de former sa demande en cour," pp. 101–102; 1621 edn]. [Montesquieu's quotation is not exact.]

[317] The change was imperceptible. One could still find peers so employed in the time of [Jean] Boutillier, who was alive in 1402, the date of his last testament, who reports [*Le Grand Coustumier, La Somme rural*] this formula in bk. 1, tit. 21. [tit. 21, "Apres ensuit de former sa demande en cour," pp. 101–102; 1621 edn]: "Your honor, in my high, middle and low justices, which I have in such and such a place [there are] court, pleas, bailliffs, feudal men, and sergeants" [O.F.]. But at that time only feudal matters were judged by peers. Ibid., bk. 1, tit. 1, p. 16 [bk. 1, tit. 3, "Des jurisdicions," p. 16; 1621 edn].

[318] As appears by the formula of the letters given by the lord, reported by [Jean] Boutillier, *Le Grand Coustumier, La Somme rural*, bk. 1, tit. 14 [bk. 1, tit. 14; pp. 65–66; 1621 edn]. It is further proven by Beaumanoir, *Coûtumes de Beauvaisis*, ch. 1, "On Bailiffs" [#23]. They performed only the procedure. "The bailiff is sworn in the presence of the men to take down the words of those who plead and must ask the parties if they want to be judged [*avoir droit*] according to the reasons they have given; and if they say "yes sir," the bailiff must constrain the men to give the judgment." See also *Les Etablissements de Saint Louis*, bk. 1, chap. 105 [1.111], bk. 2, chap. 15 [2.16; p. 378; 1881 edn]: "When the judge ought not give the judgment" [O.F.].

[u] *prud'hommes*.

capitularies, and in the first writers on practice under the Capetians.[319] The contrary abuse, which occured only in local justices, was moderated, and in a way corrected, by the introduction in several places of a judge's lieutenant, whom the judge consulted and who represented the former chivalrous men, and by the obligation of the judge to select two graduates in law in cases that could warrant a corporal penalty; finally it was nullified by the extreme ease of appeals.

[319] Beaumanoir [*Coûtumes de Beauvaisis*], chap. 67, p. 336 [#1883]; and chap. 61, pp. 315 and 316 [#1760]. *Les Etablissements de Saint Louis*, bk. 2, chap. 15 [2.16].

CHAPTER 43
Continuation of the same subject

Thus it was not a law that prohibited the lords from holding their courts themselves; it was not a law that abolished the functions of the peers in them; there was no law that ordered the creation of the bailiffs; it was not from a law that they had the right to judge. All this happened gradually and by the force of the things. The knowledge of Roman right, of the decisions of the courts, of that body of recently recorded customs, required a study of which the nobles and the illiterate were not capable.

The only ordinance that we have about this[320] is the one that obliged the lords to choose their bailiffs from the order of laity. This has been mistakenly regarded as the law creating them, but it says only what it says. In addition, it fixes what it prescribes by the reasons it gives for it: "In order that the bailiffs may be punished for their breaches of trust they must be drawn from the order of laity."[321] One knows the privileges of ecclesiastics at this time.

One must not believe that the rights the lords formerly enjoyed and which they no longer enjoy were taken away from them by usurpations; a number of these rights were lost through neglect, and others were abandoned because as various changes were introduced over the course of several centuries, they could not continue to exist along with these changes.

[320] It is for the year 1287.
[321] "So that, if in that place they commit a crime, superiors could punish them" [L.]. [*Recueil général des anciennes lois françaises*, #283.1; 2, 678].

CHAPTER 44

On proof by witnesses

Judges, whose only rules were the usages, ordinarily held inquests by means of witnesses into each question that was presented.

As judicial combat came to be used less, the inquests were made in writing. But an oral proof written down remains only an oral proof; this only increased the expense of the proceedings. Regulations were made rendering most of these inquests useless;[322] public registers were established which gave proof of most of the facts: nobility, age, legitimacy, marriage. Writing is a witness difficult to corrupt. One had customs put in writing. All this was quite reasonable; it is easier to go and look at the baptismal register to see if Peter is the son of Paul than to try to prove this fact by a lengthy inquest. When there are a very great number of usages in a country, it is easier to write them all in a code than to oblige individuals to give proof of each usage. Finally, that famous ordinance was made that prohibited the acceptance of proof by witnesses for a debt of more than one hundred pounds unless there was already some proof in writing.

[322] See how age and kinship were proven: *Les Etablissements de Saint Louis*, bk. 1, chaps. 71 and 72 [1.78–79].

CHAPTER 45

On customs in France

France was regulated by unwritten customs, as I have said, and the particular usages of each lordship formed the civil right. Each lordship had its civil right, as Beaumanoir says,[323] and so specific was this right that this author, whom one should consider as the luminary of that time and a great one, says that he does not believe that in the whole kingdom any two lordships were governed in every point by the same law.

This prodigious diversity had a first origin and it had a second. For the first, one can recall what I have mentioned earlier in the chapter on local customs,[324] and for the second, it is found in the various outcomes

[323] [Beaumanoir] *Coûtumes de Beauvaisis*, "Prologue" [#7].

[324] [Bk. 28] chap. 12.

of judicial combats, as continuous accidental situations naturally introduced new usages.

These customs were preserved in the memory of old men, gradually laws or written customs were formed.

1. In the beginning of the reign of the Capetians,[325] the kings gave particular charters and even general ones in the way I have already explained; such are the establishments of Philip Augustus and those made by Saint Louis. The great vassals together with the lords who depended on them likewise gave in the assizes of their duchies or countries certain charters or establishments, according to the circumstances; such were the assizes of Geoffroi, Count of Brittany, on the division of the nobles; the customs of Normandy, granted by Duke Raoul; the customs of Champagne, given by King Thibaut; the laws of Simon, Count of Montfort, and others. This produced some written laws that were even more general than the ones already in existence.

2. At the beginning of the reign of the Capetians, almost all the common people were serfs. Many reasons obliged the kings and the lords to free them.

When the lords freed their serfs, they gave them goods; they had to give them civil laws to regulate the disposition of these goods. When the lords freed their serfs, they gave up goods; the rights that the lords reserved to themselves as equivalents to their goods had, therefore, to be regulated. Both of these things were regulated by the charters freeing them; these charters formed a part of our customs, and this part was put in writing.

3. In the reign of Saint Louis and the following reigns, able practitioners such as Defontaines, Beaumanoir, and others put in writing the customs of their bailiwicks. Their purpose was to give a judicial practice rather than the usage of their times with respect to the disposition of goods. But everything is in them, and though these individual authors had no authority except from the truth and the public knowledge about the things they said, one cannot doubt that they served well in the rebirth of our French right. Such was, at that time, our written customary right.

Next came the great period. Charles VII and his successors had the various local customs throughout the kingdom put in writing and prescribed formalities that were to be observed in their transcription.

[325] See Laurière's *Recueil des Ordonnances*.

Now, as this transcription was done by provinces and as in each lordship depositions were given, in the general assembly of the province, about the written or unwritten usages of each place, one sought to make the customs more general, as far as this could be done without injuring the interests of individuals which were protected.[326v] Thus, our customs assumed three characteristics: they were written down, they were more general, and they received the stamp of royal authority.

When many of these customs were rewritten, certain changes were made, either by removing all that was not compatible with current jurisprudence, or by adding certain things drawn from that jurisprudence.

Though we consider customary right to imply a kind of opposition to Roman right, so that these two rights divide the territories, it is nevertheless true that a number of provisions of Roman right entered our customs, especially when new transcriptions were made of them at times that are not so distant from our own when that right was the object of knowledge of all those who were destined for civil employment, in times when one did not glory in being ignorant of what one should know, when quickness of spirit served better to learn one's profession than to engage in it, and when being continually amused was not even the attribute of women.

I could have elaborated even further at the end of this book and, by going into greater detail, could have followed all the imperceptible changes that have formed the great body of our French jurisprudence since the introduction of appeals. But I would have put a great work into another work. I am like the antiquarian who left his country, arrived in Egypt, glanced at the pyramids, and headed back.[327]

[326] It was done in this way, as is noted in the work of [Gaspard Thaumas de] la Thaumassière, *Les Anciennes et Nouvelles Coûtumes locales de Berry, et celles de Lorris commentées*. See chap. 3 [pt. 1, chap. 3; pp. 4–5; 1629 edn].

[327] In [Joseph Addison] *The Spectator* [#1, March 1, 1711].

[v] The depository of the laws. See 2.4 (note [j], bk. 2).

BOOK 29
On the way to compose the laws

CHAPTER I
On the spirit of the legislator

I say it, and it seems to me that I have written this work only to prove it: the spirit of moderation should be that of the legislator; the political good, like the moral good, is always found between two limits. Here is an example.

The formalities of justice are necessary to liberty. But, their number could be so great that it would run counter to the end of the very laws establishing them: suits[a] would be interminable; the ownership of goods would remain uncertain; one of the parties would be given the goods of the other without examination, or both would be ruined by the examination.

Citizens would lose their liberty and their security; accusers would no longer have the means to convict nor the accused, a means to vindicate themselves.

[a] *affaires.* See note [c], bk. 2; note [j], bk. 28.

CHAPTER 2
Continuation of the same subject

Caecilius, according to Aulus Gellius,[1] speaking on that law of the Twelve Tables that permitted the creditor to cut the insolvent debtor to pieces, justifies the law by its very atrocity, which prevented one's borrowing beyond one's abilities.[2] Shall the cruellest laws, therefore,

[1] [*NA*] bk. 20, chap. 1 [20.1.39–52].
[2] Caecilius states that he had neither seen nor read of this penalty being inflicted; indeed, it

be the best? Shall the excess be the good, and all the relations between things be destroyed?

is likely that it was never established. The opinion of a number of jurists, that the Law of Twelve Tables spoke only of the division of the price paid for the debtor, is very possible.

CHAPTER 3

That laws which seem to diverge from the aims of the legislator often conform to them

The law of Solon, which declared infamous all those who took no part in a sedition, has appeared extraordinary, but one must attend to the circumstances of Greece at that time. Greece was divided into very small states; in a republic tormented by civil discord it was to be feared that the most prudent people would take cover and that things would thereby be carried to an extreme.

In the seditions that occurred in these small states, the bulk of the town entered the quarrel, or began it. In our great monarchies the parties are formed by a few, and the people want to lead a life of inaction. In this case it is natural to incorporate the seditious men into the bulk of the citizens, not the bulk of the citizens into the seditious men; in the former, the small number of wise and tranquil people must be made to go among the seditious men; thus it is that the fermentation of one liquor can be checked by a single drop of a different one.

CHAPTER 4

On laws that run counter to the aims of the legislator

There are laws that the legislator has understood so poorly that they are even contrary to the end he himself has proposed. Those who established for the French that when one of two claimants to a benefice dies, the benefice remains with the survivor, doubtless sought to quell disputes. But a contrary effect results from it: one sees ecclesiastics, like mastiffs, attack each other and fight to the death.

CHAPTER 5

Continuation of the same subject

The law I shall mention occurs in this oath that has been preserved for us by Aeschines.[3] "I swear that I will never destroy a town of the Amphictyons and that I will not divert its running water; if any people dare do such a thing, I shall declare war on them, and I shall destroy their towns." The last article of this law, which seems to confirm the first, is in reality contrary to it. The Amphictyonic league wants the Greek towns never to be destroyed, and this law opens the door to the destruction of these towns. In order for the Greeks to establish a good right of nations, they had to become accustomed to thinking it an atrocious thing to destroy a Greek town; therefore, they should not destroy even destroyers. The law of the Amphictyons was just, but it was imprudent. This is proved by the very abuse of it that occurred. Did not Philip give himself the power to destroy towns on the pretext that they had violated the laws of the Greeks? The Amphictyons could have inflicted other penalties: ordering, for example, that a certain number of magistrates in the town of the destroyers or of leaders of the violating army would be punished by death; that the destroyers would cease for a time to enjoy the privileges of Greeks; that they would pay a fine until the town was reestablished. Above all, the law should have addressed the reparation of the damage.

[3][Aeschines] *De falsa legatione* [*On the Embassy* 115].

CHAPTER 6

That laws that appear the same do not always have the same effect

Caesar forbade men to keep more than sixty sesterces in their houses.[4] In Rome this law was regarded as quite proper for reconciling debtors and creditors because, by obliging the wealthy to lend to the poor, it put the latter in a position to satisfy the wealthy. A similar law, made in

[4]Cass. Dio, bk. 41 [41.38]. [This should be 60,000, not 60, sesterces.]

France at the time of the System,[b] was catastrophic; this is because the circumstances in which it was made were frightful. After removing all the means of investing one's silver, even the recourse of keeping it at home was taken away; this was equivalent to taking it away by violence.[c] Caesar made his law so that silver would circulate among the people; the minister of France made his so that silver would be collected in a single hand. The first gave lands or mortgages on individuals for silver; the second offered for silver, bills that had no value and which could by their nature have none, because his law obliged one to take them.

[b] Of John Law. [c] See 22.10.

CHAPTER 7

Continuation of the same subject. Necessity for composing the laws well

The law of ostracism was established in Athens, Argos, and Syracuse.[5] In Syracuse it produced a thousand ills because it was made without prudence. The principal citizens banished each other by holding a fig leaf in their hand,[6] so that those of some merit no longer took part in public business. In Athens, where the legislator felt the extension and limits that he should give to his law, ostracism was a remarkable thing; only a single person was subjected to it; there had to be such a great number of votes that it was difficult for any one to be exiled unless his absence was necessary.

One could banish only every five years: indeed, as soon as ostracism was practiced only against a great personage who inspired fear in his fellow citizens, it should not have been an everyday business.

[5] Aristotle, *Republic* [*Politics*], bk. 5, chap. 3 [1302b18–19].

[6] Plutarch, *Life of Dionysius*. [Plutarch did not write a life of Dionysius of Syracuse. He wrote a life of Dion, an adviser to Dionysius, but does not describe the Syracusan form of ostracism, called petalism. A source for this information is Diodorus Siculus, 11.87.]

CHAPTER 8

That laws that appear the same have not always had the same motive

France accepts most of the Roman laws on substitutions; but in France, substitutions have a motive altogether different from that of the Romans. For them an inheritance was bound with certain sacrifices to be made by the heir and were ruled by pontifical right.[7] This is why they considered it dishonorable to die without an heir and took their slaves for heirs or devised substitutions. The vulgar substitution, the first devised and applicable only when the appointed heir would not accept the inheritance, is a great proof of this; its purpose was not to perpetuate the inheritance in a family of the same name, but to find someone who would accept the inheritance.

[7]When the inheritance was too burdened, one could avoid the right of the pontiffs by certain sales, hence the phrase *sine sacris haereditas*: without sanctified heirs.

CHAPTER 9

That, without having the same motive, both Greek and Roman laws punished the killing of oneself

"A man," says Plato,[8] "who killed the one with whom he is most closely linked, that is, himself, not by order of the magistrate, or to avoid ignominy, but from weakness, will be punished." Roman law punished this act, when it was done not from weakness of soul, from boredom with life, or from an incapacity to suffer sorrow, but from despair over some crime. The Roman law absolved in the case where the Greek condemned and condemned in the case where the latter absolved.

Plato's law was formed along the lines of the institutions of the Lacedaemonians, where the orders of the magistrate were completely absolute, where ignominy was the greatest misfortune, and weakness the greatest crime. Roman law abandoned all these fine ideas; it was a fiscal law only.

At the time of the republic, there was no law in Rome punishing

[8][Plato] *Laws*, bk. 9 [873c–d].

those who killed themselves; this act is always taken in stride by the historians, and one never sees a punishment for those who did it.

At the time of the first emperors, the great families of Rome were constantly exterminated by judgments. The custom of preventing condemnation by voluntary death was introduced. It offered a great advantage. One gained the honor of a burial and the execution of one's testament;[9] this came from Rome's having no civil law against those who killed themselves. But when the emperors became as avaricious as they had been cruel, they no longer left to those of whom they wanted to be rid the means of preserving their goods, and they declared that it would be a crime to take one's life out of remorse for another crime.

What I say of the motive of the emperors is so true that they agreed that the goods of those who killed themselves should not be confiscated when the crime for which they killed themselves was not subject to confiscation.[10]

[9] "Those who decided on their own [to commit suicide] had their bodies buried and their wills respected; this was the reward for making haste" [L.] Tacitus [*Annales*, 6, 29].

[10] Rescript of the Emperor Pius, in Law 3, paras. 1–2 [*Corpus Juris Civilis, Digest* 48.21.3.1–2], *de bonis eorum qui ante sententiam vel mortem sibi consciverunt vel accusatorem corruperunt.*

CHAPTER 10

That laws that seem contradictory are sometimes derived from the same spirit

Today one goes into the house of a man to summon him to judgment; this could not be done among the Romans.[11]

A summons to judgment was a violent action,[12] a kind of physical constraint,[13] and one could no more enter the house of a man to summon him to judgment than one can today go into his house to physically constrain a man condemned only for civil debts.

The Roman laws[14] and ours equally admit the principle that each

[11] Law 18 [*Corpus Juris Civilis, Digest* 2.4.21, 22]; *in jus vocando.*

[12] See the Law of the Twelve Tables [*XII Tables, Unplaced Fragments*, 5, i.e., Cicero, *De republica* 2.31.54].

[13] "He hastened him to Court" [L.]. Horace, *Satires* 9 [1.9.77]. This is why one could not summon to judgment those to whom a certain respect was owed.

[14] See Law 18 [*Corpus Juris Civilis, Digest* 2.4.18, 21, 22]; *in jus vocando.*

citizen's house is his sanctuary and that he should not be done violence in it.

CHAPTER II

In what way two different laws can be compared

In France the penalty for false witnesses is capital; in England it is not. In order to judge which of these two laws is better, one must add that in France criminals are put to the question, in England, they are not; and one must also say that in France the accused does not produce his own witnesses, and it is very rare to admit what are called mitigating circumstances;[d] that in England one receives testimony from both parties. The three French laws form a well-linked, consistent system; the three English laws form one that is no less so. The English law, which does not admit putting criminals to the question, has only slight expectations of drawing from the accused a confession of his crime; it summons outside testimonies then from every quarter, and it does not dare discourage them by the fear of a capital penalty. The French law, which has an additional recourse, does not so greatly fear intimidating the witnesses; on the contrary, reason demands that it intimidate them: the law hears the witnesses of one side only;[15] they are those produced by the public party, and the fate of the accused depends on their testimony alone. But in England, one accepts witnesses from both sides, and the business is, so to speak, argued out between them. Therefore, false witnesses can be less dangerous there; the accused has a recourse against false witness, whereas French law gives none. Thus, in order to judge which of these laws is more in conformity with reason, they must not be compared one by one; they must be taken all together and compared together.

[15] Under the old French jurisprudence, witnesses were heard from both parts. Thus one can see, in *Les Etablissements de Saint Louis*, bk. 1, chap. 7 [1.9], that the penalty against false witnesses, in a matter of justice, was pecuniary.

---

[d] *les faits justificatifs*.

CHAPTER 12

That laws that seem alike are sometimes really different

Greek and Roman laws punished the receiver of stolen goods as they did the robber;[16] French law does the same. The first were reasonable; the latter is not. Among the Greeks and Romans, since the robber was condemned to a pecuniary penalty, one had to punish the receiver with the same penalty, for a man who contributes in any way whatever to this damage should repair it. But as among us the penalty for robbery is capital, it has not been possible to punish the receiver like the robber without carrying things to excess. The one who receives stolen goods can on a thousand occasions receive them innocently, the one who robs is always guilty; the former prevents conviction for the crime already committed, the latter commits the crime; all is passive in the one, there is action in the other; the robber must overcome more obstacles and his soul must have been hardened against the laws for a longer time.

The jurists went further: they regarded the receiver as more odious than the robber,[17] for without him, they say, the robbery could not be hidden for long. This, again, could be good so long as the penalty was pecuniary; it was a question of damage, and ordinarily the receiver was more in a position to make reparation; but when the penalty became capital, one should have been ruled by other principles.

[16] Law 1 [*Corpus Juris Civilis, Digest* 47.16]; *de receptatoribus*.
[17] Law 1 [*Corpus Juris Civilis, Digest* 47.16]; *de receptatoribus*.

CHAPTER 13

That laws must not be separated from the purpose for which they are made. On the Roman laws about robbery

When the robber was caught with stolen goods before he had put them where he had decided to hide them, it was called a manifest robbery among the Romans; when the robber was discovered only afterwards, it was a non-manifest robbery.

The law of the Twelve Tables ordered that the manifest robber be whipped and reduced to servitude if he were an adult, or only whipped if he were not an adult; it condemned the non-manifest robber only to paying twice the value of the stolen thing.

When the Porcian law had abolished the usage of whipping citizens and reducing them to servitude, the manifest robber was condemned to a payment of quadruple the value,[18] and the non-manifest robber continued to be punished with a payment of double.

It seems odd that the laws put such a difference in the status of these two crimes and in the penalty they inflicted for them; indeed, whether the robber was caught before or after carrying the stolen goods to the place of destination was a circumstance which did not change the nature of the crime. I cannot doubt that the whole theory of the Roman laws on robbery was drawn from Lacedaemonian institutions. Lycurgus, with a view to endowing his citizens with cunning, trickery, and quickness, wanted the children to be trained in petty theft and be severely whipped if they were caught; among the Greeks and later among the Romans, this established a great difference between manifest robbery and non-manifest robbery.[19]

Among the Romans the slave who had robbed was thrown off the Tarpeian rock. Here it was not a question of the Lacedaemonian institutions; the laws of Lycurgus on robbery had not been made for slaves; deviating from them on this point was to follow them.

In Rome, when someone who was not of age was caught in a robbery, the praetor had him whipped at his will, as was done in Lacedaemonia. All this came from a more distant past. The Lacedaemonians had drawn these usages from the Cretans, and Plato,[20] who wants to prove that the Cretan institutions were made for war, cites this one: "The faculty of bearing pain in individual combats and in petty thefts that have to be concealed."

As civil laws depend on political laws because they are made for one society, it would be well if, when one wants to transfer a civil law from one nation to another, one examines beforehand whether they both have the same institutions and the same political right.

Thus, when the laws on robbery passed from the Cretans to the Lacedaemonians, as they passed to them along with the government

[18] See what is said by Favorinus according to Aulus Gellius [*NA*], bk. 20, chap. 1 [20.1.9–19].

[19] Compare what Plutarch says in *Vit. Lycurgus* [17–18.3] with the laws in the *Digest* [*Corpus Juris Civilis*, *Digest* 47, 2 (2, 3)]; *de furtis* and the *Institutes*, bk. 4, tit. 1, paras. 1–3 [*Corpus Juris Civilis*, *Institutes* 4.1.1–3; *de obligationibus quae ex delicto nascuntur*].

[20] [Plato] *Laws*, bk. 1 [633b].

and even the constitution, these laws were as sensible for one of these peoples as they were for the other. But when they were carried from Lacedaemonia to Rome, as they did not find the same constitution, they were always foreign to it and had no link with the other civil laws of the Romans.

CHAPTER 14

That laws must not be separated from the circumstances in which they were made

An Athenian law wanted all the useless people to be put to death when the town was besieged.[21] This was an abominable political law which was a consequence of an abominable right of nations. Among the Greeks, the inhabitants of a captured town lost their civil liberty and were sold as slaves; the capture of a town brought about its entire destruction. And this is the origin not only of these unyielding defenses and unnatural actions, but also of the atrocious laws that were sometimes made.

The Roman laws wanted doctors to be punishable for their negligence or incompetence.[22] In this case, they condemned a doctor to deportation when his rank was somewhat elevated and condemned him to death when his rank was lower. It is otherwise with our laws. The Roman laws were not made in the same circumstances as ours; in Rome, those who wanted to meddle in medicine did; but, among us, doctors are obliged to study and to take certain degrees, so they are deemed to know their art.

[21] "Those useless on account of age are to be killed" [L.]. Syrianus, *Scholia ad Hermogenis* [*Commentarium in librum "Peri staseon"*; p. 167, #16–25].

[22] [*Corpus Juris Civilis, Digest* 48.8 (3.5)] *ad legem Corneliam de sicariis et venefis*; *Institutes*, bk. 4, tit. 3, para. 7 [*Corpus Juris Civilis, Institutes* 4.3.7]; *de lege Aquilia*.

CHAPTER 15

That it is sometimes well for a law to correct itself

The law of the Twelve Tables permitted one to kill someone who robbed at night,[23] as well as someone who robbed during the day who, upon being followed, put up a defense; but it wanted the one who killed the robber to cry out and summon the citizens,[24] and this is a thing that laws which permit one to do justice oneself should always require. It is the cry of innocence which, at the moment of action, summons witnesses, summons judges. The people must know about the action and must know of it at the moment it is done; at a time when everything speaks, appearances, faces, passions, silences, and when every word condemns or justifies. A law that can become so contrary to the security and the liberty of the citizens should be executed in the presence of the citizens.

[23] See law 4 [*Corpus Juris Civilis, Digest* 9.2.4(1)]; *ad Legem Aquiliam.*

[24] Ibid. [*Corpus Juris Civilis, Digest* 9.2.4(1); *ad Legem Aquiliam*]. See the decree of Tassillon added to the *Lex Baiuwariorum*, art. 4 [*Additiones legis Baiuwariorum, Additio quinta* 4.3]; *de popularibus legibus*.

CHAPTER 16

Things to observe in the composition of laws

Those who have a comprehensive enough genius to be able to give laws to their own nation or to another should pay certain attentions to the way they are formed.

Their style should be concise. The laws of the Twelve Tables are a model of precision; children learned them by heart.[25] The *Novellae* of Justinian are so diffuse that they had to be abridged.[26]

The style of the laws should be simple; direct expression is always better understood than indirect. There is no majesty in the laws of the Eastern Empire; its princes are made to speak like rhetoricians. When the style of the laws is inflated, they are regarded only as a work of ostentation.

[25] "As required songs" [L.]. Cicero, *De legibus*, bk. 2 [2.23.59].

[26] This was the work of Irnerius.

It is essential for the words of the laws to awaken the same ideas in all men. Cardinal Richelieu agreed that one could accuse a minister before the king,[27] but he wanted one to be punished if the things one proved were not worthy of consideration, which kept everyone from speaking any truth whatsoever against the minister because what is worthy of consideration is entirely relative and what is worthy of consideration for one is not so for another.

The law of Honorius punished by death any one who bought as a serf a freed man and any who wanted to cause him distress.[28] Such a vague expression must not be used; the distress one causes a man depends entirely on the degree of his sensitivity.

When the law has to impose some measure,[e] one must, as much as possible, avoid doing so at a price in silver. A thousand causes change the value of the money, and with the same denomination one no longer has the same thing. One knows the story of the impertinent man in Rome[29] who slapped everyone he met and had them given the twenty-five sous of the law of Twelve Tables.

When the ideas of things have been well fixed in a law, one must not return to vague expressions. In the criminal ordinance of Louis XIV,[30] after an exact enumeration of royal cases, these words are added, "And those the royal judges have judged in all times"; this brings back the arbitrariness that had just been left behind.

Charles VII says that he learns that parties make an appeal three, four, and six months after the judgment, contrary to the custom in the countries of customary law;[31] he orders them to appeal immediately unless there is a fraud or deceit by the prosecutor[32] or a great and obvious cause to take up the appeal. The conclusion of this law destroys

[27] *Testament politique* [Cardinal Richelieu, pt. 1, chap. 8, sec. 7, p. 316; 1947 edn].

[28] "Or whoever might wish to disquiet one who had been granted emancipation" [L.], *Codex Theodosianus. Constitutiones Sirmondianae*, vol. 1, p. 737 [tit. 19, deemed spurious, not included in the standard edition, Mommsen, 1905].

[29] Aulus Gellius [*NA*], bk. 20, chap. 1 [20.1.13].

[30] In the testimony for this ordinance one can find their motives for it [1670. August. *Recueil général des anciennes lois françaises, Bourbons*, #623, tit. 1, "De la compétence des juges," #11; 18, 374]. [It should be noted that M.'s quotation is not from the law in question, but represents his own interpretation; see the note at the passage, 18, 374.]

[31] In his ordinance of Montel-les-Tours, in 1453 [Laurière, 14, 284, Charles VII. *Recueil général des anciennes lois françaises*, #213, art. 18; 9, 212].

[32] One could punish the prosecutor without the necessity for disturbing public order.

[e] The French word is *vexation*, here meaning a kind of tax, although we usually translate it as "harassment."

its beginning, and it destroyed it so well that subsequently one pursued appeals for thirty years.[33]

The law of the Lombards does not want a woman who has taken the habit of a religious order, although she has not taken her vows, to be able to marry,[34] "for," it says, "if a spouse who has engaged a woman to himself only by a ring cannot without committing a crime marry another, there is even stronger reason for the spouse of god or the blessed virgin . . ." I say that in laws one must reason from reality to reality and not from reality to figure or from figure to reality.

A law of Constantine wants the testimony of the bishop alone to suffice, without other witnesses being heard.[35] This prince took a short cut: he judged the business by persons and persons by their rank.

The laws should not be subtle; they are made for people of middling understanding; they are not an art of logic but the simple reasoning of a father of the family.

When exceptions, limitations, modifications, are not necessary in a law, it is much better not to include them in it. Such details plunge one into new details.

One must not make a change in a law without a sufficient reason. Justinian ordered that a husband could be repudiated without the wife losing her dowry, if he had not been able to consummate the marriage in two years.[36] He changed the law and gave three years to the poor unfortunate man.[37] But, in such a case, two years is as good as three and three is no better than two.

When one goes so far as to give a reason for a law, this reason must be worthy of it. A Roman law decides that a blind person cannot plead because he cannot see the ornaments of the magistracy.[38] To give such a bad reason when so many good ones present themselves must have been deliberate.

The jurist Paul says that the child is born perfect in the seventh month and that the ratio of Pythagorean numbers seems to prove it.[39] It

[33] The ordinance of 1667 made rulings about this [1667. April, *Recueil général des anciennes lois françaises, Bourbons*, #503, 18, 103–180].

[34] [*Leges Langobardum*] bk. 2, tit. 37 [2.37.1, Liut. 30].

[35] In the *Codex Theodosianus. Constitutiones Sirmondianae*, vol. 1 [tit. 1, p. 477; 1952 edn].

[36] Law 1, *Code* [*Corpus Juris Civilis, Code* 5.17.10]; *de repudiis et iudicio et moribus sublato.*

[37] See *Authentica, sed hodie* [*Corpus Juris Civilis, Novellae* 22.6; *Code* 5.17.10]; at *Code de repudiis et iudicio et moribus sublato.*

[38] Law 1 [*Corpus Juris Civilis, Digest* 3.1.1]; *de postulando.*

[39] [Paul the Jurist] *Sententiarum*, bk. 4, tit. 9 [4.9.5].

is singular to judge these things by the ratio of Pythagorean numbers.[f]

Some French jurists have said that, when the king acquired a country, the churches there became subject to the right of regale, because the king's crown is round. I shall not discuss at all the rights of the king, or whether, in this case, the reason of the civil or of the ecclesiastical law should yield to the reason of the political law; but I shall say that such respectable rights should be defended by serious maxims. Who has ever seen the real rights of a rank founded on the configuration of the sign of that rank?

Davila[40] says that Charles IX was declared of age in the *parlement* of Rouen at the beginning of his fourteenth year, because the laws want one to reckon the time from moment to moment where the restitution and administration of the ward's goods are concerned; but, where the acquisition of honors is concerned, it regards the year begun as a year completed. I take care not to censure a provision which does not yet seem to have had drawbacks; I shall only say that the reason alleged by the Chancelier de l'Hôpital was not the true one; the governing of peoples is far from being only an honor.

In the matter of presumption, that of law is better than that of man. French law regards as fraudulent all acts done by a merchant in the ten days preceding his bankruptcy;[41] this is a presumption of law. Roman law inflicted penalties on the husband who kept his wife after her adultery, unless he determined to do so from fear of the outcome of a suit or from neglect of his own shame, and this is the presumption of man. The judge had to presume the motives for the husband's conduct and determine it by a very obscure way of thinking. When the judge presumes, judgments become arbitrary; when the law presumes, it gives a fixed rule to the judge.

The law of Plato, as I have said, wanted one to punish the one who killed himself not to avoid ignominy, but from weakness.[42] This law was defective because in the only case where one could not draw from the criminal the admission of the motive that made him act, it wanted the judge to base his determination on these motives.

[40] [Enrico Caterina Davila] *Dell'istoria delle guerre civili di Francia*, p. 96 [bk. 3; 1, 281–282; 1825 edn].

[41] It is from the month of November, 1702 [November 18, 1702, *Recueil général des anciennes lois françaises*, *Bourbons*, #1833; 20, 419–421].

[42] [Plato] *Laws*, bk. 9 [873c–d].

[f] The word *raison* denotes both "reason" and "ratio."

As useless laws weaken necessary laws, those that can be evaded weaken legislation. A law should have its effect, and departures from it must not be permitted by some private agreement.

The Falcidian law ordered among the Romans that the heir would always have a fourth of the inheritance; another law[43] permitted the testator to prohibit the heir from keeping this fourth part; this is trifling with the laws. The Falcidian law became useless for, if the testator wanted to favor his heir, the latter had no need of the Falcidian law, and if he did not want to favor his heir, he prohibited his heir from making use of the Falcidian law.

One must take care that laws are conceived so as not to run counter to the nature of things. In the proscription of the Prince of Orange, Philip II promised to give to the one who killed him, or to his heirs, twenty-five thousand ecus and nobility, and this on the word of the king and as servant of god. Nobility promised for such an action! Such an action ordered in one's capacity as a servant of god! All this upsets equally the ideas of honor, those of morality, and those of religion.

It is rare that one must prohibit something that is not bad on the pretense of an imagined perfection.

There must be a certain candor in the laws. Made to punish the wickedness of men, they should have the greatest innocence themselves. One can see in the law of the Visigoths that ridiculous requirement by which the Jews were obliged to eat everything accompanying the pork, but not the pork itself.[44] This was a great cruelty: they were subjected to a law contrary to their own; they were allowed to keep of their own only that which could be a sign by which they could be recognized.

[43] *Authentica, sed sum testator* [*Corpus Juris Civilis, Novellae* 1.2, 3; *Code*, 6.50.7].
[44] [*Lex Wisigothorum*] bk. 12, tit. 2, para. 16 [12.2.16].

CHAPTER 17

A bad way of giving laws

The Roman emperors, like our princes, manifested their wills by decrees and edicts, but, as our princes do not, they permitted judges or single individuals to interrogate them by letter on their disputes, and their replies were called rescripts. The decretals of the popes are, properly speaking, rescripts. One senses that this is a bad sort of legislation. Those who demand laws in this way are bad guides for the legislator; the facts are always poorly presented. Trajan, says Julius Capitolinus,[45] often refused to give these sorts of rescripts, so that a decision, and often a particular favor, would not be extended to all cases. Macrinus had decided to abolish all these rescripts;[46] he could not suffer one to regard as laws the responses of Commodus, Caracalla, and all those other incompetent princes. Justinian thought otherwise, and he filled his compilation with them.

I would want those who read Roman laws to distinguish well these sorts of assumptions from senatus-consults, plebiscites, general constitutions of the emperors, and all the laws founded on the nature of things, on the frailty of women, on the weakness of minors, and on the public utility.

[45] See Julius Capitolinus, *Opillius Macrinus* [13.1].
[46] Ibid. [Julius Capitolinus, *Opillius Macrinus* 13.1].

CHAPTER 18
On ideas of uniformity

There are certain ideas of uniformity that sometimes seize great spirits (for they touched Charlemagne), but that infallibly strike small ones. They find in it a kind of perfection they recognize because it is impossible not to discover it: in the police the same weights, in commerce the same measures, in the state the same laws and the same religion in every part of it. But is this always and without exception appropriate? Is the ill of changing always less than the ill of suffering? And does not the greatness of genius consist rather in knowing in which cases there must be uniformity and in which differences? In China, the Chinese are governed by Chinese ceremonies, and the Tartars by Tartar ceremonies; they are, however, the people in the world which most have tranquility as their purpose. When the citizens observe the laws, what does it matter if they observe the same ones?

CHAPTER 19

On legislators

Aristotle sometimes wanted to satisfy his jealousy of Plato, sometimes his passion for Alexander. Plato was indignant at the tyranny of the people of Athens. Machiavelli was full of his idol, Duke Valentino. Thomas More, who spoke rather of what he had read than of what he had thought, wanted to govern all states with the simplicity of a Greek town.[47] Harrington saw only the republic of England, while a crowd of writers found disorder wherever they did not see a crown. The laws always meet the passions and prejudices of the legislator. Sometimes they pass through and are colored; sometimes they remain there and are incorporated.

[47] In his *Utopia* [Thomas More, *Utopia*, bk. 2, pp. 39–40; 1975 edn].

BOOK 30

The theory of the feudal laws among the Franks in their relation with the establishment of the monarchy

CHAPTER I

On feudal laws

I would believe there was an imperfection in my work if I did not mention an event which happened once in the world and which will perhaps never happen again, if I did not speak of those laws which were seen to appear in a moment in all of Europe without connection with those known until then, of those laws which did infinite good and ill, which left rights when domain was ceded, which diminished the whole of the weight of lordship by giving many people various kinds of lordship over the same thing or the same persons, which set various limits to empire that was too extensive, which produced rule with an inclination to anarchy and anarchy with a tendency to order and harmony.

This would require a work expressly for that purpose, but, given the nature of this one, one will find here these laws as I have come to view them rather than as I have dealt with them.

The spectacle of the feudal laws is a fine one. An old oak tree stands;[1] from afar the eye sees its leaves; coming closer it sees the trunk, but it does not perceive the roots; to find them the ground must be dug up.

[1] "As much as the top reached to the heavens above, by so much did the roots extend to Tartarus" [L.]. Virgil [*Aeneid* 4.445–446].

CHAPTER 2

On the sources of the feudal laws

The peoples who conquered the Roman empire were from Germany. Although few old authors described their mores for us, we have two of great weight. Caesar, while waging war on the Germans, described the mores of the Germans,[2] and he regulated some of his enterprises by their mores.[3] A few pages of Caesar's on this subject are volumes.

Tacitus wrote a work expressly for that purpose on the mores of the Germans. This work is short, but it is the work of Tacitus who summarized everything because he saw everything.

These two authors are in such agreement with the codes of laws of the barbarian peoples that we have that, while reading Caesar and Tacitus, one finds these codes everywhere and while reading these codes one finds Caesar and Tacitus everywhere.

For if in the search for the feudal laws I find myself in a dark labyrinth full of paths and detours, I believe that I hold the end of the thread and that I can walk.

[2] [Gaius Julius Caesar, *De bello Gallico*] bk. 6 [4.1–10].
[3] His retreat from Germany, for instance. Ibid. [Gaius Julius Caesar, *De bello Gallico* 4.17–20.]

CHAPTER 3

The origin of vassalage

Caesar says that "the Germans did not apply themselves to agriculture; most of them lived on milk, cheese, and meat; no one had lands or boundaries of his own; the princes and magistrates of each nation gave individuals the portion of land they wanted, in the place they wanted, and obliged them to go elsewhere the next year."[4] Tacitus says that "each prince had a troop of people who were attached to him and who followed him."[5] This author, who in his own language gives them a

[4] [Gaius Julius Caesar] *De bello Gallico*, bk. 6 [6.22]. Tacitus, *Germania* [31] adds: "They have neither house, nor land, nor employment, for they are supported by whomever they come upon" [L.].
[5] [Tacitus] *Germania* [13].

name related to their state, calls them *companions*.[6] There was a singular emulation among them to obtain some distinction from the prince and there was a like emulation among the princes for the number and bravery of their companions.[7] "It is," adds Tacitus, "rank, it is power, to be always surrounded by a crowd of young people one has chosen; it is an ornament in peace, it is a bulwark in war. If one surpasses the others in the number and courage of one's companions, one is famous in one's own nation and among the neighboring peoples; one receives presents; embassies come from everywhere. Reputation often decides war. In combat it is shameful for the prince to be inferior in courage; it is shameful for the troops not to equal the valor of the prince; it is an eternal infamy to outlive him. One's most sacred engagement is to defend him. If one city is in peace, the princes go to those that are waging war; in this war they keep a great number of friends. The latter receive from them war horses and terrifying javelins. Meals, inelegant but large, are a kind of pay for them. The prince supports his liberalities only by wars and rapine. You could persuade them to work the land and wait out the year far less than you could persuade them to challenge the enemy and be wounded; they will not acquire by sweat what they can obtain by blood."

Thus, among the Germans, there were vassals but not fiefs. There were no fiefs because the princes had no lands to give, or rather, fiefs were war horses, weapons, and meals. There were vassals because there were faithful men who were bound by their word, who were engaged for war, and who did almost the same service that was later done for fiefs.

[6] *Comites* [companions].

[7] Ibid. [Tacitus, *Germania* 13, 14].

CHAPTER 4

Continuation of the same subject

Caesar[8] says that "when one of the princes declared to the assembly that he had formed a plan for some expedition and asked for followers, those who approved the leader and the enterprise rose and offered their help. They were praised by the multitude. But, if they did not fulfill

[8] [Gaius Julius Caesar] *De bello Gallico*, bk. 6 [6.23.7–8].

their engagement, they lost the confidence of the public and were regarded as deserters and traitors."

What Caesar says here and what we have said in the preceding chapter, following Tacitus, is the seed of the history of the reign of the Merovingians.

One must not be astonished that for each expedition, the kings should have had to remake new armies, persuade new troops, and engage new people, that they had to lay out much in order to acquire much, that they acquired constantly by the division of lands and spoils and that they constantly gave away these lands and spoils, that their domain grew continually and diminished constantly, that a father who gave one of his children a kingdom always united it with a treasury;[9] that the treasury of the king was regarded as necessary to the monarchy, and that a king could not, even for the dowry of his daughter, share it with outsiders without the consent of the other kings.[10] The pace of the monarchy was set by springs that had always to be rewound.

[9]See *Gesta Dagoberti I, Regis Francorum* [31; *MGH*, *Scriptorum rerum Merovingicarum*, vol. 2, p. 412].

[10]See Gregory of Tours [*Historia ecclesiastica Francorum*], bk. 6 [6.45], on the marriage of Chilperic's daughter. Childebert sent embassies to him to say he could give none of the towns of his father's kingdom to his daughter, none of his treasure or any of his serfs, his horses, his knights, his trains of oxen, or anything else.

CHAPTER 5
On the conquest of the Franks

It is not true that the Franks, on entering Gaul, occupied all the lands of the country in order to make fiefs for them. Some people have thought thus, because they have seen that near the end of the reign of the Carolingians almost all the land had become fiefs, under-fiefs, or dependencies of one or the other, but this had particular causes that will subsequently be explained.

The consequence they have wanted to draw, that the barbarians made a general regulation establishing servitude to the land[a] everywhere, is no less false than the principle. If, at a time when fiefs

[a]*servitude de la glèbe*. See 13.3 (p. 215), where Montesquieu speaks of *esclavage de la glèbe*, and 30.10 (note [b], bk. 30).

were revocable, all the lands of the kingdom had been fiefs or dependencies of fiefs, and all the men of the kingdom had been vassals or serfs dependent on them, since the one who has the goods always also has the power, the king, who would continually have had the disposition of the fiefs, that is, of the only property, would have had a power as arbitrary as is that of the sultan of Turkey; this upsets all of history.

CHAPTER 6

On the Goths, Burgundians, and Franks

Gaul was invaded by the Germanic nations. The Visigoths occupied Narbonne and almost all of the south; the Burgundians were established in the part to the east; and the Franks conquered almost all the rest.

There must be no doubt that during their conquests these barbarians preserved the mores, inclinations, and usages they had in their own country, because a nation does not change its way of thinking and acting in an instant. In Germany these peoples cultivated the land but little. It appears, according to Tacitus and Caesar, that they applied themselves earnestly to pastoral life; thus almost all the provisions of the law codes of the barbarians concerned herds. Roricon, who wrote history among the Franks, was a herdsman.

CHAPTER 7

Different ways of dividing the lands

As, on various pretexts, the Goths and the Burgundians had entered the interior of the empire, the Romans were obliged to provide for their sustenance in order to check their devastations. First they gave them grain;[11] subsequently, they preferred to give them land. The emperors, or the Roman magistrates in their name, made agreements with them

[11] See Zosimus [*Historiae*], bk. 5 [5.48, Bekker, p. 315] on the distribution of the grain requested by Alaric.

on the division of the country,[12] as is seen in the chronicles and in the codes of the Visigoths[13] and the Burgundians.[14]

The Franks did not follow the same plan. No trace of such a division of lands is found in the Salic and Ripuarians laws. They conquered; they took what they wanted, and they made regulations only among themselves.

Therefore, let us distinguish the procedure of the Burgundians and the Visigoths in Gaul, of these same Visigoths in Spain, and of the auxiliary soldiers under Romulus Augustulus and Odoacer in Italy,[15] from that of the Franks in Gaul and the Vandals in Africa.[16] The first made agreements with the former inhabitants, and consequently a division of the lands with them; the second did none of this.

[12]"[In the year 456] the Burgundians occupied part of Gaul, and they divided the lands with the senators of Gaul" [L.]. Marius, Bishop of Avenches, *Chronica*, *anno* 456 [*MGH*, *Auctorum antiquissimorum*, vol. 11, *Chronica minora*, vol. 2, p. 232].

[13][*Lex Wisigothorum*] bk. 10, tit. 1, paras. 8, 9, and 16 [10.1.8, 9, 16].

[14][*Leges Burgundionum*] chap. 54, paras. 1 and 2 [54.1–2]; and this division continued to exist in the time of Louis the Pious, as appears by his capitulary of the year 829, which was inserted into the *Leges Burgundionum*, tit. 79, para. 1 [79.1].

[15]See Procopius, *The Gothic War* [5.1.4–8; 5.11, 12].

[16][Procopius] *The Vandalic Wars* [3.3.1–3; 3.5.12–17; 4.14.8–10].

CHAPTER 8

Continuation of the same subject

What gives the idea of a great usurpation of Roman lands by the barbarians is that one finds in the laws of the Visigoths and the Burgundians that these two peoples had two-thirds of the lands; but the two-thirds were only in certain districts assigned to them.

In the law of the Burgundians, Gundobad says that his people received two-thirds of the lands at their establishment,[17] and in the second supplement to this law it is said that no more than one-half would be given to those who later came into their country.[18] Therefore,

[17]"At that time it was granted that our people would receive one-third of the slaves and two-thirds of the lands" [L.]. *Leges Burgundionum*, tit. 54, para. 1 [54.1].

[18]"That nothing more may be required by the Burgundians who have come later, other than the present requirement of half the land" [L.]. [*Leges Burgundionum*, second supplement] art. 11 [*Constitutiones extravagantes* 21.12].

not all the lands had been divided in the beginning between the Romans and the Burgundians.

One finds the same expressions in the texts of these two regulations; each explains the other. And, just as the second cannot be understood to refer to a universal division of lands, one cannot give this meaning to the first.

The Franks acted with the same moderation as the Burgundians; they did not despoil the Romans throughout the extent of their conquests. What would they have done with so much land? They took what suited them and left the rest.

CHAPTER 9

The just application of the law of the Burgundians and that of the Visigoths on the division of lands

One must consider that these divisions were not made in a tyrannical spirit, but with the idea of providing for the mutual needs of the two peoples who were to inhabit the same country.

The Burgundian law wants every Burgundian to be received as a guest in a Roman's home. This is in conformity with the mores of the Germans who, in the account of Tacitus,[19] were the people in the world who most liked to practice hospitality.

The law wants the Burgundians to have two-thirds of the lands and one-third of the serfs. It followed the genius of the two peoples, and it conformed to the way they gained their sustenance. The Burgundian who grazed his herds needed much land and few serfs, and the great work of cultivating the land required the Romans to have less land and a greater number of serfs. The woods were divided in half because their needs in this regard were the same.

One sees in the code of the Burgundians[20] that each barbarian was paired with a Roman. Therefore, the division was not general, but the number of Romans who gave a share was equal to the number of Burgundians who received it. The Roman was injured as little as possible. The Burgundian, warrior, hunter, and herdsman, did not

[19] [Tacitus] *Germania* [21].

[20] And in that of the Visigoths [*Lex Wisigothorum* 10.1.8–9].

disdain taking fallow land; the Roman kept the lands most appropriate for cultivation; the herds of the Burgundian fertilized the field of the Roman.

CHAPTER 10

On servitudes

It is said in the law of the Burgundians[21] that, when these peoples established themselves in Gaul, they received two-thirds of the lands and one-third of the serfs. Therefore, servitude to the land[b] was established in this part of Gaul before the Burgundians entered it.[22]

The law of the Burgundians, enacting over the two nations, formally distinguishes in each of them nobles, freemen, and serfs.[23] Therefore, servitude was not a thing peculiar to the Romans, or liberty and nobility a thing peculiar to the barbarians.

This same law says that if a Burgundian freed man did not give a certain sum to his master, or receive a third share from a Roman, he was still counted as a member of the family of his master.[24] Therefore, the Roman property owner was free because he was not in the family of another; he was free because his third was a sign of liberty.

One has only to open the Salic and Ripuarian laws to see that the Romans no more lived in servitude among the Franks than among the other conquerors of Gaul.

The Count of Boulainvilliers has fallen short in the chief point of his system; he has not proven that the Franks made a general regulation that put the Romans into a kind of servitude.[c]

As his work is written with no art and as he speaks in it with that simplicity, frankness, and innocence of the old nobility from which he came, everyone is able to judge both the fine things he says and the

[21] [*Leges Burgundionum*] tit. 54 [54].
[22] This is confirmed by the whole title of the *Code* [*Corpus Juris Civilis*, *Code* 11.48]: *de agricolis censitis vel colonis*.
[23] "If someone knocks out the teeth of a Burgundian aristocrat or of a Roman noble" [L.], tit. 26, para. 1 [26.1]; and "If an ordinary freeborn person either Burgundian or Roman" [L.], ibid., para. 2 [*Leges Burgundionum* 26.2].
[24] [*Leges Burgundionum*] tit. 57 [57].

[b] *servitude de la glèbe*. Here this servitude is identified as serfdom.
[c] Henri Boulainvilliers, *Histoire de l'ancien gouvernement de la France*.

errors into which he falls. Thus, I shall not examine it. I shall say only that he had more spirit than enlightenment and more enlightenment than knowledge, but this knowledge was not despicable because he knew well the great things about our history and our laws.

The Count of Boulainvilliers and the Abbé Dubos have each made a system, the one seeming to be a conspiracy against the third estate, and the other a conspiracy against the nobility. When the Sun gave his chariot to Phaeton to drive, he said to him: "If you climb too high, you will burn the celestial residence; if you drop too low, you will reduce the earth to ashes. Do not go too far to the right, or you will fall into the constellation of the Serpent; do not go too far to the left, or you will go into that of the Altar: stay between the two."[25]

[25] "Do not go too low, or go too high through the ethereal region. If you rise too much, you will burn the celestial covering; if you fall too much, you will burn the earth. Go the middle way: it is the safest. Neither turn yourself too far to the right towards the coiling Serpent, nor guide your wheel to the left side where the Altar lies. Keep yourself between the two" [L.]. Ovid, *Metamorphoses* 2 [2.135–140].

CHAPTER II

Continuation of the same subject

What has given the idea of a general ruling made at the time of the conquest is that there were a prodigious number of servitudes in France toward the beginning of the reign of the Capetians and that, as the continuous progress of these servitudes was not noticed, one has imagined in a hazy past a general law that never existed.

At the beginning of the reign of the Merovingians, there was an infinite number of freemen, among both the Franks and the Romans; but the number of serfs increased so much that at the beginning of the reign of the Capetians, all the plowmen and almost all the inhabitants of towns were serfs,[26] and whereas in the towns, at the beginning of the Merovingian reign, there was nearly the same administration as among the Romans, bodies of bourgeoisie, a senate, and judicial courts, one finds near the beginning of the reign of the Capetians scarcely anything but a lord and serfs.

[26] While Gaul was under the domination of the Romans, they formed particular bodies: they were ordinarily freed men or descendants of freed men.

When the Franks, Burgundians, and Goths invaded, they took all the gold, silver, furniture, clothing, men, women, and boys, that the army could carry; everything was put together and the army divided it.[27] The entire body of history proves that after the first establishment, that is, after the first ravages, they reached a settlement with the inhabitants and left them all their political and civil rights. This was the right of nations in those times; everything was taken in war, everything was granted in peace. If it had not been so, how would we find in the Salic and Burgundian laws so many provisions in contradiction to the general servitude of men?

But that which conquest did not do was done by this same right of nations,[28] which continued to exist after the conquest. Resistance, rebellion, the taking of towns, brought with them the servitude of the inhabitants. And as, aside from the wars waged between the different conquering nations, among the Franks in particular the various divisions of the monarchy constantly gave rise to civil wars between brothers or nephews in which this right of nations was always practiced, servitudes became more general in France than in the other countries; and this is, I believe, one of the causes of the difference between our French laws and those of Italy and Spain concerning the rights of lords.

Conquest was the business of but a moment, and the right of nations that was applied to it produced some servitudes. The same right used for several centuries extended servitudes prodigiously.

Theodoric,[29] believing that the peoples of Auvergne were not faithful to him, said to the Franks of his division: "Follow me, I shall lead you to a country where you will have gold, silver, captives, clothing, and herds in abundance, and you will bring all its men to your country."

After the peace that was made between Guntram and Chilperic,[30] as those who laid siege to Bourges were ordered to return, they took away so much booty that they left almost no men or herds in the country.

When Theodoric, King of Italy, whose spirit and policy was always to distinguish himself from the other barbarian kings, sent his army to Gaul, he wrote to the general:[31] "I want Roman laws to be followed and you must return fugitive slaves to their masters; the defender of liberty

[27] See Gregory of Tours [*Historia ecclesiastica Francorum*], bk. 2, chap. 27 [2.27]; Aimoin of Fleury-sur-Loire [*Historia Francorum*], bk. 1, chap. 12 [1.12].

[28] See the *Lives of the Saints*, cited below, n. 34.

[29] Gregory of Tours [*Historia ecclesiastica Francorum*] bk. 3 [3.11].

[30] Gregory of Tours [*Historia ecclesiastica Francorum*], bk. 6, chap. 31 [6.31].

[31] Cassiodorus [*Variae*], bk. 3, letter 43 [3.43].

should not favor the abandonment of servitude. Let the other kings delight in pillaging and ruining the towns they have taken; we want to vanquish in such a way that our subjects complain of their having been subjected so late." It is clear that he wanted to make odious the kings of the Franks and the Burgundians and that he alluded to their right of nations.

This right lasted into the reign of the Carolingians. After the army of Pepin had been in Aquitaine, it returned to France laden with an infinite number of spoils and serfs, according to the *Annals* of Metz.[32]

I could cite innumerable authorities.[33] And as tender charity was stirred by these misfortunes, as a number of holy bishops, seeing the captives shackled two by two, used the silver of the churches and even sold the sacred vessels to buy back those whom they could, as holy monks threw themselves into this task, one finds the greatest clarifications on this subject in the lives of the saints.[34] Although one can reproach the authors of these lives for having sometimes been a little too credulous concerning the things god certainly did if they were in the order of his designs, one cannot fail to find considerable enlightenment in these lives about the mores and usages of those times.

When one examines the records of our history and our laws, it seems that everything is a sea and that the sea lacks even shores.[35] All these cold, dry, insipid, and harsh writings must be read, must be devoured, as the fable tells us Saturn devoured stones.

An infinity of lands that freemen made productive became subject to mortmain.[36] When a country lost the freemen who had lived there, those who had many serfs took or had ceded to themselves great territories and built villages on them, as is seen in various charters. On the other hand, the freemen who had cultivated the arts became serfs

[32] For the year 763. "There was countless booty and captives: the entire army returned to France wealthy" [L.]. [*Annales Mettenses*, *763* (761); *MGH* SS. 1, 334].

[33] *Annales Fuldenses* 739 [*MGH* SS. 1, 345]; Paulus Diaconus, *Langobardum Historia*, bk. 3, 30 [3.30] and bk. 4, 1 [4.1]; and the lives of the saints cited in the following note.

[34] [References in this note are to volumes in the *Recueil des historiens des Gaules et de la France*, 1869 edn; each citation can lead to the complete text in the lives of the saints collected by the Bollandists, Maurists, and Gregory of Tours.] See the lives of St. Epiphanius [2, 370], St. Eptadius [3, 380–381], St. Caesarius [3, 384–385], St. Fidolus [3, 406–407], St. Partianus [3, 409], St. Treverius [3, 411–412], St. Eusichius [3, 428–430], St. Luidgerius [2, 611–632; 3, 643; 5, 449–450; *MGH* SS. 2], the miracles of St. Julianus [2, 466–467].

[35] "Shores were lacking to the sea" [L.]. Ovid [*Metamorphoses*], bk. 1 [1.293].

[36] Even the colonists were not all serfs; see laws 18 and 23 of the *Code* [*Corpus Juris Civilis*, *Code* 11.48.18, 23]; *de agricolis censitis vel colonis*, and law 20 of the same title [11.48.20].

who had to exercise them. Servitude gave back to the arts and to tilling what had been taken from them.

It was usual to give these lands to the churches to be held for the census, for the owners of lands believed that by their servitude they participated in the saintliness of the churches.

CHAPTER 12

That the lands divided by the barbarians did not pay taxes

Simple, poor, free, warlike, and pastoral peoples who were without industry and who were attached to their lands only by their reed huts[37] followed their leaders in order to get booty and not in order to pay or to levy taxes. The art of abusive taxation[d] is always invented afterwards, when men begin to enjoy the felicity of the other arts.

The transitory tax of a jug of wine for each arpent of land,[38] one of the harassments imposed by Chilperic and Fredegunde, concerned only the Romans. Indeed, the Franks, not the ecclesiastics who in those times were all Romans, tore up the rolls of these assessments.[39] This distressing tax principally affected the inhabitants of the towns;[40] now, almost all towns were inhabited by Romans.

Gregory of Tours says that after the death of Chilperic a certain judge was obliged to take refuge in a church for having in the reign of that prince subjected to taxation Franks who in Childebert's time were freeborn: "*multos de Francis qui, tempore Childeberti regis, ingenui fuerant, publico tributo subegit.*"[41e] Therefore, the Franks who were not serfs did not pay taxes.

[37] See Gregory of Tours [*Historia ecclesiastica Francorum*], bk. 2 [2.8, 27, e.g.].

[38] Ibid. [Gregory of Tours, *Historia ecclesiastica Francorum*], bk. 5 [5.28].

[39] This appears throughout the *Historia* of Gregory of Tours. The same Gregory asks of a certain Vulfolaic how he had been able to enter the clergy, as he was a Lombard. Gregory of Tours [*Historia ecclesiastica Francorum*], bk. 8 [8.15].

[40] "This tribute was introduced throughout all the cities of Gaul" [L.]. *Vita Aridii Abbatis Lemovicini* [#38; *MGH*, *Scriptorum rerum Merovingicarum*, tom. 3, p. 593; *Acta sanctorum Ordinis S. Benedicti*, Saec I, 349–352, *Acta sanct.* Aug. tom. 5, 178–194].

[41] [Gregory of Tours, *Historia ecclesiastica Francorum*] bk. 7 [7.15].

[d] *maltôte.* See note [d], bk. 25.

[e] "who in the time of King Childebert exacted public taxes from many Franks who were freeborn." Montesquieu here gives the Latin he translated in the preceding clause.

Any grammarian would pale at seeing how this passage was interpreted by the Abbé Dubos.[42] He remarks that in those times, freed men were also called freeborn. Thereupon, he translates the Latin word *ingenui* by these words: *affranchis de tributs* [those freed from taxes]; an expression which can be used in French as one says *affranchis de soins* [those freed from cares], and *affranchis de peines* [those freed from penalties]; but in Latin, *ingenui a tributis* [the members of the class of freedmen from taxes], *libertini a tributis* [the member of the class of freemen from taxes], *manumissi tributorum* [the emancipated men from taxes], would be monstrous expressions.

Parthenius, says Gregory of Tours,[43] feared he would be put to death by the Franks for having imposed taxes on them. The Abbé Dubos, pressed by this passage, coolly assumes that which is in question; it was, he says, an additional burden.[44]

One sees in the laws of the Visigoths[45] that, when a barbarian occupied the land of a Roman, the judge obliged him to sell it in order for this land to continue to be tributary; therefore, the barbarians paid no taxes on lands.[46]

The Abbé Dubos,[47] who needed the Visigoths to pay taxes,[48] departs from the literal and spiritual meaning of the law and imagines, solely because he imagines, that there was between the establishment of the Goths and this law an increase in taxes which concerned only the Romans. But it is permitted only to Father Hardouin thus to exercise an arbitrary power over the facts.

[42] [Jean Baptiste Dubos] *Histoire critique de l'établissement de la monarchie française*, vol. 3, chap. 14, p. 515 [bk. 6, chap. 14; 4, 372–373; 1742 edn].

[43] [Gregory of Tours, *Historia ecclesiastica Francorum*] bk. 3, chap. 36 [3.36].

[44] [Jean Baptiste Dubos, *Histoire critique de l'établissement de la monarchie française*] vol. 3, p. 514 [bk. 6, chap. 14; 4, 371; 1742 edn].

[45] "Judges [. . .] and the subordinates of a count should take away Roman lands [*tertias*] from those who hold them by usurpation, and they should restore those exactions due from the Romans without delay so that the Treasury may in no way be harmed" [L.]. [*Lex Wisigothorum*] bk. 10, tit. 1, chap. 14 [10.1.16].

[46] The Vandals paid none in Africa. Procopius, *The Vandalic Wars*, bks. 1 and 2 [3.5.12–17]; [Landolfi Sagacis] *Historia Romana*, bk. 16, p. 106 [18.13]. Note that those who conquered Africa were a combination of Vandals and Franks. [Landolfus Sagax] *Historia Romana*, bk. 14, p. 94 [14.8–9].

[47] [Jean Baptiste Dubos] *Histoire critique de l'établissement de la monarchie française*, vol. 3, chap. 14, p. 510 [bk. 6, chap. 14; 4.365–367; 1742 edn].

[48] It rests on another law of the Visigoths [*Lex Wisigothorum*], bk. 10, tit. 1, art. 11 [10.1.16], which proves absolutely nothing; it says only that the one who received land from a lord, on the condition that rent be paid, should pay it.

The Abbé Dubos[49] seeks laws in the Justinian Code[50] to prove that the military benefices among the Romans were subject to taxation; from which he concludes that it was the same for fiefs or benefices among the Franks. But the opinion that our fiefs originated in this establishment of the Romans is condemned today; it was accredited only at the time when Roman history was known and our own very little known and when our old records were buried in dust.

The Abbé Dubos is wrong to cite Cassiodorus and to use what happened in Italy and in the part of Gaul subjected to Theodoric to inform us of usage among the Franks; these are things that must not be confused. I shall someday show in a separate work that the plan of the monarchy of the Ostrogoths was entirely different from the plan of all the ones founded in those times by the other barbarian peoples, and that far from being able to say that something was a usage among the Franks because it was among the Ostrogoths, one is, on the contrary, quite correct in thinking that a thing practiced among the Ostrogoths would not be practiced among the Franks.

What is done most reluctantly by those whose spirit floats in vast erudition is to seek their proofs in the places that are not foreign to the subject and to find, as the astronomers would say, the sun's position.

The Abbé Dubos abuses capitularies as he does history and the laws of the barbarian peoples. When he wants the Franks to have paid taxes, he applies to freemen what can be understood only of serfs;[51] when he wants to speak of their soldiery, he applies to serfs what could concern only freemen.[52]

[49] [Jean Baptiste Dubos, *Histoire critique de l'établissement de la monarchie française*] vol. 3, p. 511 [bk. 6, chap. 14; 4, 367–368; 1742 edn].

[50] Law 3, tit. 74, bk. 11 [*Corpus Juris Civilis, Code* 11.74.3; *de collatione fundorum fiscalium vel rei privatae dominicae vel civitatem vel temporum*].

[51] [Jean Baptiste Dubos] *Histoire critique de l'établissement de la monarchie française*, vol. 3, chap. 14, p. 513 [bk. 6, chap. 14; 4, 369–370; 1742 edn], in which he cites art. 28 of the *Edict of Pistes*, 864 [*CRF* 273.28]; see chapter 18 below.

[52] Ibid. [Jean Baptiste Dubos, *Etablissement de la monarchie française*], vol. 3, chap. 4, p. 298 [bk. 6, chap. 14; 4, 120–122; 1742 edn].

CHAPTER 13

What burdens were borne by the Romans and the Gauls in the monarchy of the Franks

I could examine whether the Romans and the defeated Gauls continued to pay the burdens[f] to which they had been subject under the emperors. But in order to move more rapidly, I shall content myself with saying that if they paid them at first, they were soon exempted from them and that these taxes were changed into a military service; and I admit that I can scarcely conceive how the Franks could at first have been so fond of abusive taxation[g] and could suddenly have appeared so far from it.

A capitulary of Louis the Pious explains very well to us the state of the freemen of the Frankish monarchy.[53] Some bands of Goths or Iberians fleeing the oppression of the Moors were received in the lands of Louis.[54] The agreement made with them indicates that, like other freemen, they would go to the army with their count, that in the outpost they would stand guard and go on patrol on the orders of this same count,[55] and that they would give horses and chariots for vehicles to the deputies of the king and to the ambassadors who came from his court or went to him,[56] and besides, that they would not be constrained to pay any other census and that they would be treated like other freemen.

One cannot say that these were new usages introduced at the beginning of the reign of the Carolingians; they must have belonged at least to the middle or the end of that of the Merovingians. A capitulary of 864 says expressly that it was an old custom for freemen to perform military service and further to pay for the horses and vehicles of which

[53] Of the year 815, chap. 1 [*Praeceptem primum pro Hispanis 815*; *CRF*, 132.1]. It is in conformity with the capitulary of Charles the Bald of the year 844, arts. 1 and 2 [*Praeceptem primum pro Hispanis 844*; *CRF*, 256.1–2].

[54] "On behalf of those staying in Spain, in parts of Aquitania, Septimania, and Provence" [L.]. Ibid. [*Praeceptem primum pro Hispanis 815*; *CRF*, 132, "Preface"].

[55] "Keeping watch, and scouting, which is called *wacta*" [L.]. Ibid. [*Praeceptem primum pro Hispanis 815*; *CRF*, 132.1].

[56] They were not obliged to give any to the count. Ibid., art. 5 [*Praeceptem primum pro Hispanis 815*; *CRF*, 132.5].

[f] See note [a], bk. 13.
[g] *maltôte*. See note [d], bk. 25.

we have spoken,[57] burdens that were particular to them and from which those who possessed fiefs were exempt, as I shall prove later.

This is not all: there was a regulation that scarcely permitted subjecting those freemen to taxes.[58] He who had four manors[59] was always obliged to go to war; he who had only three was paired with a freeman who had only one; the latter defrayed the expense by a quarter and stayed at home. Similarly, two freemen who each had two manors were paired; half the expense of the man who went was defrayed by the one who remained.

There is more: we have an infinity of charters in which the privileges of fiefs are given to lands or districts possessed by freemen, of which I shall later speak at length in what follows.[60] These lands were exempted from all the burdens required of them by the counts and the other officers of the king, and, as these burdens are enumerated in detail and as there is no question of taxes in them, it is obvious that they were not levied.

It was easy for the abusive taxation of the Romans to fall of itself in the Frankish monarchy; it was a very complicated art which entered into neither the ideas nor the plan of these simple peoples. If the Tartars overran Europe today, they would have to have much experience of public business before they understood what a tax-farmer[h] is.

The unknown author of the *Life* of Louis the Pious said of the counts and other officers of the nation of Franks established by Charlemagne in Aquitaine that he gave them the defense of the frontiers, the military power, and the management of the domains belonging to the crown.[61] This shows the state of the revenues of the Carolingian princes. The prince had kept domains and made them productive with his slaves.

[57] "That the Franks of a *pagus* who have a horse go with their own count amongst the host" [L.]. It is forbidden to the counts to take away their horses; "for they would not be able to join the host or provide the post horse requisitioned in accord with the ancient customs" [L.]. *Edictum Pistense 864* [*CRF*, 273.26] in the Baluze edition, p. 186.

[58] Capitulary of Charlemagne, of the year 812, chap. 1 [*Capitulare primum et secundum anni 812*, *CRF*, 50.1]; *Edictum Pistense 864*, art. 27 [*CRF*, 273.27; see also 186.7].

[59] *Quatuor mansos.* It seems to me that what was called *mansus* was a certain portion of land attached to a manse where there were slaves; witness the capitulary of the year 853, *Apud Silvacum*, tit. 14 [*CRF*, 260.2], against those who drove slaves off their *mansus*.

[60] See below, chap. 20 of this book.

[61] In Duchesne, tom. 2, p. 287 [Anonymous, "Astronomous," *Vita Hludowici Imperatoris*, chap. 3, *anno* 778].

[h] The word here is *financier*, one who manages the finances of the king, a tax-farmer. See note [b], bk. 3.

But the indictions, the capitation, and the other imposts[i] levied in the time of the emperors on the person or the goods of freemen had been changed into an obligation to defend the frontiers or to go to war.

One can see in this same history[62] that, when Louis the Pious went to meet his father in Germany, this prince asked him how he could be so poor, for he was a king; that Louis replied he was a king in name only and the lords held almost all his domains; that Charlemagne, fearing this young prince might lose their affection if he himself took back what he had thoughtlessly given away, sent commissioners to reestablish things.

The bishops, writing to Louis, brother of Charles the Bald, said to him: "Take care of your lands so that you will not be obliged to travel constantly and stay in the households of ecclesiastics and tire their serfs with your vehicles."[63] They further said, "See to it that you have enough to live on and to receive embassies." It is obvious that kings' revenues at that time lay in their domains.[64j]

[62] In Duchesne, tom. 2, p. 89 [289] [Anonymous, "Astronomous," *Vita Hludowici Imperatoris*, chap. 6, *anno* 795].

[63] See the capitulary of the year 858, art. 14 [*Epistola episcoporum ad Ludowicum Regum 858*, *CRF*, 297.14].

[64] They continued to levy some tolls [*droits*] on rivers when there was a bridge or a ford.

[i] Here is the explanation of *impôt*, "impost."

[j] Royal domains were also called *fisci*. See note [b], bk. 3.

CHAPTER 14

On what was called the "census"

When the barbarians left their country, they wanted to put their usages into writing, but as they found it difficult to write German words with Roman letters, these laws were written in Latin.

In the confusion of the conquest and its progression most things changed their nature; in order to express them one has to use the old Latin words that were the most closely related to the new usages. Thus, what could elicit the idea of the old census of the Romans[65] was named

[65] The *census* was such a generic word that it was used to refer to the tolls for rivers, when there was a bridge or a ferry. *See Capitulare tertium, anni 803*, Baluze edition, p. 395, art. 1 [*CRF*, 57.7]; and *Capitulare quartum, anni 819*, p. 616, art. 5 [*CRF*, 141.4]. Also called by

census, tributum,[k] and when things had no relation whatever to them, one expressed as one could German words with Roman letters; thus was formed the word *fredum*, of which I shall speak at length in later chapters.

As the words *census* and *tributum* were thus used in an arbitrary way, this has cast some obscurity into the meaning that they had under the Merovingians and Carolingians; and when modern authors[66] with particular systems have found these words in the writings of that time, they have judged that what was called the *census* was precisely the Roman census and they have drawn this consequence from it, that the kings of the Merovingian and Carolingian reigns took the place of the Roman emperors and changed nothing in their administration.[67] And, as certain rights levied under the Carolingians were, by chance and certain modifications, converted into other rights,[68] modern authors have concluded that these rights were the Roman census; and, as they have seen that with the modern regulations the domain of the crown became absolutely inalienable, they have said that those rights, which represented the Roman census and which do not form a part of this domain, were pure usurpations. I shall say nothing of the other consequences.

To carry back to distant centuries the ideas of the century in which one lives is of all sources of error the most fertile. To those people who want to render all the earlier centuries modern, I shall say what the priests of Egypt said to Solon: "O Athenians, you are nothing but children!"

this name were the vehicles furnished by the freemen to the king or his envoys, as appears in the capitulary of Charles the Bald, of the year 865, art. 8 [*Apud Tusiacum 865*, art. 8; *CRF*, 274.8].

[66] The Abbé Dubos, and those who have followed him.

[67] See the weakness of the reasons of the Abbé Dubos, *Histoire critique de l'établissement de la monarchie française*, vol. 3, bk. 6, chap. 14 [bk. 6, chap. 14; 4, 337–338; 1742 edn]; especially the induction he makes from a passage of Gregory of Tours concerning a contention between Gregory's church and King Charibert.

[68] By emancipations, for example.

[k] *Census*, italicized, indicates Montesquieu's use of the Latin word *census*; "census" translates the French word *cens*; *tributum*, italicized, indicates the Latin word *tributum*; "tax" translates the French word *tribut*.

CHAPTER 15

That what was called the "census" was levied only on serfs and not on freemen

The king, the ecclesiastics, and the lords each levied regular taxes on the serfs of their domains. I prove it in regard to the king, by the capitulary *de Villis*; in regard to ecclesiastics, by the codes of laws of the barbarians;[69] in regard to the lords, by the regulations that Charlemagne made for them.[70]

These taxes were called *census*: they were economic and not fiscal rights; they were exclusively private ground rents, not public burdens.[l]

I say that what was called the *census* was a tax levied on the serfs. I prove it by a formula from Marculf, which is a permission from the king for one to become a cleric provided that one was freeborn and was not enrolled in the register of the census.[71] I prove it also by a commission that Charlemagne gave to a count he sent into the regions of Saxony;[72] it contains the freeing of the Saxons because they had embraced Christianity; and this is, properly speaking, a charter establishing them as freeborn.[73] This prince reestablishes their first civil liberty and exempts them from paying the census.[74] Therefore, these things were the same: to be a serf and to pay the census; to be free and not to pay it.

By a kind of letters-patent from the same prince on behalf of the Spaniards who had been received into the monarchy,[75] counts were prohibited from requiring any census for them and from taking their lands away. It is known that foreigners arriving in France were treated like serfs, and as Charlemagne wanted them to be regarded as freemen

[69] *Leges Alamannorum*, chap. 22 [A21; B22]; and *Lex Baiuwariorum*, tit. 1, chap. 14 [1.13], in which one finds the rulings the ecclesiastics made for their estate.

[70] Bk. 5, chap. 303 of the *Capitularies* [*Capitularia spuria. Benedictae levitae* 1.303].

[71] "If this man is really free born and not registered in the public census" [L.], bk. 1, form. 19 [*Marculfi Formulae* 1.19].

[72] In 789. Baluze edn, vol. 1, p. 250 [*Praeceptum pro trutmanno comite.* Walter, *Corpus Iuris Germania Antiqui*, 2, 103–104. *MGH* considers this law spurious].

[73] "This sworn and attested document establishes their personal status as freemen" [L.]. Ibid. [Walter, *Corpus Iuris Germania Antiqui*, 2, 104.]

[74] "Giving them all their former liberties, and all are freed from the census" [L.]. Ibid. [Walter, 2, 103.]

[75] *Praeceptem pro Hispanis 812*, Baluze edn, vol. 1, p. 500 [*CRF*, 76].

[l] *des redevances uniquement privées, et non pas des charges publiques.*

because he wanted them to own their lands,[m] he prohibited requiring the census of them.

A capitulary of Charles the Bald, given in favor of these same Spaniards,[76] wants them to be treated as were the other Franks and prohibits exacting a census from them; therefore freemen did not pay it.

Article 30 of the Edict of Pistes[n] reforms the abuse by which many colonists belonging to the king or to the church sold the dependent lands of their manors to ecclesiastics or to people of their condition and kept for themselves only a small dwelling, with the result that they could no longer be asked to pay the census; and it orders that the first state of things be reestablished; therefore, the census was a tax taken from slaves.

A further result is that there was no general census in the monarchy, and this is clear from a great number of texts. For what would the capitulary,[77] "We want the royal census required in all the places where formerly it was required legitimately,"[78] mean? What would be the meaning of the one[79] in which Charlemagne orders his deputies in the provinces to make an exact study of every census which had formerly belonged to the king's domain,[80] and the one[81] in which he disposes of the census paid by those from whom it was required?[82] What meaning is to be given to this other one[83] which reads, "If someone has acquired tributary land on which we were accustomed to levy the census,"[84] or

[76] [*Praeceptem confirmationis pro Hispanis 844*, Baluze edn, vol. 2, arts. 1 and 2, p. 27 [*CRF*, 256.1–2].

[77] *Capitulare tertium anni 805*, arts. 10 and 22 [*CRF* 44.20, 22], inserted by Anzegise, bk. 3, art. 15 [*CRF*, 183, 3.15]. This is in conformity with that of Charles the Bald, *Apud Attiniacum 854*, art. 6 [*CRF*, 261.6].

[78] "From whatever place it was exacted legitimately" [L.]. Ibid. [*CRF*, 183, 3.15].

[79] [*Capitulare tertium*] *anni 812*, arts. 10, 11, Baluze edn, vol. 1, p. 498 [*CRF*, 80.10,11].

[80] "Whatever place of old they had been accustomed to come to [*CRF* reads *exier*, to exact; Beluze reads *venire*] the king's portion" [L.]. *Capitulare tertium anni 812*, arts. 10, 11 [*CRF*, 80.10].

[81] *Capitulare secundum anni 813*, art. 6, Baluze edn, vol. 1, p. 508 [*CRF*, 77.6].

[82] "From those places where the census was exacted" [L.]. *Capitulare secundum anni 813*, art. 6 [*CRF* 77.6].

[83] Book IV of the Capitularies, art. 37 [*CRF*, 183.4.35], which was added to the *Leges Langobardum*.

[84] "If some tributary land is acquired upon which it was the custom to exact the census as our portion" [L.] [M. reads *census*; Baluze and *CRF* read *tributum*]. Bk. IV of the Capitularies, art. 37 [*CRF*, 183.4.35].

---

[m] *qu'ils eussent la propriété de leurs terres.*

[n] These laws appear in *Capitularia regum Francorum* 273.30.

finally to this other one[85] in which Charles the Bald speaks of the "lands of the census" whose census had belonged to the king from the most remote times?[86]

Notice that there are some texts which at first seem contrary to what I have said and which nevertheless confirm it. It has been seen above that freemen in the monarchy were obliged only to provide certain vehicles. The capitulary I have just cited calls this *census*[87] and opposes it to the census paid by serfs.

In addition, the Edict of Pistes[88] speaks of those free men[o] who had to pay the royal census by head and for their cottages, and who had sold themselves during the famine.[89] The king wants to buy them back. This is because those who were freed by letters of the king[90] did not ordinarily acquire a full and entire liberty[91] but paid *census in capite*, and these are the people referred to here.

Therefore, one must rid oneself of the idea of a general and universal census derived from the police of the Romans and from which it is assumed that the rights of the lords were similarly derived by usurpations. What was called census in the French monarchy, independent of the abuse this word has seen, was a particular right[p] levied on serfs by masters.

I beg the reader's pardon for the deadly boredom that so many citations must give him; I would be briefer if I did not still find in front of me the book, *The Establishment of the French Monarchy in Gaul* by Abbé Dubos. Nothing pushes back the progress of knowledge like a bad work by a famous author, because before instructing, one must begin by correcting the mistakes.

[85] 805 [865], art. 8 [*Apud Tusiacum 865*, art. 8, *CRF*, 274.8].

[86] "Where the census has been exacted as the King's portion from of old" [L.]. 805 [865], art. 8 [*Apud Tusiacum 865*, art. 8, *CRF*, 274.8].

[87] "The census or requisitioned post horse which should be paid by Frankish serfs to the royal power" [L.]. [*Apud Tusiacum 865*, *CRF*, 274.8].

[88] *Edictum Pistense 864*, art. 34, Baluze edn, p. 192 [*CRF*, 273.34].

[89] "Of those Frankish serfs who pay to the royal census as a bondsman paying poll-money and for his minor estates" [L.]. Ibid. [*Edictum Pistense 864*; *CRF*, 273.34].

[90] Article 28 of the same Edict explains all this [*Edictum Pistense 864*, art. 28, *CRF*, 273.28]. It even makes a distinction between the Roman freed man and the Frankish freed man; and one can see that the census was not a general one. This must be read.

[91] As appears by a Capitulary of Charlemagne, 813, already cited [*Capitularia secundum anni 813*; *CRF*, 77.6].

[o] *hommes francs.*

[p] This *droit*, "right," is in effect a tax, a "duty."

CHAPTER 16
On leudes or vassals

I have spoken of those volunteers among the Germans who followed princes in their enterprises. The same usage remained after the conquest. Tacitus designates them by the name "companions";[92] the Salic law by that of "men who give fealty to the king";[93] the formulas of Marculf[94] by that of "antrustions of the king";[95] our first historians by that of "leudes," "the faithful"[96] and later historians by that of "vassals and lords."[97q]

One finds in the Salic and Ripuarian laws an infinite number of provisions for the Franks and only a few for the antrustions. The provisions concerning the antrustions are different from those made for the other Franks; everywhere the goods of the Franks are regulated and nothing is said of those of the antrustions: this is a result of the goods of the latter being regulated by political law rather than civil law and being the share that fell to an army and not the patrimony of a family.

Various writers at various periods have called the goods reserved for the leudes "goods of the fisc,"[98] "benefices," "honors," "fiefs."[r]

It cannot be doubted that fiefs were at first revocable.[99] One can see in Gregory of Tours[100] that everything that Sunnegisil and Gallomagnus had had from the fisc was taken away from them and that they

[92] *Comites*: companions [Tacitus, *Germania*, 13].
[93] "Those who are armed retainers [*truste*] of the king" [L.] [*Lex Salica* 44.4; D69.4, S11.4; M. is actually quoting *ex Ribuaria* 11.1].
[94] *Marculfi Formulae*, bk. 1, form. 18 [1.18].
[95] From the word *trew*, which means "faithful" among the Germans, and among the English, "true."
[96] *Leudes, fideles*.
[97] *Vassali, seniores*.
[98] *Fiscalia*. See formula 14 of Marculf, bk. 1 [*Marculfi Formulae* 1.14]. It is said, in the life of Saint Maur, "He gave a fisc" [L.] [e.g., *Recueil des historiens des Gaules et de la France*, 3, 417B; 1869 edn] and in the *Annales Mettenses*, *anno* 747 [*MGH* SS. 1, 330]: "He gave him a retinue and many fiscs" [L.]. Goods intended for the maintenance of the royal family were called *regalia*.
[99] See *De feudis*, bk. 1, tit. 1 [1.1] and [Jacques] Cujas on this book [for text and commentary].
[100] [Gregory of Tours, *Historia ecclesiastica francorum*] bk. 9, chap. 38 [9.38].

[q] These quotation marks are not in the text.
[r] Here is something of a definition of the scope of the connotation of *biens* for the leudes. The quotation marks, again, are not in the text.

were left with only what they held as property.[s] When Guntram put his nephew Childebert on the throne, he met secretly with him and indicated to him those to whom he should give fiefs and those from whom he should take them away.[101] In a formula of Marculf, the king gave not only the benefices that his fisc held, but also those that another had held.[102] The law of the Lombards contrasts benefices with property.[103] The historians, the formulas, the codes of the different barbarian peoples, all the remaining records are unanimous. Finally, from those who wrote the book *On Fiefs*,[104] we learn that at first the lords could take fiefs away at will, that later they secured them for a year,[105] and afterward gave them for life.

101 "Those whom he should honor with gifts, and those who should be banished from office [honors]" [L.]. Ibid. [Gregory of Tours, *Historia ecclesiastica francorum*], bk. 7 [7.33.]

102 "That such and such a person be recognized to hold this position as part of a benefice from another, or as a part of our *fisc* [treasury]" [L.]. Bk. 1, form. 30 [*Marculfi Formulae* 1.30].

103 [*Leges Langobardorum*] bk. 3, tit. 8, para. 3 [Lud. 30 (pap.)].

104 [Jacques Cujas] *De feudis*, bk. 1, tit. 1 [1.1].

105 It was a kind of precarious possession that the lord renewed or did not renew, the following year, as [Jacques] Cujas has observed.

s *en propriété.*

CHAPTER 17

On the military service of freemen

Two kinds of men were held to military service: vassal leudes or under-vassals, who were obliged to do it as a consequence of their fief, and freemen who were Franks, Romans, and Gauls, who served under the count and were led by him and his officers.

The men who, on the one hand, had neither benefices nor fiefs and who, on the other, were not subject to serfdom were called freemen; the lands they possessed were what were called allodial lands.

The counts gathered the freemen together and led them to war;[106] they had officers under them they called *vicariae*,[107] and, as all the

106 See the capitulary of Charlemagne, *Capitulare primum anni 812*, arts. 3 and 4, Baluze edn, vol. 1, p. 491 [*CRF* 50.3–4]; and the *Edictum Pistense 864*, art. 26, vol. 2, p. 186 [*CRF*, 273.26].

107 "And each count has *vicariae* and *centenae* with him" [L.]. Bk. 2, art. 28 of the Capitularies [*CRF*, 183.2.28].

freemen were divided into *centenae*, which formed what was called a borough, the counts had also under them officers called *centenarii*, who led the freemen of the borough,[108] or their *centenae*, to war.[t]

The division by *centenae* is later than the establishment of the Franks in Gaul. It was made by Clotaire and Childebert with a view to obliging each district to be responsible for the robberies it might have; this is seen in the decrees of these princes.[109] A similar police is still observed today in England.

As the counts led the freemen to war, the leudes also led their vassals or under-vassals, and the bishops or abbots, or their protectors,[110] led theirs.[111]

The bishops were quite confused; they were not in agreement about what they were to do.[112] They asked Charlemagne not to oblige them to go to war any longer, and when they had obtained this, they complained that they had been made to lose public regard, and this prince was obliged to justify his intentions in this respect. Be that as it may, when the time came that they no longer went to war, I do not see that their vassals were led to war by the counts; on the contrary, one sees that the kings or the bishops chose one of the faithful[u] to lead them.[113]

In a capitulary of Louis the Pious,[114] the king distinguishes three sorts of vassals: those of the king, those of the bishops, and those of the count. The vassals of a leud or lord were led to war by the count only when some employment in the household of the king kept these leudes from leading them themselves.[115]

[108] They were called *compagenses*.

[109] *Pactus Childeberti I et Chlotharii, 595*, art. 1 [*CRF*, 3.9]. See the Baluze edn, p. 20. These rules were no doubt made by agreement.

[110] *Advocati*.

[111] *Capitulare primum anni 812*, arts. 1 and 5, Baluze edition, vol. 1, p. 490 [*CRF*, 50.1, 5].

[112] See the capitulary of the year 803, given at Worms; Baluze edn, pp. 408 and 410, *Capitulare octavum anni 803* (Worms). [Considered spurious by *MGH*; *Corpus Juris Germanici Antiqui*, ed. F. Walter, 2, 193–194; 1824 edn]; *Recueil des historiens des Gaules et de la France*, 5, 668–672; 1869 ed.]

[113] Baluze edn, p. 409 *Capitulare octavum anni 803* (*Worms*). [See previous footnote. F. Walter, 2, 193, 1824 edn], and, under Charles the Bald, *Concilio in Verno palatio 845*, art. 8, Baluze edn, vol. 2 [*CRF*, 291.8].

[114] *Capitulare quintum anni 819*, art. 27, Baluze edn, p. 618 [*CRF*, 141.27].

[115] "Concerning those vassals who serve the lord's household and who are recognized to have certain benefices; it is decreed that those who remain in the imperial household do not retain

[t] Here, as elsewhere, we have used the original Latin words, rather than trying to translate Gallicisms into English.

[u] See the definition at the beginning of 30.16.

But who led the leudes to war? There is no doubt it was the king, who was always at the head of his faithful. This is why one always sees in the capitularies an opposition between the vassals of the king and those of the bishops.[116] Our courageous, proud, and magnanimous kings surely did not enter the army to put themselves at the head of the ecclesiastical soldiery; they surely did not choose these people to vanquish or die with.

But these leudes likewise led their vassals and under-vassals, and this is shown very well in the capitulary in which Charlemagne orders each freeman who had four manors, whether as his own property or as someone's benefice, to go against the enemy or to follow the lord.[117] It is evident that Charlemagne means that the one who had only one plot of his own entered the soldiery of his count and that the one who held a benefice from a lord went with him.

However, the Abbé Dubos claims that when the capitularies mention men who were dependent on a particular lord, only serfs are in question,[118] and his claim is founded on the law of the Visigoths and the practice of the people. It would be better founded on the capitularies themselves. The one I have just cited expressly contradicts this. The treaty between Charles the Bald and his brothers speak likewise of freemen who can make their choice between a lord or the king, and this provision is in conformity with many others.

Therefore, one can say that there were three kinds of soldiery: that of the leudes or the faithful of the king, who themselves had others of the faithful dependent upon them; that of the bishops or other ecclesiastics and of their vassals; and finally that of the count who led the freemen.

I do not say that the vassals could not be subject to the count, for those who have a particular command are dependent on those who have a more general one.

One sees that the count and the deputies of the king could even make

with them their vassals; these instead are permitted to go to war with the count of their county" [L.]. *Capitulare secundum anni 812*, art. 7, Baluze edn, vol. 1, p. 494 [*CRF*, 74.7].

116 "As to our men and those of the bishops and abbots, who have either benefices or an estate of their own . . ." [L.]. *Capitulare primum anni 812*, art. 5 [*CRF*, 50.5], Baluze edn, vol. 1, p. 490.

117 "That any freeman who has four *manses* of his own or has them as a benefice from another, he should prepare himself and go himself to the host, either with his lord [or with his count]" [L.]. *Capitulare primum anni 812*, Baluze edn, p. 490 [*CRF*, 50.1].

118 [Jean Baptiste Dubos, *Etablissement de la monarchie française*], vol. 3, bk. 6, chap. 4, p. 299 [4, 120–121; 1742 edn].

them pay the ban, that is, a fine, if they had not fulfilled the engagements of their fief.

Likewise, if the vassals of the king pillaged, they were subject to correction by the count unless they preferred to submit to that of the king.[119]

[119] Capitulary of 882, art. 11, *Apud Vernis Palatium* (884), Baluze edn, vol. 2, p. 17 [*CRF*, 287.2].

CHAPTER 18
On double service

It was a fundamental principle of the monarchy that those who were under someone's military power were also under his civil jurisdiction; thus, the capitulary of Louis the Pious in 815[120] made the count's military power and his civil jurisdiction over freemen go together, thus the *placita* of the count[121] who led the freemen to war were called the *placita*[v] of freemen,[122] from which doubtless resulted the maxim that it was only in the count's *placita* and not in those of his officers that one could judge questions of liberty. Thus, the count did not lead the vassals of the bishops or abbots to war[123] because they were not under his civil jurisdiction; thus he did not lead the under-vassals of the leudes; thus the glossary of the English laws[124] tells us that those whom the Saxons called coples were styled by the Normans *comtes* or *campagnons*, because they divided the judicial fines with the king;[125]

[120] [*Praeceptem primum pro Hispanis 815*] arts. 1 and 2 [*CRF*, 132.1–2]; and the *Concilio in verno Palatio 845*, art. 8 [*CRF*, 291.8]. Baluze edn, vol. 2, p. 17.

[121] Pleas or assizes.

[122] Capitularies, bk. 4, art. 57 *Ansegisi Capitularum* [*CRF*, 183.4.55]; and *Capitulare quintum anni 819*, art. 14, Baluze edn, vol. 1, p. 615 [*CRF*, 141.14].

[123] See above, notes 111 and 116.

[124] Which is found in William Lambarde, 'Αρχαιονομια *sive De priscis anglorum legibus* ["Explicatio" s.p., 1568 edn; pp. 217–224, 1644 edn].

[125] [William Lambarde, 'Αρχαιονομια *sive De priscis anglorum legibus*]: *satrapia* ["Explicatio" at paragraph with side note "churle, Earle"]; p. 221, 1644 edn [M. has erred here. He misread *eorle* and transcribed it as *cople*.]

[v] See note [t] above.

thus we see in all times that the obligation of each vassal to his lord[126] was to bear arms and to judge his peers in his lord's court.[127]

One of the reasons that attached the right of justice to the right of leading to war was that the one who led to war also saw to the payment of the rights of the fisc, which consisted in certain services of vehicles due from freemen and, in general, in certain judicial profits of which I shall speak shortly.

The lords had the right to render justice in their fief on the same principle that made the counts have the right to render it in their county, and, indeed, as different times brought changes, the counties always followed the changes occurring in the fiefs; both were governed by the same plan and by the same ideas. In a word, the counts were leudes in their counties; the leudes were counts in their lordships.

The idea that counts were officers of justice and that dukes were military officers is not correct.[w] Both were equally military and civil officers;[128] the whole difference was that the duke had several counts under him, though there were counts who had no duke over them, as we learn from Fredegar.[129]

One will perhaps believe that the government of the Franks was at that time very harsh because the officers had simultaneously military power, civil power, and even fiscal power over the subjects: a thing that I have said in the preceding books is one of the distinctive marks of despotism.

But it must not be thought that the counts judged alone and rendered justice as do the pashas in Turkey;[130] in order to judge suits they held a kind of day-court or assizes[131] to which the notables were convoked.

To understand what concerns judgments in the formulas, in the laws of the barbarians, and in the capitularies, I shall say that the functions of

[126] *Assises du Royaume de Jérusalem*, chap. 221, 222 [1, 561–597; 1973 edn].

[127] The ecclesiastical advocates [*advocati*] were in charge of their court of pleas and their militia as well.

[128] See *Marculfi Formulae*, bk. 1, form. 8 [1.8], which contains the letters granted to a duke, patrician, or count, giving them civil jurisdiction and fiscal administration.

[129] [Fredegarius] *Chronicon*, *anno* 636, chap. 78 [78].

[130] See Gregory of Tours [*Historia ecclesiastica Francorum*], bk. 5, *anno* 580 [5.48].

[131] *Mallum* [see bk. 30, n. 121].

[w] *juste.*

the count,[132] of the *grafia*, and of the *centenarius* were the same, that the judges, the *rachinburgii*, and the *echevins* were the same persons under different names;[x] these were the adjuncts of the count, and he usually had seven of them, and, as he had to have no fewer than twelve persons in order to judge,[133] he filled out the number with notables.[134]

But whoever had the jurisdiction, whether king, count, *grafia*, *centenarius*, lords, or ecclesiastics, they never judged alone; and this usage, which had its origins in the forests of Germany, continued when the fiefs took a new form.

As for fiscal power, it was such that the count could scarcely abuse it. The rights of the prince in regard to freemen were so simple that they consisted, as I have said, only in certain vehicles required on certain public occasions;[135] and as for judicial rights, there were laws which prevented corruptions.[136]

[132] Add here what I have said in bk. 28, chap. 28; and bk. 31, chap. 8.
[133] For this whole topic, see the capitularies of Louis the Pious, *Capitula legis Salicae addenda*, art. 2 [*CRF*, 144.2]; and the formula for judgments given by [Charles] Du Cange [*Glossarium mediae et infimae latinitatis*] under *boni homines* [1,698–699; 1954 edn].
[134] *Per bonos homines*: "men qualified to act as a witness or an assessor in court." See the *Cartae Senonicae*, chap. 51 [51].
[135] And some tolls [*droits*] on rivers, which I have mentioned.
[136] See *Lex Ribuaria*, tit. 89 [91]; *Leges Langobardorum*, bk. 2, tit. 52, para. 9 [Kar. 88 (pap.)].

[x] See note [t] above.

CHAPTER 19

On settlements among the barbarian peoples

As it is impossible to inquire further into our political right if one does not know perfectly the laws and the mores of the German peoples, I shall pause for a moment to pursue the study of their mores and their laws.

It appears in Tacitus that the Germans knew only two capital crimes: they hung traitors and drowned cowards; these were the only public crimes. When a man had done some wrong to another, the relatives of the offended or injured person entered the quarrel, and hatred was soothed by a satisfaction. This satisfaction concerned the one who had been offended if he could accept it, and the relatives, if the injury or the wrong was common to them both, or if by the death of the one who had been offended or hurt, the satisfaction had devolved upon them.[137]

According to Tacitus, these satisfactions were made by a reciprocal agreement between the parties; thus in the codes of the barbarian peoples these satisfactions are called settlements.[y]

I find that only the law of the Frisians[138] left the people in a situation in which each enemy family was in the state of nature, so to speak, and in which, without the restraint of any political or civil law, it could exact its vengeance according to its fancy until it was satisfied. Even this law was tempered; it was established that the one whose life was demanded would have peace in his house,[139] that he would have it while going to and from church and to the place were judgments were rendered.

The compilers of the Salic laws cite an old usage of the Franks[140] by which the one who had exhumed a corpse to despoil it was banished from the society of men until the relatives consented to his return, and as before that time all, even his wife, were forbidden to give him bread or to accept him in his house, such a man was, with respect to the others, and the others were, with respect to him, in the state of nature until this state came to an end with a settlement.

With these exceptions, one can see that the wise men of the various barbarian nations thought they themselves should do what was too slow and too dangerous to be expected from a reciprocal agreement of both parties. They were heedful to put a just price on the settlement that was to be accepted by the one who had been injured or wronged. All these barbarian laws have an admirable precision on the subject: cases are carefully distinguished,[141] circumstances are weighed; the law puts itself in the place of the offended man and asks for him the satisfaction that, in a cool moment, he himself would have demanded.

By establishing these laws, the German peoples came out of that

[137] "It is necessary that they undertake the feuds as well as the friendships of their father and relatives. However, these feuds do not continue implacably since even a murder is expiated by a certain number of cattle and sheep; and the whole household receives this with satisfaction" [L.]. Tacitus, *Germania* [21].

[138] See this law on murder *Lex Frisionum* [2.11], and on stealing *Additio sapientum, Wulemarus* [9].

[139] [*Lex Frisionum*] *Additio sapientum, Wulemarus*, tit. 1, para. 1 [1.1].

[140] *Lex Salica*, tit. 58, para. 1 [D100.2; S17.2]; tit. 17, para. 3 [D18; S20.2].

[141] See especially titles 3 through 7, *Lex Salica* [D3–7; S49–54], which concern thefts of animals.

---

[y] Here Montesquieu defines *compositions*, "settlements."

state of nature in which it seems they still were at the time of Tacitus.

Rotharis declared, in the law of the Lombards, that he had increased the settlements for wounds over those of the old custom, so that when the wounded man was satisfied, enmities could cease.[142] Indeed, among the Lombards, a poor people who had enriched themselves by the conquest of Italy, the old settlements had become frivolous and reconciliations were no longer made. I do not doubt that this consideration obliged the other leaders of conquering nations to make the various codes of laws that we have today.

The principal settlement was the one that the murderer was to pay to the relatives of the dead man. Differences of conditions made for differences in settlements;[143] thus, in the law of the Angles, the settlement was six hundred sous for the death of an atheling, two hundred for that of a free man, and thirty for that of a serf. Therefore, the size of the settlement established on the head of a man was one of his great prerogatives for, besides distinguishing his person, it established a greater security for him among the violent nations.

The law of the Bavarians gives us a good sense of this;[144] it gives the names of the Bavarian families who accepted a double settlement because they were the first families after the Agilofingi.[145] The Agilofingi belonged to the ducal house,[z] and the duke was chosen from among them; they had a quadruple settlement. The settlement for the duke was a third more than that established for the Agilofingi. "Because he is a duke," the law said, "he is given a greater honor than his relatives."

All these settlements were fixed for a price in silver. But as these peoples, especially while they stayed in Germany, had scarcely any silver, they could give livestock, grain, furniture, weapons, dogs, hunting birds, lands, and so forth.[146] The law often even fixed the value

142 [*Leges Langobardorum*], bk. 1, tit. 7, para. 15 [Roth. 57–58].

143 See the *Lex Angliorum et Werinorum hoc est Thuringorum*, tit. 1, paras. 1, 2, 4 [1–3]; ibid., tits. 5 and 6 [9–10]; *Lex Baiuwariorum*, tit. 1, chaps. 8 and 9 [1.8, 9]; and *Lex Frisionum*, tit. 15 [15].

144 [*Lex Baiuwariorum*] tit. 2, chap. 20 [3].

145 Ibid. [*Lex Baiuwariorum*, 3]: Hozidra, Ozza, Sagana, Habilingua, Anniena.

146 Thus the law of Ina esteemed life at a certain sum of silver or a certain portion of land. [William Lambarde], 'Αρχαιονομια (*Archaionomia*), *sive De priscis anglorum legibus*. "Legis Inae Regis," tit. *De villico regis* [fol. 5. #19; 1568 edn.]

z *race*.

of these things,[147] which explains how, with so little silver, they had so many pecuniary penalties.

Therefore, these laws sought to mark precisely the differences in wrongs, injuries, and crimes, in order for each man to know exactly to what degree he had been wounded or offended, in order for him to know exactly the reparation he should accept and above all for him to know he should accept no more.

From this point of view, one conceives that anyone who avenged himself after accepting the satisfaction committed a crime. This crime contained an offense against the public no less than an offense against an individual; it was scorn for the law itself. The legislators did not fail to punish this crime.[148]

There was another crime that was regarded as especially dangerous,[149] when these people lost something of their spirit of independence in civil government and when the kings applied themselves to putting a better police in the state: this crime was that of not wanting to give or accept satisfaction. We see in various law codes of the barbarians that the legislators made it an obligation to do so.[150] Indeed, the one who refused to accept satisfaction wanted to preserve his right of vengeance; the one who refused to give it left his right of vengeance to the offended man, and this is what the wise people had reformed in the institutions of the Germans, which invited the making of a settlement but did not oblige one to do so.

I have just mentioned a text of the Salic law in which the legislator

[147] See the *Leges Saxonum*, which even makes this same determination for many peoples, chap. 18 [66]. See also the *Lex Ribuaria*, tit. 36, par. 11 [40.11]; the *Lex Baiuwariorum*, tit. 1, paras. 10 and 11 [1.9–10]: "If he has no gold, then by his flocks, slaves, land, etc." [L.].

[148] See the *Leges Langobardum*, bk. 1, tit. 25, para. 21 [Roth. 271]; ibid., bk. 1, tit. 9, paras. 8 and 34 [Roth 143; Lud. 13 (pap.)]; ibid., para. 38 [Loth. 92 (pap.)] and the capitulary of Charlemagne [*Capitulare primum*] *anni 802*, chap. 32 [*CRF*, 33.32], containing an instruction given to those whom he sent into the provinces.

[149] See in Gregory of Tours [*Historia ecclesiastica Francorum*] bk. 7, chap. 47 [7.47] the details of a lawsuit in which one party loses half the settlement that had been adjudged to him, for having taken justice himself, instead of accepting the satisfaction, despite any injury he might have suffered afterwards.

[150] See the *Leges Saxonum*, chap. 3, para. 4 [27]; the *Leges Langobardum*, bk. 1, tit. 37, paras. 1 and 2 [Kar. 19–20 (pap.)]; and *Leges Alamannorum*, tit. 45, 1–2 [A44.1–2; B45.1–2]. The last of these permitted one to do justice for himself on the spot and at that very moment. See also the capitularies of Charlemagne *Capitulare anni 779*, chap. 22 [*CRF*, 20.22]; *Capitulare anni 802*, chap. 32 [*CRF*, 33.32] and *Capitulare secondum anni 805*, chap. 5 [*CRF*, 44.5].

left it to the liberty of the offended one to accept or not to accept the satisfaction; this law banned from the commerce of men anyone who had robbed a corpse until the relatives, accepting the satisfaction, had asked that he might live among men.[151] Respect for holy things made those who drew up the Salic laws change nothing of the former usage.

It would have been unjust to grant a settlement to the relatives of a robber killed in the act of robbery, or to those of a wife who had been sent back home after a separation for the crime of adultery. The law of the Bavarians gave no settlement in cases like these, and it punished relatives who pursued vengeance for them.[152]

It is not rare to find in the law codes of the barbarians settlements for involuntary actions. The law of the Lombards is almost always sensible; in this case it wanted one to settle in accord with one's generosity and for relatives to be unable to pursue vengeance any longer.[153]

Clotaire II made a wise decree: he forbade the one who had been robbed to accept his settlement in secret[154] and without the order of the judge. The motive for this law will be seen shortly.

[151] The compilers of the *Lex Ribuaria* seemed to have modified this. See tit. 85 [88].

[152] See the decree of Tassillon [*Lex Baiuwariorum, Additio quinta*]; *de popularibus legibus*, arts. 3, 4, 10, 26, 19 [4, 3, 10, 16, 19]; *Lex Angliorum et Werinorum hoc est Thuringorum*, tit. 7, para. 4 [29].

[153] [*Leges Langobardum*] bk. 1, tit. 9, para. 4 [Roth. 75].

[154] *Pactus pro tenore pacis Childeberti et Chlotharii, circa an. 593*, and *Decretio Chlotharii II regis circa 595*, chap. 11 [*CRF*, 3.3, 13]

CHAPTER 20

On what has since been called the justice of the lords

Besides the settlement that was to pay relatives for murders, wrongs, and injuries, one had also to pay a certain right[aa] that the law codes of the barbarians called *fredum*.[155] I shall speak of it at length, and, in order to give an idea of it, I shall say that it is compensation for protection granted from the right of vengeance. Even today *fred* means "peace" in Swedish.

[155] When the law did not determine it, it was ordinarily the third of what one gave for the settlement, as appears in the *Lex Ribuaria*, chap. 89 [91], which is explained by *Capitulare 813*, Baluze edn, vol. 1, p. 512 [*Lex Francorum Chamavorum* 3].

[aa] See note [p] above.

Among these violent nations, rendering justice was nothing other than granting to him who had committed an offense one's protection from the vengeance of him who had received it, and obliging the latter to accept the satisfaction that was his due so that, among the Germans, unlike all other peoples, justice was rendered to protect the criminal from the one he had offended.

The law codes of the barbarians give us the cases in which these *freda* were to be levied. In those where relatives could not take vengeance, they give no *fredum*; indeed, where there was no vengeance, there could not be any right of protection from vengeance. Thus in the law of the Lombards,[156] if someone unintentionally killed a freeman, he paid the value of the dead man without the *fredum*, because, as he had killed him unintentionally, it was not a case where the relatives had a right of vengeance. Thus, in the law of the Ripuarians,[157] when a man was killed by a piece of wood or a thing made by hand, the thing or the wood was considered to be guilty, and the relatives took it for their own use, without being able to exact a *fredum*.

Likewise, when a beast had killed a man, the same law established a settlement without the *fredum*,[158] because no offense had been committed against the relatives of the dead man.

Finally, by the Salic law,[159] a child under the age of twelve who had committed some infraction paid the settlement without the *fredum*; as he could not yet bear arms, his was not a case for which the injured party or his relatives could seek vengeance.

It was the guilty man who paid the *fredum* for the peace and security that he had lost because of the excesses he had committed and that he could recover by protection; but a child did not lose this security; he was not a man and could not be put outside the society of men.

This *fredum* was a local right for the one who judged in the territory.[160] The law of the Ripuarians, however, prohibited his exacting it himself;[161] the law wanted the party that had won to receive it and carry it to the fisc in order, so the law says, for peace to be eternal among the Ripuarians.

156 [*Leges Langobardorum*] bk. 1, tit. 9, para. 17 [Roth. 387] Lindenbrog edn.

157 [*Lex Ribuaria*] tit. 70 [73].

158 [*Lex Ribuaria*] tit. 46 [48]. See also *Leges Langobardorum*, bk. 1, chap. 21, para. 3, Lindenbrog edn [Roth. 326]: *si caballus cum pede*, etc.

159 [*Lex Salica*] tit. 28, para. 6 [D34].

160 As appears by the *Decretio Chlothariis II regis circa 595* [*CRF*, 3.16], "The *fredus* is reserved for the judge of that *Pagus*" [L.].

161 [*Lex Ribuaria*] tit. 89 [91].

The size of the *fredum* was proportional to the size of the protection;[162] thus the *fredum* for protection by the king was larger than the one granted for protection by the count and the other judges.

In this already I see the rise of justice of the lords. The fiefs included great territories, as is shown in an infinite number of records. I have already proven that the kings placed no levy on the lands that were in the Frankish share; still less could they reserve for themselves rights on the fiefs. Those who obtained them had in this respect the most extensive enjoyment of them; they drew all the fruits and all the emoluments from them; and, as one of the most considerable was the judicial profit (*freda*), which was accepted according to the usages of the Franks,[163] it followed that the one who had the fief also had the justice, whose exercise was only in the settlements paid to the relatives and the profits owed to the lord. The justice was nothing other than the right to see that settlements in accord with the law were paid and to exact fines in accord with the law.[bb]

One sees that fiefs had this right in the formulas that bear the confirmation or the transmission in perpetuity of a fief in favor of a leud or one of the faithful[164] or of the privileges of fiefs in favor of the churches.[165] This appears again in an infinity of charters prohibiting the judges or officers of the king from entering the territory to exercise any act of justice whatever or to require any judicial emolument whatever.[166] As soon as the royal judges could no longer make any exactions in a district, they no longer entered the district, and those to whom this district remained performed the function of the royal judges.

Royal judges are forbidden to oblige the parties to give securities in

[162] *Capitulare primum incerti anni*, chap. 57, Baluze edn, vol. 1, p. 515 [*CRF*, 35.57]. And it must be noted that what was called *fredum* or *faida* [in Baluze *feida*] in the documents of the Merovingians was called *bannum* in those of the Carolingians, as appears by the *Capitulario de partibus Saxoniae, anni 789* [*CRF*, 26.16, 31, e.g.].

[163] See the capitulary of Charlemagne, *Capitulare de villis* [*CRF*, 32.4], where he puts these *freda* among the great revenues of what were called *villae* or domains of the king.

[164] See *Marculfi Formulae*, bk. 1, form. 3, 4, and 17 [1.3, 4, 17].

[165] Ibid. [*Marculfi Formulae*], form. 2, 3, and 4 [1.2, 3, 4].

[166] See the collections of these charters, especially the one that is at the end of the fifth volume of the *Historiens de France* of the Benedictine Fathers [*Recueil des historiens des Gaules et de la France*, 5; De diplomata, 5, 712–778; 1869 edn; see *MGH*, *Diplomatum Karolinorum*].

[bb] Here Montesquieu defines the "justices of the lords."

order to appear before them; therefore, it was for the one who received the territory to exact them. It is said that the king's deputies could no longer ask for lodging; indeed, they no longer had any function there.

Therefore, the justice was, in the old fiefs and in the new ones, a right inherent in the fief itself, a lucrative right that was part of it. This is why in every age it has been regarded thus, whence was born the principle that justices are patrimonial in France.

Some have believed that the justices had their origin in the freeing of their serfs by the kings and lords. But the German nations and those descended from them are not the only ones who have freed slaves, yet they are the only ones who have established justices that were patrimonial. The formulas of Marculf, moreover, show us freemen dependent on these justices in earliest times;[167] therefore, the serfs were under this justice because they were in the territory, and they were not the origin of the fiefs, for they were enveloped in the fief.

Others have taken a shorter route: they say that the lords usurped the justices and that that says everything. But are the peoples who came here from Germany the only ones on earth who usurped the rights of princes? History clearly teaches us that other peoples have made attempts against their sovereigns, but this has not been seen to give rise to what has been called justices of the lords. The origin should have been sought in the usages and customs of the Germans.

I pray that one look at the way Loyseau[168] assumes the lords proceeded to form and usurp their various justices. They must have been the most subtle peoples in the world, and they must have stolen not as soldiers pillage, but as village judges and prosectuors steal from one another. One would have to say that these warriors, in all the particular provinces of the kingdom and in so many kingdoms, made a general political system. Loyseau makes them reason as he himself reasoned in his study.

I shall say it again: if the justice were not a dependency of the fief,

[167] See [*Marculfi Formulae*] bk. 1, form. 3, 4 and 14 [1.3, 4, 14]; and the charter of 771 of Charlemagne, in [Edmund] Martenne [*Thesaurus novos anecdotorum*], vol. 1, collect. 11 [1.10–11]; "In particular we order that no public justice . . . [approach] the men of the Church and monastery of Morback, whether freeborn or slave, and those who remain on their lands, etc." [L.]. [*MGH*, *Diplomatum Karolinorum*, #64].

[168] Charles Loyseau, *Traité des justices de village* ["Discours de l'abus de Iustices de Village"; 1666 edn].

why can one see everywhere that service for the fief was to serve the king or the lord, both in their courts and in their wars?[169][cc]

[169] See [Charles] du Change [*Glossarium mediae et infimae latinitatis*] for *hominium* [4, 215–216; 1954 edn].

[cc] This question mark is not in our French text.

CHAPTER 21

On the territorial justice of the churches

The churches acquired very considerable goods. We see that the kings gave them great fiscs, that is, great fiefs, and we find justices established at first in the domains of these churches. What would have been the origin of such an extraordinary privilege? It was in the nature of the thing given; ecclesiastical goods had this privilege because it was not taken away from them. A fisc was given to the church, and it retained the prerogatives it would have had if one had given it to a leud; thus it was subject to the service that the state would have drawn from it if it had been granted to the laity, as has already been seen.

Therefore, churches had the right to have settlements paid in their territory and to exact the *fredum*, and, as these rights necessarily carried with them that of preventing the royal officers from entering the territory to exact these *freda* and from exercising any act of justice, the right of the ecclesiastics to render justice in their territory was called *immunity*, in the language of the formulas,[170] charters, and capitularies.

The law of the Ripuarians[171] prohibits the freed men of the churches[172] from holding an assembly in which justice is rendered,[173] except in the church were they were freed. Therefore, the churches had justices even over freemen and held their audiences[dd] for them from the earliest times of the monarchy.

[170] See *Marculfi Formulae*, bk. 1, form. 3 and 4 [1.3, 4].
[171] "Nowhere except in the Church where they were freed may they seek justice [*mallum*]" [L.]. [*Lex Ribuaria*] tit. 58, para. 1 [61.1]. See also para. 19, Lindenbrog edn [61.19].
[172] *Tabulariis*.
[173] *Mallum*. [See bk. 30, n. 131.]

[dd] *plaids*. This French word is related to the *placites*, or *placita* in 30.18.

I find in the *Lives of the Saints*[174] that Clovis gave a holy personage power over a territory of six leagues of country and that he wanted him to be free of any jurisdiction whatsoever. I believe indeed that this is a falsehood, but it is a very old falsehood; the foundation for the life and the lie is related to the mores and laws of the time, and it is these mores and these laws that are sought here.[175]

Clotaire II orders the bishop or important men who possessed lands in distant countries to choose from that place itself those who were to render justice or receive its emoluments.[176]

The same prince regulates the competence of the judges of the church and that of his own officers.[177] Charlemagne's capitulary of 802 prescribes to the bishops and abbots the qualifications their officers of justice should have. Another[178] by the same prince forbids royal officers to exercise any jurisdiction over those who cultivate the ecclesiastical lands,[179] unless the condition had been taken up fraudulently and in order to be exempt from public burdens. The bishops assembled in Rheims declared that the vassals of the churches were within their immunity.[180] Charlemagne's capitulary of 806 wants the churches to have criminal and civil justice over all those who live in their territory.[181] Finally, the capitulary of Charles the Bald dis-

174 [*Acta sanctorum Maii tomus tertius*] 16 Maii. *De sancto Germerio Episcopo Tolosae in Gallia, Vita* [#6–7; 16 Maii, 3, 590c–d].

175 See also [*Acta sanctorum, Januarii, tomus primus*] *De S. Melanio, Rhedonensi Episc.* [6 Januarii, 1, 327–334, esp. p. 329; *MGH, SS. Merov.* 3 30] and [*Januarii tomus secundus*] *De S. Deicolo sive, Abbate Lutrens in Burgundie* [18 Januarii; 2, 563–574, esp. pp. 569–574].

176 In the *Concilium Parisiense, 614* (615), art. 19 [*CRF*, 9.19; *Concilia Galliae* A511–A695, p. 285]: "Bishops or the powerful, who possess lands in other regions, ought not to appoint as judges or as commissioners those who are not from that place, to attend to and to render justice there" [L.]. See also art. 12 [*CRF*, 9.12].

177 *Concilium Parisiense, 614*, art. 5 [*CRF*, 9.5; *Concilia Galliae* A511–A695, Corpus Christianorum, Series Latina, vol. 148A, p. 283].

178 *Leges Langobardorum*, bk. 2, tit. 44, chap. 2, Lindenbrog edn [Kar. 99 (pap.)].

179 "That servants, the half-free, those manumitted or under contract from of old, or those recently . . ." [L.]. [This quotation is the beginning of the law; it is to identify the location rather than to specify the evidence.] Ibid. [*Leges Langobardum*, Kar. 99 (pap.)].

180 *Epistola Episcoporum ad Ludowicum regem 858*, art. 7, p. 108 [*CRF*, 297.7]: "Those estates and patrimonies where clerics live, these and their persons are under a consecrated immunity different from that which military vassals owe" [L.].

181 *Capitula ad legem Baiwariorum addita*, art. 7. See also art. 3, Lindenbrog edn, p. 444 [*CRF*, 69.4; 69.11]. "First of all it is ordered that churches have justice over those who live in and beside the church and in its power, in respect to life [by paying gold rather than suffering capital punishment] as well as to money and property" [L.]

tinguishes between the jurisdictions of the king, those of the lords, and those of the churches;[182] and I shall say no more about them.

[182] *Capitula data in synodo apud Carisiacum 857*, art. 4, Baluze edn, p. 96; *CRF*, 267.4].

CHAPTER 22

That the justices were established before the end of the reign of the Carolingians

It has been said that it was at the time of the disorder under the Carolingians that the vassals arrogated justice to themselves within their fiefs: making a general proposition has been preferred to examining it; it has been easier to say that the vassals did not possess it than to discover how they possessed it. But the justices do not owe their origin to usurpations; they derive from the first establishment and not from its corruption.

"He who kills a freeman," it is said in the law of the Bavarians,[183] "will pay the settlement to his relatives if he has any, and if he has none at all, he will pay it to the duke or to the one to whom he has petitioned during his life." One knows what it was to petition for a benefice.

"The one whose slave has been taken," says the law of the Alemanni,[184] "will go to the prince to whom the abductor is subject in order to obtain the settlement."

"If a *centenarius*," it is said in the decree of Childebert,[185] "finds a robber in another *centena* than his own or within the boundaries of our faithful and does not drive him away, he will represent the robber or will purge himself with an oath." Therefore, there was a difference between the territory of the *centenarii* and that of the faithful.

This decree of Childebert explains the constitution of Clotaire[186] of

[183] [*Lex Baiuwariorum*] tit. 3, chap. 13, Lindenbrog edn [4.28].

[184] [*Leges Alamannorum*] tit. 85 [A82, B85].

[185] *Decretio Childeberti regis circa 595*, arts. 11, 12, Baluze edn, p. 19 [*CRF*, 7.11, 12]: "Let similar conditions obtain if a *centenarius* has followed and found tracks in another's *centena*, or if it happens within the boundaries of our *fideles*, and he makes no effort to expel him from the other *centaine*, either consider him in association with the robber, etc." [L.].

[186] [*Decretio Childeberti regis circa 595*] art. 2, 3 [*CRF*, 3.9]: "If the tracks of a robber are ascertained, and whether he be present or far away, he should be punished. And if the one who pursues this thief catches him, then he ought to receive for himself the entire

the same year, which, given for the same case and about the same deed, differs only in its terms, as the constitution called *in truste* what the decree called *in terminus fidelium nostrorum*. M. Bignon and M. du Cange,[187] who believed that *in truste* meant the domain of another king, missed the mark.

In a constitution of Pepin,[188] King of Italy, made as much for the Franks as for the Lombards, this prince, after imposing penalties on the counts and other royal officers who betray their trust in the exercise of justice, or who delay in rendering it, orders[189] that if a Frank or a Lombard who has a fief does not want to render justice, the judge of his district will suspend the exercise of his fief and that in this interval the judge or his deputy will render justice.

A capitulary of Charlemagne[190] proves that the kings did not levy the *freda* everywhere. Another from the same prince[191] shows us that the feudal regulations and the feudal court were already established. When he who has a fief does not render justice, or keeps it from being rendered, another capitulary from Louis the Pious wants one to have free quarters in his house until justice is rendered.[192] I shall also cite two capitularies of Charles the Bald, one from 861,[193] in which particular jurisdictions are seen to be established with judges and officers under them, the other from 864,[194] in which he makes

settlement. However, if the thief is found out by a *trustus*, he ought to receive half of the composition, and exact from the robber the death penalty" [L.].

[187] See [Charles Du Cange] *Glossarium mediae et infimae latinitatis*, for *trustis* [8, 200–201; 1954 edn].

[188] Inserted in the *Leges Langobardum*, bk. 2, tit. 52, para. 14. It is the capitulary of 793, Baluze edn, p. 544, art. 10 [Pip. 7 (pap.)].

[189] "If perchance a Frank or a Lombard holding a benefice does not wish to render justice, that judge who is in his employ may, in the meanwhile, oppose that benefice; thus he or his envoy may render justice" [L.] [*Leges Langobardorum*, Pip. 7 (pap.)]. See also the same in *Leges Langobardorum*, bk. 2, art. 52, para. 2 [Kar. 18 (pap.)], which relates to the capitulary of Charlemagne [*Capitulare anni*] *779*, art. 21 [*CRF*, 20.21].

[190] *Capitulare tertium anni 812*, art. 10 [*CRF*, 80.10].

[191] *Capitulare secundum anni 813*, arts. 14 and 20, p. 509 [*CRF*, 77.14, 20].

[192] "If someone who is an envoy, or a bishop, abbot, or whoever has been provided with honor and estate, and who prohibits or does not wish to render justice, then those seeking it ought to live off his substance until he renders justice there" [L.]. *Capitulare quintum anni 819*, art. 23 [*CRF*, 141.23], Baluze edn, p. 617.

[193] *Edictum in Carisiaco 861*, Baluze edn, vol. 2, p. 152 [*CRF*, 271]: "whatever advocate in respect to his legal work . . . if he is found to have done something contrary to our ban in assembly or with ministers of his legal work . . . he is to be punished" [L.].

[194] *Edictum Pistense 864*, art. 18, Baluze edn, vol. 2, p. 181 [*Edictum Pistense 864*; *CRF*, 273.18]: "If from our fisc or some other immunity, or the power of some authority or proprietor he flees, etc." [L.]

the distinction between his own lordships and those of individuals.

One sees no original concessions of fiefs because they were established by the division known to have been made among the victors. Therefore, one cannot prove by original contracts that justices were attached to fiefs in the beginning; but if in the formulas of confirmations or transmissions in perpetuity of these fiefs one finds, as has been said, that a justice was established, this right of justice had to have been of the nature of the fief and one of its principal prerogatives.

We have a greater number of records establishing the patrimonial justice of the churches in their territory than ones proving the justice of the benefices or fiefs of the leudes or faithful for two reasons: first, because most of the remaining records were preserved or collected by monks for the use of their monasteries; second, because, as the patrimony of the churches was formed by individual concessions and was a kind of derogation from the established order, there had to be charters for it, whereas the concessions made to the leudes being consequences of the political order, there was no need to have and even less need to preserve a particular charter. Even the kings were often satisfied with simple transmission by scepters,[ee] as appears in the life of Saint Maur.

But the third formula of Marculf[195] proves quite well to us that the privilege of immunity and consequently that of the justice were common to the ecclesiastical and secular men, as it is made for both. It is the same in the constitution of Clotaire II.[196]

[195] "We trust our kingdom shall increase in its great monuments [temples], so we shall grant suitable favors [*beneficia*] to ecclesiastical establishments, or whatever you might want to mention here, with a benevolent purpose" [L.]. [*Marculfi Formulae*] bk. 1 [1.3].

[196] It was cited in the preceding chapter, *Episcopi vel potentes* [n. 176].

[ee] In this expression *tradition* means "transmission."

CHAPTER 23

The general idea of the book, on the establishment of the French monarchy in Gaul, by the Abbé Dubos

It is well, before finishing this book, for me to examine briefly the work by the Abbé Dubos, because my ideas are perpetually contrary to his and because, if he has found out the truth, I have not.

This work has seduced many people because it is written with much art, because what is in question is eternally assumed, because the more one lacks proof the more one multiplies probabilities, because an infinity of conjectures are set up as principles and other conjectures are drawn from them as consequences. The reader forgets that he has doubted and begins to believe. And, as an endless erudition is placed, not in the system but beside it, the spirit is distracted by secondary things and no longer concentrates on the principal one. So much research, moreover, does not permit one to imagine that nothing was found; the length of the voyage makes one believe one has finally arrived.

But when one examines it closely, it appears as an immense colossus with feet of clay, and it is because the feet are of clay that the colossus is immense. If the system of the Abbé Dubos had had a good foundation, he would not have been obliged to make three deadening volumes to prove it; he would have found everything in his subject and, without going to the ends of the earth to seek what was remote, reason itself would have taken up the charge of placing this truth in the chain of other truths. History and our laws would have said to him, "Do not take so much trouble; we shall testify for you."

CHAPTER 24

Continuation of the same subject. A reflection on the foundation of the system

The Abbé Dubos wants to remove any idea that the Franks entered Gaul as conquerors; according to him our kings, summoned by the peoples, did nothing but take the place and succeed to the rights of the Roman Emperors.

This claim cannot apply to the time when Clovis, entering Gaul, sacked and took the towns; nor can it be applied to the time when he defied Syagrius, the Roman officer, and conquered the country he held; therefore, it can relate only to the time when Clovis, who had become master of a great part of Gaul by violence, would have been summoned by the choice and the love of the peoples to dominate the rest of the country. And it is not enough for Clovis to have been accepted – he had to have been summoned; the Abbé Dubos must prove that the peoples preferred living under the domination of Clovis to living under that of the Romans or under their own laws. Now, the Romans of the part of Gaul that had not yet been invaded by the barbarians were of two sorts according to the Abbé Dubos: some were of the Armorican Federation and had driven out the officers of the emperor in order to defend themselves from the barbarians and govern themselves by their own laws; the others obeyed the Roman officers. Now, does Abbé Dubos prove that the Romans who were still subject to the empire summoned Clovis? Not at all. Does he prove that the republic of the Armoricans summoned Clovis and even made some treaty with him? Again, not at all. Far from his being able to tell us the fate of this republic, he cannot even demonstrate its existence; and, although he follows it from the time of Honorius to the conquest of Clovis, although he relates to it all the events of those times with remarkable art, it remains invisible in the authors he cites. For there is a considerable difference between proving, by a passage from Zosimus,[197] that, under the empire of Honorius, the Armorican region and the other Gallic provinces rebelled and formed a kind of republic[198] and showing that, despite Gaul's many pacifications, the Armoricans always formed a particular republic that continued to exist until the conquest of Clovis. He would need very strong and exact proofs, however, to establish his system. For, when one sees a conqueror enter a state and subject a great part of it by force and violence and when one sees shortly thereafter the whole state subjected, with history telling nothing about how it happened, one has good reason[ff] to believe that the matter ended as it began.

[197] [Zosimus] *Historiae*, bk. 6 [6.5, p. 322 Bekker].

[198] "The entirety of Armoricum and the other provinces of Gaul" [L.]. Ibid. [Zosimus, *Historiae* 6.5, p. 322, Bekker.]

[ff] *un très juste sujet.*

It is easy to see that once this point is missed, the whole of the Abbé Dubos's system crumbles from top to bottom, and every time he draws some consequence from this principle, that Gaul was not conquered by the Franks but that the Franks were summoned by the Romans, one will always be able to deny it.

The Abbé Dubos proves his principles by the Roman ranks with which Clovis was invested; he wants Clovis to have succeeded Childeric, his father, in the post of master of the soldiery. But these two posts are purely of his own creation. The letter from Saint Rémi to Clovis on which he founds his principle[199] is nothing but a congratulatory note on his accession to the throne. When the purpose of a writing is known, why give it one that is not?

Clovis, near the end of his reign, was made consul by the emperor Anastasius, but what right could a simple one-year authority give him? It is likely, says the Abbé Dubos, that in the same document the emperor Anastasius made Clovis proconsul. And for myself, I shall say that it is likely that he did not. Concerning a fact that is founded on nothing, the authority of the one who denies it is equal to the authority of the one who alleges it. I even have a reason for this. Gregory of Tours, who speaks of the consulate, says nothing about the proconsulate. This proconsulate would have been for only about six months. Clovis died a year and a half after being made consul; it is not possible to make the proconsul a hereditary post. Finally, when the consulate and, if one wants, the proconsulate, were given to him, he was already master of the monarchy and all his rights were established.

The second proof alleged by the Abbé Dubos is the emperor Justinian's assignment to the children and grandchildren of Clovis of all the rights of dominion over Gaul. I could say a great deal about this assignment. One can judge its importance for the Frankish kings by the way they executed its conditions. The Frankish kings were, moreover, masters of Gaul; they were peaceful sovereigns: Justinian did not possess an inch of land there; the Western empire had long since been destroyed, and the Eastern emperor had a right over Gaul only as the representative of the Western emperor; these were rights on top of rights. The Frankish monarchy was already founded; the regulation of its establishment was complete; the reciprocal rights of persons and of the various nations living under the monarchy were agreed upon; the

[199] [Jean Baptiste] Dubos [*Histoire critique de l'établissement de la monarchie française*] vol. 2, bk. 3, chap. 18, p. 270 [bk. 3, chap. 18; 2, 494–497; 1742 edn].

laws of each nation were given and even put into writing. What did this foreign assignment of rights do to an establishment already formed?

What does the Abbé Dubos mean by referring to the oratory of the bishops, who, in the disorder, the confusion, the total collapse of the state, and the ravages of the conquest, sought to flatter the victor? What does flattery assume but the weakness of the one who is obliged to flatter? What do rhetoric and poetry prove but the very use of these arts? Who would not be stunned to see Gregory of Tours yet say, after speaking of the murders done by Clovis, that god humbled his enemies every day because he walked in his paths? Who can doubt that the clergy were quite satisfied with Clovis's conversion and that they even found great advantages in it? But at the same time, who can doubt that the peoples suffered all the misfortunes of the conquest and that the Roman government yielded to the German government? The Franks did not want, and were not even able, to change everything, and few victors indeed have had this mania. But in order for all the consequences of the Abbé Dubos to be true, they would have had not only to change nothing among the Romans, but also to change themselves.

I might undertake to prove in the same way, following the method of the Abbé Dubos, that the Greeks did not conquer Persia. First, I would speak of the treaties that some of their towns made with the Persians; I would mention the Greeks were in the pay of the Persians as the Franks were in the pay of the Romans. For if Alexander entered the country of the Persians, besieged, took and destroyed the town of Tyre, it was a particular business like that of Syagrius. But see how the high priest of the Jews comes to meet him; listen to the oracle of Jupiter Ammon; remember what had been predicted at Gordium; see all the towns run out, so to speak, to meet him; see the satraps and the important men crowd forward. He is dressed in the Persian manner; it is the consular robe of Clovis. Does not Darius offer him half his kingdom? Is Darius not killed as a tyrant? Do not the mother and wife of Darius mourn the death of Alexander? Were Quintus Curtius, Arrian, or Plutarch, Alexander's contemporaries? Has not printing given us the enlightenment those authors lacked?[200] This is the story of *The Establishment of the French Monarchy in Gaul.*

[200]See [Jean Baptiste] Dubos, [*Histoire critique de l'établissement de la monarchie française*] "Discours préliminaire."

CHAPTER 25

On the French nobility

The Abbé Dubos maintains that in the early time of our monarchy there was but one order of citizens among the Franks. This claim, insulting to the blood of our first families, would be no less harmful to the three great houses that have reigned over us in turn. If it were so, the origin of their greatness would not go back to be lost in oblivion, in darkness, and in time; history would illuminate the centuries when they would have been common families and, in order for Chilperic, Pepin, and Hugh Capet to be gentlemen, one would have to seek their origin among the Romans or the Saxons, that is, among the subjected nations.

The Abbé Dubos founds his opinion on the Salic law.[201] This law makes it clear, he says, that there were not two orders of citizens among the Franks. The law gave two hundred sous in settlement for the death of any Frank whatsoever;[202] but it distinguished, among the Romans, between the king's companion for whose death it gave three hundred sous in settlement, the Roman proprietor to whom it gave one hundred, and the Roman tributary to whom it gave only forty-five. And, as the difference in settlements was the principal distinction, he concludes that there was only one order of citizens among the Franks, and three among the Romans.

It is surprising that his error should not itself have made him discover his error. Indeed, it would have been quite extraordinary for the noble Romans who lived under the domination of the Franks to have had a larger settlement and to have been more important personages than the most illustrious Franks and their greatest captains. What likelihood is there that the victorious people would have had so little respect for themselves and so much for the vanquished people? In addition, the Abbé Dubos cites the laws of the other barbarian nations, which prove that there were different orders of citizens among them. It would be quite extraordinary if precisely this general rule had been absent among the Franks. This should have made him think that he had misunderstood or had wrongly applied the texts of the Salic law, which is indeed what happened.

[201] See [Jean Baptiste Dubos] *Histoire critique de l'établissement de la monarchie française*, vol. 3, bk. 6, chap. 4, p. 304 [bk. 6, chap. 4; 4, 127–129; 1742 edn].
[202] He cites [*Lex Salica*] tit. 44 [D69; S11], and *Lex Ribuaria*, tits. 7 and 36 [7, 40].

One can find, on opening this law, that the settlement for the death of an antrustion, that is, of a faithful or vassal of the king, was six hundred sous[203] and that the one for the death of a Roman, a companion of the king, was only three hundred.[204] One finds in it[205] that the settlement for the death of a simple Frank was two hundred sous[206] and that the one for a Roman of an ordinary condition was only a hundred.[207] One paid also for the death of a tributary Roman, a kind of serf or freedman, a settlement of forty-five sous;[208] but I shall not speak of this, or of the one for the death of a Frankish serf or a Frankish freed man; it is not a question here of this third order of persons.

What does the Abbé Dubos do? He does not mention the first order of persons among the Franks, that is, the article concerning the antrustions, and then, comparing the ordinary Frank for whose death two hundred sous in settlement was paid with the ones he calls the three orders among the Romans and for whose deaths differing settlements were paid, he finds that there was but a single order of citizens among the Franks and three among the Romans.

As, according to him, there was but a single order of persons among the Franks, it would have been well for there to have been only one also among the Burgundians because their kingdom formed one of the principal parts of our monarchy. But in their codes there are three sorts of settlements: one for the Burgundian or Roman noble, another for the Burgundian or Roman of middling condition, and the third for those who were of a lower condition in the two nations.[209] The Abbé Dubos has not cited this law.

It is singular to see how he escapes from these passages that press him from every side.[210] Does one speak to him of the important men, of

[203] "Who is a *trustus* of the lord" [L.]. [*Lex Salica*] tit. 44, para. 4 [D69.4; S11.4]; this relates to *Marculfi Formulae*, form. 13 [1.18]. See also *Lex Salica*, tit. 66, arts. 3 and 4 [D89.3–4; S31.3–4]; and tit. 74 [D69; S11]; and the *Lex Ribuaria*, tit. 11 [11] and the capitulary of Charles the Bald, *Apud Carisiacum 877*, chap. 20 [*CRF*, 281.20].

[204] *Lex Salica*, tit. 44, para. 6 [D69.6; S11.6].

[205] Ibid., para. 4 [*Lex Salica* D69.4; S11.4].

[206] Ibid., para. 1 [*Lex Salica* D69.1; S11.1].

[207] Ibid., tit. 44, para. 15 [*Lex Salica* D69.7; S11.7].

[208] Ibid., para. 7 [*Lex Salica* D69.8; S11.8].

[209] "If someone, even if it be by chance, knocks out the teeth of a Burgundian aristocrat [*optimati*] or of a Roman noble, he will be compelled to pay out 25 solidi; (2) for an ordinary freeborn person, either Burgundian or Roman, if a tooth be knocked out, it will be settled by 10 solidi; (3) for the lower orders, 5 solidi" [L.] *Leges Burgundionum*, tit. 26, arts. 1, 2, 3 [26.1–3].

[210] [Jean Baptiste Dubos] *Histoire critique de l'établissement de la monarchie française*, vol. 3, bk. 6, chaps. 4, 5 [bk. 6, chaps. 4, 5; 1742 edn].

lords, or of nobles? These are, he says, simply distinctions and not distinctions of order; they are things of courtesy and not prerogatives in the law: or else, he says, the people spoken of were the king's council; they could even be Romans; but still there was but a single order of citizens among the Franks. On the other hand, if some Frank of a lower rank is mentioned, he is a serf,[211] and he interprets the decree of Childebert in this way. It is necessary for me to pause a bit over this decree. The Abbé Dubos has made it well known because he has used it to prove two things: one, that all the settlements to be found in the laws of the barbarians were but civil interests added to corporal penalties,[212] which altogether reverses all the old records; the other, that all freemen were judged directly and immediately by the king,[213] which is contradicted by an infinity of passages and authorities that make known to us the judicial order in those times.[214]

It is said in this decree, made by an assembly of the nation, that if the judge finds a well-known robber he will have him bound up to be sent before the king, if he is a Frank (*Francus*) but if he is a weaker person (*debilior persona*), he will be hanged on the spot.[215] According to the Abbé Dubos, *Francus* is a freeman, *debilior persona* is a serf. I shall lay aside for a moment the question of what the word *Francus* can mean here, and I shall begin by examining what one can understand by these words, *a weaker person*. I say that, in whatever language it may be, any comparative assumes necessarily three terms, the greatest, the lesser, and the least. If it were here a question only of freemen and serfs, one would have said *a serf* and not *a man of lesser power*. Thus *debilior persona* does not here mean a serf at all, but a person who must have a serf beneath him. This assumed, *Francus* will not mean a freeman, but a powerful man, and *Francus* is taken here in this acceptation, because

[211] [Jean Baptiste Dubos] *Histoire critique de l'établissement de la monarchie française* vol. 3, chap. 5, pp. 319 and 320 [bk. 6, chap. 5; 4, 145–146; 1742 edn].

[212] Ibid. [Jean Baptiste Dubos, *Histoire critique de l'établissement de la monarchie française*, vol. 3], bk. 6, chap. 4, pp. 307 and 308 [4, 129–131; 1742 edn].

[213] Ibid. [Jean Baptiste Dubos, *Histoire critique de l'établissement de la monarchie française*], p. 309 [bk. 6, chap. 4; 4, 131–132; 1742 edn]; and in the following chapter, pp. 319 and 320 [bk. 6, chap. 5; 4, 145–146; 1742 edn].

[214] See bk. 28, chap. 28, and bk. 31, chap. 8.

[215] "Thus it is agreed at Cologne, and so we command that whatever judge gives heed to a criminal robber, walks into his house, and makes a bond with him; if this one be a Frank, let him be brought to our presence, and if he be a lesser person, let him be hanged in that place" [L.]. [*Pactus pro tenore pacis Childeberti et Chlotharii. circa anno 593*], Baluze edn, vol. 1, p. 19, [*CRF*, 7.8].

among the Franks there were always those who had a greater power in the state and who were more difficult for the judge or count to correct. This explanation agrees with a great number of capitularies which give the instances in which criminals could be referred to the king and those in which they could not.[216]

One finds in the life of Louis the Pious, written by Thegan,[217] that the bishops, especially those who had been serfs and those who had been born among the barbarians, were the principal authors of the humbling of the emperor. Thegan reproaches Hebon, whom this prince had taken out of servitude and made Archbishop of Rheims, thus: "What a reward the emperor has received for so many good deeds![218] He made you free and not noble; he could not make you noble after giving you liberty."

This speech, which so formally proves two orders of citizen, does not bother the Abbé Dubos. He replies thus:[219] "This passage does not mean that Louis the Pious was not able to put Hebon into the order of nobles. Hebon, as Archbishop of Rheims, would have been of the first order, higher than that of the nobility." I leave the reader to decide whether this passage does not mean that; I leave him to judge if it is here a question of a priority of the clergy over the nobility. "This passage proves only," continues the Abbé Dubos,[220] "that the citizens born free were called noble men; in the usage of the world noble man and man born free have long meant the same thing." What! From the fact that in our modern times some of the bourgeois[gg] have styled themselves noble men, a passage in the life of Louis the Pious will be applied to these kinds of people! "Perhaps also," he goes on to say,[221] "Hebon was not a slave in the Frankish nation, but in the Saxon nation or in another Germanic nation where the citizens were divided into

[216] See Book 28, chapter 28, and Book 31, chapter 8 of this work.

[217] [Thegan, *Vita Hludowici Imperatoris*] chaps. 43 and 44 [*anno* 833].

[218] "What a repayment you have returned! He made you free men, not noble, since that was impossible after freeing you" [L.] [Thegan, *Vita Hludowici Imperatoris*, chap. 44, *anno* 833].

[219] [Jean Baptiste Dubos] *Histoire critique de l'établissement de la monarchie française*, vol. 3, bk. 6, chap. 4, p. 316 [bk. 6, chap. 4; 4, 140; 1742 edn].

[220] Ibid. [Jean Baptiste Dubos, *Histoire critique de l'établissement de la monarchie française*, bk. 6, chap. 4; 4, 140–141; 1742 edn].

[221] Ibid. [Jean Baptiste Dubos, *Histoire critique de l'établissement de la monarchie française*, bk. 6, chap. 4; 4, 141; 1742 edn].

[gg] Townsmen.

several orders." Thus, because of the *perhaps* of the Abbé Dubos, there were no nobles in the Frankish nation. But he has never more wrongly applied a *perhaps*. One has just seen that Thegan[222] distinguishes, among the bishops who had been opposed to Louis the Pious, some who had been serfs and some who came from a barbarian nation. Hebon belonged to the first group, and not the second. I do not know how one can say, moreover, that a serf such as Hebon could have been Saxon or German; a serf has no family and, consequently, no nation. Louis the Pious freed Hebon, and, as the freed serfs took the law of their master, Hebon became a Frank and not a Saxon or a German.

I have just made my attack; I must defend myself. One will tell me that the body of the antrustions indeed formed an order in the state distinct from that of the freemen but that, as fiefs were alienable at first and given in perpetuity later, this could not form a nobility by descent, since these prerogatives were not at all attached to a hereditary fief. It is this objection that doubtless made M. de Valois think that there was but a single order of citizen among the Franks: a feeling that the Abbé Dubos took from him and which he has absolutely ruined with his bad proofs. Be that as it may, it is not the Abbé Dubos who could have raised this objection. For, having given three orders of Roman nobility and styled the first "guest at the king's table," he could not have said that this title marked a nobility by descent more than did that of antrustion. But a direct reply is necessary. The antrustions or faithful were not such because they had a fief, but they were given fiefs because they were the antrustions or faithful. One will recall what I have said in the early chapters of this book: therefore, they did not have the same fief they had later; but if they did not have that one, they had another, and, because fiefs were given at birth, because they were often given in assemblies of the nation, and finally, because, as it was in the interest of the nobles to have them, it was also in the interest of the king to give them to them. These families were distinguished by their rank as the faithful and by the prerogatives of being able to petition for a fief. I shall show in the following book[223] how, in the circumstances of those times, there were freemen who were admitted to the enjoyment of this great prerogative and consequently were admitted entry to the order of the

[222] "All the bishops were angry with Louis, and most of all those of servile origin whom he had so honored, these and those of the barbarian nations brought him to this end" [L.]. [Thegan] *Vita Hludowici Imperatoris*, chaps. 43–44 [*anno* 833].

[223] [Bk. 31] chap. 23.

nobility. It was not thus in the time of Guntram and Childebert, his nephew, and it was thus in the time of Charlemagne. But though, from the time of this prince, freemen were not disqualified from possessing fiefs, it appears, by the previously cited passage of Thegan, that freed serfs were absolutely excluded from it. Will the Abbé Dubos,[224] who goes to Turkey to give us an idea of what the old French nobility was like, tell us that anyone has ever complained in Turkey that people of common birth were raised to honors and ranks, as one complained under the reigns of Louis the Pious and Charles the Bald? No one complained in the time of Charlemagne because this prince always distinguished the old families from the new ones, which Louis the Pious and Charles the Bald did not.

The public should not forget that it is indebted to Abbé Dubos for a number of excellent compositions. It is on these fine works that it should judge him and not on this one. The Abbé Dubos has fallen here into grave errors, because he had the Count of Boulainvilliers more in view than his subject. I shall draw from all my criticism but this reflection: if this great man has erred, what should I not fear?

[224] [Jean Baptiste Dubos] *Histoire critique de l'établissement de la monarchie française*, tom. 3, bk. 6, chap. 4, p. 302 [bk. 6, chap. 4; 4, 125; 1742 edn].

BOOK 31

The theory of the feudal laws among the Franks in their relation to the revolutions of their monarchy

CHAPTER I

Changes in the offices and fiefs

At first counts were sent to their districts only for a year; they soon bought the continuation of their offices. An example of this is found as early as the reign of Clovis's grandchildren. A certain Peonius was the count in the town of Auxerre;[1] he sent his son Mummolus to Guntram with silver, in order that he would be continued in Guntram's employ; the son gave the silver on his own behalf and obtained his father's place. Kings had already begun to corrupt their own favors.

Though by the law of the kingdom fiefs were revocable, nevertheless they were neither given nor taken away capriciously and arbitrarily, and this was usually one of the principal topics considered in the assemblies of the nation. One can readily think that corruption crept in on this point, as it had crept in on the other, and that one continued one's possession of fiefs in exchange for silver just as one continued one's possession of counties.

I shall show later in this book[2] that, independently of the gifts princes made for a limited time, there were others they made for all time. It sometimes happened that the court wanted to revoke gifts that had been made; this set up a general discontent in the nation, and one soon saw arise from it that revolution famous in the history of France, whose first period included the astonishing spectacle of the punishment of Brunhilda.

At first it appears extraordinary that this queen, daughter, sister, and

[1]Gregory of Tours [*Historia ecclesiastica Francorum*], bk. 4, chap. 42 [4.42].
[2][Bk. 31], chap. 7.

mother of so many kings, who is famous even today for works worthy of a Roman aedile or proconsul, who was born with a remarkable genius for affairs, and was endowed with qualities which had so long been respected, should suddenly have found herself exposed to such long, shameful, and cruel punishments[3] by a king whose authority in his nation was quite poorly consolidated,[4] unless for some particular cause she had fallen into disgrace with the nation. Clotaire reproached her with the death of ten kings,[5] but two of them he himself had put to death; the death of certain others was the crime of fate or that of the wickedness of another queen; and a nation which had let Fredegunde die in her bed, which had even opposed punishing her dreadful crimes,[6] must have been very cool about those of Brunhilda.

She was put on a camel and paraded through the whole army: a sure mark of her having fallen into disgrace with this army. Fredegar says that Protadius, the favorite of Brunhilda, took goods from the lords and filled the fisc with them, that he humbled the nobility, and that no one could be sure of keeping the position he had.[7] The army conspired against him, he was stabbed in his tent; and, whether because of the vengeance she took for his death[8] or because she followed the same plan, Brunhilda became daily more odious to the nation.[9]

Clotaire, ambitious to reign alone, and filled with the most awful vengeance, sure of perishing if Brunhilda's children gained the upper hand, entered into a conspiracy in spite of himself, and whether he was incompetent or forced by circumstances, he became Brunhilda's accuser and made a frightful example of this queen.

Warnachar had been the soul of the plot against Brunhilda; he was made Mayor of Burgundy; he exacted from Clotaire that he would not be displaced during his life.[10] In this way, the mayor could no longer be

[3] Fredegarius, *Chronicon* [*anno 613*], chap. 42 [42].
[4] Clotaire II, son of Chilperic and father of Dagobert.
[5] Fredegarius, *Chronicon* [*anno 613*], chap. 42 [42].
[6] Gregory of Tours, [*Historia ecclesiastica Francorum*], bk. 8, chap. 31 [8.31].
[7] Fredegarius, *Chronicon, anno 605*, chap. 27 [27]: "He was vicious and unreasonable with some people, drawing so much into the Treasury and snatching away people's possessions so as to fill up the Treasury . . . thus no one would be able to acquire the dignity which he had grabbed or take it away from him" [L.].
[8] Ibid. [Fredegarius, *Chronicon*], *anno* 607, chap. 28 [28].
[9] Ibid. [Fredegarius, *Chronicon*], *anno* 613, chap. 41 [41]: "The Burgundian nobles [*farones*: clansmen or officials], the bishops as well as the lords, held Brunhilda in fear and hatred, taking counsel, etc." [L.].
[10] Fredegarius, *Chronicon, anno* 613, chap. 42 [42]: "when Clotaire had sworn he would never degrade [depose] him in his lifetime" [L.].

in the situation of the French lords, and this authority began to make itself independent of the royal authority.

The fatal regency of Brunhilda had especially enraged the nation. While the laws continued in force, no one could complain that a fief had been taken away from him, for the law did not give it to him forever, but when fiefs were given by avarice, bad practices, and corruption, one complained of being deprived wrongly of that which had often been acquired in the same way. Perhaps if the public good had been the motive for the revocation of the gifts, nothing would have been said; but one displayed order without hiding the corruption, one claimed the right of the fisc, only to waste the goods of the fisc according to one's fancy; gifts were no longer either the reward for, or in expectation of, services. Brunhilda, her spirit corrupt, wanted to correct the abuses of the old corruption. Her caprices were not those of a weak spirit; the leudes and the great officers believed themselves ruined; they brought about her ruin.

We are far from having all the acts that were passed in those times, and the chroniclers, who knew of their time more or less what villagers know today of ours, have little to offer. However, we have a constitution of Clotaire, given in the council of Paris[11] to reform abuses,[12] which shows that this prince put an end to the complaints that had given rise to the revolution. On the one hand, he confirms in it all the gifts that had been made or confirmed by the kings, his predecessors,[13] and on the other, he orders that all that had been taken away from his leudes, or faithful, should be returned to them.[14]

This was not the only concession the king made in this council. He wanted what had been done against the privileges of the ecclesiastics to be corrected;[15] he moderated the influence of the court in the elections of bishoprics.[16] The king similarly reformed the business of the fisc; he

[11] Some time after the torture of Brunhilda in 615. See the Baluze edn, p. 21 [*Edictum Chlotharii II. a. 595, Capitularia regum Francorum* 9].

[12] Ibid. [*Edictum Chlotharii II. a. 595*], art. 16 [*Capitularia regum Francorum* 9, Preface]: "Before it happens that God disperses by violence those things which were done or arranged contrary to a reasonable order, we ordain, Christ willing, that by this edict to amend this course of things in a general way" [L.].

[13] Ibid. [*Edictum Chlotharii II.* a. 595], art. 16 [*Capitularia regum Francorum* 9.16].

[14] Ibid. [*Edictum Chlotharii II. a. 595*], art. 17 [*Capitularia regum Francorum* 9.17].

[15] [*Edictum Chlotharii II. a. 595, Capitularia regum Francorum* 9 Preface; see Concilium Parisiense art. 1, *Concilia Galliae* A511–A695, p. 275]: "This which for a time has been overlooked, henceforth will be continuously inspected" [L.].

[16] Ibid. [*Edictum Chlotharii II. a. 595*], art. 1 [*Capitularia regum Francorum* 9.1]: "When a

wanted all the new censuses removed,[17] and no toll[a] levied that had been established after the death of Guntram, Sigebert, and Chilperic;[18] that is, he abolished all that had been done during the regencies of Fredegunde and Brunhilda; he prohibited his men from leading his herds into forests belonging to individuals;[19] and we shall see shortly that the reform was still more widespread and extended to civil business.

bishop retires, the one chosen in his place ought to be appointed by the Metropolitan, along with the inhabitants of the province; he should be chosen by the clergy and the people; and if he be a worthy person he will be ordained by the prince; or, if indeed he be chosen from the palace, he will be ordained on account of his personal learning and merit" [L.].

[17] [*Edictum Chlotharii II. a. 595*] art. 8 [*Capitularia regum Francorum* 9.8]. "Wherever the new census has been added to in an impious manner [. . .], it will be emended" [L.].

[18] Ibid. [*Edictum Chlotharii II. a. 595*], art. 9 [*Capitularia regum Francorum* 9.9.]

[19] Ibid. [*Edictum Chlotharii II. a. 595*], art. 21 [*Capitularia regum Francorum* 9.21.]

[a] *droit de passage.*

CHAPTER 2

How the civil government was reformed

Before then the nation had shown signs of impatience and flightiness in the choice or the conduct of its masters; one had seen it rule on differences between its masters and impose on them the necessity of peace. But the nation then did what had not been seen before: it looked over its present situation, it examined its laws coolly, it provided for their deficiency, it checked violence, it regulated power.

The masculine, bold, and insolent regencies of Fredegunde and Brunhilda had less stunned this nation than warned it. Fredegunde had defended her wickedness by wickedness itself; she had vindicated[b] poison and murders by poison and murders; she had conducted herself so that her outrages were even more individual than public. Fredegunde did more evil; Brunhilda made yet more evils feared. In this crisis the nation was not satisfied to put order into the feudal government: it also wanted to secure its civil government, for the latter was still

[b] The French word is *justifier*, which we customarily translate "vindicate," but here the relation to *juste* reminds one of the retaliatory justice of Book 1.

more corrupt than the former, and this corruption was the more dangerous as it was older and, in a way, involved the abuse of mores more than the abuse of laws.

The history of Gregory of Tours and other records show us, on the one hand, a ferocious and barbarous nation; and, on the other, kings who were no less so. These princes were murderous, unjust, and cruel because the whole nation was. If Christianity sometimes seemed to soften them, it was only through the terror that Christianity gives the guilty. The churches defended themselves from them by the miracles and prodigies of their saints. The kings were not sacrilegious because they dreaded the penalties for sacrilege, but, in other areas, they committed, both in anger and in cold blood, all sorts of crimes and injustices because they did not see the hand of the divinity so present in these crimes and these injustices. The Franks, as I have said, tolerated murderous kings because they were murderous themselves; they were not struck by the injustices and pillaging of their kings because they too plundered and were unjust. There were many laws established, but the kings rendered them useless by certain letters called *precepts*,[20c] which reversed these same laws; these were nearly like the rescripts of the Roman emperors, either because the kings took this usage from them or because they drew it from the depths of their own nature. One sees in Gregory of Tours that they murdered coolly and put the accused to death before they had even been heard; they gave precepts in order to make illicit marriages;[21] they gave them to transfer inheritances; they gave them to remove the right of relatives; they gave them for marrying nuns. They did not, in truth, make laws on their own initiative, but they suspended the practice of the ones that were made.

The edict of Clotaire redressed all grievances. One could no longer be condemned without being heard;[22] relatives were always to inherit according to the order established by the law;[23] all precepts for marrying girls, widows, or nuns were nullified, and those who had

[20] These were orders that the king sent to judges, for them to do or permit certain things contrary to the law.

[21] See Gregory of Tours [*Historia ecclesiastica Francorum*], bk. 4, p. 227 [4.46]. The histories and the charters are full of this; and the extent of these abuses appears especially in the *Edictum Chlotharii II. a. 515* [*Capitularia regum Francorum* 9], given in order to reform them. See the Baluze edn, vol. 1, p. 22.

[22] [*Edictum Chlotharii II. a. 595*] art. 22 [*Capitularia regum Francorum* 9.22].

[23] Ibid. [*Edictum Chlotharii II. a. 595*], art. 6 [*Capitularia regum Francorum* 9.6].

[c] *preceptions*.

obtained and made use of such precepts were punished severely.[24] We would know perhaps more exactly what was enacted concerning these precepts if Article 13 of this decree and the following two articles had not been lost over time. We have only the first words of Article 13, which orders the precepts to be observed; this cannot mean the ones he had just abolished by the same law. We have another constitution from the same prince, related to his edict and likewise correcting, point by point, all the abuses of the precepts.[25]

It is true that M. Baluze, finding this constitution without the date or the place it was given, has attributed it to Clotaire I. It is from Clotaire II. I shall give three reasons for this.

1. It states there that the king will preserve the immunities granted to the churches by his father and grandfather.[26] What immunities could Childeric, grandfather of Clotaire I, who was not yet Christian and who lived before the founding of the monarchy, have granted the churches? But if one attributes this decree to Clotaire II, one will find his grandfather to be Clotaire I, who himself gave immense gifts to the churches in order to atone for the death of his son Chram, whom he had burned with his wife and children.

2. The abuses that this constitution corrects lasted after the death of Clotaire I, and reached their peak during the weak reign of Guntram, the cruel one of Chilperic, and the detestable regencies of Fredegunde and Brunhilda. Now, how could the nation have suffered grievances so solemnly proscribed without ever crying out against their continual return? How could they not have done then what they did when they pressed Chilperic II, who had taken up the old violent ways again,[27] to order that law and customs should be followed in judgments, as they had been in former times?[28]

Finally, this constitution, made to redress grievances, cannot belong to Clotaire I, because there were no complaints in this regard during

[24] Ibid. [*Edictum Chlotharii II. a. 595*], art. 18 [*Capitularia regum Francorum* 9.18.]

[25] In the Baluze edn, vol. 1, p. 7 [*Chlotharii regis constitutio generalis. circa 560; Capitularia regum Francorum* 8]. [M.'s argument has received general acceptance, but the issue is still controversial.]

[26] In the preceding book, I have spoken about these immunities, which were concessions of judicial rights and which contained prohibitions against the royal judges performing any function in that territory, and thus were the equivalent of the setting up or concession of a fief.

[27] He began his reign about 670.

[28] See the Life of Saint Leger [*Vita S. Luidgeri*, a. 776, bk. 1, 17; *MGH*, SS. 2, 409].

his reign and because his authority was consolidated in the kingdom, especially at the date given for this constitution, whereas it accords very well with the events that occurred in the reign of Clotaire II, which caused a revolution in the political state of the kingdom. History must be illuminated by laws, and laws by history.

CHAPTER 3

The authority of the mayors of the palace

I have said that Clotaire II had promised not to remove Warnachar from the position of mayor during his lifetime. This revolution had another effect: until this time, the mayor was the mayor of the king, and he became the mayor of the kingdom; formerly the king had chosen him, now the nation chose him. Before the revolution, Protadius had been made mayor by Theodoric,[29] and Landeric by Fredegunde,[30] but afterwards the nation was in possession of their election.[31]

Thus one must not confuse, as others have, these mayors of the palace with those who had this rank before the death of Brunhilda, the mayors of the kings with the mayors of the kingdom. One sees in the law of the Burgundians that among them the post of mayor was not one of the highest in the state;[32] nor was it one of the most eminent among the first Frankish kings.[33]

Clotaire reassured those who held posts and fiefs; and, after the death of Warnachar, when this prince asked the lords assembled at Troyes whom they wanted to put in his place, they all cried out that they would not elect anyone and, asking for his favor, they put themselves in his hands.[34]

[29] Fredegarius [*Chronicon*], a. 605, chap. 27 [27]: "At the prompting of Brunhilda, Theodoric being bidden, etc." [L.].

[30] *Gesta regum Francorum*, chap. 36 [*Liber historiae Francorum* 35; *MGH*, SS. Merov. 2, 304].

[31] See Fredegarius, *Chronicon*, a. 626, chap. 54, and *Continuationes* a. 695, chap. 101 [6]; a. 715, chap. 105 [8]. Aimoinus [*Historiae Francorum*], bk. 4, chap. 15 [4.15]. Einhard, *Vita Karoli Magni*, chap. 48 [48.1–2]. *Gesta regum Francorum*, chap. 45 [*Liber historiae Francorum* 45; *MGH* SS. Merov. 2, 318].

[32] See *Leges Burgundionum*, Preface [#5]; *Second Supplement*, tit. 13 [*Constitutiones extravagantes* 21.14].

[33] See Gregory of Tours [*Historia ecclesiastica Francorum*], bk. 9, chap. 36 [9.36].

[34] Fredegarius, *Chronicon*, a. 626, chap. 56 [54]: "In this same year Clotaire assembled the

Dagobert united the whole monarchy, as had his father; the nation relied on him and did not give him a mayor. This prince felt himself at liberty, and being reassured, besides, by his victories, he went back to the plan of Brunhilda. But this led him to such failures that the leudes of Austrasia let themselves be defeated by the Slavs[35] and returned home, and the marches of Austrasia were left prey to the barbarians.

He decided to propose that the Austrasians cede Austrasia to his son Sigebert with a treasury and put the government of the kingdom and the palace in the hands of Cunibert, bishop of Cologne, and of Duke Adalgisel. Fredegar does not go into detail about the agreements made at that time; but the king confirmed them all by his charters, and Austrasia was immediately out of danger.[36]

Dagobert, feeling death was near, commended his wife Nentechilde and his son Clovis to Aega. The leudes of Neustria and Burgundy chose this young prince for their king.[37] Aega and Nentechilde governed the palace;[38] they returned all the goods Dagobert had taken,[39] and the complaints ceased in Neustria and Burgundy, as they had ceased in Austrasia.

After the death of Aega, Queen Nentechilde made the lords of Burgundy promise to elect Floachad their mayor.[40] He sent to the bishops and the principal lords of the kingdom of Burgundy letters in which he promised them he would preserve their honors, and their ranks forever, that is during their lives.[41] He confirmed his word by an oath. It is from this time that the author of the *Book of Mayors of the Royal*

Burgundian princes and lords at Troyes and asked if they might wish, now that Warnachar was dead, to raise another to the same level as his honors; but all unanimously denied that they wished to elect a Mayor of the Palace, vigorously seeking the grace from the king to transact business with him" [L.].

[35] Fredegarius, *Chronicon*, a. 630, chap. 68 [68]: "The victory by the Wends over the Franks was well deserved, but it was obtained not so much by the boldness of the Slavs as by the senseless actions of the Austrasians, who saw themselves hated and being constantly robbed by Dagobert" [L.].

[36] Ibid. [Fredegarius, *Chronicon*], a. 632, chap. 75 [75]: "Thereafter it became known that the Austrasians were useful in defending the boundaries of the Kingdom of the Franks against the Wends" [L.].

[37] Ibid. [Fredegarius, *Chronicon*], a. 638, chap. 79 [79].

[38] Ibid. [Fredegarius, *Chronicon*, a. 638, 79.]

[39] Ibid. [Fredegarius, *Chronicon*], a. 639, chap. 80 [80].

[40] Fredegarius, *Chronicon*, a. 641, chap. 89 [89].

[41] Ibid. [Fredegarius, *Chronicon*, a. 641, 89]: "Floachad swore by the sacraments in a letter to all the lords of the Burgundian Kingdom and also to the priests, to protect in perpetuity their degrees of honor and dignity" [L.].

House dates the beginning of the administration of the kingdom by mayors of the palace.[42]

Fredegar, a Burgundian, has given greater detail about the mayors of Burgundy in the time of the revolution of which we speak than about the mayors of Austrasia and Neustria, but the agreements made in Burgundy were, for the same reasons, made in Neustria and in Austrasia.

The nation believed that it was safer to put power in the hands of a mayor whom it elected and on whom it could impose conditions than in those of a king, whose power was hereditary.

[42] *De majoribus domus regiae* [in *Recueil des historiens des Gaules et de la France*, 2, 699, 1869 edn]: "In short, at the time of Clovis, who was the son of the illustrious King Dagobert and true father of Theodoric [i.e., "true," because Theodoric was a bastard], the Frankish Kingdom began to appoint the Mayors of the Household" [L.].

CHAPTER 4

What the genius of the nation was in regard to mayors

A government in which the nation had a king and elected someone who was to exercise royal power seems very extraordinary, but I believe that the Franks, independent of the circumstances in which they found themselves, took their ideas about this from a distant past.

They were descended from the Germans, of whom Tacitus says that in their choice of a king they determined according to nobility, and in their choice of leader, according to virtue.[43] These were the Merovingian kings and the mayors of the palace; the first were hereditary and the second were elected.

One cannot doubt that most of these princes, who, in the assembly of the nation, rose and proposed themselves as leaders of some expedition to all those who wanted to follow them, for the most part united in their person both the authority of the king and the power of the mayor. Their nobility had given them royalty, and as their virtue caused them to be followed by a number of volunteers who chose them as leader, it gave them the power of the mayor. By their royal dignity our first kings were at the head of the tribunals and assemblies and gave laws with the

[43] [Tacitus] *Germania* [7]: "They chose their kings with respect to their nobility of birth, their generals for their strength [*virtute*]" [L.].

consent of these assemblies; by their dignity as duke or leader, they made expeditions and commanded armies.

In order to know the genius of the first Franks in this respect, one has only to look at the conduct of Arbogast, of the Frankish nation, to whom Valentinian gave the command of the army.[44] He enclosed the emperor in the palace; he permitted absolutely no one to speak to him of any civil or military business. Arbogast did at that time what the Pepins did later.

[44] See Sulpicius Alexander, in Gregory of Tours [*Historia ecclesiastica Francorum*], bk. 2 [2.9].

CHAPTER 5

How the mayors obtained the command of the armies

When its kings commanded armies, the nation did not think of choosing a leader for itself. Clovis and his four sons were at the head of the French and led them from victory to victory. Thibaut, son of Theudebert, a young, weak, and sickly prince, was the first king to remain in the palace.[45] He refused to make an expedition to Italy against Narses, and to his shame the Franks choose two leaders to lead them there.[46] Of the four children of Clotaire I, Guntram was the one who most neglected commanding the armies;[47] other kings followed his example; and in order to put the command in other hands without peril they gave it to several leaders or dukes.[48]

Innumerable drawbacks rose from this: discipline vanished, obedience was unknown; the armies were deadly only in their own country; they were burdened with spoils before they arrived among the enemy. One finds in Gregory of Tours a vivid picture of these evils.[49]

[45] In 552.

[46] Gregory of Tours, [*Historia ecclesiastica Francorum*], bk. 4, chap. 9 [4.9]: "Although it was in no way pleasing to their king, they entered into the war in an alliance with Lothair and Buccelin" [L.]. Agathias [*Historiarum*], bk. 1 [1.6].

[47] Guntram did not even join the expedition against Gundovald, who called himself son of Clotaire and claimed his part of the kingdom.

[48] Sometimes they were twenty in number. See Gregory of Tours [*Historia ecclesiastica Francorum*], bk. 5, chap. 27 [5.26]; bk. 8, chaps. 18, 30 [8.18, 30]; bk. 10, chap. 3 [10.3]. Dagobert, who had no mayor in Burgundy, had the same policy, and sent against the Gascons ten dukes and a number of counts who had no dukes above them. Fredegarius, *Chronicon*, a. 636, chap. 78 [78].

[49] Gregory of Tours [*Historia ecclesiastica Francorum*], bk. 8, chap. 30 [8.30]; bk. 10, chap. 3 [10.3].

"How shall we gain the victory," said Guntram, "we who do not preserve what our fathers gained? Our nation is no longer the same . . ."[50] Curious thing, it had been in decline since the time of Clovis's grandsons!

Therefore, it was natural to settle upon a single duke, a duke who had authority over that infinite multitude of lords and leudes who no longer recognized their engagements, a duke who reestablished military discipline and who led against the enemy a nation who by then knew only how to wage war against itself. The power was given to the mayors of the palace.

The first function of the mayors of the palace was the government of the economy of the royal house. Concurrently with other officers, they had the political government of the fiefs,[51] and, finally, they made disposition of them alone. They also had the administration of the business of war and the command of the armies, and these two functions were necessarily linked with the other two. In those times it was more difficult to assemble armies than to command them, and who but the one who dispensed favors could have this authority? In this independent and warlike nation, one had to invite rather than to constrain; one had to give, or offer expectation of, fiefs vacated by the death of their possessor, to reward constantly, to make preferences feared; therefore, the one who superintended the palace had to be the general of the army.

[50] Ibid. [Gregory of Tours, *Historia ecclesiastica Francorum* 8.30].
[51] See *Leges Burgundionum, Second Supplement*, tit. 13 [*Constitutiones extravagantes* 21.14] and Gregory of Tours [*Historia ecclesiastica Francorum*], bk. 9, chap. 36 [9.36].

CHAPTER 6

Second period of decline of the Merovingian kings

After the punishment of Brunhilda, the mayors were the administrators of the kingdom under the kings; and, although they were in charge of war, the kings were nevertheless at the head of the armies, and the mayor and the nation fought under them. But the victory of Duke Pepin over Theodoric and his mayor[52] completed the degradation of the

[52] See *Annales Mettenses*, a. 687, 688 [687] [*MGH*, SS. 1, 316–317].

kings;[53] the victory of Charles Martel over Chilperic and his mayor Rainfroy[54] confirmed this degradation. Austrasia triumphed twice over Neustrasia and Burgundy, and as the mayoralty of Austrasia was virtually attached to the family of the Pepins, this mayoralty rose above all the other mayoralties, and this house above all the other houses. The victors feared that some man in good standing would seize the king's person to provoke trouble. They kept the kings in a royal house as in a kind of prison.[55] Once a year they were shown to the people. There they made ordinances,[56] but these were the mayor's; they replied to ambassadors, but they were the mayor's replies. Historians tell us that at this time the mayors governed the kings who were subject to them.[57]

The delirium of the nation for the family of Pepin went so far that they elected as mayor one of his grandchildren who was still a child;[58] it established him mayor over a certain Dagobert, and put one phantom on top of another.

[53] Ibid. [*Annales Mettenses*], a. 695 [693] [*MGH*, SS. 1, 321]: "on that one has been imposed the name of 'king,' but the other shall have the privileges of the entire kingdom" [L.].

[54] Ibid. [*Annales Mettenses*], a. 719 [718, *MGH*, SS. 1, 324–325].

[55] *Annales Mettenses*, a. 719 [718 *MGH*, SS. 1, 324]: "He conceded his seat [throne] and the royalty under his power" [L.].

[56] [Hariulphe] *Chronicon Centulense*, bk. 2 [2.1; p. 49; 1894 edn]: "So that he answered what he had been taught, or rather commanded, just as if it were given by his own power" [L.].

[57] *Annales Mettenses*, a. 691 [693] [*MGH*, SS. 1, 321]: "This year of the principate of Pepin over Theodoric" [L.]. *Annales laurissenses minores* [A.680, 687; *MGH*, SS. 1, 114]: "Pepin, leader of the Franks, held the Kingdom of the Franks for 27 years having kings as his subjects" [L.].

[58] Fredegarius [*Chronicon*], *Continuationes* 714, chap. 104 [7]: "His (Grimoald's) young son Theudoald was made Mayor of the Palace in his place by the command of King Dagobert" [L.].

CHAPTER 7

On the great offices and fiefs under the mayors of the palace

The mayors of the palace took care not to reestablish the revocability of posts and offices; they ruled only by the protection that they granted the nobility in this regard; thus, the great offices continued to be given for life and this usage grew ever stronger.

But I have some particular reflections to make concerning fiefs. I do not doubt that, beginning at this time, most of them had become hereditary.

In the treaty of Andelot,[59] Guntram and his nephew Childebert undertook to maintain the liberalities given to the leudes and the churches by the kings who preceded them; and queens, daughters, and widows of kings were permitted to bequeath by testament and forever the things they held from the fisc.[60]

Marculf wrote his formulas in the time of the mayors.[61] In many of them one sees the king making gifts to a person and to his heirs,[62] and, as the formulas are images of the ordinary actions of life, they prove that, by the end of the reign of the Merovingians, a part of the fiefs had already passed to the heirs. At that time they were far from having the idea of an inalienable domain; this is a very modern thing, which was then known neither in theory nor in practice.

One will soon see factual proofs of this, and if I refer to a time when there were neither benefices for the army nor funds for its upkeep, one will surely have to agree that the former benefices had been alienated. This is the time of Charles Martel, who founded new fiefs, a time that must be distinguished from the first ones.

When the kings began to make gifts forever, either because of the corruption which slipped into the government, or because of the constitution itself which obliged kings to reward constantly, it was natural that they should have begun to give fiefs in perpetuity, rather than counties. To do without a few pieces of land was of little moment, to give up great offices was to lose power itself.

[59] Reported by Gregory of Tours [*Historia ecclesiastica Francorum*], bk. 9 [9.20]. See also *Edictum Chlotharii. a. 615*, art. 16 [*Capitularia regum Francorum* 9.16].

[60] [Gregory of Tours, *Historia ecclesiastica Francorum* 9.20]: "If by their own free will they wish to make something the property of another, or wish to confer it upon another, be it land, revenues, monies, it will be guarded and preserved in perpetuity" [L.].

[61] See [*Marculfi Formulae*] bk. 1, 24 and 34 [1.24.34].

[62] [*Marculfi Formulae*] bk. 1, 14 [1.14] which applies equally to fiscal goods given directly for ever or [those] given at first as a benefice and later for ever: "Thus it was formerly held by him or our fisc" [L.]. See also ibid., 17 [*Marculfi Formulae* 1.17].

CHAPTER 8

How the allods[d] were changed into fiefs

The way of changing an allod into a fief is found in a formula of Marculf.[63] One gave one's land to the king; he returned it to the giver as a usufruct or benefice, and recommended his heirs to the king.

In order to discover the reasons for a man thus to change the nature of his allod, I must seek, as in the very depths, the old prerogatives of that nobility which for eleven centuries has been covered with dust, blood, and sweat.

Those who held fiefs had great advantages. The settlement for injuries done them was much greater than that for freemen. It seems, according to the formulas of Marculf, that a privilege of the king's vassal was that whoever might kill him would pay six hundred sous in settlement. This privilege was established by the Salic law[64] and by that of the Ripuarians;[65] and whereas these two laws ordered a payment of six hundred sous for the death of the king's vassal, they gave only two hundred for the death of a freeborn person, a Frank, a barbarian, or a man living under the Salic law, and only a hundred for that of a Roman.[66]

This was not the only privilege of the king's vassals. One must know that, when a man cited for judgment did not present himself or did not obey the orders of the judges, he was called before the king;[67] and if he persisted in his contumacy, he was put beyond the protection of the king, and could not be received in one's home, or even given bread:[68] now, if he were of an ordinary condition, his goods were confiscated,[69] but if he were a vassal of the king they were not.[70] The first, by his contumacy, was considered to be convicted of the crime, and not the

[63] [*Marculfi Formulae*] bk. 1.13 [1.13].

[64] [*Lex Salica*] 44 [D69; S11]. See also tit. 66, 3–4 [*Lex Salica* D72; S8; see also *Pactus legis Salicae* 63.1–2] and 74 [*Pactus lex Salica* 70].

[65] [*Lex Ribuaria*] tit. 11 [11].

[66] See the *Lex Ribuaria* 7 [7]; and *Lex salica* 44.1, 4 [D69.1.4; S11.1, 4].

[67] *Lex Salica* 59 [D91; S2. See also *Pactus legis Salicae* 56]; 76 [*Pactus legis Salicae* 73].

[68] *Lex Salica* 59 "outside the community of the king" [L.]. [D91; S2. See also *Pactus legis Salicae* 56.5]; 76 [*Pactus legis Salicae* 73.6].

[69] *Lex Salica* 59.1 [D91.1; S2].

[70] Ibid. [*Pactus legis Salicae*], 76.1 [73.6].

[d] The allods were freeholds.

second. The former was subjected to proof by boiling water for the slightest crimes;[71] the latter was condemned to it only in the case of murder.[72] Finally, a vassal of the king could not be constrained to swear an oath against another vassal.[73] These privileges kept increasing, and in the capitulary of Carloman the vassals of the king are paid the honor of not being obliged to take oaths themselves, but rather of being able to have their vassals speak for them.[74] In addition, when the one who had these honors did not enter the army, his penalty was to abstain from meat and wine for as long as he had been absent from service; but the freeman who had not followed the count[75] owed a settlement of sixty sous and was put into servitude until he had paid it.[76]

Therefore, it is easy to think that the Franks and even more so the Romans who were not vassals of the king sought to become vassals; and so that they would not be deprived of their domains, one devised the usage of giving one's allod to the king, accepting it from him as a fief, and recommending one's heirs to him. This usage lasted, but it occurred chiefly in the time of the disorders under the Carolingians, when everyone needed a protector and wanted to join with other lords and enter, so to speak, into the feudal monarchy because they no longer had a political monarchy.[77]

This continued under the Capetians, as is seen in many charters,[78] either by one's giving one's allod and taking it back by the same act, or by declaring it an allod and recognizing it as a fief. These fiefs were called *fiefs de reprise*.[e]

This does not mean that those who had fiefs governed them as a good father does his family; and though freemen sought fiefs vigorously, they handled these kinds of goods the way usufructs are

[71] Ibid. [*Lex Salicae*], 56 [D89; S31; *Pactus legis Salicae* 53]; 59 [D91; S2; *Pactus legis Salicae* 56; see also 73].

[72] Ibid. [*Pactus legis Salicae*], 76.1 [73.6].

[73] Ibid. [*Pactus legis Salicae*], 76.2 [73.7–8].

[74] *Apud Vernis palatium 883*, arts. 4, 11 [*Capitularia regum Francorum* 287.4, 11].

[75] Charlemagne's Capitulary. *Capitulare secundum anni* 812, arts. 1, 3 [*Capitularia regum Francorum* 74.1, 3].

[76] *Heribannum*.

[77] In [Charles] Du Cange [*Glossarium mediae et infimae latinitatis*], at *Alodis* [1, 196; 1954 edn], Lambert d'Ardres says, "He left it to heirs who were not weak" [L.].

[78] See the ones [Charles] Du Cange cites under *Alodis* [1, 197–198; 1954 edn, *Glossarium mediae et infimae latinitatis*] and those reported by [Auguste] Galland, *Du franc-aleu et origine des droits seigneuriaux, avec les lois données au pays d'Albigeois*, p. 14 [c. 1].

[e] Fiefs that were taken back.

administered today. This is why Charlemagne, the most vigilant and attentive prince we have had, made many regulations[79] to keep them from degrading fiefs in favor of their own properties. This proves only that in his time most benefices were still for life, and that consequently one took more care of allods than of benefices, but this did not keep one from preferring vassalage to the king to being a freeman. One could have reasons for disposing of a certain particular portion of a fief, but one did not want to lose the rank itself.

I know too that Charlemagne complained in a capitulary[80] that in certain places there were people who gave their fiefs as property and later bought them back as property. But I do not say that they preferred property to a usufruct; I say only that, when they could make of a freehold a fief that would pass to their heirs, which is the case in the formula I have mentioned, there were great advantages in doing so.

[79] *Capitulare secundum anni 802*, art. 10 [*Capitularia regum Francorum* 34.10]; *Capitulare septimum anni 803*, art. 3 [*Capitularia regum Francorum* 59.3]; *Capitulare primum* incerti anni, art. 49 [*Capitularia regum Francorum* 35.49]; *Capitulare [quintum] anni 806*, art. 7 [*Capitularia regum Francorum* 46.7].

[80] *Capitulare quintum anni 806*, art. 8 [*Capitularia regum Francorum* 46.8].

CHAPTER 9

How ecclesiastical goods were converted into fiefs

The goods of the fisc should have had no other destination than to serve as gifts the kings could make to encourage the Franks to new expeditions, which increased the goods of the fisc[f] as well, and this was, as I have said, the spirit of the nation; but gifts took another direction. We have a speech of Chilperic,[81] the grandson of Clovis, who even then complained that almost all his goods had been given to the churches. "Our fisc has become poor," he said; "our wealth has been transferred to the churches;[82] now only the bishops reign; they are great and we are great no longer."

[81] In Gregory of Tours [*Historia ecclesiastica Francorum*], bk. 6, chap. 46 [6.46].

[82] This made him annul testaments made in favor of churches and even the donations made by his father; Guntram reestablished them and even made new donations. Gregory of Tours [*Historia ecclesiastica Francorum*], bk. 7, chap. 7 [7.7].

[f] *biens fiscaux.*

This was why mayors, who did not dare to attack the lords, despoiled the churches; and one of the reasons that Pepin alleged for entering Neustria[83] was that he had been invited there by the ecclesiastics to check the expeditions of the kings, that is, of the mayors, who were depriving the church of all its goods.

The mayors of Austrasia, that is the house of the Pepins, had treated the church with more moderation than had been done in Neustria and in Burgundy, and this is very clear in our chronicles,[84] where the monks never tire of admiring the devotion and liberality of the Pepins. They themselves had occupied the highest positions in the church. "A crow does not pluck out the eyes of another crow," as Chilperic said to the bishops.[85]

Pepin brought Neustria and Burgundy into subjection; but, as he had used the pretext of the oppression of the churches to destroy the mayors and kings, he could no longer despoil them without contradicting his own title and showing that he was mocking the nation. But the conquest of two great kingdoms and the destruction of the opposing party furnished him sufficient means to satisfy his captains.

Pepin made himself master of the monarchy by protecting the clergy; Charles Martel, his son, could maintain himself only by oppressing them. As this prince saw that part of the royal goods and part of the goods of the fisc had been given for life or as property to the nobility, and that the clergy, who received from the hand of the rich and poor alike, had even acquired a great part of the allods, he despoiled the churches; and, as the fiefs of the first division no longer existed, he formed fiefs a second time.[86] He took for himself and his captains the goods of churches and even the churches, and put an end to an abuse which, unlike ordinary evils, was the easier to cure for being so extreme.

[83] See the *Annales Mettenses* 687 [690] [*MGH*, SS. 1, 318]: "I was aroused, in the first place, by the priests and servants of God who often approached me on account of the unjust sufferings done the patrimonies [of the Church]" [L.].

[84] Ibid. [*Annales Mettenses*, e.g. *anno* 691; 1,320; *MGH*, SS.1].

[85] In Gregory of Tours [*Historia ecclesiastica Francorum* 5.18].

[86] [Hariulphe] *Chronicon Centulense*, bk. 2 [2.1; p. 48, 1894 edn]; "Charles [. . .,] removing jurisdiction [property] from the ecclesiastics, appropriated this real estate to the fisc, then distributed it to his soldiers" [L.].

CHAPTER 10
The wealth of the clergy

The clergy received so much during the reigns of the Merovingians, Carolingians, and the Capetians that they must have been given the whole of the goods of the kingdom several times. But, if the kings, the nobility, and the people found the means of giving them all their goods, they nevertheless found the means of taking them back. Under the Merovingians, piety founded churches, but the military spirit gave them to military men who divided them among their children. How many lands left the revenue of the clergy! The Carolingian kings opened their hands and were again immensely liberal; the Normans arrived, pillaged and ravaged, persecuted the priests and monks above all, sought out the abbeys and every religious place, and looked for whatever religious place they could find, for they attributed to the ecclesiastics both the destruction of their idols and all the violence of Charlemagne, who had obliged the Normans repeatedly to take refuge in the North. These were hatreds that forty or fifty years could not make them forget. In this state of things, what a quantity of goods the clergy lost! There were scarcely any ecclesiastics to ask for their return. It remained, therefore, for the piety of the Capetians to make enough foundations and grants of land; the opinions that had been published and believed in those times would have deprived the laity of all their goods, if they had been sufficiently honest people. But if the ecclesiastics were ambitious, so were the laity; if the dying person gave something, the heir wanted to take it back. One sees only quarrels between lords and bishops, between gentlemen and abbots; and vigorous pressure must have been put on ecclesiastics, because they were obliged to put themselves under the protection of certain lords, who defended them for a time and oppressed them ever after.

A better police, which was becoming established under the Capetians, already permitted the ecclesiastics to increase their goods. The Calvinists appeared and had everything of gold and silver in the churches made into money. How could the clergy have secured their fortune? Their very existence was not secure. They treated controversial matters, and one burned their archives. What use was it to ask from an ever impoverished nobility the return of that which it no longer had, or which it had mortgaged in a thousand ways? The clergy have always acquired, they have always returned, and they still acquire.

CHAPTER II

The state of Europe at the time of Charles Martel

Charles Martel, who undertook to despoil the clergy, was in the most fortunate circumstances: he was feared and loved by the warriors, and he worked for them; he had the pretext of his wars against the Saracens;[87] however hated he might have been by the clergy, he had no need of them; the Pope, to whom he was necessary, opened his arms to him; one knows the celebrated embassy sent to him by Gregory III.[88] These two powers were closely united because they could not do without each other; the Pope needed the Franks to support him against the Lombards and the Greeks; Charles Martel needed the Pope in order to humble the Greeks, to embarrass the Lombards, to make himself more respectable at home, and to accredit his titles and those his children might take.[89] Therefore, he could not fail in his enterprise.

Saint Eucher, Bishop of Orleans, had a vision that astonished the princes. On this topic I must relate the letter that the bishops, assembled at Rheims, wrote to Louis the German,[90] who had entered the lands of Charles the Bald, because the letter very aptly shows us what was, at that time, the state of things and the situation of men's spirits. The bishops say[91] that "when Saint Eucher was snatched up to heaven, he saw Charles Martel tormented in the bottom of hell by the

[87] See the *Annales Mettenses* [714–741, *MGH*, SS. 1, 322–327].

[88] *Annales Mettenses, anno 741* [*MGH*, SS. 1, 326]: "Gregory sent a letter to him above all and included a resolution from the Prince of the Romans, that the Roman people did indeed wish to turn to his protection and unequalled clemency and to leave the dominion of the Emperor" [L.]. Fredegarius [*Chronicon, Continuationes*, 110 [22]]: "He proposed a pact that he would withdraw from the Imperial side" [L.].

[89] One can see, in the authors of those times, the impression that the authority of so many popes made on the spirit of the French. Though King Pepin had already been crowned by the Bishop of Baience, he regarded the unction he had received from Pope Stephen as a thing which confirmed him in all his rights.

[90] *Apud Carisiacum, 858*, Baluze edn, vol. 2, p. 101 [*Epistola episcoporum ad Ludowicum regum 858, Capitularia regum Francorum* 297].

[91] *Apud Carisiacum, 858*, Baluze edn, vol. 2, art. 7, p. 109 [*Epistola episcoporum ad Ludowicum regum 858, Capitularia regum Francorum* 297.7].

order of the saints who are to be with Christ at the Last Judgment; that he had been condemned to this penalty before that time for having despoiled the churches of their goods and for having in this way become guilty of all the sins of those who had given them; that King Pepin held a council on this subject; that he caused to be returned to the churches all the ecclesiastical goods he could obtain; that, as he could recover only part of them because of his quarrels with Vaifre, Duke of Aquitaine, he had letters called *precarium* written in favor of the churches for the remainder[92] and he ruled that the laity would pay a tithe on the goods it held from the churches and twelve deniers for each house; that Charlemagne did not give away the goods of the Church; that he made, on the contrary, a capitulary in which he promised, for himself and his successors, never to give them away; that all they propose is in writing; and that several had even heard it told to Louis the Pious, father of two kings."

The regulation of King Pepin of which the bishops speak was made in the council at Leptines.[93] The Church found this advantage in it, that those who had received some of its goods now held them but precariously and that, besides, it received the tithe and twelve deniers for each dwelling that had belonged to it. But this was a palliative remedy and the ill still remained.

Even this was contradictory and Pepin was obliged to make another capitulary,[94] in which he enjoined those who held these benefices to pay this tithe and fee and even to keep up the houses of the bishop or the monastery on penalty of losing the goods given them. Charlemagne renewed Pepin's regulations.[95]

That the bishops say in this same letter that Charlemagne promised

[92] [Jacques] Cujas, *De feudis*, bk. 1 [1.1; p. 597; 1868 edn]: "Precarial tenure, whose use has been conceded by prayer" [L.]. I find in a charter of King Pepin, dated at the third year of his reign, that this prince was not the first to establish these letters called *precarium*; he cites one made by the mayor Ebroin, and continued since. See the charter of this king in *Recueil des historiens des Gaules et de la France*, by the Benedictine Fathers, vol. 5, art. 6 [92. ann. 754; 5, 701; 1869 edn].

[93] In 743. See *Capitularies*, bk. 5, art. 3, Baluze edn, p. 825 [*MGH*, *Capitularia spuria. Benedictae levitae* 1.3].

[94] [*Capitulare Mettense*, 756, art. 4 [*Capitularia spuria. Benedictae levitae* 1.13].

[95] See his *Capitulare octavum anni 803 (Worms)*, Baluze edn, p. 411 [considered spurious by *MGH*; F. Walter, 2, 194; 1824 edn; see *Recueil des historiens des Gaules et de la France*, 5, 671–672; 1869 edn], in which he rules on the contract *precarium*; and that of Frankfort, of 794, p. 267, art. 24, on the repairs of houses, *Capitulare Francofordiense*, *794*, p. 267, art. 24 [*Capitularia regum Francorum* 28.26]; and that of 800, p. 330, *Edictum dominicum de honore episcopis praestando circa 800* [*Capitularia regum Francorum* 97].

for himself and his successors no longer to divide the goods of the churches among the warriors is consistent with the capitulary of this prince, given in Aix-la-Chapelle in 803, made to calm the terrors of ecclesiastics on this matter; but the gifts already made continued to exist.[96] The bishops add, and with reason, that Louis the Pious followed the conduct of Charlemagne and did not give the goods of the church to the soldiers.

Nevertheless, the former abuses went so far that, under the children of Louis the Pious, the laity established priests in its churches, or drove them out, without the consent of the bishops.[97] The churches were divided among the heirs,[98] and when they were not kept up in a seemly way, the bishops had no other recourse than to remove the relics.[99]

The capitulary given at Compiègne establishes that the king's deputy might inspect any monastery with the bishop,[100] on notice to and in the presence of the one who held it,[101] and this general regulation proves that the abuse was general.

It was not that laws were lacking for the restitution of church goods. When the pope reproached the bishops for their neglect of the reestablishment of monasteries, they wrote to Charles the Bald that this reproach did not concern them because they were not guilty of it, and they informed him of what had been promised, resolved, and enacted in so many assemblies of the nation.[102] Indeed, they cite nine of them.

They continued to quarrel. The Normans arrived and made them all agree.

[96] As appears from the preceding note and from the capitulary of King Pepin, King of Italy, in which it is said that the king would give in fief the monasteries to those who would commend themselves for fiefs. It is added to the *Leges Langobardorum*, bk. 3, tit. 1, para. 30 [31] [Pip. 29 (31) (pap.)] and to the *Lex Salica*, collection of the laws of Pepin, in Eckhart, p. 195 [1720 edn], tit. 26, art. 4.

[97] See the constitution of Lothair I, in the *Leges Langobardorum*, bk. 3, tit. 1, para. 43 [Loth. 44 (43) (pap.)].

[98] Ibid., para. 44. [*Leges Langobardorum*, bk. 3.1.44 [Loth. 45 (44) (pap.)].

[99] Ibid. [*Leges Langobardorum*, Loth. 45 (44) (pap.).]

[100] Given the 28th year of the reign of Charles the Bald, 868, Baluze edn, p. 203 [*Apud Compendium 868*; *Capitularia regum Francorum* 259].

[101] [*Apud Compendium 868*; *Capitularia regum Francorum* 259.1]; "With the advice and consent of him who maintains the place" [L.].

[102] *Concilium apud Bonolium 856* [*Capitularia regum Francorum* 295], 16th year of Charles the Bald, Baluze edn, p. 78.

CHAPTER 12

The establishment of tithes

The regulations made under King Pepin had given the church the expectation of relief rather than actual relief, and, just as Charles Martel had found the whole public patrimony in the hands of the ecclesiastics, Charlemagne found the goods of the ecclesiastics in the hands of the warriors. One could not make the latter restore what they had been given, and the circumstances at that time rendered the thing even more impractical than it was by its nature. On the other hand, Christianity was not to perish for lack of ministers, temples, and instructions.[103]

This was why Charlemagne established tithes,[104] a new kind of good, whose advantage to the clergy was that later usurpations would be more easily recognizable, as they were given exclusively to the church.

Some have wanted to give much earlier dates to this establishment, but the authorities they cite seem to me to testify against those who allege them. The constitution of Clotaire[105] says only that certain tithes would not be levied on the goods of the church.[106] Far from the church's levying tithes in those times, its only intention was to be exempted from them. The second council of Macon,[107] held in 585, which orders tithes to be paid, says that, in truth, they had been paid in

[103] In the civil wars that sprang up at the time of Charles Martel, the goods of the Church of Rheims were given to the laity. The clergy was left to "subsist as it could," as it is said in the Life of Saint Rémy. [Laurentius] Surius, vol. 1, p. 279 [*De probatis sanctorum*, 1, 279; Tome 1, Januarii et Februarii; this is Hincmar's life of St. Rémy; see *Acta Sanctorum*, 1. Oct. Primus, p. 131; 1866 edn; *MGH* considers it spurious, but quotes the passage to which M. refers, Auct. Ant. IV. Pars Posterior, p. XXIII.]

[104] *Leges Langobardum*, bk. 3, tit. 1, paras. 1, 2 [Kar. 7, 60 (pap.)].

[105] It is the one I have mentioned in chap. 4 above, to be found in the Capitularies, Baluze edn, vol. 1, art. 11, p. 9 [*Chlotharii regia constitutio generalis. circa 560*, *Capitularia regum Francorum* 8.11].

[106] "We concede to the Church the tithes on farm land, pastures, and of pigs; no tax collector or tither may collect the possessions of the Church" [L.] [*Capitulare de villis; Capitularia regum Francorum* 32.36]. The capitulary of Charlemagne of the year 800, Baluze edn, p. 336, explains clearly what sort of tithe it was from which Clotaire exempted the Church; it was a tenth of the pigs put out for fattening in the king's forests, and Charlemagne wants his judges to pay it like the others, in order to set an example. It can be seen that it was a seigneurial or economic right.

[107] [Council of Macon] Jacques Sirmond, *Concilia antiqua Galliae*, Canon V [1, 384; 1970 edn, *Concilia Galliae A. 511–A. 695*, Concil Matisconense, A. 585, #5, Corpus Christianorum, Series Latina, vol. 148A, p. 241].

former times; but it also says that they were no longer paid at that time.

Who can doubt that before Charlemagne one had opened the Bible and preached the gifts and offerings of Leviticus? But I say that prior to this prince tithes may have been preached, but they were not established.

I have said that the regulations made under King Pepin had subjected those who possessed ecclesiastical goods as fiefs to paying tithes and making reparations to churches. It was a great deal to oblige the principal men of the nation to set an example by a law whose justice could not be disputed.

Charlemagne did more, and one sees by the capitulary *de Villis*[108] that he obliged his own lands to pay tithes; this was also a great example.

But the common people are scarcely able to abandon their interests for an example. The synod of Frankfurt[109] gave them a more pressing motive to pay the tithes. A capitulary made there said that, in the last famine, empty husks of grain were found, that they had been devoured by devils whose voices had been heard reproaching them for not having paid the tithe;[110] and, consequently, all those who held ecclesiastical goods were ordered to pay the tithe, and, as a further consequence, everyone was ordered to do so.

Charlemagne's project did not succeed at first; this burden seemed overwhelming.[111] Among the Jews the payment of tithes was a part of the founding plan of their republic, but here the payment of tithes was a burden independent of those established by the monarchy. One can see in the provisions added to the law of the Lombards[112] the difficulty there was in having the tithes accepted in civil law; one can judge by the different canons of the councils how difficult it was to have them accepted in ecclesiastical law.

108 [*Capitulare de villis*] art. 6, Baluze edn, p. 332 [*Capitularia regum Francorum* 32.6]. It was given in 800.

109 Held under Charlemagne in 794 [*Capitulare Francofordiense. 794, Capitularia regum Francorum* 28].

110 [*Capitularia Francofordiense. 794, 23. Capitularia regum Francorum* 28.25] Baluze edn, p. 267, art. 23: "We have received information that in that year in which a severe famine spread, an abundance of worthless crops was devoured by demons, and voices of reproach were heard" [L.].

111 See among others the capitulary of Louis the Pious in 829, Baluze edn, p. 663, against those who, with the aim of not paying the tithe, did not cultivate their lands, and art. 5 [*Capitulare Wormatiense 829. Capitula pro lege habenda. Capitularia regum Francorum* 191.5]: "The ninths and the tenths [tithes] about which our father and ourselves have made frequent admonitions in diverse resolutions" [L.].

112 Among others, that of Lothair [*Leges Langobardorum*], bk. 3, tit. 3, chap. 6 [Loth. 43 (pap.)].

The people finally consented to pay tithes on the condition that they could redeem them.[g] The constitution of Louis the Pious[113] and that of Emperor Lothair,[114] his son, did not permit this.

The laws of Charlemagne on the establishment of tithes were the work of necessity; religion alone had a part in it, and superstition none.

The famous division that he made of tithes into four parts, for the building of churches, for the poor, for the bishop, and for the clerics,[115] proves that he wanted to give the church the fixed and permanent estate it had lost.

His testament shows that he wanted to remedy completely the evils that his grandfather, Charles Martel, had done.[116] He divided his movable goods into three equal parts; he wanted two of them to be divided into twenty-one parts for the twenty-one archbishops' sees of his empire; each part was to be subdivided between the archbishop's see and the bishoprics dependent upon it. He divided the remaining third into four parts; he gave one part to his children and his grandchildren, another was added to the two-thirds already given, and the two remaining were used in pious works. It seemed that he regarded the immense gift he had just given to the churches less as a religious act than as a political dispensation.

[113] *Capitulare Wormatiense 829. Capitula pro lege habenda*, art. 7, Baluze edn, vol. 1, p. 663 [*Capitularia regum Francorum* 191.7].

[114] *Leges Langobardorum*, bk. 3, tit. 3, para. 8. [Loth. 48 (pap.)].

[115] *Leges Langobardorum*, bk. 3, tit. 3, para. 4 [Kar. 94 (pap.)].

[116] It is a kind of codicil reported by Einhard [*Vita Karoli Magni*, chap. 33], and which differs from the testament itself that is found in Goldast and Baluze.

[g] The verb *racheter*, "to buy back," "to redeem," is related to the *rachat*, the "redemption" or "repurchase" that often had to be paid by each new heir to a fief to his overlord to buy back his fief.

CHAPTER 13

On elections of bishops and abbots

As the churches had become poor, kings gave up electing to the bishoprics and to other ecclesiastical benefices.[117] Princes were less involved with naming someone to them; their authority was less frequently claimed by the candidates. Thus, the Church received a kind of compensation for the goods that had been taken away from it.

And if Louis the Pious left to the Roman people the right to elect popes,[118] it was a result of the general spirit of his time; one acted toward the archbishop's see in Rome as toward the others.

[117] See the capitulary of Charlemagne of 803, art. 2, Baluze edn, p. 379 [see Walter, 2, 171; see also 2, 177 and *CRF* 42.2]; and the edict of Louis the Pious of 834 found in [Melchior] Goldast, *Constitutiones imperiales*, vol. 1 [Lud. Pii, 834, 1, 188–189; 1974 edn].

[118] This is said in the famous canon. *Ego Ludovicus*, which is obviously forged. It is in the edition of Baluze, p. 591, for the year 817 [*Decretum confirmationis Paschali factae 817, Capitularia regum Francorum* 172].

CHAPTER 14

On the fiefs of Charles Martel

I shall not say whether, when Charles Martel gave the goods of the church in fief, he gave them for life or in perpetuity. All that I know is that in the time of Charlemagne[119] and Lothair I,[120] there were these sorts of goods, which passed to heirs and were divided among them.

I find in addition that a part was given as allod and the rest as fief.[121]

I have said that owners of allods were subject to service like those who possessed fiefs. That was no doubt partly why Charles Martel gave goods as allods and as fiefs.

[119] As appears in *Capitulare episcoporum*, art. 17 of 801, in Baluze, vol. 1, p. 360 [*Capitularia regum Francorum* 36.17].

[120] See his constitution inserted in the *Leges Langobardorum*, bk. 3, tit. 1, para. 44 [*Loth.* 45 (44) (pap.)].

[121] See the constitution cited above; and the capitulary of Charles the Bald for 846, chap. 20, *In villa sparnaco* [*Capitularia regum Francorum* 293.20], Baluze edn, vol. 2, p. 31; and *Synodus Suessionensis 853*, art 3, 5 [*Capitularia regum Francorum* 258.3, 5], Baluze edn, vol. 2, p. 54; and *Apud Attiniacum 854*, art. 10 [*Capitularia regum Francorum* 261.10], Baluze edn, vol. 2, p. 70. See also the *Capitulare primum* incerti anni, arts. 49, 56 [*Capitularia regum Francorum* 35.49, 56], Baluze edn, vol. 1, p. 519.

CHAPTER 15

Continuation of the same subject

It must be observed that, as fiefs had been changed into goods of the church, and the goods of the church into fiefs, fiefs and the goods of the church each took something from the nature of the other. Thus, the goods of the church had the privileges of fiefs, and the fiefs had the privileges of the goods of the church; such were the honorary rights that were seen to appear in those times in churches.[122] And, as these rights have always been attached to the high justice, in preference to what we today call the fief, it follows that patrimonial justices were established at the same time as these rights.

[122] See the Capitularies, bk. 5, art. 44 [*Capitularia spuria. Benedictae levitae* 1.44]; and the Edict of Pistes, 866, arts. 8 and 9 [*Capitularia regum Francorum* 273.8, 9], in which are seen the honorific rights of the lords established as they are today.

CHAPTER 16

Confusion between royalty and mayoralty. The Carolingians

The order of the subject has made me disturb the order of time; and I have spoken of Charlemagne before speaking of that famous period of the transfer of the crown to the Carolingians, which was made under King Pepin: a thing which, unlike ordinary events, is perhaps more noticed today than it was even at the time it happened.

Kings had no authority, but they had a name; the title of king was hereditary, and that of mayor was elective. Although mayors in later times had put on the throne the Merovingian whom they wanted, they had not taken a king from another family, and the old law which gave the crown to a certain family was not yet erased from the hearts of the Franks. The person of the king was almost unknown in the monarchy, but royalty was not. Pepin, son of Charles Martel, believed that it was appropriate to blend these two titles, a confusion that would always leave some uncertainty as to whether the new royalty was hereditary or not; and this sufficed for the one who joined great power with royalty.

At that moment mayoral authority was joined to royal authority. In the mixture of these two authorities, a kind of reconciliation occurred. The mayor had been elective, and the king hereditary: the crown, at the beginning of the reign of the Carolingians, was elected because the people did the choosing; it was hereditary because they always chose from the same family.[123]

Father Le Cointe, in spite of the testimony of all the records,[124] denies that the Pope authorized this great change;[125] he reasons by saying the Pope would have done an injustice. And it is admirable to see a historian judge of what men have done by what they should have done! With this way of reasoning, there would be no more history.

Be that as it may, it is certain that, from the moment of the victory of Duke Pepin, his family reigned and the Merovingians reigned no longer. When his grandson Pepin was crowned king, it was only one more ceremony and one less phantom: he acquired nothing by it except royal attire; nothing changed in the nation.

I have said this in order to fix the moment of the revolution so that one does not make the mistake of regarding as a revolution that which was only a consequence of the revolution.

When Hugh Capet, the first Capetian, was crowned king, there was a greater change because the state passed from anarchy to some kind of government, but when Pepin took the crown, it was a passage from one government to the same government.

When Pepin was crowned king, he changed the name only, but when Hugh Capet was crowned king, things changed, because a great fief, united with the crown, brought an end to anarchy.

When Pepin was crowned king, the title of king was united to the greatest office; when Hugh Capet was crowned, the title of king was united to the greatest fief.

[123] See the Testament of Charlemagne; and the division that Louis the Pious made for his children at the Assembly of Estates held at Quierzy, reported by [Melchior] Goldast [*Constitutiones imperiales*, 1, 145; 2, 19; quotation is from 2, 19, #3; also in *CRF* 45, 194]: "He whom the people wish to choose, that he succeed his father in the royal inheritance" [L.].

[124] *Fragmentum Historicum auctoris incerti, a Dagoberto I. usque ad Pipinum Regem*, [*Recueil des historiens des Gaules et de la France*, 2, 694; 1869 edn]; and [Hariulphe] *Chronicon Centulense 754* [2.6; pp. 50–51; 1894 edn].

[125] [Charles Le Cointe], *Annales ecclesiastici Francorum*, vol. 2, p. 319 [5, 319; Anno 752, #1]: "This story was invented after Pepin's death, and is much opposed to the equity and sanctity of Pope Zachary" [L.].

CHAPTER 17

A particular matter in the election of the Carolingian kings

One sees in the formula for the consecration of Pepin[126] that Charles and Carloman were also anointed and blessed and that the French lords were obliged on penalty of interdiction and excommunication never to elect anyone other than a Carolingian.[127]

It seems, according to the testaments of Charlemagne and Louis the Pious, that the Franks chose between the children of kings, which is closely related to the clause mentioned earlier. And when the empire passed to another house than that of Charlemagne, the faculty of electing, which had been restricted and conditional, became pure and simple, and one departed from the former constitution.

Pepin, feeling his end near, convoked the ecclesiastical and lay lords at Saint-Denis[128] and divided his kingdom between his two sons, Charles and Carloman. We do not have the acts of that assembly, but one finds what happened there in the author of the old historical collection edited by Canisius,[129] and in that of the *Annals* of Metz, as M. Baluze has observed.[130] I see there two somewhat contradictory things: that he made the division with the consent of the important men, and then that he made it by a paternal right. This proves what I have said, that the right of the people during the reign of this house was to elect from within the family; it was, properly speaking, a right to exclude rather than a right to elect.

This kind of right of election is confirmed by the records of the Carolingians. Such is the capitulary on the division of the empire that Charlemagne made among his three children, in which, after the division was formed, he says that, "if one of the three brothers has a son and the people want to elect him to succeed to his father's kingdom, his uncles will consent to it."[131]

[126] *Recueil des historiens des Gaules et de la France*, vol. 5, p. 9 [9–10]. [The *Clausula de Pepini* can also be found in *MGH*, SS. Merov., t. 1, pars 2, pp. 465–466.]

[127] Ibid., p. 10 [*Recueil des historiens des Gaules et de la France* 5, 10; *MGH*, SS. Merov., t. 1, pars. 2, p. 466]: "They never presume to elect a king from any other lineage than this one" [L.]

[128] In 768.

[129] [Henricus Canisius] *Lectionis antiquae*, vol. 2 [vol. 2, pt. 1, *Ex Toromacho*, anno 768, p. 225; 1725].

[130] [Etienne Baluze] *Capitularia*, 1, 188. [This is an historical note of Baluze, not a law text.]

[131] *Capitulare primum anni 806 (divisio)*, Baluze edn, p. 439, art. 5 [*Capitularia regum Francorum* 45.5].

This same provision is found in the division that Louis the Pious made among his three children, Pepin, Louis, and Charles, in 837 at the assembly of Aix-la-Chapelle,[132] and also in another division by the same emperor made twenty years earlier between Lothair, Pepin, and Louis.[133] One can also see the oath that Louis the Stammerer made in Compiègne when he was crowned. "I, Louis, constituted king by the mercy of god and the election of the people, do promise . . ."[134] What I say is confirmed by the acts of the Council of Valence, held in 890 for the election of Louis, son of Boso, to the kingdom of Arles.[135] Louis was elected to it, and the principal reasons given for his election were that he was of the imperial family,[136] that Charles the Fat had given him the rank of king, and that the emperor Arnulf had invested him by the scepter and by the attendance of his ambassadors. The kingdom of Arles, like the others previously a part of or dependent on Charlemagne's empire, was elective and hereditary.

[132] In [Melchior] Goldast, *Constitutiones imperiales*, vol. 2, p. 19 [2, 19; 1974 edn; also in *CRF* 194].

[133] [*Charta divisionis imperii. 817*], art. 14, Baluze edn, p. 574 [*Capitularia regum Francorum* 136.14]: "If one of them dies and leaves behind legitimate children, he ought not to divide his power among them; rather, the people assemble together and should choose whom the lord desires; the older brother should support him in this rank as a brother and son" [L.].

[134] *Ludowici II. coronatio Compendii 877*, Baluze edn, p. 272 [*Capitularia regum Francorum* 283. (A)].

[135] In [Jean] Dumont, *Corps universel diplomatique du droit des gens*, tome 1, art. 36 [1, art. 36; 1726–1731 edn].

[136] Through the female line.

CHAPTER 18

Charlemagne

Charlemagne thought that he would keep the power of the nobility within its limits and curtail the oppression of the clergy and freemen. He so tempered the orders of the state that they were counter-balanced and that he remained the master. Everything was united by the force of his genius. He constantly led the nobility from expedition to expedition; he did not leave them time to form designs, and he occupied them entirely in following his. The empire was maintained by the greatness of the leader; the prince was great, the man was greater. The kings, his children, were his first subjects, the instruments of his power, and models of obedience. He made admirable regulations; he did more, he had them executed. His genius spread over all the parts of the empire. One sees in the laws of this prince a spirit of foresight that includes everything and a certain force that carries everything along. Pretexts for avoiding duties are removed; negligences corrected, abuses reformed or foreseen.[137] He knew how to punish; he knew still better how to pardon. Vast in his plans, simple in executing them, he, more than anyone, had to a high degree the art of doing the greatest things with ease and the difficult ones promptly. He traveled constantly over his vast empire, offering his hand wherever he happened to be. Matters of business arose everywhere, and he brought them to a conclusion everywhere. Never did a prince better know how to brave danger; never did a prince better know how to avoid it. He mocked all perils, and particularly those which great conquerors almost always undergo; I mean conspiracies. This prodigious prince was extremely moderate; his character was gentle, his manners simple; he loved to live among the people of his court. He was perhaps too susceptible to pleasure with women, but a prince who always governed by himself and who spent his life working can deserve more excuses. He regulated his expenditures admirably; he developed his domains wisely, attentively, and economically; the father of a family could learn from his laws how to govern his household.[138] One sees in his capitularies the pure and sacred source from which he drew his wealth. I shall say only one word more: he ordered that the eggs from the farmyards of his domains and the unused vegetables of his gardens should be sold,[139] and he distributed among his peoples all the wealth of the Lombards and the immense treasuries of those Huns who had despoiled the universe.

[137] See his *Capitulare tertium anni 811*, arts. 1–8, p. 486 [*Capitularia regum Francorum* 73.1–8] and *Capitulare primum anni 812*, art. 1, p. 490 [*Capitularia regum Francorum* 50.1]; and *Capitulare secundum anni 813*, arts. 9, 11, p. 494 [*Capitularia regum Francorum* 74.9, 11] and others.

[138] See the *Capitulare de villis 800* [*Capitulare regum Francorum* 32]; *Capitulare secundum anni 813*, art. 6, 19 [*Capitularia regum Francorum* 77.6.19]; and *Capitularies*, bk. 5, art. 303 [*Capitularia spuria. Benedictae levitae* 1.303].

[139] *Capitulare de Villis*, 800, art. 39 [*CRF* 32.39]. See the entire capitulary, which is a masterpiece of prudence, good administration and economy.

CHAPTER 19

Continuation of the same subject

Charlemagne and his early successors feared that those whom they placed in distant spots would be inclined to revolt; they believed they would find more docility among the ecclesiastics; thus they set up in Germany a great number of bishoprics and joined great fiefs to them.[140] It seems, according to some of the charters, that the clauses containing the prerogatives of those fiefs were no different from those that were ordinarily put in such grants,[141] though today one sees the principal ecclesiastics of Germany invested with sovereign power. Be that as it may, these were the principal pieces they moved forward against the Saxons. What Charlemagne and his successors could not expect from the indolence and negligence of a leud, they believed they should expect from the zeal and active attention of a bishop; besides, such a vassal, far from using subject peoples against them would, on the contrary, need them for support against his peoples.

[140] See, among others, the *Praeceptum de institutione episcopatus Bremensis a. 789*, Baluze edn, p. 245. [Considered spurious by *MGH*; see *MGH*, *Die Urkunden der Karolinger*, vol. 1, #245, pp. 344–346].

[141] For example, the prohibition against royal judges entering the territory, to exact the *freda* and other rights. I have spoken of this at length in the preceding book.

CHAPTER 20

Louis the Pious

When Augustus was in Egypt, he had the tomb of Alexander opened; he was asked if he wanted to open those of the Ptolemies; he said that he had wanted to see the king, and not the dead: thus, in the history of the Carolingians one seeks Pepin and Charlemagne; one wants to see kings and not the dead.

A prince, the puppet of his passions and the dupe even of his virtues, a prince who knew neither his strength nor his weakness, who did not know how to gain for himself either fear or love, who had few vices in his heart but all sorts of failings in his spirit, took in his hands the reins of empire that Charlemagne had held.

At the time when the universe is in tears for the death of his father, in that instant of shock when everyone asks for Charles and finds him no more, in the time when he hastens to fill his place, he sent ahead some he trusted to arrest those who had contributed to the disorderly conduct of his sisters. This caused bloody tragedies.[142] These were hasty acts of imprudence. He began to avenge domestic crimes before arriving at the palace and stirred spirits to rebellion before becoming master.

He put out the eyes of Bernard, king of Italy, his nephew, who had come to plead for his clemency and who died a few days later; that multiplied his enemies. His fear of them made him decide to have his brothers stripped of their goods; this further increased the number of his enemies. He was much reproached on these last two points;[143] one did not fail to say that he had broken his oath and the solemn promises he had made to his father on the day of his coronation.[144]

After the death of the Empress Irmengarde, by whom he had three children, he married Judith; he had a son by her; and soon, blending the compliances of an old husband with the weaknesses of an old king, he put a disorder into his family that brought on the fall of the monarchy.

He constantly changed the divisions he made for his children. However, these divisions had been confirmed in turn by his oaths, by those of his children, and by those of the lords. It seems he wanted to tempt the fealty of his subjects; to seek to put confusion, scruples, and ambiguities into their obedience; to confound the various rights of princes, especially at a time when, as fortresses were few, the first rampart of authority was fealty promised and fealty received.

In order to maintain their shares the emperor's children solicited the clergy and gave them rights unheard of until then. These rights were specious; the clergy were brought in as a guarantee of that thing which one had wanted authorized. Agobard explained to Louis the Pious that he had sent Lothair to Rome to be declared emperor; that Lothair had made divisions among his children after having consulted heaven in

[142] In the collection of Duchesne, vol. 2, p. 295. Anonymous ["Astronomous"], *Vita Hludowici imperatoris* [anno 814, chap. 21].

[143] See the testimony of his degradation, in the collection of Duchesne, vol. 2, p. 333 [*CRF* 197].

[144] In the Duchesne collection, vol. 2, p. 276. Thegan, *Vita Hludowici Imperatoris* [chap. 6, a. 813]. He ordered him to show an unlimited clemency, "unfailing mercy" [L.] for his sisters, brothers, and nephews.

three days of fasting and prayers.[145] What could a superstitious prince do, especially when attacked by superstition itself? One senses that sovereign authority was twice thwarted, by the imprisonment of this prince and by his public penitence. One had wanted to degrade the king; one degraded royalty.

At first one can scarcely understand how a prince who had a number of good qualities, who did not lack enlightenment, who naturally loved the good, and to put it briefly, who was the son of Charlemagne, could have enemies so numerous, so violent, so irreconcilable, so eager to offend him, so insolent in his humiliation, so determined to ruin him;[146] and they would have ruined him irremediably the second time, if his children, fundamentally more honest people than they, had been able to follow out a project and agree on something.

[145] See his letters [Agobard, *Opera, Flebilis epistola. De divisione*. See Baluze's note, Migne PL 104, p. 288].

[146] See the testimony of his degradation in the collection of Duchesne, vol. 2, p. 331 [*CRF* 197]. See also the life written by Thegan. [Anonymous "Astronomous," *Vita Hludowici Imperatoris*, a. 830, chap. 44], "He was oppressed by so much hatred that his very life grieved him," [L.] says the anonymous author in Duchesne, vol. 2, p. 307.

CHAPTER 21
Continuation of the same subject

The strength that Charlemagne had put into the nation lasted well enough under Louis the Pious for the state to maintain its greatness and be respected by foreigners. The prince's spirit was weak, but his was a warrior nation. Authority within was being ruined while power abroad did not appear to diminish.

Charles Martel, Pepin, and Charlemagne governed the monarchy in succession. The first flattered the avarice of the soldiers; the other two, that of the clergy; Louis the Pious made them both discontented.

In the French constitution, the king, the nobility, and the clergy held all the power of the state in their hands. Charles Martel, Pepin, and Charlemagne sometimes joined their interests with one of the two parties in order to contain the other, and almost always with both of them; but Louis the Pious detached both of these bodies from himself. He antagonized the bishops by regulations that they saw as rigid because he went further than they themselves wanted to go. There are very good laws made in an inappropriate way. The bishops, accustomed in these times to go to war against the Saracens and the Saxons, were far from having the monastic spirit.[147] On the other hand, as he had lost confidence in his nobility, he elevated people from nothing.[148] He deprived the nobility of their positions, dismissed them from the palace, and called in outsiders.[149] He separated himself from these two bodies; he was abandoned by them.

[147] "Then the bishops and clerics began to stop wearing their belts and the golden cross-belts, on which were hung knives set with precious stones, their clothing of exquisite taste, and those spurs whose ornaments weighed down their heels. But the Enemy of human kind would not suffer such devotion, and made the ecclesiastics of all orders rise up and bring on war." Anonymous ["Astronomous"], *Vita Hludowici Imperatoris* [chaps. 28–29, *anno* 817]; in the Duchesne collection, vol. 2, p. 298.

[148] Thegan [*Vita Hludowici Imperatoris*, chap. 50, anno 834] says that what was done rarely under Charlemagne was commonly done under Louis.

[149] Intending to contain the nobility, he took as his chamberlain a certain Bernard, who brought them to despair. [On Bernard, see Nithard, *Historiarum* 1. 3.]

CHAPTER 22

Continuation of the same subject

But what weakened the monarchy above all was that this prince dissipated its domains.[150] It is at this point that one should listen to Nithard, one of our most judicious historians, grandson of Charlemagne, who was attached to the party of Louis the Pious and who wrote his history on orders from Charles the Bald.

He says that "a certain Adalhard had had for some time such an empire over the emperor's spirit that this prince followed his will in all things, that at the instigation of this favorite he had given the goods of the fisc to all who had wanted them,[151] and in that way he had reduced the republic to nothing."[152] Thus, he did throughout the empire what I have noted that he did in Aquitaine;[153] something Charlemagne redressed and no one redressed again.

[150] Thegan, *Vita Hludowici Imperatoris* [chap. 19, a. 817]: "He handed over to his *fideles* as a perpetual possession the royal estates which had been his own, his grandfathers', and his most remote ancestors'; he did this for a long time" [L.].

[151] Nithard [*Historiarum*], bk. 4, at the end [4.6]: "He persuaded him to distribute liberties here, public revenues there, among his own [Adalhard's] followers" [L.].

[152] Ibid. [Nithard, *Historiarum* 4.6]: "he all but destroyed the state" [L.].

[153] See bk. 30, chap. 13.

The state had been drained when Charles Martel came to be mayor, and one was in such circumstances that it was no longer a question of an act of authority to reestablish the state.

The fisc was so poor that under Charles the Bald honors were maintained for no one,[h] and no one was accorded security except for silver;[154] the Normans were permitted to escape for silver when they could have been destroyed,[155] and Hincmar's first counsel to Louis the Stammerer was to ask in an assembly for the wherewithal to support the expenses of his household.

[154] Hincmarus of Reims [*Opera, Opuscula et epistolae*], First letter to Louis the Stammerer [10.8].

[155] See the fragment of the *Chronicon S. Sergii Andegavensis*, in Duchesne, vol. 2, p. 401 [*Acta sanctorum*, Junii, tome 6, "Appendix ad diem XXV Junii"; tome 6, 246; 1715 edn; 7, 682–684; 1867 edn].

[h] That is, no one was paid from the public treasury. See 31.1.

CHAPTER 23

Continuation of the same subject

The clergy had cause to repent of the protection they had granted the children of Louis the Pious. This prince, as I have said, had never given the goods of the Church by precept to the laity,[156] but soon Lothair in Italy and Pepin in Aquitaine abandoned the plan of Charlemagne and went back to that of Charles Martel. The ecclesiastics had recourse to the emperor against his children, but they themselves had weakened the authority they appealed to. In Aquitaine, there was some compliance; in Italy, there was no obedience.

The civil wars that had disturbed the life of Louis the Pious were the seeds of those that followed his death. The three brothers, Lothair, Louis, and Charles, each sought to attract the important men to his party and to make of them his creatures. They gave to those who wanted to follow them precepts for the goods of the church, and in order to win over the nobility they delivered the clergy to them.

One sees in the capitularies that these princes were obliged to cede to importunate demands and that what they did not want to give was

[156] See what the bishops say in *Synodus ad Teudonis villam 845*, art. 4 [*Capitularia regum Francorum* 227.4].

often taken from them;[157] one sees in them that the clergy believed itself more oppressed by the nobility than by the kings. It also appears that Charles the Bald attacked the patrimony of the clergy the most,[158] either because he was the most provoked by them because they had degraded his father on his account, or because he was the most timid. Be that as it may, one sees in the capitularies the continual quarrels between the clergy who demanded their goods and the nobility who refused, avoided, or deferred returning them, with the kings between the two of them.[159]

The state of things in those times is a spectacle worthy of pity. Whereas Louis the Pious had made immense gifts to the churches from his domains, his children distributed the goods of the clergy to the laity. Often the same hand that founded new abbeys despoiled the old ones. The clergy did not have a fixed estate. Its goods were taken away from it; it regained them; but the crown always lost.

Toward the end of the reign of Charles the Bald and after this reign, it was scarcely any longer a question of quarrels between clergy and laity over the restitution of the goods of the church. The bishops were indeed still grumbling when they wrote their remonstrances to Charles

[157] See *Synodus ad teudonis villam 845*, arts. 3, 4 [*Capitularia regum Francorum* 227.3, 4] which very well describes the state of things, as well as the one of the same year, *Concilium in verno palatio 845*, art. 12 [*Capitularia regum Francorum* 291.12]; and *Synodis Belvacensis 845*, arts. 3, 4, 6 [*Capitularia regum Francorum* 292.3, 4, 6]; and the capitulary *in villa Sparnaco, 846*, art. 20 [*CRF* 293.20]; and the letter to Louis the German from the bishops assembled at Rheims, *Epistola episcoporum ad Ludowicum regem 858*, art. 8 [*Capitularia regum Francorum* 297.8].

[158] See the capitulary *in villa Sparnaco, 846*, arts. 20, 21, 22 [*Capitularia regum Francorum* 293.20, 21, 22]. The nobility had caused the king to be irritated with the bishops, so he drove them from the assembly: a few canons chosen from the synods were declared to be the only ones that would be observed; they were granted only what it was impossible to refuse them. See also the letter written by the assembled bishops to Louis the German in 858, *Epistola episcoporum ad Ludowicum regem 858*, art. 8 [*Capitularia regum Francorum* 297.8]; and the *Edictum Pistense 864*, art. 5 [*Capitularia regum Francorum* 273.5].

[159] See the same capitulary *in villa Sparnaco* 846 [*Capitularia regum Francorum* 293.20, 21, 22]. See also the capitulary of the assembly *Conventus apud Marsnam I. 847*, art. 4 [*Capitularia regum Francorum* 204.4], in which the clergy fell back to demanding that possession should be returned to them of all they had enjoyed in the reign of Louis the Pious. See also the capitulary of 851 *Conventus apud Marsnam II. 851*, art. 6, 7 [*Capitularia regum Francorum* 205, 6, 7], which maintains the nobility and the clergy in their possessions; and *Apud Bonolium 856* [*Capitularia regum Francorum* 295], which is a remonstrance of the bishops to the king concerning the fact that after so many laws had been made, the evils had not been repaired; and finally, the letter written by the bishops assembled at Rheims to Louis the German [*Epistola episcoporum ad Ludowicum regem 858*], art. 8 [*Capitularia regum Francorum* 297.8].

the Bald, which are found in the capitulary of 856 and in the letter they wrote to Louis the German in 858,[160] but they proposed things and they claimed promises that had been evaded so many times that one sees they had no expectation of obtaining them.

The only question that remained was to redress in general the wrongs done in the church and in the state.[161] The kings promised not to take away from the leudes their freemen, and no longer to give ecclesiastical goods by precept,[162] so that the interests of the clergy and of the nobility appeared to unite them.

The foreign ravages by the Normans, as I have said, contributed much to bringing these quarrels to an end.

The kings, daily more discredited, both for the causes I have given and for those I shall give, believed they had no choice but to put themselves in the hands of the ecclesiastics. But the clergy had weakened the kings, and the kings had weakened the clergy.

In vain did Charles the Bald and his successors appeal to the clergy to sustain the state and prevent its fall,[163] in vain did they use the respect the peoples had for this body to maintain the respect the people should have had for them;[164] in vain did they seek to give authority to their laws by the authority of the canons,[165] in vain did they join ecclesiastical penalties to civil penalties;[166] in vain, to counter-balance the authority

[160] [*Epistola episcoporum ad Ludowicum regem 858*], art. 8 [*Capitularia regum Francorum* 297.8].

[161] See *Conventus apud Marsnam II. 851*, arts. 6, 7 [*Capitularia regem Francorum* 205.6, 7].

[162] Charles the Bald, in the synod of Soissons, says that "he had promised the bishops that he would no longer give *precepts* for the goods of the Church." *Capitularia* of 853, art. 11 [*Capitularia regem Francorum* 259.11], Baluze edn, vol. 2, p. 56.

[163] See in Nithard [*Historiarum*], bk. 4 [4.3], how, after the flight of Lothair, the kings Louis and Charles consulted the bishops to learn if they could reclaim and divide the abandoned kingdom. Indeed, as the bishops formed among themselves a more unified body than the leudes, it suited these princes to assure their rights by a resolution of the bishops, which could engage all the other lords to follow them.

[164] See the capitulary of Charles the Bald *apud Saponarias, 859* [*Libellus proclamationes adversus Wenilonem*], art. 3 [*Capitularia regum Francorum* 300.3]: "Venilon, whom I had made Archbishop of Sens, crowned me; and I ought not to have been dismissed from the kingdom by anyone and certainly not without a hearing and audience from the bishops by whose ministry I was consecrated king. For they are called the thrones of God in which God sits, and His justice is discerned through them; I was and at present am prepared to submit to their paternal corrections and judicial castigations." [L.].

[165] See the capitulary of Charles the Bald *Synodus Carisiaca 857*, arts. 1–4, 7, Baluze edn, vol. 2, p. 88 [*Capitularia regum Francorum* 266.1–4, 7].

[166] See the *Synodus Pistensis 862*, art. 4 [*Capitularia regum Francorum* 272.4]; and the capitulary of Carloman and of Louis II, *Apud Vernis palatium 883*, arts. 4, 5 [*Capitularia regum Francorum* 287.4.5].

of the count, did they give each bishop the rank of deputy to the provinces:[167] it was impossible for the clergy to redress the evil they had done, and that strange misfortune of which I shall soon speak made for the fall of the crown.

[167] Capitulary *Synodus Pontigonensis 876*, under Charles the Bald, art. 12, Baluze edn [*Capitularia regum Francorum* 221.12].

CHAPTER 24

That freemen became qualified to possess fiefs

I have said that freemen went to war under their count, and that vassals went under their lord. This made the orders of the state balance each other, and though the leudes had vassals under them, they could be restrained by the count, who was at the head of all the freemen in the monarchy.

At first,[168] these freemen could not petition for a fief, but subsequently they could, and I find that this change occurred between the reign of Guntram and that of Charlemagne. I prove it by the comparison one can make of the treaty of Andelot[169] agreed to by Guntram, Childebert, and the Queen Brunhilda with the division made by Charlemagne for his children, and a similar division made by Louis the Pious.[170] These three acts contain very similar provisions in regard to vassals, and, as the same points were regulated in very nearly the same circumstances, the spirit and the letter of the three treaties are nearly the same in this regard.

But in what concerns freemen there is a major difference. The treaty of Andelot does not say that they could petition for a fief; whereas, one finds in the divisions of Charlemagne and of Louis clauses expressly made so that they could petition: this shows that after the treaty of Andelot a new usage was introduced by which freemen became qualified for this great prerogative.

This must have happened when Charles Martel distributed the

[168] See what I have said above, bk. 30, last chapter, toward the end.
[169] Of 587, in Gregory of Tours [*Historia ecclesiastica Francorum*], bk. 9 [9.20].
[170] See the following chapter, in which I speak at greater length of these divisions, and the notes in which they are cited.

goods of the church to his soldiers, partly in fief and partly as allod, bringing about a kind of revolution in the feudal laws. It is likely that nobles who already had fiefs found it more advantageous to receive the new gifts as allods, and that the freemen were only too happy to receive them as fiefs.

CHAPTER 25

THE PRINCIPAL CAUSE FOR THE WEAKENING OF THE CAROLINGIANS. *The change in the freeholds*

Charlemagne, in the division of which I have spoken in the preceding chapter,[171] ruled that after his death the men of each king would receive benefices in the kingdom of their king, but not in the kingdom of another king;[172] whereas one would preserve one's allods in any kingdom whatever. But he adds that any freeman could, after the death of his lord, commend himself[i] for a fief in the three kingdoms to whomever he wanted just like one who had never had a lord.[173] One finds the same provisions in the division made by Louis the Pious to his children in 817.[174]

But although freemen petitioned for a fief, the soldiery of the count was not weakened by it; a freeman still had to contribute for his allod and get people ready to do the service belonging to the fief in the ratio of one man for four manors, or else he got a man ready to serve the fief for

[171] Of 806, between Charles, Pepin, and Louis. It is reported by [Melchior] Goldast [*Constitutiones imperiales*, 1, 145; 1974 edn; *Capitulare primum anni 806 divisio*; *Capitularia regum Francorum* 45] and by Baluze, vol. 1, p. 439.

[172] Art. 9, p. 443. Which is in conformity with the treaty of Andelot, in Gregory of Tours [*Historia ecclesiastica Francorum*], bk. 9 [9.20].

[173] Art. 10. And this is not mentioned in the treaty of Andelot. [Gregory of Tours, *Historia ecclesiastica Francorum* 9.20.]

[174] In Baluze, vol. 1, p. 174 [574] [*Charta divisionis imperii 817*, art. 9, *Capitularia regum Francorum*, 136.9]: "A freeman who does not have a lord may commend himself to any of these three brothers whom he might wish" [L.]. See also the division made by the same emperor, in 837, art. 6, Baluze edn, p. 686 [*Capitularia regum Francorum* 194.6].

[i] *se recommander* means "to put oneself under the protection of," or, as we still say, "to commend oneself to the Lord."

him; and as some abuses were introduced thereby, they were corrected, as appears in the constitutions of Charlemagne[175] and in that of Pepin, King of Italy,[176] which explain each other.

What the historians have said, that the battle of Fontenay caused the ruin of the monarchy, is quite true, but let me be permitted to look briefly at the lamentable consequences of this day.

Sometime after this battle, the three brothers, Lothair, Louis, and Charles, made a treaty in which I find clauses that must have changed the whole of the French political state.[177]

In the proclamation[178] Charles made to the people about the part of this treaty which concerned them, he says that every freeman could choose the lord he wanted, whether the king or another lord.[179] Before this treaty, the freeman could petition for a fief, but his allod would always remain in the immediate power of the king, that is, under the jurisdiction of the count; and he depended on the lord to whom he had petitioned only by reason of the fief that he had obtained from him. After this treaty, every freeman could subject his allod to the king or to another lord, as he chose. It is not a question of those who petitioned for a fief but of those who changed their allod into a fief, and left, so to speak, the civil jurisdiction in order to enter the power of the king or of the lord they wanted to choose.

Thus, those who were formerly directly under the power of the king, insofar as they were freemen under the count, became imperceptibly vassals of one another, for each freeman could choose the lord he wanted, whether the king or another lord.

2. If a man changed a land he possessed in perpetuity into a fief, these new fiefs could no longer be for life. Thus, we see shortly thereafter a general law giving the fiefs to the children of the possessor;

[175] *Capitulare tertium anni 811*, arts. 7, 8, Baluze edn, vol. 1, p. 486 [*Capitularia regum Francorum* 73.7–9] and *Capitulare primum anni 812*, art. 1, ibid., p. 490 [*Capitularia regum Francorum* 50.1]: "That any freeman who has four *manses* of his own, or has them as a benefice from another, should prepare and go himself to the host, either with his lord, etc." [L.]. See also *Capitulare anni 807*, Baluze edn, vol. 1, p. 458 [*Capitularia regum Francorum* 48].

[176] Of 793, inserted in the *Leges Langobardum*, bk. 3, tit. 9, chap. 9[1] [Loth. 26].

[177] *Conventus apud Marsnam I. 847* [*CRF* 204], reported by Aubert le Mire [*Codex donationi piarum*; chap. 17; pp. 23–24; 1723 edn] and Baluze, vol. 2, p. 42.

[178] *Adnunciatio.*

[179] [*Conventus apud Marsnam I. 847*] *adnuntiatio Karoli*, art. 2 [*Capitularia regum Francorum* 204, III. 2]: "That any freeman in our kingdom may accept as his lord whomever he might wish, either ourselves, or one of our *fideles*" [L.].

this is from Charles the Bald, one of the three princes who had contracted to this.[180]

What I have said of the liberty of all men in the monarchy, after the treaty of the three brothers, to choose the lord they wanted from among the king and the other lords, is confirmed by acts passed after that time.

In Charlemagne's time, when a vassal had received a thing from a lord, even if it was worth only a sou, he could not leave him.[181] But under Charles the Bald vassals could follow their interests or their caprice with impunity, and this prince expresses himself so strongly on this point that he seems rather to invite them to enjoy this liberty than to restrict it.[182] In Charlemagne's time, benefices were personal rather than real; later they become real rather than personal.

[180] *Apud Carisiacum 877*, tit. 53 [52], arts. 9, 10 [*Capitularia regum Francorum* 281.9, 10; quotation is from 9]: "It is to be done in a similar way by our vassals" [L.]. This capitulary relates to another of the same year and place, *Apud Carisiacum 877*, art. 3 [*Capitularia regum Francorum* 282.3].

[181] Capitulary of Aix-La-Chapelle [*Capitulare secundum anni*] *813*, art. 16 [*Capitularia regum Francorum* 77.16]: "That no one ought to renounce his lord after he has accepted the value of one solidus from him" [L.]. And *Capitulare Pippini regis Italiae 783*, art. 5 [*Capitularia regum Francorum* 94.5].

[182] See *Ad Francos et Aquitanos missa de Carisiaco 856*, arts. 10, 13, Baluze edn, vol. 2, p. 83 [*Capitularia regum Francorum* 262.10, 13], in which the king and the ecclesiastical and lay lords agreed on this: "If there be some of you whose lord does not please you, and it appear that it would be better with another lord if you were permitted to beg this of him, you may come to him, and he may grant you a leave of absence with a tranquil and calm mind . . . and if God favor him, he may be able to beg this from the other lord and thus have peace" [L.].

CHAPTER 26
Change in fiefs

Fiefs underwent no less a change than did allods. One sees by the capitulary of Compiègne, made under King Pepin,[183] that those to whom the king gave a benefice themselves gave a part of this benefice to various vassals, but these parts were not distinct from the whole. The king took them back when he took the whole, and on the death of the leud the vassal also lost his under-fief; a new beneficiary came who in

[183] *Capitulare Compendiense 757*, art. 6, Baluze edn, p. 181 [*Capitularia regum Francorum* 15.9].

turn established new under-vassals. Thus, the under-fief was not at all a dependency of the fief; it was the person who was dependent. In this way, the under-vassal reverted to the king because he was not attached to the vassal forever, and the under-fief reverted likewise to the king because it was the fief itself and not a dependency of the fief.

Such was the under-vassalage when fiefs were revocable; such was it also when fiefs were for life. This changed when the fief passed to the heirs and the under-fiefs were passed in the same way. What the king had held without mediation was no longer held except by mediation, and royal power was, so to speak, pushed back a degree, sometimes two, and often more.

One sees in the books *On Fiefs*[184] that, although the vassals of the king could give land as a fief, that is, as an under-fief of the king, nevertheless these under-vassals or petty vavasors could not likewise give land as a fief, so that what they had given they could always take back. Besides, such a concession did not pass to the children as did fiefs, because it was supposedly not made according to the law of fiefs.

If one compares the state of the under-vassalage at the time when the two senators of Milan wrote these books, with its state at the time of King Pepin, one will find that these under-fiefs kept their primitive nature longer than the fiefs.[185]

But when these senators wrote, one had made such general exceptions to this rule as to reduce it almost to nothing. For if one who had received a fief from a petty vavasor had followed him to Rome on an expedition, one acquired all the rights of a vassal; in the same way, if one had given silver to the petty vavasor in order to obtain the fief, the latter could not take it away from one, or keep one from handing it down to one's son until he had returned his silver to him.[186] Finally, this rule was no longer followed in the senate of Milan.[187]

[184] [Jacques Cujas, *De feudis*] bk. 1.1 [1.1].
[185] At least in Italy and Germany.
[186] [Jacques Cujas] *De feudis*, bk. 1, chap. 1 [1.1].
[187] Ibid. [Jacques Cujas, *De feudis* 1.1.]

CHAPTER 27

Another change in the fiefs

In Charlemagne's time,[188] one was obliged under threat of great penalties to go to the convocation for any war whatever; excuses were not accepted, and the count who exempted someone would himself be punished. But the treaty of the three brothers[189] put a restriction that took the nobility out of the king's hand, so to speak;[190] one was no longer expected to follow the king to war, except when that war was defensive. One was free in other wars to follow one's lord or to look after one's business. This treaty is related to another made five years before between the two brothers Charles the Bald and Louis, King of Germany, by which these two brothers excused their vassals from following them to war in the case of some expedition against each other, a thing to which the two princes swore and to which they made both armies swear.[191]

The death of a hundred thousand Frenchmen at the battle of Fontenay made the remaining nobility think that they would finally be exterminated by the quarrels of these kings over their shares and that the ambition and jealousy of these kings would spill all the blood left to be spilled.[192] A law was made providing that the nobility would not be constrained to follow the princes to war except when it was a question of defending the state against a foreign invasion. It was in use for many centuries.[193]

[188] *Capitulare primum anni 802*, art. 7, Baluze edn, p. 365 [*Capitularia regum Francorum* 33.7].

[189] *Conventus apud Marsnam I. 847*, Baluze edn, p. 42 [*Capitularia regum Francorum* 204].

[190] Ibid., art. 5, p. 44. [*Conventus apud Marsnam I. 847*, *Capitularia regum Francorum* 204. III. 5]: "We wish that each of our men, in whatever kingdom he might be, may go with his lord to the Host, or go about his own business, unless there be that kind of invasion of a kingdom which is called *lantweri* [the time when one must defend the homeland]; he will then be needed, and all people must repel it together" [L.].

[191] *Conventus apud Argentoratum 842*, Baluze edn, vol. 2, p. 39 [*Capitularia regum Francorum* 247].

[192] Indeed it was the nobility who made this treaty. See Nithard [*Historiarum*], bk. 4. [On the slaughter at Fontenay see 3.1; also 4.7.]

[193] See the law of Guido, king of the Romans, among those that were added to the Salic Law and to the *Leges Langobardorum*, tit. 6, para. 2 in Eckart [bk. 3.13.3 (Wid. 4 (pap.)) or *Capitularia regum Francorum* 224.4].

CHAPTER 28

Changes that occurred in the great offices and in the fiefs

It seemed that everything took on a particular vice and was corrupted at the same time. I have said that in the early times many fiefs were alienable in perpetuity; but these were particular cases, and fiefs in general still preserved their proper nature; and if the crown had lost fiefs, it substituted others for them. I have also said that the crown had never alienated the great offices in perpetuity.[194]

But Charles the Bald made a general regulation that affected the great offices and the fiefs equally; he established in his capitularies that the counties would be given to the children of the count, and he wanted this regulation to apply also to fiefs.[195]

It will soon be seen that this regulation was more broadly extended so that the great offices and the fiefs passed to more distant relatives. It followed that most of the lords who had formerly answered immediately to the crown answered to it only mediately. These counts who had formerly rendered justice in the king's audiences,[j] these counts who led freemen to war, stood between the king and his freemen, and power was pushed back yet another degree.

There is more: it seems, according to the capitularies, that the counts had had benefices attached to their county and vassals under them.[196] When the counties became hereditary, these vassals of the count were no longer immediate vassals of the king; the benefices attached to the counties were no longer the benefices of the king; the counts became more powerful because the vassals they already had put them in a position to procure others.

[194] Some authors have said that the county of Toulouse was given by Charles Martel, and passed from heir to heir to the last Raymond; but if this is so, it was the result of some circumstances that had required choosing the counts of Toulouse from among the children of the last possessor.

[195] See *Apud Carisiacum 877*, tit. 53 [52], arts. 9, 10 [*Capitularia regum Francorum* 281.9–10]. This capitulary relates to another of the same year and place [*Apud Carisiacum 877*], art. 3 [*Capitularia regum Francorum* 282.3].

[196] *Capitulare tertium anni 812*, art. 7 [*Capitularia regum Francorum* 80.7]; and *Praeceptem primum pro Hispanis 815*, art. 6 [*Capitularia regum Francorum* 132.6]; *Capitularies* 5.228 [*Capitularia spuria. Benedictae levitae* 1.228]; and *Apud Pistas 869*, art. 2 [*Capitularia regum Francorum* 275.2]; and *Apud Carisiacum 877* [*Capitularia regum Francorum* 281.13], art. 13 Baluze edn.

---

[j] See note [dd], bk. 30.

In order to get a good sense of the weakness that resulted at the end of the reign of the Carolingians, one has only to see what happened at the beginning of the reign of the Capetians when the multiplication of under-fiefs was the despair of the great vassals.

It was a custom of the kingdom that, when the elder sons had given shares to the younger ones, the latter paid homage for them to the former,[197] so that the dominant lord no longer held them except as under-fiefs. Philip Augustus, the Duke of Burgundy, the counts of Nevers, of Boulogne, of Saint-Paul, of Dampierre, and the other lords declared that from then on, whether the fief was divided by inheritance or otherwise, the whole would always be the dependency of the same lord, without any lord in between.[198] This ordinance was not generally followed, for as I have said elsewhere, it was impossible to make general ordinances in those times, but many of our customs were set by it.

[197] As appears in Otto of Freising, *Gesta Friderici I Imperatoris*, bk. 2, chap. 29 [2.48].
[198] See the ordinance of Philippe Augustus of 1209, in the new collection [*Recueil général des anciennes lois françaises*, *Capétians*, #108, 1; 203–204; Laurière, 1, 29–30].

CHAPTER 29

On the nature of fiefs after the reign of Charles the Bald

I have said that Charles the Bald wanted an office or fief to pass from the man who had held it to his surviving son. It would be difficult to follow the progress of the abuses resulting from this and from the extension given to this law in each country. I find in the books *On Fiefs*[199] that in the beginning of the reign of Emperor Conrad II, the fiefs in the countries he dominated did not pass to the grandsons; they passed only to that child of the last possessor the lord had chosen:[200] thus, the fiefs were given by a kind of election that the lord made among his children.

I have explained in Chapter 17 of this book how, under the Carolingians, the crown was in certain respects hereditary. It was hereditary because kings were always taken from this family;[k] it was

[199] [Jacques Cujas, *De feudis*] bk. 1, tit. 1 [1.1].
[200] Ibid. [Jacques Cujas, *De feudis*, 1.1; 8, 596; 1868 edn]: "So it came about that it devolved to the son whom the lord wished to confirm in the benefice" [L.].

[k] *race.*, See note [d], bk. 18.

hereditary also because the children inherited; it was elective because the people chose among the children. As things follow one another and as one political law is always related to another political law, the same spirit was followed in the inheritance of fiefs that had been followed in the succession to the crown.[201] Thus, the fiefs passed to the children, both by the right of inheritance and by the right of election, and each fief was, like the crown, elective and hereditary.

This right of election held by the person of the lord did not exist[202] at the time of the authors of the books *On Fiefs*,[203] that is, during the reign of the emperor Frederic I.

[201] At least in Italy and Germany.
[202] [Jacques Cujas] *De feudis*, bk. 1, tit. 1 [8, 596, 1868 edn]: "Thus nowadays that it comes to all equally" [L.].
[203] Gerardus Niger and Aubertus de Orto.

CHAPTER 30
Continuation of the same subject

It is said in the books *On Fiefs*[204] that, when Emperor Conrad left for Rome, the faithful who were in his service asked him to make a law so that the fiefs that passed to the childen would also pass to the grandchildren and that one whose brother had died without legitimate heirs could inherit the fief that had belonged to their common father; this was granted.

It goes on to say, and it must be remembered that those who speak lived in the time of Emperor Frederic I,[205] that "the old jurists had always held that the inheritance of fiefs in a collateral line did not pass beyond full brothers; although in modern times one would have carried it as far as the seventh degree, for by the new right, one had carried it in direct line to infinity."[206] It is thus that the law of Conrad was gradually extended.

When all these things are assumed, a simple reading of the history of France will show that the perpetuity of fiefs was established earlier in France than in Germany. When Emperor Conrad II began his reign in

[204] [Jacques Cujas] *De feudis*, bk. 1, tit. 1 [1.1].
[205] [Jacques] Cujas has indeed proven it.
[206] [Jacques Cujas], *De feudis*, bk. 1, tit. 1 [1.1].

1024, things were still in Germany as they had been in France in the reign of Charles the Bald, who died in 877. But in France after the reign of Charles the Bald so many changes were made that Charles the Simple was not in a position to dispute with a foreign house his incontestable rights to empire and, finally, in the time of Hugh Capet, the reigning house, stripped of all its domains, could not even support the crown.

In France the weak spirit of Charles the Bald put an equal weakness in the state. But as his brother, Louis the German, and some of those who succeeded him, had greater qualities, their state sustained its strength for a longer time.

What am I saying? Perhaps the phlegmatic humor, and, if I dare say it, the immutability of the spirit of the German nation resisted longer than the French nation this arrangement in which fiefs, as if by a natural tendency, were perpetuated in families.

I add that the kingdom of Germany was not devastated, and, so to speak, wiped out, as was that of France by the particular kind of war that the Normans and Saracens waged over it. There was less wealth in Germany, there were fewer towns to sack, fewer coasts to travel along, more marshes to cross, more forests to penetrate. The princes who did not see the state ready to fall at every instant had less need of their vassals, that is, they depended less on them. And it is likely that if the emperors of Germany had not been obliged to go to Rome to be crowned and make continual expeditions in Italy, their fiefs would have preserved their primitive nature even longer.

CHAPTER 31

How the empire left the house of Charlemagne

The empire which, to the prejudice of the branch of Charles the Bald, had already given to the bastards of the branch of Louis the German,[207] passed again into a foreign house, with the election of Conrad, duke of Franconia, in 912. The branch that reigned in France and that could scarcely dispute over villages was still less in a position to dispute over the empire. We have an agreement passed between Charles the Simple

[207] Arnoul, and his son Louis IV.

and Emperor Henry I, who succeeded Conrad. It is called the pact of Bonn.[208] The two princes met on a ship in the middle of the Rhine and swore eternal friendship. A very good *mezzo termine* was used. Charles took the title of King of Western France, and Henry that of King of Eastern France. Charles made the contract with the King of Germany and not with the emperor.

[208] Of 926, reported by Aubert Le Mire, *Codex Donationum Piarum*, chap. 27 [chap. 29; pp. 37–38; 1723 edn] [*MGH*, LL. 2. Constitutiones].

CHAPTER 32

How the crown of France passed to the house of Hugh Capet

The inheritance of fiefs and the general establishment of under-fiefs extinguished political government and formed feudal government. Instead of that innumerable multitude of vassals kings had had, they now had only a few on whom the others depended. Kings had almost no more direct authority: a power that had to pass through so many other powers and through such great powers was checked or lost before reaching its goal. Such great vassals no longer obeyed, and they even used their under-vassals in order not to obey any longer. The kings, deprived of their domains and reduced to the towns of Rheims and Laon, were at their mercy. The tree spread its branches too far, and the top dried out. The kingdom was without a domain, as the empire is today. One gave the crown to one of the most powerful vassals.

The Normans ravaged the kingdom; they came on a kind of raft and in small craft, entered the mouths of the rivers, went upstream, and devastated the country along the banks. The towns of Orleans and Paris checked these bandits,[209] and they could advance neither on the Seine nor on the Loire. Hugh Capet, who possessed these two towns, held in his hands the two keys to the unhappy vestiges of the kingdom; a crown was conferred upon him that he alone was in a position to defend. In the same way later, the empire was given to the house that held the boundaries firm against the Turks.

The empire had left the house of Charlemagne at the time when it

[209] See the capitulary of Charles the Bald, *Apud Carisiacum 877* [*Capitularis regum Francorum*, 281.27], on the importance of Paris, Saint Denis, and the châteaux on the Loire at that time.

was established that the inheritance of fiefs was the result of an act of condescension.[l] This was a usage lasting even longer among the Germans than among the French;[210] it made the Empire, considered as a fief, elective. Whereas, when the French crown left the house of Charlemagne, fiefs were really hereditary in this kingdom; the crown, like a great fief, was also.

Moreover, it has been a mistake to ascribe to the exact moment of this revolution all the changes that had happened, or which happened later. Everything was reduced to two events: the reigning family changed, and the crown was united with a great fief.

[210] See above, ch. 30.

[l] That is, inheritance of fiefs was the result of an act of subordination, of commending oneself to the king and of the king's condescension. See note [i] above.

CHAPTER 33
Some consequences of the perpetuity of fiefs

It followed from the perpetuity of fiefs that the right of the eldest, or of primogeniture, was established among the French. It was not known among the Merovingians:[211] the crown was divided between these brothers, and allods were similarly divided; but fiefs, revocable or for life, not being an object of inheritance, could not be an object of division.

Under the Carolingians, the title of emperor held by Louis the Pious, with which he honored his eldest son Lothair, made him devise for this prince a kind of precedence over his younger brothers. The two kings were to go to the emperor each year, carry presents to him, and receive larger ones from him; they were to confer with him on common business.[212] This is what gave Lothair those ambitions that brought him so little success. When Agobard wrote for this prince,[213] he cited the provision of the emperor himself, who had associated Lothair with

[211] See *Lex Salica* [D93; S34] and *Lex Ribuaria* [57] under the title on allods.

[212] See the capitulary *Charta divisionis imperii. 817* [*Capitularia regum Francorum* 136], which contains the first division made by Louis the Pious among his children.

[213] See his two letters on this subject, of which one is titled *De divisione imperii* [Agobard, *Opera*, *Flebilis epistola*, *De divisione imperii*, *De comparatione utriusque regiminis*, PL 104, 287–298, *MGH Epp* 5].

the empire after god had been consulted by three days of fasting and with the celebration of masses, by prayers and alms, after the nation had given him its oath which it could not violate, and after he had sent Lothair to Rome to be confirmed by the pope. He gives weight to all this, and not to the right of the eldest. He says, indeed, that the emperor had designated a division to the younger children and that he had preferred the eldest, but to say that he had preferred the eldest is to say at the same time that he could have preferred the younger ones.

But when fiefs became hereditary, the right of the eldest was established in the inheritance of fiefs, and for the same reason in that of the crown, the great fief. The old law that formed divisions no longer existed; as the fiefs were burdened with a service, the possessor had to be in a position to perform it. A right of primogeniture was established; and the reasoning of the feudal law forced that of the political or civil law.

As fiefs passed to the possessor's children, the lords lost the liberty to dispose of them, and in order to be compensated for them, they established a right that was called the right of redemption,[m] of which our customs speak, which was paid first in the direct line and which through usage came to be paid only in the collateral line.

Soon fiefs could be transferred to outsiders as a patrimonial good. That gave rise to the right of permissions and sales,[n] established in almost the whole kingdom. These rights were arbitrary at first, but when the practice of granting these permissions became general, they were fixed in each region.

The right of redemption had to be paid with each change of heir and was at first even paid in the direct line.[214] The most general custom had fixed it at a year's revenue. That was onerous and inconvenient for the vassal, and the fief became, so to speak, in debt. It often happened in the act of homage that the lord would demand for the redemption only a certain sum of silver,[215] which, by the changes which occurred in monies, became of no importance; thus the right of redemption is today

[214] See the ordinance of Philip Augustus of 1209, on fiefs [*Recueil général des anciennes lois françaises, Capetiens,* [illegible]108, 1: 203–204; Laurière, 1, 29–30].

[215] One finds in the charters a number of these conventions, as in the capitulary of Vendome, and that of the abbey of St. Cyprian in Poitou, from which [Auguste] Galland has given us some extracts [*Du Franc-aleu et origine des droits seigneuriaux, avec les lois données au pays d'Albigeois*], p. 55 [chap. 6; pp. 70–71; 1637 edn].

[m] *droit de rachat.* [n] *droit de lods et vents.*

reduced almost to nothing, whereas that of permissions and sales has continued to exist to its full extent. As the latter right concerns neither the vassal nor his heirs but is a fortuitous case which could have been neither foreseen nor expected, one did not make these sorts of stipulations, and one continued to pay a certain portion of the price.

When fiefs were for life, one could not give a part of one's fief so as to have it always as an under-fief; it would have been absurd for the simple holder of a usufruct to have disposed of the ownership of the thing. But, when fiefs became perpetual, this was permitted,[216] with certain restrictions set by customs,[217] and was called parting one's fief.[o]

Once the perpetuity of fiefs caused the right of redemption to be established daughters could inherit a fief in the absence of males. For when the lord gave the fief to the daughter, he multiplied the instances of his right of redemption because the husband had to pay it as well as the wife.[218] This arrangement could not apply to the crown, for as it was not answerable to anyone, there could be no right of redemption for it.

The daughter of William V, Count of Toulouse, did not inherit the county. Later, Eleanor inherited Aquitaine, and Mathilda, Normandy, and the right of inheritance of daughters in those times seemed so well established that Louis the Young, after the dissolution of his marriage with Eleanor, made no difficulty about returning Guienne to her. As these two examples came very soon after the first, the general law which called women to inherit fiefs must have been introduced later in the county of Toulouse than in the other provinces of the kingdom.[219]

The constitutions of the various kingdoms of Europe followed the actual state of these fiefs when these kingdoms were founded. Women inherited neither the crown of France nor the Empire because, when the two monarchies were established, women could not inherit fiefs, but women inherited in kingdoms whose establishment was later than that of the perpetuity of fiefs, such as those founded by the Norman conquests, those that were founded by the conquests made against the Moors, and still others, beyond the boundaries of Germany and in

[216] But the fief cannot be abridged, that is, have a portion of it abolished.
[217] They specified the portion that one could make use of.
[218] This is why the lord constrained a widow to remarry.
[219] The majority of the great Houses had their particular laws of succession. See what Mr. Thaumassière tells us about the Houses of Berry.

[o] *jouer de son fief.*

quite modern times, which were in some fashion reborn with the establishment of Christianity.

When fiefs were revocable, they were given to people who were in a position to give service for them, and there was no question about minors; but, when they were perpetual, lords took the fief until the one who was to hold the fief came of age, either to increase their profits or to have the ward raised in the exercise of arms.[220] This is what our customs call the *garde-noble*,[p] which is founded on other principles than those of guardianship and is entirely distinct from it.

When fiefs were for life, one petitioned for a fief, and real transmission,[q] which was done by scepter, confirmed the fief as homage does today. We do not see that the counts, or even the deputies of the king, received homages in the provinces, and this function is not found in the commissions of these officers, which have been preserved for us in the capitularies. Indeed they sometimes made all the subjects swear the oath of fealty,[221] but this oath was scarcely an homage of the same nature as those that were subsequently established; in these, the oath of fealty was an action joined to the homage, sometimes following and sometimes preceding it, and did not apply in all the homages; it was less solemn than the homage and was entirely distinct from it.[222]

The counts and the deputies of the king still, on occasion, made the vassals whose fealty was suspect give an assurance that was called

[220] One can see in the capitulary *Apud Carisiacum 877*, art. 3 [*Capitularia regum Francorum* 282.3], Baluze edn, vol. 2, p. 269, the moment when the kings had their fiefs administered in order to protect them for the minors; an example that was followed by the lords and originated what we call the garde-noble.

[221] The formula is found in *Capitulare secundum anni 802*, art. 11 [*Capitularia regum Francorum* 34; 1, 101–102]. See also *Apud Attinacum 854*, art. 13 [*Capitularia regum Francorum* 261.13 at the end, 2, 278] and others.

[222] [Charles] Du Cange [*Glossarium mediae et infimae latinitatis*], at "hominum," p. 1163 [4, 216–220; 1954 edn] and "fidelitas," p. 474 [3, 487–489, esp. 488; 1954 edn], cites the charters of old homages in which these differences are to be found, and a great number of authorities that can be consulted. In the homage, the vassal put his hand in the lord's and took an oath: the oath of fidelity was made by swearing on the Gospels. The homage was made on one's knees; the oath of fealty was taken while standing. Only the lord could receive the homage; but his officers could take the oath of fealty. See [Sir Thomas] Littleton [*Anciennes loix des Français conservées dans les coûtumes angloises*] [bk. 2, "De féauté," #91–92]; 1, 123–126; 1779 edn]. *Foi et hommage* means "fealty and homage."

[p] This is the guardianship of the nobleman's children.
[q] *tradition.*

firmitas,[223] but this assurance could not have been an homage because kings gave it to each other.[224]

Even if the Abbé Suger speaks of a throne of Dagobert, where, according to the report of antiquity, the kings of France were accustomed to receive homages from the lords,[225] it is clear that he is using here the ideas and the language of his time.

When fiefs passed to heirs, the acknowledgment[r] of the vassal, which in early times was only an occasional thing, became a regular act: it was made in a more striking way; it was filled with more formalities because it was to carry the remembrance of the reciprocal duties of the lord and the vassal down through the ages.

I could believe that homages began to be established in the time of King Pepin, which is when I have said many benefices were given in perpetuity; but I would believe it with reservation and only on the assumption that the authors of the old annals of the Franks were not ignorant men, who, when describing the ceremonies for the act of fealty that Tassilon, Duke of Bavaria, made to Pepin,[226] spoke according to the usages that they saw practiced in their own time.[227]

[223] Capitulary of Charles the Bald, *Post reditum a Confluentibus 860*, art. 3, Baluze edn, p. 145 [*Capitularia regum Francorum* 270.A3].

[224] Ibid. [*Post reditum a confluentibus 860*], art. 1 [*Capitularia regum Francorum* 270.A1].

[225] [Suger, Abbot of St. Denis] *De rebus in administratione sua gestis* [chap. 34, p. 204, Paris, 1867 edn].

[226] [*Annales rerum Francicarum quae a Pippino et Carlo Magno*] *anno* 757, chap. 17 [in *Recueil des historiens des Gaules et de la France* 5, 34].

[227] [*Annales rerum Francicarum quae a Pippino et Carlo Magno, anno* 757, in *Recueil des historiens des Gaules et de la France* 5, 34]: "Tassilio came seeking to commend himself into vassalage by his own hand; he swore many and countless oaths, placing his hand on the relics of the saints, and he promised fealty to Pepin" [L.]. It would seem that there were both a homage and an oath of fealty. See [above] note 222.

[r] *la reconnaissance.* See 1.1 (note [g], bk. 1).

CHAPTER 34
Continuation of the same subject

When fiefs were revocable or for life, they scarcely belonged to any but the political laws; this is why in the civil laws of those times so little mention is made of the laws of fiefs. But, when they became hereditary, they could be given, sold, or given as legacies, and they belonged to both the political and civil laws. The fief, considered as an obligation to military service, was a concern of political right; considered as a kind of good in commerce, it was a concern of civil right. This gave rise to the civil laws on fiefs.

As fiefs had become hereditary, laws concerning the order of inheritance had to be relative to the perpetuity of fiefs. Thus was established, in spite of the provision of Roman right and the Salic law,[228] this rule of French right, *propres ne remontent point.*[229s] The fief had to be served, but a grandfather or a great-uncle would have been a bad vassal to give to the lord; thus from the first this regulation applied only to fiefs, as we learn from Boutillier.[230]

As fiefs had become hereditary, the lords, who were to see that service was done for the fief, required that daughters who were to inherit the fief,[231] and I believe, sometimes, males, could not marry without their consent, so that marriage contracts became for the nobles a feudal provision and a civil provision. In such an act, made under the eyes of the lord, provisions were made for the future inheritance with a view to the heirs' being able to serve the fiefs; thus, only nobles were at first at liberty to provide for future inheritances by marriage contract, as Bohier[232] and Aufrerius[233] have remarked.

It goes without saying that redemption by one of the lineage, founded on the old right of relatives, which is a mystery of our old French jurisprudence that I do not have time to develop, could not be applied to fiefs before they became perpetual.

Italiam, Italiam, . . .[234] I close the treatise on fiefs where most authors have begun it.

[228] Under the title "Allods" [*Lex Salica* (D93; S34)].

[229] [Jacques Cujas] *De feudis*, bk. 4, tit. 59 [4.59].

[230] [Jean Boutillier] *Somme rural*, bk. 1, tit. 76, p. 447 ["Des héritages eschéans à plusieurs enfans," p. 447, 1621 edn].

[231] According to an ordinance of St. Louis of 1246, made to state the customs of Anjou and Maine, those who lease from a daughter who stands to inherit the fief will give assurance to the lord that she will marry only with the lord's consent [*Recueil général des anciennes lois françaises*, #161, 1; 249–251; Laurière, 1. 58–60].

[232] [France. Parlement (Bordeaux)], *Decisiones Burdegalensis* [Nicolas de Bohier], 155. 8 [155.8]; and 204. 38 [204.38] [1620 edn].

[233] [Toulouse (Archbishopric)], *De cii Capelle Tholose* [Stephanus Aufrerius], Ques. #453 [1.171r–173g; 1531 edn].

[234] [Virgil] *Aeneid*, bk. 3, line 523 [3.523].

[s] Property cannot be passed back to persons of the preceding generation.

Bibliography

Acominatus, Nicetas, Choniates. *Historia*, Corpus fontium historiae Byzantinae, XI.1, Ser. Berolinensis, Berlin, De Gruyter, 1975

Acta sanctorum, Paris, 1863–

Acta sanctorum Ordinis S. Benedicti (Benedictines. Congregation de St. Maur)

Addison, Joseph, 1672–1719. *Remarks on Several Parts of Italy in the Years 1701, 1702, 1703*, vol. 2 of *The Miscellaneous Works of Joseph Addison*, ed. A. C. Guthkelch, London, Bell, 1914

Spectator

Aeschines, 389–314 B.C. *Oratio de falsa legatione* (*On the Embassy*)

Agathius, Scholasticus, d. 582. *Historiarum*

Agobard (Saint, Archbishop of Lyons), d. 840. *Opera*, Migne PL 104; *MGH*, Epp. 5, 150–239

Aimoinus, monk of Fleury, d. *ca.* 1010. *Historiae Francorum*, Migne PL 139

Amelot de la Houssaye, Abraham Nicolas, 1634–1706. *Histoire du gouvernement de Venise*, Lyons, J. Certe, 1740

Ammianus Marcellinus, 320–390. *Res gestae*

Andocides, 439–390 B.C. *Orationes*

Annales Fuldenses. *MGH*, SS. 1

Annales laurissenses minores. *MGH*, SS. 1

Annales Mettenses. *MGH*, SS. 1

Anson, George, Baron, 1697–1762 (compilation by Richard Walter, 1716–?1785). *A Voyage Round the World in the Years MDCCXL, I, II, III, IV*, London, Oxford University Press, 1974

Apollonius Rhodius. *Argonautica*

Appian, of Alexandria (Appianus). *Roman History* (*Historia Romana*). *The Civil Wars*, *The Wars with Mithridates*

Aristides, Aelius. *Orationes*

Aristotle (Aristoteles). *De mirabilibus auscultationibus*

Oeconomica

Politics (*Politica*)

Arrian (Arrianus, Flavius). *Anabasis*

Indica

Asconius Pedianus, Quintus. *Scholia Sangallensia Ciceronis*, in vol. 2 of *Ciceronis orationum scholiastae*

Assises du Royaume de Jérusalem (Jerusalem (Latin Kingdom, 1099–1244)). Ed. V. Foucher, Genève, Slatkine Reprints, 1973

Athenaeus Naucratia, *fl.* 3rd century, *Deipnosophistae*

Aubigné, Théodore Agrippa d', 1552–1630. *Histoire universale*, Genève, Droz, 1981–

Augustan History: *see* Julius Capitolinus and Flavius Vopiscus

Augustine (Augustinus, Aurelius, Saint, Bishop of Hippo, 354–430). *De civitate Dei*

Avienus, Rufus Festus. *Carmina*, bk. IV, *Orae maritimae*

Baluze, Etienne, 1630–1718. *Capitularia regum francorum*, Paris, Muguet, 1677. *See also Capitularia regum Francorum*

Barbeyrac, Jean, 1674–1744. *Histoire des anciens traitez. Supplément au Corps universel diplomatique du droit des gens*. Amsterdam, Janssons à Waesberge, 1739

Bartholin, Thomas, 1659–1690. *Antiquitatum Danicarum de causis contemptae a Danis adhuc gentilibus mortis*, Hafniae, J. P. Bockenhoffer, 1689

Bayle, Pierre, 1647–1706. *Nouvelles lettres de l'auteur de la Critique de l'histoire du Calvinisme*, vol. 2 of *Oeuvres diverses*, Hildesheim, Georg Olms, 1964. Reprint of 1727 edn.

Pensées diverses à l'occasion d'une comète, Continuation des Pensées diverses, vol. 3 of *Oeuvres diverses*. Reprint of 1727 edn.

Beaumanoir. *Coutumes de Beauvaisis*: *see* Philippe de Remi, Sire de Beaumanoir

Bernier, François, 1620–1688. *Travels in the Mogul Empire (A.D. 1656–1688)*, trans. Archibald Constable, London, Oxford University Press, 1916

Bible

Bibliothèque Angloise, ou Histoire littéraire de la Grande Bretagne. 15 vols., Amsterdam, La veuve de Paul Marret, 1717–1728

Bochart, Samuel, 1599–1667. *Geographia sacra seu Phaleg et Canaan*, Leyden, Boutesteyn, 1707

Bodin, Jean, 1530–1596. *The Six Bookes of a Commonweale*, ed. Kenneth D. McRae, Cambridge, Mass., Harvard University Press, 1962

Boulainvilliers, Henri, Comte de, 1658–1722. *Histoire de l'ancien gouvernement de la France*. 3 vols., La Haye, 1727.

La Vie de Mahomed, Amsterdam, P. Humbert, 1731

Boutillier, Jean. *La Grand Coustumier et practique du droict civil et canon observé en France* (*La Somme rural*), ed. L. Charondas le Caron, Paris, N. Buon, 1621

Brussel, Nicolas, d. 1750. *Nouvel examen de l'usage général des fiefs en France pendant le XI. le XII. le XIII. & le XIV. siècle*, 2 vols., Paris, C. Prud'homme, 1727

Budé, Guillaume, 1468–1540. *De asse et partibus eius*, in *Opera omnia*, vol. 2, Farnborough, Gregg, 1966; reprint of 1557 Basle edition

Burman, Pieter, 1668–1741. *Vectigalia populi romani*, Leyden, Conrad and George Wishoff, 1734

Burnet, Gilbert, Bishop of Salisbury, 1643–1715. *The History of the Reformation*

of the Church of England, Farnborough, Gregg, 1969; reprint of Oxford, Clarendon Press, 1865
Caesar, Gaius Julius. *De bello civili*
De bello Gallico
Canisius, Henricus, d. 1610. *Lectionis antiquae* (*Thesaurus monumentorum*) Antwerp, Wetstenios, 1725
Capitolinus, Julius, *fl.* 300, *Maximini duo*
Opilius Macrinus
Capitularia regum Francorum (France. Laws, statutes, etc. to 987). *MGH*, LL., Cap. Migne PL 97
Capitularia spuria. Benedictae levitae, qui dicitur, capitularium collectio. MGH, LL., tom. II, Pars altera
Cartae Senonicae. MGH, LL. Form
Cassiodorus (Cassiodorus Senator, Flavius Magnus Aurelius), *ca.* 487–*ca.* 580. *Variae*
Cassius Dio Cocceianus. *Historia Romana*
Catel, Guillaume, 1560–1626. *Mémoires de l'histoire du Languedoc*. Tolose, A. Colomiez, 1633
Chardin, Sir John, 1643–1713. *Voyages en Perse et autres lieux de l'Orient*, 10 vols., Paris, Le Normant, 1811
Cicero, Marcus Tullius. *Opera*. For individual works see "Index of Citations"
Codex Theodosianus. *The Theodosian Code and Novels and the Sirmondian Constitutions*, trans. Clyde Pharr (Princeton: Princeton University Press, 1952)
Concilia Galliae A.511–A.695. Corpus Christianorum, Series Latina, vol. 148A
Corpus Iuris Canonici. Decretalium collectiones. (Catholic Church, Corpus Iuris Canonici)
Decretum Magistri Gratiani (Catholic Church, Corpus Iuris Canonici)
Corpus Iuris Civilis. Iustiniani Institutiones (*Institutes*)
Digesta (*Digest* or *Pandects*)
Codex Iustiniani (*Code*)
Novellae (*Novels*)
Authentica (*Authentics*)
Courmenin, Louis Deshayes, Baron de, d. 1632. *Voiage de Levant*, Paris, 1632
Cousin, Louis, 1627–1707. *Histoire de Constantinople*: *see* Leo the Grammarian
Cujas, Jacques, 1522–1590. *De feudis*, in *Opera omnia*, vol. 8, Prati, Marghieri, 1859–1871
Observationum et emendationum libri XXVIII, in *Opera omnia*, vol. 1, Prati, Marghieri, 1859–1871
Cyril, St. (Cyrillus, Saint, Patriarch of Alexandria, 370(*ca.*)–444. *Epistolae*, Migne PG 77
Dampier, William, 1652–1715. *Dampier's Voyages*, 2 vols., London, E. Grant Richards, 1906
Davila, Enrico Caterina, 1576–1631. *Dell'istoria delle guerre civili di Francia*, vol. 1, Milano, Società de' classici italiani, 1825
Demosthenes. *Orationes*
Diodorus Siculus. *Bibliotheca historica*

Dionysius of Halicarnassus. *Antiquitates Romanae* (*Archaeologia romano*)
Opuscula critica et rhetorica. De antiquis oratoribus

Dodwell, Henry, 1641–1711. *Dissertatio de Arriani Nearcho*, in Arrian, *Indica*, ed. F. Schmeider, Magdeburg, Gebauer, 1798, pp. 233–254

Dubos, Jean Baptiste, 1670–1742. *Histoire critique de l'établissement de la monarchie française dans les baules*, 4 vols., Paris, Didot, 1742

Du Cange, Charles Du Fresne, Sieur, 1610–1688. *Glossarium mediae et infimae latinitatis*, 10 vols. in 5, Graz, Austria, Akademische Druck-U. Verlagsanstalt, 1954

Du Chesne, André, 1584–1640. *Historiae francorum scriptores coetanei*, 5 vols., Paris, Cramoisy, 1636–1649

Du Halde, Jean Baptiste, 1674–1743. *Description géographique, historique, chronologique et physique de l'Empire de la Chine et de la Tartarie Chinoise*, Paris, P. G. Le Mercier, 1735, indicated by "P"; La Haye, H. Scheurieer, 1736, indicated by "H"; London, S. Watts, 1736, indicated by "L."

Dumont, Jean, baron de Carlscroon, d. 1726. *Corps universel diplomatique du droit des gens*, Amsterdam, Brunel, 1726–1731

Dupin, Louis Ellies, 1657–1719. *Nouvelle bibliothèque des auteurs ecclesiastiques*, 19 vols. in 10, Paris, Pralard, 1691–1715

Du Tillet, Jean, seigneur de la Bussière, d. 1570, *Recueil des rois de France*, Paris, Mettayer, 1618

Ebülgazi Bahadir Han, Khan of Khorezm, 1603–1663. *Histoire généalogique des Tatars*, ed. Bentinck, Leyden, A. Kallewier, 1726
Histoire des Mongols et des Tatares, Paris, 1970

Eckhart, Johann Georg von 1674–1730. *Leges Francorum salicae et ripuariae*, Frankfurt, Foersteri, 1720

Einhard, 770(*ca.*)–840. *Vita Karoli Magni*, *MGH*, SS. 2, Migne PL 97

Les Establissements de Saint Louis (France. Laws, statutes, etc. 1226–1270 (Louis IX)). Ed. P. Viollet, 4 vols., Paris, Renouard, 1881–1886

Eusebius Pamphili, Bishop of Caesarea. *Chronicon bipartitum*, London, Milford, 1923
De praeparationis evangelicae

Evagrius Scholasticus, b. 536? *Historia ecclesiastica*, 1979 reprint of London, Methuen, 1898 edn

Florus, Lucius Annaeus. *Epitome rerum romanorum*

Fontaines, Pierre de, d. *ca.* 1289. *Le Conseil*, Paris, 1846

Forbin, Claude, comte de, 1656–1733. *Mémoires*, in Petitot, *Nouvelle collection des mémoires relatifs à l'histoire de France*, ser. 2, vols. 74–75, Paris, 1829; and in Michaud, vol. 33, Paris, 1857

Formulae Salicae Lindenbrogianae. MGH, LL. Form

Formulae Turonenses vulgo Sirmondicae dictae. MGH, LL. Form

Fortunatianus, Chirius, 5th cent. *Artis rhetoricae*, in *Rhetores Latini minores*, Leipzig, Teubner, 1863

France. *Parlement* (Bordeaux). *Decisiones Burdegalenses*, by Nicolas de Bohier, 1469–1539, Lyons, Albert, 1620

Fredegarius, Scholasticus, 7th cent. (*Fredegarii Chronicon*) *Chronicon*, *MGH*, SS. Merov.

Freinsheim, Johann, 1608–1660. *Supplementorum Livianorum libri*, Amsterdam, Wetstenium & G. Smith, 1738–1746

Frézier, Amédée François, 1682–1773. *Relation du voyage de la mer du Sud, du Chili, du Pérou, et du Brésil*, Amsterdam, P. Humbert, 1717

Gage, Thomas, 1603?–1656. *Travels in the New World*, Norman, University of Oklahoma Press, 1958; London, Clark, 1699

Gaius. *Institutionum epitome*, *FIRA*

Galen (Galenus). *Galeni paraphrastae Menodoti adhortatio ad artes addiscendas* (*Protreptikos logos*), Kuehn edn, 1821

Galland, Auguste, *ca.* 1570. *Du franc-aleu et origine des droits seigneuriaux, avec les lois données au pays d'Albigeois*, Paris, 1637

Garcilaso de la Vega, el Inca, 1539–1616. *Royal Commentaries of the Incas and General History of Peru*, 2 vols., Austin, University of Texas Press, 1966

Gellius, Aulus. *Noctes Atticae*

Gesta Dagoberti I. Regis Francorum. *MGH*, SS. Merov., t. 2

Giraldi, Lilio Gregorio, 1479–1552. *De deis gentium*. Basle, Oporinum, 1548
Opera omnia, New York, Garland, 1976, reprint of 1548 edn.

Godefroy, Jacques, 1587–1652. *Fragmenta legis Juliae et Papiae*, Heidelberg, Lancellot, 1617

Goldast, Melchior, 1578–1635. *Collectio constitutionum imperialium*, 4 vols., Darmstadt, W. Germany, Scientia Verlag, 1974; reprint of 1713 edn.

Gravina, Giovanni Vincenzo, 1664–1717. *Opera seu originum iuris civilis libri tres quibus accedunt de romano imperio*, Venice, Piteri 1739

Gregory of Tours (Gregorius, saint, Bishop of Tours, 538–594). *Historia ecclesiastica Francorum*, *MGH*, SS. Merov., 1, Migne PL 71

Guillet de Saint-Georges, Georges, 1625?–1705. *Lacédémone ancienne et nouvelle*, 2 vols., Paris, J. Ribou, 1676

Hariulphe, abbé de Saint-Pierre d'Oudenbourg, d. 1143. *Chronicon Centulense*, Paris, 1894; Migne PL 104

Harmenopoulos, Konstantinos, d. 1380? *Manuale legum sive hexabiblos*

Harrington, James, 1611–1677. *Oceana*, Cambridge, 1977; first published 1656

Henault, Charles Jean François, 1685–1770. *Nouvel abrégé chronologique de l'histoire de France*, Paris, Proux, 1836

Herodianus. *Ab excessu divi Marci libri octo*

Herodotus. *The Persian Wars*

Hincmarus, Archbishop of Reims, d. 882. *Opera*, Migne PL 125–126

Hobbes, Thomas, 1588–1679. *Leviathan*, London, Oxford University Press, 1967; first published 1651

Homer (Homerus). *Iliad*

Horace (Horatius Flaccus, Quintus). *Epistolae*
Satires

Hyde, Thomas, 1636–1703. *Historia religionis veterum Persarum*, Oxford, 1700

Isidore of Seville (Isidorus, saint, bishop of Seville, d. 636). *Historia Gothorum Wandalorum Sueborum*, Leiden, Brill, 1970; *MGH*, Auct., tom. 11, Chron. 2

Janiçon, François Michel, 1674–1730. *Etat présent de la république des Provinces-Unies*, 2 vols., Le Haye, J. van Duren, 1729–1730

Jobert, Louis. *The Knowledge of Medals*, 2nd edn., London, E. Curll and T. Caldecott 1715

Jordanes, 6th cent. *De summo temporum vel origine actibusque gentis romanorum*, *MGH*, Auct., tom. 5, pt. 1

Getica, *MGH*, Auct., tom. 5, pt. 1

Josephus, Flavius. *Contra Apionem*

Journal des Sçavans

Julianus Apostata, emperor of Rome, A.D. 331–363. *Caesares*

Julianus, saint, Bishop of Toledo, d. 690. *Historia Wambae*, Migne PL 96; *MGH*, SS. Merov., tom. 5. Corpus Christianorum, Series Latina, 115

Justin (Justinus, Marcus Junianus). *Epitoma historiarum Philippicarum*

Juvenal (Juvenalis, Decimus Junius). *Saturarum* (*Satires*)

Kaempfer, Engelbert, 1651–1716. *The History of Japan together with a Description of the Kingdom of Siam, 1690–1692*, 3 vols., trans. from the Dutch by J. G. Scheuchzer, Glasgow, James MacLehose and sons, 1906

Kircher, Athanasius, 1602–1680. *La Chine illustrée*, Amsterdam, Jansson à Waesberge, 1670

Koran

Krusinski, Judasz Tadeusz, 1675–1756. *Histoire de la derniere revolution de Perse*, trans. Jean Antoine Du Cerceau, 1670–1730, Paris, Briasson, 1728

Labat, Jean Baptiste, 1663–1738. *Nouveau voyage aux isles de l'Amérique*, Paris, Giffart, 1722

Nouvelle relation de l'Afrique Occidentale, Paris, Cavelier, 1728

La Loubère, Simon de, 1642–1729. *The Kingdom of Siam*, New York, Oxford University Press, 1969; reprint of 1693 edn

Lambarde, William, 1536–1601. *'Αρχαιονομια (Archaionomia), sive de priscis anglorum legibus*, 1568. Also in Beda Venerabilis, 673–735. *Historia ecclesiasticae.* London, Bee, 1644

Landulfus, Sagax. *Historia Romana* (*Historia miscella*), ed. A. Crivellucci, Rome, Senato, 1912

La Roche Flavin, Bernard de. *Des parlements de France*, Genève, M. Berjon, 1621

Laugier de Tassy, *fl.* 1720. *Histoire du royaume d'Alger*, 1720

Laurière, Eusèbe Jacob de, 1659–1728. *Ordonnances des rois de France de la troisième race*, 22 vols., Paris, 1723–1849. *See also Recueil général des anciennes lois francaises*

Le Clerc, Jean, 1657–1736. *Histoire des Provinces-Unies des Pais-Bas*, 2 vols., Amsterdam, Chatelain, 1737–1738

Le Cointe, Charles, 1611–1681. *Annales ecclesiastici Francorum*, 8 vols., Paris, Typographia regia, 1665–1683

Leges Alamannorum. *MGH*, LL. 4

Leges Burgundionum. (*Lex Burgundionum*). *MGH*, LL. 2; *MGH*, LL. Nat. 2, pt. 1
Leges XII Tabularum and *Leges Regiae*. *FIRA*
Leges Langobardorum. *MGH*, LL. 4 ("pap." indicates that the reference is from *Liber legis Langobardorum Papiensis*, also in *MGH*, LL. 4); (Roth. = Rothari Regis Edictus; Grim. = Grimoaldus Rex; Liut. = Liutprandi Leges et Notitiae; Rach. = Ratchis; Kar. = Karolus Magnus; Pip. = Pippinus Rex; Lud. = Ludovicus Pius; Loth. = Lotharius; Wid. = Wido; Otto I = Otto I (Primus); Hein. I = Heinricus I, Imperator
Leges Saxonum (*Lex Saxonum*). *MGH*, LL. 5
Leibniz, Gottfried Wilhelm Freiherr von, 1646–1716. *De origine Francorum*, Frankfurt, Foersteri, 1720
Scriptores rerum Brunsvicensium, 3 vols., Hanover, Foersteri, 1707–1711
Le Mire, Aubert, 1573–1640. *Codex donatione piarum*, vol. 1 of *Opera diplomatica et historica*, Louvain, Denique, 1723
Leo the Grammarian (Leo, Grammaticus). *Chronographia*, CSHB 44, Migne PG 108
Leti, Gregorio, 1630–1701. *The Life of Sixtus V*, English trans. by Ellis Farneworth, Dublin, W. Colles, 1779
Lettres édifiantes et curieuses (Jesuits. Letters from the Missions)
Lex Angliorum et Werinorum hoc est Thuringorum. *MGH*, LL. 5
Lex Baiuwariorum (*Lex Baiuvariorum*). *MGH*, LL. Nat. 3
Lex Francorum Chamavorum. *MGH*, LL. 5
Lex Frisionum. *MGH*, LL. 3
Lex Ribuaria (Ripuarian Law). *MGH*, LL. Nat. 3, pt. 2
Lex Salica (*Salic Law*). *MGH*, LL. Nat. 4, pt. 2
Lex Thuringorum; *see Lex Angliorum et Werinorum hoc est Thuringorum*
Lex Wisigothorum (Visigoths. Laws, statutes, etc.). *MGH*, LL. 1
Libanius. *Declamations*
Liber Augustalis or the Constitutions of Melfi (1231) (Naples (Kingdom). Laws, Statutes, etc.) *MGH*, LL. 2; Eng. trans. by James M. Powell, Syracuse, N.Y., Syracuse University Press, 1971
Liber historiae Francorum (*Gesta regum Francorum*). *MGH*, SS. Merov., 2
Lindenbrog, Friedrich, 1573–1648. *Leges Francorum Salicae et Ripuarium*, Frankfurt, Foersteri, 1720
Littleton, Thomas, Sir, 1402–1481. *Anciennes Loix des Françoises conservées dans les coutumes angloises*, Rouen, Le Boucher, 1779
Livy (Livius Titus). *Ab urbe condita*
Loyseau, Charles, 1566–1627. *Discours de l'abus des Iustices de Village*, Paris, la veufve Aubouyn, 1666
Lucretius (Lucretius Carus, Titus). *De rerum natura*
Lysias. *Orationes*
Machiavelli, Niccolò, 1469–1527. *Discorsi sopra la prima deca di Tito Livio* (*The Discourses*)
Le istorie fiorentine (*The History of Florence*)
Mandeville, Bernard, 1670–1733. *The Fable of the Bees*, Oxford, Clarendon Press, 1924

Marca, Pierre de, archbishop, 1594–1662. *Marca Hispanica*, Paris, Muguet, 1688

Marculfi Formulae (Marculfus, 7th cent.) *MGH*, LL. Form.; Migne PL 87 (For *Appendix Marculfi, see Cartae Senonicae*)

Marius, Bishop of Avenches, d. 593 or 594. *Chronica*, *MGH*, Auct., 11. *Chronica minora*, 2

Martène, Edmund, 1654–1739, and Ursin Durand, 1701–1773. *Thesauros novos anecdotorum*, Paris, Delaulpe, 1717.

Martial (Martialis, Marcus Valerius). *Epigrammaton* (*Epigrams*)

Mela, Pomponius. *De situ orbis libri III*

Milton, John, 1608–1674. *Paradise Lost*, New York, Odyssey Press, 1958

Montesquieu, Charles Louis de Secondat, Baron de la Brède et, 1689–1755.
Considerations on the Causes of the Greatness of the Romans and their Decline, trans. David Lowenthal, Ithaca, N.Y., Cornell University Press, 1965
Defense of "The Spirit of the Laws," in Masson edition, vol. 1
Persian Letters

Montrésor, Claude de Bourdeille, Comte de, 1606?–1663. *Memoirs*, 2 vols., Cologne, Sambix, 1723

Monumenta Germaniae historica
Constitutiones et acta regum Germanicorum, LL. 2
Diplomatum Karolinorum
Scriptorum rerum Merovingicarum
Die Urkunden der Karolinger

More, Sir Thomas, saint, 1478–1535. *Utopia*, New Haven, Conn., Yale University Press, 1975

Mosaicarum et Romanorum legum collatio. FIRA

Nazarius, rhetor, *fl.* 22. *Panegyricus Constantinii*, in *XII Panegyrici Latini*, Oxford, Oxford University Press, 1964

Nepos, Cornelius, *Liber de excellentibus ducibus exterrarum gentium*

Nicholas of Damascus (Nicolaus Damascenus). *Fragments*, *FGrH*

Nithard, d. 844? *Historiarum*, *MGH*, SS. 2

Nouveau mémoire des missions de la Compagnie de Jésus dans le Levant (Jesuits. Letters from the Missions)

Novellae Leonis (Byzantine Empire. Laws, statutes, etc. 886–911 (Leo VI, the Wise))

Otto, Bishop of Freising, d. 1158. *Gesta Friderici I Imperatoris*. *MGH*, SS. 20

Ovid (Ovidius Naso, Publius). *Metamorphoses*

Pactus legis Salicae. MGH, LL. Nat. 4, pt. 1

Paul the Jurist (Paulus, Julius). *Sententiarum, FIRA*

Paulus, Diaconus, 720 *ca.*–797? *Historia Langobardum*, Migne PL 95, *MGH*, SS. Lang

Perry, John, 1670–1732. *The State of Russia under the Present Czar*, London, Cass, 1967

Philippe de Remi, Sire de Beaumanoir, d. 1296. *Coutumes de Beauvaisis*, Paris, 1970; reprint of 1859–1900 edn

Philo Judaeus. *De specialibus legibus*

Philostratus, Flavius. *Vitae sophistarum*

Photius (Photius I, saint, Patriarch of Constantinople, *ca.* 820–*ca.* 891). *Bibliotheca*
Plato. *Critias*
Epistolae
Laws
Republic
Pliny the Elder (Plinius Secundus, Caius). *Naturalis historia*
Pliny the Younger (Plinius Caecilius Secundus, Caius). *Panegyricus*
Plutarch (Plutarchus). *Moralia*
Parallel Lives (Vitae parallelae). For individual lives see "Index of Citations"
Pollux, Julius, of Naucratis, *ca.* 130–188. *Onomasticon*
Polnoe sobranie zakanov Rossiiskoi imperii s 1649 goda (Russia. Laws, statutes, etc.)
Polybius. *Historiae*
Prideaux, Humphrey, 1648–1724. *The Old and New Testament Connected in the History of the Jews*, London, W. Baynes, 1831
The True Nature of Imposture Fully Displayed in the Life of Mahomet, London, Curll and Hooke, 1718
Priscus, Panites. *Fragments*, CSHB 14, Migne PG 113
Procopius of Caesarea. *Anecdota sive Historia arcana* (*The Secret History*)
The Gothic Wars (bks. V–IX of *History of the Wars*)
The Persian Wars (bks. I and II of *History of the Wars*)
The Vandalic Wars (bks. III and IV of *History of the Wars*)
Ptolemy, Claudius (Ptolemaeus, Claudius). *Geographica*, Leipzig, C. Nobbe, 1887
Pufendorf, Samuel, Freiherr von, 1632–1694. *Histoire de Suède*, continued by J. B. Des Roches de Parthenay, 3 vols. Amsterdam, Chatelain, 1748
Introduction à l'histoire générale et politique de l'univers, Latin edn. 1700. Translated and continued by Antoine M. Augustin Bruzen de la Martinière, Amsterdam, Chatelain, 1743
Pyrard, Francois, *ca.* 1570–1621. *Voyage*, trans. Albert Gray, 3 vols., Hakluyt Society, 76, 77, 80, London, Hakluyt Society, 1887–1890
Quintilian (Quintilianus, Marcus Fabius). *Instituto oratoria*
Rageau, François, d. 1605. *Glossaire du droit francais*. Paris, 1704
Recueil de voyages au Nord (Bernard, Jean Frédéric, d. 1752, edn)
Recueil des historiens des Gaules et de la France. Ed. Martin Bouguet, 1685–1754, Paris, 1869
Recueil des voyages qui ont servi à l'établissement de la Compagnie des Indes. (Renneville, René Augustin Constantin de, 1650–1723, edn), 5 vols., Paris, 1702–1706; 7 vols., Amsterdam, 1725
Recueil général des anciennes lois françaises (France. Laws, statutes, etc.). Ed. Jacques Isambert et al. (This work has superseded Laurière's *Recueil des Ordonnances des Rois de France de la Troisième Race*.)
Renaudot, Eusybe, 1646–1720, ed. and trans. (Hasan ibn Yazid Abu Zaid al Sirafi authored the Arabic original). *Anciennes relations des Indes et de la Chine*, Paris, Coignard, 1718

Retz, Cardinal d[illegible] (R[illegible]ean François Paul de Gondi, Cardinal de, 1613–1679), *Mémoires*, [illegible]is, Gallimard, 1961

Richelieu, Cardinal (Richelieu, Arman Jean du Plessis, Cardinal, Duc de, 1585–1642). *Testament politique*, ed. Louis André, Paris, Robert Laffont, 1947

Rousset de Missy, Jean, 1686–1762. *Le Procès entre l'Espagne et Grande-Bretagne*, vol. 13 (Supplement) (1756) of *Recueil historique d'actes*, La Haye, H. Scheurleer, 1728–1760

Rudbeck, Olof, 1630–1702. *Atlantica*, vol. 4 of *Atland*, Uppsala, Curio, 1675–1679, Stockholm, Alqvist Wiksells, 1938

Rycaut, Paul, Sir, 1628–1700. *The History of the Present State of the Ottoman Empire*, London, Cleave, 1703

Sallust (Sallustius Crispus, Caius) *Catilina*

Jugurtha

Santorio, Santorio, 1561–1636. *De medicina statica aphorismi*, Naples, 1784

Savot, Louis, 1579–1640. *Discours sur les medailles antiques*, Paris, Cramoisy, 1627

Scylax. *Periplus Scylacis Caryandensis*, in *Geographi Graeci minores*, vol. 1

Seneca (Seneca, Lucius Annaeus). *Apokolokyntosis* (*The Pumpkinization of the Divine Claudius*)

De beneficiis

Tragedies. Troades

Sextus Empiricus. *Pyrrhoneia*

Shaw, Thomas, 1694–1751. *Travels or Observations Relating to Several Parts of Barbary and the Levant*, Oxford, The Theatre, 1738

Simocatta, Theophylactus. *Historiarum*, CSHB 22

Sirmond, Jacques, 1559–1651. *Concilia antiqua Galliae*, 4 vols., Aalen, W. Germany, Scientia Verlag, 1970, reprint of Paris, Cramoisy, 1629–1666 edn. *See also Concilia Galliae.*

Smith, William, *fl.* 1726. *A New Voyage to Guinea*, London, Cass, 1967, reprint of 1744 edn.

Socrates Scholasticus, *ca.* 379–440. *Historia ecclesiastica*

Solis y Rivadeneyra, Antoine de, 1610–1686. *History of the Conquest of Mexico by the Spaniards*, New York, AMS Press, 1973, reprint of 1753 edn

Sophocles. *Oedipus at Colonus*

Sozomen (Sozomenus, Hermias, 5th cent.). *Historia ecclesiastica*

The Statutes of the Realm (Great Britain. Laws, statutes, etc.). 1963 reprint edn

Stephanus of Byzantium. *Ethnika*

Stow, John, 1525?–1605. *The Survey of London*, London, Dent, 1929

Strabo. *Geographica*

Suetonius (Suetonius, Tranquillus, C.). *Vitae duodecim Caesarum*

Suger, abbot of Saint Denis, 1081–1151. *De rebus administratione sua gestis*, in *Oeuvres complètes*, Paris, Renouard, 1867, Migne PL 186

Suidas. *Lexicon*

Surius, Laurentius, 1522–1578. *De probatis sanctorum*, Coloniae Agrippianae, G. Calenium Haeredes Quentelios, 1576–1586

Syrianus. *Scholia ad Hermogenis* (*Commentarium in librum 'Peri staseon'*)

Tacitus, Cornelius. *Agricola*

Annales

Germania

Tavernier, Jean Baptiste, Baron d'Aubonne, 1605–1689. *Travels in India*, trans. V. Ball, 2 vols., London, Macmillan, 1889

Tertullian (Tertullianus, Quintus Septimius Florens). *Apologeticus*

Thaumas de la Thaumassière, Gaspard, Sieur du Puy-Ferrand, d. 1712? *Les Anciennes et Nouvelles Coutumes locales de Berry, et celles de Lorris commentées*, Paris, 1692

Thegan, chorepiscopus of Treves, d. *ca.* 850. *Vita Hludowici Imperatoris*, Migne PL 106; *MGH*, SS. 2

Theophilus, antecessor. *Institutes* (*Paraphrasis Graeca Institutionum Caesarearum*)

Theophrastus, *Fragmenta*, Paris, Wimmer, 1866

Thucydides. *The Peloponnesian War*

Toulouse (Archdiocese) *Deci. capelle Tholose* (by Stephanus Aufrerius) Lyons, Giuncti, 1531

Tournefort, Joseph Pitton, 1656–1708. *Relation d'un voyage du Levant*: *see* Louis Des Hayes Courmenin

Ulpian (Ulpianus, Domitius). *Fragmenta*, *FIRA*

Valerius Maximus. *Factorum et dictorum memorabilium*

Velleius Paterculus, Caius. *Historiae Romanae ad M. Minucium consulem*

Victor, Sextus Aurelius. *De Caesaribus*

Virgil (Vergilius Maro, Publius). *Aeneid*

Vita Aridii Abbatis Lemovicini. *MGH*, SS. Merov., 3

Vita Hludowici Imperatoris. "Astronomous," *fl.* 814–840, supposed author. *MGH*, SS. 2

Vita S. Liudgeri. *MGH*, SS. 2

Vopiscus, Flavius. *Probus*

Tacitus

Walter, Ferdinand, 1794–1879. *Corpus Iuris germania antiqui*, Berlin, Reimer, 1824 (or consult Migne PL 97). *See also Capitularia regum francorum*

Xenophon. *The Constitution of the Lacedaemonians*

Hellenica

Hiero

Oeconomica

Symposium

Ways and Means

Xenophon, "The Old Oligarch." *The Constitution of Athens*

Xiphilinus, Joannes, the Younger: *see* Cassius Dio Cocceianus

Zonaras, Joannes, 12th cent. *Epitomae historiarum*, CSHB 41–42

Zosimus, historian. *Historiae*, CSHB 30

Index of names and places

Index of works cited

CAMBRIDGE TEXTS IN THE HISTORY OF POLITICAL THOUGHT

Titles published in the series thus far

ARISTOTLE *The Politics* and *The Constitution of Athens* (edited by Stephen Everson)

ARNOLD *Culture and Anarchy and other writings* (edited by Stefan Collini)

ASTELL *Political Writings* (edited by Patricia Springborg)

AUGUSTINE *The City of God against the Pagans* (edited by R. W. Dyson)

AUSTIN *The Province of Jurisprudence Determined* (edited by Wilfrid E. Rumble)

BACON *The History of the Reign of King Henry VII* (edited by Brian Vickers)

BAKUNIN *Statism and Anarchy* (edited by Marshall Shatz)

BAXTER *A Holy Commonwealth* (edited by William Lamont)

BECCARIA *On Crimes and Punishments and other writings* (edited by Richard Bellamy)

BENTHAM *A Fragment on Government* (introduction by Ross Harrison)

BERNSTEIN *The Preconditions of Socialism* (edited by Henry Tudor)

BODIN *On Sovereignty* (edited by Julian H. Franklin)

BOLINGBROKE *Political Writings* (edited by David Armitage)

BOSSUET *Politics Drawn from the Very Words of Holy Scripture* (edited by Patrick Riley)

The British Idealists (edited by David Boucher)

BURKE *Pre-Revolutionary Writings* (edited by Ian Harris)

CHRISTINE DE PIZAN *The Book of the Body Politic* (edited by Kate Langdon Forhan)

CICERO *On Duties* (edited by M. T. Griffin and E. M. Atkins)

Conciliarism and Papalism (edited by J. H. Burns and Thomas M. Izbicki)

CONSTANT *Political Writings* (edited by Biancamaria Fontana)

DANTE *Monarchy* (edited by Prue Shaw)

DIDEROT *Political Writings* (edited by John Hope Mason and Robert Wokler)

The Dutch Revolt (edited by Martin van Gelderen)

The Early Political Writings of the German Romantics (edited by Frederick C. Beiser)

Early Greek Political Thought from Homer to the Sophists (edited by Michael Gagarin and Paul Woodruff)

The English Levellers (edited by Andrew Sharp)

ERASMUS *The Education of a Christian Prince* (edited by Lisa Jardine)

FERGUSON *An Essay on the History of Civil Society* (edited by Fania Oz-Salzberger)

FILMER *Patriarcha and Other Writings* (edited by Johann P. Sommerville)

FLETCHER *Political Works* (edited by John Robertson)

SIR JOHN FORTESCUE *On the Laws and Governance of England* (edited by Shelley Lockwood)

FOURIER *The Theory of the Four Movements* (edited by Gareth Stedman Jones and Ian Patterson)

GRAMSCI *Pre-Prison Writings* (edited by Richard Bellamy)

GUICCIARDINI *Dialogue on the Government of Florence* (edited by Alison Brown)

HARRINGTON *A Commonwealth of Oceana* and *A System of Politics* (edited by J. G. A. Pocock)

HEGEL *Elements of the Philosophy of Right* (edited by Allen W. Wood and H. B. Nisbet)

HOBBES *On the Citizen* (edited by Michael Silverthorne and Richard Tuck)

HOBBES *Leviathan* (edited by Richard Tuck)

HOBHOUSE *Liberalism and Other Writings* (edited by James Meadowcroft)

HOOKER *Of the Laws of Ecclesiastical Polity* (edited by A. S. McGrade)

HUME *Political Essays* (edited by Knud Haakonssen)

KING JAMES VI AND I *Political Writings* (edited by Johann P. Sommerville)

JOHN OF SALISBURY *Policraticus* (edited by Cary Nederman)

KANT *Political Writings* (edited by H. S. Reiss and H. B. Nisbet)

KNOX *On Rebellion* (edited by Roger A. Mason)

KROPOTKIN *The Conquest of Bread and other writings* (edited by Marshall Shatz)

LAWSON *Politica sacra et civilis* (edited by Conal Condren)

LEIBNIZ *Political Writings* (edited by Patrick Riley)

LOCKE *Political Essays* (edited by Mark Goldie)

LOCKE *Two Treatises of Government* (edited by Peter Laslett)

LOYSEAU *A Treatise of Orders and Plain Dignities* (edited by Howell A. Lloyd)

Luther and Calvin on Secular Authority (edited by Harro Höpfl)

MACHIAVELLI *The Prince* (edited by Quentin Skinner and Russell Price)

de MAISTRE *Considerations on France* (edited by Isaiah Berlin and Richard Lebrun)

MALTHUS *An Essay on the Principle of Population* (edited by Donald Winch)

MARSIGLIO OF PADUA *Defensor minor* and *De translatione Imperii* (edited by Cary Nederman)

MARX *Early Political Writings* (edited by Joseph O'Malley)

MARX *Later Political Writings* (edited by Terrell Carver)

JAMES MILL *Political Writings* (edited by Terence Ball)

J. S. MILL *On Liberty*, with *The Subjection of Women* and *Chapters on Socialism* (edited by Stefan Collini)

MILTON *Political Writings* (edited by Martin Dzelzainis)

MONTESQUIEU *The Spirit of the Laws* (edited by Anne M. Cohler, Basia Carolyn Miller and Harold Samuel Stone)

MORE *Utopia* (edited by George M. Logan and Robert M. Adams)

MORRIS *News from Nowhere* (edited by Krishan Kumar)

NICHOLAS OF CUSA *The Catholic Concordance* (edited by Paul E. Sigmund)

NIETZSCHE *On the Genealogy of Morality* (edited by Keith Ansell-Pearson)

PAINE *Political Writings* (edited by Bruce Kuklick)

PLATO *Statesman* (edited by Julia Annas and Robin Waterfield)

PRICE *Political Writings* (edited by D. O. Thomas)

PRIESTLEY *Political Writings* (edited by Peter Miller)

PROUDHON *What is Property?* (edited by Donald R. Kelley and Bonnie G. Smith)

PUFENDORF *On the Duty of Man and Citizen according to Natural Law* (edited by James Tully)

The Radical Reformation (edited by Michael G. Baylor)

ROUSSEAU *The* Discourses *and other early political writings* (edited by Victor Gourevitch)

ROUSSEAU *The* Social Contract *and other later political writings* (edited by Victor Gourevitch)

SENECA *Moral and Political Essays* (edited by John Cooper and John Procope)

SIDNEY *Court Maxims* (edited by Hans W. Blom, Eco Haitsma Mulier and Ronald Janse)

SPENCER *The Man versus the State* and *The Proper Sphere of Government* (edited by John Offer)

STIRNER *The Ego and Its Own* (edited by David Leopold)

THOREAU *Political Writings* (edited by Nancy Rosenblum)

Utopias of the British Enlightenment (edited by Gregory Claeys)

VITORIA *Political Writings* (edited by Anthony Pagden and Jeremy Lawrance)

VOLTAIRE *Political Writings* (edited by David Williams)

WEBER *Political Writings* (edited by Peter Lassman and Ronald Speirs)

WILLIAM OF OCKHAM *A Short Discourse on Tyrannical Government* (edited by A. S. McGrade and John Kilcullen)

WILLIAM OF OCKHAM *A Letter to the Friars Minor and other writings* (edited by A. S. McGrade and John Kilcullen)

WOLLSTONECRAFT *A Vindication of the Rights of Men* and *A Vindication of the Rights of Woman* (edited by Sylvana Tomaselli)